Adventure Guide to
Puerto Rico
4th Edition

Kurt Pitzer & Tara Stevens

HUNTER

HUNTER PUBLISHING, INC.
130 Campus Drive
Edison, NJ 08818-7816
☎ 732-225-1900 / 800-255-0343 / fax 732-417-1744
www.hunterpublishing.com
comments@hunterpublishing.com

IN THE UNITED KINGDOM:
Windsor Books International
The Boundary, Wheatley Road, Garsington
Oxford, OX44 9EJ England
☎ 01865-361122 / fax 01865-361133

ISBN 1-58843-116-9
© 2001 Hunter Publishing, Inc.

This and other Hunter travel guides are also available as e-books in a variety of digital formats through our online partners, including Amazon.com, BarnesandNoble.com, and eBooks.com.

All rights reserved. No part of this publication may be reproduced, stored in a retrieval system, or transmitted in any form, or by any means, electronic, mechanical, photocopying, recording, or otherwise, without the written permission of the publisher.

This guide focuses on recreational activities. As all such activities contain elements of risk, the publisher, author, affiliated individuals and companies disclaim any responsibility for any injury, harm, or illness that may occur to anyone through, or by use of, the information in this book. Every effort was made to insure the accuracy of information in this book, but the publisher and author do not assume, and hereby disclaim, any liability for loss or damage caused by errors, omissions, misleading information or potential travel problems caused by this guide, even if such errors or omissions result from negligence, accident or any other cause.

Cover: Beach in Puerto Rico, © Wendell Metzen / IndexStock

Interior photographs provided by the
Puerto Rico Tourism Company (PRTC), unless otherwise indicated

Maps by Lissa K. Dailey and Kim André,
© 2001 Hunter Publishing, Inc.

Indexed by Nancy Wolff

CONTENTS

Introduction — 1
- The Land — 1
- History — 3
- Government — 11
- The Economy — 13
- Climate — 14
- Flora & Fauna — 15
- The People — 22
- Language — 24
- Religion — 25
- Music & Dance — 28
- Art & Culture — 31
- Food: A Taste of Puerto Rico — 34
- Festivals & Events — 37
- Getting Here — 40
- Getting Around — 42
- Where To Stay — 44
- Where To Eat — 49
- Adventures — 50
- Eco-Travel — 59
- Shopping — 59
- Travel Information — 62
- Travel Directory — 70

San Juan & Environs — 73
- History — 74
- Getting Here — 77
- Getting Around — 78
- Mail & Communications — 81
- Touring & Sightseeing — 82
- Adventures — 97
- Eco-Travel — 104
- Where To Stay — 105
- Where To Eat — 111
- Entertainment & Nightlife — 121
- Leisure & Shopping — 127

North Coast — 131
- Getting Here & Getting Around — 131
- Touring & Sightseeing — 133
- Adventures — 143
- Eco-Travel — 153
- Where To Stay — 156
- Where To Eat — 160

West Coast — 165
- Getting Here & Getting Around — 165
- Mail & Communications — 168
- Touring & Sightseeing — 168
- Adventures — 182
- Eco-Travel — 197
- Isla Mona — 198
- Where To Stay — 204
- Where To Eat — 210
- Nightlife — 214

South Coast — 215
- Getting Here & Getting Around — 215
- Communications & Information Sources — 216
- Touring & Sightseeing — 218
- Adventures — 237
- Eco-Travel — 250
- Where To Stay — 255
- Where To Eat — 261
- Nightlife — 266

Central Mountains — 269
- Getting Here & Getting Around — 269
- Communications — 270
- Touring & Sightseeing — 270
- Adventures — 280
- Where To Stay — 288
- Where To Eat — 294

East Coast — 299
- Getting Here & Getting Around — 299
- Communications — 302
- Touring & Sightseeing — 302
- Adventures — 312
- Eco-Travel — 324
- Where To Stay — 335
- Where To Eat — 339

Vieques Island & Culebra Island — 345
- *Overview* — 345
- *Vieques* — 346
  - History — 347
  - Getting Here — 349
  - Getting Around — 351
  - Communications & Information — 352
  - Touring & Sightseeing — 354
  - Adventures — 358
  - Where To Stay — 365
  - Where To Eat — 368
  - Nightlife — 371

Culebra	371
History	373
Flora & Fauna	375
Getting Here	376
Getting Around	378
Communications & Information	379
Touring & Sightseeing	380
Adventures	385
Eco-Travel	392
Where To Stay	393
Where To Eat	396
Spanish Phrases	399
Bibliography	409
Index	413

MAPS

The Caribbean	viii
Puerto Rico	2
San Juan Metro Area	72
Old San Juan	83
Condado	92
The North Coast	132
The West Coast	164
Rincón	172
Rincón Surf Beaches	193
Isla Mona	199
The South Coast	217
Ponce	227
Guanica Trails	239
The Central Mountains	268
Toro Negro Hiking Trails	283
The East Coast	298
El Yunque	328
El Yunque Hiking Trails	332
Vieques	356
Isabel Segunda	355
Esperanza	357
Culebra	372
Dewey	381

ACKNOWLEDGMENTS

The level of detail in this book would have been nearly impossible to achieve without the help of countless residents of Puerto Rico who took interest in our work, shared their knowledge and help and became our friends as we explored the island. We would especially like to single out a few people for thanks: Shane Dennis, for his unceasing hospitality; Yvonne Torres and Annette Blasini, who shared, among other things, their unique views on island life; Alexandra Encarnación; Tom Darby; Hilda Quiñones; Mark and Lenora Turney; Bill and T. Conner; Omar Torres; Steve-o and Lenny, who provided many insights and good times between the rigors of research; Roberto Bonilla, for his knowledge of Taino lore; Amanda Robles, for her expertise on island cuisine and restaurants; Oscar and Sylvia Blasini, for their helpful tips; Rebecca Toser for her priceless insight into Puerto Rican slang; and Richard Druitt, a valuable resource for all sorts of adventure. A big shout out and many thanks to the boys at Taino Divers – Carson, Jari, Bundy and Matt – for teaching us the underwater magic of scuba and other adventures in floating and submersion. We would also like to thank Ada Santos and Ana Marie Fournier at the Puerto Rico Tourism Company and Carlos Weber Lopez and Debbie Molina Ramos at the San Juan Dept. of Tourism for their professional advice and help.

ABOUT THE AUTHORS

Tara Stevens' nearly insatiable appetite for travel began at age 17, when she took up residence in a tent on the Pembrokeshire coastal path of her native Wales. Among other adventures, she has hitchhiked through Turkey, ridden buses from India to Nepal, navigated the Río Magdalena in northern Colombia and played poker with the elderly women who live in the Peruvian sand dunes of Huacachina. In Ecuador, she worked as travel editor on the Quito-based publication *Q*. She has served as sub-editor for the Copenhagen-based design magazine *CPH Living*, contributes regularly to *PR Week* in London, and consults for several global brands in Denmark.

Kurt Pitzer has worked as a correspondent for newspapers and magazines such as *The Boston Globe*, *Los Angeles Times*, and *People* for the past decade. He has covered stories ranging in topic from Balkan conflict to city politics. His travels and reporting have taken him on extensive journeys throughout Western, Eastern and Central Europe and the Americas. His adventures include building a bamboo hut and living with the Karen people in the northern Thai mountains, teaching journalism in Elsinore, Denmark, and commercial long-line fishing in the Caribbean, Atlantic and Pacific waters. He lives in Spain.

Caribbean Islands

Introduction

The Land

The main island of Puerto Rico is about 100 miles long and 35 miles wide, roughly the size of Yellowstone Park or the state of Delaware. It's the farthest east of the four major islands that form the **Greater Antilles**, which includes Cuba, Jamaica and Hispaniola (Haiti and Dominican Republic). In terms of geologic time, the Caribbean islands are relatively young. A mere 200 million years ago, as dinosaurs roamed the super-continents, the tectonic plates of North and South America separated, and a rectangular chunk of the east Pacific plate – now known as the Caribbean plate – knotted itself between them. Over the epochs, the Caribbean plate began to shift north, creating pressure zones in the **Puerto Rican Trench**, which, at 28,000 feet, is the deepest spot in the Atlantic Ocean. The result was a series of violent volcanic eruptions depositing heaps of magma and ash over the ocean floor. Puerto Rico emerged from the sea about 135 million years ago. Ensuing tectonic motion folded piles of debris into the mountains of the **Cordillera Central**, which forms about 60% of Puerto Rico's land mass and runs like a spine from the rain forest of El Yunque to the hills of Rincón. Due to heavy rainfall, most of the mountain range is thick with vegetation, including El Yunque, the only rain forest in US territory. At its most dramatic, the Cordillera Central rises sharply into jagged peaks that would exceed Mt. Everest in height, if measured from the ocean floor. From sea level, Puerto Rico's highest peak – **Cerro de Punta** – measures 4,389 feet.

IN THIS CHAPTER
- The Land
- History
- Government
- The Economy
- Climate
- Flora & Fauna
- The People
- Language
- Religion & Spirituality
- Music & Dance
- Arts & Culture
- Food
- Festivals & Events
- Getting Here
- Getting Around
- Where To Stay
- Where To Eat
- Adventures
- Eco-Travel
- Shopping
- Travel Information
- Travel Directory

Northeastern Puerto Rico is known as **karst country**, characterized by weird limestone formations and the thick, electric-green carpet of vegetation that covers them. Over the millions of years since Puerto Rico rose from the sea, rainwater has eroded the limestone rock into beehive-shaped *mogotes*, twisting caves, sinkholes, canyons and valleys. Occupying 617 square miles of karst country, the **Río Camuy Cave Park** is one of the largest networks of subterranean caverns, tunnels and rivers in the West-

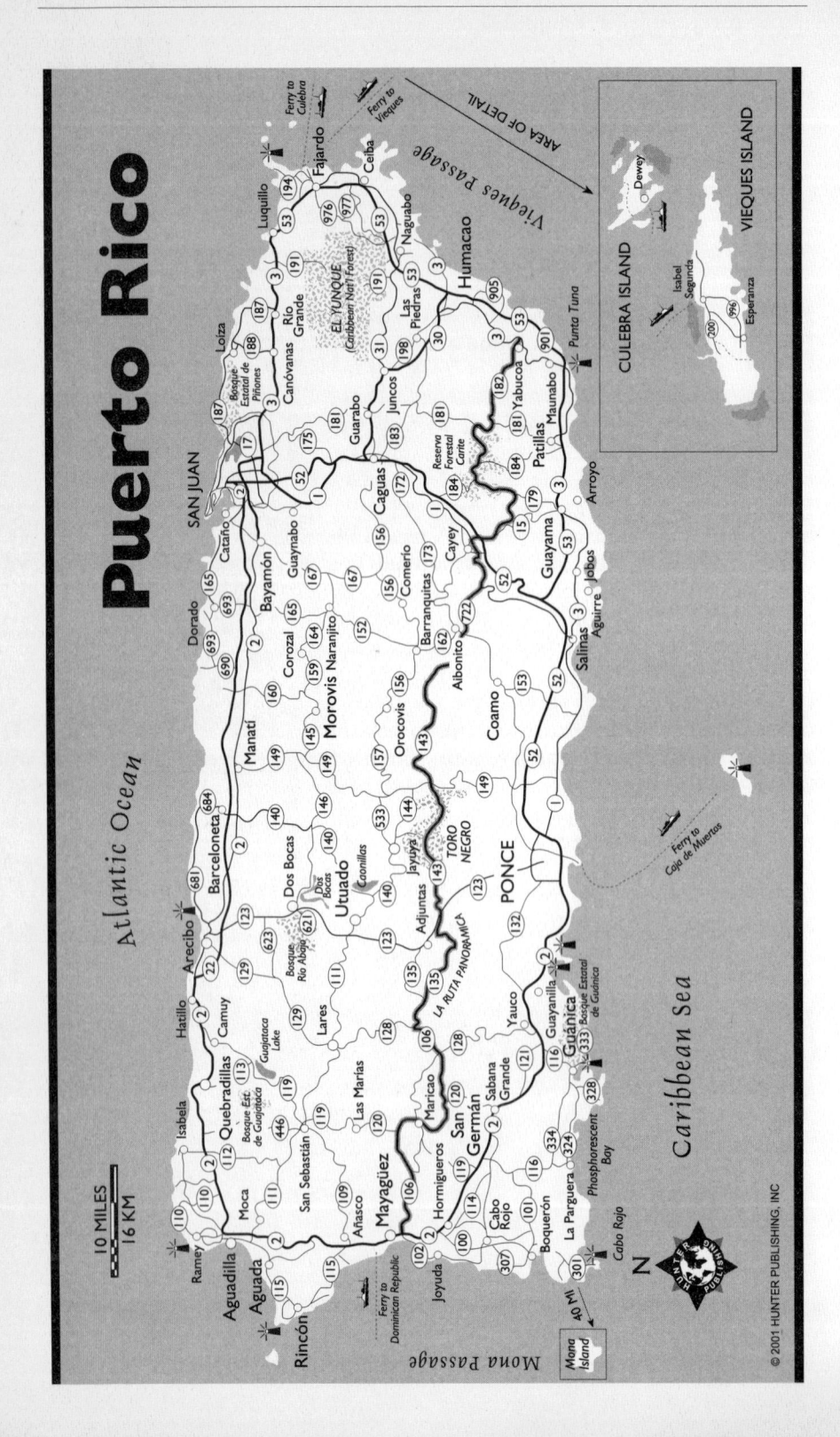

The Land

ern Hemisphere. Much of the cave system remains unexplored. On the south side of the island, the wide, arid **coastal plains** spread from the central mountains to the Caribbean Sea, and give way to an area of dry tropical forest in the southwest, characterized by blackish sands, spiny cacti and other gnarled desert plants. Mangroves and white sand beaches ring the island, and there are a number of rich coral growths. The southwest and southeastern capes rise from the sea in red cliffs. Puerto Rico is often referred to an island (including, for the sake of simplicity, in this book), which is technically inaccurate. It is an **archipelago**. Besides dozens of small cays, Puerto Rico includes four sizeable islands – Culebra and Vieques to the east and Isla Mona and Desecheo to the west.

History

In 1898 – the year the United States wrested Puerto Rico from Spain – American geologist Robert T. Hill observed that most of his fellow citizens knew less about the island "than they do about even Japan or Madagascar." Though this situation has improved somewhat today, many Americans still know shockingly little about the Caribbean commonwealth that is joined at the hip to their country. It's too bad. The history of Puerto Rico – from Taino Eden to Spanish stronghold to potential US state – has helped shape the development of the New World, and reads like a novel. Check out the *Bibliography* at the end of this book for some great works of fiction and non-fiction about the island.

■ Long Before The Conquistadors...

Although human remains recently found on Vieques suggest humans may have been there as long ago as 1700 BC, little is known of the island's first inhabitants. The first identified human visitors to the main island of Puerto Rico were nomadic relatives of Native Americans to the north, known as **Los Arcaicos**, who most likely arrived during the first century on rafts. Apparently, they didn't stick around long enough to leave more than a few stone hatchets and other traces in a cave in the Loíza Aldea area east of San Juan. Two centuries later, an Arawak Indian group known as the **Igneris** showed up in giant canoes from what is now Venezuela. Adept at pottery and fishing, they settled a few coastal areas.

The group that left the most indelible and fascinating mark on the island, however, was the **Tainos**. Migrating north along the West Indies, they landed on Puerto Rico around AD 600, according to archeologists. Also of the Arawak group, they were better at agriculture and crafting tools than their Igneri predecessors and established a rich culture in Puerto Rico and Hispaniola that would last nearly 1,000 years. Most historians agree that the Tainos numbered about 30,000 in Puerto Rico when Christopher

Columbus arrived in 1493. They called the island "Borinquén" – a word still used in various forms to designate the Puerto Rican land and people.

■ The God-Fearing Tainos

The Tainos were a relatively peaceful people who wore few or no clothes, practiced fishing and subsistence farming, and were devoutly spiritual. One of the first Spanish settlers to visit a Taino village described being amazed to see well-constructed houses of wood and straw, with walls of woven cane, surrounding a plaza. The village (empty because the residents apparently fled in terror at the sight of Spanish ships) was filled with gardens, and a well-made road led to the sea, where the natives had constructed a watchtower. This may have been a pleasure retreat for the village chief and his family, a fish-spotting platform or a guard post to warn against attacks by the fearsome Caribs, who at the time were their only enemies.

According to historical accounts written by the Spanish, the 15th century was a bad one for the Tainos. Shattering nearly 800 years of relative tranquility, the Caribs surged north from the Venezualan coast, spread through the Lesser Antilles, plundered Taino settlements and scattered their residents. By the time Columbus arrived, according to European chronicles, the Caribs had begun invading eastern Puerto Rico.

The Tainos were not great warriors, and tended to put their fate in the hands of deities, which they called *cemíes*, as well as a heavenly creator called **Yocahú**, a "good" god named **Yukiyú** and a number of lesser gods. They constantly prayed to fetishes made of wood, stone or seashells, which represented the *cemíes*. They used tobacco for mystical and medicinal purposes. Most were afraid to be alone in the dark of night, when the dead walked around in human form and could be distinguished from the living only by their lack of a navel. Each village was built around a plaza known as the *batey* – which served as ceremonial site, town hall and ballpark – where a soccer-like game between two teams was played as a religious ritual.

SUDDEN-DEATH SOCCER?

It is unknown if the Tainos practiced human sacrifice, offering the losers of their competitions to the gods as the Mayans did. But anthropologists agree that the matches were seen as a forum for the expression of divine will, and that the atmosphere at the games was deadly serious.

In what was probably the first anthropological study of the New World, a Catalonian friar named **Ramón Pané** lived with the Taino people for several years to study their customs and beliefs in order to begin converting them to Christianity. His report on Indian mythology, written in 1505, includes an uncanny prophecy. Sometime during the early 15th century, a great chief named Cazivaquel fasted for a week in order to communicate with the gods. When he emerged, he reported that a *cemí* had told him that upon his death, the new chief would rule only a short time, and that a clothed people would arrive and eventually rule the Tainos, killing many of them. The *cemí* also said that the remaining Tainos would die of hunger. At first, the Taino people believed the prophecy referred to the Caribs. But because the Caribs only plundered, they told Fr. Ramón, perhaps it instead referred to Admiral Columbus and his men.

■ The Spaniards Arrive

After first discovering the "Indies" in 1492, Christopher Columbus was named "Admiral of the Ocean Sea" by Spanish King Ferdinand and Queen Isabella and outfitted with 17 ships for a second voyage. He set sail on September 25, 1493 from Cádiz in southwestern Spain, with more than 1,200 sailors, soldiers and settlers eager for gold and riches in the unknown lands. After about two months spent crossing the Atlantic and island-hopping along the Lesser Antilles, the Spanish fleet moored in a bay off western Puerto Rico on November 19. It is unclear exactly where Columbus and his men (and they were all men) set foot the next morning. Several towns claim the honor, but it was probably a beach at either Boquerón or south of Aguadilla. They stayed just long enough to replenish their drinking water, take a quick peek around and name the island **San Juan Bautista** (John the Baptist, a favorite saint of Columbus'), before moving on to the neighboring island of Hispaniola, which would become the seat of Spanish colonial government for centuries to come.

Puerto Rico was practically ignored for 15 years after its discovery, until a lieutenant of Columbus named **Juan Ponce de León**, frustrated by poverty in Hispaniola, was granted permission to found the first European settlement in Puerto Rico. Why he chose an inhospitable swampy area in Guaynabo, which he called **Caparra**, is anyone's guess. Life for the first settlers was hellish. Beset by mosquitoes and food shortages, they tried unsuccessfully at first to convince Taino natives to grow food and mine gold for them. An edict from Queen Isabella ordered colonists to force Indians into labor, without enslaving them or resorting to cruelty. This was impossible, of course. As the number of colonists grew, however, so did the need for Indian labor and the level of brutality used against them. For several years, the Tainos grew increasingly unhappy with the god-like, clothed invaders, who beat or killed them if they resisted work and stole their women to serve as mistresses and wives. But by the time they realized that the Spaniards were mortal, it was too late. A few Taino chiefs banded together with a small group of Caribs and rose up against the Spanish in 1511, but were crushed by the better-armed adversaries during several battles. According to at least one historical account, Ponce de León, Puerto Rico's first governor, ordered his men to shoot 6,000 Indian survivors of the confrontation. Most Indians who were not killed or captured fled to remote mountain areas or nearby islands. This produced a new labor shortage, and in 1513 the local government began to import African slaves to do the backbreaking labor necessary to establish the colony. For protection from future attacks, the settlement of Caparra was moved to a peninsula in the San Juan bay (now Old San Juan), which they called Puerto Rico (meaning "rich port").

> **DID YOU KNOW?** *The island of Puerto Rico was originally called San Juan, and the city of San Juan was called Puerto Rico. A confused Spanish mapmaker switched them by mistake in 1521, and the names stuck.*

■ The Age of Piracy

Spanish courts granted jurisdiction over all the lands discovered by Columbus to his son Diego, and a demoted Ponce de León left the island in 1513 for what is now Florida, in search of the mythical **Fountain of Youth**. He never found it, of course, and died in relative obscurity in Cuba some years later. But the island he first settled began to take on its own identity in his absence. Because nearly all settlers were men, they mixed freely with Taino women and (in later generations) the daughters of Yoruba and Mandingo slaves. Their children were of mixed ancestry, and were called *criollos*. Today, more than 60% of Puerto Ricans have some trace of Taino blood, and many share some African as well as European ancestry.

Although Spain officially controlled all gubernatorial aspects of island life, Puerto Rico never became the cash cow the crown had hoped it would. Sparsely populated and producing only meager amounts of gold, it survived as a producer of sugar, tobacco, coffee and other agricultural goods and as a trade and military center. Colonists strengthened the walls around the San Juan peninsula and constructed a fort called **El Morro**, with formidable rows of cannons and 18-foot-thick ramparts to protect the bay. The storied fort withstood waves of attacks by British and Dutch invaders, due to its awesome firepower and impregnable defenses. San Juan became a stopping-off point and safety deposit box for ships traveling between Spain and its more lucrative colonies in Mexico and Central and South America. This made the waters around Puerto Rico prime turf for pirates. Legendary **buccaneers** and **privateers** such as Henry Morgan and Francis Drake plundered countless Spanish ships around the Mona Passage and surrounding Caribbean waters, throwing trade into disarray and prompting the Spanish government to invest even more money into fortifying the San Juan bay. Away from San Juan and the eye of the throne, however, the rest of Puerto Rico developed as a rogue, if indolent, nation. Most settlements around the island were small, with residents living a hand-to-mouth lifestyle that one Spanish visitor described as "undisciplined." Due to unreasonable trade restrictions by the desperate Spanish government, Puerto Ricans turned to smuggling and illegal trade, and the lively contraband industry brought wealth to residents of far-flung island outposts such as Ponce, Cabo Rojo and Fajardo. Eventually, to avoid heavy taxation from the mother country, even residents and government officials in San Juan became *contrabandistas*. By the 18th century, practically no revenues flowed from Puerto Rico to Spain.

■ The Spanish Hold Slips Away

Her glory faded, Spain faced increasingly daunting problems at home during the 18th and 19th centuries, such as de facto rule over the country by France and costly wars fought on the French behalf. In a bid to gain at least some revenues from Puerto Rico, the Spanish crown loosened restrictions on the island's economy in the mid-1760s. Immigrants rushed to take advantage of the new economic freedom, and the island's population tripled to 150,000 within three decades. Whereas roads, schools and a coherent economy had been almost nonexistent before, the island began to pick itself up by the bootstraps as waves of new arrivals breathed new life into San Juan and the sleepy, far-flung settlements. In 1805, when British Admiral Nelson destroyed the Spanish fleet at the Battle of Trafalgar – effectively shutting down most of Spain's trade with the Americas – the Colonial hold on the island slipped to mere military and administrative capacities. In the rest of the Americas, it slipped even further. Revolutions toppled Colonial governments from Argentina to Mexico, and by the middle of the 1820s the once-glorious Spanish empire in the Americas had dwindled to two Caribbean islands – Cuba and Puerto Rico.

■ The Hammock Swingers

A few things seemed to happen all at once. Spanish purchase of Puerto Rican goods nearly ground to a halt. The United States, newly free of English rule, had money to spend. And a slave uprising in western Hispaniola (now Haiti) threw that island's lucrative sugar and rum industry into disarray and caused many plantation owners to flee to Puerto Rico. During the 19th century, the Puerto Rican economy began, slowly, to bloom, thanks in large part to growing trade with the United States, especially in sugar, tobacco and coffee. Immigrants poured in from other Caribbean islands and former Spanish colonies, and the agricultural production depended less on slavery (though the practice did exist in its most despicable form, and wasn't abolished until 1872) than on the labor of free men from across the racial spectrum. An 1830 Spanish census put the island population at roughly 325,000, with 34,000 slaves and 127,000 "free people of (all types of) color." Most of the island countryside was populated by peasants, who worked on plantations or on small farm plots around their homes. These peasants, who lived meagerly but in relative comfort, became known as ***jíbaros***. Col. George Dawson Flinter, a Spanish commander who fled to the island from Venezuela after independence, described them as follows: "They swing themselves to and fro in their hammocks all day long, smoking their cigars, and scraping a guitar."

Regardless of the accuracy of Flinter's remark, and whether or not island intellectuals of the time would have agreed, *jíbaro* peasants became the backbone of something new and growing in Puerto Rico – a sense of a national identity. With US dollars flowing in, population exploded to nearly a million people by the end of the century, and a new class of educated Puerto Ricans began to feel it was time to throw off the yoke of Spanish rule.

> **ABOUT JIBAROS:** *"Like the peasantry of Ireland, they are proverbial for their hospitality: and, like them, they are ever ready to fight on the slightest provocation."* – Col. George Dawson Flinter, describing *jíbaros*.

■ Rumblings of Independence

Desperate to maintain its last vestiges of colonial power, Spain installed a series of harsh governors loyal to the crown in Puerto Rico during the mid-1800s. They stripped islanders of many liberties and, at one point, even sought to subdue an increasingly restless populace by promoting gambling and drink. Aided by loyalist exiles from lost Spanish colonies, they were able to thwart potential revolutionary plots before they got going. As early as 1838, the colonial government executed and forced into exile leaders of an independence movement led by **Buenaventura Quiñones** – the island's first *independentista* hero. Fifteen years later, a doctor from Cabo Rojo named **Ramón Emeterio Betances** formed a secret society dedicated to the abolition of slavery, social reform and independence for the island. The government eventually forced him to flee to New York, where he and others joined forces with Cuban independence leaders in exile.

EL GRITO DE LARES
(The Cry of Lares)

In 1868, Ramón Emeterio Betances traveled to Santo Domingo to purchase weapons and supplies for a Puerto Rican uprising, but was delayed in reaching the island. Unable to contain themselves, between 600 and 1,000 Creoles from western Puerto Rico took over the town of Lares with what arms they had, and proclaimed an independent state. By the next afternoon, however, the poorly organized rebels were routed by militias and regular troops. The government quickly rounded up the insurgents (eight were killed and 20 escaped), who were jailed for only four months before being granted amnesty by a more liberal government in Spain.

■ US Certainty

During the second half of the 19th century, the United States increasingly saw Puerto Rico as more than a sugar and rum shop. The spirit of Manifest Destiny, which led the westward expansion of the country, reached a fevered pitch. US generals also worried about British takeover of a number of small islands in the Lesser Antilles. Washington, they argued, needed a foothold in the Caribbean. Tabloid newspapers openly supported the Cuban independence cause and printed graphic stories of atrocities committed by Spain. After Cuban poet and patriot José Martí sparked a revolution on his island in 1895, the stage was set for the US to intervene. Perhaps anticipating the inevitable, Spain granted autonomy to Puerto Rico and Cuba in 1897, hoping to stave off the push for full independence. It was too late. US naval forces blocked Spanish access to Cuba, and after the US battleship *Maine* mysteriously exploded and sank in the Havana Harbor in February 1898, Congress approved a resolution calling for the immediate departure of all Spanish forces from Cuba. Spain declared war. It was a short and lopsided contest that forever changed the history of both Puerto Rico and the United States. The Spanish soon surrendered Cuba and on July 25, 1898, exactly three months after the war began, US forces invaded the south shore of Puerto Rico, quickly ensuring control over the island and preempting a celebration of independence upon Spanish withdrawal there. Whereas the Cubans deserved independence, many Americans felt, Puerto Rico had not waged civil war against the Spanish and was therefore fair game. A July 11, 1898, article on the editorial page of *The New York Times* put it bluntly: "We are not pledged to give Puerto Rico independence, and she will have done nothing to entitle her to it at our hands."

THE PUERTO RICAN FLAG

Notice that the Puerto Rican flag is the exact same design as the Cuban flag, only with inverted colors (the flag of Puerto Rico has a blue triangle and red and white stripes, while the Cuban flag has a red triangle and blue and white stripes). Perhaps prophetically, pro-independence Cubans had inverted the colors from the scheme of the United States flag, and the less unanimously independence-minded Puerto Rican exiles re-inverted them. Originally, the shade of blue in the Puerto Rican flag matched that of the Cuban stripes. After the Marxist revolution in Cuba, however, the United States forced Puerto Rico to adopt the deeper shade used in the Stars and Stripes.

■ The US Gets Involved

Misgivings about US intentions before the Spanish-American War had prompted Puerto Rican emissaries to ask President McKinley for self-determination in case of Spanish withdrawal (he ignored the request). But things were changing too quickly for inexperienced and fragmented local leaders to keep up. Despite the fears of some educated islanders that they might end up trading one colonial ruler for another, most Puerto Ricans simply welcomed US troops in a state of euphoria at the end of 400 years of Spanish sovereignty. The US promised "justice and humanity," as well as wealth, according to a proclamation by the US major who led the invasion. Perhaps naively, there was a general feeling of surprise when the United States set up a military government on the island and began giving orders in the English language. Since then, US influence in Puerto Rico has often been seen as a double-edged sword. Although the *americanos* immediately began to improve schools, roads and sanitary conditions, and in 1900 set up a civilian government, they exerted de facto control of all important decisions about the island's future. The US granted citizenship to all Puerto Ricans just before World War I (partly under pressure from locals and partly to recruit soldiers for the war effort). The island's economy became wholly dependant on the fortunes of the US mother ship, and when the Depression struck, it hit Puerto Rico with whiplash force. In 1933, unemployment hit 65%. Increasingly, Puerto Ricans called for change and a reconsideration of its status – whether independence, autonomy or statehood. Demonstrations culminated on Palm Sunday in 1937, when hundreds of nationalists marched in Ponce. In a confrontation with police, 19 demonstrators were killed in what became known as the **Ponce Massacre**.

■ Political Independence

In 1947, the United States for the first time granted Puerto Ricans the right to elect their own governor. The hands-down winner was Luis Muñoz Marín, son of a former political leader and champion of the *jíbaro* peasantry. An advocate of practical change and improving living standards rather than quibbling over the island's political status, he gained the confidence of both a majority of Puerto Ricans and the US government. The island was granted a constitutional government the following year, and in 1951 residents overwhelmingly voted to become a commonwealth of the United States, a.k.a. a "free associated state" (see *Government*, page 11). Supporters of independence became increasingly marginalized and militant and, during the 1950s, nationalist radicals attacked the governor's mansion in San Juan, attempted to assassinate President Harry Truman in Washington DC and opened fire on the US House of Representatives, injuring four statesmen. The majority of Puerto Ricans, however, seemed to agree with the adage, "Better the devil you know… " – especially if he has deep pockets.

■ The Neo-Rican Explosion

When the US economy boomed during the 1950s, hundreds of thousands of Puerto Ricans took advantage of their citizenship and sought better jobs in the United States. Most settled in cities like Chicago, Miami and, especially, New York. By 1960, more than a million Puerto Rico lived on the US mainland. In New York, Spanish Harlem became a potent if entirely inaccurate symbol of Puerto Rico among an American populace that had never paid much attention to the island commonwealth but loved the musical *West Side Story*. Back home, Puerto Ricans living in New York were called *neoriqueños* and – fairly or not – were often derided for losing their *boricua* identity and giving their relatives in the Caribbean a bad name. Such derision may have been a reflexive impulse. While *americanos* may not have gained a true picture of the island through closer association with it, Puerto Ricans have during the past four decades increasingly understood and, more importantly, assimilated US culture.

Government

Of all the US territories and possessions outside the 50 states, only two – Puerto Rico and the Northern Marianas (islands just north of Guam) – are **commonwealths**. In general, commonwealths have their own constitutions and enjoy greater autonomy than the unincorporated territories (a.k.a. possessions) of the US Virgin Islands, American Samoa and Guam. Of those, Puerto Rico is by far the most populous and politically important.

As a "self-governing commonwealth in association with the United States," the government of Puerto Rico in many ways resembles that of a US state. With its own governor and two legislative chambers (House of Representatives and Senate), it controls all internal affairs, except those that fall under United States federal jurisdiction. These include citizenship, currency, highways, the postal system, Social Security, communications, agriculture, mineral resources and all things military. The major differences between Puerto Rico and an actual US state are its exemption from federal tax codes (the island has its own taxation system) and the lack of real representation in the US Congress, where Puerto Rico has one non-voting member. Puerto Ricans cannot vote in US presidential elections, and the island is denied some federal revenues given to states. Men over 18 are eligible for conscription into military service (many Puerto Ricans served in Vietnam and other wars). On the other hand, as US citizens, Puerto Ricans pay and receive Social Security, and poverty-stricken adults can receive federal welfare. The judicial system, too, somewhat resembles that of a US state, with a combination of local and federal courts that hear civil and criminal cases, according to jurisdiction. But although penal, procedural and public law is based on the US model, civil and commercial codes more resemble their Spanish counterparts.

> **DID YOU KNOW?** *Puerto Rico has its own Olympic team and competes as an independent nation in the Miss Universe pageant.*

Unlike US states, Puerto Rico is divided into **municipalities**, rather than counties, with the mayor and municipal assembly of each controlling planning and other local issues. Elections are held every four years – and are a spectacle to behold. Instead of televised debates and sound-bite advertisements, campaigning takes the form of traffic-snarling caravans and street-side rallies. Partisans with flags encourage motorists to honk their horns in support of their candidate. Pickup trucks overburdened with speaker blocks blitz residential neighborhoods, blaring slogans and patriotic salsa music, and voters are wooed with free chicken at public barbecues. Puerto Rican democracy has street party flair.

■ Politics & the Status Issue

Puerto Ricans often say that politics, not baseball, is their national sport. For proof of this, note that the island has one of the highest levels of voter participation in the world – more than 80% in recent general elections. Especially around election time, you may witness tempers flaring as ordinary folk spontaneously debate each other in the streets, cafés and bars. A few eateries around the island post signs asking their patrons to refrain from talking politics, just to keep the peace. Much of the brouhaha centers on the island's status vis-à-vis the United States. There is no greater political issue in Puerto Rico, and it is an extremely sensitive subject. Visiting *americanos* are often asked their opinion on the issue, and if you can offer a thoughtful, respectful response – along with a few informed questions – you may be rewarded with an intriguing discussion. Or you may be harangued with propaganda anyway.

Of the three major political parties, the **Popular Democratic Party** (PPD) supports maintaining autonomy without independence from the US; the **New Progressive Party** (PNP) supports full US statehood for Puerto Rico; and the **Puerto Rican Independence Party** (PIP) aims to make the island an independent state. In general, Puerto Ricans are intensely proud of their culture and its differences from that of the United States, and many are at least sentimentally independence-minded. But the ballot box is a reality check. Although the island is emotionally tied to its Latino heritage, the economy is so dependent on the United States that the majority of voters don't consider independence a real option, and the PIP has never been able to claim more than 5% of the electorate. After pro-commonwealth forces dominated Puerto Rican politics, the pro-statehood PNP won the two elections at the end of the 20th century and sponsored plebiscites on the status issue. Narrowly, the status quo was upheld. Then in 2000, partly due to controversy over the Navy's continued bombing of Vieques (see Vieques & Culebra), former San Juan Mayor Sila Calderon and her PDP allies won a landslide victory, to control the governorship and the legislature.

WILL PUERTO RICO BECOME THE 51st STATE?

If Puerto Ricans vote to join the United States, with full rights and responsibilities of a state, the matter of statehood would then pass to the US Congress.

The Economy

To oversimplify the 500-year development of the Puerto Rican economy, it has gone from sugar to rum, from rum to women's underwear and from women's underwear to Valium. Sounds like fun! But although Puerto Rico has become one of the best economies in the Caribbean, and things are still improving, it remains economically worse off than the poorest US state, Mississippi. Agriculture dominated the local livelihood from the time Spanish settlers failed to find gold until the Depression this century. A bright spot centered around the rum industry, which helped build the southern city of Ponce. During the 1930s, the Puerto Rican government invested heavily in further promoting rum trade, and the island quickly became the world's largest producer of the spirit. Today, 77% of rum sold in the United States comes from Puerto Rico.

In the 1940s, the government developed an economic plan called Operation Bootstrap – an attempt to join the industrial revolution by luring manufacturing capital with tax incentives and duty-free access to the US market. Off-island (mostly US) companies built plants to manufacture clothing, tobacco, processed food and leather, shifting jobs away from sugar plantations and coffee *fincas* (plantations). Today, Puerto Rico imports more than two-thirds of its food. Agriculture has shrunk to 1% of the Gross Domestic Product and – although the focus has shifted – manufacturing of items such as canned tuna and lingerie still plays a large part in the economy. More recently, as wages have begun to catch up to industrialized standards, the government has sought to bring to Puerto Rico more capital-intensive industries, such as **high-tech** and **pharmaceuticals** (again with tax incentives approved by the US Congress). Hewlett-Packard, for example, now operates a massive facility in Aguadilla. The Roche Products plant in Manatí produces the entire US supply of Valium, as well as Librium and other tranquilizers. In fact, local manufacturing is so strongly linked to the US market that about 90% of Puerto Rican exports are sent north to the States.

> **DID YOU KNOW?** *Although Puerto Rico's minimum wage is tied to that of the United States, average incomes are well below US averages. The average hourly wage in 1999 was $8.08, with a Gross Domestic Product per capita of $9,800. Unemployment dipped to about 10% in 1999 – the lowest level in years. However, to stay above the poverty line, roughly half of Puerto Ricans receive food stamps, according to recent figures.*

Climate

The weather is gorgeous almost every day of the year, with average temperatures of around 82° Fahrenheit, Trade winds keep the local humidity to a minimum. Like many of their Caribbean neighbors, Puerto Ricans routinely wake up and regard the sparkling sun and the tropical sea with a yawn and the adage, "Just another day in paradise." However, there are actual seasons on the island – the wet season (June through October) and a dry season (November through May), which are most evident in the mountainous and western areas. In general, the South Coast is driest. The East Coast is also predictably dry most days year-round. But you can get rained on any time of the year in the mountains. The lowest temperature ever recorded in Puerto Rico was 42° Fahrenheit, measured near Aibonito in 1911. The west tends to get more downpours during the wet season, when you can bank on a couple hours of heavy rain each afternoon. Otherwise, it's also blessed with glorious sunshine.

As in the rest of the Caribbean, the meteorological celebrity known as the hurricane puts Puerto Rican property owners on edge from mid-June until mid-November. Hurricanes form in the doldrums, a narrow equatorial belt of the Atlantic and Caribbean waters, and can move northwest, north or northeast. They often claim islands of the Antilles as their first victims. Tropical storms officially become hurricanes when wind velocity exceeds 74 mph, and are categorized by strength from one to five. A category five hurricane has wind velocities of more than 155 mph, and generally rips apart anything in its path. Hurricane Hugo caused severe damage to Puerto Rico in 1989, and parts of the island have yet to recover from destruction wreaked by Hurricane Georges in 1998.

> **DID YOU KNOW?** The word "hurricane" comes from the Taino deity Jurikan, the god of destructive winds.

Flora & Fauna

Puerto Rico is a nature-lover's dream, with thousands of acres of parkland and natural reserves. Simply getting off the highway and onto a winding mountain road will provide an unexpected feast for the eyes. Walk the cactus paths of the dry tropical forest, home to more than 700 species of birds, or lose yourself in the eerie cloud forest of Toro Negro or the rain forest of El Yunque. Kayak through mangroves in search of the elusive manatee, or plunge into the underwater world of coral gardens and sea creatures. With so much natural diversity on one rock, you're not likely to get bored. Here's an overview of what you can see.

■ Plant Life

Wet Forests

Puerto Rico was almost entirely clad in a thick, verdant forest 500 years ago. Settlement, agriculture and industry felled most of it, and although reforestation efforts since the 1970s have restored about 40% of tree cover to the island, only 1% of virgin forest remains (most of it in El Yunque). The wet forests are categorized into distinct zones, and all are crawling with rich vegetation and animal life. At its highest elevation the dwarf, or cloud, forest is usually bathed in mist, with gnarled trees stunted by the strong winds. Below this is rain forest with palm and hardwood trees tangled in ferns and vines. The only officially designated rain forest is El Yunque, although you will notice many of the same species throughout the mountainous interior. At lower elevations, subtropical wet forest, lower wet forest and subtropical moist forest climates cover most of Puerto Rico.

Tropical Dry Forests

Found mainly on the South Coast and on offshore cays and islands, Puerto Rico has some of the finest examples of tropical dry forest in the world. With rainfall as little as 20 inches a year, these areas are characterized by a tangle of leathery trees and dusty vegetation, tall cactus spears and desert blooms. It's a rare and complex ecosystem. The 1,640-acre **UN Biosphere Reserve at Guánica** has more than 700 species of plants (48 endangered and 16 endemic), and attracts botanists, ornithologists and nature-lovers from all corners of the globe. With impenetrable nesting cover, more than half the bird species in Puerto Rico are found in the island's dry forests, which crawl with land crabs, toads, lizards and about 1,000 species of insect.

> **RECOMMENDED READING:** *Herbert Raffaele's illustrated* **Guide to the Birds of Puerto Rico and the Virgin Islands** *is a valuable resource.*

Mangroves

Mangroves are a diverse group of salt-tolerant shrubs that grow along coastal tropical and sub-tropical zones, forming numerous narrow canals and channels that create a protective barrier against tropical wind and waves. Tangled knots of red, black, white and buttonwood mangroves snake their way across 22,971 acres of Puerto Rican coast, sheltering numerous migratory birds, shallow-water amphibians and fish. They are perfect spawning grounds for many species, and during hurricanes islanders stash their boats in the protective network of narrow mangrove canals and channels. Marine, animal and bird species ride out storms there, too, and ecologically mangroves are an essential barrier protecting the land mass from erosion. Despite the importance of mangrove estuaries, however, they often fall victim to developers in constant search of new coastal property to urbanize. The largest mangrove system on the island is in **Piñones**, just east of San Juan, and some of the prettiest and most user-friendly are on the south coast at the **Parguera** and **Aguirre reserves**. All are perfect for exploration by kayak.

Trees

More than 700 tree species take root in Puerto Rico, of which about 550 are indigenous to the island. El Yunque is, of course, a star attraction, with giant tree ferns and palms interwoven with the vermilion blooms of African violets and rainbow colors of orchids. On lower trails, **cecropia** trees form tunnels under a canopy of silvery-bottomed leaves. This is one of the fastest-growing species in the forest, quickly filling bald patches left behind by tropical storms and hurricanes. The majestic **tabonuco** flourishes on the "big tree trail" of El Yunque and is distinguished by the sticky, pungent white sap that oozes from its bark. Around the island, you are bound to come across the giant **ceiba** tree, which grows to hundreds of years in age and is characterized by elephantine roots that surround its base like a pile of distended legs. Another ancient is the extremely rare **guayacán**, which has wood so dense that it sinks in water; in the past its wood was used as currency. Its extract, guayacol, was once considered an effective remedy for cholera. Another tree recognized for its healing properties is the **campeche**, whose sap contains the active ingredient haematoxylin, used in treating dysentery.

A wide variety of fruit-bearing trees flourishes on the island, including the **papaya**, **breadfruit** and **plantain**. Between coconut palms along the beaches, you'll often see **almond** trees. The national tree of Puerto Rico, however, is the stunning **flamboyán**. The most common is the red-flowered variety, which can be found island-wide. When it drops its petals during summer months, whole stretches of highway become carpeted in flaming petals. Flamboyán trees with yellow or blue blossoms are more rare, and have a shorter flowering season.

> **DID YOU KNOW?** *Puerto Ricans say that when there are many avocados on the trees, the island will be safe from destructive hurricanes for another year.*

Fruit

Puerto Rico has an abundance of fruit and vegetables – some easily recognizable, others strange and unfamiliar. Depending on the time of year you visit there will always be something in season, often being sold for a pittance on the roadside. In May, **grapefruit** season is followed by the ripening of **mangos**, which pile up in great yellow heaps along the roadsides from June to the end of August. Larger, purple-tinged mangos ripen later and are less stringy than their smaller yellow cousins. **Avocados** come into season in late August, as do **breadfruit** – introduced to the island as cheap food for slave workers. The breadfruit tree has broad leaves yielding large, knobby, green fruit, which is used like plantain or potatoes in cooking. In summertime, fruit sellers line the roads with bunches of **quenepas**. Crack the hard green outer shell with your teeth to get to the slimy, ivory-colored flesh (it tends to stick to the roof of your mouth, and is an acquired taste). Quenepas are curiously addictive, however. Another common snack is the *uva caleta*, or sea grape, named for its purple skin and mildly sweet white flesh. **Plantains** are the staple fruit of the Puerto Rican diet (fried or baked), but look for the tiny banana known as the *manzano* – the sweetest variety on the island. Coconut palms and almond trees are both laden with fruit for several months beginning in late September.

■ Animal Life

Mammals

The only land-based mammal indigenous to Puerto Rico is the bat. These insect-devouring night flyers live in massive colonies in the caves of Isla Mona and the Camuy area, and outnumber humans on the island. Puerto Rico has 13 species of bats, nearly half of which are found only in the Greater Antilles: seven are insectivores, four eat fruit and one species feeds only on nectar. The **Mexican bulldog bat** (a.k.a. the fishing bat) hunts fish. Most live in the caves of the karst country (see *North Coast*, page 143), and have been given descriptive names. In the Cucaracha Cave near Aguadilla, the dominant **Jamaican long-tongued bat** lives alongside the **sooty-moustached bat** and the **Antillean ghost-faced bat**. In this cave alone, there are over 700,000 bats, and their nighttime feeding frenzy extends five miles around the cave entrance and makes for some spectacular wildlife watching (catch them at dusk). Although their main natural predator is the Puerto Rican boa, the biggest threat to the bats' survival is human encroachment. Several non-profit groups are dedicated to the protection of natural bat habitat, including **Ciudadanos del Karso**, which lobbies to conserve Puerto Rican "bat country."

All other mammal species have been introduced to Puerto Rico by human settlers, including **pigs**, **cows**, **goats** and **horses** brought by the Spanish, **mongooses** imported to control rat and snake populations (the rats were brought unintentionally, of course) and **rhesus monkeys** placed on the off-limits-to-public cays of Desecheo and Cayo Santiago for scientific experiments. Some of the species have flourished and gone wild. Pigs, for example, have run rampant on Isla Mona to an extent that hunting for them is permitted seasonally to keep their numbers down. Mongooses have thrived and now represent a nuisance to farmers.

Reptiles & Amphibians

It's often written that there are no snakes on Puerto Rico, but there are. The chance of seeing one is extremely unlikely, but not impossible. The island is home to the rare and endangered **Puerto Rican boa** and to the **Puerto Rican racer** – both found in El Yunque. **Green iguanas**, which are occasionally spotted in the Fajardo area and surrounding cays, can grow to four or more feet in length. Even more impressive in size is the **Mona iguana** (a species found only on Isla Mona). It lazes sluggishly on the beach until it is disturbed, when it can reach gazelle-like speeds. Stranger still is the **caiman**. These alligator relatives were brought to Puerto Rico as pets during the 1970s. They snapped at the fingers and toes of their owners until they were turned loose into Puerto Rico's biggest freshwater lagoon, Laguna Tortuguero. Here they have flourished and found their way onto the menus of a few local eateries. If you see one, don't try to pet it.

At the other end of the spectrum, the **coquí** is without a doubt Puerto Rico's most treasured critter. This frog, measuring just over an inch long and rarely glimpsed by the human eye, makes its presence known by a constant and enigmatic song – "koh-KEY, koh-KEY" – especially at night or after a rain shower. Island forests have as many as 10,000 coquís per acre – the highest frog population measured anywhere in the world – and you'll hear their endearing song throughout wetter parts of the island. There are well over a dozen varieties of coquí, most of which are found only in Puerto Rico.

AMPHIBIAN AEROBATICS

Forest-dwelling coquís spend the night primarily in the upper canopy, dive-bombing as far as 45 feet to the forest floor when daytime winds dry their skin. Here they are protected from breakfasting birds, and absorb moisture from the forest floor through an especially porous area of their skin. At day's end, they return to the upper canopy, where they find refuge from night-feeding tarantulas and other predators.

Insects, Etc.

This being the tropics, bugs reach bigger proportions than their European or North American counterparts. **Cockroaches** the size of linebackers, **spiders** that could cover your face (only slight exaggerations) and other unspeakable horrors lurk in dark corners. **Bees** and **fire ants** tend to be aggressive and territorial. **Mosquitoes** cling and draw blood and the kamikaze tactics of **sand flies** and **no-see-ums** are enough to drive the calmest of people into a murderous frenzy. All of these pests are relatively harmless, however, especially if you liberally apply insect repellent. Cases of malaria and other tropical fevers are as rare here as in the United States, with the exception of a few isolated instances of dengue fever, a debilitating mosquito-borne disease that can keep you in bed for up to a month.

The nastiest critter on the island is undoubtedly the poisonous **centipede**, whose sting is excruciatingly painful and potentially (though seldom) fatal. Don't mistake it for the cute and harmless millipede, which usually measures no more than an inch or two long and which curls into a tight coil if touched. The centipede can grow to ghastly lengths of a foot or more, and is instantly recognizable by its two devilish horns and quickness on its (many) feet. It is a species seldom spared by Puerto Ricans, who kill it by squashing it repeatedly with a large stone or brick, or pinning it down and slicing it to pieces with long-handled kitchen utensils.

On the other hand, the friendly *guaba* **tarantula** is the object of misplaced fear. More friend than foe, it feeds on mosquitoes, flies and other irritating insects. Among the other 15,000 or so insect species on the island, 216 species of **butterflies** and **moths** (a few as large as the palm of your hand) come in a delightfully whimsical array of colors.

Birds

Puerto Rico attracts hundreds of birdwatchers each year because of the sheer abundance of different habitats and the amazing variety (several hundred) of species that live in them. About 130 species reside in the dry forest of Guánica (a hotspot on the international birder's circuit) alone, and El Yunque rain forest is home to 60 others. Some are extremely rare, endemic and in serious danger of extinction (such as the **Puerto Rican parrot**, the national bird, and the **Puerto Rican nightjar**). **Boobies**, **brown pelicans**, **frigate birds** and other marine birds are easily seen in coastal areas. The **red-tailed hawk** coasts on thermals in mountainous areas and a number of species of **todies**, **thrashers**, **warblers** and **whippoorwills** can be spotted with a keen eye (and binoculars). See regional chapters for more specifics.

■ Marine Life

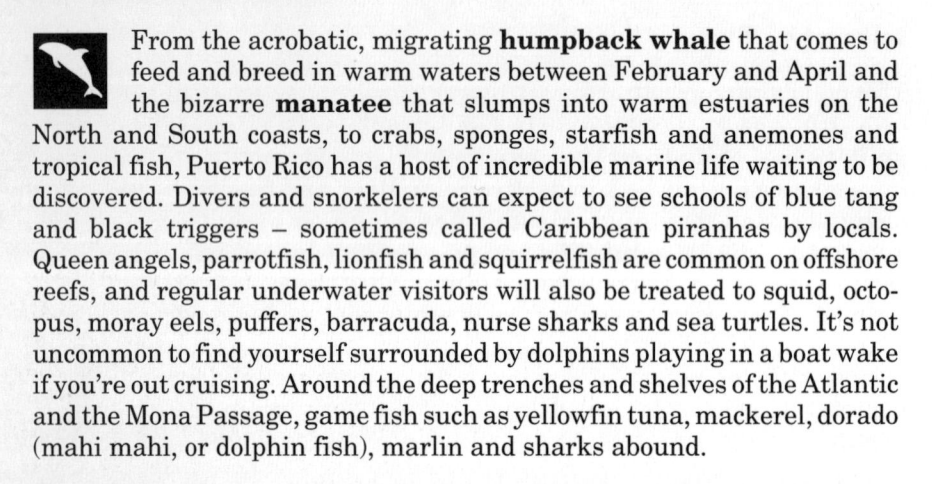

From the acrobatic, migrating **humpback whale** that comes to feed and breed in warm waters between February and April and the bizarre **manatee** that slumps into warm estuaries on the North and South coasts, to crabs, sponges, starfish and anemones and tropical fish, Puerto Rico has a host of incredible marine life waiting to be discovered. Divers and snorkelers can expect to see schools of blue tang and black triggers – sometimes called Caribbean piranhas by locals. Queen angels, parrotfish, lionfish and squirrelfish are common on offshore reefs, and regular underwater visitors will also be treated to squid, octopus, moray eels, puffers, barracuda, nurse sharks and sea turtles. It's not uncommon to find yourself surrounded by dolphins playing in a boat wake if you're out cruising. Around the deep trenches and shelves of the Atlantic and the Mona Passage, game fish such as yellowfin tuna, mackerel, dorado (mahi mahi, or dolphin fish), marlin and sharks abound.

Manatees

It is speculated that the myth of the mermaid came about as sailors of yore brought home tales from the tropics of a strange sea mammal that nursed its young like a human mother. Though no beauty (gray, wrinkled and blubbery, and commonly called the "sea cow"), the manatee shares endearing qualities with other marine mammals, frequently nuzzling each other and forming strong family bonds. Unfortunately, past hunting and present development of coastal areas has severely reduced the numbers of these loveable creatures, and all of the manatee subspecies are in peril of extinction. Shy and bulky (they can grow to 12 feet in length and weigh 1,200 pounds or more), manatees frequent warm, shallow water and feast primarily on sea-grass near freshwater estuaries.

> **TIP:** *If you hope to glimpse a manatee, one of the best places to try is the **Jobos Bay National Estuarine Research Reserve** (see page 253-254), although tracking devices have pinpointed them in spots all around the island.*

Turtles

Increasingly, conservation groups in Puerto Rico are stepping up efforts to protect endangered species, and several offshore cays and the island of Culebra have been designated as refuges for sea turtles. The hawksbill, leatherback, loggerhead, and green sea turtles all visit various Puerto Rican beaches to deposit their eggs. Birds, mongooses, marine predators and human disturbances all contribute to the high mortality rate of turtles hatched on the sands of Puerto Rico and elsewhere – only one in 1,000 or more hatchlings survives. These ancient creatures have changed little since the time of the dinosaurs. One of the most spectacular, the leatherback turtle, which nests on secluded beaches of Piñones, Isla Mona and Culebra, can weigh up to 1,400 pounds. Conservation programs are run by the US Fish & Wildlife Service in Guaynabo, ☎ 787-749-4402, and the Puerto Rico Department of Natural Resources, ☎ 787-724-8774.

Coral Reefs

The coral reef is neither fully plant nor animal nor mineral, but is one of the most important ecosystems on the planet. Think of it as a city, built up of many individuals, which functions as an organism. Coral survives on the photosynthesis of the algae within its tissue, and then returns the favor by exhaling carbon dioxide. Coral reef is found only in shallow waters, where it can receive sunlight, at temperatures above 72° Fahrenheit. The basic organisms of coral are cylindrical creatures called **polyps**, which have small mouth-like openings – the hungry inhabitants of the city. Besides using photosynthesis, coral also feeds on plankton and other minute sea life, by seizing prey between tiny tentacles and then stunning its victim with small poisonous spears called nematocysts. They may look harmless enough, but two-thirds of coral species are toxic and can have a nasty "bite."

> **CAUTION!** *Beware the orange-colored stinging coral, a.k.a.* **fire coral**, *which looks like a small, leafless tree tipped white and crawling with delicate feelers.*

The reproductive methods of coral are also somewhere between plant and animal, and they vary widely depending on the type of coral, of which there are many dozens. Some bud asexually, while others do it sexually with male polyps releasing millions of spermatozoa to fertilize female polyps. Individual polyps may live up to 1,000 years, making them some of the oldest creatures on earth, and their survival depends on maintaining huge numbers in vast colonies. When a polyp dies, it releases limestone, which forms the core structure of a coral reef. New coral polyps affix themselves to the limestone structure, literally building a living space atop a growing burial mound. The ecosystem is precariously delicate, however, and subject to environmental changes such as global warming, water pollution, coastal development, over fishing and destruction by boat anchors and tropical fish hunters. Once the number of live corals on a reef decreases past a critical point, the entire reef system is almost certainly doomed to die. According to the environmental activist group Action Atlas, an estimated 90% of coral reefs around Florida and Jamaica are either dead or dying, largely due to the effects of mass tourism and improperly treated sewage.

WHAT MUST THE NEIGHBORS THINK?

The release of clouds of coral spermatozoa, which can travel thousands of miles, is the only breeding pattern on Earth that can be seen from space.

So far, Puerto Rico has been spared the worst destruction. Next to the Cayman Islands, Puerto Rico has some of the healthiest coral reefs in the Caribbean, particularly on the West and Southwest coasts. Here you can see coral in some of its most delightful forms, many of which resemble familiar land objects. Fields of fan corals have a delicate filigreed skeleton, and grow in purple and turquoise clusters that sway in the current. Vase corals seem only to be missing bouquets of flowers, giant brain corals look like they were seized from a neurosurgeon's operating table, and elkhorn coral appear to have been lifted off the head of a stag. As you dive or snorkel, enjoy these surreal and complex creatures but, to avoid damaging them, don't touch them. As all good dive schools will tell you, when you visit a coral reef system, take only memories, and leave only bubbles.

The People

As is the case with many cultures of the world, once you say something in general about Puerto Ricans an opposing truth is likely to emerge. About four million people live on the island, and nearly two million more Puerto Ricans reside in the United States, leading some to say that there are actually two Puerto Ricos. Like US residents, Puerto Ricans shop at JCPenney and Macy's, eat at fast-food restaurants, and drive their sport utility vehicles to the mall. Yet they take pains to set themselves apart from *americano* culture. Puerto Ricans are laid-back and love nothing more than a party, but an intellectual spirit thrives, education is top priority and politics is a national sport (the island has one of the highest voter turnouts in the world). Puerto Ricans are intensely proud of their island's beauty. A Puerto Rican friend once said, "We suffer from a crisis of identity. That's what happens after 500 years without independence."

A recent "back-to-roots" movement begs the question: How do you define Puerto Rican-ness? The island's people are a mix of many cultures. Centuries ago, Spanish settlers began taking Taino brides. Many of their descendents later intermarried with African slaves. Immigrants from European countries, the United States and Asia trickled in over the years, and waves of political and economic refugees from South America, Cuba and the Dominican Republic have enriched the blend. Under the warm Caribbean sun, the country's cultural ingredients have slowly boiled down into a gumbo of outgoing people who welcome visitors and will bend over backwards to impress and help others.

Family ties are incredibly strong in Puerto Rico, where weekends typically involve animated gatherings with parents and assorted cousins, uncles, aunts and grandparents.

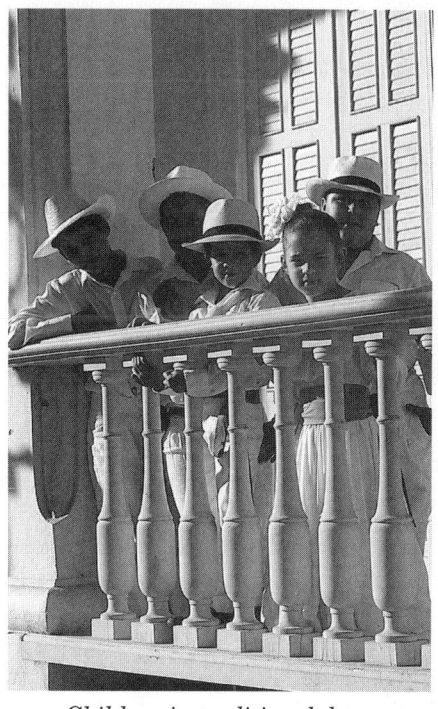

Children in traditional dress at a folkloric festival. (Bob Krist, for the PRTC)

On the other hand, some young people here complain that the family bond also wraps them under a stiflingly protective wing. Puerto Rican parents rarely encourage their children to fly off to exotic places in search of adventure and fortune. They feel it's more important to shelter them. Tellingly, most swimming pools here are constructed without a deep end.

> **DID YOU KNOW?** *A recent newspaper survey found that, despite being surrounded by the sea, only one in five Puerto Ricans could swim.*

Puerto Rican culture retains some of the chivalrous traditions of Old Spain. Men still open doors for women, for example. But feminism is alive and well in Puerto Rico and, economically and culturally, women are gaining power as fast as (and in some cases faster than) their counterparts in the US. Many women own their own businesses and, in the 2000 election, Sila Calderón became the first woman chief executive of the island.

If one must make a sweeping generalization about Puerto Ricans, however, it is that they are an outgoing, exuberant people. They love to dance, make music, show off, and flirt. They like company. At the beach, rather than spreading out in search of a private stretch of sand, they tend to crowd together into a tight knot of humanity, where they can socialize. In conversation, they make shake your hand 10 times in as many minutes. Try an experiment: find a busy sidewalk here and ask someone for directions. Scratch your head and look lost. Soon a crowd will form. Arguments may break out, as even people who have never heard of your destination start to gesture and shout things like, "Just go straight ahead, then turn lef, right, left again, go around a corner, then head left and you can't miss it!" It's as ordinary for Puerto Ricans to help a stranger as to help a friend or family member. If you come to Puerto Rico with an open mind and a generosity of spirit, you will surely meet people who will invite you into their lives, in one way or another. Accept the invitation, if you're so inclined. It's the best way to learn about who Puerto Ricans are.

SIGN LANGUAGE

It's often said that Puerto Ricans love to talk and talk. Yet, charmingly, they have developed some unique sign language for simple expressions, such as the habit of pointing at things with their lips and pressing their fingers to their cheeks to indicate that something is tasty.

Language

Due to their history, Puerto Ricans are possibly the world's most solidly bilingual people, conversing in both Spanish and English. In the San Juan area, you will find that almost everyone speaks English – often with an American accent picked up from years living in the States. Even in outlying areas, a surprising number of people can converse flawlessly in English, and the majority of the rest can manage basic communication with non-Spanish speakers. This means extra work if you come to the island hoping to improve your Spanish. Many Puerto Ricans will answer you in English even if you speak to them in their own language, for a variety of reasons. Some are eager to demonstrate that they can speak English, or to practice their skills. And most Puerto Ricans are simply used to speaking English when addressing gringos (many ex-pats can – and, sadly, have – spent years on the island without learning more of the idiom than, "*Una cerveza, por favor,*" or "*¿Donde está el baño?*"). However, a basic knowledge of Spanish is helpful, especially if you plan to travel to remote areas of La Cordillera, or if you want to experience the culture more broadly. Overall, the more Spanish you speak the more friends you are likely to make. And, importantly, even limited attempts at Spanish can show locals that you care about and respect their culture, and that you don't automatically expect them to speak the language of *los americanos*.

SPANGLISH: IDIOM OF THE FUTURE?

Many Puerto Ricans are so conversant in both Spanish and English that they mix the two languages freely, as many Latinos living in the United States do. They have also "Spanish-ized" many English words, such as *janguear* (to hang out), *chequear* (to check) and *jonrón* (a home run in baseball).

On the street and between friends, many Puerto Ricans tend to clip their pronunciation – generally favoring vowels and diphthongs over consonants, and sometimes dropping the entire beginning or ending of words. This is not done to confuse you, the visitor. It's a tendency brought to the island by early settlers from Andalusia and other poorer regions of Spain, but also influenced by the cadence of Taino and Yoruba languages. If you're standing outside a shop and an employee shouts something that sounds like TA ceh-ROW, they are most likely trying to communicate, *Está cerrado* (It's closed). Also, Puerto Ricans have a slightly irreverent love for their language, and if you stay on the island long enough you'll get acquainted with their colorful, evolving slang (see *Spanish Words & Phrases*, at the end of this book).

Religion

■ Catholicism

Beginning with Columbus' second voyage in 1493, Spanish monarchs began sending priests to the New World to convert "heathen" Amerindians to Roman Catholicism. In 1519, Puerto Rico became the first papal see in the Americas and, for a short time, the New World headquarters for the Spanish Inquisition. But partly due to lack of funding, the Catholic Church in general failed to inspire the islanders, and in the process alienated many by denying them priesthood. Consequently, people took a relatively halfhearted view of it, and in some places characteristics of tribal rituals became woven into the established dogma. When the US gained control of Puerto Rico it separated the church from the state and allowed freedom to worship any faith. Officially, 85% of the population is still Roman Catholic and, although many are deep believers, the practice is generally less fervent than in the more dogmatic churches of Italy or Spain.

■ Evangelical Churches

If you happen to be walking along the street and hear strange whooping and ecstatic singing coming from a corner house, it is probably not a wild teenage party but the worshipful incantations common in more than 1,500 **evangelical churches** that have sprung up in Puerto Rico since the Americans arrived in 1898. Today, 8% of Puerto Ricans are members of Protestant congregations, and 3% practice a different belief system, which includes Jews and Muslims. Fewer than 3% of Puerto Ricans state that they are not religious.

■ Spirituality & the Occult

To a large extent, Puerto Rico is more a spiritual nation than a religious one, with lingering belief in spirits worshipped by Taino and African ancestors – like the Taino spirit *Jupías*, who haunts the dreams of mortals. *Curanderos* or **espiritistas** (healers) are consulted regularly on the subjects of money and marriage, health and happiness, blessings and revenge, to name a few. *Botánicas*, the stores that supply herbs and potions essential to Puerto Rican spiritual rituals, can be found in almost every town. The practice is fairly tame, however. If you're hoping to find bare-breasted women anointing themselves with chicken blood and sticking pins into voodoo effigies, you'll be disappointed. The wildest Puerto Rico gets in terms of spiritual ceremony is a watered-down version of Santería, originally practiced between the 16th and 19th centuries by islanders of Cuban or African descent. The ceremony represented a kind of barter system between man and god – usually to heal the sick or bring luck and good fortune – and was not particularly sinister. Over the centuries however, interpretations of Santería have become blurred, and today it is fairly obscure and regarded with suspicion and a whiff of fear. The modern version combines a general sense of superstition with a tendency to purchase special candles and potions from *botánicas*, just in case. Add to this the Puerto Rican penchant for keeping *santos* – wooden, stone or ceramic images of Christian saints – for good luck, and you get a healthy blend of Christian superstition and Taino and African idol worship.

THINGS THAT GO BUMP IN THE NIGHT

The Bloodthirsty Chupacabra

Known as **chupacabras** (literally "goat suckers") as far away as Texas, South America and the UK, these mysterious blood-sucking monsters apparently kill by boring holes in the skull or neck of their prey and then vacuuming out the insides, leaving corpses that are nothing but a deflated sack of skin and a few bones. Few people claim to have actually seen a *chupacabra*, and descriptions of them range from a large jackal-like animal to a slimy gray humanoid, possibly visiting our planet from space or maybe the result of a botched genetic experiment. But the carnage left behind as evidence is well documented. In rural areas of Puerto Rico, hundreds of animals have been slain in this gruesome manner during the past decade, baffling police and scientists alike. Canóvanas Mayor Chemo Soto has organized a series of expeditions to photograph or capture the monster, using caged goats as bait. Although it has earned him the nickname Chemo (Indiana) Jones, Soto and his band of hunters have so far failed to bag their quarry. Every Puerto Rican is familiar with *chupacabra* attacks reported in local newspapers, however, and for farmers the fear is real. The strikes appear to be increasing in frequency. In October 2000 a *chupacabra* attack was reported in the Buena Vista area of San Antonio, with alarming signals that the monster is becoming more indiscriminate in choosing its prey. The corpses of a turkey and five ducks were reportedly found emptied of organs and body fluids, and two hens were wounded. According to witnesses, the attacker left behind "a green and yellow substance… with a gel-like appearance that smells like sulfur." Oddly, the chupacabra seems to favor attacking near towns beginning with the letter 'C', such as Caguas, Carolina, Canóvanas and Cabo Rojo.

UFO Sightings

Puerto Rico is one of the world's hotspots for reports of UFO sightings and extraterrestrial activity, and not just because the Arecibo Observatory is used by the scientists of the SETI (Search for Extra-Terrestrial Intelligence) program (see page 139 in the *North Coast* chapter). For decades, residents have claimed to witness unearthly craft hovering over such places as El Yunque rain forest, the hills above Lajas and the nearby Laguna Cartagena. According to "reliable sources" interviewed by your faithful correspondents, these places are most likely used as alien bases. Conspiracy theorists note: all are on government property! Reportedly verified by a university physicist from Mayagüez, an unclassifiable blue-green vapor began issuing from Laguna Cartagena in the 1980s, and sounds of subterranean construction have been heard intermittently ever since. Some "experts" see this as the work of an underground reptilian race that has immigrated to our planet. Other witnesses have seen slender gray creatures with almond-shaped eyes (not to be confused with *chupacabras*) near the lagoon, as well as workers wearing white Haz-Mat uniforms and CIA-looking men wearing mirrored sunglasses and carrying briefcases into the underbrush (see page 184 in the *West Coast* chapter).

Music & Dance

When people think of Puerto Rican music, they usually think of **salsa**, **merengue** and (occasionally) *bomba y plena*. These may be the most distinctive styles, but since the time of the Taino people, Puerto Ricans have created music that crosses many musical borders.

■ Classical

During the 18th and 19th centuries, wealthy landowners began sending their children who showed musical promise to study in Spain and, through a trickle-down effect, the classical overtures popularized by baroque and romantic composers began to make their way back to this Caribbean outpost. The first Puerto Rican to gain any real international recognition was composer **Manuel Tavares**, and his success inspired a small island "boom" in enthusiasm for classicists. By the 1830s, classical concerts, operas and zarzuelas (operatic comedies) were in full swing in the theaters and concert halls of San Juan.

Meanwhile, a new classical rhythm was developing in Ponce. **La Danza** was conceived by composer **Juan Morel Campos**, who had been searching for an appropriate identity for the ballroom dancing that took place every Saturday night among Ponce's elite. He came up with a unique minuet performed on the piano, and this musical tradition lives on (see *Festivals & Events*, page 231).

The next local sensation was the sumptuous voice of tenor **Antonio Paoli** (1872-1946), who is Puerto Rico's best-known opera singer. But the most famous classical musician ever to have come out of Puerto Rico was Spanish-Puerto Rican cellist **Pablo Casals**. His legacy is recognized for two weeks every June during the Pablo Casals Music Festival (see page 40), which attracts classical aficionados from all over the world.

■ Folk Music

Jíbaro-inspired bands are among the best-loved musicians on the island, especially for their upbeat ballads and *cuatro* performances, many of which mix music with storytelling. Unfortunately, they are also the most difficult to find, as they often perform only at private parties, weddings or otherwise impromptu celebrations (not unlike flamenco musicians). The best way to see and hear this type of music is to get in touch with one of the haciendas in the Cordillera Central, such as Hacienda Juanita in Maricao (☎ 787-838-2550), which often have live music on weekends. Sadly, there is no festival dedicated to *seis* or Puerto Rican folk music, but you have a very good chance of hearing it at any of the mountain festivals.

THE CUATRO

At least four instruments evolved from the six-string Spanish classical guitar: the **requinto**, the **bordunua**, the **cuatro** and **tiple**. The most popular is the *cuatro*, which has 10 strings arranged in pairs, producing a lovely sound that can swing from mournful to *alegre* in the brush of the finger. Carved from solid blocks of laurel wood, it is recognized as Puerto Rico's national instrument. Be prepared to spend hundreds of dollars if you want to own one of these.

> **TIP:** *Some of the best recorded cuatro music is performed by the* **Orquesta de Cuerdas de Puerto Rico.**

■ Sexy Salsa

As recently as the late 1980s, the youth of San Juan had almost completely assimilated the sound and culture of imported American and British rock and pop. But the past decade has brought a refreshing revival of interest in salsa, merengue and Latino music in general among young people. In the words of one 21-year-old San Juan resident, "Everybody's getting back to their roots."

Literally meaning "sauce," salsa developed in the nightclubs of New York as Puerto Rican and Cuban immigrants celebrated the end of WWII and attempted to recapture the sound of their native islands. The music comes in a number of forms, and mixes a sultry array of rhythm instruments with Afro-Caribbean musical styles. **Tito Puente**, the godfather of salsa, fused big-band jazz with the maracas, bongos, timbales, conga drums and claves of Africa and the Caribbean to create what remains the world's favorite salsa music. Although Puerto Rico has fewer salsa clubs than one might expect, plenty of bars in San Juan and around the island pump this music from the jukebox at ear-splitting volume, long into the night. Some have live music on weekends (see *Live Music*, page 124), and most town festivals have live salsa acts.

> **TIP:** *If you're looking for some "sauce" to take home, recordings by* **Willie Colón, El Gran Combo de Puerto Rico, Hector Lavoe** *and* **Celia Cruz** *are all good bets.*

■ Bomba y Plena

Even in Puerto Rico, there seems to be a lot of confusion about the origins of *bomba y plena*. This is largely because the two styles – *bomba* and *plena*

– are invariably spoken of in the same breath as if they were a single musical form. Most scholars agree that *bomba*, strictly African in origin, came out of the Yoruba slave colonies in Loíza Aldea, while *plena* seems to have been born of a coupling of Taino and Spanish rhythms emerging from Ponce.

- **Bomba** involves a drummer and a dancer who embark on an impassioned rhythmic dialogue, in which drummers slap out complex rhythms on the *tambores* (congas or barrel drums) and dancers use every muscle to writhe, wriggle, clap and stamp to the beat. Eventually, the performance takes a competitive turn, as both dancing and drumming become more and more frenzied – each trying to outdo and outlast each other. More than anything on the island, this music gives a true sense of Puerto Rico's African heritage.

- **Plena** evolved from an oral tradition in which people singing it were effectively reporting the news. Songs are usually bold and sassy (sometimes sung as duets), and deliver highly satirical accounts of the days events, particularly where politics or local gossip are concerned. Accompanied by the *güiro* (a hollow gourd with shallow ridges that is scratched with a stick), the *cuatro* (a 10-stringed guitar) and *panderos* (the tambourine), the music is as passionate as it is dramatic. In a nod to Puerto Rican diversity and cultural heritage, the two styles are often performed together. One of the best chances to see them occurs in November, at the National Bomba y Plena Festival in Ponce. *Plena* is a frequent feature of any number of local festivals (*fiestas patronales* tend to feature salsa), and variations on textbook *bomba* can often be seen on Sunday evenings at El Flamboyán in Luquillo or at the Institute of Puerto Rican Culture in San Juan.

> The best and most famous of these bomba y plena musicians and dancers are the **Cepeda** family, who continue a tradition formed more than a century ago in the slave colonies of Loíza by their forefathers. For information, ☎ 787-757-1672 or 776-3386.

■ Latin Pop

The hottest act ever born in Puerto Rico is, of course, **Ricky Martin**, who, with international superhits such as *Livin' La Vida Loca*, is probably the most famous Puerto Rican ever. His performance at the 1999 Grammys wowed musical heavyweights such as Madonna and Luciano Pavarotti and earned him the "Best Latin Pop" title. Ricky is no newcomer to fame, however. In his early teens, he performed with the boy group Menudo, and producers repeatedly chastised him for his inability to conform to the band's code of remaining static on stage. In other words, he's always been an incorrigible hip swinger. On his most recent tour, Puerto Rican newcomers **Vivanativa** came along as the opening act, and many pundits are already pegging the band to reach international stardom. Their second CD, *Viejo*, is well worth a listen (check the group's Web site, www.vivanativa.com).

IS THAT A MARACA IN YOUR POCKET, OR...

Hit some local bars (such as Café Puerto Rico in Old San Juan) on a Friday or Saturday night, and there's a good chance you'll be handed a strange-looking instrument from behind the bar (some locals bring their own instruments). This is your opportunity to join the impromptu "jam," which is a regular feature at bars featuring music, especially once a few rounds of rum have loosened the inhibitions of the audience. The **maraca** is to be shaken vigorously in time to the music. **Claves** are a Caribbean variation on Celtic spoon-playing, with two sticks tapped together to strike a beat. If you've got rhythm, you may be given the chance to try your hand on the **tambores** (barrel-shaped drums with animal hide stretched on top, and the key element of bomba), or on the **bongos**, which are small, paired drums that rest on the player's knees.

Art & Culture

■ The Art Scene

Old San Juan has a hive of small, independent art galleries, some with impressive collections of Puerto Rican and international art (see page 127). The best art collection in the Caribbean is housed in the **Museo de Arte de Ponce**, though its reputation is staked on the international collection rather than national works. Regardless, visitors interested in learning about Puerto Rican art history should keep an eye out for the work of **José Campeche** (1752-1809), a self-taught painter who became obsessed with the story of Christ and was the first Puerto Rican painter to gain any real credibility. What few people know about Campeche is that he was the son of a freed slave and several of his paintings point subtly to the true nature of colonization. The second half of the 19th century saw the birth of a style of realism called *costumbrismo* (local color), pioneered by the works of one man – **Francisco Oller**. Heavily influenced by the works of French masters Paul Cézanne and, especially, Gustave Courbet, who was his mentor and teacher during his time in

France, Oller later became known as the first Latin American Impressionist.

In the 20th century, a most striking art movement came out of **printmaking** and **poster art**. As the government embraced industry over agriculture in the 1940s, it began commissioning informational posters to spread news of a fast-changing society to a rural populace largely without radio or access to other mass media. In 1952, painter **Lorenzo Omar** took over the Division of Community Education and, along with a number of colleagues, raised the poster tradition into a real art form. Posters were made using a serigraph silkscreen printing process, and had a more artistic quality than their cousin, the lithograph. Artists such as **Rafael Tufiño** became well known throughout the island based on popular, yet exquisitely done, posters and prints. By the 1970s, however, so many Puerto Ricans had televisions at home that the need for posters evaporated, and the movement died out. Today, the posters are highly collectible. The Institute of Puerto Rican Culture and the Puerto Rican Tourism Company both have collections but, unfortunately, no public gallery space has been made available for their display. More traditional and newer art forms have blossomed in the interim, but the results have been spotty. The work of one of the better contemporary painters, **Myrna Baez**, can be seen at the **Museo de Arte de Ponce**. To see the work of current and upcoming Puerto Rican artists, check out the many small galleries around Old San Juan, such as **Atlas Art**, as well as exhibitions at the **Museo de Arte de Puerto Rico** in Santurce, which opened in 2000 (see page 93).

■ Writers & Poets

The first writing to emerge from Puerto Rico was in the form of diaries, memoirs, and especially letters sent back to Spain by early settlers. Of these, the best known include the works of Gonzalo Fernández de Oviedo, who published the *Historia General y Natural de Las Indias* (the General and Natural History of the Indies) and Fr. Bartolomé de las Casas, whose work titled the *Historia de las Indias* (History of the Indies), is one of the earliest – if overly rosy – accounts of the first years of colonization in Puerto Rico.

Right up until the early 19th century, writing continued in a pro-Spanish vein that painted highly exaggerated promotional portraits of life on the island, and left out details about the miserable poverty and high illiteracy that had been afforded by 400 years of colonial rule. New arrivals on the island translated their new world into prose and poetry, with considerable attention given to the mountain peasant, or *jíbaro*. The most famous of those stories, ***El Gíbaro***, written in 1849 by Manuel Alonso Pacheco, is a now-classic collection of poems and stories that gave the *jíbaro* the idealistic image of a folk hero. Then, in 1894, Manuel Zeno Gandía responded with a naturalistic novel titled ***La Charca*** (The Stagnant Pool). In it, he countered the romanticized image of the *jíbaro* with images of the terrible social conditions that he observed in many of Puerto Rico's simple communities. It was a gritty social commentary that gave a stab of realism to a new genre in modern Puerto Rican literature that was developing at the time, which became known as *costumbrismo* (local color).

The first truly *costumbrismo* work, however, was written by Alejandro Tapía y Rivera (1826-1882), who shocked readers with his controversial musings in a poem dedicated to Satan – the ***Sataniada***. A fire-and-brimstone tale, it was its confrontational style rather than its substance that inspired a small movement of contemporaries who liberally doused their lyrical poems with acidic political references. The most prolific was revolutionist **Lola Rodríguez de Tío** (1843-1924), whose outspokenly political poems were considered inappropriate by male critics, at a time when women still did not have the right to vote.

The short-lived Spanish-American War in 1898 marked the start of a new wave of socio-political writers, an island outgrowth of the Spanish "**Generation of '98**" movement, who focused on the conflict between Hispanic tradition and the increasing Americanization of the island. Writers and journalists such as José de Diego and especially Luis Muñoz Rivera, founder of the newspaper *La Democracia* in 1890 – which supported autonomist and liberal causes – became the movement's leaders. This theme of rival cultural influences vs. the Puerto Rican identity continues today, and it could be said that the Generation of '98 movement has never truly died in Puerto Rico. Hugely influential was **Antonio S. Pedreira** (1899-1939), a professor of Hispanic studies, who wrote a landmark work entitled ***Insularismo*** about Puerto Rican culture after 3½ decades of US political control. It unleashed a flood of works by other Puerto Ricans who, in essays, novels and poetry, explored the cultural struggle faced by the island since 1898. Notable among these works were ***La Llamarada*** – one of the best-known works in Puerto Rican literature – and ***Los Amos Benevolos*** (The Benevolent Masters), by **Enrique A. Laguerre**, born in 1906 and still kicking (see *Moca*, *West Coast* chapter, page 170).

The most distinguished Puerto Rican playwright was **René Marqués**, author of the three-act ***La Carreta*** (The Oxcart), which depicts the poor economic conditions that led to mass exodus of Puerto Ricans to the United States. Another notable novelist was **Pedro Juan Soto** (born 1928), who lived in New York, taught English, and was one of the first truly bilingual Puerto Rican writers. Among his best-known works were *Spiks* – a hard-nosed account of life in the barrio – which appeared in 1956, and *Usmail*, published in 1958. Since then, two exceptional women writers have emerged, giving a fresh perspective on the ever-present issue of identity in Puerto Rico. **Rosario Ferré** (the daughter of Ex-Governor Luis A. Ferré) penned the excellent *The House on the Lagoon*, an evocative account of a family's tumultuous history that mirrors that of Puerto Rico. From an immigrant's viewpoint, **Esmerelda Santiago** has written a modern classic entitled *When I was Puerto Rican*, which depicts her odyssey from an island childhood to a search for a "better life" in the US.

Food: A Taste of Puerto Rico

■ Spices & Seasonings

Visitors to Puerto Rico may have mixed feelings about *comida criolla* (local creole cooking). We heartily recommend it as the vestige of a culinary culture that is slowly getting buried under mushrooming fast-food outlets and restaurants serving nouveaux and international fare. At its worst, *comida criolla* can be greasy and unappealing. At its best, it blends the traditions of Taino, African and Spanish cooking to delicious result. Unlike many of the other Caribbean peoples, Puerto Ricans aren't big on explosively spicy food (although most restaurants supply *pique* hot sauce – sometimes homemade – on request. The most typical spices used are **cilantro** (a large-leafed and more aromatic member of the parsley family), garlic, onions and peppers, used to make *sofrito,* the base of nearly everything that comes out of the Puerto Rican kitchen. Meat and seafood is usually seasoned with **adobo** – similar to a very mild curry powder.

■ Rice, Beans & Vegetables

Standard daily fare for most Puerto Ricans is **arroz con habichuelas** (rice and beans), served with **tostones** (twice-fried green plantains) or **amarillos** (sweet plantains fried once) and either chicken, pork or meat. The best restaurants serve a respectable salad; otherwise, expect iceberg lettuce and bland tomatoes.

> **VEGETARIANS, TAKE NOTE:** *Vegetarian food is still a bit of a novel concept in Puerto Rico, although major towns and cities usually have at least one vegetarian lunch place and San Juan has a few great options.*

■ Meats

For a Sunday afternoon meat feast, head to more rural areas where Puerto Rican families will be tucking into **lechon asada** (spit-roasted pork) at ubiquitous *lechoneras* (especially recommended are the ones around Carite Forest, Guavate, about an hour from San Juan). If you enjoy meat, you'll love the local way of preparing pig. Marinated for two or three days and then slow-cooked over an open flame, it's served crisp and crunchy with traditional trimmings such as steamed cassava (*yucca*), *batata* (sweet potato), *calabasa* (pumpkin) and *arroz con gandules* (a yellow rice and pigeon peas). Soups and stews are also popular. Check out **caldo de gallina** or **mariscos**, a thin, watery brew made from fish or chicken stock; **sancocho**, a hearty stew made of root vegetables and usually a few chunks of ham shank; or **asopao**, a gloopy rice-based soup based on African gumbo. These are serious space fillers. If anything can be called the national dish of Puerto Rico, it's **mofongo** (mashed plantain balls flavored with pork rinds) or **mofongo relleno** (stuffed). Both are served with broth and chicken, fish or meat. The latter involves lining a 10-inch length of bamboo with mashed plantain and then stuffing it with juicy seafood, chicken, pork or beef, and baking the whole thing. If you haven't had *mofongo*, you haven't really tried Puerto Rican food.

WARNING FOR WEAK STOMACHS

Don't get *mofongo* confused with **mondongo**, a rich stew of chopped tripe and other viscera. If you're into this kind of thing, look for other Puerto Rican delicacies featuring innards, such as **cuchifrito** – pork innards stew; **gandinga** – various internal organs spiced and stir-fried; **mollejas** – intestines (pure and simple); and **morcillas** – blood sausages.

■ Fish & Seafood

Like seafood? You're on a Caribbean island, so dig in! **Dorado** (mahi-mahi), **chillo** (snapper), **cangrejo** (crab) and **langosta** (lobster) are all good local catches and usually come with a choice of sauces. **Calamares** (squid), **mejillones** (mussels) and **camarones** (shrimp) are all local favorites, even if some of these are sometimes imported. Two island sauce classics are **ajili-mojili**, a heavy-duty garlic-butter reduction, and **criollo**, a less powerful *sofrito*-based sauce with tomatoes and onions. Street stands selling sweet water **ostiones** or *ostras* (oysters) by the dozen can be found in Boquerón. The inevitable **bacalao** (salted codfish) comes in various sumptuous guises, often with a rich tomato sauce or *en escabeche* – a thoroughly delicious seafood classic inspired by *ceviche*, a recipe of cold, fried fish marinated in vinegar, oil, lime juice, peppercorns, capers, bay leaves and onions. **Serenata** is similar but made with flaked *bacalao*, and is also served cold, with an oil-and-vinegar dressing along with a salsa of onions, tomatoes and avocados. Other, and more unusual, fish or seafood you are sure to see on local menus includes **mero** (grouper), which, with its fine, stringy texture, is often ruined by overcooking, leaving an aftertaste of glue. **Chapín**, the so-called "ugliest fish in the sea," is, on the other hand, usually divine. Reputable restaurants (beware of restaurants falsely advertising *chapín*) serve it with the tail still on, resembling a drumstick. Although not technically seafood, **jueyes** (land crabs) are often stuffed into fried snacks, made into a stew or mixed into rice.

AFTER THE MEAL

Finish your meal in true Puerto Rican style, with a *tembleque* (coconut flan), *flan* (caramel custard), or **guava shells** stuffed with a mild, milky local cheese. It almost goes without saying that you should order a *café d'aquí* (local coffee) to wash down the sweets.

■ The Coffee of Popes & Kings

If you enjoy a good cup of coffee, you're in for a treat. Puerto Rico is home to some of the finest java in the world. Revered by connoisseurs, **Alto Grande** is one of only three coffees on earth given the "Super-Premium" title (the others are Jamaican Blue Mountain and Hawaiian Kona). Over the last hundred years, Alto Grande has been the preferred "cup-a-Joe" for many kings and queens of Europe. It is the coffee of choice by none other than the Pope, and Alto Grande coffeemakers have promoted their product as "The Vatican's Choice." One Puerto Rican mail-order company that supplies it is **Green Island Co.**, ☎ 877-567-5282, www.gicco.com.

■ Street Food

For cheap eats, Puerto Rican street food is a bargain. In general, street food here is safe (if laden with calories and fats) and partaking of it is one of the best ways to get to know the locals. Roadside stands selling pinchos (meat on a stick) and other snacks can be found all over the island, especially on weekends and holidays. They attract Puerto Ricans of all stripes. So get yourself a cold beer, and join in. Here's a basic street-food menu to get you started:

- *Alcapurrias:* Banana-shaped pockets of mashed plantain or cassava, stuffed with meat or *jueyes* (land crabs), then deep-fried.
- *Bacalaítos:* Slabs of codfish crumbs fried in a deep coating of greasy batter. Very popular.
- *Empanadillas:* Usually delicious thin pockets of fried plantain or dough surrounding lobster, crab, conch or meat.
- *Papa Relleno:* Balls of mashed potato surrounding a hearty nugget of ground beef, dipped in egg and deep-fried.
- *Pasteles:* A Puerto Rican tamale, consisting of mashed plantain stuffed with a semi-sweet filling of chickpeas, raisins, roasted peppers, and ground meat. They are then wrapped in a banana leaf and boiled for an hour.
- *Piononos:* Slivers of ripe plantain wrapped around a ball of seasoned meat or cheese, then deep-fried.

- **Pinchos**: As common in Puerto Rico as a hotdog cart in New York City, these sticks of grilled meat or fish are usually coated in spicy or BBQ sauce and topped with a slice of bread.
- **Sorullos**: Fat fingers of cornmeal, fried and usually served with a squirt of Russian dressing.

Rum Dummying

Genuine Puerto Rican rum is widely considered the best in the world. There are various brands and distillations ranging from pure, clear *cristal* (usually mixed with Coke or fruit juice or added to piña coladas) to *añejo*, a smooth golden variety poured over ice, and rich, spicy dark and flavored rums. Though Bacardí is the most famous rum associated with Puerto Rico, it is Cuban, not Puerto Rican, in origin (see San Juan, page 96). If you want the real deal, buy **Don Q** (founded by the Seralles family in Ponce), the favorite of local rum-heads. Don Q supplies the entire range of inebriants. Also, look out for the butterscotch-flavored **Don Juan** (also of the Serralles empire), which, mixed in equal parts with Don Q *cristal*, forms a formidable shot called "Double-D" (ask for it in Rincón, if nowhere else).

Beware the local hooch called *cañita*. Strong and likely to make you get naked in public, it's a real "moonshine" shocker made over the course of several days, with sugarcane fermenting in coconut shells, using methods supplied by the devil.

OFF THE WAGON

There is nothing like the taste of cold, green coconut water straight from the fruit to reassure that you really are in paradise. *Cocos fríos* are sold from roadside wagons near most beachside areas, and sipping virgin coconut milk through a straw can refresh you, especially after a rum-fueled night of debauchery. Coconut refreshment also takes the form of *piraguas* – paper cups filled with shaved ice and drenched in sweet, sticky coconut cordials. If you dislike coconut, piraguas are usually also available in blueberry, mango and tamarind, among other flavors.

Festivals & Events

Like most of their Caribbean neighbors, Puerto Ricans use almost any excuse to declare a holiday. American holidays, such as Labor Day, the Fourth of July and the birthday of Martin Luther King Jr. and US presidents are celebrated, of course. But so are Spanish holidays, days devoted to Catholic saints, and recently concocted "holidays" to honor Puerto Rican friendship with neighboring islands and certain dates important to island history. With 78 municipalities – each with their own *fiestas patronales* (patron saint festivals) – it's a wonder anything ever gets done. But somehow, Puerto Ricans manage to fit a solid amount of work in between fiestas. As a visitor, you should be able to find a celebration of something almost any time of year. Following are a few highlights of local festivities. For more information, contact the **Puerto Rico Tourism Company**, ☎ 800-223-6530; www.prtourism.com.

■ January

San Sebastián Street Festival – Crazy days in mid-month on the streets of Old San Juan. Expect music and dancing, parades and processions, copious amounts of food and drink, and plenty of shameless goings on. ☎ 787-722-1709 or 723-7800.

■ February

Maricao Coffee Festival – This is a good place to get in touch with Puerto Rico's own brand of folk music – especially the *seis* – and hang out with country folk. Sadly, Hurricane Georges in 1998 so damaged coffee crops in this region that it may take few years to get the coffee-plantation part of the festival back to normal. The festival is a traditional tribute to mountain life. ☎ 787-838-2290.

RAVE ON

February 2000 marked Puerto Rico's first-ever electronic dance music festival. We're talking rave-dance culture introduced to the island in big-tent style (with other psychedelic weirdness!). The setting was the weird karst country around Ciales (near Manatí). The event, called *El Cuco*, attracted DJs from the UK, US, Germany and France, with ravers attending from as far away as Israel and Poland. More events are promised. But, as usual, this type of event is strictly underground. Check out www.tsunami-trance.com for more information, or ask around in the clubs of Old San Juan, because this ever-changing information ain't going to be published in no travel book.

■ February/March

Ponce Carnaval takes place the week before Lent, and is one of the biggest, brightest, loudest and liveliest festivals on the island. It may not match the fervor of Río, New Orleans at Mardi Gras or Vegas on a good night, but the show is impressive with masked *vejigantes* (devils) swooping through the streets as inebriated revelers swarm the sidewalks. ☎ 787-841-8044, ext. 261.

■ March

Dulce Sueño Paso Fino Fair, Guayama – If you want to see the ballet-stepping waltz of local Paso Fino horses in competition, don't miss this two-day equestrian fair. ☎ 787-864-0600.

■ May/June

Puerto Rico Heineken Jazz Fest, San Juan – Local and international performers take to the stage at this predominantly Latin jazz festival. In 2000 the event celebrated its 10-year anniversary and now attracts 15,000 jazz fans a year. It takes place for four days at the Sixto Escobar Park (near the Normandie and Hilton Hotels in Condado). ☎ 787-277-9200.

■ June

Pablo Casals Festival, Bayamón – Aficionados of classical music time their vacations to coincide with this respected event. It promises two weeks of performances by leading symphony orchestras, conductors and soloists from all over the world, and is one of the foremost events of its kind

Masked festival dancers in Ponce.
(Bob Krist, for the PRTC)

in the Americas. Most of the concerts are staged at the Luis A. Ferré Center. ☎ 787-724-4747 or 721-7727.

San Juan Bautista Day, San Juan – This is one of the most important *fiestas patronales,* notable for its midnight ceremony. Puerto Ricans flock to the beaches where, on the stroke of 12:00, they walk backwards into the sea seven times to invite good luck for the year ahead and wash away bad luck from the year before. The beaches in Condado and Isla Verde are packed with midnight beach parties, but no matter where you are there's likely to be something going on, as the whole island seems to have picked up on this most endearing of customs. ☎ 787-721-2400.

■ July

St. James Festival, Loíza Aldea – Another raucous fiesta where masked *vejigantes* take center stage. This festival, celebrating Puerto Rico's African heritage, is wild, wacky and theatrical and is widely considered the best on the island. ☎ 787-876-3570.

■ August

International Billfish Tournament, Club Náutico de San Juan – This is one of the world's longest-running premier game-fishing events. It costs around $400 to enter, but winners reap the rewards with as much as $20,000 in prize money for blue marlin reaching upwards of 900 lbs. ☎ 787-722-0177 or 722-0190.

■ November

National Bomba y Plena Festival, Ponce – Prepare to don your glad rags and shake on down to the beat of drummers and singers who come from all over the island to perform. ☎ 787-841-8044.

La Festival Indígena, Jayuya – For visitors in search of the singing, dancing, *cuatro*-playing *jíbaros*, be sure to come for at least one day of this traditional folk festival. ☎ 787-828-1241.

Getting Here

■ By Air

You will probably arrive on a flight from a major US or European city into the **Luis Muñoz Marín International Airport** in San Juan. Most major carriers have flights, and it's a hub for American Airlines, with connections to other Caribbean islands. TWA also offers a near-daily (check schedules, as they're subject to change) red-eye flight from Newark, New Jersey to Aguadilla, arriving at 2 a.m. – the only other destination for flights from abroad. This flight is highly recommended if you're planning to stay on the west coast and your visit is for a week or less, since the road trip from San Juan to Rincón or Mayagüez can take three hours or more.

Airports

San Juan
Aeropuerto Int'l Luis Muñoz Marín . . . . ☎ 787-791-3840

Aguadilla
Aeropuerto Rafael Hernández . . . . ☎ 787-891-2286

Mayagüez
Aeropuerto Eugenio María de Hostos . . . . . ☎ 787-833-0148

Ponce
Aeropuerto Mercedita . . . . ☎ 787-842-6292

Fajardo
Aeropuerto Diego Jiménez Torres . . . . ☎ 787-860-3110

Vieques
Aeropuerto Antonion Rivera Rodríguez . . . ☎ 787-741-0515

Culebra
Aeropuerto Benjamín Rivera Noriega . . . . . ☎ 787-742-0022

Airlines

Air St. Thomas . . . . ☎ 787-791-4898 / 800-522-3084
American Airlines / Eagle . . . ☎ 787-749-1747 / 800-433-7300
British Airways . . . . ☎ 787-723-4327 / 800-247-9297
Continental Airlines . . . . ☎ 787-793-7373 / 800-525-0280
Martin Air . . . . ☎ 787-723-7474
Northwest Airlines . . . . ☎ 787-253-0206 / 800-225-2525
PRINair . . . . ☎ 787-890-1630
TWA . . . . ☎ 787-253-0440 / 800-221-2000
United Airlines . . . . ☎ 787-253-2776 / 800-426-5561
Vieques Air-Link . . . . ☎ 787-722-3736

Inter-Island Flights

A number of private charter airlines island-hop to other Caribbean destinations. **Inter Island Express**, ☎ 888-253-4556, www.interislandexpress.com, offers first-class service from Puerto Rico to destinations such as St. Barths and Nevis, among others. **Charter Flights Caribbean Inc.**, ☎ 787-791-1240, 810-1362, or 398-3181, www. guiapr.com/charterflights, offers daily departures to St. Thomas, St. Croix, Beef Island and Virgin Gorda. Executive plane and helicopter charters all over the Caribbean are available from **Caribbean Helicorp Inc.**, ☎ 787-722-1984, www.caribhelicorp.com, e-mail ninov@ibm.net.

■ By Sea

Often used as a gateway to the rest of the Caribbean, San Juan is the largest home-based cruise port in the world, home to 28 resident vessels with new ships arriving or passing through each year. High season can see up to 10 to 12 cruise ships at a time, the largest of which can host up to 2,000 seafaring folk, and discussions to expand portage in the next four to five years are already underway. Around 1.2 million cruise passengers visit San Juan each year, each spending between $90 and $150 every time they step ashore. It's no wonder, then, that cruising is one of Puerto Rico's most lucrative assets, or that Old San Juan is booming.

Getting Around

■ By Car

If you plan to go adventuring around the island, and don't have local friends to chauffeur you, you'll probably want to rent a car. All major rental car agencies have offices at the airport and in the larger cities. Phone numbers are listed in the following chapters. Economy cars can usually be rented for $25 to $30 per day, not including insurance, which we recommend you get.

> **TIP:** *Due to the high rate of car theft in Puerto Rico, get full insurance for peace of mind. Also, if possible, avoid renting a Toyota Tercel or a Mitsubishi Mirage, the two most-stolen models on the island, according to police. Avoid parking in isolated areas, and hide all items of value, including sunglasses and cigarettes.*

Road rules are basically the same as in the United States. Note, however, that while speed limits are posted in miles per hour, road signs list distances in kilometers (one kilometer = .62 mile). When a sign says your destination is 10 km. away, it's just over six miles. Highways 22, 52 and 53 are **toll roads**, so keep a couple of dollars of change on hand for these. Most tolls cost between 35¢ and 70¢ – the price is marked when you come into the turnstile. If you don't have change, simply merge to one of the right-hand lanes marked with a "C" and attendants will change bills for you.

Driving Etiquette

If you are used to driving among predictably law-abiding fellow motorists in the US or northern Europe, consider the following. While it doesn't compare to the madcap road-rally style practiced in India, Russia, or uncountable other countries, the Puerto Rican method of driving tends toward mild anarchy. Speeding past traffic on the shoulder of a road or is perfectly acceptable. If you see an ambulance or police car flashing lights behind you, this is an opportunity to let them pass and then tailgate at breakneck speed. Merging into a thoroughfare from a side road is simply a matter of nosing your automobile into traffic until a generous fellow traveler waves you in or until you force them to a screeching halt. A general rule: let ambitious drivers pass in front of you, and smile and wave when the favor is returned.

MILEAGE CHART

Distances are shown in miles	AGUADILLA	BARCELONETA	CAGUAS	CAYEY	DORADO	FAJARDO	HUMACAO	LOIZA	MANATI	MAYAGUEZ	NAGUABO	PONCE	QUEBRADILLAS	SALINAS	SAN GERMAN	SAN JUAN	UTUADO	YABUCOA
AGUADILLA		47	90	103	70	112	108	99	50	17	112	63	18	87	31	81	43	115
BARCELONETA	47		45	58	25	67	62	54	5	65	67	63	30	63	78	36	31	70
CAGUAS	90	45		13	27	36	18	28	40	100	24	53	73	29	87	18	74	26
CAYEY	103	58	13		40	50	31	41	53	86	37	40	86	16	74	30	72	39
DORADO	70	25	27	40		51	45	35	20	87	51	79	53	56	101	17	56	52
FAJARDO	112	67	36	50	51		22	23	63	129	13	89	97	65	125	34	97	31
HUMACAO	108	62	18	31	45	22		29	58	117	10	71	90	47	105	34	92	10
LOIZA	99	54	28	41	35	23	29		49	116	35	81	82	57	115	19	83	39
MANATI	50	5	40	53	20	63	58	49		67	62	51	33	58	81	31	34	64
MAYAGUEZ	17	65	100	86	87	129	117	116	67		123	46	34	70	14	98	49	110
NAGUABO	112	67	24	37	51	13	10	35	62	123		77	95	53	111	39	96	20
PONCE	63	63	53	40	79	89	71	81	51	46	77		67	24	34	70	32	64
QUEBRADILLAS	18	30	73	86	53	97	90	82	33	34	95	67		91	48	64	35	98
SALINAS	87	63	29	16	56	65	47	57	58	70	53	24	91		58	46	56	40
SAN GERMAN	31	78	87	74	101	125	105	115	81	14	111	34	48	58		104	66	98
SAN JUAN	81	36	18	30	17	34	34	19	31	98	39	70	64	46	104		65	43
UTUADO	43	31	74	72	56	97	92	83	34	49	96	32	35	56	66	65		96
YABUCOA	115	70	26	39	52	31	10	39	64	110	20	64	98	40	98	43	96	

■ Public Transportation

Upon arrival, traveling by car becomes almost obligatory. However, with a healthy amount of creativity and patience, it is possible to navigate the island by public buses, known as ***públicos***. These are actually taxi-bus hybrids: vans that seat 12 to 15 people and have their place of origin and destination printed at the top of the windshield. Most make short hops of 15 miles or less, but the price is right. One-way travel often costs less than $5. You can either stand at a roadside and flag them down or catch one at a station (most are located at the central plaza of every major town). Depending on the driver and the other passengers, you can usually ask to be dropped off at the location of your choice, provided it isn't too far off route. From there you're pretty much on your own, because taxis are scarce outside of San Juan and Ponce. **Taxis** are as expensive as in major US cities, and usually hard to find outside metropolitan areas. However, it's a good way to get from the airport to your hotel in greater San Juan. Finally, if you plan to stay exclusively within the Old San Juan-Condado area, it is also possible to get around by **bicycle** and save a load of cash.

Where To Stay

According to José Corujo, executive director of the Puerto Rican Tourism Company, hotel room space in Puerto Rico increased by more than 25% in the year 2000 alone – from 12,000 to 16,000 rooms. And that's just hotels! You'll notice a building frenzy all along the coast, with no signs of slowing. Thankfully, a great many island spots remain quiet and uncrowded, even on the coast. So, whether you are looking to cram yourself in with the masses or escape to a remote hideaway (or anything in between), the *Where To Stay* sections in the regional chapters should point you in the right direction.

ACCOMMODATIONS PRICE KEY
Rates are per room, per night, for double occupancy. Single occupancy may or may not get you a discount, so ask when making a reservation. Breakfast included where noted. Taxes and services charges are additional.
$ . . . . Up to $50
$$. . . . . $50 to $100
$$$. . . . . $101 to $150
$$$$ . . . . $150 and up

Overall, expect to pay at least $60 a night, even for the most basic of accommodations. You may get a better deal during low season (late spring and summer months), but this is increasingly unlikely as Puerto Rico becomes more and more popular as a year-round tourist destination.

> **ROOM TAX AND SERVICE CHARGES:** *Unless otherwise stated, expect to be charged a room tax of 11% in hotels with a casino, 9% in smaller hotels without a casino, and 7% in small hotels, guest houses and paradores. Some hotels and guest houses may also add a 10% to 15% service charge to the final bill.*

■ Types of Accommodations

A variety of types of accommodations, listed in the regional chapters, may be broken down as follows.

Hotels

Every coastline has at least one **luxury hotel**, some vast and sprawling, others small and exclusive. Nearly all cost at least $250 a night, and include beach access, swimming pools, recreation areas, fine dining, bars, casinos and organized tours. In other words, most are all-inclusive. Great for honeymooners, couples in search of a decadent, romantic getaway or anyone used to sitting in the lap of luxury.

Chain hotels (Marriott, Holiday Inn, etc.) are usually high-rise, and have at least 100 rooms and lots of facilities, such as swimming pools, game rooms, at least one bar and restaurant and usually a casino. Often you can get good package and family deals in these places. Unfortunately the size makes them rather impersonal. Major hotel chains are the same all over the world – big on business, low on character.

Guest Houses

We prefer smaller, independently run guest houses, where the experience more resembles an intimate weekend spent with friends. The best of these are bursting with character, with sitting rooms, galleries, flowering gardens or comfortable terraces and patios. The only drawback is that, due to their size, the best ones are often full if you don't book well in advance. Usually, it's much easier to get rooms here on non-holiday weekdays.

Paradores

Paradores are government-sponsored inns dotted about the island. They cost about the same as guest houses. Puerto Rico's tourist authorities are inordinately proud of these places, but if you're used to the system of *paradores* in Spain, you're in for a major disappointment. Many are run-down or simply characterless, and some are so dismal that you'd be better off stringing a hammock between a couple of palm trees. The few exceptions are mountain retreats such as Hacienda Juanita in Maricao (page

291), or La Casa Grande near Utuado (page 291). Otherwise, we've seen little of which to be proud.

Bargain Accommodations

The most basic type of accommodations (apart from camping) is the **Centro Vacacional** (holiday center). Catering mainly to budget-conscious Puerto Rican families, these are bare-bones cabins or villas that sleep six or more for around $60 a night. If you have a group of travelers together, it's a great bargain, and many *centros vacacionales* are in prime locations. All have cooking and barbecue facilities, but you need to bring your own sheets and blankets (these can usually be rented from the office, but call first to be sure), as well as cooking utensils.

Another budget option – and a kinky one – is to catch eight hours of sleep at one of the island's **motels**. In Puerto Rico, "motel" means "love motel," where illicit affairs are conducted in the most discreet way possible. Many are tucked away on back roads, and look like storage units due to the roll-down shutters that cover the garage entrances. Here's how it works: Drive in, pay the attendant $20 to $25 in cash (usually for six or eight hours), and then pull your car into one of the empty garages. The attendant will shut the garage door behind you. Now that you and your companion are hidden from sight, enter the adjacent windowless bedroom chamber, where you'll find a large, usually cleanly made bed, a shower and a TV that invariably features porn movies. Perfect for adventurous couples who need only a place to catch a few hours of sleep and, um, relax.

OUR TOP 10 (OKAY, 11) PLACES TO STAY

These were chosen for their combination of charm, location and price, and are listed in geographical order, starting from Old San Juan and moving counter-clockwise around the island. We were trying to keep it to 10, but found it necessary to add just one more!

- **The Gallery Inn** ($$$-$$$$). An old Spanish mansion with incredible views in Old San Juan, it edged out the more traditional Hotel El Convento for us, due to its eccentric charm and the warmth of its hosts (page 105).

- **Guest House Old San Juan** ($). Somewhat grungy, this is one of the cheapest places to stay in Puerto Rico, and it's right in the heart of the colonial quarter, with a couple of cool balcony rooms for $35 a night! (page 106.)

- **At Wind Chimes Inn** ($$). A block from the beach, this Spanish villa-style guest house easily wins over the competition in Condado for its soulful use of space and light, and other classy touches (page 107).

- **Villas del Mar Hau** ($$$-$$$$). With adorable beachfront cottages on one of the best stretches of beach on the island, this one's a no-brainer (page 158).

- **The Horned Dorset Primavera** ($$$$). Private plunge pools, plenty of marble, and glorious balconies overlooking the sea in Rincón draw stars and starlets to this five-star retreat, which is often named as the finest hotel-restaurant in the Caribbean (page 206).

- **Mary Lee's by the Sea** ($$$-$$$$). An enchanted garden getaway for self-sufficient travelers, the lifelong work of Mary Lee overlooks the Caribbean coastline and the tropical dry forest of Guánica (page 257).

- **Hotel La Casa Grande** ($$). Morning yoga on a lovingly converted coffee farm, plenty of hammocks, and dense greenery make this mountain retreat near Lago Caonillas relaxation central (page 291).

- **La Casona de Guavate & Posada El Castillo** ($). For sheer wackiness and bargain "luxury" tents (with Astroturf and lanterns), schedule a visit to this oddity on the edge of the Carite forest (page 289).

- **Casa Cubuy Eco-Lodge** ($$). Spartan rooms with amazing views on the south side of El Yunque attract travelers seeking a jungle getaway and great hiking (page 336).

- **Inn On The Blue Horizon** ($$$$). Delightful cottages and main house at a jaw-droppingly beautiful seaside cliff in Vieques, with postcard views, savannah grass, friendly people and more than a touch of class (page 365).

- **Culebra Island Villas** ($$-$$$). A pretty villa complex right on one of the world's greatest stretches of sand, Flamenco Beach (page 394).

Camping

There are two kinds of camping on the island – the official kind and the unofficial kind. Official campsites provide toilets, showers and possibly a place to get a meal and a hot cup of coffee, as well as barbecue areas, picnic tables and sometimes covered space under which to pitch a tent. Some of these get overrun on weekends, as family camping getaways are popular with locals. Along the **Ruta Panorámica** (see the *Central Mountains* chapter), you'll find lovely forest campsites. Some beach campsites are located along the coast of the main island and in Culebra and Vieques. The normal cost to pitch a tent is $10 per night. Be aware that you may need a permit or a reservation to stay at some of these places, and none are worry-free in terms of theft (see *Crime*, page 62). Unofficially, the adventurous traveler should feel free to camp anywhere it seems okay to do so – you may or may not get moved along in the morning. Serious refuge seekers should head to the rain forest (see **El Yunque**, pages 325-334) or to one of many hidden beaches (especially along the East Coast). If you really want to remove yourself from civilization, find a fisherman to take you to a remote cay and pick you up in the morning. See also **Caja de Muertos** (page 253) or **Mona Island** (pages 202-203) for ideal camping escapes.

If their camping system seems a bit bureaucratic, don't be put off. Many camping spots have offices on site (usually open weekends), particularly those under the Department of Natural Resources administration. Even if you show up unannounced, turn on the charm and it's unlikely you'll be refused. Private campgrounds are listed under *Where To Stay* in each chapter.

CAMPING ADMINISTRATION OFFICES

- **Fomento Recreativo**, ☎ 787-724-2500, PO Box 902-2089, San Juan, PR 00904-2089, for reservations. This government-run agency deals with campgrounds and cabins at Luquillo Beach, Seven Seas (Fajardo), Punta Guilarte (Arroyo), Monte del Estado (Maricao), Boquerón, Tres Hermanos (Anasco) and Rincón.

- **Negociado del Servicio Forestal**, ☎ 787-724-3724/3647, fax 721-5984, PO Box 906-6600, Puerta de Tierra, San Juan, PR 00906-6600, is part of the Departmento de Recursos Naturales y Ambientales (DRNA) and administers seven campgrounds, including Mona Island. If you want help in planning your camping trip or need suggestions on where to go, visit their offices at Club Náutico, Dos Hermanos Bridge, en route into Old San Juan.

- **Department of Natural Resources**, ☎ 787-724-3724, Division of Forest Land Use Permits, PO Box 5887, Puerta de Tierra, San Juan, PR 00906, has jurisdiction over Carite Forest, Toro Negro Forest Reserve, Guilarte (Carr. 131 and Carr. 518), Coamo Hot Springs, Susúa Forest, Guánica Forest, Guajataca Forest, Río Abajo Forest and Cambalache Beach.

- **US Forest Service**, ☎ 787-888-1880, takes care of camping in El Yunque. Or you can get a permit from the Palo Colorado Visitor Center, Carr. 191, Km. 8.9, soon after you enter the rain forest. You must be there before 4 p.m.

- **Autoridad de Conservación y Desarrollo de Culebra (ACC)**, PO Box 217, Culebra, PR 00775, ☎ 787-742-0700, administers the campgrounds on Flamenco Beach.

Where To Eat

If fine dining is an integral part of your vacation, center yourself near San Juan. Rapidly gaining a reputation as the gastronomic center of the Caribbean, **Old San Juan** has an unbeatable variety of offerings (including the only Thai, Vietnamese and Romanian restaurants on the island), much of which is top class. You'll find innovative French, Italian, international and Creole cuisine budding all over the old city. There are also some exceptional places to dine, dotted around the island. Fresh seafood is obviously the strong point of many menus, and a few towns (such as **Joyuda** on the west coast) have pinned their livelihood to restaurants serving the catch of the day. Unfortunately, top-notch Puerto Rican food (the kind *abuela* – grandmother – used to make) can be difficult to find. Often, the best finds are outside of San Juan, tucked away in some obscure town or village. Canteen-style eateries are great for quick, authentic and cheap lunches, and roadside cafés – particularly *lechoneras* (which offer barbecued pork and chicken) – serve up some of the best budget nosh on the island.

OUR TOP 10 RESTAURANTS

From spare-no-expense gourmet restaurants to local Creole eateries, the following list highlights some of the top eateries on the island. Many fine San Juan restaurants are not on this list because we've tried to cover a large geographic area.

- **The Parrot Club** (page 111) maintains its reputation as the trendiest eatery in Old San Juan with great *nuevo Latino* cooking and excellent people watching.

- **Café Zaguan** (page 113), a pleasant sidewalk café in the historic quarter, serves excellent fajitas, *ceviche* and tuna steaks for some of the city's best prices.

- **Kaplash** (page 210), in Rincón, makes the Top 10 for its always-tasty (and cheap) seafood *empanadillas* on a cliff-top perch – a good choice for lunch.

- **The Horned Dorset Primavera** (page 211), also in Rincón, fully deserves its reputation as the best restaurant in Puerto Rico, and possibly the Caribbean.

- **Cilantro's** (page 261), in San Germán, is another great *nuevo Latino* eatery, with inventive dishes served in the patios of a renovated Catalan mansion.

- **Mark's at the Meliá** (page 263), in Ponce in the old Hotel Meliá, spotlights chef Mark, a fusion cook with an imaginative handle on local produce.

- **El Dujo** (page 295), near Jayuya, serves up some of the island's best Puerto Rican food in a fun Bedouin tent atmosphere.

- **El Tenedor** (page 342), just 30 minutes from metropolitan San Juan, is a gourmet grill set in a converted rum distillery. It's a favorite with locals.

- **Café Blu** (page 368), at the Inn On The Blue Horizon in Vieques, is easily one of the top restaurants in Puerto Rico, whether you're into mushrooms, seafood or fine meats.

- **Oasis** (page 370), at Water's Edge in Vieques, throws caution to the wind with an eclectic menu of Thai-inspired stews and exotic meats in a casual atmosphere.

Look for restaurants affiliated with the ***Mesones Gastronómicas*** program – a government-sponsored initiative to "protect, maintain and promote" the best in Puerto Rican cuisine. So far, there are 43 participating restaurants across the island, which nominally represent the best food from that area. On the whole, they're not bad and usually reasonably priced. Snack shacks and roach coaches can be found everywhere. And for fast-food junkies, yellow and red painted outlets appear like a rash on every major highway, main street and shopping mall on the island. In this book, we have refrained from listing fast-food and chain restaurants.

Adventures

Adventures are covered in detail within each chapter, and organized by the type of activity. Below is a brief summary of what's available.

On Foot

Hiking

Plan a trek through **El Yunque** rain forest (page 325-334) or the **Cordillera Central** (pages 280-287), where you can feel lost in a Jurassic world of giant ferns and strange rain forest foliage while occasionally catching glimpses of the distant sea through the mist. Trails are safe and generally well maintained, especially in El Yunque, which is the most visited tourist site on the island outside of Old San Juan. In the Cordillera Central, summit through dwarf trees of the cloud forest to the island's highest point (4,389 feet above sea level) and other peaks for astounding 360° views. There are dozens of routes, accessible and remote, suiting almost every level of exertion, with waterfalls and swimming holes along the way. For the longer, tougher trails we definitely recommend lightweight, waterproof boots. The mountain areas can get damp and spooky with mist, and warm rain commonly bathes the forest canopy. Also, bring plenty of drinking water, as the mild humidity can open the pores and dehydrate you. Consider a combined hiking/camping trip for maximum mountain time, especially in La Cordillera. Other hikes abound in the island's many reserves and nature parks (see *Eco-Travel*, below). For more mild-mannered strolls, almost every coastal area of Puerto Rico is ideal for long **beach walks** along connecting coves and bays. Richard and "Rubio" Druitt of **Island Walkers**, ☎ 787-887-4359, www.islandwalkers.com, are an excellent resource for serious hikers.

Caving

Ever been rappelling down a cave wall into an underground river, and then been carried along by the current into an exotic, open-air forest paradise? If you have, you're already familiar with the adrenaline rush. If not, hook up with the only adventure operator that does full-day trips to the caverns at **Camuy** (North Coast). Tyrolean descents, dramatic sinkholes, underground pools and bizarre calcite formations await! If you're a spelunking nut and want to explore the caves by yourself (only a fraction of the system has been mapped), check with **Aventuras Tierra Adentro** (page 144) in San Juan for some guidance before gearing up and heading underground. It's easy to get lost if you're on your own and don't know where you're going.

For a more mellow experience, there is a guided walk-in tour of a few Camuy caverns that is more theme park in nature, with a mini-train to easy pathways and tour guides who explain to visitors the karstic limestone rock formation. On **Isla Mona**, you're on your own to explore some of the weirdest caves to be found anywhere. Ruins of a century-old German bat guano mining enterprise, Taino petroglyphs painted on the walls, underground snorkeling and diving, cliff-side cavern outlets and rumors of hidden pirate treasure make the dozen-plus caves on this surreal island one of the greatest adventures in the Caribbean. Check with **Taino Divers** (page 190) in Rincón for other charters that run to Isla Mona for more details.

Golf

Puerto Rico is sometimes called the "Palm Springs of the Caribbean," because it has 14 18-hole courses and four nine-hole courses, many of which are spectacular. Most overlook the sea. Of note are courses at some of the island's finest luxury resort hotels, such as the **Conquistador** in Fajardo, the **Doral Resort at Palmas Del Mar** near Humacao, the **Hyatt Regency Cerromar** in Dorado and the **Westin Río Mar** near Luquillo.

> **TIP:** *Hole 13 at the **Hyatt Dorado Beach** course in Dorado was ranked as one of the world's 10 best by none other than Jack Nicklaus.*

The public **Bahia Beach Plantation** in Río Grande has three beachfront holes, 75 acres of lakes, views of El Yunque rain forest and three finishing holes that rank among the toughest on the island. Most of the best courses are within an hour's drive from San Juan, and are open to the public at limited times.

OUR TOP 10 ADVENTURES

- **Mona Island:** The ultimate castaway fantasy can be had on the deserted, prehistoric Isla de Mona, where you can explore caves, dive, snorkel in amazing waters and camp under the stars (West Coast).

- **Tracking Tainos:** In the dramatic and mysterious karst country, follow eco-guides through ancient rivers and along forest paths used by the island's first inhabitants (Central Mountains).

- **Camuy Caves:** Go for the thrill of rappelling and body rafting, or take the mellower guided tour through the burrowing system of caves and rivers – one of the largest in the world! (North Coast).

- **Walking Old San Juan:** Discover colonial history while walking the enchanting streets of Old San Juan (San Juan & Environs).

- **Hiking El Yunque:** Within its incredible biodiversity, the only rain forest in US territory has many natural pools and waterfalls, where you can swim and shower under the canopy of a tropical paradise (East Coast).

- **Desecheo Island:** Explore the surreal underwater realm around Isla de Desecheo, just a short boat ride from Rincón (West Coast).

- **Culebra Sun Worshipping:** Escape to the one of the "Last Virgins," as Vieques and Culebra are sometimes called, find a spot on one of the world's most gorgeous beaches and do nothing. Absolutely nothing (Vieques & Culebra).

- **Bioluminescent Swims:** You and about a trillion micro-organisms make a natural light show at Mosquito Bay – probably the world's finest bioluminescent lagoon – where eco-guides explain all (Vieques & Culebra).

- **Sub-Tropical Fun:** Learn to windsurf, ocean kayak and mountain bike through the Guánica sub-tropical dry forest and around offshore mangrove cays (South Coast).

■ **Sun-Dappled Horseback Rides:** At the prettiest deserted beaches in the northwest, ride fine horses along the sand and through almond groves, stopping for a swim in the warm ocean and a hike along some cliffs (North Coast).

■ On Horseback

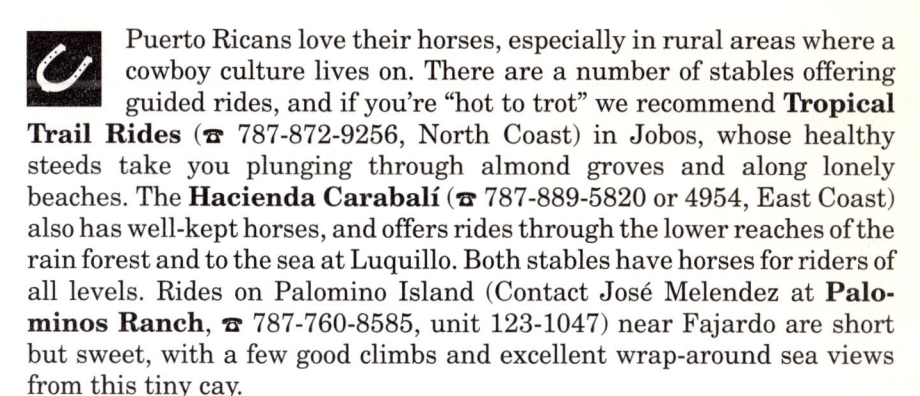

Puerto Ricans love their horses, especially in rural areas where a cowboy culture lives on. There are a number of stables offering guided rides, and if you're "hot to trot" we recommend **Tropical Trail Rides** (☎ 787-872-9256, North Coast) in Jobos, whose healthy steeds take you plunging through almond groves and along lonely beaches. The **Hacienda Carabalí** (☎ 787-889-5820 or 4954, East Coast) also has well-kept horses, and offers rides through the lower reaches of the rain forest and to the sea at Luquillo. Both stables have horses for riders of all levels. Rides on Palomino Island (Contact José Melendez at **Palominos Ranch**, ☎ 787-760-8585, unit 123-1047) near Fajardo are short but sweet, with a few good climbs and excellent wrap-around sea views from this tiny cay.

■ On Wheels

Cycling & Mountain Biking

Around San Juan you'll find several well-kept and easy biking paths that can take you along seaside ruins of Spanish colonial forts to the old part of the city, through the beachfront palm groves of **Piñones** or around **Isla de Cabras** near the Bacardí rum factory. Check out **Condado Bicycle**, ☎ 787-722-6288, in Condado, or **Bike Stop**, ☎ 787-782-2282, in Río Piedras for more information.

During the second week of every May, more than 100 athletes from clubs in Puerto Rico and the Caribbean gather for the **Cycling Competition** in Sabana Grande. Otherwise, road cycling on the island is spotty at best. We don't advise cycling around the island – the roads are too narrow and the traffic is too erratic. But there are some great mountain biking trails. One island favorite is at **Bosque Cambaleche** in Arecibo (North Coast), with a five-mile advanced course that features challenging ups and a few pulse-pounding single-track downs, as well as trails for more modest cyclers. Other favorite rides in Puerto Rico are **Las Pardas** in Guánica (South Coast), **El Viadon** in Cabo Rojo and around **Puntas** in Rincón (West Coast), and the easy ride through central **Aguirre** on the South Coast. Bike tour operators such as Bike Stop, Condado Bicycle and Isabela Mountain Bike offer all-inclusive day and overnight trips with gear rentals and meals included. Most can also provide maps and rent you bikes and racks if you'd prefer to go it alone.

Driving

Driving the **Ruta Panorámica** along the spine of La Cordillera Central (central mountains) is a pilgrimage of beauty for motorists. Beware: It's not for the faint of heart. Roads snake through hairpin mountain curves and rockslides are not uncommon during the rainy summer season. But the rewards include simultaneous views of the Atlantic and Caribbean, stop-offs at dwarf rain forests and strange tropical highland outposts, and visits to the "pure" *jíbaro*-culture interior.

On Water

Swimming & Sun Worshipping

Considering the startling fact that (according to a recent newspaper survey) only one in five Puerto Ricans can swim, it's easy to understand why so many public beaches are located on shallow, sandy shores with calm waters. If you don't mind (especially weekend) crowds, beaches such as **Luquillo** (East Coast), **El Combate** (West Coast) **Ocean Park** and **Isla Verde** (San Juan) are a swimmer's dream, with waves no bigger than ripples and rent-able float toys for open-water novices. If you are comfortable in the water, the whole island is your oyster. There's a good beach every few miles along most of the coastline and, of course, on the islands of Culebra and Vieques. See the following chapters for beach-by-beach reviews. Currents in some areas around the island can be strong, so be sure to check before getting in over your head.

Surfing

Ever since the World Surfing Championships were held in Rincón in 1968, Puerto Rico has been a temporary home to an annual migration of wave seekers. The best months to come are November through March, when swells along the northwest corner of the island can reach up to 25-30 feet and things get a little hairy. Most of the gringo surfers flock to **Puntas** in Rincón (West Coast) and the stretches of sand between **Aguadilla** and **Isabela** (West and North coasts). Locals surf there too, and all along the north coast and even a few spots on the east coast. Swells can get big at a couple of breaks around **Arecibo**, and there's a small but thriving surf scene around **La Pared** in Luquillo. Surf shops near all the spots listed above rent out surfboards by the day, and you'll find plenty of like-minded souls around with whom to compare notes and gripe about how etiquette on the water just isn't what it used to be.

Diving & Snorkeling

It is often said that scuba diving is the closest you can come to space exploration, and not just because of the incredible feeling of weightlessness under water or the silence that envelops the exaggerated sound of your breathing. Life down there is simply another planet, filled with strange and whimsically shaped creatures painted in impossible colors and spectrum-defying hues. Blessed with some of the best diving in the Caribbean, Puerto Rico has a few truly world-class sites, such as the otherworldly **Isla Mona** (with visibility of up to 200 feet), the waters around **Desecheo Island** (West Coast), the infinite Wall near **Parguera** (South Coast) and around **Vieques** and **Culebra** islands. In general, the farther you get from the Puerto Rican mainland the better the visibility, since river runoff from the mountains tends to cloud coastal waters. Still, even diving or snorkeling off certain beaches is better than anything to be found in the United States. Great snorkeling destinations include the cays near **Fajardo** and **Culebra** and a number of shoreline reefs along the northwest corner of the island.

If you are a certified scuba diver, be sure to bring your PADI or SSI card because the reputable dive shops will ask to see it. If you're not certified, Puerto Rico is an excellent place to learn. Most dive shops around the island offer courses for $300-$350, which includes classroom and confined-water training and four open-water dives. Many shops also offer one-tank "discover" dives for the uninitiated, with a capable instructor at your side the whole way.

> **TIP:** *Divers with the bends no longer have to fly to Florida to find a decompression chamber. The new **Hyperbaric Medical Facility** in San Juan is one of the best in the world and is the largest in Latin America;* ☎ *787-281-2794/2797.*

Kayaks, Surf Bikes & Other Beach Toys

You'll find plastic kayaks for rent at many of the island's large public beaches, where you can paddle around outside the swimming areas. For a more peaceful experience, try kayaking through the labyrinthine mangroves at **Parguera**, **Aguirre** (South Coast), **Laguna de Condado** (San Juan) or **Las Cabezas de San Juan** near Fajardo. Another way to play off the beach is by riding the kayak-bicycle hybrid known as the "surf bike," a new invention that is beginning to pop up in surfing and kayak shops island-wide. A more nefarious machine, the personal watercraft (Jet Ski is one brand name), shatters tranquility wherever it goes. Unfortunately, this evil toy is hugely popular in Puerto Rico. We recommend against using them because they disturb wildlife in and out of the water and are a danger and a nuisance to humans. If you absolutely must ride one, try to stick to the waters around San Juan, which already suffer from enough noise pollution that the waspy whine of your engine will make little difference.

Whale Watching

Families of endangered humpback whales pass through the **Mona Passage** and the waters around **Vieques** and **Culebra** every year between January and April, to breed in the warm Caribbean waters. A few west coast charter companies offer half- or full-day trips to see these magnificent creatures, and the Puntas lighthouse in Rincón is one of the only passive (from land) whale-watching parks in the world.

Fishing

The waters around the **Puerto Rican Trench** – where submerged cliffs measuring thousands of feet drop to an eventual depth of 28,000 feet – make the island ideal blue marlin country, especially in the months of July through October. Tournaments abound, especially during marlin season, including the **International Billfish Tournament** (early September), which organizers claim is the longest running consecutively held big-game fishing event in the world. For tournament information, contact Club Naútico in San Juan, ☎ 787-722-0177. Sportfishing charter operations can be found dotted along all four coasts, and backwater fishing is also hugely popular, with some hotspots for bonefish, tarpon, snook and jacks.

BACKWATER FISHING - SEASONAL CATCHES

	BONEFISH	TARPON	SNOOK	JACK CREVALLE
JAN	★★	★★★★	★★★	★★★★
FEB	★	★★★★	★★★★	★★★★
MAR	★	★★★★	★★★★	★★★
APR	★	★★★★	★★★★	★★
MAY	★	★★★★	★★★	★★
JUN	★	★★★	★★	★★
JUL	★	★★	★★	★★
AUG	★★	★★	★★	★★
SEP	★★★	★★	★★	★★
OCT	★★★★	★★★	★★	★★★
NOV	★★★★	★★★★	★★	★★★★
DEC	★★★	★★★★	★★	★★★★

★ = FAIR   ★★ = GOOD   ★★★ = GREAT   ★★★★ = PEAK

DEEP-WATER FISHING – SEASONAL CATCHES

	BLUE MARLIN	BLUE MARLIN ON FLY	WHITE MARLIN	MAHI-MAHI	WAHOO	SAIL-FISH
JAN	★★	★★	★	★★★★	★★★	★★★★
FEB	★★	★★	★	★★★★	★★	★★★★
MAR	★★	★★	★★	★★★★	★★	★★★
APR	★★	★★	★★★	★★★	★★	★★
MAY	★★	★★	★★★★	★★	★★	★
JUN	★★★	★★	★★★★	★★	★★	★
JUL	★★★★	★★★	★★★	★★	★★	★
AUG	★★★★	★★★★	★★	★★	★★	★★
SEP	★★★★	★★★★	★	★★	★★★	★★★
OCT	★★★	★★★★	★	★★★	★★★★	★★★★
NOV	★★	★★★	★	★★★★	★★★★	★★★★
DEC	★★	★★	★	★★★★	★★★★	★★★★

★ = FAIR   ★★ = GOOD   ★★★ = GREAT   ★★★★ = PEAK

Source: Capt. Omar Orraca, www.fishinginpuertorico.com. Used with permission.

Sailing

Cut loose and let the Caribbean winds push you out to sea, and you may want to never return! Puerto Rico is a fine beginning or end point for a sailing charter – whether it's a one-day excursion or a weeks-long voyage to distant and exotic isles. Dozens of companies operate crewed and non-crewed charters out of the **Puerto Real** marina in Fajardo (one of the largest marinas in the Caribbean), **Club Nautico** in San Juan, and the southern towns of **Salinas** and **Parguera**. Salinas is by far the prettiest marina. Day excursions are especially popular from **Villa Marina** in the Fajardo area, where catamarans take large groups on snorkeling/sailing trips to a string of nearby cays. To charter your own (non-crewed) boat, be sure to bring some written documentation, such as a captain's license or proof of enrollment in a sailing school (documented experience). Smaller crafts may be rented without documents, but some owners may ask you to somehow demonstrate your knowledge of sailing.

■ Spectator Sports & Activities

Goose-Stepping Horses

Paso Fino horses – the darlings of teenagers and men throughout rural Puerto Rican towns – are known for their fine bone structure, elegant profile and distinctive gait. Named for their high "fine step," Paso Finos were brought to the island in the 1500s by the first wave of conquistadors and are direct descendants of the world-famous Andalusian horses of southern Spain. Their lineage can be traced as far back as the Mongols, who introduced a swift battle horse to the Arab countries about 800 years ago, producing a new breed called the Berberisco (Berber) in North Africa. From there, the breed was introduced to Spain. Today there are more than 7,000 registered Paso Finos in Puerto Rico, the best of which are essentially show horses that – after centuries of breeding, competition and racing – emerged as symbols of wealth and entertainment for the upper classes. The majority, however, are ridden for fun and as transportation by would-be street cowboys. The **Dulce Sueño Paso Fino Fair** (see *Festivals & Events*, page 39) is the most important show and takes place in Guayama for two days in early March. Another good event, the **Fiesta La Candelaria**, happens the first weekend in February in Manatí. Contact the Manatí City Hall, ☎ 787-854-2868, for more information. For those intent on gambling outside the casinos, traditional horse racing also takes place on Wednesdays, Fridays, Sundays and holidays at **El Combate** in Canóvanas (Hwy. 3, Km. 5.5), which locals claim to be one of the prettiest racetracks in the hemisphere.

Gladiator Birds

Many people might think of **cockfighting** as a cruel blood sport enjoyable only to sadists and barbarians, but as in many Caribbean islands it's extremely popular in Puerto Rico. To its followers, *la pelea de gallos* is not a sport, but an *afición* – an activity of passion. On Friday evenings and Sundays, hordes of (mostly) men, young and old, throng to small arenas scattered throughout the island, many bringing their own roosters. The atmosphere is informal and congenial yet highly charged. Once all the *galleros* have arrived, roosters in hand, they mingle around calling out the weights of their birds in order to match them for a fight. The roosters are then classified. Their innermost "thumb" talons are clipped and replaced with sharp plastic barbs, in order to even the playing field between birds with naturally long and short talons. The object of the match is to stab, peck and kill, of course. But the real drama is between the spectators, who place bets by shouting across the ring. At the more prestigious events, sums lost and won can reach tens of thousands of dollars. Losing roosters are unceremoniously dumped in the trash. The largest cockfighting arena on the island is **Club Gallistico de Puerto Rico**, ☎ 787-791-1557; Isla Verde Ave. Open 2 p.m. to 9 p.m. Elsewhere on the island it's best to show up late to these fights. As many as 34 matches can drag on for up to six hours, and the most intense action usually comes near the end.

Eco-Travel

Eco-travel means traveling with an interest in and a respect for the natural environment. Almost all travel should be eco-travel. In this book, we've designated adventures as "eco-travel" when they fall within governmental natural reserves, forests or parkland, or if they are especially focused on the appreciation of nature. Eco-travel is as much a responsibility as an opportunity. It means that you leave a place in the same or a better state than you found it. Respect for trails, the protection of the environment and packing out trash are fundamental. For its size and population, Puerto Rico has an incredible number and range of eco-travel destinations. See following chapters for more details.

Shopping

Though Puerto Rico is chock full of strip malls and American-style shopping centers, the most invigorating shopping experience is in Old San Juan, where you can find anything from elegant European designer outlets to funky fashion and craft shops, and from stores hawking pungent cigars, Panama hats and rum to cheesy kiosks selling gaudy fridge magnets and T-shirts.

■ Foodstuffs

You won't find better **rum** for a lower price anywhere in the world. Islanders consider Don Q the best, available in *cristal*, *añejo* and dark. For specialty or rare rums try any of several shops on Calle Fortaleza in San Juan.

Coffee is another obvious treat to take back home, and many of the island coffee farms make gift packages of their finest roasts. The best and most expensive coffees are Alto Grande (deemed one of the world's three greatest beans) and Yauco, but if you want to go for something a bit cheaper Yaucono is also good and is what many locals drink.

Hot sauce – though rarely eaten by islanders – is a Caribbean fixture, and a few small enterprises brew salsas made of fiery local chili peppers, mangos, pineapples and other fruits with a distinctive flavor sure to keep the heat burning long after you return home. Virgin Fire is a Rincón-based manufacturer, producing hot sauces with cool names like Dragon's Breath and Pineapple Sizzle. Buy them individually or in special gift packs from shops all over the island.

■ Cigars

Because the same import/export laws apply to Puerto Rico as to the US, it's very difficult to get hold of a good *Cubano* (unless you buy them illegally, or take a side trip to the Dominican Republic). However, Puerto Rican **cigar** bars and shops stock plenty of brands rolled on the island and elsewhere to please all but the most discerning aficionado. Take home a local cigar, and you've got a souvenir of a bit of history.

Despite the tobacco industry's decline, a culture of cigar smoking persists and local production continues. Smokers should look for the cigars of Enrique Velázquez, owner of **EMV International House of Cigars**, 1203 Americo Miranda, Perparto Metropolitano, ☎ 787-782-6871 or 783-5116, fax 787-781-0069, e-mail emvcigar@coqui.net. His locally produced cigars – Señor Velázquez Selectos – are widely considered among the best in Puerto Rico. The shop has a special smoker's suite and free espresso for visitors wishing to try before they buy. **Club Jibarito**, Calle Cristo, ☎ 787-724-7797, fax 787-724-4358, e-mail jibarito@tld.net, is the height of cigar luxury, also with a smokers' room and a range of gentleman's gifts. Many of the big hotels have cigar bars.

CIGAR-MAKING WAS AN EDUCATION

During the 18th and 19th centuries, when tobacco production peaked in Puerto Rico, owners of large plantations took the commendable action of employing "readers" to alleviate the monotony of cigar rolling. In a time of no television or radio, readers were among the few educated men on the island and would pass the day reading out loud from whatever newspaper was available, at the same time providing some semblance of an education to the workers. By the time the production of cigars and other agricultural goods began to be phased out to make room for the Industrial Revolution, "rollers" were the most literate and well-informed rural workers on island. They quickly rose to positions of leadership in newly formed labor organizations, and some of today's Puerto Rican union leaders are grandsons and granddaughters of yesterday's cigar rollers.

■ Panama Hats

Though not strictly Puerto Rican, Panama and Borsalino hats are widely worn among rural gentlemen and are available for purchase in Old San Juan, starting at about $25 and reaching well in excess of $500. You will see several shops on Calle Fortaleza selling tailored hats. The best is **Olé**, ☎ 787-724-2445, fax 722-5304. They will block your hat to exactly fit the size of your head and have a good range of styles.

■ Folk Art

Puerto Rican arts and crafts are available in contemporary and antique forms, and the discerning shopper can pick up some real bargains. **Santos** are carved religious figures – usually wooden – and few traditional Puerto Rican homes are without at least one. You will often see lighted candles flickering on shrines laden with offerings to the various saints, most commonly St. Anthony or one of the virgins. Warding off evil and bringing good fortune to their believers, *santos* are immensely important to superstitious islanders, so much so that these days ceremonies held at home in honor of the saints sometimes replace Mass.

In San Juan, **Puerto Rico Arts & Crafts** on Calle Fortaleza, ☎ 787-725-5596, is a good outlet for all Puerto Rican crafts, including *santos*, along with the **Popular Arts and Crafts Center** on Calle Cristo, ☎ 787-722-0621. The **Fomento Económica Artesanía Offices**, ☎ 787-758-4747, provides lists of *santeros* (*santos* carvers). **Olé**, also on Calle Fortaleza, ☎ 787-724-2445, has an interesting collection and is one of the better places to get a bargain if you're in the market for antiques.

Puerto Rican woodcarver. (Sandra Reus, for the PRTC)

Brightly colored, papier-mâché **carnival masks** from Ponce or carved and painted **coconut husks** from Loíza capture the festive spirit of the island. The carved coconut husks are available almost exclusively from the town of Loíza, but the devilish horned faces of the Ponce carnival are widely sold in sizes ranging from matchbox to mammoth. You'll find them in shops on Calle Fortaleza in San Juan.

If you think lace is a gift only for granny, think again. Puerto Rican *mundillo* **lace** is making a big comeback in the shape of elegant bed and table linens, and is eagerly sought by collectors. **The Folk Arts Center** at the Dominican Convent, Calle Norzagaray in Old San Juan, ☎ 787-722-0621, has a fine display of this delicate craft as well as information on where and what to buy. Enthusiasts should try to make the trip to the center of lace making – a small town called **Moca** on the west coast – or go to the **Weaving Festival** held at the end of April in Isabela (call the city hall in Isabella for more information; ☎ 787-872-6400).

■ Unique Items

For something completely different, **The Butterfly People**, Calle Fortaleza, Old San Juan, ☎ 787-723-2432, fax 723-2201, www.butterflypeople.com, e-mail info@butterflypeople.com, has the largest collection of mounted butterflies in the world. Gathered from natural deaths (according to the owners) from all over the world, the butterflies are carefully wrapped in waxed paper and sent to San Juan, where butterfly artist Attenaire Purinton creates a pallet of the most intense and luminous colors on Earth. From single species to whole compositions of 30 or more butterflies, these are some of the most magnificent artworks in Puerto Rico.

Travel Information

■ When To Go

The mild Puerto Rican climate lends itself to vacation getaways year round. The height of the tourist season is between November and March, when sun-starved northerners head south for sun, sand and waves. You'll find that many prices quoted during the high season decrease by to 20-30% the rest of the year. Puerto Ricans take their vacations during the summer months, and reservations at top inns, restaurants and attractions may be scarcer from mid-June to mid-August. From late August until early November, prices drop significantly and the island becomes noticeably sleepier. Remember that planning a vacation during hurricane season (June 15-November 15) involves an element of risk.

■ Crime

Puerto Rico has a definite crime problem, with an average of more than two murders a day, rampant drug trafficking and high rates of break-ins and other offenses. You'll see bars on the windows of most houses in poorer urban areas, and newspapers are full of sensational crime reporting. Despite this, visitors should feel safe in Puerto Rico. Violent crime is almost completely kept within the boundaries of poor urban areas, where it is usually drug-related, gang-on-gang attacks. Violence is almost unheard of in tourist areas and towns, where police presence is extremely visible due to the importance of tourism to the Puerto Rican economy. You'll find that police officers are friendly and helpful, especially to visitors. Rural areas are pretty safe, too, probably because residents of small towns all know each other and it's hard to get away with anything there.

KEEPING SAFE

The only real dangers to tourists are theft and muggings. Using common sense, you can avoid these.

- Keep valuables locked up.
- Don't sling your purse or wallet on a bar.
- Park your rental car in public parking lots or in other places where it's not likely to be stolen.
- Leave nothing of any value (including cigarettes and sunglasses) where it can be seen inside your car when you park.

A few popular beaches have gained a reputation as late-night mugging areas (Condado and Isla Verde are often mentioned), but we've never encountered or heard of any problems that should prevent you from taking a moonlit stroll by the sea. Keep your wits about you, and if you ever are the victim of a mugging, don't resist. Muggers are usually desperate or strung out on drugs, and some carry weapons. Just give them your wallet. As a general rule, if you are in an area with other people around, you're usually safe. If for some reason you ever should need help, gallant Puerto Ricans are quick to come to your aid.

> **TOURIST POLICE:** *If you need assistance In the Condado or Isla Verde areas outside San Juan, contact the Tourist Police (contact numbers on page 70), who specialize in dealing with typical tourist complaints, from stolen bags to more serious problems. Officers speak English, and visitors will probably find their complaints dealt with more quickly and efficiently than through the regular police department.*

FOR EMERGENCIES, DIAL 9-1-1

As in the United States, the toll-free number to dial in case of an emergency is 911.

■ Traveling With Kids

Puerto Rico is extremely kid-friendly, with endless activities designed for whole families. It's also a relatively safe place to bring a child, with few dangerous animals or insects (on land). The disease rate is low, and you won't have to worry about your child coming home with some weird tropical infection. If your kids are aged between five and 12, it may be worth staying in one of the big resort hotels, as many offer family packages with reliable "kids' clubs," which give you a chance to sneak off with a clear conscience. Kids' clubs usually cost between $25 and $35 a day with activities and lunch included. Most resorts also have plenty of game rooms, sports facilities and discos to keep teenagers occupied.

Many adventures in Puerto Rico are just as much fun for kids as they are for adults, including subterranean treks into the Río Camuy Cave Park, hikes and picnics in El Yunque or the endless supply of water adventures. For entertainment tailored directly to children, **Cascadas Water Park** (☎ 787-891-1005) near Aguadilla has flumes and dizzying aqua chutes, but it's open only during the summer months. In the San Juan area, **Plaza Acuática**, ☎ 787-754-9800 (opposite Plaza las Américas) has slides, rapids and mini-golf. The safest beaches for kids are the public ones. Invariably they have very calm water and an area cordoned off for swimmers, but lifeguards are rare so keep an eye on your brood. Adventurous kids might like to try something new such as the **Bubblemakers** program, teaching kids aged eight and older how to scuba dive. Many dive shops offer this course.

In Cupey, **Solid Rock**, ☎ 787-751-1512, a climbing gym, boasts 14,000 feet of artificial rock walls, and welcomes children as young as three. Indoor activities for kids include **Luis A. Ferré Science Park**, in Bayamón, ☎ 787-740-6868. Immensely popular, it has seven themed museums – all with interactive displays – a zoo, kiddies' park and great picnic areas. In Old San Juan, **Museo del Niño** on Calle Cristo, ☎ 787-722-3791, is one of a rare breed of museums designed especially with children in mind. On Sunday afternoons between 4 p.m. and 5 p.m. a **children's theater** takes place on the Paseo La Pincesa, also in Old San Juan, ☎ 787-723-0692 for details.

■ Special Needs

Women Travelers

There is absolutely nothing that should discourage confident women travelers from going it alone or with other women in Puerto Rico. This is a progressive, well-educated society and, contrary to the bogus Latino cultural stereotype, women are not subject to male dominance or much harassment. Many local women have high-powered careers, and choose not to get married or have children. Male machismo is quickly becoming a creature of the past, if for no other reason than the fact that women will no longer put up with it. Most Puerto Rican men are extremely polite and chivalrous, and genuinely interested in talking to foreigners of both sexes. Women traveling alone may get special attention from men but, well, they're men, aren't they? That said, there are always a few rotten apples who try to spoil the reputation of the rest. The occasional cretin still practices the habit of "hissing" at women they find attractive, and though this is not particularly threatening, it can be annoying. All you can really do is ignore it and avoid a confrontation. In terms of safety, the same rules apply here as anywhere else in the world. Don't go walking on unlit, empty beaches or parks alone at night, avoid dark streets and alleyways, lock car doors if you're driving alone and don't pick up hitchhikers. Above all, retain your sense of humor. This will always relieve a potentially bad situation more effectively than a temper tantrum. For women's resources, try **Women in Action Entertainment Group**, PO Box 11850, Suite 301, San Juan, PR 00922-1850, ☎ 787-723-4538.

Gay & Lesbian Travelers

There is probably no better destination for gay and lesbian travelers in the Caribbean than Puerto Rico, and nowhere more so than in San Juan (see pages 108-109). The Condado strip and nearby Ocean Park are just as steamy as Puerto Vallarta, Mexico, without the redneck factor. For a completely over-the-top, decadent gay holiday, you're probably best off finding accommodations in the middle of the action. Condado has a few hip nightclubs, wonderful food, beachfront villas and beautiful people. Being gay in Puerto Rico really isn't an issue, providing you're not traveling to remote areas with your partner and making a spectacle of yourselves in local straight bars. Old San Juan is probably less gay-oriented than Condado, and the rest of the island is more conservative than Old San Juan. However, most Puerto Ricans are open-minded and extremely friendly to strangers, and there's really no reason why you shouldn't have a ball wherever you go.

We definitely recommend taking time out from the party to explore the island. You'll find gay-friendly hotspots outside of San Juan, too (San Juan hangouts are listed on page 126). On the east coast, **Bebo's Pub**, Carr. 187 in Piñones, has DJs, with drag acts and strippers on weekends. **Mirabueno**, ☎ 787-809-5809, Carr. 3, Int. 967, in Río Grande, is a small, gay-friendly Spanish restaurant, with live drumming intermittently. On the south coast, the most popular gay venue in Ponce is **The Cave**, ☎ 787-840-5461, Barrio Tenerías, which also features drag acts and strippers. A more mainstream crowd hangs out at **Michaelangelo's**, ☎ 787-844-2914, Carr. 10. Heading west to the student town of San Germán, check out **Norman's Bar**, Barrio Maresúa, Carr. 318, or **The World**, ☎ 787-264-2002, Carr 360. Both have occasional drag shows. En route from kayaking adventures in La Parguera (or secluded sunbathing at one of the cays midweek), stop in Lajas at **Milagro's Place**, Carr. 116, for a cocktail and a chat with the locals.

On the west coast, Boquerón has a couple of mixed-crowd bars. The **Fish Net** is a typical seafood joint by day but packs in local revelers at night, and **Shamar** (a bit more ambient) is right on the beach. **El Quinque Pub de Confe Jr.**, Barrio Carreras (near Añasco), comes recommended. In Rincón, Deirdre and Layla at **Café con Leche** (in the center of town), will welcome you with open arms (as will all their customers). It's a before- and after-hours place hauling in a mixed crowd of late-night drinkers along with gay regulars from the west coast. Movie nights on Wednesdays show anything from *The Adventures of Priscilla, Queen of the Desert* to *Pulp Fiction*. Prepare to party till dawn, and give the girls our best regards when you do. In Jobos, **Villa Ricomar**, Carr. 459, has pool tables and occasional drag shows, strippers and DJs.

The only gay-friendly spot we've heard of on the north coast is **El Diamante** in Morovis, with music and dancing. In the central mountains, **Kenny's**, Carr. 360 in Caguas, is another drag hall with billiards and lively music. Gay and lesbian travelers might also consider a hopping over to Culebra or, especially, Vieques, which are both extremely popular destinations.

GAY & LESBIAN RESOURCES

- The **Atlantic Beach Hotel**, ☎ 787-721-6900, Calle Vendig, Condado, and **Scriptum Books**, ☎ 787-724-1123, 1129 Ashford Avenue, Condado, are both excellent resources for getting the lowdown on gay events and activities during your stay.

- Another good resource is the **Gay Pride Coalition**, PO Box 8836, Fernandez Juncos Station, Santurce, PR 00911, ☎ 787-261-2590.

- If you're a student, the University of Puerto Rico can you put you in touch with gay and lesbian groups. Try the **College Community Pro Gay Equality Group**, ☎ 787-764-0000, ext. 6389, Río Piedras Campus, or the **Gay and Lesbian Support Group**, ☎ 787-764-0000, ext. 5683 / 5684, also Río Piedras. Ask about any similar groups that may be operating out of R.U.M. (University of Mayagüez).

- Lesbian moms can write to **Lesbian Mothers**, PO Box 1003, Old San Juan, PR 00902, for information on meeting other women and what to do in Puerto Rico with a kid in tow.

- Apparently, there is a scuba diving club for the gay and lesbian community, called **Breeze Divers**, ☎ 787-282-7184. We couldn't get through to them, but maybe you'll have better luck.

- Finally, should you find yourself the victim of violence or any other violation of your basic human rights contact the **Human Rights Foundation**, ☎ 787-289-2407, fax 731-6757, 1357 Ashford Avenue, Box 402, San Juan, PR 00907-1432.

Travelers With Disabilities

This is neither the best nor the worst place in the world for travelers with disabilities, although standards may seem a bit lax compared to those set by the United States and northern Europe. Compared to other Caribbean islands, however, it's a breeze. Federal law dictates that all public buildings must have wheelchair access and all of the big chain hotels have rooms and toilets specifically designed for their guests with such needs. The **Hyatt Dorado Beach Resort,** ☎ 787-796-1234, on the breezy north coast, comes highly recommended, with facilities such as a shuttle bus with wheelchair lift.

For adventures, we recommend the following excursions: **El Yunque**, which has a wheelchair-accessible visitor center, with "best-of" examples from the rain forest, and wheelchair-friendly bus tours; and **Luquillo Beach**, which has wide concrete paths through groves of seaside palm trees. In San Juan, **Wheelchair Getaway**, ☎ 800-868-8028, cell 787-378-9192, takes vans with space for two wheelchairs each on excellent tours of the old city and the Bacardí rum factory, as well as to the rain forest. Full transport is available between the airport, hotels and cruise ships.

Some of the smaller guest houses around the island also have facilities designed with wheelchair travelers in mind (see the *Where To Stay* sections in each chapter). Access to some of the restaurants, particularly in Old San Juan, could prove a bit tricky, as many are small with narrow courtyards and little space between tables. But Puerto Rican hospitality being what it is, you will usually find restaurant owners and their staff more than happy to try and accommodate you, especially if you give some advance notice.

Support Groups

Help for addicts: If you've kicked and need a meeting, check out **Narcotics Anonymous,** Grace Lutheran Church, 150 De Parke St., Santurce, PR, ☎ 787-763-5919. They can also point the way to Alcoholics Anonymous meetings.

■ Money & Costs

The currency of Puerto Rico is the US dollar. Cost-wise, the island is on par with most of the United States and southern Europe. During peak season (December to April) prices rise by up to 25%, but even at low season, the cheapest accommodations hover around the $60-80 mark. If your budget is really tight but you're determined to go, consider camping and cooking for yourself – or looking for long-term rental on a house. If money is no object, then Puerto Rico offers an infinite variety of beachfront hotels – from the action-packed Condado strip in San Juan to the isolated shores of Bosque Estatal de Guánica to mountain retreats in the numerous coffee plantations and sugar haciendas hidden in the island's mountainous center. On the whole, however, plan on spending between $50 and $200 a day.

> **TIP:** *Travelers' checks are accepted almost everywhere, and even small towns have automatic teller machines where you can get cash.*

The easiest way to cover your costs while traveling is with a credit card. There are ATMs (called ATH in Puerto Rico) in every town and on most major high streets in the city. Visitors will also find that most hotels, guest houses and restaurants (even the small ones) accept all or most major credit cards. Travelers checks can be used almost as freely as cash, or changed at banks, including **Banco Popular**, ☎ 787-724-3659 (this 24-hour number gives locations), the **Thomas Cook Foreign Exchange** at the Luis Muñoz Marín Airport, ☎ 787-791-2233 (open 9 a.m. to 8 p.m.), and most major hotels.

Tipping

As in the US, tipping is par for the course, and visitors should bear in mind that bar and waitstaff rely on tips for their income. Sometimes a 15% gratuity will be automatically added to your bill. Otherwise, a tip of 15 to 20% is customary.

Wiring Cash

Western Union, ☎ 800-325-4045, has outlets at Pueblo Xtra supermarkets island-wide, and other locations.

Customs

Puerto Rico falls under the jurisdiction of US Customs and the US Department of Agriculture. Generally, you're more likely to have your baggage checked traveling from Puerto Rico to the mainland US than the other way around. From abroad, expect to be inspected as rigorously as you would be upon entering the continental United States. Remember to leave agricultural products at home. Tobacco products, alcohol, canned goods and dried foods are usually exempt from customs restrictions.

Communications

Telephones

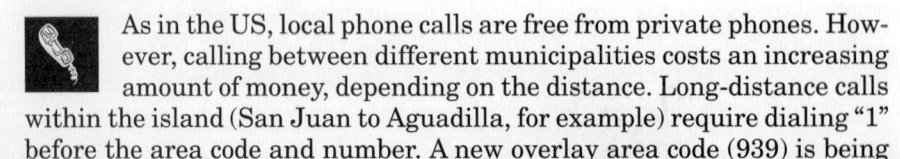

As in the US, local phone calls are free from private phones. However, calling between different municipalities costs an increasing amount of money, depending on the distance. Long-distance calls within the island (San Juan to Aguadilla, for example) require dialing "1" before the area code and number. A new overlay area code (939) is being implemented for new numbers sometime in 2001. Most numbers, however, will have the area code of 787. When calling to the United States and Europe from Puerto Rico, you'll enjoy savings if you purchase a phone calling card, easily available throughout Puerto Rico at drugstores, major supermarkests, internet cafés, and other stores (we recommend the Walgreens card). Most phone calling cards bought in the US will work in Puerto Rico.

E-mail & Internet Access

Internet use is beginning to boom here. AOL, CompuServe and other large servers now have dial-up numbers in San Juan. You will find several Internet cafés in San Juan and increasing numbers scattered around the island, particularly in main tourist areas. (These are listed at the beginning of each chapter.) On average, expect to pay at least $3 to $5 for half an hour online. If you travel with your own laptop, data-port access costs about the same at a cybercafé. Most of the major hotels now have business facilities that can be used by non-residents, but these are significantly more expensive.

Mail

Puerto Rico is part of the **United States Postal Service** system. You will find blue mailboxes and post offices in every town.

■ Newspapers & Magazines

The only English language newspaper in Puerto Rico (and the only one to win a Pulitzer prize) is the *San Juan Star*. The reporting is fairly good, though news buffs may find it a little thin in details. In San Juan you can usually pick up a copy of *The New York Times*, *The Miami Herald* and *USA Today* from bookstores such as Borders in Plaza las Américas, and Pueblo Xtra Supermarkets (the most convenient is on Calle Wilson and De Diego, Santurce).

There are also several free publications worth browsing through on arrival. *Que Pasa* is a bi-monthly publication (available from the front desk of most hotels and guest houses) with extensive and up-to-date listings pages for hotels, restaurants and places to hang out and have fun. *Where – San Juan* (available from the concierge at most big hotels) is monthly and has good filler stories on the latest and greatest things around town. *Bienvenidos* (some good feature stories on island heritage, food and drink) and pocket-sized *Places to Go* are both annual publications with lots of useful information.

Travel Directory

General Information

Directory Assistance .... ☎ 411
Talking Clock .... ☎ 787-728-9595
Weather................................... ☎ 787-766-7777
PR Tourism Company .... ☎ 787-721-2400 or 800-233-6530

Lost Or Stolen Credit Cards/Travelers Checks

American Express......................... ☎ 800-327-1267
MasterCard............................... ☎ 800-307-7309
Visa .... ☎ 800-847-2911

Emergencies & Medical Assistance

Emergencies..911
Police, San Juan (non-emergency)............ ☎ 787-793-1234
Fire / Ambulance.......................................911
Tourist Police, Condado .... ☎ 787-726-7020
Tourist Police, Isla Verde .... ☎ 787-728-4770
Air Ambulance Service ..... ☎ 787-756-3424 / 877-AEROMED
Medical Emergency/Paramedics:
  San Juan .... ☎ 787-744-2222
  Elsewhere............................. ☎ 787-754-2550
Wheelchair Rental, San Juan .. ☎ 787-726-4023 / 800-868-8028
Río Piedras Medical Center, Emergency....... ☎ 787-777-3535
Cardiovascular Center, Río Piedras........... ☎ 787-754-8500
Centro Medíco de Puerto Rico, Emergency..... ☎ 787-754-3533
Río Piedras Pediatric Hospital............... ☎ 787-777-3535
Ashford Presbyterian Community
  Hospital, Condado .... ☎ 787-721-2160
Pavía Hospital, Santurce .... ☎ 787-727-6060
Hospital Dr. Gubern, Fajardo .... ☎ 787-863-0924
Hospital Bella Vista, Mayagüez.............. ☎ 787-834-6000
Hospital de Dama, Ponce .... ☎ 787-840-8686

Conservation & Environmentalism

Conservation Trust of Puerto Rico............ ☎ 787-722-5834
Natural History Society of Puerto Rico........ ☎ 787-726-5488
Puerto Rican Conservation Foundation .... ☎ 787-763-9875
Caribbean Environmental Information......... ☎ 787-751-0239
Committee to Save Guánica................... ☎ 787-821-2302

Helpful Web Sites

Web sites for hotels, guest houses, restaurants and adventure facilities are listed in the relevant chapters. For general information, check out the following:

- **www.prtourism.com** – Puerto Rico Tourism Company
- **www.sanjuan.org** – San Juan tourism info
- **www.fideicomiso.org** – Conservation Trust of Puerto Rico
- **www.travelmaps.com** – Maps of Puerto Rico
- **www.prhtasmallhotels.com** – Puerto Rican Hotels and Tourism Association site, listing various small hotels, including some with rock-bottom prices.
- **www.woofbyte.com/puertorico** – An up-to-date site for lesbian and gay accommodations, restaurants, clubs and bars.
- **www.greenheads.com/adventours** – Excellent adventure travel information about Puerto Rico.
- **www.gicco.com** – Puerto Rican coffees

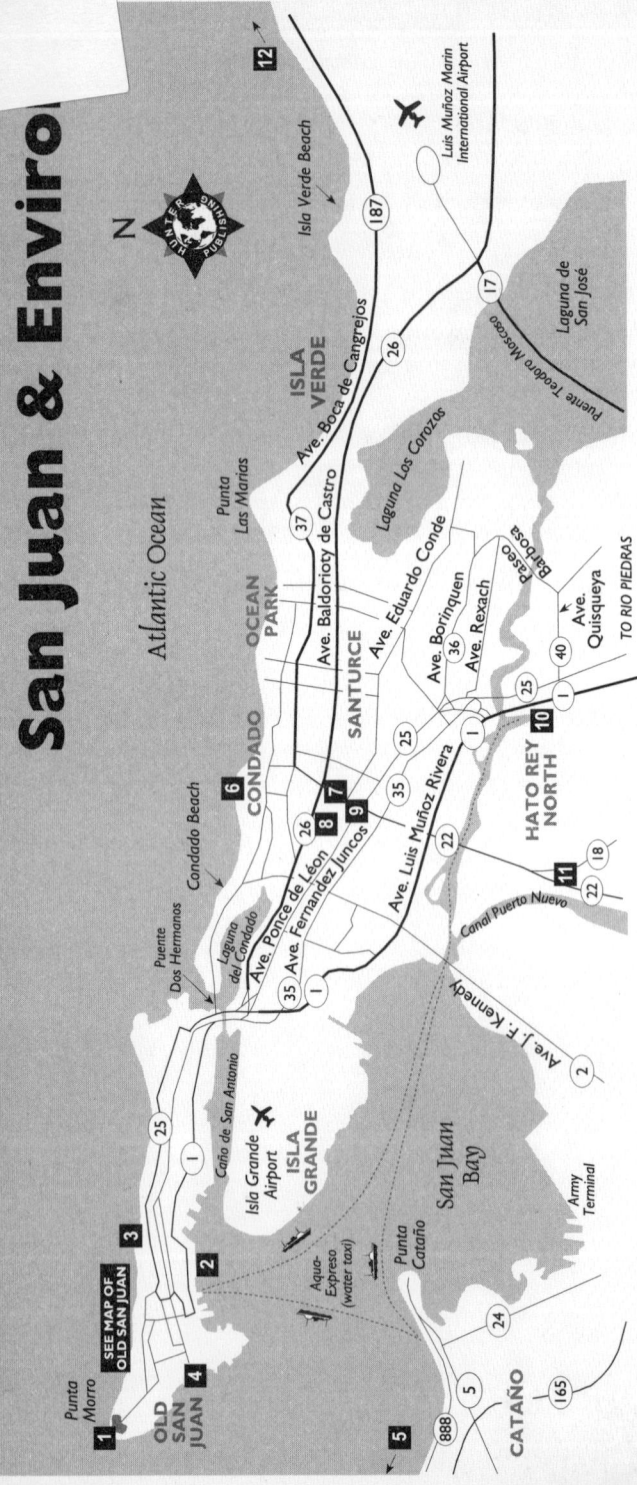

San Juan & Environs

1. Castillo San Felipe El Morro
2. Cruise ship and ferry docks
3. Fuerto San Cristobal
4. La Fortaleza
5. Bacardí Rum Distillery; Isla de Cabras; El Cañuelo Fort
6. Ashford Memorial Hospital
7. Museo de Arte de Puerto Rico
8. Plaza Mercado
9. Centro de Bellas Artes Luis A. Ferré
10. Aqua-Expreso Terminal
11. Plaza Las Americas Mall
12. Piñones State Forest

1 MILE
1.6 KM

© 2001 HUNTER PUBLISHING, INC

San Juan & Environs

San Juan is the oldest city in US territory, and the second-oldest in the Americas, and stakes its claim as the cultural and economic hub of the Caribbean. With high-end designer and jewelry shops, more than 30 limousine services in the phone book and more banks than you would want to count, it displays all the trappings of the wealthiest large city of the Antilles. It is also probably the world's greatest example of combined 20th-century North American and Spanish colonial influences – from the paella served at the Marriott and other high-rise hotels in Condado and Isla Verde, to the historic neighborhood of Old San Juan, where Chryslers and Buicks squeeze cautiously through cobblestone streets built just wide enough for the axle of a Spanish carriage.

IN THIS CHAPTER
- Old San Juan
- Condado
- Ocean Park
- Santurce
- Isla Verde
- Piñones
- Hato Rey
- Río Piedras
- Cataño
- El Cañuelo & the Isla de Cabas Peninsula
- Caparra

Despite outside influences, the allure of San Juan today is pure Puerto Rican. The city breathes – practically pants – with the energy of a cosmopolitan center flourishing in the gentle climate of the Caribbean. A new style called *nuevo Latino* is reinvented daily by those who create music, art and cuisine here, making San Juan one of the most happening cities in the Americas. From the colonial tourist center of Old San Juan to the beach neighborhoods of Condado, Ocean Park, Isla Verde and beyond, the city has treasures, both obvious and hidden, to delight any traveler.

Nearly two million people live in the greater metropolitan area and, like any city its size, San Juan has its share of problems. Many of the outlying areas have grown too quickly for responsible planning. Traffic reaches nightmare proportions at rush hour, and housing projects in poorer areas suffer from the related afflictions of drugs and gang violence. On the other hand, San Juan has undertaken an incredible renaissance during the past 15 years. Recently little more than a slummy relic of colonial power, Viejo San Juan – and increasingly the rest of the city – has transformed itself from a conquistador-era military outpost into the single most visited tourist site in the Caribbean.

Many visitors think of San Juan as one big beach with an appendage of charming old buildings. And while it's true that a visitor can spend a weeklong vacation doing nothing but lie in a chaise longue, soaking up sun and rum punches until the casinos reopen, there is much more to do. Hopefully, readers of this book will take the time to explore the fascinating culture of San Juan, and use it as a staging area for explorations of the island at large.

History

■ The Safest Harbor

In 1508, when the Spanish Crown granted Juan Ponce de León permission to colonize Puerto Rico, the island's first governor settled uncomfortably on the marshy banks of a small river in what is today the commercial Guaynabo district of the city. After several years of malaria outbreaks and harassment by Indians, he and a few dozen surviving settlers wisely began relocating in 1511 to a more defensible spear of land, what is now **Old San Juan**. Jutting out into the Atlantic Ocean and protecting a natural bay, the San Juan peninsula was quickly recognized for its potential as a military stronghold in the New World. In 1533, Spanish reinforcements built **La Fortaleza**, which today functions as the governor's seat, and six years later began construction of a massive fort – **El Morro** – at the peninsular tip, with ramparts up to 140 feet above the Atlantic Ocean, to guard over the entrance to the fledgling port.

La Fortaleza.
(PRTC)

■ Would-Be Conquerors

The scarcity of gold on the island failed to dissuade prospectors from stopping here, and soon the little port known as Puerto Rico (in the early days the name San Juan referred to the whole island) became a thriving supply and trade center for ore seekers en route to or from more remote regions of the Americas. Because of its location and protected harbor, it also became a "strong box" for Spanish gold in transit. Of course, this also made it irresistible to British, French and Dutch admirals in search of booty. In 1595 – only seven years after the defeat of the Spanish Armada off the British coast – the fearsome **Sir Francis Drake** attacked El Morro in what would be his last expedition. Frustrated by the firepower from the imposing fort, El Draque (as the Spanish called him) never gained a foothold on the island and died of plague aboard his ship soon afterwards. Three years later, **Sir George Clifford**, Count of Cumberland, laid siege to the city and managed to conquer some outlying areas, but was unable to take El Morro. Five months after the siege began, dysentery forced Clifford and his men to abandon their quest for the coveted port. The most devastating attack on San Juan came at the hands of Dutch General **Boudewin Hendricks**, who invaded the island by land with an overwhelming force in 1625. Though the Dutch quickly took over the city of San Juan, they too failed to crack El Morro, from which they were subject to constant counter-attack. Without control of the fort, Henricks realized, there was no control of the island. Frustrated, the Dutch troops burned San Juan and left.

■ The City Walls

After the Dutch left it in ruins, King Philip IV of Spain ordered the fortification of the entire city. Soon, 42-foot-high walls of sandstone brick – with a thickness of up to 20 feet in some places – surrounded the peninsula, with a few entrances, such as **Puerta de San Juan**, built to withstand almost any attack. At the neck of the headland, Irish-born engineers employed by the Spanish king designed the ingenious **Fuerte San Cristóbal** to protect the city from land invasions. By 1771, one hundred years later, ramparts extended between the two forts, making what is now Old San Juan practically impregnable. The last major attack on the city, by British **Lt. General Ralph Abercromby** in 1797, was such a dismal failure that in the future foreign ships would simply avoid San Juan.

A royal dictate requiring San Juan to trade only with Spanish ships increased the isolation of the city from outside influences. And while San Juan was designated the first papal see in the New World and remained a crucial stronghold of Spanish influence, rival cities such as Ponce and San Germán on the other side of the island thrived on smuggling and slowly sapped the economic strength of the capital. Waves of wealthy fugitives from revolutions in Haiti, the Dominican Republic, Venezuela and elsewhere breathed some new cultural life into San Juan during the 18th and 19th centuries. But by the end of the 19th century, the city represented fading Spanish power in the Americas, and the once-influential residents of this fortress city could only watch helplessly as events began to overtake them.

■ The American Century

After nearly 400 years, the only successful assault on El Morro ended with more of a whimper than a bang. Despite a few rounds of cannon fire between the old fort and US battleships, the heavy fighting of the 1898 **Spanish-American War** took place in Cuba. When it was over, defeated Spanish forces glumly handed over the keys to San Juan to the United States in a ceremony at La Fortaleza on October 18, 1898. At the time, the population of San Juan was estimated at about 12,000. Slowly at first, the city began to grow as North American influence opened it to increasing trade. World War II drew increased US attention to the strategic location of the island, and investment poured in from the north. It may have happened too fast. As poor farmers and agricultural workers flocked to San Juan to apply for new jobs offered by US-based manufacturers, roads and housing complexes spread at a pace that outstripped long-term planning efforts. North American residents and visitors preferred the beachside communities of Condado and Isla Verde, where they built high-rise luxury hotels that marked the beginning of the San Juan tourism industry. Moneyed East Coast residents seeking a sunny week away from the cold at home began to arrive in droves. These early visitors generally stayed within the confines of the all-inclusive hotels, however, and tourism revenues left the island almost as quickly as they arrived. Meanwhile, Old San Juan languished in terms of tourism, and until recently was better known for its seedy faded glory than as a classy, forward-thinking travel destination.

■ The Renaissance of San Juan

Since the late 20th century, the city of San Juan has undertaken an impressive face-lift of the historic quarter that could serve as a model for city planners everywhere. It goes well beyond the fresh coats of paint that brighten the pastel façades of the townhouses in Old San Juan. Ashford Avenue in Condado has undergone a major renovation, and an urban train is planned that should ease travel within Viejo San Juan. Ordinances against drinking in the streets, as well as proactive police efforts and noise and pollution control have changed the atmosphere from a rowdy town of students, pimps and drug dealers to a zone more conducive to families and tourists. The art galleries, restaurants, cafés, theme bars and shops that swell the storefronts help keep tourist revenues on the island. Cruise ship passengers by the thousands disembark to find a sparkling old city with restored colonial plazas and freshly washed cobblestones, with (as it's often said) block for block more entertainment value than Manhattan. Old San Juan hasn't completely lost its edge, though. The district around La

Perla still teems with enough drug dealers and shady characters to entertain the most adventurous of night-prowlers. And the bars and small dance clubs still get wild on a Friday night.

Getting Here

■ By Air

The **Aeropuerto Internacional de Luis Muñoz Marín** in Isla Verde is the base for nearly all flights to and from Puerto Rico. For flights to and from Vieques, Culebra and other provincial island airports, small carriers such as **Vieques Air Link**, ☎ 787-722-3736 or 888-901-9247, and **M&N Aviation**, ☎ 787-722-5980, use the **Aeropuerto de Isla Grande**, just across the bay from Puerta de Tierra. Helicopter flights also depart from Isla Grande.

Airport Ground Transportation

Most of the upper-end hotels provide airport pickup and drop-off service on request. Otherwise, if you don't rent a car at the airport, **taxis** are the quickest, but most expensive, way to get where you're going. For those traveling light or on a strict budget, **buses** to and from the *parada* at the arrivals concourse will get you to Old San Juan, with stops in Isla Verde and Santurce, where you can switch buses for destinations in Ocean Park and Condado. The line to the airport is designated on bus maps as A5. Airport **shuttles** and *públicos* (public buses) abound at the airport, and you can usually team up with other travelers headed your way to share costs. When full of passengers, most independent shuttles cost less than $5 per person to points in San Juan. Look for the kiosks outside the arrivals area.

■ By Ship

San Juan has one of the largest cruise ship ports in the Caribbean, hosting more than 1.2 million passengers a year, who use it both as a terminus and a port of call. Many passengers begin or end their cruise here, and we recommend allowing time to spend at least a couple of days in the city enjoying the vast array of international dining options, nightclubs, bars, cafés, casinos and shopping that Puerto Rico's capital city has to offer.

The port snuggles up against the walls of the old city and, although the town seems very close to the port (and very small at only seven blocks deep), be aware that the streets of Old San Juan are very steep. Visitors who have difficulty getting around can make use of the free trolley system that stops outside the terminus.

> **TIP:** *It's not worth getting a cab around Old San Juan, and chances are you'll have difficulty finding one.*

Cruise ships vary greatly in size (carrying anywhere from a few hundred to 2,000 passengers), price, and facilities, and it pays to shop around. Contact a travel agent specializing in cruises, or check out www.cruisemates.com – an on-line magazine for cruise aficionados packed with news and features that offers advice for families, kids, teens, and gay and lesbian cruisers. Another good site to try is www.porthole.com.

MAJOR CRUISE LINES CALLING AT SAN JUAN		
Carnival Cruise Lines	☎ 800-327-9501	www.carnival.com
Celebrity Cruises	☎ 800-437-3111	www.celebritycruises.com
Costa Cruise Lines	☎ 800-462-6782	www.costacruises.com
Crystal Cruises	☎ 800-446-6620	www.crystalcruises.com
Holland America Line	☎ 800-426-0327	www.hollandamerica.com
Norwegian Cruise Line	☎ 800-327-7030	www.ncl.com
Princess Cruise Line	☎ 800-774-6237	www.princess.com
Radisson Seven Seas Cruises	☎ 800-477-7500	www.rssc.com
Royal Caribbean Int'l	☎ 800-327-6700	www.royalcaribbean.com

> **RECOMMENDED READING:** *Cruisers stopping at Puerto Rico will find valuable information in* Cruising the Caribbean, 3rd Edition, *by Laura and Diane Rapp;* Frommer's 2001 Caribbean Cruises and Ports of Call, *by Heidi Sarna; and* Puerto Rico and US Virgin Islands Guide, *by Janet Groene and Gordon Groene.*

Getting Around

■ Buses

The **Autoridad Metropolitana de Autobuses** has lines that run throughout the greater metropolitan area of San Juan. This is a viable, if slow, way to get around. Mercifully, the buses are air conditioned and generally in good condition. Bring your own quarters (each line costs 25¢), because change is not given on the buses! The station in **Old San Juan** is next to the marina on the ground floor of the beige-colored parking garage, just below the municipal tourism office (not La Casita). The Santurce station, called **Parada 18**, is located on Avenida Fernandez Juncos. The **Isla Verde** station is next to the Isla Verde Mall just outside the international airport, and links to the arrivals concourse. Near the University of Puerto Rico, the **Río Piedras** station has connections to farther flung stations throughout the metropolitan area. This is also the station where you'll find several *públicos* that run to points around the island.

Some of the more useful lines are: **B21**, which runs from Old San Juan through Condado, past the Centro de Bellas Artes and ends at Parada 18 in Santurce. **A5**, which runs from Old San Juan through Santurce and Ocean Park and ends at Isla Verde. From here you can catch line **B40** to Piñones. **M lines** connect Old San Juan and Hato Rey, following much the same route as A5. From Hato Rey, you can catch the **M2** bus to the shopping mall and movie theaters of Plaza Las Americas. Be aware that routes are subject to change, so check the map posted at (some) stations or ask the driver before boarding.

THE OLD-FASHIONED WAY

If you're not in a hurry to get somewhere, a restored trolley-style bus takes passengers free of charge around the main streets of Old San Juan. Just hop on whenever it stops. Or climb aboard a Spanish *calesa* (horse and carriage) at Pier 1 at the harbor, and take a romantic tour around the old city.

■ Taxi Services

Fares

Ask the taxi driver the approximate fare to your destination before entering a cab, even if he or she is using a meter. Try to pay little or no more than the following:

- **Zone 1** – Airport to Isla Verde, $8
- **Zone 2** – Airport to Condado/Miramar, $12
- **Zone 3** – Airport to Piers in Old San Juan, $16
- **Zone 4** – Old San Juan Area, $6
- **Zone 5** – Piers to Puerta Tierra, $6
- **Zone 6** – Piers to Condado/Miramar, $10
- **Zone 7** – Piers to Isla Verde, $16

Taxi Companies

AA American Taxi	☎ 787-982-3466
Astro Taxi	☎ 787-727-8888 or 8889
Major Taxi Cabs	☎ 787-725-2870
Metro Taxi Cabs	☎ 787-725-2870
Rochdale Taxi Cabs	☎ 787-721-1900
Asociación Taxis de Carolina	☎ 787-762-6066
Asociación Taxis de Cataño/Levittown	☎ 787-795-5286
Coop. Servicio Capetillo	☎ 787-758-7000

■ Rental Cars

TIP: *An astonishing number of guest house owners have tales of guests whose vacations were ruined by car theft. Fully insure your rental. Car theft is a thriving industry in Puerto Rico.*

RENTAL CAR AGENCIES

AAA Car Rental	☎ 787-791-1465
Alamo Rent a Car	☎ 787-753-2265
Avis	☎ 787-253-5919 / 5918 / 5924 / 5926
Budget Rent-A-Car	☎ 787-791-3600
Economy Car Rental	☎ 787-784-0741
Champion Car Rental	☎ 787-782-3232
Charlie Car Rental	☎ 787-728-2418
Discount Car Rental	☎ 787-726-1460
Dollar Rent a Car	☎ 787-725-5350
L&M Car & Truck Rental	☎ 787-791-1160
Moto-Rental Plus	☎ 787-727-4449
National Car Rental	☎ 787-791-1805
Nelly Rent a Car	☎ 787-725-0504
Target Rent a Car	☎ 787-728-1447
Thrifty Car Rental	☎ 787-253-2525
Vias Car Rental	☎ 787-796-6404

Parking

In Old San Juan, you'll find two large parking structures on Calle Recinto Sur as you come into town. Parking costs $1.25 for the first hour, 50¢ for additional hours. If you're staying in San Juan longer than a week or two, consider a monthly pass for $65, available at the parking lot offices on ground level. At the upper end of town, **Calle Norzagaray** is a good place to look for street parking. A parking lot beneath **Parque de Bene-**

ficencia between the Puerto Rican Institute of Culture and the Museo de las Américas puts you conveniently close to the nighttime hub of Calle San Sebastián.

■ Scooters

Navigating the city by scooter can be a kick, and city roads can take you all the way through Condado and Isla Verde to Piñones (scooters are not allowed on expressways). In Old San Juan, **Wheels For Fun**, ☎ 787-725-2782, Calle O'Donnel 204 (near Plaza Colón) rents out scooters by the hour or by the day. The following rates include scooter, helmet, lock, map and a tank of gas: $20 for one hour; $35 for two hours; $45 for three hours; or $55 per day. Scooters can take two passengers ($5 for an extra helmet) and must be returned by 6 p.m., or there's a $35 late fee.

■ Bicycles

Great for getting around San Juan, bicycles are available for hourly or daily rental from several locations. **Condado Bicycle**, ☎ 787-722-6288, 1106 Ashford Ave. (across the street from La Concha Hotel) in Condado, e-mail condadob@coqui.net, has good rates, sturdy bikes and a friendly staff that offers excellent tips on where to bike (see *On Wheels*, page 99). Open 365 days a year from 10 a.m. to 6 p.m., they'll outfit you with wheels, a helmet, lock and map for: $8 per hour; $20 per day; or $24 for 24 hours. In Old San Juan, **Wheels For Fun**, ☎ 787-725-2782, Calle O'Donnel #204, has similar rates, but apparently discourages overnight rentals.

TRAIN AROUND THE CORNER

A planned commuter rail system is optimistically scheduled to open by 2002. For more information, contact the Department of Transportation, ☎ 787-765-0927/765-8831.

Mail & Communications

Post offices are located at 153 Calle Fortaleza, ☎ 787-723-1277, in Old San Juan, and on Loíza Street, ☎ 787-727-2452, in Condado, as well as the airport, Plaza Las Américas and many other locations around the city.

E-mail access in Old San Juan is available at **Soapy's Station** in the Wyndham Hotel, Calle La Marina, e-mail skytalk@isla.net, for $6 an hour; it is open daily from 10 a.m. to 10 p.m. Soapy's tends to get busy, especially when cruise ships come in. **The Cybernet Café**, ☎ 787-791-3138, 5575

Isla Verde Ave., is a chilled-out cyber zone, where you can listen to reggae and salsa while checking e-mail. It's also open daily 10 a.m. to 10 p.m., and costs $8 per hour for access. Most large hotels have e-mail access at business centers, though it's usually more expensive.

Touring & Sightseeing

■ Old San Juan

As the Caribbean sun strikes its first assault on the bright townhouses of Old San Juan, the seductive smell of coffee and fresh-baking bread leaks from the doors of the city's bakeries. The historic quarter lurches awake. A queue of cars forms outside the multi-story parking lots, as city employees and other commuters press into town. On a street corner facing the port, a vendor hawks African masks, pretending to carve them by hand for the sake of passersby. In the Plaza de Salvador Brau, next to the Church of San Francisco, foursomes of retirees sit on stone benches, slapping dominoes onto a table. Leaning over her balcony to attach a laundry line, a young woman pauses to call down to her lover on the narrow cobblestone street. The deep moan of a ship's horn announces the arrival of a cruise line, and several hundred map-wielding passengers spill down the gangplank onto Plaza del Puerto. Already, it's hot. The *piragua* man is doing brisk business, selling shaved ice cones by the dozen. Lunch hours are long, and the courtyards and patios of the old city's eateries throng with diners who linger over coffee until mid-afternoon.

Later, when the sun finally softens and dips below Isla de Cabras across the bay, a different city comes alive. Couples stroll arm in arm along Calle Norzagaray, for views of El Morro and the Atlantic. Restaurants and art galleries fill with patrons who dress to be seen. The after-dinner crowd hits bars and clubs along Calle San Sebastian, which invite customers with dueling blasts of salsa music.

Every moment in Old San Juan is a snapshot for the senses. The best way to experience the historic quarter is to slowly explore its narrow passageways, stopping whenever a detail inspires you. Take a walking tour of Old San Juan (see *Adventures On Foot*), which has been designated a World Heritage Site by the United Nations.

A tourist information center for the **Puerto Rican Tourism Company** is housed at La Casita ("little house"), at Plaza Dársenas (on Calle Commercio in front of the federal building)), ☎ 787-722-1709. It is open daily from 8:30 a.m. to 9 p.m. (closes at 5.30 p.m. Thursday and Friday), and is a logical place to start your tour. Depending on the mood of the staff member you encounter, you may or may not get the information you need. Our advice for dealing with the tourism office: Stuff your pockets with flyers, have a

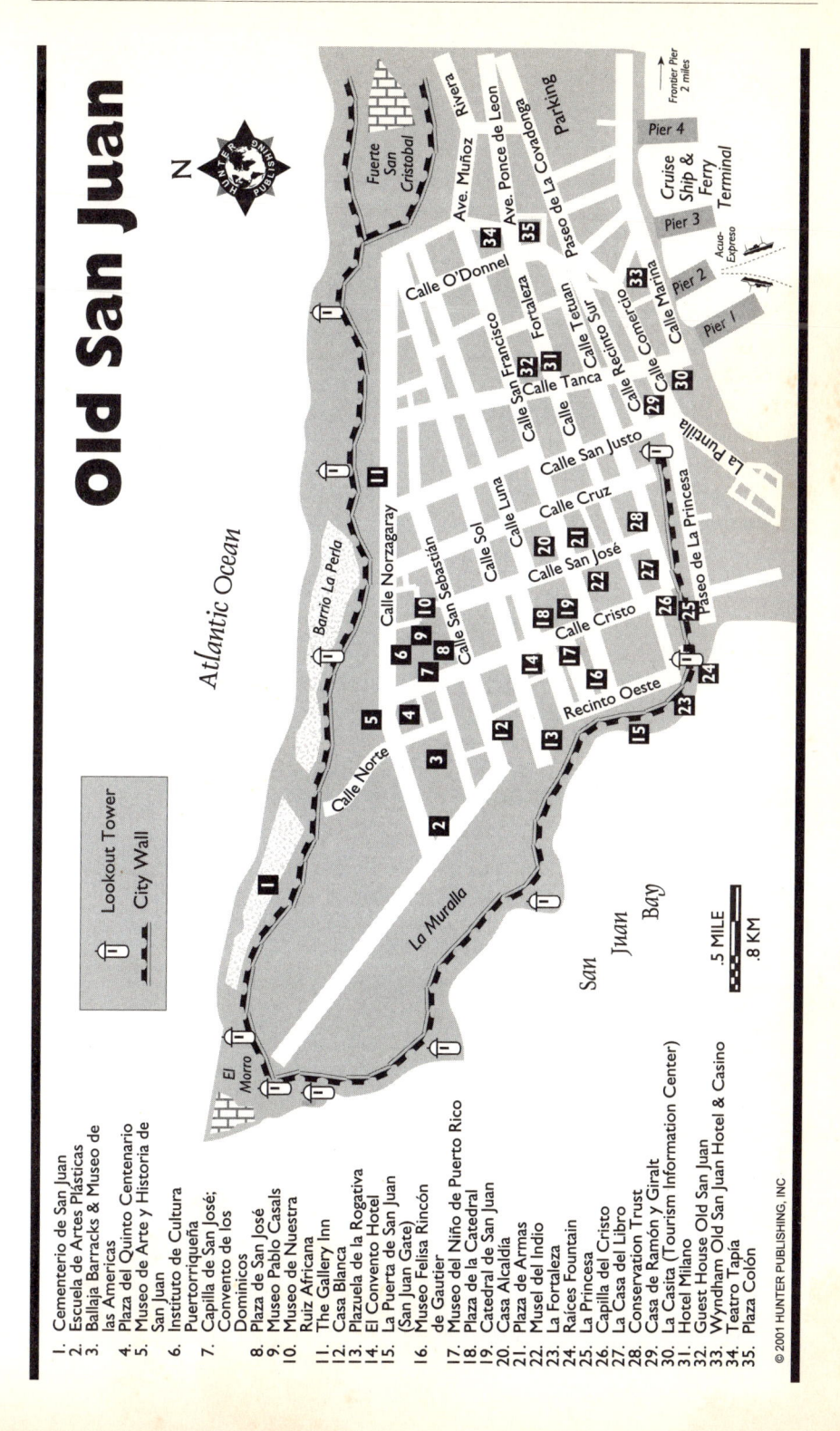

Old San Juan

- ↥ Lookout Tower
- ▬ ▬ City Wall

1. Cementerio de San Juan
2. Escuela de Artes Plásticas
3. Ballajá Barracks & Museo de las Americas
4. Plaza del Quinto Centenario
5. Museo de Arte y Historia de San Juan
6. Instituto de Cultura Puertorriqueña
7. Capilla de San José; Convento de los Dominicos
8. Plaza de San José
9. Museo Pablo Casals
10. Museo de Nuestra Ruiz Africana
11. The Gallery Inn
12. Casa Blanca
13. Plazuela de la Rogativa
14. El Convento Hotel
15. La Puerta de San Juan (San Juan Gate)
16. Museo Felisa Rincón de Gautier
17. Museo del Niño de Puerto Rico
18. Plaza de la Catedral
19. Catedral de San Juan
20. Casa Alcaldía
21. Plaza de Armas
22. Musel del Indio
23. La Fortaleza
24. Raíces Fountain
25. La Princesa
26. Capilla del Cristo
27. La Casa del Libro
28. Conservation Trust
29. Casa de Ramón y Giralt
30. La Casita (Tourism Information Center)
31. Hotel Milano
32. Guest House Old San Juan
33. Wyndham Old San Juan Hotel & Casino
34. Teatro Tapia
35. Plaza Colón

© 2001 HUNTER PUBLISHING, INC

shot of rum on the house and set out on your colonial adventure. Don't miss the following highlights.

PASEO LA PRINCESA – Leaving La Casita, thread your way through the knot of *piragua* carts to a long, cobblestone avenue lined with park benches, running perpendicular to the city wall. Here you'll find the forbidding gray structure of a former jail, **La Princesa**, currently headquarters for the Puerto Rican Tourism Company, ☎ 787-721-2400. There is a permanent exhibition of contemporary Puerto Rican art (open weekdays from 9 a.m. to noon, and 1 p.m. to 4 p.m.). On the waterfront, the strange **Raíces Fountain** includes statues of a fallen horse, several naked maidens and a dolphin.

LA MURALLA (CITY WALL) - It took residents more than a century to build this monster wall of sandstone blocks, some of which measure more than 20 feet thick, making the city impregnable. Continue past the red-painted San Juan Gate to walk the full length of the eastern section of La Muralla, ending below the ramparts of El Morro. The 15-foot turrets – once used to defend the city – are now mostly inhabited by teenage Romeos and Juliets at lunchtime.

> **TIP:** *Although the little sand beaches around La Muralla may tempt you for a swim, be warned that the water here is more polluted than it looks and the currents are strong.*

LA PUERTA DE SAN JUAN - The San Juan Gate is one of three remaining portals into the old city (the other two are at the cemetery east of El Morro and at La Perla) and was the official passenger entrance to Old San Juan during the 18th and 19th centuries. During this era, new arrivals would disembark across a plaza, now covered by the streets of Caleta de las Monjas and Caleta de San Juan, to the cathedral, where they would give praise for their safe passage across the Atlantic Ocean.

MUSEO FELISA RINCÓN DE GAUTIER - This striking pink home on the corner of Caleta de San Juan, with its blooming balconies and ornate ironwork, was for 22 years (1946-1968) home to San Juan's most beloved mayor and one of the most famous women's libbers of the 20th century. Affectionately called Doña Fela by Puerto Ricans, Felisa embarked on a series of civic exploits that earned her hundreds of diplomas, plaques and certificates, and in 1954 she was awarded the title of "Woman of the Americas." Guided tours of her home/museum, ☎ 787-723-1897, are available Monday through Friday, 9 a.m. to 4 p.m.

PLAZUELA DE LA ROGATIVA - According to legend, in 1797 an astonishing event took place in San Juan that would secure Spanish rule for another hundred years and banish the idea that women are the weaker sex. The Caribbean seas were rife with rival European powers and San Juan, a gateway between the Atlantic and the Caribbean, was a particularly desirable port to conquer. With a 60-ship flotilla and 8,000 men, British Lt. Gen. Ralph Abercromby assaulted the storied city at the same moment that the island's governor languished on his deathbed, unable to call defenses to his aid. Nearly hopeless, the bishop and the women of the town took to the streets, wielding torches, chanting wildly and tolling the cathedral bells so incessantly that it seemed reinforcements had arrived. Seeing this from his ship, so the story goes, Abercromby abandoned his attack plans. The statue at this plaza is dedicated to the bishop and the torch-wielding women of San Juan. It is possibly the most stirring monument in Puerto Rico.

PLAZA DE LA CATEDRAL - Fronting the San Juan Cathedral and the children's museum, this plaza now showcases the works of sculptor Jorge Zenos – called simply "cat," "rooster" and "boat." In previous centuries, the plaza extended all the way from the cathedral to the San Juan gate.

MUSEO DEL NIÑO DE PUERTO RICO - Adjacent to Hotel El Convento, this children's museum features exhibits in the Spanish language only, although this shouldn't deter gringo kids from enjoying it. Dedicated entirely to kindergarten-age whim, it includes three levels of games and educational interactive displays, with pint-size go-karts, fancy dress-up areas and a mysteriously popular dentist's chair. The staff is well versed in child's play, and can take over while you sightsee nearby. For more information, contact them at ☎ 787-722-3791, fax 723-2058, www.museodelninopr.org. The museum is open Tuesday through Thursday, 9 a.m. to 3 p.m.; Friday, 9 a.m. to 5 p.m.; and Saturday and Sunday, 12.30 p.m. to 5 p.m. Entrance costs $2.50.

CATEDRAL DE SAN JUAN - Although sometimes naively compared by locals to the grandeur of the cathedral in Seville (see the plaque across the street), the San Juan Cathedral is nevertheless one of the finest religious structures in the Caribbean. Commissioned in 1521 by the first bishop of San Juan, Alonso Manso, the original church was little more than a flimsy shack. When it was demolished by a hurricane five years later, settlers quickly erected a stone replacement in the style of the cathedral in Seville, just in time for the first ordination of a bishop in the New World, in 1529. Restoration over the years has left it with a largely neo-classical façade, although a few original gothic-style details remain, including the archways and balustrades. A marble tombstone dedicated to Juan Ponce de León looms over the north wing. Mass and blessings are doled out from the southern chapel. Unfortunately, votive candles have been replaced by cheesy electric lights, which may be lit via switch for $1. It's open Monday through Sunday, 8.30 a.m to 4 p.m.

CAPILLA DEL CRISTO - Two versions survive of the legend surrounding this tiny cliff-top chapel next to Parque de las Palomas (Pigeons' Park) at the lower end of Calle Cristo. Both involve a young man who accidentally hurtled over the cliff after a horse race during the San Juan Bautista celebrations. One version says that the altar guards against future bad luck. Others say that, according to eyewitnesses, a spectator called out to Christ as the young horseman plummeted over the cliff, and that divine intervention miraculously saved his life. Either way, believers still make the pilgrimage to this chapel to pay homage to divine powers that either did or didn't save the life of a young caballero. Capilla De Cristo is open Tuesdays between 10 a.m. and 3.30 p.m.

LA CASA DEL LIBRO - This incredible treasure on Calle Cristo is home to written texts that span more than 500 years of literature, memoirs and other documents. Check out the texts signed by Los Reyes Catolicos – Spanish monarchs Isabela and Ferdinand – and marvel at a few manuscripts dating back more than 2,000 years. Open 11 a.m. to 4.30 p.m., Tuesday to Saturday. Free admission. ☎ 787-723-0354.

EL MORRO - Several football fields' worth of grass separate the battlements of San Juan from the rest of San Juan, and stepping back the traveler might imagine the carnage that took place on this seemingly oversized putting green during centuries past. This was a cleverly designed last line of defense. A dry moat made it impossible for advancing armies to see, let alone penetrate, the fortress walls on approach. Luckless infantrymen or cavalry were completely exposed to Spanish light arms and cannon fire on this deadly fairway. The seaward approach was even more treacherous. Six levels of cannon shafts and bombproof vaults rising 140-feet from the rocky headland made invasions by sea virtually impossible. In 1540, the original *garita* (sentry box) was so small that it could mount only four cannons. As San Juan increasingly became a target for raids and invasions, settlers quickly realized their hopes of survival depended on the construction of a massive fortress to guard the bay. Italian engineer **Bautista Antonelli** conceived the original design in the 16th century. But the awesome structure that stands today was the work of Irishman **Thomas O'Daly**, who masterminded the re-fortification of San Juan during the final 25 years of the 18th century. During WWI, as a precautionary move, US forces modernized many of Old San Juan's bunkers and batteries for 20th-century use, and El Morro itself became part of a massive administrative, housing and hospital complex called **Fort Brooke**. During WWII, both fortresses – El Morro and San Cristóbal – were used as secret command

A teenage Romeo and Juliet steal a kiss at El Morro. (PRTC)

and communication centers. One can only imagine what the next 500 years will bring. Visitors are free to roam the ramparts, the gunrooms and chambers, tunnels, arcades and courtyards that for the past half-millennium have stood undefeated. Open 9 a.m. to 5 p.m. daily. Spanish-language tours depart 10 a.m. and 2 p.m.; English tours start at 11 a.m. and 3 p.m. $2 adults, $1 senior citizens and children. ☎ 787-729-6960.

CASA ROSADA - "Pink House" seems an unlikely name for a stern military barracks but, after all, it was built by the same people who don ballet slippers before fighting bulls. Constructed in the late 19th century, this handsome mansion is lodged between the vast green lawns of El Morro and the entrance to San Juan harbor. It now houses a fancy day-care center for the children of government workers. The chimney stacks rising up from under the hill belonged to the gunpowder magazine, Polovorín de Santa Elena.

CEMENTERIO DE SAN JUAN - On the eastern corner of the glacis of El Morro, the cemetery of Old San Juan is one of the oldest post-Columbian burial sites in the Americas, and one of the most prestigious. Many of the graves are those of early colonizers, though the most famous tomb is that of Pedro Albizu Campos, who fought for independence in the early 1900s. To avoid ghosts, ghouls and junkies, visit this place with a buddy, especially after dark.

LA PERLA - With one of the grittiest reputations in Puerto Rico, La Perla (The Pearl) is well known as a reliable place to score drugs and get into trouble. Seen from the streets above, it might appear to be a quaint fishing community built next to the sea. From the water, it looks like a pleasant jumble of colorful matchbox homes. But enter its 500-year old gates and you'll find yourself more popular than a beauty queen in a prison yard, as young street salesmen brandishing bags of pot, powder and pills rush up shouting "*¿Que quiere? ¿Que quiere, amigo?*" Novelist Oscar Lewis put La Perla on the international map in his 1966 *La Vida*, a grim tale of drugs and prostitution in this *barrio* (neighborhood) and a precursor to all the talk of "livin' la vida loca." San Juan residents will warn you that this is the most dangerous part of the city and to just stay away, especially at night. The truth is La Perla carries a ghetto stigma that belies a fascinating community of ordinary people, as well as a few derelicts, struggling to survive. Not the best place in the world to flash a Rolex, it's also not as perilous as other *sanjuaneros* make it seem. Residents are for the most part extremely friendly and, if nothing else, the "market" ensures the safety of its potential customers.

ESCUELA DE ARTES PLÁSTICAS - Facing El Morro, the School of Plastic Arts was the first institution of learning dedicated to the arts in Puerto Rico. Originally built as a hospital for the mentally ill, it was used to treat soldiers injured in the neighboring Dominican Republic war before its completion in 1872. Student workshops offer a window onto the state of contemporary Latin Expressionism. Monthly exhibitions coincide with

Noches de Galerías ("gallery nights"; see page 128), and at lunchtime this is a good place to meet young bohemians around the front courtyard.

PLAZA DEL QUINTO CENTENARIO – This multi-level plaza was conceived as part of festivities surrounding the 500-year anniversary of the arrival of Columbus. It's a prime spot for watching tall ships come into port after the long race across the Atlantic, with a view over the ocean and El Morro. At a cost of over $10 million, however, it seems like a monumental waste of money. The plaza is dominated by a totem pole that serves no cultural or historical purpose, and two stave-carrying bronze goats adorn the lower steps.

INSTITUTO DE CULTURA PUERTORRIQUEÑA – Located next to the Capilla de San Juan, this is an excellent place to pick up information (mostly in Spanish) on Puerto Rican culture, new museums and other places of interest. Staff members are generally far better informed than their counterparts at the Puerto Rico Tourism Company. The institute also houses a small but interesting collection of pre-Columbian artifacts and occasionally hosts photographic or art exhibitions. The shop has a great selection of Puerto Rican gifts for sale. Open Tuesday through Sunday, 9 a.m. to 5 p.m. Entry is free. ☎ 787-724-0700.

BALLAJA BARRACKS & MUSEO DE LAS AMÉRICAS – This neoclassical quadrangle built around a colossal courtyard was erected between 1854 and 1864 to house approximately 1,000 men – the last and largest military headquarters of Spain in the Western Hemisphere. Covering 7,700 square meters, it somberly contrasts with the brightly colored houses of Calle San Sebastián and gives little hint of the wealth of art and culture inside. The museum opened in 1992, with nine second-floor galleries that show permanent and temporary exhibitions. The highlight has to be the collection of folk arts spanning the American continents from Vermont to Argentina. On display are traditional dress, heathen masks, musical instruments and other folkloric curiosities that thread together cultures covering many centuries and thousands of miles. The most recent arrival to the museum pays tribute to the influence of African heritage on the culture of Puerto Rico. On the last Tuesday of each month, exhibitions at the Museo de las Américas are often the highlight of the Noches de Galerías in Old San Juan. Hours are Tuesday to Friday, 10 a.m. to 4 p.m., and weekends from 11 a.m. to 5 p.m. Guided tours are available in English and Spanish (call for schedule), and entrance is free. ☎ 787-724-5052.

PLAZA DE SAN JOSÉ – Once reputed as party central, this plaza at the top of Calle Cristo has become more civilized in recent years, although on weekend nights it still gets packed with the overflow from the bars and bistros on Calle San Sebastián. Home to three of the cultural treasures of Old San Juan – the Capilla de San José, Museo Pablo Casals and Museo de Nuestra Raíz Africana – it transforms into a bustling arts and crafts fair during the monthly Noche de Galerías.

CAPILLA DE SAN JOSÉ – Gleaming white, the San Juan Chapel is the second oldest church in the Western Hemisphere, and a fine example of gothic architecture that far surpasses the cathedral. Descendents of Juan Ponce de León worshipped here for nearly two centuries, and during that time his grandson, Juan Ponce de León II, recovered the remains of the island's founding governor from Havana and had them brought to Capillo de San José for entombment. More than 350 years later, however, city officials moved Ponce de León's remains to the city cathedral, where they have stayed since the late 19th century. Another outrage occurred in 1972, when a Flemish carving of the Virgin of Bethlehem – brought to the island in 1511 – disappeared. She has never been found. Open weekdays, 7 a.m. to 3 p.m. (closed Thursday), and Saturdays from 8 a.m. to 1 p.m.

MUSEO PABLO CASALS – The museum in this small 18th-century building pays tribute to the life and music of the legendary Spanish cellist who lived his final years in Puerto Rico. Fans of classical music relive highlights of Casals Music Festivals past and view or listen to hundreds of videos and audiotapes recorded in the museum's music room since 1957. The legacy of Casals lives on in the Puerto Rican Symphony Orchestra, the Conservatory of Music and the Children's Special String Program. Open Tuesday to Saturday, 9:30 a.m. to 4:45 p.m. Tuesday to Saturday, ☎ 787-723-9185. $1 adults / 50¢ children.

MUSEO DE NUESTRA RAÍZ AFRICANA – Opened in late 1999, this excellent museum displays artifacts of African arts, crafts and culture and a thought-provoking commentary on the role of African people in the development of Puerto Rican society. From the disturbing life-size mockup of slave quarters on ships bound for America, to a sales receipt for a "thick-lipped" 10-year-old boy, juxtaposed with a newspaper clipping announcing the abolition of slavery on March, 22, 1873, the curators offer a penetrating insight into the crime that built the New World. On a lighter note, *bomba* performances are staged here most Friday evenings, and workshops on drum-making and playing and dancing *bomba* are held throughout the year. Open Tuesday through Saturday, 9:30 a.m. to 5 p.m., and Sunday from 11 a.m. to 5 p.m. Museum entrance is free. ☎ 787-724-0700 ext: 4239.

CASA BLANCA – Inconspicuously positioned at the west end of Calle San Sebastián, the "White House" of Puerto Rico was for more than 200 years the residence of descendents of Juan Ponce de León. The founding governor's son-in-law, García Troche, originally built the fortress-like mansion as a precursor to La Fortaleza, to defend his family and neighbors against attacks by indigenous people and marauders. After the construction of a proper fort in 1533, Casa Blanca served as a residence until the family sold it in 1779 to the government, which returned it to martial service. After the Spanish-American War, it became the official residence of the commander of US armed forces, and remained military property until 1967. Today, Casa Blanca is a tranquil oasis of terraced gardens, waterways and a few monuments, including a colonial-era sentry box and, ironically, Indian petroglyphs. The house features an ethnographic museum (call for opening hours), and the garden is open daily ($2 for adults, free for senior citizens and kids) from 8 a.m. to 5 p.m. ☎ 787-724-5477.

CONVENTO DE LOS DOMINICOS - Built in the 16th century for Dominican nuns, this convent has been beautifully restored. A shrine to the Virgin Mary presides over a courtyard used for occasional outdoor music concerts. Indoors you'll find a top-rate shop run by the Puerto Rican Institute of Culture (see *Shopping*) and a space used for the annual Festival of Puerto Rican Music in November. For upcoming events: ☎ 787-721-6866.

MUSEO DE ARTE E HISTORIA DE SAN JUAN - Next to the Dominican convent on Calle Norzagaray, the official museum of San Juan overlooks a former market square. A half-hour documentary, in Spanish and English, sheds light on the making of San Juan. The museum is open Tuesday through Sunday, 8.30 a.m. to 3:45 p.m. (lunch break from noon to 1 p.m.) and Saturday 10 a.m. to 5 p.m. ☎ 787-724-1875.

MUSEO DEL INDIO - One of the most obscure museums in Old San Juan, this hole in the wall on 119 Calle San José is easily missed. However, it has a remarkable collection of Taino Indian *cemíes* and other anthropological artifacts. Tours by arrangement, in English and Spanish, begin at 9 a.m. and end when the museum closes at 4.30 p.m., except at lunch hour. ☎ 787-721-2864.

PLAZA DE ARMAS - The central plaza of Old San Juan is nearly always alive, and is a logical navigational center for your explorations of the historic quarter. Surrounded by the grand façades of government buildings, several fast-food outlets and the Puerto Rico Drugstore, this sunlit cobblestone square, plagued by pigeons, seems almost European. Shopping aside, travelers seek out this plaza for the green kiosk that serves cups of extra-strength espresso. This is where many city residents begin and end their day.

CASA ALCALDÍA - On the north side of Plaza de Armas, City Hall has a small tourist office and occasional exhibitions. For a quick view of the interior, use the back entrance on Calle Luna.

LA FORTALEZA - Otherwise known as Santa Catalina Palace, La Fortaleza has been the residence of the governor of Puerto Rico since the 17th century, though its historical significance is military. Built in 1533 as the city's first real fort, La Forteleza was taken by enemy forces only twice – in 1598 by George Clifford, the Earl of Cumberland, and in 1625 by a Dutch general who burned the city in his wake, partially destroying the fort. Rebuilt in the 1640s, the stark military façade over the following centuries sprouted neo-classical arches, columns and balustrades, and was embellished with fine tiles and inlays befitting a palace for its gubernatorial occupants. The *jardín hundido* (sunken garden) and the dungeons draw most attention from visitors. La Fortaleza remains a functioning government office (like the White House in Washington DC), so call in advance for tour times. ☎ 787-721-7000, ext. 2111.

Fuerte San Cristóbal.
(Bob Krist, for the PRTC)

FUERTE SAN CRISTÓBAL - Of all the Spanish-built fortifications in the Americas, Fuerte San Cristóbal was the largest. Built during the late 17th century by an Irish engineer, to protect the city from land invasions, the fort used a principle best described as defense-in-depth; the fortress worked much like a Russian doll, each wall knocked down by enemy soldiers would present yet another wall in their path. Certain details of the history of San Cristóbal remain mysterious. On the walls of a dungeon below the fort, visitors can still see the outlines of five Spanish galleons etched into stone. Historians believe a Spanish inmate, convicted of mutiny, may have scrawled this crude artwork as he awaited execution. Open daily from 9 a.m. to 5 p.m., entrance to the fort costs $2 for adults and $1 for senior citizens and children (free with a ticket to El Morro). Forty-minute tours, in Spanish and English, are well worth the time. ☎ 787-729-6777.

PLAZA COLÓN - At one of the original gateways to the city, this traffic-clogged plaza continues to play the role of sentry of Old San Juan. With its statue of Christopher Columbus and prominent location, it's a popular filming location for television advertisements, and a good place to wind up your tour of the historic city with a glass of rum punch and a plate of *frituritas* from Café Puerto Rico, or a fresh slice of spinach quiche and fresh-squeezed juice from Café Berlin.

TEATRO TAPIA - Built in 1830 as the city's first performing arts theater, the Tapia Theater was originally envisioned as something far more elaborate than its current incarnation. Unfortunately, the military concerns of the old city forced budget cuts and a more conservative design for this early monument to Puerto Rican culture. It must be something of a thorn in the side of San Juan that the theater in Ponce is much more grand. Still, it's worth a visit. ☎ 787-722-0407, for upcoming events.

CASA DE RAMÓN Y GIRALT – Another restored home with an exhibition of Taino artifacts, Casa Ramón y Giralt also serves as the headquarters of the Conservation Trust of Puerto Rico. This is the former residence of Don Ramón Power y Giralt, who joined the Spanish navy and at the end of the 18th century fought against Napoleon. Elected as the representative of Puerto Rico in the Spanish courts, he helped persuade Spanish officials to loosen restrictions on the colony during the early 19th century. Casa staff are knowledgeable and helpful, and from here visitors can arrange trips to Hacienda Buena Vista, Ponce and Las Cabezas de San Juan. Open Tuesday to Saturday, from 10 a.m. to 4 p.m. ☎ 787-722-5834.

■ Condado, Ocean Park & Santurce

On the ocean side of Hwy. 26, also known as Avenida Baldorioty de Castro, **Condado** is an extremely popular tourist area that bustles with restaurants, hotels and wide sandy beaches. The western end begins at Puente Dos Hermanos, which connects the island of Puerta de Tierra and Old San Juan to mainland Puerto Rico, and runs along the either side of the main thoroughfare, Ashford Avenue, to Ocean Park. The area is packed with little guest houses and a few large hotels, including a Marriott, with casinos, exotic eateries, funky shops and some wild nightspots. The gay scene thrives here, and the tourist crowd is a healthy mix of young couples and families of all stripes.

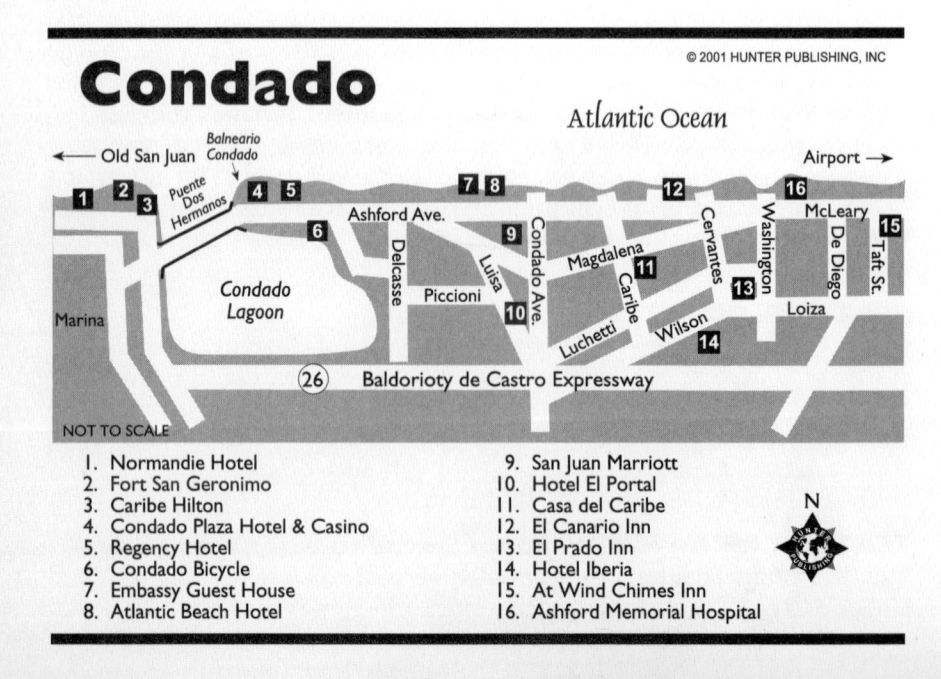

Condado
© 2001 HUNTER PUBLISHING, INC

1. Normandie Hotel
2. Fort San Geronimo
3. Caribe Hilton
4. Condado Plaza Hotel & Casino
5. Regency Hotel
6. Condado Bicycle
7. Embassy Guest House
8. Atlantic Beach Hotel
9. San Juan Marriott
10. Hotel El Portal
11. Casa del Caribe
12. El Canario Inn
13. El Prado Inn
14. Hotel Iberia
15. At Wind Chimes Inn
16. Ashford Memorial Hospital

Just east of Condado, the quieter neighborhood of **Ocean Park** is protected from high-rise development by a municipal code barring the construction of buildings taller than three stories. Many visitors prefer to stay in the mellower guest houses in this residential area, most of which face a wide, clean beach.

On the other side of Avenida Baldorioty de Castro, **Santurce** could hardly be more different. A flourishing business and residential area during the mid-20th century, it quickly declined into a gritty neighborhood of poorer families and hoodlums as business owners flocked to the new commercial center in Hato Rey. During the past few years, however, Santurce has begun to experience something of a revival, thanks to increased police presence, the opening of the **Museo de Arte de Puerto Rico** and a civic revival that has included the makeover of the popular **Plaza Mercado** open-air market on Calle Canals, with dozens of stalls vending fruit and vegetables, meats and cheeses, flowers, sandwiches and coffee. Especially if you're staying in Condado, Plaza Mercado is definitely worth a stop, especially early in the morning for picnic supplies. You'll know you've found it when you see the large metallic avocados out front.

THE MUSEO DE ARTE DE PUERTO RICO

Reviewed by art historian Lenora Turney

Opened in 2000, the **Museo de Arte de Puerto Rico**, ☎ 787-977-6277, 299 De Diego Ave., www.mapr.org, is a rare jewel in an otherwise unseemly neighborhood. Its grand scale, neo-classical façade and spacious interiors cleverly incorporate parts of the former Santurce Surgical Hospital, for which the structure was originally built. Some of the most impressive works on display are those created just for the museum. A magical, five-acre sculpture garden with lily pond is truly one of the most beautiful public spaces in Puerto Rico. Well-lit exhibition areas, high ceilings, graceful arches and highly polished floors are features of the five-floor museum, which highlights the evolution of Puerto Rican art from the 16th century to the present. Two 5,000-square-foot galleries host local and international shows. Be sure to visit the 400-seat theater, where the curtain is made of six giant panels of hand-stitched *mundillo* lace, sewn together to depict two hands and a map of the world. Sit on one of eight benches carved of cedar and mahogany into organic shapes, which harmonize with specially designed engravings at the landing of each stairway. Exploring the Museo de Arte de Puerto Rico is a relaxing and enjoyable way to learn about the history of Puerto Rican art. It also features a restaurant and a small museum well stocked with works of Puerto Rican artisans. Open Tuesday to Sunday, 10 a.m. to 5 p.m., and Wednesdays from 10 a.m. to 8 p.m. (closed Mondays). Admission is $5 for adults, $3 for children under 12 and $2.50 for people with disabilities and anyone over 60.

Isla Verde

Since the first high-rise hotels opened here in the late 1950s and early 1960s, this strip of beachfront has provided US residents with a convenient getaway for gambling and sunbathing. Right next to the airport, much of Isla Verde conspicuously lacks any hint of Puerto Rican flavor. But the skyscraping hotels often offer good package deals, and Isla Verde remains a popular holiday resort town.

> **TIP:** *Avoid the charmless areas directly adjacent to Avenida Baldorioty de Castro in Isla Verde, which are crammed with fast-food outlets and auto parts stores.*

Piñones

Piñones is one of the most idyllic spots near the San Juan metropolitan area, blessed with more than five miles of gorgeous sand beaches and a seaside road that winds through thick palm groves, almond trees and an important wildlife area. Though only 15 minutes by car from downtown San Juan, it feels like a different world. Stop at a roadside shack for the chilled juice of *coco frío* straight from the coconut, or at one of the many food stalls and outdoor restaurants selling live oysters, clams and other seafood right next to the beach. From eastbound Hwy. 26 in Isla Verde, take the Carr. 187 exit just before reaching the international airport.

At the western end of Piñones, you'll pass **Punta Cangrejos**, **Punta Maldonado** and the **Laguna Torrecilla**, a bioluminescent lagoon surrounded by mangrove and pine and a vital nesting ground for migratory birds and other wildlife. An excellent bike trail winds through the natural area and along a strand of beach. Soon you'll reach "downtown" Piñones, a cluster of wooden restaurants and food stalls right on the beach.

GETTING HERE BY BUS OR BIKE

Piñones is one of the few outlying points of interest easily reached from San Juan by bus or bicycle. From the central bus station in San Juan, look for the B40, A7 or M7 buses. Be sure to confirm with the driver before getting aboard. You'll find bike rentals at **El Pulpo Loco** in "downtown" Piñones, or rent from **Condado Bicycle** (☎ 787-722-6288, 1106 Ashford Ave.) and ride about an hour along the beach until you get here.

With the Piñones State Forest on one side and the Atlantic Ocean on the other, the ride along Carr. 187 is one of the most scenic in Puerto Rico. East of the restaurant area, you'll find plenty of opportunities to exit the main road on the seaward side and drive along sandy paths next to the sea, where you can park and access nearly empty beaches. Carr. 187 finally veers away from the water at **Punta Vacia Talega**, a popular picnic spot for humans and birds alike, with great views and, for now, virgin landscape. Unfortunately for nature lovers, private developers who own much of the land here hope to turn this lovely point into a hotel-condo complex someday. Continuing on Carr. 187 will take you to Loíza Aldea (page 302).

■ Hato Rey & Río Piedras

Southeast of Old San Juan on Hwy. 1 (Avenida Luis Muñoz Rivera) or Hwy. 25 (Avenida Ponce de León), the city's financial district, Hato Rey, gleams with high-rise glass buildings. There is little to do here except lunch at one of the swanky eateries and watch businessmen talk money into their cell phones. The Plaza Las Américas shopping mall here is just like its US counterparts, with most of the same retail outlets and a cinema complex showing Hollywood blockbusters.

Farther south, Río Piedras is home to the University of Puerto Rico. The large student population has given rise to a few trendy bars and nightclubs, and daytime highlights include a trip to the **Jardín Botánico**, ☎ 787-250-0000, ext. 6580, or 767-1710/763-4408, a lush, 75-acre botanical garden on Avenida Luis Muñoz Rivera. Part of the Estación Experimental Agricola in Mayagüez (and therefore part of the University of Puerto Rico), the gardens are well suited for visitors interested in tropical greenery. Walkways and a small trolley connect areas landscaped with ponds, oriental bridges and hundreds of species of tropical and subtropical plants and trees. Stop for a picnic (alcoholic beverages are not permitted on the grounds) under the shade of a cinnamon or nutmeg tree. Be sure to check out the awe-inspiring, giant lobster-claw plants and the Jardín Monet. Orchid lovers may phone ahead for access to a protected orchid garden housing more than 30,000 of the delicate flowers. Also in the university district, the biggest, freshest fruit and vegetable market in San Juan, **Mercado de Río Piedras**, has entirely taken over Paseo José de Diego, and is a fun place to haggle over bananas and zeppelin-sized watermelon. Afterwards, head to the **Museo de Antropología, Historia y Arte**, ☎ 787-764-0000, at the university, where all the treasures unearthed during archaeological digs end up if they don't find their way into permanent collections elsewhere. Opening hours are fairly erratic, so call in advance.

■ Cataño

Mention Cataño to most *sanjuaneros* and the response will likely be a sigh, a shake of the head or a disgusted scoff. Poor Cataño has long been the neglected sister across the bay from the Old San Juan, choked by industry and depressing housing developments. The best thing about Cataño is the peninsular view eastward over the San Juan Bay. Gazing in any other direction, you'll see nothing but urban blight, warehouses and the factory smokestacks of Bayamón to the west. The vast majority of travelers visit Cataño for only one reason – the **Bacardí Rum Distillery**. Many San Juan tour operators and large hotels include the Bacardí plant in their tours of the city, because it includes a pleasant ferry ride across the bay and the sampling of rum, which tends to put guests in a good mood. Other than the Isla de Cabras peninsula, the only other curiosity in Cataño would be the controversial pyramid-shaped library where, critics jokingly contend, "the books fall off the shelves." There may be some hope for Cataño yet, however. Rejuvenation efforts near the waterfront have attracted a few restaurant owners and plans are in the works for a giant statue of Christopher Columbus (taller than the Statue of Liberty) on **Isla de Cabras**.

Distillery Tour

Take the free ferry to Cataño from La Lancha at Pier 2 in Old San Juan, Monday to Saturday, every half-hour from 8:30 a.m. to 4:30 p.m. (coinciding with the Bacardí tour hours). While crossing the bay, you'll see the six-story, bubblegum pink Bacardí distillation tower, known as the Cathedral of Rum. From the Cataño ferry terminal, catch a $2 *público* to the distillery. Visitors often appreciate that the free tours of the rum facilities begin with a sampling of the product under a huge, yellow bat-shaped canopy (the Bacardí emblem is a bat), which adds a rosy glow to the tram ride around the 127 acres of the distillery. The Bacardí plant has a fine exhibition of Puerto Rican arts and crafts, and every December hosts the **Bacardí Artisans Fair**, which claims to be the largest such event in the Caribbean. For more information, contact the Bacardí distillery, ☎ 787-788-1500.

THE WORLD'S FAVORITE RUM

The Bacardí family began producing rum in Cuba in the late 19th century, and moved its operation to Puerto Rico during the 1930s for easier access to the US market. Today, the Bacardí Rum Distillery in Cataño produces more than 100,000 gallons or rum per day – making it by far the world's largest producer.

■ El Cañuelo & The Isla de Cabras Peninsula

The long western lip at the mouth of the San Juan Bay, Isla de Cabras (Goats Island), and the little fort of El Cañuelo formed a crucial part of the defense of the city during Spanish rule. Originally built of wood in the late 1500s, El Cañuelo was briefly occupied by the Dutch in 1625. Afterward, realizing the importance of the location, the Spanish built a small masonry fort that today stands abandoned. Cannon fire from El Cañuelo and El

Morro caught enemy ships in a deadly crossfire that effectively removed the threat of sea attack on San Juan. To reach Isla de Cabras from downtown San Juan, take Carr. 165 past the federal prison to Carr. 180 (just west of the Bacardí Rum Distillery). You may smell noxious fumes as you pass a thermo-electrical plant and a detergent manufacturer, before reaching the Cañuelo Recreation Area, which is nothing more than a couple of forlorn picnic areas and decrepit basketball courts with rusting, netless hoops. A fenced-off police post and a couple dozen mangy stray dogs inhabit the end of the peninsula. The square edifice of El Cañuelo (there is no entrance) abuts the water, surrounded by trash and tangles of old fishing line. This depressing scene is offset by a gorgeous view across the bay. Nearby, a few local fishermen on a rock jetty cast their lines – wistfully it seems – over the water toward stately El Morro and the cheerful buildings of Old San Juan.

■ Caparra

The last tourist site in the San Juan area was the first settlement established by Juan Ponce de León upon arrival to Puerto Rico in 1508. It's as unlikely a destination for travelers today as it was for the capital of the island 500 years ago. Ponce de León and his small band of settlers lasted three years on this swampy hole in what is now **Guaynabo** before malaria and Indian attacks forced them to relocate to present day Old San Juan. Unearthed in 1936, the remains of the site are little more than a few foundations of original buildings – a footnote to the island's history located in one of its most featureless and most commercial areas – on Km. 6.6 of Hwy. 2. A small **museum**, ☎ 787-781-4795, has a few Taino Indian artifacts and is open irregularly. Entrance to the site is free, but call ahead to make sure it's open.

Adventures

■ On Foot

Walking Tours in Old San Juan

Walking the historic quarter with a guide who knows the secrets and legends surrounding the sights can make the city come alive, and gives you a chance to have questions answered on the spot. All of the tours suggested below feature bilingual guides who speak English as well as any *estadounidense* (American) or Brit. Some of the best guides for historic tours are **Gonzalo De León**, ☎ 787-253-2571, or with María Pla at **Colonial Adventures Old San Juan**, ☎ 787-793-2992. Book with them at least a day or two in advance.

Many San Juan area hotels offer guided tours of Old San Juan, with varying levels of competence and knowledge. Most cost $30 or more per person, and include transport to and from the sponsor hotel. However, for free, you can join a historical walking tour sponsored by the **City of San Juan**, by calling Carlos Lopez Weber at the *municipio*, ☎ 787-721-6363, ext. 279, for reservations (at least one day in advance recommended). A bilingual guide will lead you to highlights of the gothic 16th-century structures and more modern buildings, including City Hall, the Capilla de Cristo, Calle Cristo, San Juan Bautista Cathedral, El Convento Hotel, La Rogativa and the San Juan port. Although the cathedral is the only building you'll enter on this tour of more than an hour, the guides are knowledgeable and this is a great way to get oriented. Groups have a minimum of 10 and a maximum of 24 people. Meet at the Tourism Information Center inside City Hall on San Francisco Street, in front of Plaza de Armas. Tours begin weekdays at 1:30 p.m. and Mondays at 10 a.m. and 1:30 p.m.

Legends of Puerto Rico, ☎ 787-531-9060, offers longer and more inventive tours, developed by Debbie Molina Ramos, a great storyteller who is as passionate about her subject matter as she is professional. Her **Historical Zone Walks**, on Saturdays at 10 a.m., include the historical highlights of Old San Juan, including a guided trip through the colorful past of El Morro fort. The 2½-hour journey costs $25 per person. On Wednesdays at dusk, **Walk Among the Dead** is "the ideal tour for spooky stories and shadow lovers!" By the light of torches made from gourds, you'll prowl the narrow cobblestone alleys and the ancient promenade leading to the old fort, and hear history told from an eerie point of view. On this tour, every story ends with a death or tragedy. About three hours long, it costs $39 per person. On Tuesdays, Thursdays, Fridays and Saturdays, **San Juan Nights** finds the action of the evening. Meet up with Debbie and the others on your tour of four to 14 people at the Don Q house near the port (rum tasting optional), and then head to one of Old San Juan's trendiest restaurants for dinner and an informative, merry meal. After dinner, your party hits the town, visiting the bar or bistro offering the best live music that night. The tour meets at nightfall and costs $30 per person (you pay your way for food, etc.). **Treasures of Old San Juan** combines a leisurely walk through the quarter, historical narrations and several "treasure hunts," in which stories and legends of Puerto Rico are told using craft works of local artisans, which are hidden in strategic locations for the group to find. And it's finders/keepers. Available upon request, it costs $35 per person. Except for San Juan Nights, the Legends of Puerto Rico tours operate with a minimum 10 and maximum 26 people, and flexible hours are available for booking by large groups.

Tennis

Isla Verde Country Club, ☎ 787-727-6490/624-3208, behind (but not part of) the Green Isle Inn, has four well-kept and lighted courts open to the public, a pro shop and lessons available. Open daily from 8 a.m. to 10 p.m., court fees for non-members are $4 per hour per person, plus $2 per hour for lights, if you play after dark. Also try **Pito Gonzalez Tennis Academy**, ☎ 787-763-1014, 260 Hostos in Hato Rey, which has eight courts, pro shop, showers and offers instruction. The following places have higher rates (up to $20 per hour): the **Caribe Hilton**, ☎ 787-721-0303, has six courts; the **Condado Plaza Hotel & Casino**, ☎ 787-721-1000, has two courts; and **El San Juan Hotel & Casino**, ☎ 787-791-1000, has two courts.

■ On Wheels

Bicycling

VIEJO SAN JUAN - A scenic bike tour is a perfect way to see the highlights of **Old San Juan** without hiking the whole thing. Start at the Puente Dos Hermanos bridge, which connects Condado and Puerta de Tierra. Keep to the right (it is legal to ride on the sidewalk, too) for excellent cliff-top views over the ocean, all the way to Plaza Colón and the heart of the old city. At Plaza Colón, turn right and ride or walk uphill to the San Cristóbal fort, then continue along Calle Norzagaray to get to El Morro. Riding is permitted on the paved path leading out to El Morro, but not on the grass. The streets around the point have the best riding, with views westward over San Juan Bay to Isla de Cabras. Enjoy!

THE PIÑONES PATH - Opened in 2000, this $7 million bike path through Piñones is one of the best-conceived adventure routes in Puerto Rico. Also known as the **Paseo Tablado**, the trail leads past lagoons surrounded by mangrove and pines, through palm groves and along the beach, with many places to stop for a swim, a cold *coco frío* or a *pincho* snack. The Department of Roads plans to eventually extend this path all the way to Old San Juan, and it's already possible to continue from it in either direction on your own initiative. You'll find the beginning of the bike path well marked just before you cross the bridge into Piñones on Carr. 187. The path runs through mangrove growth and along the ocean, cutting back and forth across Carr. 187 to the inland side, where bikers weave through trees on a flat surface that makes for easy riding. If you continue riding along Carr. 187 past the end of the official path, you'll come to some more excellent beaches and, eventually, **Loíza**. For a longer journey (about 20 miles each way), start this ride in Condado and follow the shore through Ocean Park and Isla Verde to the beginning of the path.

PARQUE LINEAL MARTÍ COLL - This easy one-mile bike and jogging path runs through the heart of metropolitan San Juan, along a bridge above the Caño de Martín Peña waterway between the Parque Central and the Aqua Expreso. Because it is near Condado, consider combining this ride with a tour of Old San Juan or the longer trip to Piñones. Start at the Parque Central (expect a small parking fee if you bring a car) or the Aqua Expreso (free parking), and make the two-way ride. Also consider combining this ride with the ferry to Cataño or Old San Juan.

> **TIP:** *Avoid this path after 5 p.m. on weekdays, because the sidewalks get crowded with after-work joggers.*

BIKE RENTALS & SHOPS

For an all-around great bike rental experience, check out **Condado Bicycle**, ☎ 787-722-6288, 1106 Ashford Ave. (across the street from La Concha Hotel) in Condado, e-mail condadob@coqui.net. Open 365 days a year from 10 a.m. to 6 p.m., they'll outfit you with wheels, a helmet, lock and map for: $8 per hour; $20 per day; or $24 for 24 hours. Condado Bicycle also organizes all-inclusive group trips for downhill mountain biking madness throughout the island.

In Carolina/Isla Verde and Piñones, **Adrenalina**, ☎ 787-727-1233, 4770 Isla Verde Ave. (look for Andy's Café), has more than 40 bikes – including tandems – most of which are kept at El Pulpo Loco in "downtown" Piñones. To rent one, either show up in Piñones or call Paul at Adrenalina. He provides free pickup and delivery from your hotel to the bikes, included in the rental price, which is $10 for an hour or $20 for the day. Tandem bikes are available for $20/$40 per hour/day; baby trailers for $10 per day. In Old San Juan, **Wheels For Fun**, ☎ 787-725-2782, Calle O'Donnel 204, has similar rates, but apparently discourages overnight rentals. In Puerto Nuevo, near Plaza Las Américas, **Bike Stop**, ☎ 787-782-2282, 513 Andalusia Ave., organizes personalized mountain biking adventures island-wide for small groups (ask for Ivan). Bike Stop does not offer daily bike rental.

■ On Water

Swimming & Sunbathing

CONDADO – Condado is divided into two beaches. The *balneario*, or official public beach, is a crescent of sand that faces Fuerte San Gerónimo across the Condado Lagoon, on the east end of the Puente Dos Hermanos. It's a great beach for kids because the rocky point shelters the bay from large surf and ensures near-glassy conditions. Farther east, a wide stretch of sand runs along the Atlantic seaboard of **Condado**, in front of a string of hotels that includes the Ramada, the Condado Beach, La Concha and the Marriott. The sand here is generally clean, and during peak season it can get crammed with local boogie boarders and hotel guests splayed out on lounge chairs like shish kebabs on the grill.

> **CAUTION:** *Swimmers should be aware that the Condado currents sometimes get strong, and on breezy days strong trade winds kick sand in your face (another reason to rent a lounge chair).*

OCEAN PARK – Quieter and prettier, the beach along Ocean Park is great for both swimming and catching rays. Formerly known as a hangout for drug dealers, users and drunks, Ocean Park has undergone such a radical municipal uplift – including daily cleaning by the city – that it is now probably the best beach in San Juan. Normally calm waters near the shore and a sand bottom make it a good swimming beach. A couple of tranquil seaside guest houses serve grilled seafood and vegetarian food overlooking the beach, and you may find a volleyball game to join at Ocean Park, especially on weekends. Farther east, **Punta Las Marías** is a popular surfing and windsurfing break, with a small but thriving surf community nearby and lots of little bars near the sand.

ISLA VERDE – Of all beaches in Puerto Rico, Isla Verde most resembles Miami Beach, with a wide strip of sand under high-rise condos and hotels. Although you'll see fewer silicone hard-bodies strutting here, Isla Verde remains the most popular beach in San Juan, with plenty of places to get lunch and a cocktail or rent watersports equipment. Beware the personal watercraft menace. Toward the eastern point, especially on weekends, families stake out their turf with hammocks, tents and barbecues under a clump of palm trees that has so far been spared the bulldozer.

PIÑONES – For more deserted stretches of sand, head for Piñones, a mostly undeveloped paradise just 10 minutes from the airport. Acres of palm groves line the shore, where occasional vendors sell fried Puerto Rican finger foods and *coco frío*. When you pass the "downtown" Piñones area of restaurants and wooden shacks vending live oysters, clams and barbecued *pinchos* (meat on a stick), look for a place to turn toward the shore on a sandy road. The stretch of sand all the way to Punta Vacia Talega is good for beachcombing and a swim. A few sharp lava reefs fringe some of the beaches here and the water can be somewhat difficult to get into. **Punta La Talega** is the most idyllic spot, but can get crowded on weekends.

> **THEFT WARNING:** *Piñones has a reputation for car break-ins, so don't leave anything of value inside and be sure to lock up.*

Parasailing

Located behind the Wyndham Old San Juan Hotel & Casino, **San Juan Water Fun,** ☎ 787-643-4510/931-4510, offers parasailing, banana boat rides and sailboat rides daily between 10 a.m. and 5 p.m. Parasailing (in which you are strapped into a parachute and pulled by a powerboat) costs $45 per flier, for a ride of eight to 10 minutes. Jet Ski rental costs $50 for a half-hour.

Deep-Sea & Light Tackle Fishing

Within quick striking distance from San Juan are some of the island's best blue water and fly-fishing spots. The ocean trench north of the city is alive with game fish such as wahoo, dorado (dolphin fish), tuna, marlin and other billfish. Inshore, light tackle fishermen flock to **Laguna de Torrecilla** and **Laguna Piñones** for tarpon, snook, snapper, grouper and king mackerel. Captain José Campos of **Puerto Rico Angling**, ☎ 787-724-2079, who holds a title for a record-breaking 93-pound king mackerel, will show you the good water. The company is based at the Boca de Cangrejos marina (between Isla Verde and Piñones). Campos offers charters on his fully rigged 31-foot Bertram for $375 half-day, or $575 full day, including snacks, water, tackle and bait. Inshore fishing is done aboard his 16-foot Carolina skiff, and is catch-and-release.

Captain Joe Castillo of **Castillo Water Sports**, ☎ 787-791-6195 or 727-6087, offers deep-sea fishing from the San Juan Bay marina, for $1,000 full day and $700 half-day. Light tackle tarpon fishing from the Catillo skiff at Boca de Cangrejos costs $275/$325 for two/three people for a half-day. Captain Omar Orraca of **Caribbean Outfitters**, ☎ 787-396-8346, www.fishinginpuertorico.com, has similar rates for deep-sea and backcountry fishing.

Diving & Snorkeling

You have to be truly dedicated or desperate to dive around the San Juan metropolitan area, where winds chop up the water and visibility is often poor. Only one operator offers regular diving off the shores of San Juan. Behind the Normandie Hotel in Puerta de Tierra, Karen and Tony Vega at **Caribe Aquatic Adventures**, ☎ 787-724-1882, fax 723-6770, www.caribeaquaticadventure.com, will take you right off the beach to explore a 30-foot-deep lava reef, with caves, tunnels and overhangs. This is a breeding and feeding area for chubs, tangs, parrotfish and French angels, many of which are accustomed to being fed by hand, as well as octopus, squid and lobsters. Visibility is normally only about 20 feet, however, and on good days reaches no more than 35 feet. The dive is offered daily at 9:30 a.m., 11 a.m., 2:30 p.m. and 4 p.m. to certified and resort (no previous experience) divers, for $80 and $100 respectively (less if you have your own BCD and regulator). Caribe Aquatic also runs trips to Palominito Island on the east coast, including transportation and dive equipment.

Several charter outfits based in San Juan specialize in dive trips to other parts of Puerto Rico, including transportation (see other chapters for more information on local dives). For dives on the east side of the island, try Luis and Danielle Torres at **Mundo Submarino**, ☎ 787-791-5764, fax 791-

1690, located at the Laguna Gardens Shopping Center in Isla Verde, www.mundosubmarino.net, e-mail mundosubmarino@tld.net. Trips to dive sites between Fajardo and Culebra cost between $110 and $125 for a two-tank dive, including lunch, cold drinks and transportation from San Juan to the dock in Fajardo and back again. Maximum boatload is six people. Luis and Danielle also offer PADI open-water certification courses, including classroom training, equipment and four boat dives. At **Scuba Centro**, ☎ 787-781-8086, fax 791-8981, 1156 F.D. Roosevelt Ave. in Hato Rey, www.scubacentro.com, Jaime offers two-tank dives in the eastern and southeastern waters of Puerto Rico, including Vieques and Culebra, for $49, plus $30 for equipment rental. Rafael Ocasio at **La Casa del Buzo**, ☎/fax 787-753-3528, e-mail buzo3@tld.net, offers trips all around Puerto Rico for good rates, as well as classes from open water certification to instructor, and equipment sales rental and repairs.

Surfing & Windsurfing

Between October and late April, the waves around San Juan get crazy with surf-seekers. The best waves are generally east of Isla Verde, but breaks all along the San Juan coastline attract surfers and windsurfers alike. There is little competition between the two, since windsurfers usually stay out of the water until it's too windy for the surfers. Some of the best spots are listed below.

- **La Concha** - In front of La Concha in Condado, this shore break with sand bottom can get nasty with a lot of power behind the waves. The outer reef breaks here when the sea is big.

- **Pine Grove** - In front of the Ritz-Carlton at the west end of Isla Verde, this shore break with a sand bottom is where *sanjuaneros* have learned to surf for decades. Seas are usually one to five feet during season.

- **Aviones** - Right off Piñones, this is one of the most popular surf spots in Puerto Rico. With a reef break close to shore, it offers consistent waves, even when they are small. Faces can reach 10 feet.

Rent boards for $25 per day from **Wave Rider**, ☎ 787-722-7103, next to the Caribe Hilton in Puerta De Tierra, www.waveriderpr.com. For surf and windsurf rentals, check out **Cool Runnings**, 2421 Laurel Street in Punta Las Marias. If you're interested in kite surfing, ask around at Cool Runnings or call Pedro Rodriguez, ☎ 787-374-5329.

A half-dozen excellent windsurfing spots between Condado and Isla Verde draw board sailors from all over the world during winter and spring months, with waves occasionally up to 20 feet or more for riding and jumping. During summer months, slalom and racing conditions prevail, with steady trade winds averaging 12 to 18 knots. For rentals and more information, stop in on local windsurfing aficionado Jaime Torres at **Velauno**, ☎ 787-727-0883/728-8716, 2434 Loiza Street in the Punta Las Marias

Shopping Center (near Cool Runnings), www.velauno.com. If you've never tried windsurfing but always wanted to learn, Velauno offers windsurfing instruction for $45 per hour, or $150 for a four-hour course. You'll also find windsurfing rentals and instructors at some of the larger resort hotels, usually for higher rates.

Eco-Travel

■ Piñones State Forest

The Piñones area is the nearest natural area to San Juan, and contains the largest mangrove network in Puerto Rico as well as a diverse network of waterways, beaches, dunes and palm groves. The lagoons of Torrecilla and Piñones harbor at least 38 species of fish, as well as a **bioluminescent bay** – in which tiny organisms known as dinoflagellates feed on decomposing mangrove litter and light up the water in a swath of blue-green light when disturbed. Unfortunately, Piñones has fallen victim to enough ambient light and pollution to somewhat dim the brilliance of the bioluminescence. For a more dramatic underwater light show, head to Bahía Mosquito on Vieques Island or to Parguera on the south coast.

At least 46 bird species find shelter in the Piñones State Forest, including the white-breasted heron, blue heron, royal heron, owls and brown pelicans. The latter put on an impressive late afternoon show at Punta Vacia Talega, where they dive-bomb the water for fish. Near the little islet of **Carmelita**, you may see the unforgettable sight of herons up to their knees in brackish mangrove, fishing with their long, serrated bills. During summer, **sea turtles** crawl up onto the beaches of Piñones to lay their eggs (watch your step!).

Because the forest is situated across the road from some gorgeous swimming beaches and seafood shacks, it makes an excellent eco-travel daytrip. One of the best ways to appreciate the park is to bike along the new path (see *On Wheels*). Another is by kayak with Gary Horne at **Tortuga Kayak**, ☎ 787-725-5169, www.kayak-pr.com, e-mail kayakpr@worldnet.att.net. Operating 365 days a year, Gary takes groups of up to 20 two-person kayaks on a four-hour tour of Piñones Lagoon and surrounding waters. You'll find yourself paddling under freshwater trails canopied by mangroves. The red and black mangrove ecosystem is home to dozens of species of migrating ducks, turkey vultures, herons and osprey. More unforgettable still, you will almost certainly see **green tree iguanas**, which can measure up to six feet in length, lounging in the sun and devouring the vitamin-rich mangrove leaves. (Gary says in one day he and his guests counted 250 of these giant lizards). After a guided educational tour through the mangroves, the kayaking ends at a beach near Boca de

Cangrejos, for lunch and a swim. A snorkeling spot nearby features a small forest of fan corals and tropical fish. Tortugas Kayak provides snorkeling equipment, and the entire trip, including transportation to and from San Juan and lunch, costs a reasonable $45 per person. Ask Gary about other kayaking trips to mountain lakes and cays off the southern and eastern coasts of Puerto Rico, including the trip to Monkey Island.

Where To Stay

Choose your accommodations in the San Juan area based on whether you'd rather be a few steps from the beach or right in the heart of the colonial center. Either way, you're within quick striking distance of the other. Old San Juan and Condado are both good places to stay in the thick of the restaurants and nightlife of the capital city.

ACCOMMODATIONS PRICE KEY

Rates are per room, per night, for double occupancy. Single occupancy may or may not get you a discount, so ask when making a reservation. Breakfast included where noted.

$	Up to $50
$$	$50 to $100
$$$	$101 to $150
$$$$	$150 and up

■ Old San Juan

One of most charming places to stay anywhere is **The Gallery Inn**, ☎ 787-722-1808, fax 724-7360, 204-6 Norzagaray, www.thegalleryinn.com. It is a treasure trove of art and antiques, music and sculpture, overlooking Old San Juan and the seas beyond. Twenty-two unique rooms in this labyrinthine 18th-century home have been designed by artist/owners Jan D'Esopo and Manuco Gandía to balance luxury with eccentric appeal. Guests enjoy the many terraces and salons. Invisible fingers play the Steinway grand in the music room; the doll-house room has a library for quiet reading; the wine cellar and banqueting room are excellent private party venues; and the upper deck has the best 360° views in the old city. Join other guests downstairs in the foyer at sundown, where Jan, Manuco and half a dozen noisy tropical birds make merry with fine wine in a garden of sculptures and antique furniture. Book early, as do the many guests who make return visits to this little wonderland. Phones, a/c and custom details. $$$-$$$$

The **Hotel El Convento**, ☎ 787-723-9020 or 800-468-2779, 100 Cristo, fax 721-2877, www.elconvento.com, e-mail elconvento@aol.com, is more classically gorgeous, if less eccentric and personal. Built in a four-story quadrangle, with long arcades and tiled floors, right in the heart of Old San Juan, Hotel El Convento includes a small pool and Jacuzzi with views over the rooftops of Old San Juan, a gym, several courtyard restaurants and designer shops in its arcades. Its 57 bedrooms feature mahogany beams and handcrafted furniture, with color schemes from sunset yellow to marine blues. Each has a/c, TV and VCR, a full stereo system, refrigerator, two-line telephones, bathrobes and plenty of luxury details. $$$$, including continental breakfast, afternoon wine and hors d'oeuvres.

At the **Wyndham Old San Juan Hotel and Casino**, ☎ 787-721-5100, 100 Brumbaugh St. and La Marina, guests get an unparalleled view of the cruise ships with resort-type accommodations and facilities. $$$$

A welcome newcomer to the historic district, **Hotel Milano**, ☎ 787-729-9050, on Calle Fortaleza 307, is a comfortable mid-range option with some good views over the harbor from some rooms. A popular rooftop bar and restaurant adds to the allure. $$-$$$

An amazing and rare bargain, **Guest House Old San Juan**, ☎ 787-722 5436, Calle Tanca 205, is somewhat run-down and crumbling, but fairly clean. Rooms in the interior have no windows, and for a few dollars more you can request one of the excellent rooms with balconies overlooking Calle Tanca – the best deal in the city. Each floor has two shared bathrooms. If possible, book balcony rooms in advance. This guest house accepts cash only. $.

Another good deal, the **Caleta Guest House**, 725-5347, 11 Caleta de las Monjas, www.thecaleta.com, has rooms with balconies and bay view. $$-$$$. Owner Michael Giessler also has furnished interior rooms to rent for $475 to $750 per month and vacation rental apartments for between $450 and $900 per week.

■ Puerta de Tierra

In the Puerta de Tierra area, the **Caribe Hilton**, ☎ 787-721-0303, Calle Rosales, San Gerónimo Grounds, www.caribe.hilton.com, imported sand to build a small private beach, and is popular with business travelers and families. Its "Vacation Station" program keeps kids busy while parents work, sightsee or relax by the pool or sea. All 645 rooms have a/c, cable TV and telephones, and facilities include a new full service spa, nightclub and three restaurants. $$$$. Next door, the **Radisson Normandie Hotel**, ☎ 787-729-2929, fax 729-3083, Muñoz Rivera and Calle Rosales, has 180 rooms (115 of which are junior suites) built in Art Deco style to recall the famous French ocean liner *Normandie*. Though lacking a beach, the hotel does have a beachfront swimming pool and dive shop. All rooms have a/c and cable TV. $$$$.

> **LOOKING TO BUY?** *Roca Realty,* ☎ 787-723-3966, *and* **Wilton Cancel Realty,** ☎ 787-721-1040, *both specialize in finding homes in the area.*

■ Condado

High End

Just across the Puente Dos Hermanos from Puerta de Tierra, the distinguished **Condado Plaza Hotel & Casino**, ☎ 787-721-1000, has 570 rooms that tend to be more refined than those of its neighbors. The newly renovated Italian marble lobby includes chandeliers, mosaics and a luxury ambiance befitting film stars. With three pools (one of them saltwater), numerous water sports and fitness programs, five restaurants and the largest casino in Puerto Rico, this place is for hedonists who want to be near the center of town. $$$$

Slightly less glamorous is the **Regency Hotel**, ☎ 787-721-0505, which has 127 rooms in a 10-story complex, each with its own private balcony and all modern conveniences. Suites on the second to the 10th floors have full kitchens, living and dining areas and large balconies. Fine dining restaurant and piano bar in the lobby. $$$-$$$$

Commanding a large chunk of Condado Beach, the **San Juan Marriott Resort & Stellaris Casino**, ☎ 787-722-7000, 1309 Ashford Ave., has all the luxuries of a modern resort, including a busy beachfront pool surrounded by palm trees, pagodas and bridges, and beach bar. Tennis courts, gym, a couple of restaurants (with 24-hour room service) and a business center are also available. The 525 rooms are modern, with dual telephone lines, voicemail and private balconies, but essentially lacking in character. In fact, there's little to distinguish this Marriott from others around the world, except for its location and the fact that it won the Puerto Rico 2000 Excellence Award. $$$$

Mid-Range & Budget

By far the prettiest guest house in Condado is the Mediterranean-style **At Wind Chimes Inn**, ☎ 787-727-4153 or 728-0671, fax 728-0641, on the corner of Ashford Avenue and Taft Street, with cheery, tiled rooms, sunflower fabrics and bamboo furniture. Interior patios keep the rest of San Juan at bay, with interconnecting balconies and walkways that lead to alcoves for reading or terraces for sunning yourself. Just a block from the beach (where Condado and Ocean Park meet) in the metropolitan area, At Wind Chimes Inn also has a swimming pool with waterfall, and a patio bar fashioned from half a sailboat. All rooms have a/c, phone, cable TV, and a few have kitchenettes. This tasteful guest house is easily one of the island's top accommodations for location, comfort, ambiance and price and is fully booked much of the time. Book early. $$

Under the same management as At Wind Chimes Inn, **Casa del Caribe**, ☎ 787-722-7139, 57 Caribe St., is a slightly more humble version with a small shady courtyard, also just a block and a half from the beach. Thirteen rooms each have cable TV, phones and a/c with a choice of king, queen, twin or full-size beds. One advantage of staying here is its proximity to the Ashford strip and the nocturnal adventures it inspires. $$

El Prado Inn, ☎ 787-728-5925 or 899-468-4521, 1350 Calle Luchetti, is a decent and reasonably priced B&B less than a minute from the action in Condado. It has a small pool and 22 rooms with a/c, cable TV, ceiling fans and parking. $$

El Canario Inns, www.canariohotels.com, has three guest houses (25 to 40 rooms each) located in the Condado area, all with basic accommodations including continental breakfast, the morning paper, a/c, cable TV and telephone. Of the three, **El Canario Inn**, ☎ 787-722-3861, 1317 Ashford Ave., seems the nicest, with a pleasant red-brick courtyard but no view, and rooms on the avenue are noisy. $$-$$$

The **Hotel El Consulado**, ☎ 787-289-9191, fax 723-8665, 1110 Ashford Ave., Condado, is a good-looking European-style B&B near shops, nightclubs, restaurants and casinos on the Condado strip. Its 29 rooms are spacious with a/c, cable TV and telephone. $$-$$$

The **Atlantic Beach Hotel**, ☎ 787-721-6900, 1 Vendig St., is popular with gay couples and others, situated right on the Condado beach, with a rooftop terrace and Jacuzzi. Its 37 comfortable but unremarkable rooms have all necessary conveniences. Also at the hotel are a decent restaurant and a bar that hosts outlandish entertainment in the form of drag shows, strippers and DJs most nights of the week. $$-$$$

The **Embassy Guest House**, ☎ 787-725-8284, 1126 Sea View Street, has cheap rooms, but be warned: one guest complained she felt she had to put on flip-flops just to walk from the bed to the bathroom. $-$$

Hotel Iberia, ☎ 787-723-0200, 1464 Wilson Ave., is three blocks from the beach, on a relatively quiet thoroughfare. It is a simple townhouse with no frills. All 32 rooms have a/c and cable TV and access to the rooftop terrace. A small Spanish-style restaurant is attached. $$. Similarly, **Hotel El Portal**, ☎ 787-721-9010, 76 Condado Ave., is 2½ blocks from the beach and close to restaurants and larger hotels. All 48 rooms have queen or twin beds, refrigerator, cable TV, a/c, and include continental breakfast on the sundeck. Other budget options include **Hotel Miramar**, ☎ 787-722-6239, 606 Ponce de León Ave., and **Hotel Olimpo Court**, ☎ 787-724-0600, 603 Miramar Ave., in case other places listed above are fully booked. $$

■ Ocean Park

The beachfront **Numero 1 Guest House**, ☎ 787-726-5010, 1 Santa Ana St., has gone from strength to strength since it opened eight years ago, attracting praise from various glossy travel magazines, *The New York*

Times, the *Washington Post* and others. Surrounded by tropical gardens and abutting the beach, all 13 elegantly decorated rooms have a view of some kind, a/c, ceiling fans, mini-bar and queen- or king-size beds. With a swimming pool, ocean-view terrace and its top-class restaurant, Pamela's (see *Places to Eat*), it's little wonder guests return often to this quiet paradise. $$-$$$$, including breakfast.

A self-described "alternative" guest house, **Ocean Walk Guest House**, ☎ 787-728-0855, 726-0445, or 800-468-0615, 1 Atlantic Place, is a converted Spanish-style home situated right on the beach, with a bar practically spilling onto the sand. Though much of the clientele is gay and lesbian, all comers are welcome. Slightly faded, its swimming pool and barbecue still pack in a lively crowd. $$-$$$

A block from the sand, the similar **Ocean Park Beach Inn**, ☎ 787-728-7418, 3 Elena St., is one of the most intimate guest houses around, with private entrances to each of the rooms and views of the ocean or the garden. $$$

Hostería Del Mar, ☎ 787-727-3302 or 727-0631, fax 268-0772, 1 Calle Tapia, e-mail hosteria@caribe.net, has sundecks on the beach and a breezy restaurant and bar overlooking the sea. Bedrooms have a/c, cable TV and telephone (some with oceanfront balconies), and are built around a small courtyard. Several suites have kitchenettes. $$-$$$.

Tres Palmas Inn, ☎ 787-727-4617, fax 727-5434, 2212 Park Blvd. (Punta Las Marías), is a quiet, family-oriented B&B on the beach. There's also a swimming pool and Jacuzzi with ocean views. Rooms are recently renovated with a/c, cable TV, telephone and a range of sleeping arrangements for couples or families. $$-$$$

■ Isla Verde

High End

The Ritz-Carlton San Juan Hotel & Casino, ☎ 787-253-1700, 6961 Los Gobernadores Ave., has everything you would expect of this luxury chain: impeccable service, glamorous surroundings and high tea in the afternoons. Occupying eight acres of pristine beach along the Isla Verde waterfront, the Ritz-Carlton is the envy of many competing high-class hotels. The Vineyard restaurant is probably the most elegant eatery in Isla Verde, and the hotel's spa is likely the most luxurious in the city. The 414 guestrooms, four garden-view suites and one Ritz-Carlton suite all come with the graceful amenities one demands when putting on the Ritz. $$$$

What past visitors may remember as the San Juan Grand is now the **Inter-Continental San Juan Resort & Casino**, ☎ 787-791-6100 or 800-443-2009, 5961 Ave. Isla Verde, www.interconti.com. It still commands an excellent position on the beach, with Venetian balconies, marble goddesses, a funky discotheque and several restaurants. Many of the rooms are oceanfront, and all have a/c, cable TV and telephones. As resort hotels go, this is one of the best. $$$$

Embassy Suites Hotel & Casino San Juan, ☎ 787-791-0505, 8000 Tartak St., www.embassysuitessanjuan.com, has 300 two-room suites in a high rise built around a lush tropical atrium and lagoon-style swimming pool. Included in the room price are a cooked-to-order breakfast and a two-hour open bar every day. $$$$

ESJ Towers, ☎ 787-791-5151, ext. 44, 800-468-2026, 6165 Isla Verde Ave., is a good choice for independent travelers on an open budget. Furnished apartments come with fully equipped kitchenettes (there is also a luncheon restaurant and cocktail bar), cable TV, direct dial phone and voicemail, maid service and a fitness center, pool and Jacuzzi. The price includes indoor parking. $$$$

Mid-Range & Budget

Overlooking the sea, **Hotel La Playa**, ☎ 787-791-1115/7298, 6 Calle Amapola, www.hotellaplaya.com, e-mail manager@hotellaplaya.com, is a small hotel that seems miles away from the bright lights of Isla Verde. Part of its charm is a sundeck that stretches over the ocean, and an open-air restaurant and bar serving drinks and canapés. $$$. Next door, the **Empress Ocean Front Hotel**, ☎ 787-791-3083, 2 Amapola St., has an even better view of both Piñones and coastal San Juan, from its seemingly endless deck. Since swimming along the coast here is discouraged, the owners have incorporated a lovely pool into the deck. $$$

El Patio Guest House, ☎ 787-726-6953, DO-87 3rd St., Villamar Ext., is one of the best deals in Isla Verde for self-sufficient travelers. A small, family-run outfit in a residential neighborhood, it has 14 rooms with a/c, refrigerator, cable TV, swimming pool and the use of a communal kitchen. Just three blocks from the beach, its only drawback is that the largest available beds are doubles. $$

Casa De Playa, ☎ 787-728-9779 or 800-916-2272, 86 Isla Verde Ave., is a good deal right on the beach. All rooms come with a kitchenette, a/c, cable TV and direct dial telephones. $$-$$$.

The **Borinquen Royal Guest House**, ☎ 787-728-8400, fax 268-2411, 58 Isla Verde Ave., is a block from the beach, with modern facilities, just five minutes from the airport. $$

On a quiet, residential street, **Hotel Mario's**, ☎ 787-791-6868, 2 Rosa St., has 50 no frills rooms with a/c and cable TV, just a block from the beach. $$. Now under the same ownership, **The Green Isle Inn and Casa Mathiesen**, ☎ 787-726-4330 or 8662, 36 Calle Uno, Villamar Sector, have reasonable rates and basic rooms with a/c, cable TV, telephone, refrigerator and cooking facilities. Ask for a room away from the traffic on Calle Uno, to avoid sleepless nights. $$

Rentals

Green Island Realty, ☎ 787-791-1237, on Isla Verde Avenue and Tartak Street, offers an extensive range of vacation apartments in the Condado and Isla Verde areas, including short- and long-term rentals, furnished or unfurnished, from humble studios to three-bedroom penthouses with swimming pool. Expect to pay between $420 and $1,500 a week. This is apparently the only rental agency in the area that accepts all major credit cards.

Where To Eat

Increasingly recognized as *the* food destination of the Caribbean, San Juan has enough restaurants, cafés and bars to keep critics busy for a year. The wide range of eateries features everything from *comida criolla* to nueva Latina to a host of international and specialty gourmet restaurants. Below are our recommendations. For a more extensive list (though without reviews), pick up a copy of *Tables; Puerto Rico's Guide to Great Dining*, ☎ 787-723-9394/722-6652, www.tables-pr.com, available at $1.50 from large supermarkets and newsstands. ¡Buen Provecho!

■ Old San Juan

Fine Dining

The best sushi restaurant in Puerto Rico is **Yukiyu**, ☎ 787-722-1423, 311 Recinto Sur. It also gets top marks for authentic décor: paper screens, antique kimonos and funky geometric tableware. Fish is usually top grade and more varied than at other sushi restaurants on the island. Expect to spend $30 a head for sushi and drinks. The lunch special costs $19. Open daily from noon to past midnight.

At the only Romanian restaurant in Puerto Rico (and perhaps the Caribbean), **Transylvania**, ☎ 787-977-2328, 317 Recinto Sur, sink your fangs into Vlad-inspired dishes such as *mititei-Rumanian delight* (sausages made on the premises), $8; beef stroganoff with egg noodles, $24.95; and *sarmale in foii de varza* (cabbage stuffed with pork, beef and rice, served with polenta and sour cream), $16.75. Stick to the excellent Romanian dishes at Transylvania, as the other items on the menu are relatively unspectacular.

Probably the most famous and trendy restaurant in the old city is **The Parrot Club**, ☎ 787-725-7370, 363 Fortaleza, www.parrotclub.com. It is often credited with starting the "boom" of nouvelle cuisine in San Juan. In terms of dining, this is the best place to see and be seen in the historic quarter. Owner Emelio has put together a menu that screams for attention, including gourmet crab cake appetizers, cured lamb broiled on a sugarcane spear and the house special: sushi-grade tuna broiled with a dark rum and orange essence sauce over yucca and cassava mash. Because reservations are not taken, you may find yourself waiting a half-hour or more at the bar, where you can knock back the famous "Parrot Passion" cocktails. Main dishes cost between $15 and $30. Open daily from about 6 p.m. to midnight (a bit later on weekends) and for Sunday brunch from noon to 4 p.m. Across the street, Emilio's second restaurant, **Dragonfly**, ☎ 787-977-3961, 364 Fortaleza, is equally popular, drawing locals and tourists alike to sample chef Roberto Treviño's alchemy of Asian and Caribbean flavors. Try halibut ceviche with ginger, coconut milk and scallions for $14, Abuelo Wong's sweet and sour crispy snapper for $13, or, Mongolian beef wrapped in *mu shu* tortillas for $15. Small and elegant, Dragonfly is definitely worth a visit.

Another fire-and-spice eatery nearby is **Tantra**, ☎ 787-977-8141, 356 Fortaleza, Puerto Rico's only Indian restaurant. You'll find curries, breads and tandoori grills in an atmosphere enhanced by silks and draperies, scattered cushions and the scent of fruit tobacco smoked as an after-dinner treat through a hookah pipe. A taste of the Raj doesn't come cheap – a basket of assorted breads costs $10, curries between $15 (for vegetarian) and $28 (assorted meat preparations). Open Tuesday through Sunday, 6 p.m. to midnight. The more affordable lunch menu is available from noon to 3 p.m.

For classy French cuisine, **Trois Cent Onze**, ☎ 787-725-7959, 311 Fortaleza, offers a truly elegant experience with tuxedoed waiters presiding over immaculate linen-clothed tables, romantic candlelight and live music played on a grand piano. Open Monday to Thursday, 11.30 a.m. to midnight; Friday and Saturday, 11.30 a.m. to 1 a.m. Entrées cost between $15 and $25. A four-course chef's menu is also available for around $25 a head.

The oldest restaurant in the Puerto Rico (founded in 1848), **La Mallorquina**, ☎ 787-722-3261, 207 San Justo, serves fine *criollo* cuisine in a classy dining area that opens onto the street. This restaurant has served more celebrity guests than any other in San Juan. Open Monday to Saturday, 11.30 a.m. to 10 p.m.

At the Hotel Milano, **Panorama**, ☎ 787-729 9050, 307 Calle Fortaleza, offers rooftop dining, with great views over the San Juan Bay. Lunchtime specials are a good deal at $8 to $10, and the dinner menu revolves around classics like paella Panorama with codfish, clams and shrimp, and the more exotic-sounding seafood festival with red Creole sauce, for between $18 and $25 a plate. For a more lustful diversion, check out **La Ostra Cosa**, ☎ 787-722-2672, 154 Cristo, which specializes in oysters and other aphrodisiacs served in a patio under the stars. Expect to spend $30 apiece for this seduction.

La Querencia, ☎ 787-725-1304, 100 De La Cruz, has rapidly gained the respect of local gourmets for its intimate courtyard setting and *criollo* food with a French twist. Dishes start around $15.

Casual

Calle Recinto Sur features restaurants serving such diverse international cuisines as Thai and Vietnamese (the only such eateries on the island), Chinese, Japanese Italian, Mexican and French. At one of our favorites, **Al Dente**, ☎ 787-723-7303, 309 Recinto Sur, owner and chef Giancarlo Amenta packs in pasta lovers with his genuine Italian hospitality and fine food to match. Open Monday to Saturday, 6 to 11 p.m. Main courses cost between $12 and $18. Nearby, the **Vietnam Palace Seafood Restaurant**, ☎ 787-723-7539, Recinto Sur, features dishes like shaken beef and beef sautéed with lemongrass over rice noodles for about $10 each. Open 11 a.m. to 11 p.m. Next door, the **Royal Thai Restaurant**, ☎ 787-725-8424 or 8401 imports ingredients (including the chicken) from New York. Connoisseurs of Thai food may find the dishes a bit ordinary, but classics such as green curry and jasmine rice, soups and stir-fries are still delicious. Entrées will set you back $10 to $15.

For outdoor dining, **Café Zaguan**, ☎ 787-724-3376, Calle Tetuan, is hosted with pizzazz by owners Billy and Diana. Stop by for wraps, salads and soups for lunch (daily 9.30 a.m. to 4 p.m.). Dinner favorites, served Tuesday to Saturday, 6 p.m. to midnight (Fridays are the most popular here), include sesame-crusted, rare-seared tuna and chicken fajitas for two. If you like ceviche, Billy's version is king. Vegetarian dishes on request. With prices generally lower than the fancier restaurants one block away on Calle Fortaleza, it's one of our favorite spots, and was the restaurant of choice of Gene Hackman and Morgan Freeman during the filming of *Under Suspicion* in 2000. Sharing the same outdoor dining space, **Il Grottino**, ☎ 787-723-8653, 361 Calle Tetuan, bakes gourmet pizza in a clay oven, for between $15 and $20, as well as other Italian dishes. Fine dining upstairs includes a wine list with 415 vintages. Open Monday to Friday, noon to 3 p.m. and 6 p.m. to 1 a.m.; Saturdays from 6 p.m. to 1 a.m.

Specializing in French/Mexican cuisine, Amanda Robles of **Amanda's**, ☎ 787-722-0187, 424 Norzagaray, has been voted one of the top 10 chefs in San Juan. Her *pollo a la Mexicana* is drenched in a magnificent 29-ingredient *mole* sauce. Other specialties include *camarones Acapulco* and an inventive vegetarian selection. Cocktails are also a high point here, and many visitors stop by just to sip a frappé at this turquoise and pink perch overlooking the sea. Add your comments to Amanda's visitor's book! Dishes range in price from $12 to $20.

Casa Borinquen, ☎ 787-722-7070, fax 722-7150, 109 San Sebastián, gets rave reviews for its reasonably priced, creative Puerto Rican cooking. Feast on pork loin glazed in mango sauce, shrimp with cilantro and coconut and cassava stuffed with crabmeat, for $15 to $20. Rich and creamy *asopao* (rice stew with seafood or poultry), also available in vegetarian form, is cheaper. There's a 30-minute waiting time for this dish.

Café Berlin, ☎ 787-722-5205, is a popular outdoor eating spot overlooking Plaza Colón. It has excellent home-baked breads, pies and pastries, along with a small but inventive menu of dishes such as stuffed chayote (a small green squash). They also sell a small range of health foods, dried pulses, soups and other snacks. Most plates cost about $10.

The **Hotel El Convento** has three sidewalk café-style eateries, all with good wine lists and reasonably priced lunch menus.

Budget

At **Tío Danny's Deli-Restaurant,** ☎ 787-723-0322, 313 Fortaleza St., Danny specializes in traditional Puerto Rican fare, with breakfast, lunch and dinner served buffet style in a patio with plastic tables and umbrellas. This is a lunchtime favorite with *sanjuaneros*. Try the *serenata* (codfish salad), *masitas de cerdo* (fried diced pork) with rice and beans and *tostones* (twice-fried green plantains). Danny also serves a selection of deli-style sandwiches and salads, and the menu changes somewhat daily. Open from 6 a.m. to 11 p.m. daily, with lunches in the $6 range and dinners from about $8 to $15.

For vegetarian fast food, the Hare Krishna cafeteria, **Gopal,** ☎ 787-724-0229, 201 Calle Tetuán, offers a selection of healthy meals, to the sound of Hindi pop songs, for less than $5 (includes three dishes and a drink). It's open for lunch Monday to Friday, 11.30 a.m. to 3 p.m.

The friendly atmosphere at **Café Puerto Rico,** ☎ 787-724-2281, on Calle O'Donnel 208 in Plaza Colon, draws locals and travelers alike for an excellent *tapas* menu and Puerto Rican specialties such as *asopao*. Try the *frituritas* plate to sample a great selection of island appetizers, or the Spanish sausage cooked in red wine. Most appetizers are $5 to $7, and entrées are upwards of $10. The kitchen is open Monday to Saturday, 11 a.m. to 11 p.m., Sunday 11 a.m. to 9 p.m. The upstairs bar stays open until the party dies down.

For authentic local fare, **Restaurante El Jibarito,** ☎ 787-725-8375, 280 Calle Sol, serves tasty Puerto Rican food with the pride of a Puerto Rican grandmother cooking for her family. Entrées between $7 and $15.

Sanjuaneros flock to **Café Mallorca,** ☎ 787-724-4607, 400 Calle San Francisco, after Sunday morning mass for hot chocolate and *mallorcas* (a delicious pastry from the Spanish island of the same name). You'll no doubt encounter Bruno, who has been waiting tables here for the past 37 years and, with a passion for the menu, will tell indecisive customers exactly what they should eat. Coffee and a pastry costs less than $5, and giant fruit salads, ham, pancakes and eggs are also available. Open 365 days a year, 7 a.m. to 8 p.m. One block up, **La Bombonera,** ☎ 787-722-

0658, 259 Calle San Fransisco, is another famous breakfast haunt that has lured crowds for more than 100 years. Patrons often form long lines here for *mallorcas* and other pastries straight from the oven. With most breakfasts and lunches costing less than $7, it's open daily 7.30 a.m. to 8 p.m.

The Caribbean Deli, ☎ 787-725-6696, 205 Calle Tanca, is perfect for lunch on the go, with a variety of *criollo* specials for around $7 and wraps or soup and salad for $5. Open Monday to Thursday, 11 a.m. to 7 p.m.; Friday and Saturday 11 a.m. to 5 p.m.

Arepas y Mucho Mas, ☎ 787-724-7776, 366 Calle San Francisco, serves traditional Venzuelan food like *pabellon* (black beans, shredded and stewed meat, sweet plantains and cheese) from a living-room-style restaurant. Give-away prices combined with delicious home-cooked fare draw big crowds.

With shaded garden dining, **La Princesa Café**, ☎ 787-724-2930, Paseo de la Princesa, offers a basic but pleasant lunch menu, and you can usually get a plate of rice and beans for about $5. Open Monday to Wednesday, 9 a.m. to 4 p.m; Thursday and Friday, 9 a.m. to midnight; Saturdays, 4 p.m. to midnight; and Sundays, noon to midnight.

At the **Escuela de Artes Plásticas**, a hole-in-the-wall eatery in the front courtyard dishes out chicken, ribs and vegetarian dishes with rice and beans for less than $5, and you can picnic with students on the lawn overlooking El Morro. Open weekdays between 11 a.m. and 2.30 p.m.

Few tourists set foot in **La Sombrilla**, ☎ 787-638-6240, which has only two tables surrounded by shelves of booze, but this place gives a flavor of what Old San Juan used to be like. The daily menu of *pasteles*, steaks or pork chops, with *arroz con gandules,* costs as little as $5. Opening hours are at the whim of the owner.

Finally, if you're melting under the sun and only a liter of ice cream will do, fear not: **Ben & Jerry's**, ☎ 787-723-6313, 61 Calle Cristo, the dairy duo from Vermont, has a fully stocked ice-cream parlor in the heart of Old San Juan.

■ Condado & Santurce

Fine Dining

Popular for business lunches, **Cherry Blossom**, ☎ 787-723-7300, 1309 Ashford Ave. (at the Marriott Hotel, Condado), has a good-quality sushi bar and a vast teppanyaki grill, where chefs prepare food with the flourish and precision of knife throwers. An à la carte sushi meal easily reaches $25. Open Monday to Friday, noon to 3 p.m.; Monday to Saturday, 5:30 p.m. to midnight; and Sunday 1 p.m. to 5.30 p.m.

Àjili Mójili, ☎ 787-725-9195, 1052 Ashford Ave., Condado, is probably the most popular destination for tourists seeking "true" Puerto Rican cuisine. Although it attempts to reach gourmet standards (and succeeds in terms of price, with entrées from $18 to $30!), take heed that this is not a spot favored by locals. Superior Puerto Rican food for a fraction of the cost can be found elsewhere. Open daily from noon to 3 p.m., and 6 p.m. to 11 p.m.; closed Sundays.

For upscale Puerto Rican food, you'll do better to visit **Pikayo**, ☎ 787-721-6194, Hotel Tanamá, 1 Joffre Street, Condado, or at its new second location at Museo de Arte de Puerto Rico. Chef Wilo Benet is critically acclaimed throughout the island for his fusion of local ingredients with international flair. Open Monday to Saturday, 6 p.m. to 10.30 p.m. (and for lunch at the museum). Main courses are $15 to $30.

Hermes Creative Cuisine, ☎ 787-723-5151, 1108 Ashford Ave., Condado, elaborates on meat and fish classics. The menu changes every two months, but you can expect rarities such as lamb chops with goat cheese and tequila sauce and venison filets. Entrées cost about $30.

Located in a beautifully restored Spanish home in Santurce, **La Casona,** ☎ 787-727-2717 or 3229, 609 San Jorge, Esquina Fernández Juncos, has some of the most elegant dining in the metropolitan area. Choose to sit in a dusky, fully stocked wine cellar or one of seven more formal dining areas. With excellent filet mignon and seafood, it's open Monday to Friday, noon to 3 p.m. and 6 p.m. to 11.30 p.m., and Saturdays for dinner only.

Casual

Marisquería Miró, ☎ 787-723-9593, 76 Condado Ave. at the Hotel El Portal, Condado,, has won the "Tenedor de Honor" (Fork of Honor) award every year since it opened in 1986, for perfectly cooked fish dishes. Highlights include halibut with *cabrales* cheese, grilled sea bass and seafood with black rice. Most dishes cost less than $20. Open for lunch and dinner Tuesday to Thursday 11 a.m. to 10.30 p.m., Friday and Saturday 11 a.m. to 11 p.m. and Sunday 11 a.m. to 10 p.m.

Marisquería La Dorada, ☎ 787-722-9583, 1105 Esq. Magdalena in Condado, also has an excellent reputation for Puerto Rican seafood dishes at comparable prices. More casual, **Red Snapper**, ☎ 787-722-3699, 1120 Ashford Ave., Condado, does a tasty seafood *mofongo*, and is known for its selection of jazz recordings. Also less than $20 an entrée. If this all sounds a bit fishy, **Danny's International Pizzería y Cafetería**, ☎ 787-724-0501, 1352 Ashford, also in Condado, has recently doubled in size to make room for ever-growing numbers of fans. A large pizza with three or four toppings costs around $18. Across the street, **Vía Appia**, ☎ 787-735-8711, 1350 Ashford Ave., is another popular Italian eatery with an authentic atmosphere.

Go Mexican at **Don Andrés**, ☎ 787-723-0223, 1350 Ashford Ave. in Condado, on a Thursday, Friday or Saturday evening and you'll likely be treated to live mariachi music by owner Armando Ramos and his amigos. "I love to sing for my guests!" he says, bursting into song to prove it. Fajitas, burritos and enchiladas cost between $10 and $15.

La Patiserrie Francés, ☎ 787-728-5508, 1504 Ashford Ave., Condado, is the best place on the island for freshly baked baguettes, spinach-and-feta-stuffed croissants and eggs Florentine on weekends. Sandwiches and gourmet salads cost up to $7.

Three Cuban restaurants called **Metropol**, ☎ 787-268-3045, 105 Avenida de Diego (in Condado), serve consistently pleasing Cuban fare to hungry patrons. A whole Cornish hen stuffed with *congri* (black beans and rice) costs $9; the "Cuban Fiesta," consisting of a lot of just about everything on the menu, is just $10. The other two branches are in Isla Verde, ☎ 787-791-4046, and Hato Rey, ☎ 787-751-4022.

The only Greek restaurant in the area is the tiny, easily missed **Fleria**, ☎ 787-268-0010, 1754 Loíza St., Santurce, Try mousaka, dolmades and tzatziki. Portions are small but reasonable, with entrées generally under $10. Open daily 11.30 a.m. to 11 p.m.

For fresh fish and seafood across from the open-air market in Santurce, **Tasca El Pescador**, ☎ 787-721-0995, 178 Calle Dos Hermanos, is a popular local spot for lunch and dinner. Main courses with Puerto Rican side dishes cost $11 to $15.

Budget

For a healthy and cheap lunch, **Salud**, ☎ 787-722-0911, 1350 Ashford Ave., a small café behind a health food store, serves homemade soups, salads, sprouts and fresh squeezed juices for between $5 and $7.

If you don't mind eating in a heavily air-conditioned supermarket, **Pueblo Xtra Supermarket**, at the intersection of Calle Wilson and De Diego, Santurce, has a deli with cheap lunches such as lasagna, roast chicken, and rice and beans, for about $5.

Seldom discovered by tourists, **Pomarrosas**, ☎ 787-268-6270, Hwy. 26, Santurce (next door to Target Car Rental), serves Puerto Rican fare in a dining area crammed with local antiques, including ancient cameras, bicycles, tools, toys and portraits of Taino Indians, Puerto Rican luminaries and baseball players. Dishes and cold beer are served on wooden plates and in tin cups. Try fricassee of guinea hen or sautéed rabbit for $11, or *churrasco* steak or chicken for $7. Open Monday to Friday from 11 a.m., Saturday and Sunday from 1 p.m., until the last diner leaves.

■ Ocean Park

Fine Dining

Pamela's, ☎ 787-726-5010, 1 Santa Ana St. at Numero 1 Guest House, features the magic of esteemed San Juan chef Esteban Torres, who specializes in Caribbean fusion cuisine. The oceanfront restaurant has indoor and outdoor dining. Lunch specials (a bargain at $8 to $12) include trout with apples, roasted bell peppers and wasabi dressing, and barbecue shrimp with coconut *arepas* and spicy black bean sauce. Dinner appetizers include crab cakes with a lemon-lime aioli, and plantain-encrusted calamari with toasted peanut and chili vinaigrette, for around $12. Entrées include grilled prawns in coconut curry sauce, island-spiced pork loin with pineapple sweet and sour sauce, and "catch of the day," for $20 to $30.

Casual

Dunbar's, ☎ 787-728-2920, 1954 McLeary Avenue, is hugely popular for gourmet pub food. Rare seared tuna sandwiches (don't ask for it well done, or you won't be served!) and Mediterranean salads sprinkled with pine nuts, sun-dried tomatoes and goat cheese cost less than $12. Evening entrées range from $12 to $18, and are consistently good, and Sunday brunch featuring fresh oysters and breakfast favorites packs in locals and travelers alike. Open Monday to Thursday and Sundays, from 11.30 a.m. to midnight; and Fridays and Saturdays from 5 p.m. to 1 a.m.

Carnivores indulge at Argentinean steak house **Che's**, ☎ 787-726-7202, 35 Caoba St. in Punta Las Marías, which has won awards for its *parillada*, *churrasco*, and *chimichurri* meat dishes, as well as its massive steak grill for two. Most entrées cost $15 and up.

Hostería Del Mar, ☎ 787-727-3302 or 0631, 1 Tapia Street (see *Where to Stay*) on the beach, has an appealing vegetarian/macrobiotic menu, including ayurvedic and vegan dishes. Most combination plates cost about $12.

Budget

Cafeteria-style **Kasalta**, ☎ 787-727-7340, 1999 McLeary St., has long been a local favorite for great Spanish-style lunches, pastries and strong coffee, for as little as $7. Open daily 6 a.m. to 10 p.m.

La Casita Blanca, ☎ 787-726-5501, Calle Tapia, is another *criollo* luncheon favorite, and was featured in the news during the 2000 gubernatorial campaign when leading candidates Sila Calderon and Carlos Pesquera stopped in for a "peace lunch" together. Dishes range between $7 and $15. Open Monday to Thursday, 11:30 a.m. to 7 p.m.; Fridays and Saturdays, 11:30 a.m. to 10 p.m.; and Sundays from noon to 5 p.m.

■ Isla Verde

Fine Dining

The Vineyard, ☎ 787-253-1700, at the Ritz-Carlton Hotel, is probably the best restaurant in a resort hotel in San Juan, with a wine list comprehensive enough to earn it an Award of Excellence from *Wine Spectator* magazine two years in a row. The food, though excellent, comes in nouvelle portions and costs a small fortune.

Several good restaurants are at the Wyndham El San Juan Hotel and Casino, ☎ 787-791-1000, ext. 5 (for dining reservations), including **Yamato**, ☎ 787-791-8152, a basic sushi bar with excellent seaweed salad. Another is **Back Street Hong Kong**, ☎ 787-791-2035 or 1224, a theme restaurant (a la Las Vegas) where street signs in Chinese and oriental style bridges and back-alley décor add kitsch appeal to an excellent, if pricey, menu.

Ruth's Chris Steak House, ☎ 787-253-1717, Ave. de Isla Verde, offers top-grade surf and turf, including filet mignon, Maine lobster and an extensive wine list.

Casual

The **Outback Steak House**, ☎ 787-791-4679, Embassy Suites Hotel, 8000 Tartak Street, attracts a fun, young crowd with steaks grilled Aussie style, "bloomin' onions" (giant onions breaded and deep-fried in beer batter), and plenty of Foster's beer. Entrées cost $10 to $23. Another theme steak house is **The Ranch**, ☎ 787-791-1000, ext. 5, at the Wyndham El San Juan Hotel & Casino. You'll see line-dancing waiters, mechanical bulls, horseshoe pits and western movies. Ribs come $14.50 for a half rack, $25 for full.

Basilico, ☎ 787-727-6380, 2 J.M. Tartak St. (at the Colonial Hotel), has one of the finest views in Isla Verde from its ground-floor restaurant and 11th-floor terrace, with a menu that leans toward northern Italian.

Many diners at **La Marina Del Curro**, ☎ 787-728-3628, Marginal de la Baldorioty, Villamar-Isla Verde #11, are staying at the Green Isle Inn nearby and are too lazy to look for a restaurant farther away. Decent food is let down by side dishes of over-boiled vegetables, and most dishes cost $18 or more. The chef has twice won awards for the world's largest paella.

Budget

Homemade pasta at **Tiramisu**, ☎ 787-726-3162, Marginal Villamar, C-19 Isla Verde, keeps this low-key family-style restaurant bustling with satisfied return customers. Try spinach-and-ricotta-stuffed ravioli, eggplant Parmesan or penne with smoked salmon and vodka. Open weekdays until

10 p.m. and Friday and Saturday until 11 p.m. Most pasta dishes cost less than $12.

Inexpensive Mexican food and live music nightly make **Lupi's**, ☎ 787-253-1664, Carr. 187, almost as attractive as its twin restaurant in Old San Juan.

Bagelfields, ☎ 787-253-3633, 6070 Ave. de Isla Verde, serves bagels with cream cheese, lox and all other trimmings to visitors jonesing for New York, with prices between $4 and $7.

> **TIP:** *Picnickers can stock up at **Grande Supermarket**, 3102 Ave. de Isla Verde, which is open 24 hours and has small deli and bakery departments.*

■ Hato Rey & Río Piedras

In Hato Rey, **Jerusalem**, ☎ 787-764-3265, G-1 Calle O'Neil, serves an excellent Middle Eastern appetizer platter with hummus, falafel, kalamata olives, feta cheese, eggplant dip and pita bread, for around $10, as well as main dishes for up to $20. Open Monday to Thursday and Saturdays, 11 a.m. to 10:30 p.m., Fridays and Sundays from 11:30 a.m. to 11 p.m., it features belly dancers on weekend nights.

Vegetarians can fill up on "live" and organic foods for around $7 a plate at either **Natural Organics**, ☎ 787-756-6760, 214 Eleanor Roosevelt Ave., Hato Rey, or **Garden of Health**, ☎ 787-282-7023, Royal Bank Center Lobby, 255 Ponce de León Ave., Hato Rey (in the financial sector). Both are closed in the evening.

For eat-in or take-out, **Café Valencia**, ☎ 787-764-3790, 1000 Muñoz Rivera Ave., Río Piedras, has a loyal following for seafood and paellas *valencianas*, for about $15. Open Monday to Thursday and Sundays, 11:30 a.m. to midnight, Fridays from 11:30 a.m. to 2 a.m. and Sundays 5 p.m. to 2 a.m.

El Mesón, ☎ 787-765-2183, 1668 Paraná Street, Río Piedras, does a good range of vegetarian soups, salads and sandwiches, for about $5 to $7.

For Irish beer and pub food, **Shannan's Pub**, ☎ 787-281-8466, 496 Bore Street, in Río Piedras, serves Guinness, bangers and mash and other bar favorites Monday to Friday, 11:30 a.m. to 1 a.m., Saturdays and Sundays to 2:30 a.m.

Entertainment & Nightlife

■ Theater & Concerts

The **Centro de Bellas Artes Luis A. Ferré** (Fine Arts Center), ☎ 787-725-7353, 7358 or 7334, Ave. Ponce de León (stop 22), Santurce, is Puerto Rico's Carnegie Hall or La Scala – an award-winning center with three theaters, including the Antonio Paoli Festival Room, home to the Puerto Rican Symphony Orchestra. Performances range from classical to country-western music, ballet, modern dance and theater (Spanish or English). Longer-term listings can be found in *Que Pasa* magazine. For shorter-run events check weekend sections of local newspapers or call the box office (above). Look for live music performances at the **Muñoz Marín Amphitheater**, ☎ 787-728-2022, Muñoz Marín Park, in Hato Rey. It's the best venue on the island.

■ Movies

You'll find cinema complexes showing Hollywood blockbusters around the city, especially in malls, such as Plaza Las Americas, Hato Rey; Plaza del Sol, Bayamón and Plaza Carolinas. Check listings in the *San Juan Star* or other newspapers. Two smaller theaters often have more interesting (and sometimes local or European) films. **Metro**, ☎ 787-722-0465, Ave. Ponce de León is in Santurce near the Condado hotels, and the **Fine Arts Cinema**, ☎ 787-721-4288, Ave. Ponce de León, is Puerto Rico's best independent cinema.

■ Bars

Old San Juan

Old San Juan has enough bars to make your mind spin, but here are a few to get you started. Bar central is **Calle San Sebastián**, where weekend nights get going at about 10:30 p.m. **Nono's**, ☎ 787-725-7819, 100 San Sebastián (on Plaza San José), is one of the old city's most famous bars, swarmed by local and visiting barflies alike. A good place to meet strangers, it has pool tables upstairs. Usually open daily 11 a.m. to late. Slightly more upscale, **Amadeus**, ☎ 787-722-8635, 106 San Sebastián, features classical music, aged rums and cigars.

El Batey, Calle Cristo, is a small bar of legend because it invites patrons to graffiti the walls of its dungeon-like rooms (feel free to add your own two cents worth if you can find any free wall space), and can get smoky and raucous as the evening churns into night. Across the street, **Café Bohemio**, ☎ 787-723-9200, 100 Calle Cristo, is more for the beautiful people – a civilized Mediterranean-style patio café with a good wine list and tasty hors d'oeuvres, crowded with well-heeled *sanjuaneros* on weekend evenings. Farther down the street, **Maria's**, ☎ 787-721-1678, 204 Calle Cristo, is the place for big fruity Mexican-style cocktails, and often fills with cruise passengers when the ships come in.

On Plaza Colón, **Café Puerto Rico**, ☎ 787-724-2281, 208 Calle O'Donnel, has been around for over 70 years, and is frequented by a great mix of people – San Juan literati, students, musicians and a few travelers. Be sure to try Ray's rum punch – a heady mixture of papaya, mango, pineapple, *acerola* and enough rum to float a battleship. On weekend nights, the intimate upstairs bar opens for live music, with audience participation welcome!

> **HOME-BREWED COINTREAU:** *If you can't beg a glass from Ray's stash at Café Puerto Rico, here is his "secret" recipe for homemade Cointreau. Take one liter of white rum, one pound of sugar and three whole oranges in good condition; place ingredients in a glass jar; let mixture stand for three or four days. Serve over ice.*

Philistines in search of trademark T-shirts and memorabilia will find **Hard Rock Café**, ☎ 787-724-7625, at 253 Recinto Sur. Youngish visitors will need ID to get in, and the vibe is, of course, rock and roll. Open Monday to Sunday, 11.30 a.m. to 2 a.m. For a similarly gringo environment, **Hooters**, ☎ 787-722-9464, 413 San Francisco, caters to a young crowd, with dinner and drinks served by women wearing little orange shorts.

In the Puerta de Tierra neighborhood, the Caribe Hilton has a new bar called **Moonlight**, ☎ 787-721-0303, with music is from the '70s, '80s and '90s, but no dance floor. It's open Fridays and Saturdays only, from 9 p.m. to 3 a.m.

THE PIÑA COLADA FLAP

A plaque outside a bar named **Barranchina**, ☎ 787-725-1044, on Calle Fortaleza, credits its former bartender, Don Ramón Portas Mingot, with inventing this creamy cocktail in 1963. The **Caribe Hilton**, however, claims the piña colada was born at its Beachcomber Bar on August 15, 1954, at the hands of bartender Ramón "Monchito" Marrero. One thing is for sure: The Caribe Hilton served early versions of the rum-coconut-pineapple concoction to visiting celebrities that included John Wayne, Charlton Heston, Elizabeth Taylor and Joan Collins.

Condado, Ocean Park & Isla Verde

Il Grottino Wine Bar, ☎ 787-723-0499, 1372 Ashford Ave., is a civilized cocktail lounge with a small bar cleverly obscured by a flower garden that, despite traffic, still attracts hummingbirds and butterflies in the early evening. There's a 200-bottle wine list from which to choose. Open Monday to Saturday from 6 p.m. to late.

Dunbar's, ☎ 787-728-2920, 1954 McLeary St. in Ocean Park, is the liveliest pub in this part of town, packed to the gills with a young international crowd on weekends, when the party nearly spills into the street, and music from the '70s and '80s pumps long into the night.

Mango's Café, ☎ 787-727-9328, 2421 Laurel St., Punta Las Marías, is known for reggae on weekends and a more eclectic crowd. **Pepíns Café**, ☎ 787-728-6280, 2479 Loíza St., a popular tapas bar, caters to an elegant crowd of mostly over-25s, with Latin jazz and piano music. Open Tuesday to Friday from 5 p.m. and Saturday from 7 p.m. until late.

Beer connoisseurs will rejoice at the only microbrewery in town, **Borinquen Grill & Brewing Co**, ☎ 787-268-1900 or 800-877-BREW, 4800 Ave. de Isla Verde, e-mail borinquengrill@yahoo.com. Flavorful varieties brewed on the premises include coquí amber lager, Taino pale ale, *rubia* pilsner, honey-wheat ale and a stout.

The **Oyster Bar**, ☎ 787-726-2161, also on Avenida de Isla Verde, hosts a Mardi Gras festival in March and continues apace the rest of the year by encouraging patrons to gulp oysters, suck crawfish heads and down "hurricane" drinks in rapid succession. Open daily until late, this is a favorite among full-on party animals. More sophisticated revelers may enjoy a mellow aged rum or glass of champagne at the **Lobby Lounge**, ☎ 787-253-1700, ext. 4270, 6961 Los Gobernadores Ave. (at the Ritz-Carlton), to the strains of classical and jazz, and occasionally salsa music when the bartender feels risqué.

Piñones

On Fridays, Saturdays and Sundays, the little beach bars and restaurants of Piñones explode with action, as Puerto Ricans young and old head here for barbecue food, fried snacks, cheap beer and a beach party vibe. Unfortunately, some guidebooks and other tourist literature warn visitors away from Piñones at night, because it has had a reputation for rowdiness and some crime. However, providing you obey basic rules of caution (lock your car, don't wander off alone into dark areas, etc.) you should feel free to join some of the best times in town. Just east of the Punta Cangrejos bridge on Carr. 187, you'll begin to see the barbecues and many cars. Park in a busy area and explore! For live music and good food, we recommend **Soleil Beach Club and Bistro**, ☎ 787-253-1033, with Latin jazz, calypso, salsa, Spanish rock and blues on weekends.

■ Live Music

Bar Rumba, ☎ 787-725-4407, 152 Calle San Sebastián, is the best-loved live music venue in Old San Juan, often hosting stars of the Puerto Rican rumba and salsa circuit. Old timers and trendy youngsters alike give it their all on the dance floor, and this is the best place in town to get an impromptu lesson in salsa or rumba technique. Open Tuesday to Sunday, 7 p.m. to late (arrive after 10 p.m. to see it in full swing).

Café ? (also known as Café Pregunta) ☎ 787-723-5467 or 531-4180, 157 Calle San José, attracts a young crowd of students and young professionals, with merengue and salsa most nights, live *bomba* on Wednesdays, jazz on Saturdays. Expect this place to be packed well into the wee hours, with carryings-on getting wilder as the night progresses. Open Monday to Saturday from 7 p.m.

Lupi's Mexican Grill and Sports Cantina, ☎ 787-722-1874, 313 Recinto Sur (with a sister location on Avenida de Isla Verde) has nightly live music – usually local bands playing rock, pop and salsa – and gets packed with a young crowd on weekends. Open daily 11 a.m. to 1 a.m.

For diners, the **Parrot Club**, ☎ 787-725-7370, 363 Calle Fortaleza, usually features live jazz, rumba and salsa music on Tuesdays, Thursdays and Saturdays, until midnight.

Rarely visited by tourists, the newly renovated **Plaza Mercado** (see page 93) on Calle Canals in Santurce often transforms into an outdoor dancehall on Friday and Saturday evenings, when local acts take over the bandstand. Great Puerto Rican flavor!

Sit-down diners are serenaded by strolling Latin guitarists in the quiet ambience of **Havana's Café**, ☎ 787-725-0888, 409 Del Parque St., Santurce, on Fridays and Saturdays. Music starts 7 p.m. On Friday nights, salsa and merengue bands get people dancing at the Marriott Hotel, ☎ 787-722-7000, 1309 Ashford Ave. in Condado.

> **¡BAILA BOMBA!** *Make your own bomba drum out of a rum barrel, learn to play it and grind to the rhythm at* **Museo de Nuestra Raíz Africana**, ☎ *787-724-0700, ext. 4239, Plaza San José, Old San Juan. Live bomba music is on offer many Friday evenings (call for information and tickets).*

■ Nightclubs

Old San Juan

Dance is the focus at the three-level **Club Lazer**, ☎ 787-721-4479, 251 Cruz St., www.clublazer.com, on Mondays and Tuesdays from 8 p.m.,

Thursdays from 9 p.m., and Fridays and Saturdays from 10 p.m. On weekends its mostly dance, trance and techno, with a state-of-the-art light show and a roof-top terrace for cooling off between grooves; mid-week the music is more varied. On a smaller scale, **The Gallery Café**, ☎ 787-725-8676, 305 Calle Fortaleza, has a more underground scene, catering to slightly older, more selective club-goers who appreciate the creative wizardry of local DJs.

Bahía Seaport, ☎ 787-724-6222, on the waterfront in Puerta de Tierra, has live entertainment Wednesday to Saturday, often with a cover charge of $10 at the door. The atmosphere and type of entertainment is subject to frequent change, and attracts an elegant Puerto Rican crowd (the *gente buena* comes out for special events). The dress code is smart, with no jeans or tennis shoes. Opening hours vary, so it's best to call ahead.

Santurce

Formerly the popular Egipto Club, **Stargate**, ☎ 787-725-4664, 1 Ave. R.H. Todd, has a haphazard Egyptian/futuristic theme (silver-painted mummies and sphinxes), where the entrance is bizarrely called the Gate of Terror. Despite the "yikes – no concept!" atmosphere of the place and the cover charge of $10 or more (steep by Puerto Rican standards), this place remains popular with young people who dance to '70s, '80s and salsa music. Open Thursday to Sunday, 9 p.m. to 4 a.m.

Hip clubbers go to **Asylum**, ☎ 787-723-3258, 1320 Ave. Ponce de León, located in a converted theater, where the stage is used for a variety of acts from cabaret, fashion shows, performance art and comedians on Sundays. The music leans toward cool experimental and underground dance.

Isla Verde

Merengue and salsa bands regularly top the bill at **Chico Bar**, ☎ 787-791-1000, at the Wyndham El San Juan Hotel, and is preferred by an over-30 crowd. Open Wednesday to Sunday, 9 p.m. to 1 a.m. **Martini's Night Club**, ☎ 787-791-6100, at the Inter-Continental San Juan, mixes dance music and salsa, and features live shows on Mondays and Tuesday from 10 p.m. The disco is open Thursdays and Fridays from 9 p.m., and Saturdays from 11 p.m.

Babylon, ☎ 787-791-2781 or 791-1000, at the Wyndham El San Juan Hotel & Casino, gets down on weekends with an older spectrum of disco-loving club-goers. Open Thursday to Saturday, from 9 p.m. **Area 51**, ☎ 787-728-3730, D-11 Ave. de Isla Verde, doles out free shots to get customers in the mood for a disco celebration every Friday and Saturday night from 9 p.m. Guests must be over 23.

GAY & LESBIAN SPOTS IN SAN JUAN

The increasing number of gay-oriented destinations in San Juan include: **Steamworks,** ☎ 787-725-4993, 205 Luna St., Old San Juan, a no-girls bathhouse; **The New Bachelor,** ☎ 787-721-3945, 112 Condado Avenue, a low-key disco; the **Downstairs Bar,** 6 Condado Ave. (at Condado Inn); the **Beachside Bar,** ☎ 787-721-6900, 1 Vendig St. (at the Atlantic Beach Hotel), with an intermittent drag scene; **Eros,** ☎ 787-722-1131, 1257 Ave. Ponce de León, with the most outrageous dance, drag and strip acts in the area; **Junior's Bar,** ☎ 787-723-9477, 602 Condado St., with drag shows and strippers on weekends; **La Laguna Club,** ☎ 787-722-1131, 53 Barranquitas St., which stays open late with a mixed crowd; and **Cups,** ☎ 787-268-3570, 1708 San Marcos St., a girls' girls hangout with a laid-back mixed crowd.

■ Casinos

Lose Your Shirt (and More) in Puerto Rico!

Many people regard gambling as a fundamental evil, and look upon those who gamble as degenerate pariahs. Nonsense, we say! Gaming is a great and worthy pastime. Nothing could be more glamorous than laughing at the loss of $100. And nothing feels better than winning it back. Although San Juan is no Las Vegas, most large hotels have casinos, many of which have tables with stakes low enough even for the most timid novice. Puerto Rican casinos are open to anyone over the age of 18, and some have 24-hours licenses. Players nearly always drink for free. Just wave your hand in the air, and if you're betting (or losing) lots of money, a waitress will come promptly! For the uninitiated, here are a few tips on what and how to play.

- **PAI GOW POKER** - This card game combines elements of the ancient Chinese game *pai gow* with traditional poker. Basically, you play two hands at once, with all 52 cards of the deck plus jokers, which can be used as an ace or to complete a straight, flush or straight flush. Each player receives seven cards, which they must split into two hands – a high hand (five cards) and a low hand (two cards). Both hands must be higher than the dealers' to win. Unusually, in this game, the dealer may explain the ranking order of the cards and help you arrange your hands.

- **CARIBBEAN STUD** - A tropical name for five-card stud poker. Players bet (use the ante circle) and receive five cards face down. The dealer takes four cards face down, one card exposed. After examining your cards you can either play or fold. If you fold you loose your ante. If you play, you must double your original bet, known as a back bet. When all the players have made their decisions, the dealer reveals his or her cards, but can play only with an ace, king or higher in hand. The game continues, as in poker. If your cards beat the dealer's, you receive even money on the ante bet and a bonus (according to the ranking order of the hand) on the back bet. For example, a pair may receive even money on the back bet, while a royal flush pays out 100-1.

- **ROULETTE** - One of the easiest games in the casino, roulette relies more on Lady Luck than on skill (although roulette addicts would never admit so). Simply place your chips on numbers that seem "lucky" on the board and let the croupier do the rest. Or choose a color – red or black. Use the force! The silver ball comes to rest as the wheel slows, determining the winner. Wager chips until the croupier indicates no more bets.

- **BLACKJACK - A.K.A. "21"** - You're dealt two cards face up. The dealer gets one card face up and the other face down. Now the calculation begins. Are you closer to 21 (without going higher) than the dealer? Basically, you'll do well by assuming the dealer's hidden card is worth 10. And the usual rule is that the dealer must draw over a minimum total of 16. So if the dealer has a showing card of two to five, hold. If this is new to you, make sure you join a table in the middle and not in the crucial first or last player positions. In blackjack, you can play as a team against the dealer. This game inspires camaraderie.

Leisure & Shopping

■ Art Galleries

Atlas Art, ☎ 787-723-9987, 208 Calle Cristo, e-mail atlasartosj@yunque.net, is the prettiest and best-stocked gallery in San Juan, with local and international works, including Viktor Shvaiko, Thomas McKnight and Gaugy. One of the highlights is a world-class collection of etchings, lino prints and bronze sculptures by Spanish artist Angel Botello, who used the building as an apartment and studio late in his life. Also on view are the works of contemporary Puerto Rican artists such as Roberto Parrilla, who turns period photographs into abstract expressions. Open Monday to Saturday, 10 a.m. to 6 p.m., Sundays 11 a.m. to 6 p.m.

Galería Botello (previously at Atlas Art), ☎ 787-754-7430, fax 250-8274, 314 F.D. Roosevelt Avenue, Hato Rey, www.botello.com, retains many works of its original artists, as well as a definitive collection of the Spanish master whose works captivate audiences worldwide with colorful depictions of humanity. Open Monday to Saturday, 10 a.m. to 6 p.m.

The **Frank Meisler Gallery**, ☎ 787-722-7698, 101 Calle Fortaleza, showcases works of the master of humorous sculpture, which have been received as gifts by US presidents and world leaders. The delightfully quirky **Galería San Juan**, ☎ 787-722-1808, 204 Norzagaray St., is a wonderland of art and sculpture by Jan D'Esopo and Manuco Gandía, displayed in a garden atmosphere complete with tropical birds and classical music. More conventionally, **La Galería De La Calle Cristo**, ☎ 787-977-4286, 156 Cristo (second floor), houses a colorful collection of contemporary art.

NOCHES DE GALERÍAS

On the first Tuesday of every month, *sanjuaneros* attend Noches de Galerías, during which more than 20 galleries stay open late with special exhibitions. Often, bars and restaurants nearby follow suit with live music, performance and other artistic endeavors, and the old city comes alive with the appreciation of various media from 6 p.m. to 9 p.m.

■ Spa Treatments

As the name suggests, **Zen Spa**, ☎ 787-722-8433, 1054 Ashford Ave., is a tranquil retreat offering a range of pampering, including facials, hydrotherapy, rain forest mud wraps and massage. Open Monday to Friday, 7 a.m. to 9 p.m., Saturdays 7 a.m. to 6 p.m., Sundays 9 a.m. to 6 p.m.

Le Spa Personal Fitness and Body Care, ☎ 787-722-0985 or 7000, ext. 6161, at the San Juan Marriott in Condado, offers a one-stop shop for indulgence. Choose from therapeutic body massages and treatments, aromatherapy and half- and full-day health and beauty sessions. Open from 6 a.m. to 10 p.m. daily.

■ Shopping Areas

Old San Juan has three main shopping streets that turn shopping into a colonial adventure. On Calle Fortaleza, **Joseph Machini**, ☎ 787-722-7698, 101 Calle Fortaleza, is one of the most respected designers of custom-made jewelry on the island. Vendors at **La Calle mini-mall**, 105 Calle Fortaleza, stock Puerto Rican festival masks, hand-carved *santos* and other arts, crafts and antiques. At **Heraldica**, a historical research center, ☎ 787-724-4348, 109 Calle Fortaleza, www.heraldicapr.com, staff will search your family tree while you wait.

On Calle Cristo, best known for its art galleries, a few designer shops include **Polo Ralph Lauren Factory Shop**, ☎ 787-721-4202, 201 Calle Cristo, as well as **Tommy Hilfiger**, **Speedo** and **Guess**. At **Big Planet**,

☎ 787-725-1204, 205 Calle Cristo, travelers can stock up on kit bags and tech products. The ultimate gentleman's store, **El Galpon**, ☎ 787-725-3945, 154 Calle Cristo, sells fine Suarez Panama hats and the island's best cigars. For kitchen enthusiasts, check out the shelves of **Spicy Caribe**, ☎ 787-725-4690, 154 Calle Cristo, for Caribbean cookbooks, tropical tableware and unique gourmet items. On Plaza San José, the **Puerto Rican Institute of Culture gift shop** is good for Puerto Rican musical instruments, folk music and Spanish colonial history books.

On Calle San Francisco, *sanjuaneros* get their surf wear, skateboarding threads, street fashion and piercings. For deals on sportswear, check out **Almacenes Fernandez**, ☎ 787-722-0991, 264 Calle San Francisco.

In Condado, **Ashford Avenue** may lack the quaint appeal of Old San Juan, but has some excellent shopping venues, where die-hards with plastic may find deals on Calvin Klein, Louis Vuitton, and Versace, as well as some local designer shops. One of the most interesting is **Nono Maldonado**, ☎ 787-721-0456, 1051 Ashford Ave., a leading Caribbean designer of ready-to-wear clothing for men and women.

Finally, mall addicts should look no further than **Plaza Las Américas**, ☎ 787-767-5202, F.D. Roosevelt Ave., Hato Rey, the Caribbean's largest shopping center with more than 200 stores, including the largest JCPenney store in the world, 10 movie theaters and 25 fast-food restaurants (open Monday to Saturday, 9 a.m. to 9 p.m., Sundays 11 a.m. to 5 p.m.).

> **WARNING – DESIGNER RIP-OFFS:** *As a rule, brand-name designer stores are reliable. However, buying designer brands from boutiques can be risky, and we've heard reports of garments with high-end labels falling apart soon after purchase, presumably because they are not the genuine article.*

North Coast

The star of the north coast is undoubtedly the surreal **karstic** region, where porous limestone hills have been eroded by millennia of rainfall into whimsical shapes and great cavernous pores, with sinkholes, underground streams and systems of caverns that remain only partly explored. Overgrown by subtropical forest, this landscape is a feast for the eyes and a rarity of the earth. Highlights include the **Camuy Caves**, the giant radio telescope at the **Arecibo Observatory** and three **state forests** that await the explorer. The counterpoint communities of **Dorado**, which is dominated by two Hyatt mega-resorts, and **Jobos**, with its laid-back surfer culture and quiet, unspoiled beaches, bracket the northern coastline. From San Juan, the metropolitan area dilutes westward through the charmless towns of Bayamón, Cataño, Toa Baja and Toa Alta and beyond, but once you reach either the foothills of the **Cordillera Central** or the northern coastline, the allure of the region begins to emerge. The plantain- and coffee-growing towns in the lower reaches of the central mountains give a first hint of the splendor to come. And, of course, you'll find some seductive white-sand beaches dotted between the more developed areas.

IN THIS CHAPTER
- Dorado
- Naranjito, Corozal, Morovis and Ciales
- Manatí
- Barceloneta
- Arecibo
- Hatillo
- Camuy
- Guayataca
- Isabela and Playa Jobos

Getting Here & Getting Around

The toll road of **Hwy. 22** stretches most of the way across the north coast, but unfortunately ends in **Hwy. 2**, a stoplight-clogged road that can slow traffic to the pace of a mule train. If you are heading west from San Juan along the north coast, be sure to leave before 2 p.m., or the insane rush-hour traffic will add an hour to your journey. The mountain roads between Naranjito and Bosque Río Abajo are pretty, but extremely curvy and slow, whereas **highways 149, 10 and 129** south into the hills from Hwy. 22 are open, straighter and much quicker. There are few places to rent cars along the north coast, but if you are staying in Dorado, just east of the Hyatt hotels, **Vias Car Rental**, ☎ 787-796-6404/6882, fax 796-7228, has compacts, luxury cars, pickup trucks and vans, with local pickup service.

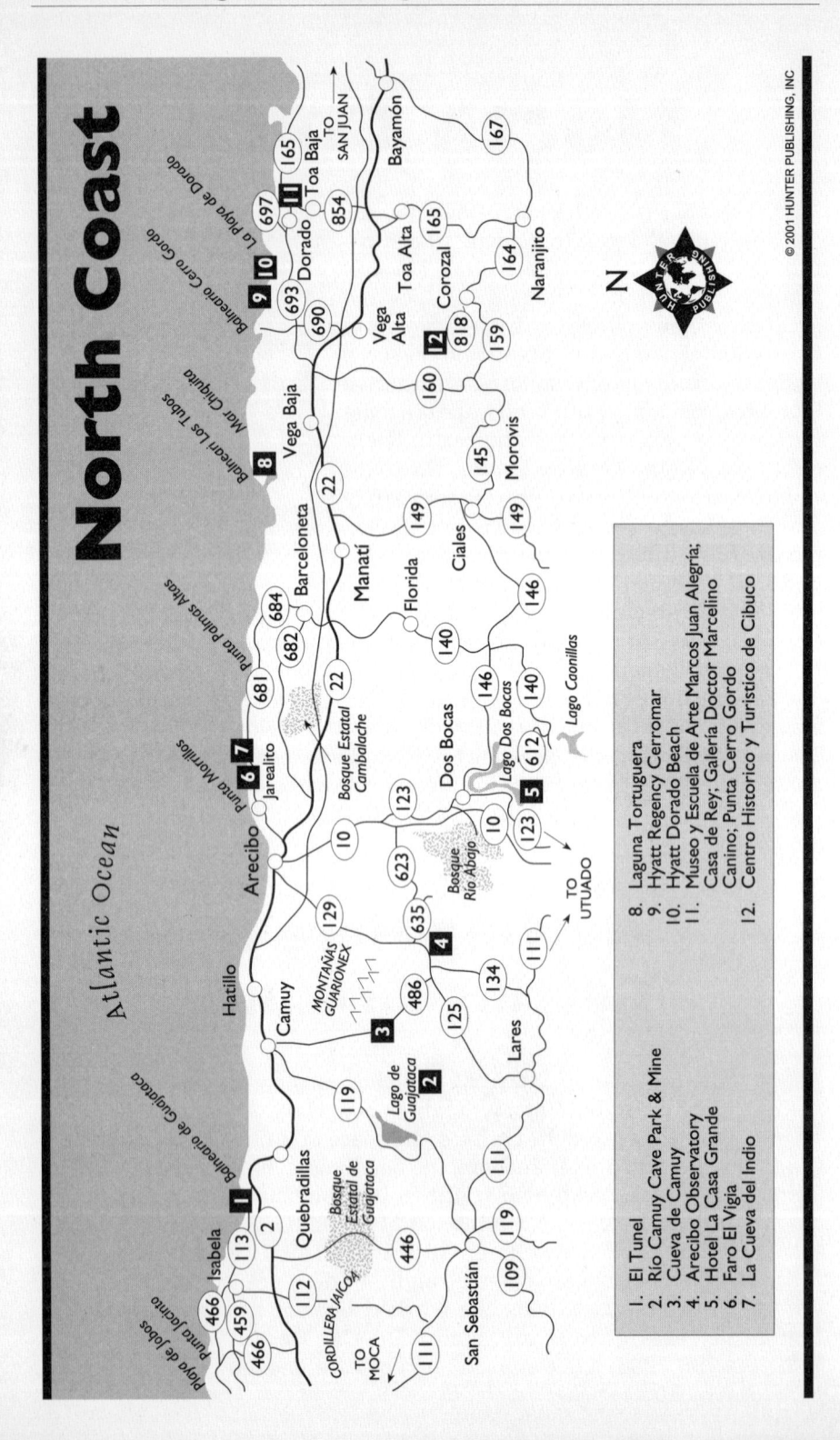

North Coast

1. El Tunel
2. Rio Camuy Cave Park & Mine
3. Cueva de Camuy
4. Arecibo Observatory
5. Hotel La Casa Grande
6. Faro El Vigía
7. La Cueva del Indio
8. Laguna Tortuguera
9. Hyatt Regency Cerromar
10. Hyatt Dorado Beach
11. Museo y Escuela de Arte Marcos Juan Alegría; Casa de Rey; Galería Doctor Marcelino Canino; Punta Cerro Gordo
12. Centro Historico y Turistico de Cibuco

© 2001 HUNTER PUBLISHING, INC

The diminutive **Nery Juarbe Municipal Airport** in Arecibo, ☎ 787-881-2072, is mainly for private traffic, with no commercial flights from beyond island borders, and unless you have your own airplane, attempting to fly into Arecibo will cost you more time than it saves. For budget travelers, though, the *público* station in Arecibo is the nerve center for the central north coast. ***Públicos*** go to and from San Juan and to most surrounding towns, including Barceloneta, Camuy and Hatillo. You'll find *público* stations in all sizeable towns, including Naranjito, Corozal, Morovis, Ciales, Manatí, Quebradillas and Isabela, with interconnecting service. The schedule is loose, and the fare between towns is usually less than $5 one way. As on the rest of the island, you'll just have to show up at the station and look for your desired destination on the front windshield of the vans. It is also possible to flag down *públicos*, but you need to be familiar with their routes.

Touring & Sightseeing

■ Dorado & Environs

Once you leave Bayamón and the San Juan metropolitan area on Hwy. 22, you'll pass the basically uninspiring towns of **Toa Alta**, **Toa Baja**, **Vega Alta**, **Vega Baja** and **Manatí** – most of which contain little more than commercial development, unsightly semi-urban housing and residential neighborhoods. You could, however, take detours to the north or south for some interesting sights. **Dorado**, meaning "golden" in Spanish, is best known for the two Hyatt mega-resorts, the **Hyatt Dorado Beach Hotel** (the oldest mega-resort on the island) and the **Hyatt Regency Cerromar**, that dominate its western end. The most unusual feature of the Cerromar is its 1,776-foot man-made river – with waterfalls, lounge caves and a swim-up bar – probably the longest freshwater swimming pool in the world. The resorts sprawl over more than 1,000 acres and include four exclusive 18-hole golf courses. Around them, turquoise and terra cotta luxury condo complexes have sprouted Palm Springs-style, with the exceptions being one painted in clownish Lego colors, and another with the vaguely forbidding name "The Clusters." On the eastern end of town, however, Dorado retains some of its own history and charm.

On the town plaza, check out the **Museo y Escuela de Arte Marcos Juan Alegría**, ☎ 787-746-1433, which exhibits works of local artists and offers classes in drawing and painting. The **Casa del Rey**, a little museum of artifacts dug up near the seaside *Ojo del Buey*, is closed for remodeling for an indefinite period of time. In the meantime, the skeleton of a Taino woman, circa AD 600-1200, and other Indian tools and shell jewelry can be viewed at the **Galería Doctor Marcelino Canino**, a tiny sea-green colored gallery on the southeast corner of the central plaza. Undiscovered until 1984, the skeleton has been determined to be that of a 15-year-old female who died of an unknown disease. Both are open from 10 a.m. to 4:30 p.m. weekdays.

Near the *Ojo del Buey* (Ox's Eye), a rock formation that looks like the head of an ox with an eyehole, **La Playa de Dorado**, the public beach, is a fine place for swimming. Poorly signposted, it can be reached by driving westward on Carr. 693 and turning right at the Gulf station. Farther west, the rocky **Punta Cerro Gordo** and adjacent public beach has a massive camping area and a budget horseback-riding outfit nearby. The area is hugely popular with locals on weekends and holidays. From Carr. 693 west, take the turnoff for Carr. 6690 northward.

■ Naranjito, Corozal, Morovis & Ciales

Visiting this string of towns tucked in the mountains above the north coast is a lovely drive, even if it doesn't quite match the splendor of the Ruta Panoramica. All four are former agricultural strongholds with pretty plazas, connected by roads that wind through the tropical forest. Each has at least one, if sometimes tenuous, claim to tourist interest. Following Carr. 167 southward from Bayamón, you wind through rolling hills with volcanic rock faces and thick vegetation, dotted with hilltop homes and *lechoneras*. On Carr. 164, **Naranjito** is a small two-road town in the valley of a normally dry riverbed, surrounded by a number of modest plantain farms. Brightly colored brick and concrete one-story homes with bars and shutters on the windows give way to a central plaza, where the main feature is the peculiar church – a huge, trapezoidal, barn-like building, painted gray and white with heavy modernistic touches. The 28,000 or so townsfolk are proud of their volleyball tradition; the local team won an unprecedented number of statewide trophies, especially in its heyday in the 1950s and 1960s, and is immortalized in bronze statues in the central plaza.

On a ridge along Carr. 164, **Corozal** is surrounded by dense greenery studded with bamboo, palms, creeper vines and wild plantains, as well as the remnants of a few sugarcane plantations. Some of the nearby hilltops afford views of much of the island, from the taller hills of the Cordillera Central in the south to the Atlantic Ocean in the north. The main point of interest for the traveler is the newly opened (December 2000) **Centro Historico y Turistico del Cibuco**, ☎ 787-859-3060, fax 859-2268 (ask for director Hiram Berrios), Carr. 818, Km. 2.5, a recreation and historical center on a picturesque old sugarcane hacienda in the Cibuca neighborhood. Along with artisan exhibitions and a shop, a lake with paddleboats, and a restaurant and cafeteria, the center includes a little museum to the region's sugarcane heritage and a wooden boardwalk that leads into a cave where you can see original Taino petroglyphs. It's open Friday to Sunday and holidays, from 10 a.m. to 6 p.m., and entrance costs $5 for adults, $3 for children. The **Festival Nacional del Plátano** (National Plantain

Festival) is held in Corozal the final weekend in September each year, during which local artisans exhibit handiwork and runners from around the island compete in the "plantain marathon."

YES, WE HAVE NO BANANAS

According to the Department of Agriculture, the municipalities of Corozal, Naranjito and Barranquitas produce more than 20 million *platanos*, or plantains, annually – roughly 60% of one of Puerto Rico's staple foods. Don't expect to peel and eat them, though. Unlike *plátanos* you'd find in Spain (bananas), the more bitter plantains must be fried or baked before consumption.

Descending through bamboo- and vine-studded forests along Carr. 159, you'll end up in the town of **Morovis**, which calls itself the "Artisan Capital of Puerto Rico." If you are interested in buying a handmade *cuatro* or *tiple* string instrument – which produce sounds unique to Puerto Rico – contact artists Julio Negrón Rivera, ☎ 787-862-0342, or Aurelio Cruz Pagán, ☎ 787-862-4583, at their homes. The city hall in Morovis, ☎ 787-862-2155, has a list of 18 local artists and phone numbers for their home studios. Unfortunately, there is no exhibition space for the town's artisans. One of the only places to view local work is (no joke) **Burger King** on Carr. 115, which has a couple of glass cases exhibiting old-style wooden toys made by Francisco Aponte Cabrera. Also on Carr. 115, just northeast of the town plaza, the bakery **Panadería La Patria** has the oldest bread oven in Puerto Rico, constructed in 1862, which churns out loaves of local favorite *pan patita echá* from its 20-foot-deep maw.

Leaving Morovis, you could head toward Orocovis, stopping at **Casa Bavaria**, a German beer garden with a great view high in the *jíbaro* hills, or continue along Carr. 159 toward **Ciales**. On this route, you'll notice that the landscape suddenly turns karstic, with greenery bearding the limestone rock faces. Ciales is a pretty country town right on the edge of the forest, but is probably best known to travelers as a stepping-off point for the mountainous area around the Toro Negro Forest Reserve (see the *Central Mountains* chapter, page 273). Driving around the area, especially southward into the mountains of La Cordillera Central, you'll find many places to stop and hike, as well as waterfalls in which to bathe.

■ Manatí & Environs

Avoid the town of **Manatí**, which is a crowded and featureless stretch of strip malls of the worst North American variety. Near Manatí, however, the Laguna Tortuguero and the Balneario Los Tubos are worth checking out if you're passing this way and not in a rush.

The **Laguna Tortuguero**, the largest freshwater lagoon on the island (about 2,200 acres), is best known as the home of the newly introduced caiman, a relative of the alligator. During the 1970s, a number of islanders bought baby caimans as a sort of macho pet. For many, the novelty soon wore off and, as the caimans grew, owners began dumping them in the lagoon, where they have flourished on a rich diet of freshwater fish. Don't expect to see one if you visit, however. They usually sleep during the day and come out to feed only at night, when the Laguna Tortuguero is closed to the public. Enter the lagoon area from Carr. 687, and a winding gravel path takes you to a bucolic spot with picnic areas and a wooden observation deck dipping into the expanse of the lagoon. Fishing and kayaking are popular activities here, but unfortunately there's no place to rent equipment so you have to bring your own. There are several walking paths in the woods surrounding the lagoon. Just ask the rangers on duty to point you in the right direction. They are friendly – ebullient even – and love to describe the dimensions of caimans they've sighted. Usually, they speak at least passable English. We advise taking exit 42 on Carr. 22 to avoid the traffic tangle in Manatí. If you take that route, a side trip along Carr. 686 yields a gorgeous stretch of road that passes **Balneario Los Tubos** toward Los Molinos. The public beach is nice, and you can park for free along several palm-lined stretches of sand just west of it. There are a couple of good surfing breaks along here, too.

■ Barceloneta & Environs

What can be said about Barceloneta? It was named after a poor seaside neighborhood of Barcelona, Spain, and is known for pineapple cultivation. What else? City officials, apparently grasping at straws for some kind of tourist interest, say that one of the most important dates in this island town was in 1938, when boxing champion Jack Dempsey paid a visit. Hmm.

The city center is crowded with pedestrians, and therefore good for people watching. Otherwise, it's completely forgettable. Nearby, however, the seldom-visited **Bosque Estatal Cambalache** contains some of the island's only surviving virgin forest, and has some excellent hiking and mountain biking trails through surreal karstic landscapes that date back to before human meddling, for a truly prehistoric feel. To get here, take Carr. 683 north from Hwy. 22, then turn right onto Carr. 682. In about 1½ miles, look for signs for the Job Corps, which is better signposted than the state forest. The driveway is the same for both. Cambalache has facilities for camping (see *Where to Stay*, page 159), and entrance and hiking are free of charge.

Barceloneta is also the inevitable beginning or end point for a marvelous drive along the coastal Carr. 681, where you'll find a few excellent beaches for swimming or surfing, a lighthouse museum (near Arecibo), and **La Cueva del Indio**, a sinkhole cave in a rock outcropping into the sea, the walls of which are covered in Taino petroglyphs (see *Adventures On Wheels*

Pineapple workers in the fields.
(PRTC)

in this chapter). From here westward and into the mountains, the terrain is one of the world's best examples of karstic landscapes – limestone rock eaten away into strange shapes by millennia of rain and seawater erosion.

■ Arecibo, Bosque Río Abajo & Environs

Despite its jurisdiction over the largest municipality in Puerto Rico and its status as the island's oldest city in its original location, the seaside town of **Arecibo** is a bummer and a good place to get stuck in traffic. Named for the Taino chief Aracibo, who ruled the area when colonists began arriving in the early 16th century, it's also called Villa del Capitan Correa, in honor of the commander of Spanish and Puerto Rican troops who foiled a British invasion in 1702. Unless you feel obliged to try the local delicacy – *empanadillas de ceti*, a fried bread pocket stuffed with newly spawned fish from the Río Arecibo estuary (local fishermen have been harvesting infant fish here since the time of the Indians) – avoid the town in favor of surrounding attractions.

North of Arecibo, take Hwy. 10 – a fast, two-lane highway cut into hundreds of feet of limestone rock – to the **Bosque Río Abajo**, one of the island's best, yet most overlooked eco-travel destinations, where you can hike 24 different trails that wind through tropical hardwood forests and karstic *mogotes* (hills) and caves. Highlights include camping under forest *bohíos* and a visit to an aviary full of endangered birds. Next to the Río

Abajo is the largest lake on the island (artificial, like most others), **Lago Dos Bocas**, which, along with the adjacent **Lago Caonillas** (*Central Mountains*, page 278), provides water to most of northwestern Puerto Rico. A ferry takes visitors on half-hour tours sponsored by the government. On weekends, the lake is a popular retreat, and four lively restaurants, accessible only by boat, open for weekend warriors and solace seekers. This area is a natural gateway for exploring the mountain areas around Jayuya, Utuado and Adjuntas.

Music of the Stars

For anyone who's ever stared at the stars in the night sky and wondered, "What's out there?" and "How might we find out?" a visit to the **Arecibo Observatory** – with the biggest radio telescope on earth – is a must. As seen on screen in *Contact*, *GoldenEye* and *The X Files*, the 1,000-foot-diameter dish sunk into a limestone cavity in the hills is awesome in itself. Built in the early 1960s, its spherical surface comprises more than 38,000 perforated aluminum panels, with a surface area of about 18 acres, or the equivalent of 26 football fields. Massive. Fixed in place, it is the most sensitive instrument of its kind, and can accurately detect radio signals up to 10 billion light years away – at the extreme edge of the universe. This means it can also take in signals that date back in time to the first moments of the Big Bang, when the universe as we know it was born.

Used around the clock by scientists from all over the world, the National Astronomy and Ionosphere Center has led the way to Nobel Prize-winning discoveries and reshaped the way astronomers look at our solar system

Arecibo Observatory.
(PRTC)

and galaxies near and far. Groundbreaking research into pulsars has been conducted here, as well as a re-mapping of local planets and the Earth's atmospheric content. And sci-fi buffs take note: It is also perhaps the greatest tool for the **Search for Extra-Terrestrial Intelligence** (SETI) scientists, who listen to the void hoping to one day get a signal from sentient beings of a faraway galaxy. So far, though, no word from the ETs. Unfortunately, the scope of the dish – monitoring a conical slice of the sky and allotted less than one percent of the bands in the radio frequency spectrum – is limited.

> **ASTRONOMER'S COMMENT:** *"We get some incredibly valuable information about a small area of the sky. But, at best, we've gathered only one leaf in a jungle."* – Arecibo Observatory staff astronomer Tapasi Ghosh

Although you probably won't see scientists at work (they're usually sitting at computer terminals and poring over inscrutable maps of radio waves), the newly opened visitor center at the observatory is extremely good. You'll want to spend an hour or two checking out the interactive displays that explain all aspects of the dynamics of the universe and the history of radio telescopy. You'll learn how radio waves emanating from space were first discovered in 1931 by a physicist from Bell Labs, who was trying to find the source of static in long-distance radio transmissions on earth. Feel free to skip the corny, 20-minute film, however. Outside the visitor center, an observation deck lets you look out on the awesome proportions of the dish. Notice the roving eyeball-like apparatus suspended above the stationary dish. This is a $25 million Gregorian reflector system (named for the 17th-century mathematician, James Gregory), completed in 1997, which boosted the telescope's versatility and sensitivity to unmatched levels. It might not look it from the observation deck, but the Gregorian dome itself is six stories high. Meteorologists, astronomers and ET seekers use data collected here for groundbreaking studies of pulsars, galaxies, planets and the spaces in between. The newly built visitor center is excellent for stargazers of all ages.

The observatory, ☎ 787-878-2612, is open to the public Wednesday to Friday, from noon to 4 p.m., and weekends and holidays from 9 a.m. to 4 p.m. Entrance costs $4 for adults, $2 for children. If you don't bring a sack lunch, hot dogs and sodas are sold on the observation deck, from which you can almost hear the ETs baying for more ketchup. The observatory is reached by following either Hwy. 10 or Carr. 129 south from Hwy. 22. It is clearly signposted via either route, but from Carr. 129, the quickest route is to take Carrs. 134, 635 and 625.

■ Hatillo

Once an area dominated by dairy farms and lush pastureland, Hatillo is a usually bypassed – though fairly charming – seaside town with an important annual festival and a growing surfer scene. Most migrant surfers skip the Hatillo area in favor of more famous points on the northwest corner of the island, but the **Los Cabros** point at the western end of town has some good breaks and was hosting a local surf championship when we visited (it's right off **Paseo del Carmen,** a blue-and-white painted boardwalk). In calmer weather and during summer, the beaches around town are good for swimming and people watching.

After Christmas (December 27 and 28), Hatillo kicks off the **Fiesta Las Máscaras** (Festival of Masks), which has been celebrated here every year for the past 175 years. The festival commemorates the Day of the Innocents, a Catholic feast remembering the children of Jerusalem who died at the hands of King Herod in his search to destroy the prophesied Messiah. It is a colorful affair – another of Puerto Rico's famous mask festivals in which participants garb themselves in bat-like cloaks and bells. Concealed behind garishly painted wire-mesh masks, they set about entertaining onlookers and collecting donations for the Catholic Church. As festival-goers are usually fueled on chicken, *arroz con habichuelas* and especially the local hooch, *ron cañita,* things can get pretty wild. From Hwy. 2, Carr. 130 leads into the main plaza of Hatillo.

Festival of the masks in Hatillo.
(Sandra Reus)

■ Camuy

Camuy is famous as the gateway for exploring the **Cuevas de Camuy** (Camuy Caves), which burrow through the porous limestone hills south of town – one of the world's three largest underground river systems (and the only such system in the world fed by two distinct rivers). Anyone interested in spelunking will find Camuy a world-class destination. Only a fraction of the cave system has been explored. The town itself is less attractive than Hatillo, however, and it is not necessary to pass through it to get to the caves. From Hwy. 2, follow Carr. 486 to the Cuevas de Camuy and, farther south, the **Río Camuy Cave Park** (see page 143).

■ Guajataca & Environs

Most of **Coastal Guajataca** remains hidden from Hwy. 2, which snakes along a cliff before cutting through the Cordillera Jaicoa. Elevated in this way, most visitors drive right past a lovely beach without noticing it. Just west of the town of Quebradillas, you'll pass the entrance to the Hotel Parador Guajataca and then Hotel Parador Vistamar. This second turnoff takes you down to the sea and **El Tunel**, a tunnel that is one of the best remnants of the railway that circumnavigated Puerto Rico during the first half of the 20th century and, more recently, has been a venue for weekend music festivals. Now that you're off Hwy. 2, stop and explore the area around the tunnel, either on foot, in your car or on a mountain bike (see *On Wheels* in this chapter). The road through the tunnel leads to **Balneario de Guajataca** – where the mouth of the Río Guajataca spills onto a chunk of palm-fringed sand popular with local surfers and sun worshipers. Most of the week, Playa Guajataca is nearly deserted, but it undergoes a transformation at the weekends when the beach turns into a mini Woodstock, with local bands and performers entertaining around the ruins of the old railway tunnel.

STOP THAT TRAIN, I WANNA GET OFF...

The train that lumbered around the Puerto Rican coastline from 1907 until the mid-1950s was notoriously slow. Since it had no dining car, passengers disembarked often, and the train almost single-handedly popularized regional island dishes, as hungry travelers feasted on *empanadillas de ceti* in Arecibo, *brazo de gitano* pastries in Mayagüez, oysters in Boquerón, etc.

The Guajataca province, in the northwest corner of the island, is rich in natural resources – especially in the **Bosque Estatal de Guajataca** – an idyllic retreat from Aguadilla, Arecibo and the infuriating stop-go of Hwy. 2. The Guajataca forest is about 20 minutes from either town. Just a few miles inland on Carr. 446, the region becomes a warren of small mountain roads through the conical *mogote* hills. Within the forest, some excellent trails through this karstic region traverse swimming holes and lead to waterfalls and the Cueva del Viento (Wind Cave). Locals consider this to be some of the best hiking on the island. You can get a map from the small information center and Department of Natural Resources office, Carr. 119, Km. 22.1, ☎ 787-896-7640. A short drive away from the forest proper (you will need to hire a car to explore this area, since *públicos* rarely travel these roads), **Lago de Guajataca** is a pretty, man-made lake best explored by kayak, and well stocked with fish for those with their own rods, reels and other gear (see *Adventures*). Drive around the lake on a weekend and you'll find hundreds of others sitting at lakeside *lechoneras* or rest stops, enjoying thrilling views of haystack-shaped hills drenched in tropical foliage. During the rest of the week, you may feel you have stumbled upon a land that humans forgot.

■ Isabela & Playa Jobos

From the town of Isabela westward through **Jobos** (pronounced HO-bohs), the coastal area is everything one could hope for in a quiet stretch of seaside, with beautiful arched coves, sand dunes, golden beaches and crystalline waters. Jobos has long been a favorite of regional surfers, who commandeer the beach for much of the winter, but for now at least it remains relatively free of the tourist throng. The words "hideaway" and "island's best-kept secret" are sometimes used to describe it, and some locals have been known to deny the existence of the place when traveling, just to keep it that way. Dotted with cottages, small inns and a few pubs and surf shops, it's a perfect escape zone for a relaxing week of water adventures or reading on the beach, or to use as a staging area for your adventures along the north and west coasts.

At the secluded **Playa Montones**, just east of town, giant boulders provide shelter from the breaking surf – a great place for kids to splash around in a natural lagoon. It's also the site of the romantic beachside cottage rentals at Villas del Mar Hau (see *Where To Stay*, page 158). Located just within the Isabela municipality, the Jobos area beaches are best reached on Carr. 4466 via Carr. 110, from either Aguadilla or Hwy. 2.

Adventures

■ On Foot

Camuy Caves: Spelunking in Style

Puerto Rico has some of the most important caves in the Western Hemisphere and, like Carlsbad Caverns in New Mexico, a few of the most spectacular ones are set up for easy viewing. The **Río Camuy Cave Park**, ☎ 787-898-3100, ext 411 (for reservations), well signposted on Route 129 near the town of Lares, offers guided tours through the Cavernas del Río Camuy and nearby sinkholes. Start your tour at the visitor's center with a short film, then board a tram through dense jungle foliage into a 200-foot sinkhole and enter Cueva Clara de Empalme. Here you'll spend 45 minutes or so on a guided walk among hulking **stalactites** and **stalagmites** – icicle-shaped formations formed by the precipitation of calcite from rainwater – dramatically flood-lit to reveal their awesome shapes.

> **DID YOU KNOW?** *For cave novices: stalactites hang from the ceiling of a cave; stalagmites rise in giant cones from the cave floor.*

The strange colors that emanate from them are caused by impurities within the calcite. Keen photographers should bring a tripod to take advantage of the excellent photo opportunities, but beware the threat of lens-besmirching guano drops from thousands of bats above. A well-worn subterranean path around giant boulders leads to a spot where the **Río Camuy** rushes past through a tunnel. Now you are witnessing one of the world's three largest underground river systems. Leaving this cave, you'll take a trolley to the yawning, 650-foot-diameter **Tres Pueblos sinkhole**. Nearby, you can see 42 Taino **petroglyphs** at the newly opened **Cathedral Cave**, and kids of all ages may enjoy searching for semi-precious stones at the **Río Camuy Mine**. The Río Camuy Cave Park is open Wednesday to Sunday and holidays, from 8 a.m. to 4 p.m. (the last trip departs at 2 p.m. for the full tour and at 3:45 p.m. for just the main cave). Entrance costs $10 for adults, $7 for children, with a $2 fee for parking. Entry is limited, and we advise avoiding the weekends so you can be in a smaller group.

WHAT DWELLS BENEATH

More than 2,000 caves have been discovered in the Camuy area, and speleological experts say this constitutes only a fraction of the system's caverns. Inhabitants discovered so far include 13 species of bat, coquí frogs, crickets and a giant, tarantula-like arachnid called the *guaba*.

Even more child-oriented is the privately-owned **Cueva de Camuy**, ☎ 787-898-2723, Route 486, Km. 1.1. It is smaller, and less interesting, but offers guided tours through a similarly floodlit stalactite and stalagmite cave, with a swimming pool and waterslide, pony rides, café and other amusements above ground. Open Monday to Saturday, it costs just a few dollars per person (entrance fees have been known to change here). Nearby is **Cueva del Infierno** (Cave of Hell) to which tours of two to three hours can be arranged by phoning ☎ 787-898-2723. Also check out **Expediciones Tanamá** (*Central Mountains*, page 283) for a more eco-warrior approach to the caves in this region.

Camuy Caves: Getting Wild and Wet

Imagine yourself rappelling hundreds of feet down into a subterranean sinkhole, emerging into a cave, then body rafting through an underground river until you shoot out through a gaping cave mouth into a natural pool surrounded by subtropical forest. Sounds cool? It is. For the true adventurer, this is the big ride. **Aventuras Tierra Adentro**, ☎ 787-766-0470, fax 754-7543, on Avenida Piñero #268-A, University Gardens, Río Piedras (San Juan), offers nail-biting, yet safe, excursions to the karstic realm, including transport and full guidance by adventure professionals who know the territory and will do just about anything to ensure the safety of their guests. Most trips cost $85 to $100 per day per person, and leave from San Juan near daybreak (returning around dusk). Participants are required to bring sturdy shoes, a change of clothes and plastic garbage bags to protect body warmth in case of an emergency. Other equipment, such as helmets, ropes, harness, lights and life vests, is included in the price of the trip. For anyone in decent physical condition, don't worry, these adventures are totally manageable and the guides are pros. Rosano Boscarín and the Aventuras Tierra Adentro crew offer the following white-knuckle trips:

- **Descending Cueva Angeles and Beyond** – An adrenaline-pumping Tyrolean descent (basically, you whiz down fixed ropes on a pulley system) over the forest canopy lands you at the mouth of a sinkhole, which is descended via a 200-foot rappel into the Angeles Cave. Once inside the cave, you'll splash around in natural pools and marvel at the bizarre, calcite wonders. Leave your best pants at home, because the next step is a body raft through a sick mudslide that lands you in the (mostly) cleansing waters of the Camuy River. Float the river through strange karstic canyons and emerge at the end of the day feeling as though you've truly accomplished something.

- **Rappelling the Tanamá** – Hook yourself like a piece of wet laundry to a clothesline, then zip down 300 feet over treetops until your guide "encourages" you to rappel into a cave and then into the brave waters of the Río Tanamá ("Butterfly River" in Taino language). From here, float the current through tall canyons and stop off at natural spring pools nearly choked by exotic vegetation. Another big adventure.

- **Tanamá 800** – Start at a lovely hiking trail near the Arecibo Observatory, then slide-descend on ropes 500 feet above the primeval karstic forest to the Tanamá River. From here, body raft through canyons and several caves. Some people say the 800-foot descent is as good as skydiving from an airplane. You be the judge.

Hiking

Three forests on the north coast have nearly 70 hiking trails between them, and it's easy to get pleasantly lost in any of them. The **Bosque Estatal de Guajataca**, ☎ 787-896-7640 (forest information), ☎ 787-896-8812 (camping), has more than 25 miles of well-maintained foot paths (40 official trails). Unfortunately, the maps provided by the Department of Natural Resources are nearly useless, so you'll be forced to explore on your own. Ask for directions to the Del Viento Cave, which harbors bats and is surrounded by a jungle nesting ground for dozens of bird species. There are also several river pools and waterfalls (see *Swimming*, below), where you can cool off midway through a hike. The **Cambalache State Forest** has short paths through virgin forest (see *Mountain Biking*, below), and the trails of the **Bosque Río Abajo** take you into the heart of karstic splendor (see *Eco-Travel* in this chapter).

Golf

The two adjacent Hyatt mega-resorts in Dorado have four great courses between them, all designed by Robert Trent Jones, making this area one of the hemisphere's top golf resort destinations. And because they are only 30 minutes from San Juan, they are some of the favorite courses of short-term visitors to the Puerto Rican capital, as well. The east and west courses at the **Hyatt Dorado Beach Resort**, ☎ 787-796-8961, fax 278-1948, carve their way through forest land and grapefruit and coconut plantations, where the only sounds you'll hear besides the wooshing of your club are waves breaking on the shore and birdsong. The par-five hole 13 has been rated by Jack Nicklaus as one of the top 10 holes in the world for its double dogleg that challenges advanced golfers to hit over a couple of ponds and reach the green in two strokes. Built in 1958, the east course has a hilly front nine and a seaside back nine; the holes on the west course see-saw back and forth near the Atlantic and include four challenging par-threes. Public play for both courses is daily from 7 a.m. to 6 p.m. The north and south courses at the **Hyatt Regency Cerromar Beach Resort**, ☎ 787-796-8915, fax 796-5562, skirt the coastline and are littered with challenging man-made water hazards and well-bunkered greens. The signature hole seven on the north course is set amid flowing tropical plants, overlooking the sea, and ends at a green beneath the seven-story resort (great if the pressure of onlookers improves your game!). Several "runway" tees have fairways of 100 yards or more, and some greens on both courses seem wide enough for the landing of a small aircraft. Public play is daily from 7:30 a.m. to 5:30 p.m.

■ On Horseback

The Beach-Lover's Romance Ride

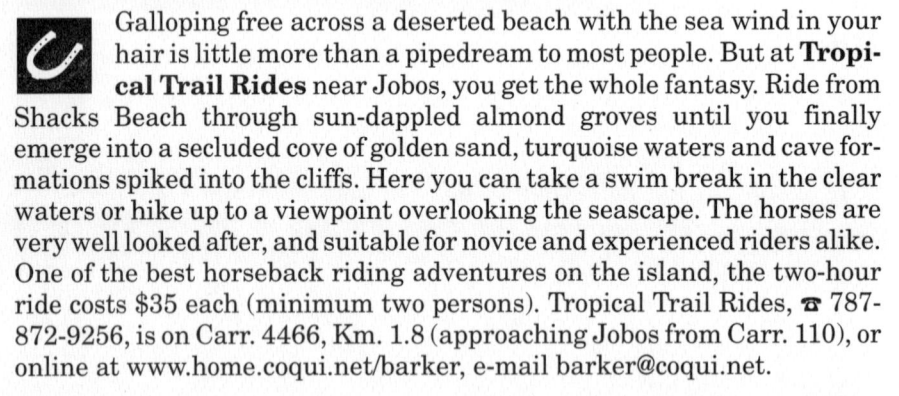

Galloping free across a deserted beach with the sea wind in your hair is little more than a pipedream to most people. But at **Tropical Trail Rides** near Jobos, you get the whole fantasy. Ride from Shacks Beach through sun-dappled almond groves until you finally emerge into a secluded cove of golden sand, turquoise waters and cave formations spiked into the cliffs. Here you can take a swim break in the clear waters or hike up to a viewpoint overlooking the seascape. The horses are very well looked after, and suitable for novice and experienced riders alike. One of the best horseback riding adventures on the island, the two-hour ride costs $35 each (minimum two persons). Tropical Trail Rides, ☎ 787-872-9256, is on Carr. 4466, Km. 1.8 (approaching Jobos from Carr. 110), or online at www.home.coqui.net/barker, e-mail barker@coqui.net.

At Cerro Gordo, a smaller operation, **Tropical Paradise Horse Rides**, ☎ 787-720-5454, also offers rides along the sandy shore. The horses here seem weaker than the strong steeds at Tropical Trail Rides in Jobos, and if you're a true equestrian, we definitely recommend making the trip to Jobos for the real thing. Tropical Paradise Horse Rides in Cerro Gordo can be found by following Carr. 690 west along the coast, then look for hand-painted signs (with a picture of a horse) in a residential neighborhood for the north spur of Carr. 690.

■ On Wheels

Mountain Biking

The subtropical **Cambalache State Forest** has a six-mile loop through ancient vegetation and surreal karstic landscape, with some great single-track downs, a few sweat-breaking ups and plenty of offshoot trails to explore. It's possibly the best ride on the island,

and the small 1,050-acre Cambalache park contains some of the island's only virgin wet forest. You start with a short uphill and then follow small yellow arrows that mark the trail. One unmarked fork in the road comes right after you pass the rusting corpse of a jeep – veer to the right here, even though this path looks less traveled. After this, the track takes you on exhilarating roller-coaster swings through the forest. You may be tempted to do this loop more than once! If you ride Cambalache on a weekday, you may have the forest pretty much to yourself. Even on weekends, traffic on the trails is one-way so you still may not encounter other riders. To get here, take Exit 64 on Hwy. 22 (westbound from San Juan), and follow Carr. 683 until you see a large pink church. Turn right and follow signs for the Job Corps (it's better signposted than the park itself). The entrance to Cambalache is at the Job Corps building.

> **CAUTION:** *You must have a permit and a helmet to ride in Cambalache, and rangers have been known to check for these at the park entrance. Permits cost just a dollar, and can be obtained from the Departamento de Recursos Naturales y Ambientales in the Puerta de Tierra neighborhood of San Juan,* ☎ *787-878-7279.*

Head for *El Tunel* in **Quebradillas** for an easy bike ride through 12 miles of karstic landscape, seaside views, plantain farms and sand dunes. Park before you reach the tunnel for the following side trip: backtrack past the water tower and cross under Hwy. 2 to a blocked-off road that marks the entrance to a plantain farm. Ride through the lovely plantain fields of the Guajataca River valley, with karstic cliffs on one side and the Guajataca River below. This is an amazing bit of scenery.

> **TIP:** *The plantain fields are a weekends-only ride, because the plantain farm is sometimes off-limits during workdays.*

Backtrack again, and then go through the tunnel. After the tunnel, you'll have two opportunities to descend the hill and cross a meadow to the beach road. The first turning requires some confidence in your downhill skills, and the second is appropriate for novice riders. Don't mind the sandy beach track. You may want to walk your bike along it, as you pass dunes and rock formations on your left. Stop and hike over the dunes and rocks to the sea – there's a swimming beach, too. Just past the almond grove, the track becomes hard-packed, and eventually leads to a paved road. On the paved road, summit the hill, pass through a little neighborhood, and then turn left on the main road which takes you downhill and finally through a slalom cut between cliffs under a canopy of trees. You'll end up at Hwy. 2 again, a short distance from where you parked. Cross the highway and bike along its shoulder back to your car. To get here, enter Guajataca on Hwy. 2 westbound, pass the Parador Guajataca and cross over a bridge. Exit immediately after the bridge, then turn left toward the ocean. You'll see a parking area at the foot of the cliff on your left.

Less than an hour from San Juan, the **Hacienda Las Marias** hosts an annual fat-tire race and is open year-round, seven days a week, from 9 a.m. to 5 p.m. The off-road trail through gorgeous terrain is only four miles long, but includes challenging ups, thrilling downhills and a couple of technical descents. Usually deserted except on weekends, when you may encounter another biker or two, the hacienda is a great place for intermediate bikers to hone their skills. You'll pay a $3 entry fee at a cantina at the farm's entrance. Just west of Vega Baja, take exit 41 to Carr. 670. Turn left at Carr. 670 until you hit Carr. 155, then turn right. When you come to Carr. 643, turn right again (westbound). Look for a small banner on your right-hand side, marking the entrance.

GEARING UP

Luis Ruiz of **Isabela Mountain Bike Tours** and his crew will organize tailor-made rides for groups up to nine or 10 people, with all equipment and transport provided, including trips along the northern coastline, from Cabo Rojo to Parguera and in the Bosque Estatal de Susua. If you are staying at a hotel between Aguadilla and Camuy, they'll even deliver bikes and helmets to you. Give them at least a day or two advance notice, however, through their hotline in Clearwater, Florida: ☎ 727-409-0842 (messages are forwarded to cell phones in Puerto Rico). Or try renting your own bikes in the San Juan area.

Scenic Drives

THE CARR. 681 COASTAL JAUNT – For one of the island's best coastal drives, including stops at secluded beaches, an Indian cave and a lighthouse museum, start westbound at Barceloneta (or eastbound at Arecibo) and follow Carr. 681 as it hugs the Atlantic shore in a region characterized by strange formations of rock and sandy beaches lined with palm and almond trees. From Barceloneta, Carr. 684 runs along the muddy Río Grande de Manatí to La Boca, a backwater pueblo that seems to lack only tumbleweeds blowing across its streets to complete the picture of desolation. But as soon as you come to **Punta Palmas Altas** (Tall Palms Point), the picture brightens. Some awesome stretches of beach and palms are dotted with colorful Caribbean cottages and gardens bursting with wild tropical flowers, especially around the Palmas Altas *barrio*. You'll find picnic-perfect plots of sand or grass, or stop at Hollow's Restaurant near the Islote neighborhood for a seafood lunch in a pretty patio across the street from the beach. This roadside has many swimming and surfing beaches.

After Punta Caracoles (Snails Point, named for its twisted rock), you may or may not see a sign for **Cueva del Indio**, but look for the large Esso gas station on the south side of the road, east of the Jarealito neighborhood. The station is a good place to leave you car (just ask permission from the attendant), due to rumors of theft in the tiny, secluded parking area for the cave. From the Esso station, cross the street and walk west about 20 yards for beach access. The cave is inside the big rock sticking out into the sea about 100 yards east of here – aim for the notch and you can't miss it. A footpath leads around behind the rock, for easier access. The glorious view from the top spans the coastline westward to Arecibo and beyond. To the east, natural arches formed by the pounding surf stick out from the karstic rock like giant claws raking the sea.

TENDERFOOT BEWARE!

Chances are that you have less rugged feet than the Taino Indians who first used this cave. Be sure to wear comfortable closed shoes, such as tennis shoes or boots, not flip-flops. The rock surface is uneven and sharp.

Rainwater and the sea have conspired to drill bizarre holes in the rock and erode it into fanciful shapes. The cave was formed in this fashion. Go halfway down, and you'll begin to see the petroglyphs left by Taino visitors hundreds of years ago – capriciously line-drawn faces with big ears and bug eyes. It's unclear for what purpose the cave was used: as a place of worship, a refuge for fishermen or just a social gathering place. "Everybody has a theory about what the drawings in that cave are for," says Hector de Jesus, the manager of the Esso station. "I prefer the mystery." Within the cave, you may come across an old beer can or some other relic left by a more modern visitor. Perhaps the Tainos used the cave for basically the same purpose: to get away from the others and have a little party!

The area around **Jarealito** would be an interesting photographic study on the risks of building homes too close to the sea. A rocky coast with a few nice beaches in between, it includes a long stretch where the distance between the road and the sea is no more than 10 yards, and yet individuals have endeavored to squeeze houses in there. Some are newly constructed and still standing, and look as though they might survive a storm or two. Many are ramshackle, abandoned and in various stages of decomposition under the weight of the elements. At Punta Morrillos, the **Faro El Vigia** (somewhat redundantly named the "Lookout Lighthouse") has been turned into a museum (stamps, paintings and sculptures by local artists) and tiny theme park overlooking the sea. Closed for renovation when we visited, it was scheduled to reopen in mid-2001, with a newly built pirate ship replica and six miniature Taino huts out front, presumably for children to play in and possibly for some "living history" events. The entrance to the lighthouse is well signposted from Carr. 681.

DRIVING AROUND GUAJATACA LAKE – Head up to Lago de Guajataca for a serene getaway on a gorgeous lake surrounded by the **Cordillera Jaicoa** to the east and the **Montañas Guarionex** to the west. As in the nearby Bosque Estatal de Guajataca, there are usually few tourists here and (especially on weekdays) you may spend a leisurely day and see few other people. On weekends, a few bars, restaurants and *lechoneras* on the water's edge get lively (one or two have dancing and live music), and you may see a few Puerto Ricans out on the lake fishing. Circumnavigating the lake by car takes less than an hour with no stops, and the drive through subtropical forest and bamboo thickets, with many lakeside views, is serenity itself. Follow Carr. 119 south from Camuy or north from San Sebastián, and circle the lake via Carr. 453 and Carr. 455, stopping for a *pincho* and a cold beer at one of the eateries overlooking the water. If you are a gringo/a, expect the proprietor and other patrons to be pleasantly surprised by your visit.

BEST SEAT IN THE HOUSE

The majority of people experience Lago de Guajataca from the shore, but the way to get the most out of a visit to the lake is by renting a kayak at the Lagovista Hotel (see *Where To Stay*) for $10 an hour, and then paddling around and out into the middle.

Unfortunately you can't swim in the lake, but it is apparently well stocked with local fish like *lobina*, *chopa*, *tucunaré* and catfish. Bring your own fishing tackle. If you haven't brought your own equipment to the island, your best bet is to find a place to rent gear in San Juan. You might also try the **Arecibo Fishing Shop Bait & Tackle**, ☎ 787-878-9024, on Carr. 681, just outside of Arecibo. The local Departamento de Recursos Naturales y Ambientales office is located in a rustic wooded area on Hwy 119, Km. 22. The rangers are friendly, but are useless in terms of helping you find fishing tackle.

■ On Water

Best Swimming Beaches

Although you can swim at many beaches on the northern coast, there are a couple of standouts for which it is worth traveling the extra mile. The first is the area around **Mar Chiquita**, just west of Laguna Tortuguero. A stretch of idyllic sand right on the edge of Carr. 686 almost demands that you stop for a dip, as palms tower over beach hideaways, where usually gentle waves ripple over the sandy shoreline.

The **Balneario Los Tubos** is the main feature of this pretty drive, but if you stop your car next to almond trees on either side of the public beach you'll find yourself in island paradise where you can easily forget that the main road is only a few yards away.

You'll also find some secluded spots near **Barrio Isolde**, along Carr. 681, between Barceloneta and Arecibo, which features swaths of sand so wide they seem to beg a football match – lonely, gorgeous with karstic outcroppings, and only the occasional boogie-boarder to contend with.

The prize for best swimming beaches along the northern coast, however, must go to the area around **Playa Jobos**, where sharp cliffs meet offshore reefs to form perfect bathing holes. Playa Jacinto, just east of Jobos, has facilities such as bathrooms, showers, etc. But if you're looking to truly break away, drive along Carr. 486 until you see any turnoff that looks good (there are many), then head down to the shore where you're likely to find a deserted beach worthy of a postcard to send home.

Forest Waterfalls

At a nameless, locals-only watering hole on the edge of the **Bosque Estatal de Guajataca**, you can strip down and swing freely across a pond surface on a rope swing, or hike upstream for more secluded river pools. It involves only a short hike from the road before you come to a series of jungle bathing areas. Take Carr. 110 south from Hwy. 2, just west of Isabela, or Carr. 111 straight eastward from Aguadilla, until you reach the town of Moca. Follow Carr. 111 eastward toward San Sebastián, and drive for about 20 minutes until you see an Esso gas station. Take a left here, continue for about half a mile and turn right after you've crossed a bridge painted green and yellow. There is also a footbridge crossing the river here. Drive through the neighborhood for about a mile and a half until you reach a row of mailboxes. Turn right again and continue past Patsy's Ponies. After approximately 100 yards you will see a vine-covered gate on the left (and a well-kept ranch opposite). A barely discernible sign reads "No Trespassing," long overgrown with creepers and vines. A gap in the fence leads to a trail that takes you to the edge of the state forest. Follow the path down to the river and the waterfall, which on a sunny day looks like a movie set for the remake of *Blue Lagoon*. Except on weekends and holidays, you'll probably have the place to yourself. There is a rope swing that will land you in the middle of the pool and, unfortunately, a bit of trash left by mindless visitors past. Bring along a trash bag and help pack it out!

Surfing

Second only to the northwestern corner around Rincón and Aguadilla in surfer lore, the north shore has some well established surfing spots with a few killer breaks, depending of course on conditions. Following is a list of hotspots. Note: Wave heights represent potential maximums, not the normal occurrence.

Around **Punta Cerro Gordo** (just west of Dorado), you'll find good left and right breaks during summertime and sometimes winter. Locals identify five separate spots along the Cerro Gordo coast (from east to west): **Ojo del Buey** breaks left and right when waves reach six to 12 feet, with a southern wind or windless conditions; **Hoyo 12** breaks left with southern winds and reaches maximum face heights of 12 feet; **Breñas**, also seven to 12 feet on a good day, breaks right; **La Pasa** breaks left and right from three to 10 feet, and with the right conditions can provide tubes; and **Snapper's**, a less shapely right break when it gets above three feet.

Near **Los Tubos** public beach (Carr. 686 north of Manatí), left-favoring reef breaks can be heavy with local waves and break-ins, getting big a few times a year. Most gringos simply refer to the area as Los Tubos, but at least three breaks known to locals (east to west) are **La Boca**, which can break left or right with an east or south wind; **Los Tubos**, which has reportedly been measured up to 25 feet, breaking both ways, with occasional strong currents; and **Pata Pata**, a left break with an east or south wind.

Along Carr. 681 almost straight out from the Río Grande de Manatí, **Machuca's** breaks right and has been known to peak at seven to 18 feet; west of Barceloneta; **Bali** (straight out from the junction of Carrs. 681 and 684) is an experts-only strong left break that can reach 10 to 18 feet. **Hollows** (east of Punta Las Tunas) is an outstanding hollow right reef break, with shallow coral. It's usually three to 10 feet on a good day. Left breaks are poorer. A number of breaks (some newly discovered) around **Arecibo** are drawing hordes of local surfers on good days. The best known is **La Marginal**, which breaks left and right with heights of eight to 25 feet. If it's big and you're just learning how to surf, stay out of the water.

> **CAUTION:** *One hears scattered reports of fights and occasional vandalism of the cars of non-locals in the Jobos surf area. Use common sense and good etiquette to avoid these situations.*

The major lure of the north coast is along the stretch from Isabela to Jobos beach. Just west of the town of Isabela, **Sal Si Puedes** is a popular left break with the swell bending around the end of a cove. Can get seven to 18 feet with a south or no wind, but it blows out easily. The next break westward, **Middles**, is unpredictable, with hollow, grinding rights and reports that it gets anywhere from three to 20 feet – also not for beginners on a big day. **The Spot**, also known as "Secret Spot," is a consistent, pitching, wedge-shaped wave that rarely exceeds seven feet, but is often good year-round. Breaks right. **Golondrinas** gets tube in a shallow left reef break next to a rock – can get up to six or seven feet. **Jobos** is a long right peaking at about six feet over a sand bottom inside. Jobos is also known for its year-round consistency. Takeoff is inside, and you may encounter some territorial disputes.

Diving & Snorkeling

Five miles west of Dorado, **Cerro Gordo Beach** is a well-traveled dive just a few yards from shore. Brain, basket and star corals host an abundance of French angels, damselfish and tropical swimmers of many different stripes, many of which are accustomed to hand feeding by divers. You'll see large colonies of sea fingers, sea fans and sponges, the occasional moray eel, sea turtle and, once in a blue moon, a manatee. With visibility usually less than 40 feet, this is a popular night dive and possibly the best spot on the north coast. **Shacks Beach**, about a mile west of the Jobos village on Carr. 4466, is one of the island's most popular dive and snorkeling sites due to its submarine caves and caverns that can be entered right off the beach. Not the best dive in Puerto Rico, it's great for beginners, and its popularity may have something to do with its accessibility. For snorkeling, hit the water and clear a few sandstone ledges as you make your way to water deep enough for swimming. Then gear up and swim out another 30 yards or so to the reef, where you'll be able to free dive among grottos packed with blue tangs, grunts and other tropical fish. Despite the easy access, it's still better to dive Shacks with a guide, because the network of undersea caves and canyons (most in less than 30 feet of water) is somewhat labyrinthine, and you'll quickly find the best spots if accompanied by someone who knows where they're going.

DIVE SHOPS

For diving here and at sites covered in the West Coast and other chapters, **La Cueva Submarina**, Carr. 466, Km. 6.3 at Playa Jobos, ☎ 787-872-1390, is a reputable outfit that visits dive sites around Aguadilla and beyond. One-tank dives cost $55 ($10 per extra tank), and it's possible for non-divers to explore some of the spots, along with an instructor, for $45. Equipment rental is a reasonable $20 if you and a buddy want to go out on your own. **Arecibo Dive Shop**, 686 Miramar Ave. in Arecibo, ☎ 787-880-3483, e-mail aredive@coqui.net, has equivalent prices for sales and rentals, and offers certification courses for anything from Open Water to Divemaster status.

Eco-Travel

■ Cambalache State Forest

Agriculture and development caused the destruction of more than 90% of Puerto Rican virgin forest, and Cambalache – a small, 1,100-acre area – is one of the few places to see vegetation in its pre-colonial splendor. Due to their relative inaccessibility, the tops of the limestone *mogotes* in this small forest serve as island refuges for plant and animal species – such as the endangered Puerto Rican boa and various bat species, a few of which can be found nowhere else on earth. The forest contains about four miles of hiking and mountain biking trails and the Cambalache Nursery, ☎ 787-881-1866, where you can see and even purchase ornamental tropical plants. It is open from Monday to Friday, 7:30 a.m. to 3 p.m.

■ Bosque Río Abajo

This was one of five state forests created by the Puerto Rico Reconstruction Administration in 1943, in a belated attempt to protect river valleys, manage what was left of prime forestland on the island, and rehabilitate endangered species. For a day or overnight trip, it's an intriguing eco-travel destination. Because the forest lacks the major tourist traffic of El Yunque or Toro Negro, on weekdays you may find yourself nearly alone in about 5,000 acres of dramatic limestone *mogotes* and karstic cliffs jutting up between 600 feet and more than 1,300 feet above sea level. The forest is dense in places with bamboo, tropical hardwoods and florid vegetation. More than 20 hiking trails summit *mogotes*, lead to a complete system of caves and wander through the forest, which includes more than 175 types of trees, including 47 species that are threatened or in danger of extinction. Island deforestation has prompted the government to try to save many native species, and the rich soil and subtropical climate in the Bosque Río Abajo provide excellent conditions for replanting exotic species. Under scientific oversight, some tree species have recovered to the extent that their wood is again being used for artisan crafts and even fence posts. Walking the forest trails, you're likely to see native **cedar** and **cork** species, **mahogany** and the giant **ceiba**, as well as the **jojoba** tree, the seeds of which are crushed to extract oil used in moisturizers. Some of the island's most prized bird species are also found in the forest, including **turtledoves**, **thrushes** and **nightingales**, and the endangered *guaraguao de bosque*, or broad-winged hawk. Since 1983 the Río Abajo forest has participated in efforts to save the **Puerto Rican parrot** from extinction. The number of parrots in the forest fluctuates, as the national bird is bred and relocated to and from El Yunque (see *El Yunque* in the East Coast chapter for more).

PARROT REVIVAL

Calling ahead for an appointment with scientists at the **Bosque Río Abajo aviary**, ☎ 787-376-6625, is probably your only chance to see the Puerto Rican parrot, brought back from the brink of extinction (there were only 13 left in the early 1970s). Thanks to the efforts of the Puerto Rican Parrot Cooperative recovery program, more than 150 green parrots now live in the Bosque Río Abajo aviary and in El Yunque. Ask for Ricardo. He may or may not be able to take you to see this nearly lost bird, depending on how the project is going and the parrots' birth cycle.

In addition to El Yunque, Bosque Río Abajo is probably the forest best equipped for the inquisitive visitor. Just inside the entrance to the forest from Hwy. 10, the **Visitor Center**, ☎ 787-817-0984, has interpretative displays and videos about the forest ecosystem in Spanish and English (they're also planning to translate written materials into Italian and German, according to one ranger). Bilingual guides are available for mini-lectures on native species, and if you have a group of four people or more they'll even take you on an eco-hike. The visitor center is open from 9 a.m. to 3 p.m., closed Sundays and holidays.

Farther into the forest, near the camping area (you'll drive on the main road through a residential neighborhood on the way), the **aviary** is open to the public the same hours as the visitor's center. Here you will find scientists engaged in species preservation, and they are usually eager to explain their work to visitors. We recommend a preliminary stop at the aviary to learn in depth about some of the species; after that, go to the visitor's center to sign up for an interpretative hike with a guide. Within the forest, you may camp under the cover of *bohíos*, and Río Abajo is one of the few state forests where you can show up without a reservation and be allowed to pitch a tent (see *Where To Stay*, page 159).

> **TIP:** *If you arrive and don't find anyone at the visitor's center or the aviary, stop by the forest office (a small hut about a hundred yards west of the visitor's center) and ask for Kike (pronounced KEE-kay) Casanova. An extremely amiable ranger, Kike may even take you hiking himself and, if you ask, might break out his boom box and teach you some salsa steps. The office, ☎ 787-880-6557, is officially open 7 a.m. to 3:30 p.m.*

Where To Stay

ACCOMMODATIONS PRICE KEY
Rates are per room, per night, double occupancy. Single occupancy may or may not get you a discount, so ask when making a reservation. Breakfast included where noted.
$ .... Up to $50
$$ .... $50 to $100
$$$ .... $101 to $150
$$$$ .... $150 and up

■ Dorado

The all-inclusive **Hyatt Dorado Beach Resort**, ☎ 787-796-1234 or 800-233-1234, has 298 units and everything one could possibly want from a mega-resort, including swimming pools, casino, access to beach and golf courses. The same is true of high-rise **Hyatt Regency Cerromar**, reached at the same phone numbers as the Hyatt Dorado. The Cerromar features what is often called the world's longest freshwater river swimming pool (1,766 feet!), and has volleyball courts, poolside bars, a casino and organized activities. It is possible to spend a week at either resort without ever knowing you're in Puerto Rico. If you are not staying at these hotels, most of their facilities are off-limits (except for the golf courses).

■ Manatí, Arecibo & Environs

On either side of the entrance to Laguna Tortuguero on Carr. 687, you'll find the **Hotel El Molino Rojo** and the **Hotel El Molino Azul**, which are not hotels at all, but the Puerto Rican breed of "love motels." For $25, you'll get a room for eight hours, a bed with clean sheets, air conditioning, showers, cable TV and, of course, porn videos. The entrance to each room is through a shuttered garage, for maximum discretion. There is no office or phone number for these *"lujosas habitaciones"* – just a couple of guys in a golf cart getting paid in cash by nervous adulterers.

At the other end of the spectrum, if you plan to stay anywhere near Bosque Río Abajo or Lago Dos Bocas, check out **Hotel La Casa Grande** (listed in the *Central Mountains* chapter).

■ Hatillo & Camuy

On Carr. 119 in Camuy (Km. 7.5), the guest house **Posada El Palomar**, ☎ 787-898-1060, has clean, fairly standard rooms (the owners say they are "romantic," but that depends on you) very near the beach, as well as a restaurant, Jacuzzi, swimming pool and indoor and outdoor games. Not a bad place to stay the night before a morning trek to the Camuy caves or the Arecibo Observatory. The facilities are fully accessible for people with disabilities. $$.

Much more generic (and right on the highway) is the **Parador El Buen Café**, ☎ 787-898-1000, on Carr. 2 just east of Hatillo, another example of the perplexingly hit-and-miss system of paradores on the island. If you want nothing more than a place to lay your head, this misnamed "country inn" has an authentic diner downstairs, parking, beds, bath and cable TV. $$.

If you're on a tight family budget, or if you want to meet Puerto Rican families on one, or if you're one of those admittedly few people who enjoy gritty seaside resorts full of children running amok, try **Punta Maracayo Camping** in Hatillo, ☎ 787-820-0274, fax 820-8404, westbound on Hwy. 2, just past El Buen Café. Look for a few *pincho* stands and roadside hawkers selling hammocks, and turn right at the giant lettered sign reading *Ampliación Complejo Turístico Municipal*. Locals know the beach as Playa Sardinera. You'll find a kiddie's park with an extremely bad replica of Mickey Mouse and a wooden boardwalk along a mediocre beach, where the main attraction is a completely sheltered cove where children may swim safely. There are several pools here, including a waterslide, open from Wednesdays to Sundays. You can camp here for $50 per weekend, provided you bring your own tent. Wooden-slat and concrete cabins that have seen better days rent for $145 per weekend for four people, $200 for eight.

■ Quebradillas

A good base for exploring the northwest, Quebradillas has several options right off the highway near the beach. Two paradores are good bets for families traveling with children. The **Hotel Parador Vistamar**, Carr. 113 N (off Hwy. 2), ☎ 787-895-2065, fax 895-2294, a stone's throw from the beach, has large comfortable rooms, some with oceanfront terraces. Boisterous kids can let off steam playing tennis, basketball or swimming in the freshwater pool. All rooms have a/c and cable TV. $$-$$$. Kids under 12 sharing a room with their parents stay free.

Nearby, and with similar facilities, the **Hotel Parador El Guajataca**, Carr. 2, ☎ 787-895-3070 (reservations only), fax 895-3589, has been around for 70 years and was the first guest house in the northwest. It has all the usual amenities, plus game room, table tennis, playground and lifeguards at the pool. For grownups, a cocktail bar, live music on weekends and room service from 7 a.m. to 8 p.m. are attractive bonuses. $$.

■ Guajataca Lake

For quieter R&R at a romantic getaway, take Carr. 119 south from Carr. 2 in Camuy until you reach Lago de Guajataca. At Km. 22, look for the left-hand fork in a small lane leading down to **Hotel Lagovista,** ☎ 787-896-5487. This quiet, country hotel on the banks of Lago de Guajataca has swimming pool, sundecks and a restaurant serving *criollo* food. You may also rent kayaks for $10 an hour. $$-$$$ (for a room with a balcony overlooking the lake). Rates may be flexible mid-week.

■ Isabela

Encroaching development is muddying so much land along this part of the coast that it could easily reach overkill in the next few years. For now however, there is only one place to stay – **Villas de Costa Dorada**, Carr. 466, Km. 0.1, Emilio González 900, ☎ 787-872-7255, fax 872-7595, www.costadoradabeach.com, a sprawling backwater retreat with wedding-cake frills and lots of romantic details. Rooms are colorful and spacious with a near constant ocean breeze coming in off the Atlantic. Be warned, however, that a major building project was going on next door when we visited, so you may want to check on it before checking in. $$$. One- to two-bedroom apartments go for between $225 and $400 a night, are clean and comfortable, and have all the necessary gadgets for self-catering.

■ Jobos

Unlike Isabela, Jobos has many incredibly serene options right on the beach, with cheaper guest houses along Carr. 4466 in the center of Jobos. The **Hotel Restaurante Ocean Front**, ☎ 787-872-0444, www.oceanfrontpr.com, has comfortable if unspectacular rooms and is right on the water, with a sundeck and grill, perfect for a sunset cocktail after a day at the beach $$.

The **Sonia Rican Guest House and Restaurant**, also on Carr. 4466, ☎ 787-872-1818, looks like a stray chunk of concrete jungle at the shore, but is clean and comfortable inside and good value for families. $$.

If you can afford the slight step up in price, two hotel/resorts in Jobos will seduce you with sublime ocean views, palm trees nodding in the breeze, soft-lit restaurants and boardwalks made for walking hand-in-hand with your mate or paramour. On the north end of Jobos on Playa Montones, **Villas del Mar Hau**, Carr. 4466, km. 8.3, ☎ 872-2045/2627, is a delightful complex of clapboard beachfront cabañas and villas leaning over a pristine stretch of beach. The larger units have porches with hammocks strung right over the sand. With a (seldom-used) swimming pool, barbecue areas, tennis, volleyball, and games room, there's plenty to keep you occupied if you get tired of building sandcastles and swimming in sapphire waters.

The gazebo-style bar and restaurant serve up tasty seafood and cocktails. $$-$$$.

Equally charming, though nearly double the price, is the **Villa Montaña Resort**, ☎ 787-872-9554 or 888-780-9195, fax 872-9553, www.villamontana.com, also on Carr. 4466, but at the south end of town. It is more resort-like, with immaculately trimmed lawns and orderly walkways. The pool and restaurant offer romantic ocean views, and if you have children you'll appreciate the safe, confined space abutting a private beach with water toys for rent. Included is a well-equipped fitness center. $$$$

■ Camping

Cerro Gordo has a massive camping area under palm trees with patches of grass, near rocky cliffs overlooking the sea. It's a short walk to a decent swimming beach, and has dozens of tent spaces that can accommodate well over 100 people. Spaces cost $13 per night, including facilities such as showers, toilets, picnic areas and lifeguards on duty at busy times. A couple of snack stands near the camping area are open on weekends, and a couple of grungy seafood bars within walking distance are often open weekdays. This place can get jam-packed on weekends, especially during summer. Follow Carr. 690 north from Hwy. 22, and you can't miss it. For reservations, call directly to the campground office, ☎ 787-883-2730 (we were told that the office hours are subject to change, so make sure to call before arriving).

The **Cambalache State Forest** has two camping areas, with combined space for 75 people, along with picnic areas, shelters, bathrooms and showers, for $10 per night. The phone number in San Juan for reservations is ☎ 787-881-1004. Take Carr. 682 to an exit marked for the Job Corps, about 10 minutes west of Barceloneta by car (the Job Corps sign faces eastbound traffic only).

The **Bosque Río Abajo** has some of the best forest camping on the island – especially during the week – among dense jungle vegetation and karstic rock cliffs. The official camping area has space for 40 people under *bohíos*, but the rangers on site would probably let you camp outside if you seem responsible and the *bohíos* are full, which often happens on weekends, holidays and during late summer. You'll find showers, toilets, barbecue areas and picnic tables here, too. The Río Abajo forest is also one of the only island forests where you make reservations directly at the on-site visitor's center, ☎ 787-817-0984, which is open from 9 a.m. to 3 p.m. The office for the forest, ☎ 787-880-6557, is officially open 7 a.m. to 3:30 p.m., and the staff there can also help you get situated.

In the Guajataca area, driving toward Lago de Guajataca on Carr. 119, you'll pass **Campamento Guajataca** ☎ 787-790-0323. Established in 1938, it is primarily a Scouts' campground with the usual facilities, including mess and games areas. It's exceptionally pretty, set in a lush landscape and sheltered by bamboo. If listening to rounds of "Ging-gang-gooly-gooly-watcha" and smelling beans baking on the campfire are not your idea of a good time, try going mid-week (not during school vacations), as private campers may stay here by arrangement.

At Km. 22 on Carr. 119, **Ninos Camping**, ☎ 787-896-9016 (next door to Lagovista), is also on the banks of the lake, with cabins and camping space, both requiring self-sufficiency. Bring food, water and charcoal for the grill. There are just three basic cabañas here, each sleeping five to seven people. It costs $175 to $200 for a weekend. Or you can pitch your own tent on the water's edge for $25 a night.

Within the Bosque Estatal de Guajataca, there are 10 campsites in an area called **La Vereda**, five miles south of Hwy. 2 on Carr. 446, for $4 per night. Permits and reservations required – call the San Juan office for forest reserves, ☎ 787-724-3724.

CRASHING ON THE SAND

Camping on the more secluded beaches of **Jobos** has long been a tradition among penniless surfers, although it is technically illegal. Some use a tent or hammock, some don't.

Where To Eat

■ Just West of San Juan

On the outskirts of the San Juan metropolitan area, the seldom-discovered **Millie's Place**, 337 Parque Street in the town of Sabana Seca, ☎ 787-784-3488, serves fresh crab raised in the back yard of the restaurant. It's a fine place for lunch if you're heading out of San Juan for points west. Also known for excellent lobster and fish, Millie's opens at 11 a.m. five days a week (closed Mondays and Tuesdays). Closing hours are 5 p.m. on Wednesday and Thursday, 10 p.m. on Friday and 6 p.m. on Saturday and Sunday.

Not far from the Hyatt Cerromar on Carr. 693, **Pepe**, ☎ 787-883-0941, is a popular seafood and steak house along the so-called Costa de Oro (Gold Coast). Open daily for lunch and dinner, from 11:30 a.m. to 10 p.m. Entrées generally cost between $12 and $20.

■ Dorado

The best restaurant in Dorado is undoubtedly **El Ladrillo**, 334 Mendez Vigo, ☎ 787-796-2120, which lures even cuisine-spoiled *sanjuaneros* with its fine steaks and seafood in a classy atmosphere. This is one of the eateries that deserves its *meson gastronomica* billing. Congenial owners Tato and Tata Maldonado started El Ladrillo in 1975 with only four tables, and now have a beautiful brick interior (*ladrillo* is Spanish for brick) that seats dozens at elegant tables surrounded by a gleaming red-tile floor and paintings by local artists on the walls. The menu includes the entire range of fish, lobster, crab and shellfish, as well as succulent US prime Angus beef and lamb cooked to order. After dinner, relax in the Spanish-style bar with a glass of cognac and a fine cigar. Entrées range in price from $10 to $34.

Farther west, on Calle Marginal C-1 (the so-called Costa de Oro), **La Terraza**, ☎ 787-796-1242, is a more casual – yet very pleasant – outdoor terrace serving *criollo* cuisine, seafood and steaks. The Creole entrées all cost $10 or less, and you'll pay under $20 for fine meats and fish (except lobster). There are several other promising-looking establishments along the main strip (Calle Mendez Vigo), and just west of town the Hyatt resorts also have a wide selection of restaurants. Almost directly across the street from El Ladrillo, the **Country Cheese Sports & Oyster Bar**, ☎ 787-278-2015, is a less expensive hotspot that features burgers, oysters and cheaper entrées and attracts a younger party crowd that boogies into the night with live music on weekends.

■ Manatí Area

Heading west from Dorado, you'll hit a culinary wasteland, with few places to recommend in the areas around Manatí and Barceloneta. But if you can't drive another mile and eschew the ever-present golden arches, try **Su Casa Steak House**, Carr. 671, Km.1 in Manatí, ☎ 787-884-0047, which is open for lunch and dinner every day except Sunday. You'll find international cuisine, seafood and, of course, steak, in a casual atmosphere, with most entrées in the $15 to $20 range.

A BAVARIAN BEER GARDEN IN JÍBARO COUNTRY

For a bizarre experience, make the trek to **Casa Bavaria**, ☎ 787-862-7818, a schnitzel house and beer garden high in the tropical hills of one of the most remote regions of Puerto Rico. It's southeast of Manatí, on Carr. 155, midway between Morovis and Orocovis (Km. 38.3). Here you can gaze out over the hills toward the distant Atlantic Ocean to the north, as you and mountain locals chow down on wiener schnitzel, homemade bratwurst and Beck's beer, to the strains of recorded oom-pah music. Owners Martina and Mike López Bolik (he's half Puerto Rican, but both were born and raised in Germany) chatter away in Bavarian dialect spiked with Puerto Rican slang. Definitely unique, it's open Thursday to Sunday for lunch and dinner.

If you drive the coastal Carr. 681 between Barceloneta and Arecibo, stop in at **Hollow's Restaurant**, Carr. 681, Km. 11.2 in Barrio Islote, ☎ 787-816-3312. This little family-run patio restaurant, with eight tables across the street from the sea, serves up seafood *mofongo*, dorado, conch, snapper, lobster, shrimp and octopus (and a couple of steak dishes for non-fish eaters) in a friendly atmosphere. A bar to the side also serves *empanadillas* and tropical drinks.

■ Lago Dos Bocas

On weekends, four adjacent lakeside restaurants are extremely popular adventure dining destinations. **Meson Don Alonso**, ☎ 787-894-0516, and **El Fogón de Abuela** (Grandma's Stove), ☎ 787-894-0470, both serve up tasty Creole cuisine at about $15 to $20 per entrée. **Rancho Marina**, ☎ 787-894-8034, and **Villa Atabeira**, ☎ 787-767-4023, also serve Puerto Rican food, and each has a few cabañas for overnight guests. The better of these is Rancho Marina, where food and drinks are often served late into the night, as long as the guests maintain a lively atmosphere. Live music is common here on weekends, and Rancho Marina occasionally has kayaks for rent in the afternoons. These are great places for lunch or dinner, but definitely call ahead for reservations. The restaurants have their own boat service for dinner guests, which runs back and forth from the main dock (the entrance is on Carr. 123, near the entrance for Bosque Río Abajo). For lunch, you may catch the public ferry from the main dock and enjoy a half-hour tour around the lake. The public ferry leaves every hour on the hour from 10 a.m. until 4 p.m. and, for early birds, at 6:30 a.m. and 8:30 a.m. Next to the main dock, the **Dos Bocas Quick Lounge** is a typical snack bar – open every day until just after sundown– with Puerto Rican *pinchos* and light fare and, on weekends, *lechon asado*. To get to the Lago Dos Bocas area, take Carr. 10 south from Arecibo to Bosque Río Abajo.

■ Hatillo

At the far western end of town there's an expensive but "cool" hang-out named **Baja Beach Restaurant & Bar**, ☎ 787-820-8773. This place recalls California, with its beachfront sundeck and bar and volleyball net just outside on the sand. A surf 'n turf dinner will set you back only about $15, but lobsters cost an unjustifiable $35 to $45 each.

You can eat much more cheaply, albeit on the roadside of Hwy. 2, at **El Buen Café**, ☎ 787-898-3495, fax 820-3013, arguably the best old-school diner in Puerto Rico. Ham and eggs will set you back a couple of bucks, the coffee is nothing to be ashamed of and the desserts (particularly the vanilla flan) are excellent. The interior features three horseshoe-shaped eating bars for an authentic soda-fountain feel. It is also a convenient pit stop if you're driving from San Juan to the west side of the island, or vice-versa, since it's located just west of the entrance to the *autopista*, Hwy. 22 (on which there are no restaurant stops all the way to San Juan).

■ Quebradillas & Guajataca

For solid Puerto Rican and Caribbean food, with many seafood options, try the **Parador Vistamar** in Quebradillas, ☎ 787-895-2065, with a casual atmosphere and excellent views of the Atlantic Ocean. It's open for breakfast, lunch and dinner, with most entrées in the $15 to $20 range. On Hwy. 2 in Quebradillas (Km. 103.8), **Casabi**, ☎ 787-895-3070, is listed as one of Puerto Rico's *mesones gastronomicos*, and serves up local *criollo* cuisine and seafood, also in the $15 to $20 range.

Fine dining is rather thin in the Guajataca area, but there are a handful of roadside barbecues with *pinchos* (meat on a stick) and *lechon asada* and bars selling freshwater fish. Consider packing a cooler and finding a secluded spot for a picnic in the open air.

■ Jobos

Most guest houses in Jobos have restaurants attached, but a couple deserve special mention. **Olas y Arena,** ☎ 787-830-8315 or 888-391-0606, part of Villas Del Mar Hau (see *Where To Stay*), serves up paella and seafood in a bamboo gazebo shaded by Casuarina pine trees. This rustic spot overlooking the beach is elegant yet informal – a perfect romantic getaway. Entrées run $15-20.

At the Villa Montaña Resort (also in *Where To Stay*), **The Eclipse** specializes in fusion cuisine, blending Asian and Caribbean accents for delightful plates. Get here early, as the kitchen closes at 9.30 p.m. Most entrées cost about $20. Driving around Jobos, you'll also find a number of less remarkable seafood eateries and beachside restaurants.

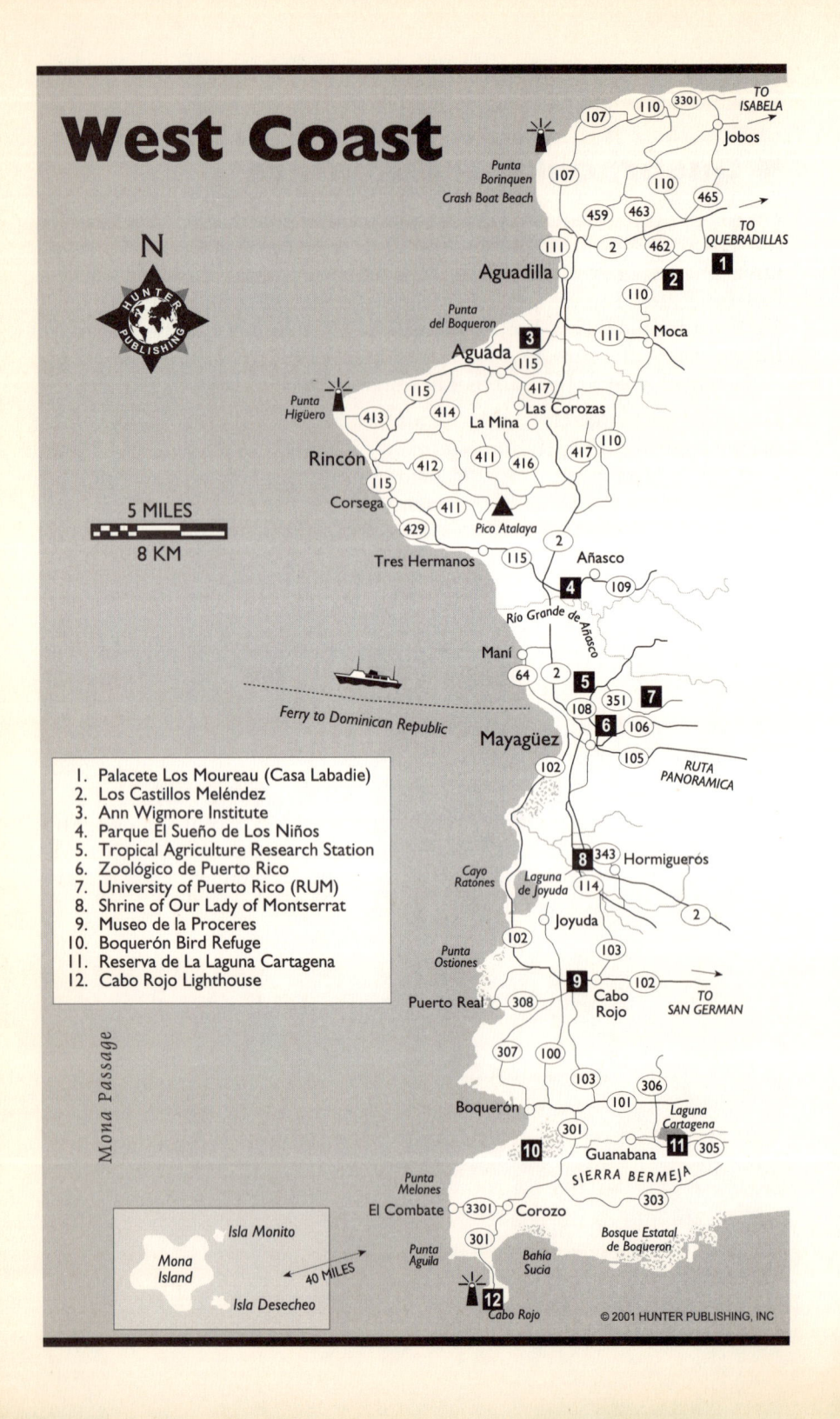

West Coast

1. Palacete Los Moureau (Casa Labadie)
2. Los Castillos Meléndez
3. Ann Wigmore Institute
4. Parque El Sueño de Los Niños
5. Tropical Agriculture Research Station
6. Zoológico de Puerto Rico
7. University of Puerto Rico (RUM)
8. Shrine of Our Lady of Montserrat
9. Museo de la Proceres
10. Boquerón Bird Refuge
11. Reserva de La Laguna Cartagena
12. Cabo Rojo Lighthouse

© 2001 HUNTER PUBLISHING, INC

West Coast

For surfers, scuba divers and seekers of tranquility and fine seafood, western Puerto Rico is home sweet home. The coastline alternates from dramatic cliffs in the northern and southern capes to luxurious beaches and little fishing villages in between, with a few stinky industrial spots to break up the bucolic monotony. Rincón, the "Malibu of the Caribbean," dominates the international tourist trade, whereas the little towns along the rest of the shore capture the weekend and spring break traffic of Puerto Rican locals. There's definitely a Wild West atmosphere here. Cowboys young and old clog traffic through every town, riding bareback on their high-stepping Paso Fino horses, seemingly oblivious to fuming motorists behind. In summer, mangos hang heavy on the trees, and red-flowered *flamboyan* trees drop a royal carpet of petals on the highways. Roadside shacks, tucked discreetly between mini-malls and KFC and Church's chicken outlets, offer genuine, old-school barbecue. And if you stop in some of the west-coast fishing villages, you'll find seafood caught mere hours earlier. But besides having fabulous beaches and ocean views, the west coast is a water-sports playground, with offshore reefs and islands that create the best conditions in Puerto Rico for surfing and scuba diving.

IN THIS CHAPTER
- Aguadilla
- Moca
- Aguada
- Rincón
- Añasco
- Mayagüez
- Cabo Rojo (the town)
- Puerto Real
- Boquerón
- Laguna Cartagena
- Cabo Rojo Peninsula
- El Combate
- Isla Mona

Getting Here & Getting Around

■ By Land

There are two ways to reach the west coast from the San Juan area – via the north coast on highways 22 and 2, or over the Cordillera mountain range and along the south coast on Hwy. 52 (connecting from Carr. 18 leaving San Juan southward). Geographically, the southern route is much longer, but because it is an expressway nearly all the way, it is smoother than the stop-and-go of much of the northern route. It is also more scenic, as it leads through the hillside towns of Caguas and Cayey and along the Caribbean coast west of Ponce. The trip generally takes just under three hours on the southern route, and a little more than two hours via the north.

Hwy. 2 extends along most of the west coast, but because only the south-coast section is an *autopista de peaje* (toll road), expect numerous stops at traffic lights in all major towns in the west. The drive from Cabo Rojo to Aguadilla can take up to an hour, depending on traffic.

> **CAUTION:** *Be careful driving the lesser roads here, especially near the coast. Many are narrow, and views of the ocean can distract motorists from the necessity of watching oncoming traffic.*

■ Rental Car Agencies & Taxis

If you arrive at along the west coast by air or sea, you will find major car rental agencies at either the Mayagüez or Aguadilla airports. Here are a few, to get you started: **Thrifty** – Mayagüez airport, ☎ 787-834-1590; **Budget** – Mayagüez airport, ☎ 787-832-4570; Aguadilla airport, ☎ 787-890-1110; **Hertz** – Aguadilla airport, ☎ 787-890-5650; Mayagüez, ☎ 787-832-3314.

Taxis are usually waiting at the airports when flights arrive. **Mr. Special** in Mayagüez, ☎ 787-832-1115 or 1154, covers most of the west coast, as does **Taxi Western** in Mayagüez, ☎ 787-832-0562, and **Mega Taxi** in Aguadilla, ☎ 787-819-1235.

■ Vans & Públicos

Public vans bring passengers from San Juan to Aguadilla or Mayagüez and back for about $15 one way, but the trip can take four hours or more. *Públicos* also run between Mayagüez, Rincón, Aguadilla and other west-coast towns, with fares usually in the $1-$6 range one way. *Público* stations are located in Mayagüez about two blocks north of Plaza Colón in Barrio Paris; in Rincón on Calle Nueva just south of the town square; and in Aguadilla in the town's central plaza.

Two independent van lines operate between San Juan and the west coast. The **Blue Line**, from the Río Piedras *público* station in San Juan to Aguadilla and back, has five morning and one afternoon departure each way, on Tuesdays, Thursdays and Saturdays. The Aguadilla station is located across from the church on the southeast corner of the town square, next to a multi-story parking garage. The full one-way trip (normally about three hours) should cost no more than $20 per person. Depending on the driver and other passengers, detours may be negotiable. The Blue Line will stop at the San Juan airport or Old San Juan on request. Information and reservations: ☎ 787-891-4550 (Aguadilla) or ☎ 787-765-7733 (Río

Piedras). Or call Yey or Henry (the drivers) on their cell phones, ☎ 787-309-0997 and ☎ 787-390-4553.

Similarly, **La Sultana** runs vans both ways between San Juan and Mayagüez, departing every two hours between 5 a.m. and 5 p.m. The Mayagüez station is on C. Doctor de Perea in Barrio Barcelona. Don't pay more than $20 for the full one-way trip of three or four hours. Information and reservations: ☎ 787-832-1041/2502 (Mayagüez) and ☎ 787-767-5205 (Río Piedras).

■ By Air

Flights are available from San Juan to the airports at Mayagüez and Aguadilla, and from Newark, New Jersey to Aguadilla (a nightly flight on TWA). Because the Newark-Aguadilla flight arrives in the wee hours of the morning (1:45 a.m. or 2:45 a.m., depending on whether the US is on Daylight Savings Time), try to arrange to be picked up by the staff of a hotel, adventure agency or a friend. Flight schedules change often, so it's best to check with a travel agency or directly with the airlines: **TWA**, ☎ 787-728-5595; **American Airlines** and **American Eagle**, ☎ 800-981-4757 or 787-749-1747.

■ By Sea

If you're up for an 11-hour ferry ride across the Pasaje de la Mona (Mona Passage), Mayagüez offers an option for cheap travel to and from the Dominican Republic capital, Santo Domingo, and the opportunity for adventure on Puerto Rico's neighbor to the west (the mountains of the interior are bigger and wilder there). With enough space for 250 cars and more than 500 passengers, the rainbow-trimmed ferry comes complete with a video casino, a seedy bar with blue velour furnishings, a cafeteria, restaurant and a theater with back-to-back movies of the Jean-Claude Van Damme variety. Cabins for two cost about $50 one-way. Otherwise, you can try to catch some sleep slouched in the uncomfortable cinema chairs, on one of four coveted couches in the reception area or on deck chairs outside (best to have a sleeping bag or a good blanket for this). Immigration can be excruciating, especially into Puerto Rico, but at least you get to witness the odd spectacle of customs officials processing immigrants in the ship's casino. Ferries leave Mayagüez on Monday, Wednesday and Friday at 8 p.m., from the **Puerto de Mayagüez**, located next to the pungent tuna-processing plants. From Hwy. 2, take Carr. 102 toward the sea less than a half-mile, then turn right on Carr. 3341. The return ferry leaves Santo Domingo on Sundays, Tuesdays and Thursdays at 8 p.m. A round-trip costs about $150 without a cabin in the summer and about $170 in winter. Bringing your car across costs about $60 extra one way. Contact **Ferries del Caribe**, ☎ 787-832-4800.

LOCAL TRAVEL AGENCIES

Agencia de Viajes Megar, ☎ 787-890-2129, at Km. 9.5 on Carr. 110 in Aguadilla, is a full-service agency, as is **Centro Viajes**, ☎ 787-891-0260, Km. 120.0 on Carr. 2, also in Aguadilla. In Mayagüez, **Sultana Travel Agency**, ☎ 787-833-5553 or 7474, at Pablo Casals 24, can help you book just about anything. **Condado Travel**, ☎ 787-831-7790, is on the north side of Mayagüez at Sam's Club in Western Plaza, Suite 155, Carr. 2. They are open every day, including Sunday afternoons.

Mail & Communications

In Boquerón, the **Punto Activo Internet Café**, Muñoz Rivera 62, ☎ 787-644-0787, has eight terminals. Internet access costs $5 for 30 minutes, $8 an hour. They are open every day from 9 a.m. to 5 p.m. (planning to extend until 9 p.m.) daily, with a pleasant environment for catching up with your e-mails or surfing the Web.

The **US Post Office**, ☎ 787-823-2625, is situated on the outskirts of town on Carr. 101. In Rincón, **Postal Plus**, on Carr. 115 south of town, has two terminals connected to the Internet, as well as photocopy, fax and long-distance phone services, ☎ 787-823-7587, fax 823-6792, e-mail postman@caribe.net.

Touring & Sightseeing

■ Aguadilla

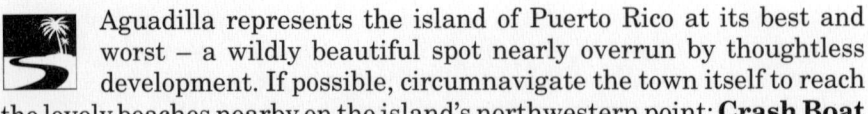

Aguadilla represents the island of Puerto Rico at its best and worst – a wildly beautiful spot nearly overrun by thoughtless development. If possible, circumnavigate the town itself to reach the lovely beaches nearby on the island's northwestern point: **Crash Boat Beach**, with its colorful fishing boats upended in front of shabby snack stands, and the secluded **Wilderness Beach** and **Shacks Beach**, both reached on turnoffs from Carr. 107R. During the week, these are excellent places to catch some rays, swim and snorkel along nearby coral reefs and old piers, and there are also some good diving and spear-fishing spots right off the coast. On weekends, though, some of the beaches can be a bit of a zoo.

If by some quirk of curiosity or boredom you find yourself venturing into the town center of Aguadilla, you might notice some signs of an ongoing $12 million municipal renovation, including a new park under construction and cosmetic attempts to restore charm to the city center. The town's most coveted historical site, however – the ***ojo de agua*** spring, where, for centuries, Taino Indians and European seamen gathered fresh water – is a lost cause. Built as a lush, Spanish-style garden a century ago, it is now hideously covered over with yellow and white concrete.

Parque Colón on Paseo Cristobal Colón follows the waterfront to the southern tip of Aguadilla along a strip of grubby looking restaurants. The park itself seems parched and dusty despite the foliage provided by mango trees and the remaining "green" spaces, and the plaza is a maze of concrete paths and picnic furniture. Garbage piles up in what would otherwise be quite a pleasant kiddies park with rope bridges, climbing frames and tree houses.

North of Aguadilla, at the sports complex on the Ramey Base, the **Punta Borínquen Golf Course** (see *On Foot*) has holes with great views and affordable rates.

The **Aguadilla Tourism Office**, ☎ 787-890-3315, is at the Rafael Hernández Airport.

ENOLA GAY WAS HERE

Before World War II, hundreds of families cultivated sugarcane, coconuts and hearts of palm on the northwestern point of Puerto Rico, and the quiet pueblo of nearby Aguadilla retained much of its Spanish colonial flavor. The US Air Force Base Ramey completely changed all that. In 1939, the Air Force purchased more than 3,500 acres of flatland overlooking the north end of the Mona Passage and built a base that became the training ground for some of the most important missions of World War II, including campaigns against Nazi airships in the European theater and bombing raids against Japanese targets, including Hiroshima and Nagasaki. The base temporarily boosted the local economy, but when military operations ceased there in 1973, it left behind a legacy of unsightly strip malls and fast-food restaurants that had sprung up to serve it. Now many of the former Air Force buildings have been converted for use by the police, Coast Guard and governmental agencies, with many of the barracks turned into low-income housing for the area's underemployed residents.

■ Moca

Named after the Taino word for the laurel-like trees that once covered the surrounding valley, the little hillside town of Moca is best known as Puerto Rico's literary city, as well as for the fine *mundillo* lace that has been made here for centuries. Make a day-trip to this pretty pueblo. Although the Moca trees have all but vanished, a lovely drive through hillsides of ver-

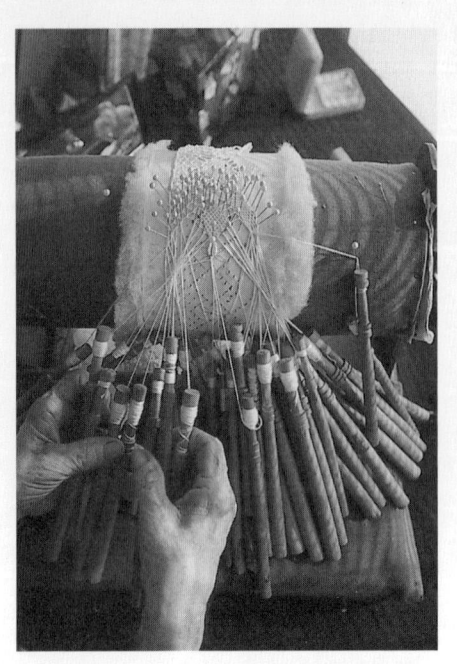

*Making mundillo lace in Moca.
(Bob Krist, for the PRTC)*

dant outcroppings and tropical flora leads you into town, where a couple of plantation castles stand out against the more modern *barrio* around them, remnants of the French colonial presence on Puerto Rico's west coast. One, **Los Castillos Meléndez**, is privately owned, but the restored grounds of **La Casa Labadie** are open to the public (see *On Foot*, page 183) and contain a library with the original manuscripts of writer Enrique A. Laguerre. Although an inordinate number of the island's writers, poets and musicians have been born in the Moca area, Laguerre is the one most likely familiar to non-Puerto Ricans. His novels, *El 30 De Febrero* and *El Fuego Y El Aire,* as well as other writings, are seminal studies of the Puerto Rican condition and history. His most famous work, *La Llamarada*, depicts the lives of *jíbaros* on the sugarcane plantations around Moca. Laguerre was nominated for the Nobel Prize for literature in 1999.

THE WORLD OF MUNDILLO

The Spanish brought the art of lace-making to Puerto Rico in the 1500s, and it is now one of the most highly prized crafts on the island. Created almost exclusively by women, "mundillo" refers to the intricate wooden apparatus – a little world unto itself – used to create the fine weave. Strands are threaded together by hand, with wooden bobbins, to make styles ranging from sturdy table linen to fine filigrees for wedding dress bodices. Visitors interested in the craft should be sure to stop in at **Doña María Lasalle's,** ☎ 787-877-2100, just around the corner from the pharmacy on Plaza Publica, where a monument honors the women of Moca who have preserved the *mundillo* tradition. Doña Maria is a living testament to the craft, and produces some of the most sought-after lace in the world (her clients include former First Lady Barbara Bush). Her tiny, one-room shop is open to the public from 10 a.m. to 4 p.m. on weekdays. To try your own hand, ask Doña María about how to participate in local workshops.

For three days at the end of June, the annual **Mundillo Festival** takes place in the central plaza of Moca. Visitors and local craftspeople come together to celebrate the old art of making bobbin lace. It's not to be missed if you have a passion for textiles. Visitors interested in going to the festival should contact the Puerto Rico Tourism Company in San Juan (☎ 787-721-2400) for dates.

■ Aguada

South of Aguadilla on Carr. 115, one of the island's oldest municipalities, Aguada, has little to offer that can't be improved upon by heading south to Rincón. The tiny seaside town is crowded and ordinary, the beaches unspectacular, their waters murky with silt and river runoff. South of Aguada, on the pretty Carr. 115, you will find an abundance of auto parts shops, backyard mechanics and roadside "roach coaches" selling barbecued chicken, pork and *empanadillas* on weekends. This stretch of highway is also home to the Ann Wigmore Institute, a live-foods health retreat (see *Where To Stay*).

■ Rincón

One of the island's hot spots for gringo tourists, Rincón gets top marks for adventure opportunities, with gorgeous stretches of beach, the best surfing in Puerto Rico, proximity to diving off Desecheo and Mona islands, whale watching and natural beauty still unspoiled by large-scale development. There are plenty of charming little guest houses and good restaurants here, a few decadent beach bars and a laid-back culture full of quirky characters and strange occurrences.

> *The word **Rincón** ("interior corner" in Spanish) is appropriate name for this chunk of land that noses out into the sea like a snout between the Aguadilla and Mayagüez bays. But the town's name actually comes from a wealthy, 16th-century sugar plantation owner named Don Gonzalo Rincón, who left his land to the local poor when he died.*

It was surfing that put Rincón on the international map. After the world surfing championships were held here in 1968, the area became a mecca for wave riders seeking a rare winter destination with nearly consistent breaks throughout the season. Of course, this isn't always the case. Recent off-years with unexpectedly calm waters have filled beachside bars with wistful surfers scanning the horizon while disconsolately gripping plastic cups of rum punch.

Surfing has been only part of the draw that has made Rincón a nesting ground for migratory North Americans, many of whom came here years

Rincón & Environs

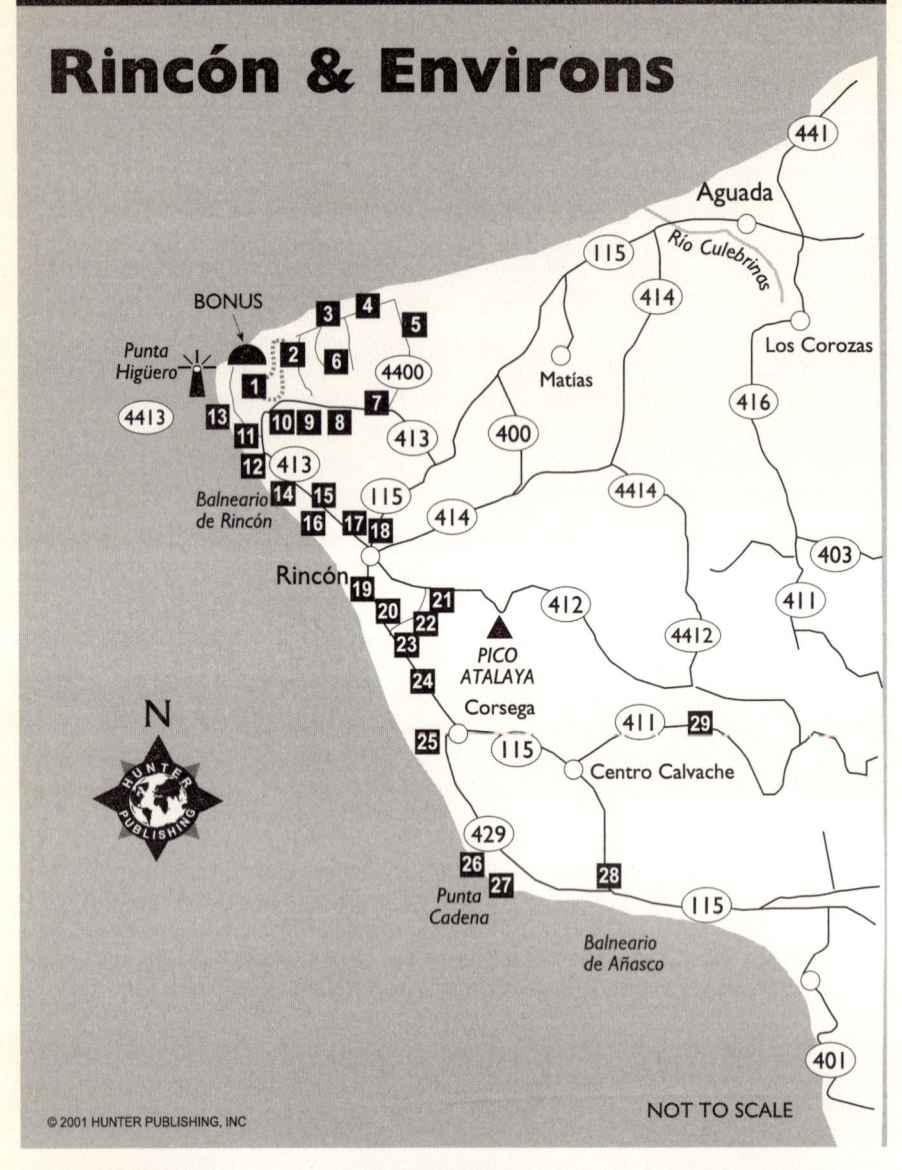

1. Mountain bike trail
2. El Flamboyán
3. Beside the Point & Larry B's
4. The Landing
5. Rincón Surf & Board
6. Sandy Beach Inn
7. Brisa's Bar
8. The Lazy Parrot
9. Tres Capitanes
10. Tres Hermanas
11. Rustic Art Gallery
12. El Faro Guest House
13. Calypso; Desecheo Dive Shop; Hot Waves Surf Shop
14. Puesta del Sol
15. Mr. Marlin
16. Taino Divers
17. Rincón Tourist Office
18. Post Office
19. Café Con Leche
20. Police Station
21. Público Terminal
22. West Coast Surf Shop; Rincón Centro del Salud (Health Center); Closeout
23. Parador Villa Antonio
24. Villa Cofresí; El Patio Familiar; El Bambino; Postal Pins
25. Coconut Palms
26. Horned Dorset Primavera
27. El Molino del Quijote
28. Kaplash
29. La Cima Burger

ago and stayed. This small town resembles one in Northern California, with residents offering in-house massage therapy, ritual healing techniques and belly dancing lessons. Though a few Puerto Ricans occasionally roll their eyes and refer to Rincón as a "gringo hell," the locals still far outnumber the settlers and the population is a healthy mix of vegetarians and hedonists from the US mainland and fun-loving *pincho* eaters from town.

DRIVING IN RINCÓN

First-time visitors to Rincón may notice the bumper stickers that read "413 – Road to Happiness" on cars hurtling along *las curvas de Rincón* – the infamous Rincón curves. Motorists should be aware that a great many *rincoeños* favor driving in the middle of the narrow roads, possibly because the stunning views of the palm-bedecked shore make it difficult to keep one's attention on the banality of driving. As a result, the 413 is the scene of many (though few fatal) bumps and grazes.

If you stay long enough, it may dawn on you that everyone in Rincón is at least slightly nuts. It's a place of many "artists" and few galleries. Hopefully, you'll meet the town's self-appointed traffic warden, named "Bienvenidos" ("Welcome"), who sports a woolen poncho, a spectacular pair of greased sideburns and a whistle with which he disorganizes parking downtown. His brother roams the streets "keeping the peace" with a plastic pistol and dime-store sheriff's badge. Stay long enough, and you'll surely witness forms of behavior unacceptable to most of society. There is talk of inbreeding and unspeakable acts taking place behind the bakery in Puntas. Rumors fly. Everybody's a town crier. A lunatic vein runs through the town. Observers point to the town's location, where the Atlantic meets the Caribbean, at the "Gateway to the Bermuda Triangle." Others say behavior has been affected by the presence of the old nuclear power reactor, called "BONUS," which pokes up from the coastline like a giant green wart.

Next to the BONUS reactor, the older **Punta Higüero Lighthouse** and adjacent environmental park (one of the only whale-watching parks in the world) provide a nice strolling area overlooking the sea. Built in 1892, the lighthouse originally used a 270-candlepower oil lamp to warn passing ships. Though keepers changed the system in 1913 to a 26,000 candlepower oil vapor system, the technological leap fell victim to the omnipotence of nature five years later, when the structure was all but destroyed in an earthquake and tidal wave. Rebuilt in 1922, it has so far lasted to this day. It was temporarily turned into a maritime museum but, unfortunately, the museum closed shortly thereafter due to lack of public interest. If you'd like to know more about the Rincón area, Hector at El Faro gift shop (near the lighthouse) is a goldmine of information.

WHAT A BONUS!

The dubiously named BONUS (Boiling Nuclear Superheater) power plant – a lime-green dome that bubbles alien pod-like out of the ground – has provoked more than a little controversy and speculation since it was built in 1962. The first nuclear reactor in Latin America, it was meant to provide energy for much of the northwest corner of Puerto Rico. It operated only sporadically for six years, until it was shut down for good due to "technical difficulties." Though the prospect of leaking radiation has prompted fears and unsubstantiated sightings of mutant fish and monstrous corals in the area, and is sometimes blamed for the erratic behavior of the locals (some even claim the ominous dome houses the bodies of, or is controlled by, extraterrestrials), most of the hubbub was probably due to government secrecy about the closure and the reactor itself. Recent Department of Energy tests have put local radiation levels well within safety standards, and vigilant environmental groups are more concerned about radiation dangers in the future than from the past. The nuclear core of the reactor and the radioactive basement of the site are encased in leak-proof cement, and BONUS has been deemed safe for public use. But environmentalists worry what might happen should the aging plant be struck by an earthquake or tsunami, both of which have hit the area in the past hundred years. The ex-mayor of Rincón had proposed turning BONUS into a rah-rah nuclear museum (presumably with photos of Einstein, photos from the history of atomic power, Johnny Atom action figures, etc.), to promote tourism. For now, the project is stymied by the arguments of La Liga Ecologica Puertorriqueña de Rincón that a natural disaster might cause a health hazard to a daily stream of visitors.

Rock embankments, called **The Spanish Wall**, along many of Rincón's beaches are all that remains of the foundation of a railroad that once almost entirely circled the island (check out Pools Beach, as well as the ocean villas surrounding the Horned Dorset hotel). Built in the early 1800s by the French when sugarcane production was a mainstay of industry here, the railroad became arguably Puerto Rico's first and last "public transport" system as sugarcane fell into decline. Elderly locals still remember the eight-hour trip from Mayagüez to San Juan as a wonderful journey around the coasts of the island. The bakery/liquor store **L'Estación** used to be the train station, and above the bar you can see black-and-white photos from steam-engine days while sipping a rum and Coke with the other riff-raff.

Information & Assistance

The staff at the **Rincón Tourist Information Center**, Carr. 413, Calle Sol, ☎ 787-823-5024, has a fairly good knowledge of the municipality and produces its own cartoonish map of Rincón.

In the event of an emergency, the **Police Station** is located on Calle Nueva near the *público* station, ☎ 787-823-2020. For medical care, contact the **Centro de Salud** (Health Center), ☎ 787-823-2795.

If you're interested in local environmental and conservation issues, **La Liga Puertorriqueña Ecologica de Rincón** meets every second Monday of the month at the Municipal Senior Citizens Center at 7 p.m., and anyone is welcome to attend. A recycling center has been set up behind the sports center on Carr. 429 in Corsega – an example of recent community initiatives to protect the natural environment in Rincón.

■ Añasco

The pretty pueblo of Añasco is southeast of Rincón, on Carr. 109 off Hwy. 2. It is seldom visited by tourists, which is a shame since it is one of the rare small towns that still captures the flavor of rural Spanish colonial architecture. The coast nearby was one of Columbus' brief stops as he explored the Puerto Rican coast in late 1493 and, although there is no museum to commemorate it, the area is steeped in history. For decades after Columbus, waves of explorers, conquistadors and merchants took refuge in the mouth of the Río Grande de Añasco (named for Spanish settler Don Luis de Añasco), and small pueblos of settlers and Indians sprang up around it. Today, the town's central plaza is the second biggest on the island, and surrounds a fountain with statues depicting three Taino Indians drowning the young Spanish conquistador Salcedo in 1511. A duplicate statue is found in the waters of the Río Grande de Añasco, just outside town.

WHERE THE GODS DIED

The motto of Añasco, "Donde Los Dioses Murieron," points to a grimly pivotal moment in the history of the indigenous Taino people. When the conquistadors first arrived, the Indians assumed them to be gods, and therefore immortal. It was in present day Añasco that this myth was shattered. In 1511, Taino Chief Uraycán, apparently feeling jilted over the settlement of his ancient homeland, ordered several young Indians to take one of Añasco's men to the river and try to drown him. After the successful murder, word spread among the Taino population that the Spanish were indeed human, giving the natives enough confidence to mount a number of small uprisings. When the Spanish, in turn, realized that the indigenous people were not simply docile slaves, they crushed them brutally.

The town is famed for *hojaldre* – a soft cake with a taste similar to gingerbread. In the morning, the whole town seems filled with its mouth-watering aroma. As with many local delicacies, the recipe for *hojaldre* is a closely guarded secret. When Señor Hojaldre first produced it fresh from the oven in 1903 and realized he was on to a winner, he took steps to ensure that the only genuine slice of *hojaldre* you're ever likely to get is from the little factory here in Añasco.

Finally, if you happen to be around after Three Kings Day in early January, the **Fiestas Patronales de St. Antonio Avart** (the patron saint festival of Añasco) is a popular nine-day party attracting thousands of revelers who come to share in the fun, music and a canoe race down the Rio Grande de Añasco. It starts January 9.

CHILDREN'S DREAM PARK

For young children, Añasco's **Parque el Sueño de los Niños**, on Carr. 109 just west of town, ☎ 787-826-6088, offers a fairy-tale castle, a movie theater specializing in Disney classics (in Spanish), a haunted house and play park with various oversized plastic toys. While it may not be Disneyland, for $10 it's not a bad back up plan if the kids are getting unruly. There's also a large outdoor swimming pool complete with wave machine (who needs the beach anyway?) where hordes of noisy teenagers flirt and hang out.

■ Mayagüez

From the word in the Taino language meaning either "place of many waters" or a type of indigenous tree, Mayagüez is the third-largest urban center in Puerto Rico, an unassuming city with a growing student population and a once-vital seaport of waning importance. For centuries it was the major point of export for coffee grown in the mountains due west, and a key link between Puerto Rico and Hispaniola (Dominican Republic). But after the US takeover of the island more than a century ago, coffee production declined and restrictions tightened on trade. An earthquake leveled much of the city in 1918, and reconstruction has captured only some of the city's former glory. During the 20th century, industrialization transformed much of Mayagüez, and new tuna canneries (Starkist, among others) dominated the coast, at one point satisfying more than half of North America's appetite for the "chicken of the sea." By now, however, about half of the canneries have closed down and the wealthy who accumulated their riches here have fled to gated, suburban mansions in the hills to the west of the city.

> **TIP:** Driving south into Mayagüez could include a coastal detour through the not-unsightly but essentially uninteresting beach town of Maní on Carr. 64. But unless you enjoy dirty port areas and the unimaginable stench around the aging tuna processing plants, avoid this back entrance to Mayagüez. In fact, avoid the port area altogether. Take Hwy. 2 into town, get off at Calle McKinley and head east several blocks into the town's Barrio Paris.

Fortunately, the expansion of the University of Puerto Rico's branch, **Recinto Universitario Mayagüez** (known as RUM, appropriately enough), has helped give the old town new flair. Students in search of cheaper housing have turned Barrio Paris into a lively quarter with a few funky shops, bookstores, restaurants and bars, all the way to the Plaza Colón, where the main attraction is a massive statue of the explorer surrounded by Taino Indians and conquistadors. There have also been a few official stabs at renovation of key structures such as government buildings and the city's main theater. After a face-lift involving more than $4 million in federal funds, the baroque/neoclassical **Teatro Yagüez** (just west of Plaza Colón) is a center for the arts and educational activities, as well as beauty pageants.

Northeast of the city center, you will find the only major zoo in Puerto Rico, the **Zoológico Zoorico** (see page 186). Nearby, at the southeast corner of the university, the **Estación Experimental Agrícola Federal** provides researchers from RUM and the US Department of Agriculture one of the best sites in the Caribbean to study indigenous crop species, hybrids and cash crops brought to the island from all over the world.

Farther west toward the docks, the supposed **red-light district** known as *Dulces Labios* ("sweet lips"!) is sordid enough, but doesn't quite live up to its suggestive name. In the past, prostitute queens sporting sequined regalia stood brazenly on street corners in this area. But today, police keep streetwalkers on the move and spread out through the city. The *barrio* is, however, the location of one of the finest bakeries in town, **Brazo Gitano Franco**, which was founded by the great-uncle of Spanish dictator Francisco Franco.

■ Hormigueros

A few miles south of Mayagüez, on Carr. 343 (signposted as Avenida Hormigueros from Hwy. 2), the town of Hormigueros is best known for its **Shrine of Our Lady of Montserrat**. Legend has it that, in the early 17th century, a local landowner named Girardo González found himself confronted by a wild, aggressive-looking bull in the hills near his home. Figuring himself a goner, he begged to the heavens: *"Favoréceme, Divina Señora de Monserrate!"* Suddenly, a "coffee-colored lady" appeared in the sky, carrying the baby Jesus. Upon seeing the vision, as the story goes, the bull dropped to its knees in supplication, allowing Gerardo González to escape. The thankful landowner founded a hermitage on the very spot. Renovated with concrete three decades ago, the yellow and white church towers over the town. The wall behind the altar was supposedly built on the exact site of the virgin's appearance. Notice the small hole left in the brickwork to allow her to enter the church should she reappear. Every year on September 8, hundreds of pilgrims still climb the steps to the church, many on their hands and knees. An oil painting inside the church depicts the miraculous event, and there is a nice view from the entrance to the shrine. If the church doesn't interest you, there's no other reason to visit Hormigueros.

■ Joyuda

Take a slow drive along Carr. 102, south from Mayagüez, to fully appreciate this string of fishing hamlets, mini piers and wooden dwellings on stilts that form what locals call the "Gold Coast of Cabo Rojo." More than two dozen seafood eateries here are extremely popular with Puerto Ricans, especially on weekends and holidays, and those on the west side of Carr. 102 have great sea views. The tiny **Cayo Ratones** (Rats Cay) just offshore is a cheap and popular spot for picnics and sunbathing. There aren't any rats on this deserted rock, just a pebbly beach, okay snorkeling and a shower and, on most weekdays, you can probably have it to yourself. It's definitely to be avoided on weekends, when local church groups and hordes of children mob the tiny cay. Look for a sign that says "Paseo En Bote" (Boat Passage) and ask for Chicharo (a weathered old guy who usually wears a faded Duran Duran T-shirt), who will take you on the half-mile trip and pick you up later for $3 per person.

■ Cabo Rojo (the town)

Not to be confused with Cabo Rojo the peninsula (see below), the town of Cabo Rojo, on Carr. 102 east of Carr. 100, is the seat of the local municipality and uninteresting except, possibly, for the **Museo de los Proceres** (Museum of Patriots). Built in 1995, the neoclassical design of the museum is meant to conjure images both of the Cabo Rojo lighthouse and, as its brochure says, "the Greek philosophy warranted by our ancestors." Inside, you'll find an odd collection of bones and artifacts from digs at Taino Indian sites, documents by local historian and philosopher Salvador Brau, portraits of local heroes and fairly unoriginal works of art by contemporary Puerto Rican artists. The staff is extremely friendly and helpful, though, and the museum has a library with historical texts about Cabo Rojo and an Internet connection that can be used by the public. The museum, ☎ 787-255-1580, is open from about 8 a.m. to 4 p.m. (closed Sundays), and is located next to the police station on the southeast end of town. The Cabo

Rojo Tourism Office is on an off-ramp on the southbound side of Carr. 100, about a mile north of Carr. 101.

■ Puerto Real

West of the Cabo Rojo pueblo, on the looping Carr. 308, the fishing village of Puerto Real produces more than a million pounds of fish per year – including the majority of seafood consumed on the west coast – despite its diminutive size. It's a pretty drive past the pastel clapboard houses along the waterfront, but unlikely to inspire more than a quick visit. If you have access to your own grill, try bargaining with some of the local fishermen as they come in from sea (early a.m.), or stop in at one of the little *pescaderías* (fish markets) for fresh dorado (mahi mahi), tuna and snapper. You can also find whale-watching charters here in season, January to April. Just north of Puerto Real, **Punta Ostiones** is a picturesque outcropping where oysters have been collected since the time of the Taino Indians.

> **SEAFOOD TIP:** *Despite its reputation as the fishing center of the west coast, Puerto Real is not the place to dine. The "restaurants" here are more like seedy drinking dens than anything else. Do as the locals do and head to the seafood strip in Joyuda instead (see* Where To Eat, *page 212).*

■ Boquerón

This pretty seaside town with its colorful main street is gaining a reputation as a party spot for well-to-do Puerto Ricans and yachters. And if the amount of big development going on here – in the form of new condos, hotels and guest houses – is anything to go by, then one can easily imagine a Boquerón tourism boom in years to come. This is one of the places on which historians claim Columbus may have landed in 1493 on his first visit to Puerto Rico. Compared to its sister town of El Combate, the center still retains some of its colonial character. North of town, on Carr. 307, the **Playa Buye** is a lovely swimming beach, and worth walking along to find a secluded cove. It's also a good place for eco-travel, with the nearby Refugio de Aves de Boquerón – a heaven for bird watchers and mangrove enthusiasts (see page 197).

■ Laguna Cartagena

This marshy lagoon along Carr. 305 is perhaps noteworthy only to UFO aficionados, to whom it is the local equivalent of Area 51, and as testimony to the Puerto Rican penchant for seeing strange visions and bizarre creatures. Though it is now fenced off and designated as a government reserve, the curious adventurer can probably find a way to explore the area and try to find out what all the extraterrestrial fuss is about (see page 184).

■ Cabo Rojo Peninsula

This wild and windswept cape was named by Christopher Columbus in 1493 as he rounded Puerto Rico's southwestern corner and noticed the limestone cliffs tinged pink with minerals, dubbing the area "Los Cabos Rojos." Settlers quickly encamped on the cape, and by 1525, had confiscated the natural salt flats from Taino Indians and converted them into an important economic resource for the fledgling Spanish colony. Today, driving out to the peninsula on Carr. 301 makes an excellent day-trip across low hills and dunes, with stunning views of the sea. Passing the tiny villages of Corozo and Pole Oleja, you'll catch glimpses of the white piles of **Las Salinas de Cabo Rojo**, the last of Puerto Rico's salt factories still in operation.

The cliffs and lighthouse at Cabo Rojo.
(Bob Krist, for the PRTC)

Follow Carr. 301 after it turns into a rough but navigable dirt path, out to **El Faro de Cabo Rojo**. Built in 1881, the lighthouse still warns passing ships of the treacherous rocks just offshore, despite its crumbling façade (although a local group plans a restoration of the lighthouse, funds are still pending). Walking or mountain-biking the paths around the lighthouse and surrounding cliffs gives the impression that you've just reached the end of the world – a barren, eerie landscape with nothing as far as the eye can see but the dark waters of the Pasaje de la Mona. It was once the perfect place for marauding pirates and other highwaymen of the sea to hide out. Notice that the cliffs are pockmarked with caves, some large enough to hide ships in. These include Las Cuevas de Cofresí, reached via a signposted road off Carr. 303, near La Parguera.

COFRESÍ AND THE PIRATES OF THE CARIBBEAN

The seamen and cutthroats who plundered their way through the Caribbean in the 17th and 18th centuries are legend: Blackbeard the psychotic; Calico Jack, who wore striped trousers and turned women into pirates; Captain Henry Morgan, namesake of the spiced rum; Captain Kidd, who inspired Robert Louis Stevenson's *Treasure Island*; and the sadistic murderer Black Bart. Puerto Rico's own homegrown buccaneer doesn't quite fit the mold – Roberto Cofresí y Ramirez de Arellano lived a century after those in the who's who of pirate lore, and his image survives as a beloved Robin Hood figure who donated much of his loot to the poor.

A native of Cabo Rojo, Cofresí was a romantic youngster and an avid reader of pirate and adventure stories. By the early 1800s, he had outfitted a pirate ship, the schooner *Ana*, and with 15 friends began years of successful raids on foreign trade ships. He darted in and out of caves and remote coves along the Puerto Rican coastline and, due to his generosity toward locals, authorities found it nearly impossible to get information about his whereabouts. In 1824, however, he stepped over the line, attacking eight trading vessels that included one US ship. In what may have been the first use of force by the United States in Puerto Rico, the US Naval forces sent a well-armed schooner to the Caribbean with the sole purpose of capturing Cofresí and his crew. After a long, fierce battle, all 16 were rounded up and sent to El Morro castle, where they were judged by the Spanish Council of War and – like all self-respecting pirates before them – were, on March 29, 1825, executed.

■ El Combate

At the end of Carr. 3301 on the Cabo Rojo peninsula is **El Combate**, Puerto Rico's longest beach, with about three miles of sand, palms and almond trees stretching as far as the eye can see. Meaning "the battle," it gets its name from a failed invasion of the peninsula in 1759 by a group of settlers to the north that hoped to take over the lucrative salt mines. Alerted by a resident to the pending attack, villagers from Boquerón, Puerto Real and El Faro area drove the invaders into the sea with machetes and axes. Since then, *caborojeños* have also been known as "*Mata con Hacha*," or "Kill with Ax" (no worries, the locals are friendly enough these days!). Today, El Combate is best known as a weekend party town, frequented by inebriated young people who seem intent on spoiling the natural beauty of the place by hurling empty beer cans and plastic cups into the bushes. Fortunately, because of the length of the beach, it is possible to escape this rather nocuous behavior by taking a hike to the far end. And if you're under 25, single and want to practice your Spanish and salsa steps, a Saturday night here may be just the thing.

■ Isla Mona

Called the "Galapagos of the Caribbean," Isla Mona rises out of the sea like a flat limestone tooth – a strange and unique island sanctuary and an explorer's dream. Very few Puerto Ricans, and even fewer foreigners, have ever been here. But scientists and well-informed adventurers visit this forgotten island, and come away with an unforgettable experience akin to traveling back millions of years in time. If you are spending more than a week in Puerto Rico, it is definitely recommended.

This mostly uninhabited natural reserve is accessible only by boat and with written permission from the government, and no more than 100 visitors are allowed on the island at a time. It has a genuinely prehistoric atmosphere, and the place is loaded with history. Weird creatures abound, such as the four-foot Mona iguana, fish-eating bats and dozens of cave-dwelling seabirds. Twisting stalactites and stalagmites strike surrealistic poses in the island's 18 cave systems, the walls of which still bear the markings of indigenous peoples, pirates and miners who took refuge there. And the underwater life that inhabits the coral reefs offshore makes Isla Mona one of the world's great diving destinations (see the *Isla Mona* section later in this chapter).

Adventures

■ On Foot

Beach Walks

Better than a treadmill, and more picturesque by far, a walk through the wet sand at water's edge can break your sweat conveniently close to the sea. The beaches at **El Combate**, **Boquerón** and **Buye** all have long stretches of sand, perfect for a long stroll. One of our favorites is from the beaches of **Rincón north to Puntas**. Start at the Black Eagle Marina (parking available), with beach access just north of the restaurant. From here you can walk northward past Steps Beach, around a cove, all the way to Maria's Beach and beyond, within constant view of Desecheo island 13 miles offshore. Pop in at the Calypso bar for a soda or a rum punch, and then double back to lose the calories as the sun sinks down.

The Moca Plantations

Driving north on Carr. 110, from Moca toward Isabela (a stretch of road called *Jardines la Sierra* because of its garden-like beauty), you'll find a French plantation-era fortress, called **Los Castillos Meléndez**, at the intersection of Carr. 4110. The three fairy-tale buildings look wildly out of place. It's privately owned and, contrary to rumor, is not open to the public, according to the municipal office and the Tourism Company.

Continue north on Carr. 110, turn right on Carr. 464 (when you see Ruben Supermarket), and the old French sugarcane plantation, **Palacete Los Moureau**, rises gloriously out of the remaining cane fields. **Casa Labadie**, as the Palacete Los Moureau is more commonly known here, comes to life under the direction of Dalme Lassalle, who will gladly show you around if you make an appointment, ☎ 787-830-2540. Originally owned by a French nobleman, the plantation was sold in the late 19th century to Juan Labadie, whose mysterious widow, Cornelia Pellot, built the French plantation house in 1905. In the process, she became firm friends with writer Enrique Laguerre and allowed him a workspace in Casa Labadie. Inspired by the place, in 1935 he wrote his most famous work here – *La Llamarada* – which documented the lives of sugarcane workers and is respected as one of the most thorough socio-cultural commentaries of the period.

> **DID YOU KNOW?** *Enrique Laguerre, who still lives and writes in Moca and occasionally visits the house that inspired so much of his work, was nominated for the Nobel Prize for literature in 1999.*

The last surviving member of the Pellot-Labadie family died in 1992, and in 1993 a devastating fire destroyed much of the original home, leaving only the stone structure in its wake. Looters took the few surviving pieces of furniture and some family relics. Since then, the Moca Administration bought the land and salvaged the building, restoring much of the original look, although the spiral staircase has been replaced with a "safer" block stairwell and a basement library has been added. The mahogany entrance is hung with pictures of Laguerre and various past and present Puerto Rican dignitaries. It includes some of Laguerre's personal collection, including first edition copies of works by Virginia Woolf and others, and Laguerre's own original manuscripts, typewritten on yellowing pages. The only remaining evidence of the life of Cornelia Labadie are her initials, cast into the awnings of the north-facing balcony doorway.

With luck, some of the history of Palacete Los Moureau will be kept alive. Current plans, however, are to turn the estate into a tourist destination with cabañas, sports facilities, its own trolley and possibly a hotel. One can only wonder at what will become of it. Hours are 8 a.m. to 4:30 p.m. Call the municipal office in the town center, ☎ 787-877-6015 or 2270, for more information.

Boquerón Bird Refuge

One of the better hikes in the west is through the **Refugio de Aves de Boquerón** (see the *Eco-Tourism* section of this chapter). As with other hiking trails, be sure to wear sturdy shoes and carry plenty of drinking water.

Cabo Rojo Lighthouse

All around the lighthouse, windswept limestone cliffs tower over the *Pasaje de la Mona* waterway and, to the south, the Caribbean Sea. A walk on the cape trails, between the salt flats and the glittering sea, has a stark romance to it. The cliffs are little more than 70 or 80 feet high, but the surf pounding on the rocks below provide more than a hint of danger. Look for caves in the rock surfaces of surrounding cliffs, which hid pirate ships centuries ago. After driving the rutted track of Carr. 301 to the peninsula (half the adventure is getting there), park next to the misnamed Bahía Sucia, which means "Dirty Bay." When you've finished exploring the cape, take a dip in its turquoise saline waters, dry off on the glistening sand and on your way back stop at a roadside snack stand for the local favorite, *tostones gigantes* (fried and salted plantain patties).

Laguna Cartagena

This little lagoon just north of the Sierra Bermeja hills has been taken over by the federal government, which claims that it has plans for a natural reserve there. Not everyone believes this line. Many residents of nearby Maguayo and Guanábana who were around then tell of alien spacecraft crash-diving into the swampy waters of the lagoon in 1987, and a few still spin tales of eerie gray creatures with almond-shaped eyes roaming the local tundra afterward. Either way, this spooky, desolate marsh can be a fun place for a day hike. The government offers little explanation for some strange relics left around the lagoon, such as small jungles of plastic pipe sticking up at odd angles from the soil, mounds of earth with skyward-facing mounting plates, wooden jetties that lead nowhere. So use your imagination. Notice the white (surrender?) flags poised above bulrushes and slimy flotsam. Below the water, it's said, an entire extraterrestrial society waits, watching and breeding.

THE SEARCH FOR INTELLIGENT LIFE

Southwestern Puerto Ricans have long had a knack for witnessing unearthly appearances, whether it was the Virgin of Montserrat in Hormigueros centuries ago or, more recently, visits by UFOs. On May 31, 1987, a rare, strong earthquake shook the Cabo Rojo area, and the Puerto Rico Seismologic Service reportedly placed the epicenter at 81,000 feet below Laguna Cartagena. Later, however, it revised its estimate, saying the epicenter was a deep fissure offshore in the Mona Channel. That official "waffling," along with witness accounts, ignited the imagination of UFO buffs and convinced many that the government is "hiding something" in Cabo Rojo. Some residents of Guanábana and Maguayo describe an explosive sound that accompanied the 1987 earthquake, and a weird, cigar-shaped craft that hovered above the lagoon during the following three days. Many claim to have seen eerie lights at night and cobalt-blue smoke issuing from fresh cracks in the earth. A few say that when they tried to get a closer look at the lake, they were turned away by well-dressed men or workers wearing anti-contamination gear. Some residents claim that UFOs have visited the area since the 1950s, and there are incidental reports of encounters with gray-colored aliens with long, spindly arms and triangular heads. If your favorite TV show is *The X-Files*, grab your camping gear and stake out the Laguna Cartagena. Who knows? You might see something.

Plenty of old cattle trails intertwine the bramble and grassy plains surrounding the lagoon, and one could spend days exploring here. Trails through red earth wind up into the uninhabited Sierra Bermeja hills. To complete the weird atmosphere, a US Air Force radar balloon hovers above, (ostensibly) watching the sea for drug smugglers. To reach the lagoon, take the pleasant country road, Carr. 305, west, until it seemingly dead-ends at Carr. 303. Turn left, and then make your first right after the little yellow bridge (about 100 yards south). Follow this (it's Carr. 305 west again) to the small village of Maguayo. A sign at the end of the village reading **Reserva de la Laguna Cartagena** marks the beginning of the trail. To get a little closer to the lagoon, you can follow the dirt path past the sign, looking for holes in the barbed wire fence.

> **TIP:** *Much of the low vegetation is interspersed with thorny hedgerows, so we recommend boots for this one.*

Puerto Rico Zoo

In Mayagüez, the only major zoo, **Zoorico Zoológico de Puerto Rico**, ☎ 787-834-8110, is home to a wide variety of animals from faraway places, including a white rhino, wart hogs, sloths, big cats, chimps, giraffes and camels. Puerto Rico's first baby camel was born in spring 2000 – the offspring of "Coke" and "Sprite" (corporate sponsorship knows no bounds here). Recent renovations have given many of the animals a generous space in which to roam, to a mix of *Jungle Book* tunes and salsa music piped over loudspeakers throughout the park. Located on Carr. 108 in Mayagüez, the zoo is open Wednesday to Sunday, 8.30 a.m. to 5 p.m. Admission for adults is $6, and children under 11 get in free.

Golf

Perched on the cliff tops north of Aguadilla, **Punta Borinquen Golf Course** was originally built for the US Air Force officers stationed at Ramey Airforce base in the 1940s, and was often used by General Dwight D. Eisenhower and other top brass. It's now a well-maintained public course, and one of the best deals on the island – the 18-hole course costs $18 for the greens fee and an additional $26 for a cart. There are no lakes, but an abundance of sand traps and a strong westerly crosswind provide an entertaining game, with magnificent views of the Atlantic Ocean and the Mona Passage. Located on Golf Street, Ramey, Aguadilla, ☎ 787-890-2987, it's open from 7 a.m. to dusk.

Club Deportivo del Oeste, Carr. 102, Joyuda, ☎ 787-851-8880, is renowned for having the most difficult opening hole on the island (a par five with a 550-yard fairway and two lakes). It is a complex nine-hole course, and its unrelenting uphill and downhill lies in the foothills of the Cordillera Central ensure a challenge for "extreme" golfers. The real attraction, though, is the coastal view. Get a mid-afternoon tee time and then hit the clubhouse to enjoy the sunset. Part of a private club, the course is open to the public from 7 a.m. to 5 p.m. with a $30 fee, including cart.

■ On Horseback

In Rincón, **Tres Hermanas** offers horseback rides on weekends from their shop on Carr. 413, ☎ 787-823-7698. Unfortunately, riding on the beach is prohibited and can get you a $500 fine, so you are restricted to the streets and foothills of Corsega. At $20 an hour, it's also rather expensive, considering what you get. We recommend riding with Tropical Trail Rides in Jobos instead (see *North Coast*, page 146).

On Wheels

Cycling & Mountain Biking

Due to the narrowness of roads and the madcap driving patterns of some motorists, we don't recommend cycling in traffic lanes, unless you feel confident in such situations. Unfortunately, there aren't any good designated cycling paths established on the west coast yet. One is planned for Rincón, along the old coastal railway, but no one expects it to be finished before the end of 2002 or later.

DOMES TRAIL IN PUNTAS – Behind the BONUS nuclear power station, a small labyrinth of single- and double-track paths is popular with mountain bikers, and is often the site of Puerto Rico's annual X-treme Games in June. If you're a true downhill junkie, you'll be a little disappointed by the level of x-tremity here. But there are some killer ocean views and a couple of short but tricky drops. With about five miles of track, it's a great course for beginners. Start at the baseball field above the Calypso Bar in Puntas (parking is available across the street from the lighthouse), and ride north across a vacant lot until you find the double track leading into the trees. The drop-offs are about a mile and a half in, right after you see the water tanks, and they can sort of leap up on you if you're at speed, so be careful. The rest of the track is mostly gentle slope. Not worth crossing the island for, but if you're in the Rincón area and have access to a mountain bike, it's a pleasant five miles.

CABO ROJO TRAILS – The same walking paths around the lighthouse in Cabo Rojo make for nice mountain biking, but don't look for many intense downhills. Basically, you hike-a-bike (carry it) up to the lighthouse and cruise along the cliffs. Great views, gentle ride.

GETTING A BIKE

Try your luck at **Ciclo Mundo**, ☎ 787-805-1820, on the first floor of Mayagüez Town Center, or **Paul Julien's Caribbean Vacation Villa**, ☎ 787-821-5364, fax 821-0681, e-mail julienpr@yahoo.com, www.viewthis.com/caribbean, on Carr. 333, San Jacinto, Guánica (South Coast).

Scooting Around Boquerón

Mopeds and Go-peds (motorized stand-up scooters) can get you around the picturesque town of Boquerón and, if you're willing to brave the country roads, the town's pretty environs. Both are available for rent by the hour from **Boquerón Skooter Rent**, ☎ 787-254-0080, cell 640-5363. You'll find them on the way into town on Muñoz Rivera, open 11 a.m. to 10 p.m.,

Thursday through Sunday. Mopeds start at $20 an hour (add $10 for each additional hour); Go-peds are $15 an hour ($8 for each additional hour).

Driving Carr. 114

Carr. 114 was one of the first established roads in Puerto Rico, and is a pretty alternative to Hwy. 2, running from just below Mayagüez to San Germán. Sugarcane carpets the valley, and you can see remnants of the 100-plus-year history of the "ancient" throughway, including two red brick buildings that once housed the road builders. Keep an eye out for a couple of plain, dome-shaped tombstones that mark the common gravesites of victims of a cholera epidemic that killed hundreds here in the 1850s. About halfway along this route, an abandoned, powder-pink hacienda, with crumbling columns and arches and long-dead rooftop terrace gardens, stands as a lone monument to a nearly forgotten plantation era.

■ On Water

Diving

Make no mistake, next to the Cayman Islands, western Puerto Rico has some of the best diving spots in the Caribbean, with a coastline dotted with walls, submarine caverns, pristine reefs and, best of all, the wild offshore islands of Desecheo and Mona. Diving around both of these islands is highly recommended for unspoiled reefs, innumerable varieties of coral, occasional big marine life and great visibility.

ISLA DESECHEO - A deserted federal preserve 13 miles west of Rincón, hump-like Desecheo is off-limits for public access. The waters around it, however, are fair game for diving. **Candyland,** popular for its live, candy-colored coral formations including brain, mushroom and barrel sponges, teems with parrotfish, grouper, shy eels and turtles and an abundance of tropicals. **Yellow Reef** consists of a series of pinnacles and swim-throughs, where shellfish and lobster lurk in the shadows. The top of the yellow-hued reef is just 20 feet from the surface, and drops to about 90 feet at the perimeter. Another favorite for grottoes, caverns and bridge-like coral formations is **Las Cuevas,** an ethereal spot where you can see barracuda, rays, crags of lobster colonies, snapper, trigger fish and weird life forms. Most dive shops in Rincón and some to the north and south regularly make the 40-minute trip to Desecheo, leaving around 8 a.m. and generally bringing you back to the dock by 2 p.m. (see *Choosing The Right Dive Shop,* below).

ISLA MONA - Hands-down the best diving in Puerto Rico, with visibility up to 200 feet, incredible rock and coral formations, deep walls and big marine life, Isla Mona is a must for serious divers. Because the island is at least four hours by boat from Puerto Rico, diving here is usually done as part of a multi-day excursion. See the Isla Mona section for more details, pages 198-204.

AROUND THE NORTHWEST CORNER - Although Desecheo and Mona usually steal the spotlight for diving off the west coast, there are a number of other reefs, coral formations, drop-offs and cathedral-like caverns a short boat ride away or accessible straight from the beach. Off-beach dives around Aguadilla include the underwater caverns at **Shacks Beach** and the reef at **Crash Boat Beach**, which is considered a good place for novice, check-out and night diving. A wall teeming with giant sponges and marine life drops to 125 feet, and a night dive here will reveal polyps stretching their multi-colored heads out of the coral to feed on plankton. These flower-like creatures should be seen and not touched, as they're often armed with stinging nematocysts. Myriad schools of fish chomp lazily on large sea vegetables, attracting predator sharks and barracuda in search of dinner. Also off Crash Boat is an artificial reef made of discarded tires. It starts in about 90 feet of water and, although there isn't much to see, some dive operators bring students here for advanced diver certification due to the depth and easy access. Check in advance, because you may be asked for an Advanced Open Water Diver certificate for these dives.

AROUND THE SOUTHWEST CORNER - South of Cabo Rojo, vertical walls that drop to around 100 feet ring a number of offshore cays. The best reef here is known as **Las Coronas** or **Cayo Ron** – a mile long with fine examples of hard and soft corals. Visibility is not quite so good here (usually about 50 feet), but you can still get a good look at what the reefs have to offer. **The Tourmarine Adventures**, Joyuda, ☎ 787-851-9259, takes certified divers out for $45 without equipment (not for novices).

SCUBA FOR KIDS

Caribbean Reef Divers, ☎ 787-254-4006 or 255-3483, runs a course for kids, called Bubblemakers. It's a unique introduction to scuba diving, designed for children between eight and 11 years old. In a swimming pool with a maximum depth of six feet, they will learn how to use the equipment and how to breathe underwater. It costs $50 and is also based at the Bahía Salinas Beach Hotel.

WRECK DIVING - Though numerous ships and aircraft have met a bitter end in Puerto Rican waters over the years, most have either disappeared, are inaccessible, or at least very difficult to get to. One outfit specializing in finding lost treasures of the deep is **Acuatica Underwater Adventures** in Aguadilla, ☎/fax 787-890-6071, e-mail aquatica@caribe.net. They make trips to the submerged wreck of a B-29 bomber that plummeted into the sea near Ramey Air Force Base in 1953. The wreck lies about 110 feet down, and the cockpit and wing are in exceptionally good condition, with other sections of the plane scattered nearby. This is a decompression dive for advanced divers only. The staff at Acuatica is also a good source of information about other wrecks in Puerto Rican waters. Wreck/boat dives cost $75, including weights, belts and two tanks (for additional equipment add $10).

CHOOSING THE RIGHT DIVE SHOP

Whether you're a beginner hoping to learn scuba or an advanced diver, the crew that takes you out on the water can make or break your experience. You need to know that the equipment you will use is well maintained, and that the divemaster is attentive to the needs of everyone in the group. Scuba diving is potentially dangerous in many different ways, and it pays to seek out a dive shop that will ensure that your trip is safe as well as fun. As a student or inexperienced diver, make sure you learn with an instructor who will work with you until you feel comfortable in the water and then stick by you every step of the way. Certified divers, too, will get more out of their dive by going out with an attentive, knowledgeable crew. Finally, don't forget the fun factor. Find people who are intelligent and great to hang out with, and your experience will be greatly enhanced in and out of the water.

For all-around quality, our favorite dive shop on the island is **Taino Divers** in Rincón. The crew – Carson, Jari, Bundy and Matt – has an unbeatable reputation for safety and knowledge. They are US Coast Guard accredited and rigorously maintain their equipment, ensuring a worry-free and fun experience. This group is an absolute pleasure to be around (you may find yourself unable to resist buying them a beer after the dive), and covers the whole spectrum of aquatic adventures, from diving and snorkeling to sportfishing, sunset cruising and excursions to Isla Mona. They also offer PADI courses from Open Water through Divemaster certification. Small, personalized classes for Open Water Diver run $350, and can be completed in three to five days, depending on the student. If you're an experienced diver, ask them about drift, cave, nighttime and deep-water dives. A two-tank dive costs $75, plus $15 for full scuba gear rental. You'll find them at Black Eagle Marina, ☎ 787-823-6429, fax 823-7243, www.tainodivers.com.

Mr. Marlin, Carr. 413 in Rincón, ☎ 787-823-5880, fax 823-5880, offers blue water hunting and more radical scuba adventures for experienced divers, such as drift diving (two-tank dives $70-$90, depending on location), where you abandon yourself to the pull of the current while the boat follows your course from above. Not for the faint of heart. Ask divemaster Scott how he got the shark bite in his BCD!

Desecheo Dive Shop, ☎ 787-823-0390, on the road to El Faro in Rincón, is another long-established charter business with a good track record. **Mona Aquatics**, next to Club Nautico in Boquerón, ☎ 787-851-2185, has a good reputation, as does **Caribbean Reef Divers** at the main dock in Puerto Real, ☎ 787-254-4006, e-mail diveprcr@coqui.net or divingjm@coqui.net. The Caribbean Reef Divers boat leaves from the picturesque Bahía Salinas Beach Hotel at El Faro in Cabo Rojo, not the Puerto Real dock. Snorkeling trips including gear and boat ride cost $35, a two-tank dive with equipment costs $85 and PADI Open Water Certification is about as cheap as you'll find, at $200.

Snorkeling

Most charter operations will take snorkelers out on dive trips, so those uncomfortable underwater can check out the reefs from the surface. A good off-the-beach snorkeling area can be found at **Steps Beach** in Rincón. A mere 10-50 yards offshore, forests of purple and green sea fan corals sway with the surf. A huge garden of elkhorn coral is home to iridescent blue hamlets, parrotfish and angelfish and schools of triggerfish with electric blue dorsal fins. Barracuda and sea turtles also regularly visit this enchanting underwater canteen. Walk northward along the beach from the Black Eagle Marina until you see an old set of concrete steps askew on the sand. It's easiest to enter the water about 75 yards south of the steps, and then swim around the point for great underwater views.

GETTING THE GEAR

Most dive shops rent fins and masks for around $25 a day, but if you plan to be on the island a while and do a lot of snorkeling (and/or diving), consider buying the basics. US Divers is a good brand costing around $50 for mask, snorkel and fins. Slightly more expensive but highly recommended by professional divers are Genesis and Sherwood, from $65 all the way up to $300 for total gearheads.

Surfing

The northwestern point of the island is known to surfers worldwide. The combination of swells that wrap around the peninsula, offshore winds and long point breaks create perfect conditions for peeling waves and long rides. Board-toting thrill-seekers usually begin arriving in Rincón and Jobos in late September for the tail end of hurricane season, which can produce a few monstrous swells, and stay through early April, when the sea generally flattens out. Here's a breakdown of the hottest surf spots.

- **Jobos** and **Surfers** beaches, in the Aguadilla area, are fairly reliable for catching a wave, with a long right break and a sand bottom. They're very popular with locals, however, and on weekends the swell is thick with water bugs all waiting for the perfect break.

- Like many of the beaches here, **Antonio's**, the site of the 1968 World Surfing Championships, was named by local surfers at the time (in this case, by Antonio Muniz, owner of The Landing restaurant and bar). Waves break on a sand beach with better rights than lefts, and average winter heights of three to seven feet.

- As its name suggests, **Sandy Beach** has a soft sand bottom, making it ideal for beginners. Waves favor a left break. You get a lot of boogie boarders around here, too.

- **Spanish Wall** and **Pools** are both small, local haunts, but neither has much of a reputation among serious surfers. **Domes**, on the other hand, has some of the most consistent waves in the area. If it's flat everywhere else, you still have a good chance of catching something here. The wave is long, so it's another good place to learn. But because of this, Domes also tends to get crowded.

Rincón is a famous surfing spot.
(PRTC)

■ **Indicators** is known for an excellent right break. However, the bottom is jagged with coral-encrusted pipes, and the break is more or less on top of the same rocks warned against by the lighthouse above. Local surfers say you should attempt this spot only if you know the area, or at least check it out with some of the local guys before hitting the water.

■ **Maria's** and **Dogman's** enjoy both left and right breaks. Locals and visiting surfers alike favor this spot for its resemblance to Hawaii's famous Pipeline. Maria's is named for the generous woman who fed hungry, penniless surfers in the '60s, when Rincón was nothing but an idyllic backwater.

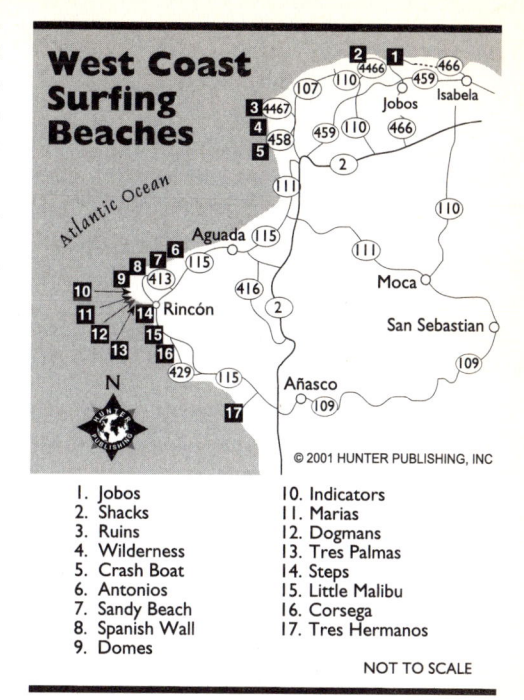

West Coast Surfing Beaches

1. Jobos
2. Shacks
3. Ruins
4. Wilderness
5. Crash Boat
6. Antonios
7. Sandy Beach
8. Spanish Wall
9. Domes
10. Indicators
11. Marias
12. Dogmans
13. Tres Palmas
14. Steps
15. Little Malibu
16. Corsega
17. Tres Hermanos

NOT TO SCALE

> **TIP:** *If you don't surf, but like to watch, Maria's Beach is probably one of the best spectator spots.*

■ **Tres Palmas** can crank out some seriously big action. Strictly for pros on heavy days, it breaks right on the biggest "out reef" in the Caribbean. With a good chance of getting caught in the "close-out" (where the wave breaks on top of you), the surf here is frequently described as "sick." On a good year, waves can reach 25-30 feet, and the terrifying drops pictured in local postcards are often of these Tres Palmas monsters.

■ **Steps** is named for a washed-away block of concrete stairs that was once part of a coastal train station but now sits incongruously in the middle of the beach. It's about 50 yards south of Tres Palmas and allows considerable speed off the break, fueled by the larger waves offshore. The elkhorn coral ridge that runs to the north, however, makes it a dangerous spot if you tend to spill.

■ **Little Malibu** is very fast, with good tubes that break in shallow water. Watch out for the fire coral lurking in the shallows here. Ouch!

SURF SHOPS

Several surf shops in town rent out boards by the day, and sell all the gear you need to look like a true grom. **West Coast Surf Shop**, ☎ 787-823-3935, www.westcoastsurf.com, is one of the biggest. Board rental (including long boards) costs $20 for 24 hours; boogie boards $10. If you're looking to learn, they can also put you in touch with a local who will show you the ropes for a token fee. There's also the way-cool **Closeout**, ☎ 787-823-2515, e-mail dicri@coqui.net, selling board shorts and fashion accessories (also skateboarding gear). **Hot Waves** at Maria's Beach is a little stall right on the action.

Swimming

As with most of the island's coastline, there is no shortage of fine beaches here for swimming and sunbathing. The shoreline at **Corsega** just south of Rincón is quiet and sheltered from the winds that create big surf to the north, and the lack of reef makes it easy on the feet. Try to position yourself somewhere between the fishing village and the Villa Cofresí hotel, for maximum space to yourself. A bit farther south on Carr. 401, the long public beach at **Tres Hermanos** is next to an open-air *pescadería*, where you can buy the catch of the day to grill later. Most boats come in before 9 a.m., though, and if you arrive late the best you'll come home with is some bait.

One of the best swimming beaches in Rincón is **Sandy Beach,** a cool spot to kick back under a palm tree with a piña colada from the bar in one hand and a good book in the other.

In Boquerón, the **public beach** is one of the best on the island, with a coconut palm grove and more sand than you can shake a stick at. It is often compared to the three-mile El Combate (we prefer Boquerón), the longest public beach in Puerto Rico. Because this weekend destination can get packed, bring a picnic and head south for a more tranquil dose of sun worship. If you take the last left turn before entering town, you can park in a dirt lot away from the hordes. Steer clear of the muddy salt flats at the far end, though, or you're likely to get your car stuck in the slick goo (as we did).

Playa Buye, off Carr. 307 between Puerto Real to Boquerón, has a shallow sandy shoal, and at some places you can wade out a hundred yards in waist-deep bathwater. At the southwestern tip of the island near El Faro in Cabo Rojo, **Bahía Salinas** and **Bahía Sucia** are fringed by stunted dry forest and mangroves and practically glow due to the high salt content in the sand and water.

HEALING WATERS

Wading through the waters of the **Corozo Salt Flats** is rumored to be comparable to bathing in the Dead Sea, and not only due to the high salt content. The rich concentration of composite minerals is said to have medicinal properties particularly beneficial to the skin and for those who suffer from allergies. The mineral-thick water includes magnesium, said to relieve asthma; bromine, for the relief of nervous tension; iodine, for an effective metabolism; sulfur, a natural disinfectant; and potassium, which helps regulate the body's water balance. The Corozo Salt Flats are found along Carr. 301, on the way to the Cabo Rojo lighthouse. For more information and easy access to good muddy water, contact the Bahía Salinas Beach Hotel at El Faro in Cabo Rojo, ☎ 787-254-1212.

Kayaking & Surf Biking

Kayak rentals are available at most public beaches and from many surf and dive shops. The going rate is $10 per hour or $40 per day for single-person kayaks (two-person kayaks are usually available, too). These aren't true long-distance, ocean-going crafts, but amateur versions (you sit on top, not in them) intended for paddling along the shore to check out the scenery. Though in Boquerón, if you're feeling energetic, it is possible to rent a kayak at the beach, paddle south for an hour or so, cross a portage and enter the mangrove bird refuge (see *Eco-Travel*, below). The Boquerón rental shop, on Calle Muñoz Rivera in town, also rents out a new apparatus – the surf bike. With a bicycle seat, pedals and handlebars mounted to a surfboard-like hull, these contraptions apparently can reach speeds of 10 mph or more on the water, depending on your energy level. In El Combate, **Israel Boat Rental** south of the town center has kayaks and *pedalos* (foot paddleboats) for $10 an hour.

Sportfishing & Deep-Sea Fishing

Blue and white marlin, yellowfin tuna, wahoo and dorado (mahi mahi) wait just offshore to test your skill (and strength) with the rod and reel. A number of charter outfits operate from Aguadilla, Rincón, Boquerón and Cabo Rojo. **Mr. Marlin** is in Rincón, on Carr. 413, just before you get into the town center, ☎ 787-823-5880, fax 823-5889. Scott, the owner/operator (several bill-fishing tournament wins under his belt earned him the name), is a renowned fisherman and a salty old sea dog if ever there was one. A self-confessed half-man, half-fish who is "happier off land than on it," he'll find the marlin if they're around. A half-day charter, including a light lunch of sandwiches, sodas and beer, costs $300, or $550 for a full day. He also offers blue water hunting.

The always-entertaining **Taino Divers** (see *Diving*, above) can hook you up with just about any fish in the water, with competitive rates, lunch and beer included. For a guaranteed good time, find them in Rincón at Black Eagle Marina, ☎ 787-823-6429, fax 823 7243.

Tourmarine Adventures, Joyuda, ☎ 787-851-9259, does deep-sea fishing charters (six people, $350 for a half-day, $500 full day) out at the Tourmarine, a drop-off about 20 miles offshore, where the sea bed plummets into the deepest part of the Mona Passage. A cheaper alternative is to go line fishing, at $25 per person.

Whale Watching

The Mona Passage west of Puerto Rico is one of the best spots in the world to view the humpback whale, a magnificent creature that comes each winter to breed in the warm Caribbean waters. Between the months of January and April, many dive and sportfishing charter boats along the western coast offer whale-watching trips. Cheaper – and kinder to the whales – is to head to the Rincón lighthouse at Punta Higüero and keep an eye on the sea: this is one of the only "passive" (on land) whale-watching parks on earth. Toward the end of the season (late February through April), parent humpbacks and their newborn young pass surprisingly close to the Rincón peninsula on their journey back north (contact **Taino Divers**, ☎ 787-823-6429, for responsible whale-watching charters).

THE "SINGING WHALE" IN PERIL

The humpback whale, characterized by its extraordinarily long, white pectoral fins, is perhaps best known for its use of complex and lengthy vocalizations – an eerie melody sung repeatedly as a means of communication – giving it the name "the singing whale." These sopranos of the deep can grow to more than 50 feet and weigh up to 30 tons. Females calve every two years, and are often accompanied on their migratory path by a male. Unlike many marine creatures that lack such guardianship, the young humpback calves stand a very good chance of survival. The greatest threat to their existence is from humans. Between 1805 and 1970, North American whalers culled between 14,000 and 18,000 humpbacks in the North Atlantic alone. By 1970, the humpback was the fourth most depleted large cetacean in the world and was finally placed on the list of endangered species. Despite illegal hunting, the greatest risk to their survival is now posed by less sinister activities, such as entanglement in fishing lines, collision with ships, recreational boating, and personal watercraft (such as Jet Skis) that disturb their breeding grounds. Ironically, as ships have become more numerous, whales have grown more used to them, often ignoring boaters at their peril. The high-pitched whine of the personal watercraft, however, is said to drive the whales into flight. The offshore Silver Bank near the Dominican Republic remains a popular humpback breeding ground because the waters are protected from boaters by a fringe reef.

See these regal mammals in a responsible way. Team up with charters that will maintain a respectful distance from the whales as they breach for air, or take advantage of the rare opportunity to see the aquatic giants from land.

Eco-Travel

■ Boquerón Bird Refuge

If you like pointing out strange birds and being able to name them in Latin, English and Spanish, or if you're one of those people who enjoys a steamy walk through mangroves, check out the **Refugio de Aves de Boquerón**. Created in 1963 to stem the draining of local wetlands for agriculture, the refuge comprises 463 acres of brackish lagoon, thick with cattails and red, white and black mangroves. It's a favorite roosting place of the endangered brown pelican and 120 other known species of birds, including the yellow-crowned night heron, the yellow warbler and many of their cousins. Four miles of pathways and boardwalk lead through this important ecosystem, allowing for an excellent walk that takes about an hour, not including stops.

Game birds and waterfowl such as the blue-winged teal, the common moorhen and the common snipe attract more than 1,000 visitors per year for hunting, which is permitted between November and January. Many more visitors come year-round, just to look at the birds, or to shoot them with cameras, not guns. The shallow lagoon, with its combination of salt water from the sea and fresh river water from the east, also sustains nine species of fish, including tarpon and snook. Fishing for them is permitted, but you'll need to bring your own gear and canoe, as nobody in the immediate area rents out equipment.

Rarely done, a kayaking tour through this tangled mangrove area could be a hoot – or a nightmarish survival experiment, depending on your temperament. Again, you'll need your own gear. The women who rent kayaks at the **Balneario Boquerón** will help organize trips if you pay extra. Otherwise, just rent a kayak for the day at the Boquerón beach, paddle south for about a mile, carry your kayak over a portage in the lagoon inlet (just right of the two egg-shaped rocks) and plunge in for some hell-bent exploring.

The easiest way to visit the refuge, of course, is to drive in and just walk around, ideally in the early morning when the sun is more forgiving. As you drive south from Boquerón on Carr. 301, watch for the sign and dirt road on your right because it's easy to miss. At the end of the short dirt road, you'll find parking and a small green office on stilts where you can sign in and collect literature and maps of the area, most of it in Spanish. Bird profiles are available in all three languages. The refuge, ☎ 787-851-4795, is open daily from 7.30 a.m. to 4 p.m.

■ Cabo Rojo National Refuge

As you head toward the lighthouse on Carr. 301, look out for the **Refugio Nacional Cabo Rojo**, near Corozo, another haunt for amateur (and professional) ornithologists. There are several trails expressly for bird-watching among the ruins of an old hacienda, where migratory ducks, herons and songbirds spend the winter. This refuge, ☎ 787-851-7297 or 7258, is open 7.30 a.m. to 4 p.m. weekdays.

■ Tropical Agriculture Research Station

The staff at this place emphatically denies that it's a botanical garden. But with an amazing collection of flora, in a beautiful setting open to the public, it should at least garner the title of botanical "find." One of the only sights in Mayagüez worth pursuing, the **Tropical Agriculture Research Station**, located next to the university (RUM) between Hwy. 2 and Carr. 108 on Carr. 65, houses a tropical plant, herb and spice collection considered to be one of the best in the western hemisphere. Landscaped gardens reveal a wealth of tropical species, such as the magnificent Puerto Rican Palm (distinguished by its silvery trunk), the amber-barked Ceylon cinnamon and the Madagascan travelers tree, as well as mace and bay rum species desperately sought by seafarers of yore. This makes an interesting stroll through the natural treasures of the tropics. The research station, ☎ 787-831-3435, is open weekdays from 7 a.m. to 4 p.m.

Isla Mona

Approached by boat, Isla Mona looms up suddenly out of the water, its sheer, 200-foot cliffs forming a seemingly unassailable plateau. Flat and sand-colored, it looks somewhat unearthly. Nearing the island, you'll notice the deep serrations that gouge the rock face from top to bottom, formed when the rock was pushed by violent tectonic plate upheaval. "God's claw marks," a frequent visitor to the island calls them.

Almost exactly midway between Puerto Rico and the Dominican Republic, Isla Mona and its tiny sister island to the north, Isla Monito (which is inaccessible, with no beachhead), are the peaks of an underwater ridge that separates the Caribbean basin from the Atlantic Ocean. The southern face of Mona plunges, in giant steps, 16,400 feet into unknowable depths.

Isla Mona

Eighty-two miles north of the island, the submarine mountain range rises from a depth of 26,410 feet, rivaling the Himalayas. This is the deepest trench in the Atlantic Ocean.

Though most of the 20-plus miles of coastline (Mona is seven miles long by four miles wide) is dominated by forbidding rock cliffs, several idyllic beaches along the southern and eastern shores provide perfect access for visitors. Camping is permitted on three beaches: Playa Pájaros, Playa del Uvero and Playa Sardinera. A double-track, concrete path connects the three camping sites to the ranger station at Playa Sardinera.

■ History

Pushed up by tectonic plate movement several million years ago, the submarine landmass that includes Isla Mona remains something of an enigma to geologists. Recent research suggests that this massive shard of rock may have split off from the plate which now forms much of western South America, millions of years ago, making its moniker "Galapagos of the Caribbean" even more appropriate.

Arawak migrants from what is now Venezuela are thought to have first inhabited Mona about 1,000 years ago, followed centuries later by the **Taino** Indians, who set up the closest thing to civilization on the wild island. Their petroglyphs are still etched into the walls of many of Mona's caves, and in the remote interior one can still find (with patience and most of a day to trek) the ruins of a Taino ball court.

Columbus stumbled upon Isla Mona on his second voyage to the Americas in 1493 and, a few years later, **Ponce de León** made a supply stop here. Future generations of explorers decimated the island's Taino population, either by direct assault or by capturing them for slave labor in Puerto Rico. By the end of the 16th century, only a handful were left, and for the next few centuries the only human visitors to Mona were pirates looking for an inhospitable spot from which to raid ships in the Mona Passage and the crews of distressed merchant vessels seeking any port in a storm. Historians have documented that hundreds of ships sank in Mona's treacherous, reef-riddled waters, and at least 11 known shipwrecks have been identified. The danger to passing ships continues. In the 1980s, two large ships – the *A Regina* and the *Alborada* – ran aground on the reef of Playa Pájaros, and the upended steel hull of the *Alborada* still pokes out of the water as a warning to sailors.

In the mid-1800s, speculators from different nations began intermittently trying to harvest the mounds of bat guano piled up in Mona's caves, and in the early 1890s, a German company set up a guano-collecting operation that lasted until the outbreak of the Second World War. In its heyday between the wars, the enterprise involved more than 600 laborers dynamiting bat droppings to fertilize the gardens of the Weimar Republic. The operation had folded, however, by the height of WWII, when a Nazi submarine torpedoed the island, apparently believing the Allies maintained a secret post there. After the war, pressure mounted to protect Isla Mona from human meddling, and in 1975 the island was finally designated a natural reserve under the Puerto Rico Department of Natural Resources. This designation protects only the island itself, not the reef or marine life of the surrounding waters.

■ Flora & Fauna

No other reef and island habitat within US jurisdiction has such a valuable diversity of species within so small an area. The 13,000 acres of the island proper, covered mostly by dry tropical forest or tropical desert, contain about 500 known plant species, dozens of which are endemic to the area.

> **CAUTION:** *A number of plants have survived Isla Mona's harsh environment by developing burrs or spikes, so dress appropriately if you intend to do any off-trail exploring.*

Nearly 100 species of birds – some strange, some common – make their home on Mona, including graceful hunters such as **hawks**, **frigate birds** and **pelicans**, and dozens of cliff dwellers, such as the **brown-breasted**

booby and its dazzlingly shod cousin, the **red-footed booby**. Some feed on fish, others on the more than 500 known insect species here. Most of the insects are harmless to humans, but some are annoying (the mosquito, the no-see-um) or worse, including three species of scorpion and a stinging centipede that can grow to more than a foot long (the barbed tail of the centipede carries the venom).

CRITTERS THAT BITE BACK

Unlike the main island of Puerto Rico, Isla Mona is the home of a few dangerous critters. **Scorpions**, **centipedes** and **black widow spiders** can pack dangerous doses of venom. **Wild pigs** may charge if cornered, as may the normally docile **Mona iguana**, which has quick, vice-like jaws and sharp teeth. In the water, caution must be exercised around **urchins**, **jellyfish**, **moray eels**, **barracudas** and some species of **sharks**. Avoiding an unfortunate encounter is easy. It is almost unheard of for any of these creatures to attack a human except in self defense. Remember that you are in their home, and always be careful where you put your hands and feet.

Goats and **feral pigs** left by would-be settlers also run wild on the island. Hunting for them is permitted in winter months to thin their numbers, especially because they like to feast on the eggs of iguanas and endangered marine turtles. More interesting, if you stay at one of the island's beaches for more than a few hours, you are sure to run across the prehistoric-looking **Mona iguana**, an endemic reptile certified as threatened under the 1973 Endangered Species Act. They are not particularly shy of humans, and may wander into your campsite in search of scraps of food. But don't be fooled by their sluggish gait. Until you have witnessed the jaw-dropping spectacle of an iguana sprinting like Ben Johnson across the beach, you may wonder how this exotic lizard has survived for millions of years.

Mona's offshore ecosystems are no less diverse and important. There are patch and fringing reefs, spur and groove systems, underwater caverns, and 23 species of coral, including abundant black corals, deep-water sponges and algal reefs, all teeming with attendant life. Tropical reef fish abound, and rays, sharks, octopus and barracuda are often seen. In winter and early spring, visitors often see **humpback whales** playing very close to Mona's shores. **Saddleback** and **spinner dolphins**, too, are common in the area.

KEEP THE REEF

Overfishing of Mona's waters by Puerto Rican and (illegally) Dominican Republic fisherman has severely depleted snapper and grouper populations and, along with damage from boat anchors and ship groundings, killed some live reef, according to Reefkeeper International. The organization is lobbying to designate Mona a "Commonwealth Marine Protected Area," which would further protect the offshore ecosystem. For more information, check out the excellent Web site www.reefkeeper.org, and look for updates on Mona issues.

Lobster is still a common find for visitors, and **queen conch** are so abundant that their sun-bleached shells litter some of the beaches. Endangered **hawksbill** and **leatherback turtles** use Isla Mona as a nesting ground, and if you ever happen to see one of these ancient creatures clawing its way up the beach, respect its privacy. Turtles are skittish about where they lay their eggs, and if startled on land they may abort their nesting. Once the mother begins laying eggs, however, she goes into a trance and you may get near enough to watch without disturbing her.

■ Getting Here

Charter Boats

The easiest and, if you plan to scuba dive, the most economical way to visit Mona is with an all-inclusive charter. Most are small boats for fewer than six or eight paying customers, depending on the size of the boat. This keeps the party intimate, and ensures that dives don't become a fin-bashing affair. Food, camping gear and other provisions are normally included, and the better charter outfits will tailor your trip to include fishing and cave exploration. We highly recommend **Taino Divers**, which runs a three-day trip for $400 per person, if you want the full four tanks of diving (the cost decreases if you plan to dive less). This fun crew always stocks soy sauce and Japanese wasabi to enhance a freshly caught tuna sashimi lunch, and guitars are welcome for campfire sing-a-longs. Check them out at the Black Eagle Marina in Rincón, ☎ 787-823-6429, fax 823 7243, www.tainodivers.com, for five-star treatment at a two-star price.

Also in Rincón, **Mr. Marlin**, Carr. 413, ☎ 787-823-5880, fax 823-5880, offers flexible Mona opportunities. Ask Scott if he'll help you spear fish or catch lobsters for dinner. If you want to plan your own Mona adventure and go it alone, fishermen in Puerto Real or Cabo Rojo will usually strike a deal to drop you off on the island and pick you up.

In Aguadilla, **Mona Aquatics**, ☎ 787-851-2185, will take you to Mona and back for $115 per person. They can provide diving equipment, camping gear and other provisions for an additional cost. Chartered flights from Aguadilla to the airstrip near the ranger station at Playa Sardinera were abandoned in late 1999, but check with the **Department of Natural Resources**, ☎ 787-724-3724, to see if they've resumed. Permission to camp must be obtained beforehand from the director of reserves and refuges, Robert Matos (or his staff), ☎ 787-724-3724.

Traveling Solo

If you're going solo to Isla Mona, you'll need to check in with rangers at Playa Sardinera upon arrival (otherwise, your charter crew should take care of this for you). Remember that the rangers are on-island for lonely two-week stints, without much human contact. An offering of a candy bar or a cold beer and some friendly conversation (especially in Spanish) could lubricate any transaction.

> **TIP:** *No matter who ferries you to the island, a few items are recommended: sun block, bug spray, a stash of bottled water and a change of long-sleeved clothing (nighttime winds can get chilly, by Caribbean standards). Also, remember to shake out sleeping bags, swimming fins, etc. before you shove your limbs in.*

■ Adventures on Isla Mona

Hiking

A visit to Isla Mona can seem like a trip to another planet and, if your schedule allows, hiking up to the island mesa will give you that solitary feeling of being in a lost world. Cement tire tracks lead to the plateau from each of the three camping beaches.

> **A WORD TO THE WISE:** *If you plan to venture off the beaten path, be sure to let someone know beforehand, bring plenty of water and, if possible, a compass. Amateur explorers have been known to get lost in the trackless wilderness, and some unfortunates have even been forced to spend fearful nights sleeping in the thicket until they can be rescued.*

Caving

The greatest on-land attractions of Mona are undoubtedly the 18 cave systems. Twisting subterranean labyrinths drop into watery sinkholes or open suddenly onto cliff sides 100 feet or more above the sea. Many of the caves were briefly inhabited long ago, so look for petroglyphs and graffiti left by Taino Indians, pirates and miners.

> **TIP:** Do not cliff-dive anywhere on Isla Mona – the water below is shallow and rocky.

Mountain Biking

Few people ever go mountain biking here, but this could give you much greater mobility on land. Ask your boat captain if you can bring a bike on board.

Diving

With some of the most pristine reef sin the Caribbean, deep walls and visibility of 150-200 feet, Isla Mona is a must for diving aficionados. Most charters to the island offer four tanks of diving per person, over the course of two days. Because of the transparency of the water, Mona is also a great spot for snorkeling.

> **TIP:** For stargazing on Isla Mona, bring along a telescope or at least binoculars. Before or after the moonset, the dead-dark island provides a chance to see the constellations un-dimmed by human torch or city light.

Where To Stay

ACCOMMODATIONS PRICE KEY

Rates are per room, per night, double occupancy. Single occupancy may or may not get you a discount, so ask when making a reservation. Breakfast included where noted.

$	Up to $50
$$	$50 to $100
$$$	$101 to $150
$$$$	$150 and up

■ Aguadilla

Aguadilla has many standard rooms with air conditioning and cable TV, if you're looking only for a place to lay your head. The **Hotel El Faro**, ☎ 787-882-8000, on Carr. 107, Km. 2.1, is a good deal and has two restaurants – one serving Italian, Mexican and *criollo* cuisine and the other serving steaks and seafood. The hotel and restaurants each received the top award in 1999 from a Spanish travel organization. It also has two swimming pools, tennis courts, short bicycle paths, a beauty salon and landscaped gardens. $$

The **Hotel & Hacienda El Pedregal**, ☎ 787-891-6068 or 882-2865, on Calle Cuesta Nueva, off Carr. 111, also has well-appointed grounds. With swimming pools and lounge chairs, a billiard terrace, game rooms and a restaurant and cocktail lounge, it's designed with families in mind. $$

Well advertised, but something of a concrete box, **La Cima Hotel & Restaurant**, ☎ 787-890-2016, 2783 or 3033, fax 890-2017, Carr. 110, e-mail lacima@caribe.net, seems to cater more to the business traveler than to tourists. Its bragging points are conference and meeting rooms (175-person capacity), business facilities and proximity to Rafael Hernández Airport and Base Ramey. $$ ($$$ for an apartment sleeping eight).

The **Cielo Mar Hotel**, ☎ 787-882-5959/5960, fax 882-5577, Ave. Montemar, #84, has panoramic views of the Pasaje de la Mona, a pool, restaurant and bar and the added bonus that all rooms have a balcony with a sea view. Ask about weekend package deals. $$$

■ Aguada

Wheatgrass colonic implant, anyone? Sprouts for breakfast, lunch and dinner? It may sound gruesome to the uninitiated, but the "living foods lifestyle" offered at the **Ann Wigmore Institute**, Carr. 115, Km. 20, has been used to treat physical and emotional illnesses ranging from obesity to chronic fatigue syndrome to cancer. Hundreds come here each year for a radical diet and learning program designed to rid the body of toxins. Not to be confused with raw foods, living foods (they're still growing when you eat them) are free of additives, preservatives and heat-tampered elements, and should be extremely easy for the body to digest and assimilate, thereby freeing the body to heal itself. The Wigmore course includes yoga, skin and body care and techniques in food preparation. The living foods lifestyle is not for everyone (it can be tremendously taxing emotionally and physically) and the Institute stresses that it is a "school for learning," not a miracle cure. A two-week program costs $864 for a shared dormitory (max 12) and $1,820 for a private room with bath. For further information, contact Ann Wigmore Institute, ☎ 787-868-6307, fax 868-2430, PO Box 429, Rincón, PR 00677, www.annwigmore.org.

Rincón

Budget Accommodations

Turn west off Carr. 413, near Las Brisas bar, and you'll come to **Rincón Surf and Board**, ☎ 787-823-0610, fax 823-6440, http://home.coqui.net/surfsup, e-mail surfsup@coqui.net; $-$$. This is one of the best places in town for the budget traveler, and if you don't mind sharing, dorms are a real bargain at $20 a bed. Another lively budget place (and a great place to meet other surfers and travelers) is the **Sandy Beach Inn**, Carr. Vista Linda (off Carr. 413 at Puntas Bakery), ☎ 787-823-1146, www.sandy-beachinn.com. It is popular with a young crowd and has one of the best restaurants in town. $-$$

Mid-Range Guest Houses

Approaching Rincón from Aguada on Carr. 413, **The Lazy Parrot**, ☎ 800-294-1752 or 787-823-0224, e-mail lazyparrotinn@juna.com, www.lazy-parrot.com, has seven rooms, each with a different tropical theme. The real highlight, though, is the charming garden with swimming pool and Jacuzzi. $$-$$$

Follow Carr. 413 down toward the ocean (turn right at the whitewashed tractor tire in Puntas) and you'll come to **Beside the Pointe**, ☎ 787-823 8550. It's right on the beach, and each room has been decorated with Disneyesque parrots, pelicans and tropical fauna. $$-$$$ (discounts in summer).

El Faro Guest House, ☎ 787-823-5247, on Carr. 413 heading into downtown Rincón, has rooms with a double and single bed, some with kitchenettes. Those with a wraparound terrace give a great view of the lighthouse and Desecheo Island. $$

Just south of Rincón, **Villa Cofresí**, ☎ 787-823-2450, on Carr. 115, www.vilacofresi.com, is named for Puerto Rico's famous pirate, and has secluded, if plain, accommodations on an excellent swimming beach. $$

The **Parador Villa Antonio**, ☎ 787-823-2645/2285, fax 823-3380, Carr. 115, Km. 12.3, www.villa-antonio.com, does a "honeymooners package" for three to four days, including a $30 dinner voucher at a local restaurant and a bottle of champagne, plus goodies. $$$+

Expensive

The **Horned Dorset Primavera**, ☎ 787-823-4030 or 4050, reservations ☎ 800-633-1857, www.horneddorset.com, Apartado 397, has been rated the best hotel/restaurant in the Caribbean three years in a row by *Condé Nast Traveler*. Truly one of a kind, this hotel does not allow mobile phones, radios or television, or children under 12, in favor of a relaxing atmosphere in which one is practically forced to read, sunbathe and luxuriate. Two swimming pools, private beach access, magnificent gardens and a beachside bar staffed by formally dressed waiters ensure that you enjoy the serene atmosphere. All rooms feature four-poster beds, marble bathrooms and either an oceanfront terrace or a deck with private plunge pool. Winter rates go from $380-$800 a night, with a minimum stay of five nights during the peak season and a week during Christmas and New Year's. It's also possible to rent the entire resort, with full service – a recent weekend wedding cost the bride's family $65,000. $$$$

Self-Catering

An increasing number of pretty beachside apartments and cabañas for rent make the Rincón area a haven for short-stay vacationers who like to cook for themselves. Tim and Michelle Brennan at **Tropicabañas**, ☎ 787-823-2967, http://home.coqui.net/getwet, e-mail getwet@coqui.net, have three very private, very secluded, fully equipped cottages (one two-bedroom, two studios) to let – all with access to Dogmans Beach (popular with surfers) for $500/$400 respectively.

Other possibilities are **Coconut Palms**, www.coconutpalmsinn.com, e-mail coconut@coqui.net, which overlooks a golden beach – a popular site for weddings and private celebrations; **Caribbean Paradise**, **Tropical Tree House** and **Casa Muneca**. Get in touch with Gail for information on these four properties, ☎ 787-823-6452, fax 823-5821. $$-$$$

■ Mayagüez

If you must stay in Mayagüez, due to either a pressing business appointment or a personal obsession with spending a night in every town, there are a few options. Budget travelers will find a good deal at the **Hotel Colegial**, ☎ 787-265-3891, overlooking the campus of the university. $$

Another cheapie is the **Hotel Embajador**, 111 Este Ramos Antonio, ☎ 787-833-3340, where Caribbean poet Derek Walcott wrote part of *Omeros*, the work that won him the Nobel Prize in 1992. $$

Downtown in Barrio Paris, the **Hotel Mayagüez Plaza** (formerly Hotel La Palma), ☎ 787-891-9191, maintains some Spanish colonial grace, with shuttered windows and iron balconies overlooking the plaza area, and is undergoing renovation. $$

For a predictable stay in a chain hotel, try the **Best Western Mayagüez Resort & Casino**, ☎ 787-832-3030, north of the city on Hwy. 2, with 20 acres of tropical gardens and, of course, gambling; $$$-$$$$. Nearby, the **Holiday Inn & Tropical Casino**, ☎ 787-833-1100, is slightly cheaper, with all the ambience of a doctor's waiting room. $$$

THE LOVE SHACK

For a spicy six hours, consider an afternoon with your companion at the **Hotel Caribbean** – a.k.a. "La Ruta del Amor" – on Carr. 114, a few miles south of Carr. 100. What appears to be an abandoned row of storage units is actually a windowless den of iniquity. Behind each shuttered garage door lurks a discrete parking space and a mirrored, red-lit bedroom with shower and X-rated movies on the TV. Just keep your car idling, and an attendant will throw open one of the garage doors with a wink and a sleazy grin. It costs $20 for six hours.

■ Joyuda

To stay in Joyuda is to have a real Puerto Rican holiday. Few foreign visitors stay here or even visit this place. One of the prettiest guest houses, with an inner courtyard, swimming pool, and bar, is the **Parador Joyuda Beach**, ☎ 787-851-5650, fax 255-3750, Carr. 102, Km. 11.7; $$. Nearby, with more resort-type features, is **Parador Perichi's**, ☎ 787-851-3131/ 800-435-7197, fax 851-0560, Carr. 102, Km. 14.3, perichi@tropicmail.com, with a steak and seafood restaurant, well-stocked bar and 49 air-conditioned rooms, each with private bath and balcony. $$

■ Boquerón

Right on the waterfront, the lively (if somewhat dingy) **El Schamar Restaurant & Hotel**, ☎ 787-851-0542, at the intersection of Muñoz Rivera and José de Diego, is fine if you want to hang out and party but, conversely, bad for anyone seeking peace and quiet. $$

The **Parador Boquemar**, ☎/fax 787-851-2158, has uninspiring but clean and comfortable rooms (deluxe rooms or suites may be worth the extra few dollars) with all modern conveniences – balconies included on second- and third-floor rooms. The hotel also has a swimming pool and restaurant. $$

Rooms at **The Cofresí Beach Club**, 57 Muñoz Rivera, ☎ 787-254-3000, fax 254-1048, http://home.coqui.net/cbcsella, e-mail cbcsella@coqui.net, are fully equipped with telephone, VCR and shared swimming pool; $$$. Boquerón is also a good place to let an apartment by the week or month. Just ask around town on arrival.

■ Cabo Rojo

The lovely **Bahía Salinas Beach Hotel**, Carr. 301, Cabo Rojo, ☎ 787-254-1212 or 800-981-7575, fax 254-1215, e-mail bahiasal@caribe.net, www.pinacolada.com/bahiahome.html, has shady garden terraces overlooking the sea and a large swimming pool and Jacuzzi area with live music on weekends. It's one of the most secluded spots on the west coast – very popular with honeymooners – and is within walking distance of the salt flats and El Faro lighthouse; $$-$$$. Caribbean Reef Divers' boat leaves from the hotel dock (see page 191), and owner/captain David Pagán can arrange fishing and diving trips.

■ Camping

Although not officially sanctioned, **Crash Boat Beach** in Aguadilla is a favorite camping spot among locals. If you pitch your tent here, we suggest doing so at one of the far ends of the beach and maintaining a low-key presence. Rincón must be one of the few places left on the planet where you can still camp on the beach for free and not get turfed off at 6 a.m.

During holidays, the beach at **Black Eagle Marina** can get crammed with the tents of young Puerto Ricans. Some of these impromptu campsites get quite lavish, with self-constructed showers and temporary mains for portable televisions, lighting and the obligatory salsa music. Feel free to join in. On weekdays, you'll probably have the whole area to yourself. Keep your tent behind the almond trees, and check in with the marina police, ☎ 787-823-3048, to let them know you're there. Nearby, another popular campsite is **Tres Hermanos** beach, where you may or may not get charged $3 to pitch a tent. The beach here is beautiful and very tranquil, but unless there are a lot of other campers, it's not as safe as the Black Eagle Marina.

At Playa Buye just north of Boquerón, the **Hacia Playa Camping al Natural**, ☎ 787-851-2923, is right on the beach. Although it's absolute mayhem on long weekends, the campground is large enough that you can probably find a slightly isolated spot. Parking costs $3, and tents and camper vans belonging to the campground go for $20 a night (you can probably pitch your own tent for a few bucks). If the office is closed on a weekday, go ahead and camp until someone asks you for money.

At **Bahía Sucia**, below the lighthouse in Cabo Rojo, charred campfire remains and a few stray tent poles indicate that this is a popular, though unofficial, camping spot. It's a perfect place for it – on a half-moon beach with lagoon-like waters, with enough surrounding bush for some cover. Be careful, as there is some risk of brush fire.

Where To Eat

■ Aguadilla

Dario's Gourmet, ☎ 787-890-6143, Carr. 110, Km. 8.8, is a favorite for excellent Creole cooking. From the outside it looks more like an English country cottage (without the thatched roof) and stands out from the rest of the Base Ramey environment.

At the intersection of Carr. 110 and Carr. 4466, a wooden Mexican joint called **Hot Chili Peppers**, has a small garden and a pleasant atmosphere. Meals range from $8 to $15.

If you need a drink and a smoke (and let's face it, you might after an hour or more in Aguadilla traffic), **The Wine Garden & Cigar Shop**, Carr. 110, Km. 8.7, Base Ramey, ☎ 787-890-0685, has a small but good selection of wines from Spain, France and Italy (by the bottle only) and Havana-style cigars from Puerto Rico and the Dominican Republic. No frills, but a couple of tables and chairs are provided so you can indulge right on the spot.

■ Rincón

With excellent views from its wraparound deck, the **Sandy Beach Inn** in Puntas, ☎ 787-823-1034, serves up succulent blue-lipped mussels in white wine, Cajun crawfish with spiced butter and pasta in a lobster, scallop and shrimp cream sauce. Portions are mammoth, and a good value at $10-$20 for an entrée.

The Lazy Parrot, Carr. 413, ☎ 787-823-5654, serves a catch-of-the-day special, as well chicken breast stuffed with roasted garlic and, on Thursdays, tuna sushi for $10-$15.

If you're on a budget, it pays to stick with local food. Several excellent and cheap places in Rincón include **El Flamboyan**, with *mofongo* for $6 and up and sea views. For fresh-fried seafood *empanadillas*, *sorullos* and other snacks, check out **El Patio Familiar** south of town on Carr. 115. Farther south on Carr. 115, **Kaplash**, ☎ 787-826-4582, has, in our opinion, the best *empanadillas* and homemade *pique* in town, for $2.50 each. Just south of the town center, **El Bambino**, ☎ 787-823-3744, Carr. 115, serves huge plates of Italian and Puerto Rican food, with a $5 lunch special on weekdays. There are also a couple of pizzerias and Chinese restaurants for cheap eats.

Romantics are sure to appreciate **El Molino del Quijote**, ☎ 787-823-4010, Carr. 429, Km. 3.3, with its seafront patio, flower garden and fountains. Open only on weekends (Fridays and Saturdays from 4 p.m. and Sundays from noon), the chef specializes in seafood paella and dorado or snapper cooked to perfection. Entrées run about $15, and the restaurant will stay open until the last customer leaves. The owner also has a couple of cabañas available for rent.

BEST IN THE CARIBBEAN

For the finest dining in Puerto Rico, don't miss the restaurant at the **Horned Dorset Primavera** in Rincón, ☎ 787-823-4030. It's consistently rated among the best in the Caribbean, and we couldn't agree more. Chef Aaron Wratten (formerly of Daniel's in Manhattan) specializes in "French cuisine with Caribbean accents" using hand-picked ingredients. Although the abundance of fresh local seafood features heavily on the menu in dishes such as *escabeche* of wahoo with yellow tomato coulis and pan-seared red snapper with citrus and chives, you can also expect to see foie gras from the Hudson Valley, New Zealand spring lamb and grilled quail with arugula and roasted mushrooms. Given advance notice, Aaron will also cater to most dietary requirements. Elegant dining at this converted hacienda by the sea costs a reasonable $64 per person for the *prix fixe* menu, and $88 for the chef's tasting menu of eight to 10 courses. Dinners are semi-formal, meaning no shorts or T-shirts.

We suggest you avoid eating at **The Landing**, off Carr. 413 (signposted from Brisas Bar), ☎ 787-823-3112/4779. It has a great position on the seafront, but we found the food to be mediocre and expensive and the service slightly above boorish. With entrées upwards of $20, think TGI Fridays at double the price. Nevertheless, it's a popular party spot, and by 11 p.m. the place is packed with cell-phone-toting young Puerto Ricans and sunburned gringos. They have live music on Saturday evenings, and closing time occasionally stretches to near dawn.

■ Añasco

If you're anywhere near Añasco, stop in for excellent Italian food at **Capriccio,** 12 Manuel Malave St, ☎ 787-826-3387. Owner and chef Roberto Rivera came from the Horned Dorset Primavera, and now serves up his own menu of classic pastas and "exotic" meats like venison, buffalo and bear, at a quarter of the price. Specialties include spaghetti marechiano (pasta with scallops, oysters, shrimp and fish of the day) and beef tenderloin, with entrées ranging in price from $7 for simple pasta dishes to $42 for châteaubriand for two people. Reservations are required, which is rare even for the best restaurants in San Juan. Open Tuesday through Sunday, noon to 9 p.m.

■ Mayagüez

One of the few reasons to visit Mayagüez is **El Estoril** on Calle Méndez Vigo, ☎ 787-834-2288 – definitely a restaurant worth making a trip. The Portuguese-born owner has restored the wood-paneled bar, stucco walls and tiled floors. Waiters in coattails serve a wonderful selection of red wines in this carnivore's paradise. Look around, and most people are tucking into the châteaubriand ($42 for two people), and one taste of this melt-in-the-mouth steak will show you why. Most entrées are between $15 and $20. Across the street, sample coffee and cakes, including the celebrated *brazo gitano,* at the **Cafeteria Brazo Gitano**, 101 Calle Méndez Vigo. It's cheap and cheerful, and if you're interested in catching up on the local gossip, this apparently is the place to do it.

On Peral Street, the **Oyster Seafood Restaurant & Bar**, ☎ 787-831-3707, www.oysterbarpr.com, is open until 3 a.m., with live music on weekends, and six different ways to serve oysters.

El Castillo Restaurant, ☎ 787-831-7575, at the Mayagüez Resort and Casino, serves international and Caribbean food, with special features all week, brunch on Sundays ($22), a "seafood festival" on Fridays ($25) and a pianist from Tuesday through Saturday for dinner.

> **TIP:** *The specialty cake of Mayagüez – the **brazo gitano** (Spanish for "gypsy arm") – is a tubular jelly roll, most often made with guava paste. Best eaten with coffee, it makes a nice gift if you're invited to someone's home for dinner.*

■ Joyuda

More than 20 seafood restaurants along Carr. 102 make Joyuda Beach the seafood strip of the west. Each makes pretty much the same claim – "*famoso por sus mariscos frescos*" (famous for the freshest seafood), and there's little to choose between them save for the ambience. *Chillo* (snapper), *mero* (grouper) and *carrucho* (conch) will be familiar to anyone who's been in Puerto Rico for more than a couple of days. Seafood junkies might want to look out for the lesser-known and famously hideous-looking *chapín* (cowfish or trunkfish). Despite its reputation as one of the ugliest fishes in the sea, locals revere the sweet, tender meat and *chapín* is considered something of a delicacy.

As a rule of thumb, any restaurant that is packed is a good bet for tasty fare. **Restaurant Raitos,** ☎ 787-851-4487, is one of the best spots for outdoor eating, with spacious gazebos overlooking Isla Ratones. They claim to have the best seafood *empanadillas* on the strip – you'll have to decide for yourself.

One of the first restaurants you'll come to on Carr. 102 driving from Mayagüez is **Los Balcones**, ☎ 787-851-6216. It's a good lunch place serving seafood in a pretty flower garden. **El Bohio**, ☎ 787-851-2755, also on Carr. 102, is built on stilts and has an impressive fish menu. Beware the brutal air conditioning and head for the covered terrace outdoors. Entrées range from $13-$30 (for broiled lobster tail). One of the more up-market eateries is **Vista Bahia Restaurant**, ☎ 787-851-4140 or 851-0512, Carr. 102, where waiters dress like cruise ship crew and the atmosphere is one of nautical luxury. Seafood and fish dishes are upwards of $16, and they stock a large selection of wines.

Toward the south end of the Carr. 102 strip, the blue-and-white painted **Casa de la Playa**, ☎ 787-851-5924, is very informal and serves Mexican and seafood at reasonable prices. Be sure to try a plate of fried *chapín*, a personal favorite, which looks like chicken legs with fins. You'll dine at a wraparound sundeck, shaded by a huge ceiba tree, facing a small dock. Be sure to wear plenty of insect repellent at dusk (or ask for some at the bar) – the bugs are ferocious.

■ Boquerón

The town center is crammed with seafood restaurants and, although none stand out in terms of fine dining, you can bet on freshness and quality fish.

> **TIP:** Whatever you do, don't pass up the street-side stalls selling fresh **oysters** (and clams) near the marina end of town. Unlike their large relatives found elsewhere on the island (often imported from the States), these oysters grow in "sweet water," where freshwater and saltwater mix in equal parts. With river water from the Río Grande flowing into the nearby mangrove, the Boquerón area is the perfect habitat for these miniature, sweet-tasting oysters. Served live, they're $4 a dozen.

At the marina end of town, at Calle José de Diego 210, ☎ 787-851-0345, the **Bahía** stands out for its odd resemblance to a Swiss chalet. Live music is often performed at the permanent, street-level stage, and the restaurant upstairs serves *capitán* (hogfish), *chapín* (cowfish) and other seafood in a variety of ways. Most entrées are between $10 and $15.

A local Dutch carpenter recommended **Galloway's** (next door to Club Nautico), ☎ 787-254-3302, but warned us it was "very expensive but great." Actually, the food is no more expensive than other places in town. But the dining room extends over the water, which could perhaps make it seem more expensive. Come here for *asopao* (gumbo) and the sunset. Dishes range from $7 to $21 for a mixed seafood platter.

Nightlife

■ Rincón

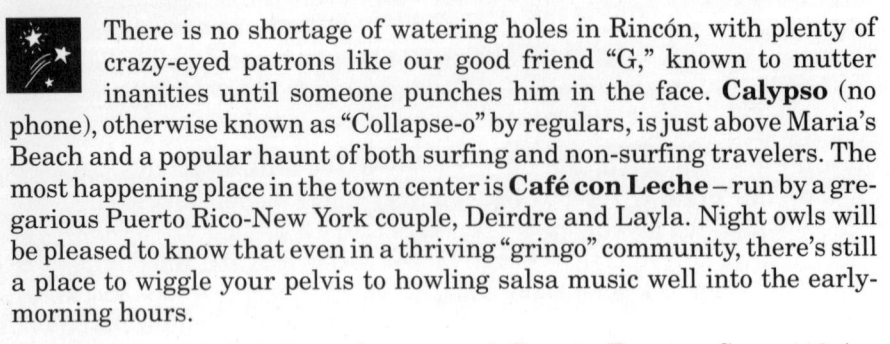

There is no shortage of watering holes in Rincón, with plenty of crazy-eyed patrons like our good friend "G," known to mutter inanities until someone punches him in the face. **Calypso** (no phone), otherwise known as "Collapse-o" by regulars, is just above Maria's Beach and a popular haunt of both surfing and non-surfing travelers. The most happening place in the town center is **Café con Leche** – run by a gregarious Puerto Rico-New York couple, Deirdre and Layla. Night owls will be pleased to know that even in a thriving "gringo" community, there's still a place to wiggle your pelvis to howling salsa music well into the early-morning hours.

The **Puesta del Sol Guesthouse and Sports Bar**, on Carr. 413 (no phone) just above Calypso, has a casual atmosphere, four pool tables and occasional live music on weekends. Rafi, the owner, plans a disco upstairs. Farther up the hill on Carr. 413, **Brisas Bar** (no phone) has more pool tables, and is rarely so crowded that you have to wait to play. The best sunset-viewing spot in town is **La Cima Burger** (no phone) with magnificent views of Mona and Monito islands on a clear day. Getting there is a steep drive up Carr. 4412 and Carr. 4411, but well worth it. Burgers, fried seafood and rum and beer are about the only things on the menu. Open daily from noon to 10 p.m.

South Coast

On the lee side of the island, shielded by the Cordillera Central, the south coast sweeps across a hot, arid strip of land between the base of the mountains and the Caribbean Sea. The island's second largest and second most important city, **Ponce**, grew up with very different traditions and history than its northern rival San Juan, and has recently undergone an excellent renovation of its historic center. Although some of the other coastal towns have fallen victim to thoughtless development, the south contains some excellent mangroves in **Parguera** and **Salinas** and, in **Guánica**, one of the world's best examples of the rare type of ecosystem known as subtropical dry forest. Excellent opportunities abound for hiking, windsurfing, scuba diving and exploring unspoiled offshore cays that emerge from transparent waters. Delve into the rich history of Ponce, visit crumbling remnants of the once-mighty sugar industry of the south, or explore the salt flats and mangrove estuaries of the Jobos Bay research reserve. With many adventures little more than an hour's drive from San Juan, a visit to the south coast is well worth the trip.

IN THIS CHAPTER
- San Germán
- La Parguera
- Ponce
- Caja de Muerto
- Coamo & the Hot Springs
- Salinas
- Aguirre
- Guayama
- Arroyo
- Patillas

Getting Here & Getting Around

From San Juan, the most direct route to the South Coast is **Hwy. 52**, and once you're out of the Río Piedras area it's clear sailing on the scenic toll road through the Cordillera Central. You can cross the island north to south in about 45 minutes and be all the way to Ponce in just over an hour. Although it may seem tempting to circle around the eastern or western coasts via **Hwy. 3** or **Hwy. 2**, both routes promise long stretches of traffic-light nightmare. Even the trip from San Juan to San Germán is twice as fast on highways 52 and 2 than via the northern coast.

■ Rental Car Agencies & Taxis

Apart from several taxi companies in Ponce, you will find it nearly impossible to get a cab in the more remote regions of the south coast. In Ponce call **Borinquen Taxi Cab**, ☎ 787-843-6000, on Calle Roosevelt, **Degetau**

Taxi Cab, ☎ 787-840-7555, at the corner of Calle Victoria and Calle Molina, **Ponce Taxi**, ☎ 787-842-3370, on the corner of Calle Méndez Vigo and Calle Villa, and **Taxi Union**, ☎ 787-840-9126, at the Centro del Sur Shopping Center.

■ Públicos

Two companies operate on the South Coast. **Choferes Unidos de Ponce**, ☎ 787-764-0540, which travels in and around Ponce, and **Línea Boricua**, ☎ 787-765-1908, which serves interior municipalities, including Lares, Jayuya, Utuado and San Sebastián. Call to check on travel times and destinations and let them know where you're staying. They will often take you door-to-door.

Communications & Information Sources

In Ponce, you can check e-mail and surf the 'Net just south of Ponce City Hall at **Navacom1**, on the corner of calles Concordia and Luna, ☎ 787-984-2169. They're open every day except Sunday from 8 a.m. to 8 p.m. In San Germán, **Password Internet Café**, on Plaza Santo Domingo facing the Porta Coeli, ☎ 787-892-4485, fax 892-4625, www.password.com, has 14 terminals and a lively student scene. Open until midnight, it costs $3 for half an hour.

Post offices are in all major towns. In **Ponce**, the USPS is at 819 Ave. Hostos and at 2340 Ave. Eduardo Ruberte; in **Guánica**, the office is at 39 Calle 13 de Marzo, Suite 101.

Ponce has two **tourism offices** on Plaza Las Delicias, one on the first floor of Fox Delícias Mall, ☎ 787-843-0465, and another above Citibank, ☎ 787-841-8044. At the latter, Judith Santos has extensive knowledge of the city and can give you the scoop on just about everything else on offer in Ponce.

Ponce's Spanish-language newspaper, *La Perla del Sur*, is good for up-to-date local information on what's going on in town. You can occasionally find the *Ponce Star* (an offshoot of the *San Juan Star*) in English, and most information at tourist sights is available in both English and Spanish. A couple of bookstores on Calle Isabel stock English-language magazines and newspapers.

Crash Boat Beach on Puerto Rico's West Coast. (PRTC)

A tranquil beach on Culebra Island. (PRTC)

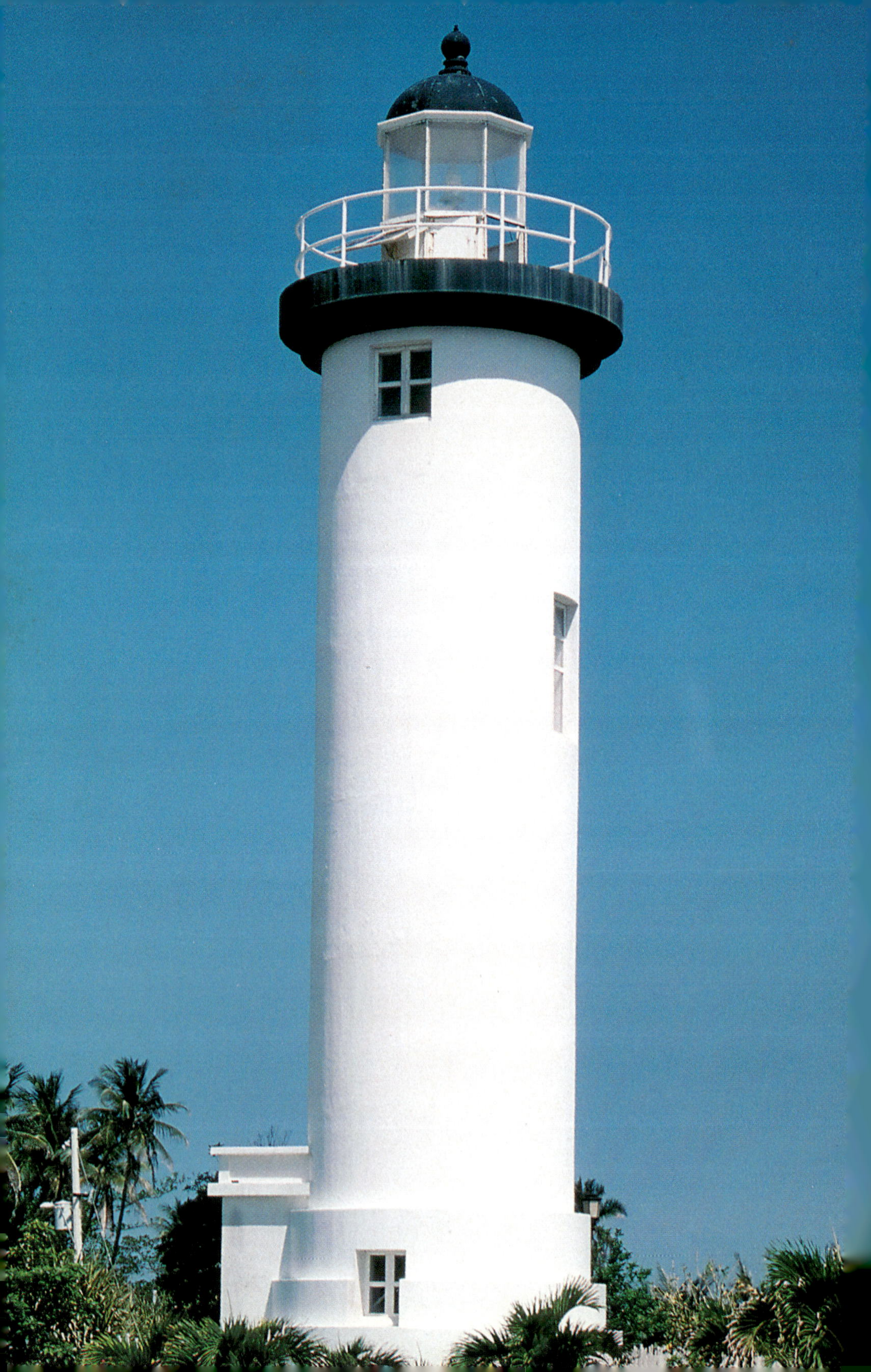

Above: *One of the many lechoneras in the Guavate area.* (© Len Kaufman, PRTC)
Opposite: *The Punta Higüero lighthouse at Rincón.* (© Len Kaufman, PRTC)
Below: *Revelers in costume at the Hatillo Festival of the Masks.* (Sandra Reus)

Above: *The colorful Parque de Bombas in Ponce.* (PRTC)
Opposite: *A house on Vieques Island.* (Joe Colon, PRTC)
Below: *Dancers at a folkloric festival in Ponce.* (Bob Krist, PRTC)

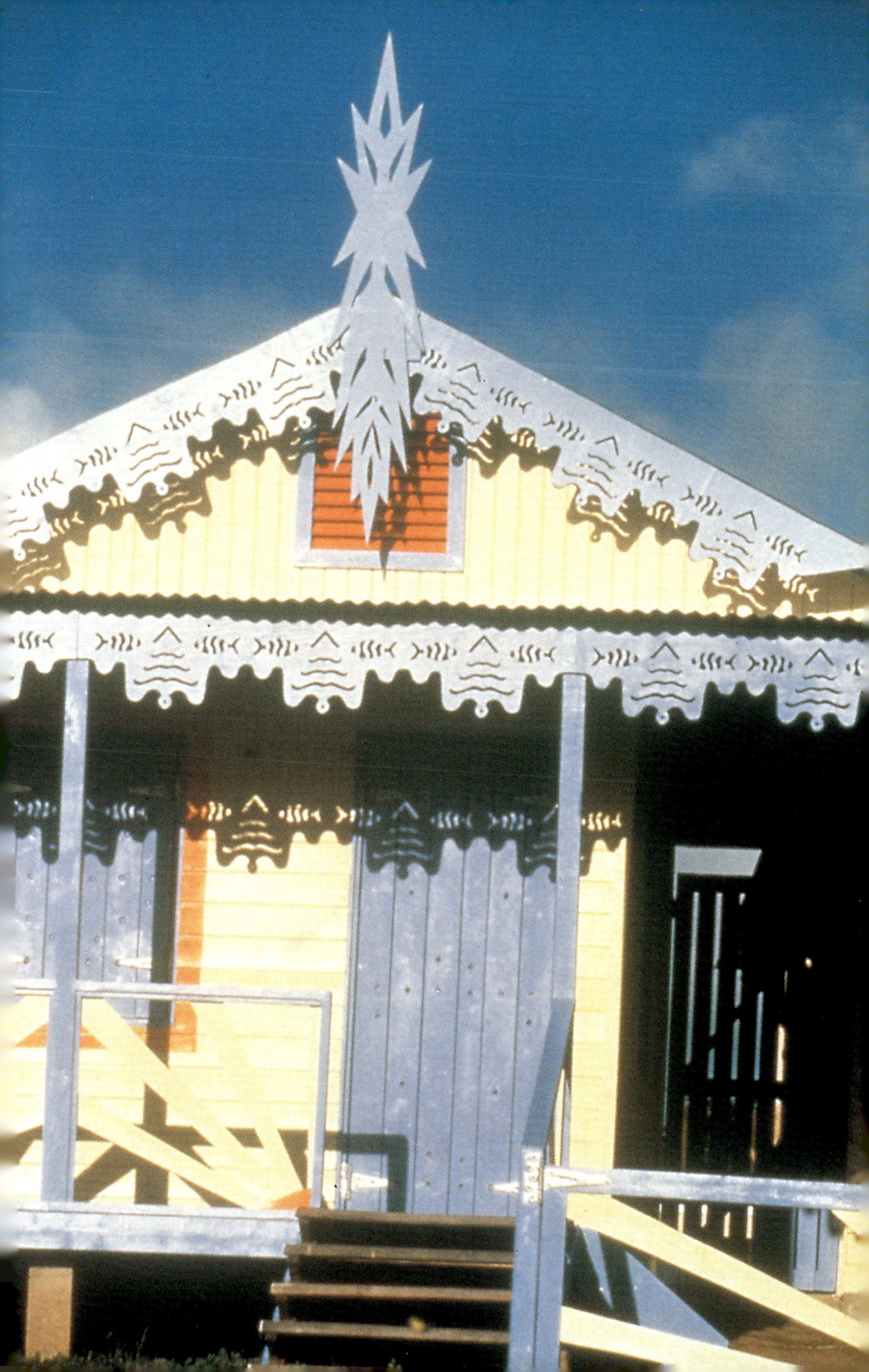

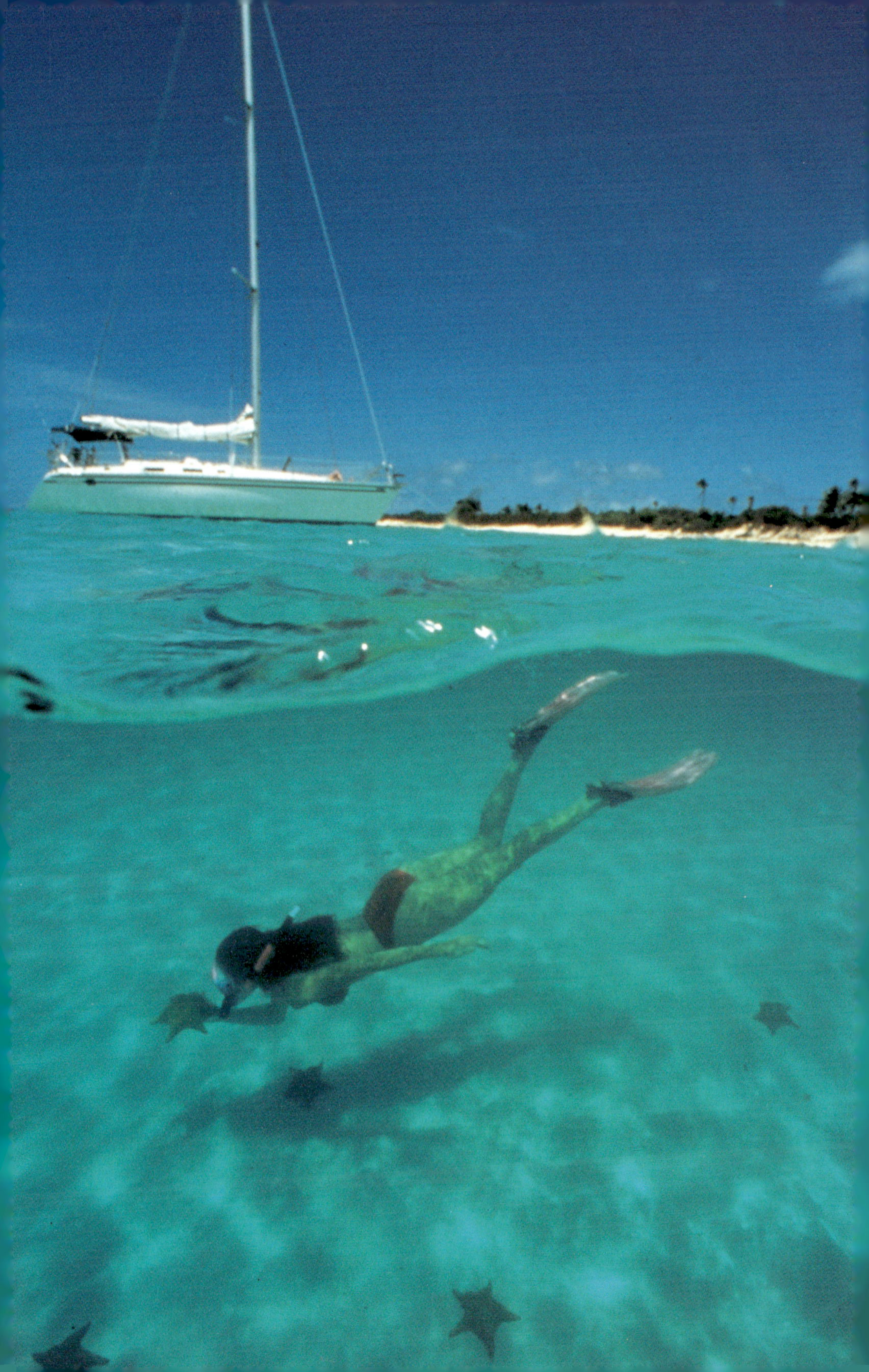

Above: *Plaza Mercado in San Juan.* (© Joe Colon, PRTC)
Opposite: *Snorkeling in Puerto Rico's crystal clear waters.* (PRTC)
Below: *A sentry box at El Morro.* (PRTC)

Above: *San Juan Gate.* (Bob Krist, PRTC)

Below: *Old San Juan.* (PRTC)

Públicos ■ 217

South Coast

10 MILES
16 KM

1. Porta Coeli Museum; Casa Morales Lugo; Plaza Francisco Quiñoñes; Catedral de San Germán de Auxerre; Casa de Ponce de León; Botanica San Miguel
2. Bahia Fosforescente (Phosphorescent Bay)
3. Bosque Estatal de Guánica (Guánica Forest)
4. Bosque Estatal de Susúa
5. Caja de Muertos (Coffin Island) Nature Reserve
6. Hacienda Buena Vista
7. Parque Ceremonial Indigena Tibes
8. El Vigia; Castillo Serrallés
9. Coamo Hot Springs
10. Campamento Santiago (Puerto Rico National Guard) Albergue Olimpico
11. Bosque Estatal de Aguirre
12. Jobos Bay National Estuarine Research Reserve
13. Casa del Gobernador
14. Casa Cautiño
15. Patronato del Museo Antigua Aduana; El Malecón (Boardwalk)

© 2001 HUNTER PUBLISHING, INC

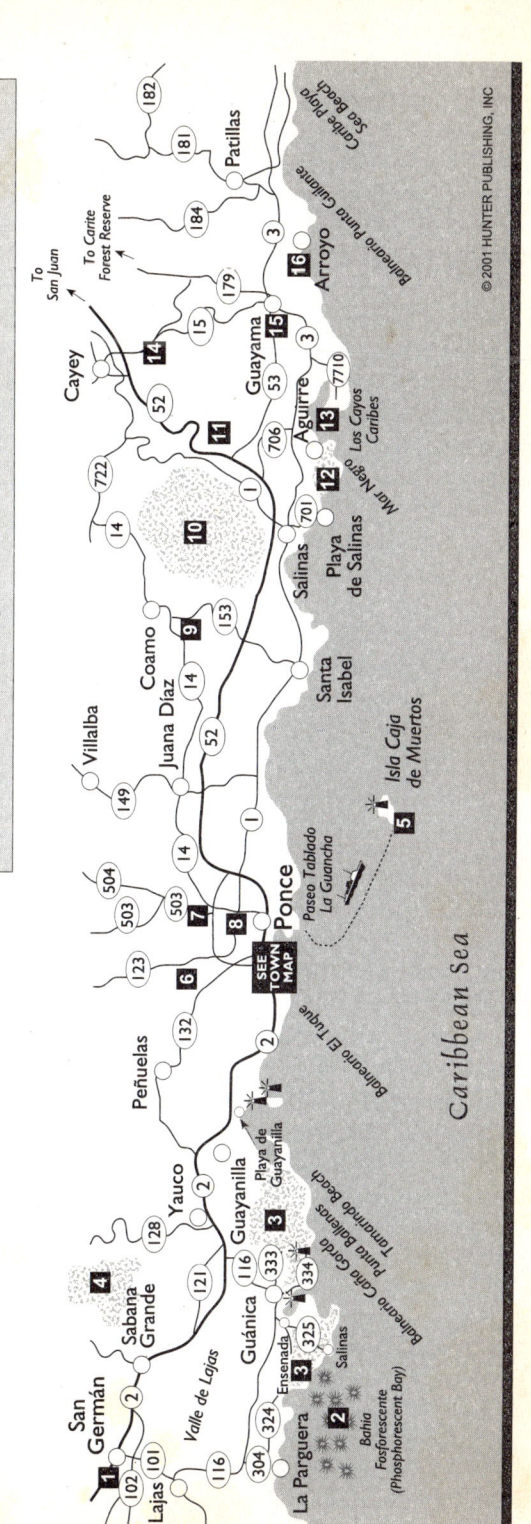

Touring & Sightseeing

■ San Germán

San Germán is Puerto Rico's second-oldest municipality and one of its most handsome. Residents often refer to their city, which is surrounded by lush green peaks, as *Ciudad de las Lomas* (City of Hills). Although it has been described as Mediterranean in flavor, the atmosphere is more like a wealthy version of an Andean town. Its array of architectural styles – from baroque, neo-classical, Victorian and Art Deco crossed with Creole and colonial structures – earns San Germán a deserved place on the National Register of Historic Places. The only other spot on the island to have earned this title is Old San Juan. Unlike Old San Juan, San Germán is quiet as a grave, receives few visitors and guards its secrets well. Many of its best sights can be viewed only from the outside. So with the exception of a couple of small museums – including **Porta Coeli**, the oldest church in the Caribbean – there is little to do here but stroll the tired cobblestone streets and try to conjure the town's rich history since its foundation in 1512.

History

In 1528, French attackers hoping to gain a foothold in Puerto Rico razed the little settlement of San Germán. After Spanish soldiers ousted the French, Dominican priests founded a monastery on the foundations of the village in 1543, and began providing education and health care – luxuries unavailable to common settlers – to rural farmers in exchange for food. This secured the resurrection of San Germán, which quickly gained a reputation as an oasis of civilization in the island's wild west. By 1573, settlers had christened the site **San Germán del Nuevo**, partly in a nod to Germaine de Foix, the second wife of King Ferdinand of Spain. Throughout the 17th and 18th centuries, the dynamic presence of the Dominican monks allowed **Porta Coeli** to prosper as a church and cultural center and, with its holdings in sugarcane, cattle and property, the monastery-based town began to attract aristocrats and wealthy landowners. By the turn of the 19th century, however, the monastery had lost much of its wealth due to a series of hurricanes and poor harvests. In 1812, monks petitioned the Spanish court to turn Porta Coeli into a university for scholars who could not afford to journey to Spain or Hispaniola, only to have the idea rejected. Penniless, the monks finally abandoned the monastery that had spawned the town. During the years to follow, municipal leaders floated several ideas for the use of Porta Coeli, including a misguided proposal to use it as a district jail. This incensed the people of San Germán, and the plan never came to fruition. By 1866, the monastery stood in ruins. Today, all that remains is the small chapel and part of the front wall, which still hold center stage in front of the town's main plaza.

Sights

A mosaic ground map on **Plazuela San Germán** clearly defines the municipalities and layout of the territory around San Germán in 1514. Walk uphill from here and you'll stand on the red bricks and blue cobbles of **Plaza Santo Domingo**, home to Porta Coeli and the center of a nearly forgotten era of wealth and opportunity. The **Museo de Arte Religioso Porta Coeli** is more impressive as the only remaining relic of the Dominican monastery and as one of the best examples of Colonial missionary architecture in the Americas, rather than for its small collection of religious items. Restored for use as a chapel in 1878, Porta Coeli was recognized as a historic monument in 1930. Lightning struck the chapel in 1948, seriously damaging the roof and causing city patriarchs to undertake permanent protection of the building. Bishop Eduard MacManus eventually donated it to the commonwealth of Puerto Rico for a dollar. The carved wooden altar was hewn in the 17th century, decorated with gold leaf until the 19th century, and still rests beneath the chapel's heavy beams of black mahogany, laurel and ausubo. Items of note include two icons of the revered virgin Nuestra Señora de Monserrate and a collection of life-size wooden *santos*.

Porta Coeli Church in San Germán. (PRTC)

Next to Porta Coeli, the Queen Anne-style **Casa Morales Lugo,** identified by a small brass placard as the private residence of Morales Lugo, is one of the finest examples of Victorian influence you are likely to see on the island. It has been occupied by Waldemar Lugo – one of Puerto Rico's preeminent artists (see his work at the Museo de Arte de Ponce) – for the past 55 years. You can't go in, but if you're lucky you might see him at work under the gables of his downstairs terrace. Walk one more block uphill to come face to face with the cathedral that presides over the shady garden of **Plaza Francisco Quiñones** and the somewhat eerie silence that characterizes the plazas of San Germán. Founded in 1739, the **Catedral de San Germán de Auxerre**, far more opulent than Porta Coeli's humble chapel, is particularly notable for a luscious trompe l'oeil fresco that graces the main nave. It is still an active parish.

The former home of Puerto Rico's first governor, **Casa de Ponce de León**, at 13 Calle Dr. Santiago Veve, has been continually occupied since it was built in the 17th century, and like the other historic *casas* of San Germán is closed to the public, although the municipality has proposed turning the Ponce de León house into a museum. Call the **San Germán City Hall**, ☎ 787-892-3500, for more information.

Up for a bit of mystical apothecary healing? Check out **Botanica San Miguel**, also on Calle Dr Santiago Veve. To many local residents, Israel, the owner, is a latter-day magician who conjures powerful potions for any number of ailments and dispenses charms to bring love, luck or riches. "People even ask me for lottery numbers," he says with a wink. "And they win!"

Nightlife & Food

Until recently, the town center would metamorphose at night as students from the **Universidad Interamericana** poured in and partied long into the night. In 1996, however, town officials imposed a midnight curfew to reduce noise and drunken behavior, and now many of the bars are shuttered or gone, sending the young at heart elsewhere (to Mayagüez, Ponce and Hormigueros, for example) to get their kicks. Even in the student quarter (at the west end of Calle Luna), the most action you're likely to see is a couple of happy-hour bars serving $1 beers and the neon lights of various fast-food outlets. Night is as quiet as day. Travelers will likely find that San Germán warrants a few hours to soak up the atmosphere. Consider timing your visit around a lunch or dinner date at **Cilantro's** (see page 261) – one of our favorite restaurants on the island, and in itself worth a visit to the city.

A BREAST OF BREAD

Like many of Puerto Rico's major towns, San Germán has its particular culinary specialty – a fist of a bread loaf exuberantly nicknamed "titty" or "hooter" bread for its knobby appearance. Most of the *panaderías* sell it, but don't expect anything as nurturing as mother's milk. It's basically *pan de agua* in a different shape.

■ La Parguera

A once-quiet fishing village turned travel destination, La Parguera these days sees more polo shirt-clad tourists grappling marlin from the deck of a fancy Bertram than it does weather-hardened locals in paint-peeling sloops. The change happened over the past century, as word spread of a magical lagoon that lit up at night, and fishermen hung up their nets in favor of ferrying visitors to see the strange bioluminescence of the **Bahía Fosforescente** (Phosphorescent Bay). Others turned to renting out kayaks or boats by the hour for exploration of the elaborate mangrove channels surrounding the town. Though fishing is no longer the means of survival for the men and women of La Parguera, the **Fiesta de San Pedro**, honoring St. Peter, the patron saint of fishermen, continues to pack the town each June. Be sure to make reservations at guest houses long in advance if you plan to visit at this time of year. For specific dates, contact the Puerto Rico Tourism Company in Cabo Rojo, ☎ 787-851-7070/ 254-1922. Despite the laid-back, small-town feel of Parguera, a couple of its bars can get wild at night, especially during the weekend. La Parguera is basically young and fun, and has much more going for it than most other small towns on the south coast. Colorful and casual, with a variety of day-trips, scuba diving and eco-excursions to choose from, it promises few dull moments, and beaches in nearby Boquerón, Cabo Rojo and Guánica compensate for the fact that Parguera doesn't have its own stretch of sand.

Guánica & The Dry Tropical Forest

When American troops first landed in Guánica to claim Puerto Rico during the Spanish-American War in 1898, they found a charming little residential community jarringly surrounded by dry, twisted scrub bent submissively under a hostile sun. As they prepared to do battle and sweated buckets in their Sears-made uniforms, they probably failed to notice the peculiar beauty of the rare dry tropical forest environment, the abundant bird life or the bright desert flowers punctuating the dusty greenery. It wasn't until 1981 that the United Nations recognized the importance of this seemingly inhospitable environment and declared it a world biosphere reserve. Encompassing 9,900 acres, Guánica is considered one of the largest and best-preserved tracts of subtropical dry forest anywhere. Scientists estimate a mere 1% of the world's subtropical dry forest remains. With 36 miles of hiking trails, 28 lonely beaches and accessible offshore cays, diving, kayaking and one of the best spots on the island for windsurfing, there's enough here to keep you busy for at least a few days.

The gloomy, industrial town of Guánica, however, has very little to recommend itself to visitors. Bypass the town center as quickly as possible on Hwy. 2 and turn south on Carr. 116 (about halfway between Mayagüez and Ponce). This is a stunning drive across coastal savannah, with the gray-green hills of Guánica on the horizon. Many of the best places to stay (a couple are within the actual dry forest) and adventure sites are a bit tricky to find (see *Adventures* and *Where To Stay* in this chapter). No overnight trip to Guánica should end without a visit to the *barrio* locals call San Jacinto and a trip by skiff (or, better, by kayak or windsurf board) to **Gilligan's Island** and **Isla Ballena** (Whale Island). If you can get to the cays' southern side, you face the wide-open Caribbean on a desolate beach you can almost certainly claim as your own. Maybe because of the secluded atmosphere, the Guánica area attracts a disproportionate number of European travelers inclined to seek out secret getaways.

Bosque Estatal de Susúa

After a couple of days exploring Guánica under the relentless sun, you may be tempted to head to the nearest mountain forest on the map to cool off. The 3,000+ acres of the **Bosque Estatal de Susúa**, ☎ 787-833-3700, stretch from dry south to the more temperate uplands near San Germán and center around a rock called *La Serpentinita* (the Little Streamer), a broken black and green formation laced with various mineral deposits. There is some decent hiking, mountain biking and camping in the Susúa forest, but if you have time we recommend that you keep driving to the Bosque Estatal de Maricao, El Toro Negro (*Central Mountains*, page 273) or the Bosque Río Abajo (*North Coast*, page 137).

Ponce

The slander was vicious. Long before we first visited Ponce, friends in San Juan told us it is a city of carjacking, mugging and unspeakable sin. Blistering temperatures, fetid air and the lack of entertainment drive residents into a violent frenzy, they said. "You'll be raked across the coals! Tarred, feathered, hung in effigy!" If you hear such ridiculous bad-mouthing from *sanjuaneros*, don't believe a word. Ponce may not have quite the cosmopolitan vogue of San Juan, but it is extremely civilized, relatively safe and – with a surprising chic of its own and numerous attractions – justifies spending a couple of days enjoying the city known as *La Perla del Sur* (the pearl of the sea). The darling and recently restored historic quarter spreads outward from the **Plaza Las Delicias** no more than three or four blocks in either direction in a mix of architectural styles, predominantly neoclassical, art deco and colonial.

Unlike San Juan, Ponce is better geared to amblers than gamblers. Pedestrian streets like Paseo Atocha have in recent years bloomed with hip fashion retailers, market stalls and food vendors. Allow plenty of time for shopping excursions. The laid back *"mañana, mañana"* attitude of most *ponceños* means that even though there may be five or six shop assistants saying, "That shirt looks great on you!" it will still take half an hour to buy it. In the evening, take a stroll along *Callejón de Amor* (Little Street of Love), when flower sellers open for business and the scent of blossoms perfume the air. And, if you happen to be in town on the last Thursday of the month, Calle Isabel closes to traffic for *Noche Romántico* – a night of romance – when café and restaurant owners bring tables and chairs onto the streets, and musicians serenade lovers throughout the night.

History

Named after **Juan Ponce de León**, shipmate of Christopher Columbus and the island's first governor, Ponce is built on a level plain from which the central Cordillera mountains rise out of the Caribbean sea in dramatic blue-hued peaks. The first settlers were Catalonian adventurers who had established themselves near the seaside mouth of the Río Jacaguas, but were driven inland to present day Ponce in 1692, after persistent attacks from pirates and fearsome Caribe Indians. For the next century, for purposes of protection, Ponce was so well hidden from the coast that crews of passing ships – friend or foe – would sail past unaware of the city's existence. The town remained a backwater until 1801, when residents established a lookout post on the northern side of **El Vigía**, the hill overlooking the town, from which they could send messages to the municipal office that a nearby ship was either an enemy or a potential trading partner. Far from the watchful eye of San Juan officials, a fledgling contraband trade sprang into being in Ponce. In 1831, the San Juan-based governor granted permission for Ponce to open an actual harbor. Thus began a rivalry between Ponce and the capital that continues even today. In those days, perhaps anticipating a threat from the southern city, the governor restricted Ponce's trading rights to Spanish ships carrying Spanish goods in order to protect interests in San Juan. Undeterred, the residents of Ponce took matters into their own hands and, isolated from San Juan by the mountains of La Cordillera, quietly got rich by trading illegally with any ship that passed its way.

Throughout the 19th century, Ponce prospered in trade and agriculture, and local merchants basically ignored authorities and the taxation requirements of San Juan. Through sheer market force, the city became an integral part of Puerto Rico's fledgling economy, headed by dynasties like the **Serrallés** family, who helped build Ponce into a city of art and culture. The Ponce aristocracy, obsessed with beautifying the city in order to match progress in San Juan, imported great paintings, music and literature from Europe and commissioned European-trained architects to build lavish homes in the center of the city. Bursting with confidence fueled by wealth, Ponce began to exert an influence that reverberated throughout the island and lured intellectuals, politicians and journalists with its reputation for liberal, free-thinking ideas – a quality none too popular with Spanish loyalists in San Juan. Early impulses to throw off the yoke of Spanish sovereignty found sympathy here. It may be unsurprising, then, that when US soldiers arrived on the south coast in 1898, Ponce officials euphorically presented them with keys to the city. The welcome may have been premature, however. It was followed by a slow dive into tragedy. After the American invasion, the city's illegal trading practices were brought to an abrupt halt. Hurricanes devastated the coffee industry, and sugar prices plummeted. In 1918, an earthquake toppled many of Ponce's finest buildings. By the time the Great Depression took hold in the 1930s, Ponce was in such bad shape that the US military completely abandoned the city in lieu of the more promising port of San Juan. In its absence, an independence movement began to take root. The next time Ponce blipped across the international radar screen, it was the result of a festering discontent that led to the bloodiest event in modern Puerto Rican history.

THE PONCE MASSACRE

I shall never forget the photograph of those cadets... standing quietly with their hands at their sides waiting to be shot – defenseless but not one of them running away. – Arthur Garfield Hays, "Defending Justice in Puerto Rico," *The Nation*, June 5, 1937

On a sweltering evening in 1935, five young members of the Nationalist Party made their way to Ponce University, where conservative students were reportedly protesting pro-independence remarks made by Nationalist Party leader Pedro Albizu Campos. Whether or not their intention was peaceful, the young activists met a grisly end. They never made it to the gathering, and the bodies of four of them were later found murdered, apparently at the hands of the police. An official investigation into the crime went nowhere. Though details are sketchy, an apparent eye-for-an-eye revenge spree ensued. A year later, Insular Police Chief Colonel Riggs was assassinated. Two young men arrested for his killing were shot while in police custody. The scandal touched every resident of Puerto Rico and even some in the continental US. With both sides baying for blood, blame was placed on National Party leader Campos, who was sentenced to six years in prison for conspiracy to overthrow the government of the United States. On Palm Sunday, March 21, 1937, in a symbolic gesture to their cause, the Nationalist movement successfully sought permission from the Ponce mayor to march along Calle Marina in peaceful protest of Campos' imprisonment. The street filled with nationalist supporters cheering young cadets and bemoaning the imprisonment of their leader. Unbeknownst to them, Governor Blanton Winship overruled the permission at the last minute and sent his chief of police, Colonel Orbeta, to stop the demonstration.

Exactly what happened next is a matter of speculation. A shot was fired, and police, apparently believing the nationalists armed, opened fire into the crowd of citizens. When the volley ended, 21 people lay dead and another 200 or so, including six police officers, were injured. Governor Winship reported to his superiors in the US that the nationalists were entirely to blame for the massacre. A federal commission found otherwise. Photographs left no doubt as to the source of the gunfire: In grainy black and white, scenes depicting policemen armed with Tommy guns, revolvers, tear gas and grenades stood in stark contrast to the young protesters, ironically dubbed the "Army of Liberation," who were clad in Sunday-school dress, unarmed and defenseless. Although no one was ever officially indicted for the crime, Governor Winship left Puerto Rico soon afterwards and never returned. Within two years, Puerto Rico had its first locally elected governor, Luis Muñoz Marín. For a fuller account, check out the **Museo de la Masacre de Ponce**, Calle Marina, ☎ 787-844-9722, open Wednesday through Sunday from 8 a.m. to 4.30 p.m.

Nearly bereft of the exotic trades that made it great, Ponce has in the past 60 years relied on the less glamorous industries of plastics and cement to keep its economy intact. As it jealously regarded the fattening of San Juan on the proceeds of post-war tourism, Ponce withered in the heat and fell silent. Until 1985, that is, when Governor Rafael Herdandez Colón (encouraged by his son, the mayor of Ponce) allocated half a billion dollars to *Ponce en Marcha* (Ponce on the Move), a program to restore the historic quarter to its former glory. Despite political bickering, it has been largely successful and led to the completion of a new highway, the restoration of many of Ponce's historic buildings and a new wave of civic pride.

For a deeper understanding of the Ponce vibe, visit the Museo de la Historia de Ponce, which details the region's history from a 135-million-year-old rock to a sugar boomtown that lifted Puerto Rico from its economic knees. Sugar makes rum and rum made Puerto Rico. A short bus ride from the museum, the family home of **Don Juan Serrallés** (see page 229) the founder of Don Q rum, is now a museum, in a neighborhood of Beverly Hills-style villas overlooking the city. From here, it's easy to see why Ponce considers itself apart from the rest of Puerto Rico. North of the city, one of the most important archaeological discoveries in Puerto Rico's history – the **Tibes Indian Ceremonial Park** – (page 229) is still being excavated. While here, you can also hop on a ferry to **Caja de Muertos** (Coffin Island – page 253), an eco-travel destination where legends of golden caskets and jewels have lured treasure hunters for over 100 years.

The Central Plaza

Getting around town is now a theme park excursion, with a "toy" train for kids and old-fashioned trolleys that tour the historic quarter, to the port and into the hills. Both travel four different routes and tours last 1½-two hours. A trip around the city center in a horse-drawn buggy runs from 8 a.m. to 8 p.m., and is free of charge. Catch these "taxis" at the Casa Alcaldía on the main square, **Plaza Las Delicias**. Any tour of Ponce logically starts here, and a stroll around the plaza and surrounding area may be just as rewarding. There are plenty of cafés and, on the north side, an excellent ice cream shop. Beautifully restored build-

The Catedral de la Nuestra Señora de la Guadalupe.
(PRTC)

ings on the plaza include the **Casa Alcaldía** – which once served the more macabre purpose of incarceration and public execution. Under the flicker of gas lamps, the *Fuente de Leones* (Fountain of Lions) glows magically at night with rainbow-colored spotlights. The **Catedral Nuestra Señora de la Guadalupe** was inspired by stories of the miracles of the *Virgen de la Guadalupe* in Mexico and, despite occasional damage done by earthquakes and other disasters, the cathedral still stands unmoved in the plaza center, with twin steeples and "jeweled" domes pointing heavenwards into the Caribbean sky. Open 6 a.m. to 3.30 p.m. weekdays, and 6 a.m. to noon weekends, ☎ 787-842-0134.

The Firehouse & Other Historic Buildings

Brochure photos don't quite prepare you for the whimsical, yet somehow classy, *Parque de Bombas* (Fire Station), ☎ 787-284-3338 or 4141, ext 342. It must have been a startling sight when it was unveiled during the 1883 World Fair. The red and black Moorish moderne design was conceived as a crowd pleaser by Maximo de Meana y Guridi, a Spanish lieutenant, who became mayor the following year and gave it to the Fire Corps as the first fire station in Puerto Rico. Open 9.30 a.m. to 6 p.m. daily, entrance is free.

An example of a rich man's fancy, circa 1900, **Casa Armstong Poventud** is generally considered to be the most beautiful example of the French neoclassical style in the city. It's now the home of the **Instituto de Cultura Puertorriqueña Sur** (☎ 787-844-2540/2420) and is a good place to pick up more in-depth cultural information on the city. Open 9 a.m. to 5 p.m. weekdays.

One of the architectural treasures of Ponce, **Teatro La Perla**, ☎ 787-843-4399, on the corner of calles Cristina and Mayor Cantera, was designed in 1864 by an Italian architect Juan Bértoly Calderoni and, like many of the important buildings damaged during the 1918 earthquake, it has been lovingly and accurately restored. Four out of six original Corinthian columns are back in place. If you're in town for the evening, find out what's playing at the theater by stopping by the box office or checking listings section of the newspaper *La Perla del Sur* or the tourist office, which is open daily 8 a.m. to 4 p.m. Popular shows are often sold out.

The Best Of The Museums

Near to the theater, the **Museo de la Historia de Ponce**, ☎ 787-844-7071, is housed within two of Ponce's most prominent former homes, Casa Salazar and Casa Zapater, on Calle Isabel. Exhibits trace the social, cultural, political and economical development of Ponce through its 300-year history. Much of it is dedicated to Ponce's nonconformist role in Puerto Rican politics, but plenty of other interesting stories abound, especially if you visit the room full of yellowing newsprint. More than 200 newspapers have been published in Ponce since the first newspaper in Puerto Rico, *El*

Historic Ponce

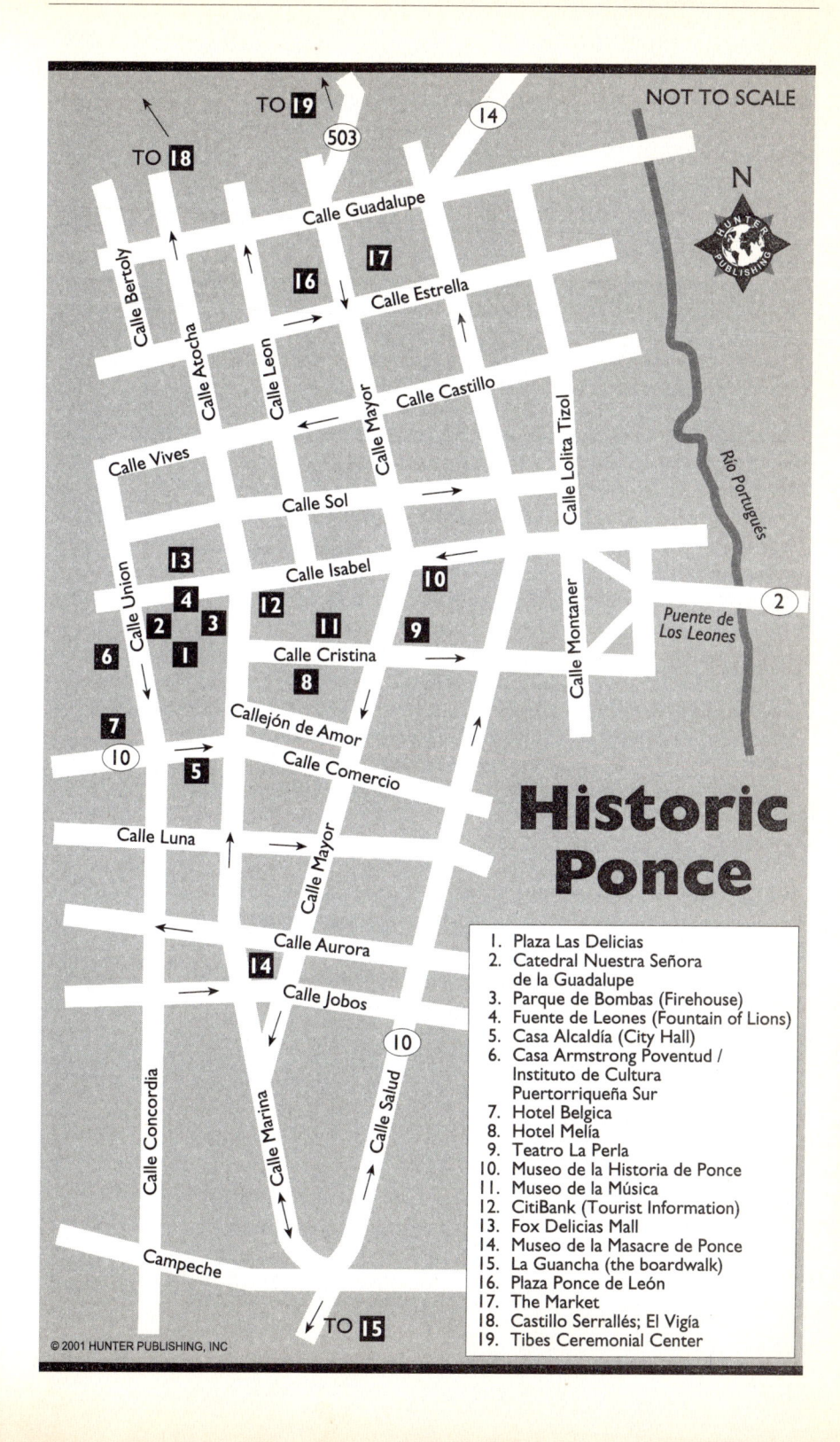

1. Plaza Las Delicias
2. Catedral Nuestra Señora de la Guadalupe
3. Parque de Bombas (Firehouse)
4. Fuente de Leones (Fountain of Lions)
5. Casa Alcaldía (City Hall)
6. Casa Armstrong Poventud / Instituto de Cultura Puertorriqueña Sur
7. Hotel Belgica
8. Hotel Melía
9. Teatro La Perla
10. Museo de la Historia de Ponce
11. Museo de la Música
12. CitiBank (Tourist Information)
13. Fox Delicias Mall
14. Museo de la Masacre de Ponce
15. La Guancha (the boardwalk)
16. Plaza Ponce de León
17. The Market
18. Castillo Serrallés; El Vigía
19. Tibes Ceremonial Center

Ponceño, was first published in 1852. For an in-depth look at Puerto Rican history, this is an unbeatable place to start. We highly recommend taking a tour with one of the well-informed and bilingual guides. The museum is open every day except Tuesday, from 10 a.m. to 6 p.m. Entrance costs $3 adults, $1 children.

Occupying most of Calle Salud, the **Museo de La Música Puertorriqueña**, ☎ 787-848-7016, is a must for anyone interested in the evolution of Puerto Rican music, with exhibits showcasing instruments and memorabilia of Taino, African and Spanish cultures and explaining the development of distinctive island grooves such as *bomba y plena* and *la danza*. It also sets the record straight on issues such as the origins of salsa music. It's open 9 a.m. to 4 p.m., Wednesday to Sunday. Admission is free.

The collection of European art at the **Museo de Arte de Ponce**, Las Américas Avenue, ☎ 787-848-0505 or 840-1510, fax 841-7309, www.museoarteponce.org, is probably the largest and most impressive in the Caribbean. Donated from the private collection of former Governor Luis A. Ferré, the permanent exhibition displays mainly European works spanning at least five centuries from medieval masters to the pre-Raphaelite movement. The highlight for most visitors is Lord Leighton's *Flaming June*, which, along with Burne-Jones' *The Sleep of King Arthur* and others, represents a solid collection of British masters. The brooding spectacle of *The Choosing of the Bride* by Makovski looms off the wall – Russian to the core! In the Puerto Rican collection, especially notable is the 1931 masterpiece *La Terraza* by Myrna Buez. You can easily lose yourself for a couple of hours here, so allow enough time. Open daily from 10 a.m. to 5 p.m.; $4 for adults, $2 for children under 12.

The Market

Like Barcelona in Spain, Ponce is a seaside city, presided over by a giant cross on a hill, that built its own beach, and has a history of bloody clashes between its resident free-thinkers and more conservative forces from a faraway capital city. The outdoor market of **Plaza Ponce de León**, ☎ 787-284-4141, hints at the Catalan soul of Ponce as it bursts with vendors selling fruits, vegetables, flowers and knickknacks. This is a good place for a cheap lunch on the go. Often referred to locally as *Plaza de los Perros* (plaza of the dogs), it used to be a meat market overrun with stray dogs scavenging for scraps and bones. City officials kicked out the dogs in 1992 and gave the plaza a face-lift. A local hangout, it provides great people watching and photo ops, located between Calle Mayor and Calle León. It seemed like a cruel blow of fate that the Caribbean town lacked its own beach, so during the renovation program several million dollars were spent to build a sandy *balneario* for beach bums, complete with a wooden boardwalk – **La Guancha** – lined with food stands and boisterous bars that pump out live salsa on weekends. During the week it's ghostly quiet.

El Vigía

Overlooking the town, El Vigía was once a crucial hilltop lookout post for spotting ships at sea. Although it is crowded with upper-class homes today, the views over the city and out to sea are still awesome. If you feel so inspired, you may climb to the top of a monstrous concrete cross, **La Cruzette del Vigía**, for $3. Or you can head downhill and see nearly the same view over a cup of coffee, from the far more pleasant surroundings of the Don Juan Café terrace at the Serrallés mansion.

The House That Rum Built

The over-the-top splendor of the **Castillo Serrallés**, ☎ 787-259-1774, fax 259-3464, demonstrates just how vast was the class divide during the Depression. Built during the 1930s for the powerful Don Q Rum dynasty – the Serrallés family – the mansion is a splendid example of the Spanish Revival period. It took four years to build – two of which were dedicated entirely to the exquisite details of the dining room – and cost the equivalent of about $85,000 to construct. Today it is estimated to be worth between $17 and $25 million. Doña Rosita, the granddaughter of Don Juan Serrallés, lived here until 1986, but eventually decided that the house was too big and sold it to the government for the bargain sum of $400,000, on condition it be turned into a museum. From the oldest piece in the mansion (a 16th-century table), to the still-functioning early British refrigerator, to Doña Rosita's wardrobe laid out by her bedside as though she had just gone to the kitchen for coffee, the details of daily life have been immaculately preserved. A small museum exhibit pays homage to the rum business that not only built the Serrallés fortune, but also turned the island's economy around. Though best known for rum, the Don Q distillery also produces wine and a delicious butterscotch-flavored liqueur called Don Juan, as well as something they proclaim to be vodka ("We call it Nikolai Vodka," our tour guide said with a straight face, "The only vodka in the world made from 100% sugarcane!"). Opening hours are Tuesday and Thursday, 9.30 a.m. to 5 p.m.; Friday, Sunday and public holidays, 9.30 a.m. to 5.30 p.m. Entrance fees are $3 for adults, $1.50 for children. Tours in Spanish or English last about 45 minutes.

Tibes Indian Ceremonial Park

In 1975, floods caused by Hurricane Eloise washed away layers of topsoil north of Ponce, revealing an Indian ceremonial site dating back to AD 700. Only five of 35 designated acres have so far been fully excavated, revealing ceremonial plazas, or *bateyes*, used by Tainos for ritual ball games similar to soccer. Also uncovered was a star-shaped formation of flat stones laid out in triangles pointing directly to the sunrise and the sunset during solstice and equinox, the meaning of which remains unclear. So far, around 140 skeletons have been dug up, most of which were found buried in the fetal position – a practice typical of the Igneri, Pre-Taino and Taino Indians who believed in reincarnation. No further digs are planned for the immediate future, although new research has detected remains of villagers' homes that, if excavated, could help establish the size of the population.

A tour of the Tibes Indian Ceremonial Park, ☎ 787-840-2255 or 5685, fax 841-0105, begins with an eight-minute video, in Spanish with English subtitles, about the discovery of the site. Pottery, agricultural tools, jewelry and other artifacts on display in a well-designed museum shed light on the cultures of the Igneri, pre-Taino and Taino civilizations. The tour continues through botanical gardens leading to a *yucayeque* (village) replica consisting of thatched *bohíos* (huts) and a *caney* (chief's "palace"), and eventually to the excavation site. Open Tuesday through Sunday, from 9 a.m. to 4 p.m., it costs $2 for adults, $1 for children. To get there, take Carr. 503 north of Ponce, then follow the signs.

Hacienda Buena Vista

Probably the best place to get a sense of 19th-century hacienda life in Puerto Rico is **Hacienda Buena Vista**, ☎ 787-722-5882 (reservations), 284-7020 (information). It was built in 1833 by members of the Vives family, who escaped to Puerto Rico during the Venezuelan revolutionary war with plenty of capital. Initially farmed by slaves, the Vives estate thrived, producing bountiful crops of cacao, corn, plantains, pineapples and coffee. Toward the end of the century, Señor Vives and his son Carlos were some of the first hacienda owners in Puerto Rico to use the new tools of the Industrial Revolution, and transformed the 500-acre estate into one of the most sophisticated working farms on the island. It fell into decline after WWII, however, and the hacienda was sold to the government in the 1950s. The Conservation Trust of Puerto Rico acquired it in 1984. Along with a splendid view from the estate house, the hacienda contains about 90 acres of sub-tropical forest on the banks of the Río Cañas, now a sanctuary for different birds and other wildlife. Visitors get the whole nine yards, as they are led through the main house, the slave quarters and the stables, to a semi-interactive tour of 19th-century agricultural tools. All of the machines on display here have been restored to full working order, including a revolutionary water mill that single-handedly doubled productivity on the farm, and corn and coffee mills. You can even try your hand at grinding coffee beans the old-fashioned way. The hacienda is open Wednesday through Sunday, but visits require a reservation. Spanish tours start at 8.30 a.m. and 10.30 a.m.; English language tours begin at 1.30 p.m. The cost is $5 for adults, $2.50 for senior citizens and $2 for children under 12. To get here, follow Carr. 10 north toward Adjuntas for about 10 minutes, and look for the signs.

Festivals & Events

Ponceños celebrate a festival of some sort every month of the year except April and August. The downtown tourist office (above Citibank) provides a full list of these, but here are some of the best. Call the tourist office (☎ 787-841-8044) for more information.

- **Carnaval** (mid- to late Feburary) – Revelers come from all over Puerto Rico to join the Ponce Carnaval the week before Ash Wednesday. The celebration dates back to when slaves and workers living near the harbor began painting their faces in garish colors to ward off demons and promote a more fruitful harvest. Over the decades, the rest of the citizenry of Ponce began to join in, adding characteristics of their own such as the crowning of the Carnaval Queen and *La Danza* (Ballroom Dancing) competitions. But it is the African-inspired festivities that set the tone from day one, with the arrival of *El Rey Momo* (Lord of Mischief), who remains disguised behind a magnificent and usually ridiculous papier-mâché mask until the last day, when the crowd may take a stab at guessing his identity. Day two kicks off with the *baile de los vejigantes* (dance of the devils), who also clad themselves in brightly colored masks that spout numerous devilish horns, and charge through the streets flapping like giant bats. Traditionally this was the exclusive privilege of the men and boys, but recent years have seen more and more girls donning their own devilish disguises. By Sunday, the historic quarter erupts with full force, as floats representing towns from all over Puerto Rico, *vejigantes*, dancers and musicians parade through the streets. Finally, Carnaval ends the way it first began, as a harvest festival. With any crop-destroying demons well banished, the ceremony turns to a ritual sardine burial (in this case, a papier-mâche fish in a paper coffin), symbolizing fertilization of the soil.

THE MAD BLADDER

The term *vejigante*, used for the devilish carnival participants in Ponce and in Loíza, originally comes from the Spanish word *vejiga*, meaning "bladder." Apparently, the revelers of yesteryear filled animal bladders (especially those of "a cloven-hoofed animal," according to tradition) with air or seeds and used these sacks to clobber unsuspecting onlookers.

- **Fiesta Nacional de La Danza** (around May 6) – One of the most formal fiestas in the Puerto Rican calendar, *La Danza* is a treat for fans of ballroom dancing. Dressed in their most elegant attire – ladies in silk and satin, gentlemen in coat and tails – couples swirl under a moonlit Plaza Las Delicias to celebrate the birthday of *La Danza* "founder" Juan Morel Campos. The local style of ballroom dancing became popular during the 1930s, when Campos was the leader of Ponce's municipal band, and the festival is usually held on or around Campos' birthday, May 6.

- **Fiestas de Bomba y Plena** (November) – This is a wonderful opportunity to witness two distinct styles of Puerto Rican music – *bomba*, a heavily African-influenced style that involves a sort of duel between drummer and dancer, and *plena*, a Spanish-influenced gossip and news bulletin expressed through music. *Plena* undoubtedly began in Ponce, while Loíza and Ponce both claim heritage rights for *bomba*. But places don't own art, people do, and the important thing is that if you make it to this festival you'll be hip-swinging all the way home.

- **Parada de Luces** (November) – If you happen to be visiting with your brood in November, this new festival (the first one was in 1999) is especially for the children of Ponce, and features cabaret dancing, clowns, lots of lights, fireworks and fun activities of the high-pitched-squeal variety.

- **Fiesta Patronales and holiday festivities** (December) – Around the holidays, the Puerto Rican penchant for partying hits full swing, and nowhere more so than in Ponce. The patron saint festival honoring the Virgin of Guadalupe kicks off in early December, followed by Las Mañanitas on December 12, when musicians march through the town center at 4 a.m. and the entire town comes out to join a procession to the cathedral. Religious events with a street party appeal take place throughout the month, culminating in the impressive *Concierto de Navidad* (Christmas Concert) and mass. *Ponceños* claim that their city has the most beautiful Christmas lights on the island.

Shopping in Ponce

Two shops worth browsing for gifts or souvenirs are located on Plaza las Delicias. **Utopía**, ☎ 787-848-8742, stocks all manner of Puerto Rican crafts (and many South American ones), along with a small selection of gourmet preserves and locally made candies. This is also a good place to buy Ponce carnival masks, which range in price from less than $10 for the smallest to $700 and up for the largest and most complex. Across the street, **Mi Coquí** sells fun gifts such as painted wooden ornaments, hammocks and grinning ceramic coquí frogs.

Isla Caja de Muertos

Driving toward Ponce from the east or west, you'll notice a large cay off the southern coast called Isla Caja de Muertos, or Coffin Island. A nature reserve, it is seldom visited by Puerto Ricans and even less so by foreigners. But it's a perfect day-trip for nature lovers and sun worshippers alike.

LEGENDS OF COFFIN ISLAND

Though there are several stories of how the island got its name (one is that an early French explorer, believed its outline looked like a coffin on a table), the most interesting involves the 19th-century Portuguese pirate, José Almeida. A former wine merchant, Almeida fell in love with a Basque lady in Curaçao, married her in St. Thomas and took her pirating with him. On their first raid, however, she refused to remain in safety below deck and was killed by a stray bullet. The distraught Almeida had her embalmed and placed in a glass box inside a copper coffin. He buried her in a cave on a deserted island near Ponce and, according to the legend, returned each month to gaze on her preserved corpse and leave part of his treasure in her grave. Almeida was caught on the Puerto Rican mainland in 1832, tried and executed by the firing squad at El Morro. Many years later, it is said, a Spanish engineer discovered the empty glass-and-bronze coffin in the cave and, identifying the cay on a map, gave it its name. If treasure was ever found here, it was kept secret.

The island was reportedly once used as a secret meeting place for about a dozen Masons, until an 1887 decree by the Spanish crown let the group meet openly. Throughout history, though, the most regular visitors to Caja de Muertos have been seabirds and hawksbill turtles, which have found the tranquil cay a safe place to lay their eggs. Since 1981, the mile-long cay has been a state nature reserve, watched over by a biologist, a ranger and other staff at all times. Small groups of visitors come mostly on weekends, either by private boat or a single day charter, to enjoy the diving, snorkeling, nature watching and hiking up to the cave of Almeida the Portuguese and the lighthouse, with its incredible wraparound views of the aquamarine reef and southern shore of Puerto Rico.

■ Coamo Hot Springs

Hot springs have been found in several places in Puerto Rico, including Ponce and Arroyo, but the only site where you can plunge in and enjoy the mineral-rich waters is in the tiny municipality of Coamo. There is very little else in Coamo: a sub-par golf course and small museum in town dedicated to the history of the area are hardly worth mentioning, so forget we did. The Coamo Hot Springs are tucked away in the dusty foothills of the Cordillera Central, where Taino Indians used them long before the arrival of the Spanish, giving rise to the claim that these are the oldest hot springs on record in the Americas. The first colonial use of the springs dates back to 1571 and, according to the promotional lore, this is the fountain of youth that Juan Ponce de León was seeking. So it is somewhat ironic that he never found them, and instead went searching in Florida.

■ Salinas

Bordered by thick palm groves and thorny scrub that resembles the Guánica dry forest, with sea views through the vegetation, Carr. 1 into Salinas is inspiring either as a drive or bike ride. This somewhat makes up for the town of Salinas, which seems grubby, run-down and hopeless. However, Salinas does have one redeeming feature in the natural, old-school **Salinas Marina**, considered by many boaters to be the best port in Puerto Rico. Surrounded by mangrove cays, some of which have small sand beaches, the marina is a world unto itself.

> **TIP:** Fans of actor Kurt Russell will be pleased to learn that the movie Captain Ron *was filmed here, largely around Cayo La Matita. This is a source of a perhaps excessive local pride, so mention that you know this bit of trivia and make new friends!*

The Salinas Marina is a tightly knit yachting community, with many reclusive international sailors anchored just offshore for months or years at a time. On weekdays, you may not meet a soul at the marina, but on weekends the place fills with Puerto Rican party boaters. During hurricane season, the surrounding mangroves are a safe haven for boaters. Due to the diversity of those who drop anchor here, Salinas is a great place to come to look for passage to other Caribbean Islands, South America or even Europe, especially in springtime when sailing conditions are best. Puerto Rican cruisers mostly occupy the 100 or so slips, and if you're cash-poor you may have luck finding work shining up brass or chrome fittings, or carrying out general maintenance. To get to the marina, follow signs to Playa Salinas on Carr. 701. Something of a rabbit warren, the town seems to have been deliberately built in concentric circles for the purpose of confusing out-of-towners. Park behind a large concrete hotel called Marina de Salinas & Posada El Náutico.

■ Aguirre

A sugar town frozen in time, the "ghost town" of Aguirre is a curiosity on an island that is one of the most densely populated landmasses in the world. An abandoned cinema, hospital, bowling alley and other boarded-up buildings lend an eerie atmosphere to this former boomtown. At times, the only evidence that Aguirre is inhabited at all are the red-and-white power plant chimneys that poke up over the palm trees as you approach town on Carr. 705. The center of Aguirre reeks of history. The year after the Spanish-American war, investors from Boston chose this spot to build a sugar-plantation community, and constructed white clapboard mansions that appear airlifted from New England. To house local workers, they built squat gray housing on the other side of the main thoroughfare. In the early 20th century, it appeared the Bostonians had found their version of El Dorado – the mill at Hacienda Aguirre pumped out so much processed sugar that investors felt compelled to build a golf course to keep themselves occupied when they weren't gloating over receipts. They bought up 12 miles of local railway, two engines and 50 wagons to bring sugarcane from surrounding plantations. When productivity mushroomed to more than 12,000 tons of sugar per year in 1902, they bought out the French Railroad Company and its tracks that ran from Guayama to Ponce. Huge revenues from sugar fattened the pockets of the gringos throughout most of the first half of the century, but as profits gradually slid into losses in recent decades the *americanos* began to flee. The last American investors left Aguirre in 1990, and already the jungle is reclaiming some of its turf. Get here with a camera before most of this weird time capsule disappears.

The road to Aguirre.
(© 2000, Tara Stevens)

Among other things, you'll find decaying clapboard mansions set back from the road into town. The best preserved is **La Casona**, a lavish 14-room mansion with landscaped gardens and spectacular views of the bay from its wraparound balcony. It was built for the president of the sugar mill and is now the private weekend retreat of a Spanish television producer. Next door, enjoy similar views from the balcony of the crumbling **American Hotel**, originally built for visiting American executives. Its social club became the first bowling alley in Puerto Rico in the 1960s and is now the home to the **Jobos Bay Natural Estuarine Research Reserve Visitors Center** (see *Eco-Travel* section).

Before it was abandoned, the town also had a hospital, movie theater, marina and Puerto Rico's oldest golf course, which is one of the only businesses still operating. Over the hill from Aguirre's town you'll find a small fishing village; a launch site for kayaking trails is scheduled to open here in the future. It's a sign that Aguirre may eventually get due recognition as a historical site. Local authorities have filed a petition to the federal government to designate Aguirre on the National Register of Historic Places.

> **TIP:** Be sure to stop by the little **Aguirre visitor center**, ☎ 853-3569/4617. Housed in the old social club/bowling alley, it has an excellent photographic exhibition documenting Aguirre's history and interactive displays about the nearby estuarine reserve. The center is usually open during normal business hours, but closes for lunch between noon and 1 p.m.

■ Guayama

Known as the City of Witches due to its long-ago population of slaves, some of whom practiced *santería* witchcraft, Guayama today is a relatively uninteresting sugar plantation has-been town that makes the questionable claim to being the "cleanest city in Puerto Rico." Surrounded by a sprawl of fast-food joints and auto parts shops, its main attraction is **Casa Cautiño**, ☎ 787-864-9083, the luxurious neo-classical home of three generations of Puerto Rican aristocrats located on the main plaza. The Cautiño family made its fortune in sugar and then lost everything when the government confiscated its property for tax evasion. The house has since become a museum, with relics from the sugar heyday, such as silver antiques, imported textiles and sumptuous carved mahogany furniture. Otherwise, the only reason to visit Guayama is for the **Dulce Sueño Horse Fair** in February, during which some of the island's best Paso Fino horses are on display (see *Festivals & Events*, page 39).

■ Arroyo

It's hard to imagine that Arroyo was once a bustling sugar port with close connections to the then-Danish islands of St. Thomas and St. Croix. A few colorful A-frame homes still stand along the shore, testimony to a mild Scandinavian influence best represented by Danish descendant Edward Lind, one of few aristocrats who actually lived here. In reality, Arroyo has always been the poorer younger sibling of Guayama, and if you found Guayama boring you can skip this overdeveloped town.

The town's main artery, Calle Morse, is home to a US Customs House that has been converted into a small museum, **Patronato del Museo Antigua Aduana**, ☎ 787-839-8096, which is open infrequently. Arroyo has also developed its own version of Ponce's boardwalk – **El Paseo Las Americas El Malecón** – as well as a free trolley service that scoots visitors around the sights in less than an hour.

> **DID YOU KNOW?** *The only significant event in Arroyo's history happened in 1859, when Samuel Morse installed the first telegraph line in Latin America at the Lind family home, Hacienda La Enriqueta, because his daughter was engaged to Edward Lind.*

■ Patillas

Also known as *La Esmerelda Del Sur*, (The Emerald of the South), the coastal area offers visitors little to do but sit in a hammock and watch the waves ripple in the sun and the palm trees rustle in the breeze. On weekends, Puerto Rican families arrive for lunchtime get-togethers. The vibe is friendly, and it's often easy to join these familial fiestas. The seafood restaurants are great places to kick back with a beer and, though they don't serve breakfast, you may catch a rare glimpse of a manatee if you're on the coast at dawn (the best place to see them is on a concrete quay near the restaurant El Mar de la Tranquilidad). A large white cross on a knoll to the left of Carr. 3 indicates the road to Patillas, but consider bypassing the town for the outlying coastal *barrios* between Patillas and Maunabo.

Adventures

■ On Foot

Hiking the Trails of Guánica Forest

The 9,900-acre Guánica forest is considered one of the largest and best-preserved tracts of subtropical dry forest anywhere (find out more about the ecological importance of the forest on page 250). Unlike hiking trails in El Yunque rain forest, Guánica is refreshingly free of swarms of tourists, paved trails and overrun picnic sites. Most of the trailheads are found near the ranger station, located in the heart of the eastern forest at the end of Carr. 334. If the station is open, stop by to chat with the friendly staff and pick up supplementary information about what to see. Trails range in challenge and length, and although the longest stretches fewer than five miles, there are enough loops and crossroads to provide hiking from mild to strenuous. Entry to the Guánica Reserve is free. For more information, call ☎ 787-821-5706, 724-3724 or 721-5495, or write to Miguel Canals, PO Box 985, Guánica, PR 00653. You can set out on your own to explore the forest trails, or take advantage of eco-tour charters in the area (see page 254).

TIP: *When hiking the trails in Guánica, it's a good idea to wear protective clothing against the spikes of certain desert plants (such as the* chicharron *– its reddish holly-shaped leaves sting like hell). Be sure to carry plenty of drinking water, since there is nowhere to stock up, and periodically douse your exposed skin with insect repellent.*

BALLENA TRAIL: An easy amble through Dominican mahogany and limestone scrub, this 1.25-mile trail is a hall-of-fame of species hardy enough to survive this climate, including cactus, century plants, *agave* (not the tequila variety) and twisted gumbo limbo trees. The star attraction is a 700-year-old Guayacán (*lignum vitae*), an evergreen leviathan distinguished by seasonal bluish flowers. The trail ends at Bahía Ballena, where you can stop for a swim before hiking back up the hill. If you venture along the shore as far as Tamarindo beach, be aware that both green and leatherback turtles lay their eggs here. A great hike.

COBANAS TRAIL: A pitted road follows a ridge for just over two miles east through a long-abandoned plantation of campeche trees, once used to treat dysentery.

CUEVA TRAIL: Flat, easy and less than a mile long, this trail winds through spectacular coastal cactus forest – prickly pear cacti grow up to about 10 feet tall here – with colorful butterflies flitting through the brush. About halfway, a limestone cave is home to two species of bat and a rare

The Guánica Caves.
(© Joe Colon, PRTC)

On Foot ◼ **239**

Guánica Forest Reserve

Paved Road
Secondary Road
Trail

1.6 KM
1 MILE

LLUBERAS
GUITARRA
MESETA
CUEVA
COBANAS
VELEZ
LLUBERAS
DINAMITA
VIGIA
GRANADOS
MURCIELAGO
FUERTE
GUTIERREZ
PARK HEADQUARTERS
BALLENA
LA HOYA
Private Property
OJO DE AGUA
HOYA HONDA
334
EL VER
PICUA
333
FUERTE
333

N

© 2001 HUNTER PUBLISHING, INC

South Coast

type of eyeless shrimp. You must get permission from the park ranger to enter.

FUERTE TRAIL: At around four miles long, with lots of dips and short climbs, this is the most demanding and most rewarding of Guánica's trails. Includes spectacular views of the bay and a visit to the ruins of Fort Caprón – an old Spanish lookout post that seems to echo with ghosts of the short-lived Spanish American War. Three short side trails lead into the only moist sections of the forest, if you want to extend your hike.

GRANADOS TRAIL: One of the most popular trails, this easy half-mile loop is shaded from the searing sun by tall mesquite, *guayacán* and violet trees and makes a convenient loop. It's excellent for bird watching, with over 40 migratory and resident species recorded in the area. Keep your eyes peeled for coral fossils embedded in the limestone.

LA HOYA TRAIL: Just under two miles, La Hoya probably offers the most variety in terms of vegetation and landscape. Yellow leafless dodder vines (reportedly used as love charms in the Antilles years ago) strangle *coccolaba* trees, and thickets of evergreen forest flourish where spring water seeps through the limestone.

LLÚBERAS TRAIL: An excellent trail for hikers who want to get a sense of the different ecosystems of the reserve; deciduous, evergreen, dry scrub and coastal forest. The five-mile trail culminates among the abandoned ruins of the once-thriving Llúberas sugar mill.

MESETA TRAIL: Follow the rugged coastline of the reserve for two miles traversing rocky headlands and sandy coves, where mangroves spread their roots into the sea. Try several unusual, edible fruits, including the Spanish dildo cactus, which produces purple fruit with black seeds, and the sea grape, with round, red-veined leaves and purple grape-like fruits. You're bound to see pelicans, white tropicbirds and possibly frigate birds hunting for fish. Tread carefully on these beaches. Turtles and the endangered *bufo lemur* crested toad hide their eggs among soft vines that send runners through the sand.

MURCIÉLAGO TRAIL: This short (about .75 mile) trail drops steeply through dry, deciduous forest and eventually into a verdant ravine. Look out for the dainty lime-green Puerto Rican tody, with its fire engine red collar, that nests here. You can pick up the somewhat overgrown Dinamita Trail here, which leads back on to Carr. 333.

OJO DE AGUA TRAIL: Freshwater springs, unique to this part of the reserve, feed the vegetation on this 1½-mile hilly hike. If you get a whiff of lemon scent, it is the *amyris* tree.

VELEZ/VIGÍA TRAIL: A good .62-mile loop leading to the highest part of the forest, Criollo II, where gigantic turkey vultures circle ominously high in the air. Watch out for a sharp drop-off on one side of the hill, or else you may become carrion for the birds.

Hiking in Jobos Bay National Estuarine Research Reserve

This least-explored of all the protected areas in Puerto Rico includes the **Bosque Estatal de Aguirre**, **Jobos Bay** itself and the **Guayama Cays**, also known as the **Los Cayos Caribes**, which wrap themselves around the bay like a string of pearls. From Salinas, the first trail you'll come across is in the **Bosque Jagueyes**, Carr. 3 (Camino La Esperanza) – a vast salt flat with a lunar vibe – worth getting off the beaten track for a "here-I-am-on-the-Moon!" vacation photo. A more "regular" hike leads through the scrubby subtropical dry forest of the Bosque Estatal De Aguirre, Carr. 7710 (off Carr. 3). Similar to Guánica, the dry forest culminates in a series of mangrove systems and lagoons. A small campsite has been developed within the forest (for serious campers who don't need showers or flush toilets), but to use it you must get a permit from the visitor's center in Aguirre town center, ☎ 787-853-4617 or 3569, fax 853-4618.

Golf

Compared to the opulent courses on the rest of the island, golfing on the South Coast is a poor man's last resort. The **Aguirre Golf Club**, ☎ 787-853-4052, on Carr. 705, was built in 1925 by a group of idle sugar barons from Boston and is the oldest course on the island. If that's a selling point, the only takers are a few wayward tourists, a handful of die-hard residents and the odd desperate adventurer. This short, unruly course is open daily from 7.30 a.m. to 6 p.m., with bargain green fees of $10 from Monday to Friday, $18 weekends and holidays. Add $12/$24 for a golf cart for 9/18 holes. No one in his or her right mind would want to play the **Coamo Springs Golf Club**, a desolate, breezeless course in the middle of what amounts to the Puerto Rican desert.

■ On Wheels

Cycling & Mountain Biking

Threaded with old fire roads and rough trails cut between coral and limestone rock, the area around **Guánica** offers white-knuckle bikers some gnarly climbs and steep downs. Paths here are still relatively uncharted, but this could change dramatically in the next few years as more and more adventure outfitters recognize the extreme-sport potential of Guánica. The area known locally as **Las Pardas** has 12 miles of excellent single-track downhill runs (as well as a few long ups) and terrific ocean scenery. You'll almost surely be on your own (watch out for rogue hikers) as you whiz through forests of cacti and vegetation that can be seen few places on earth. The starting point is not far from the town of Guánica. Head for the Ensenada neighborhood, Carr. 333, and ask for the old sugarcane processing plant (in an area sometimes referred to as Guaipao). The trail starts next to the abandoned plant, and you should find plenty of side paths to keep you busy as you head into the forest.

Another good run starts at Bahía de la Ballena (at the end of Carr. 333), and continues along clifftops to Guayanilla. Get in touch with Paul Julien at **Caribbean Vacation Villa**, ☎ 787-821-5364, for more information. Paul is constantly scouting the area for more thrilling rides, and will no doubt be able to direct you to Guánica's top spots. If you want a guide, you can negotiate a rate with him (see *On Water* in this chapter).

For novice or easygoing cyclists, the area around the nearly deserted town of **Aguirre** is a fascinating ride. Park on Carr. 706, then bike to Hwy. 3, where you turn right. Take an immediate left on a road lined with palm trees – the only route in and out of Aguirre. Keep to the left when you come to the remnants of an old gas station, pass an abandoned two-story train depot and arrive at the American Hotel. The visitor's center is next door, and the old hotel has great views of the "ghost town," estuarine landscape and the sea. This is where your bicycle exploration begins. You can get in a good 10 miles of riding in while seeing Aguirre and surrounding areas to their best advantage. From San Juan, follow Hwy. 52 south until you get to Hwy. 53. Exit on Carr. 706 and park on the side of the road just before you reach Hwy. 3.

THIRSTY IN A GHOST TOWN

Be sure to bring a plentiful water supply when riding in Aguirre or Guánica. There's no place to buy refreshments nearby, and the climate is hot and dry.

Riding The Sugar Train

Built mainly for transporting sugar around the island, this short-lived train circumnavigated the island during the first part of this century. A few older islanders have fond memories of hopping aboard for trips along the coast – either for transportation purposes or just to enjoy the scenic ride. Most of the track has given way to coastal roads and seaside developments, and the only surviving stretch of track in use – *El Tren Del Sur* – opened as a tourist attraction in 1996. This line between Arroyo and Guayama dates back to 1939 when it was part of the great Aguirre Sugar Empire, and continued until 1988, shortly before the sugar plantation breathed its last gasp. A salvaged engine and three or four carriages takes visitors on a one-hour run through 3½ miles of sugar plantations littered with the rusting skeletons of turn-of-the-century farm machinery. A planned extension would run all the way to Ponce. For more information and a timetable, ☎ 787-271-1574 (weekends only). Reached from Hwy. 3 in Arroyo, it costs $3 adults, $2 children, $1.50 senior citizens.

Stock Car Racing

Motorheads can check out the only car-racing track on the island, **Puerto Rico International Speedway**, ☎ 787-824-0020, midway between Salinas and Aguirre, Carr. 1. It attracts professional drivers from all over the world, with the fastest and most thrilling races held on weekends.

■ On Water

Water Adventures with Paul Julien

Star-struck windsurfing enthusiasts occasionally show up at **Paul Julien's Caribbean Vacation Villa** in Guánica to ask, wide-eyed, if he is indeed *the* Paul Julien. Yep, it's him. This windsurf demigod was, in the 1970s, the first person ever to surf the Colombia Gorge, has co-written a bible on learning to windsurf and currently holds several championship titles. He turned up in Guánica about a year and a half ago, drawn by what he considers the "best windsurfing conditions in Puerto Rico," and quickly set up an adventurer's paradise. Already hugely popular with athletes looking for a tropical training destination, as well as a small circle of European pleasure seekers, Paul Julien's Caribbean Vacation Villa, ☎ 787-821-5364, on Carr. 333, San Jacinto, Guánica, is truly special (see *Where To Stay*, page 257). Gregarious and passionate about adventure, Paul has almost unlimited windsurfing and kayaking equipment suitable for anyone from absolute beginners to seasoned professionals. Whether you have always wanted to learn to windsurf but never tried, or you're a seasoned veteran looking to wave-ski six- to seven-foot faces or fly-jump eight-foot swells, he's got you covered. A stable of kayaks includes racers, open-ocean surfers and family sized kayaks. He is probably the only person on the island who'll take you kayak diving (open-water C-card required) – just load up your scuba gear and drop anchor near a rarely visited reef for some seriously "off-the-beaten-path" underwater exploration. You can take advantage of his selection of surf and boogie boards (apparently there's a fairly good break out at Playa Ballena) or snorkel and scuba gear, or use his pad as a launch for rowing, fishing or mountain biking. Even if you travel with nothing but the shirt on your back, Paul provides his guests with everything from grass beach mats to dry sacks for cameras, gratis. He continues to explore the Guánica area, and you could spend weeks here embarking on a new adventure every day.

Windsurfing

For flat-water windsurfers, the south coast has many of the best spots on the island. Sheltered by mangroves and fringe reefs with scooped out bays, the surface here is almost invariably calm. For ocean-going action, you can head out past the reefs for wind and waves. Two of the most popular spots are around **Cayo Caracoles** and **Cayo Enrique**. In La Parguera, **Ventolera**, located in El Muelle Shopping Center (☎ 787-808-0396, e-mail ventolera@juno.com) rents out various high-wind boards, including Quicksilver, Blue Planet, Reef, Anarchy and Spy. The staff at Venterola will point you in the right direction to other good spots, too.

Kayaking

Kayaking off southern Puerto Rico, you can get completely lost in miles of channels formed as the woven mangroves twist their way in and along the coast. It's a low-impact way to get an intimate view of the mangrove estuaries. The best known of these curious mazes is at **La Parguera**, where you can also kayak to numerous cays and along a charming shore lined with colorful floating houses, rickety old piers and craggy beaches. Combined with an eco-tour through the mangroves and a nighttime trip to the Bahía Fosforescente, it's a full day of Huckleberry Finn-style exploration. For one or two-person kayak rentals, **Alelí Tours**, ☎ 787-899-6086, right on the Parguera dock, charges $10/$15 an hour, $30/$40 a half-day and $50/$60 a full day.

UPSTREAM, DOWNSTREAM

Before and during your kayak journey, remember to keep an eye on currents. It's always more pleasant, when you're feeling tired at the end of the trip, to return with the current, not against it.

Serious adventurers swear the best way to explore **Guánica's** outer fringes is by kayak, particularly around the peninsula of **Bahía de la Ballena**. The watery trail takes you through tangled mangrove channels and into a large hidden lagoon rarely visited by outsiders. Kayakers who reach Gilligan's Island (see *Boating*, below) can explore two shallow channels that cut across the island with the feel of a Jungle Cruise at Disneyland. On the far side of the cay (facing out to sea) a beach almost inaccessible to ferry passengers is secluded enough for skinny-dipping. Kayaks can be obtained from **Paul Julien** (above) or **Dive Copamarina** at the Copamarina Beach Resort, ☎ 787-821-0505, which rents out single/double kayaks for $12/$20 an hour, $60/$90 a day. Other water toys include hydro-bikes (a floating bicycle with propeller and pedals), water beetles (pedal-boats), sail boards, Sunfish (one-person sailboats) and little motor boats.

From **Salinas**, eight miles of deserted mangrove cays stretch all the way to Jobos Bay National Estuarine Research Reserve (below). Rent a kayak from **Marina de Salinas**, ☎ 787-824-3185, on Carr. 70, and cut loose into the mangrove maze (kayaks or hydro-bikes for $15 an hour, $50 per day). The waters here are exceptionally calm, so paddling is easy. Bring food and drinks in a waterproof bag, since there is nowhere to stop on the way. If you're up for a shorter trip, check out a small marina on the other side of the bay, known as **La Barca**, where you can lunch at a restaurant of the same name.

At the **Jobos Bay National Estuarine Reserve** (see page 253) the Kayak Trail winds its way through the Mar Negro to Los Cayos Caribes, where, if you paddle around quietly at sunrise or at sunset, you might meet up with an elusive West Indian manatee, the adorable, blubbery sea mammal that can grow to 13 feet in length and weigh as much as 3,500 lbs. About 300 live in the area, favoring the brackish waters of the mangrove channels and feeding more-or-less exclusively on the sea-grass beds that surround the cays. The sight of one of these colossal creatures frolicking in the shallows is a rare treat. The staff at the Reserve have also designed a boat trip along the **Cayo Caribe Trail** to a boardwalk built in the wetland areas around the cays for easy viewing. This is an excellent option for eco-travelers who prefer not to walk much. Contact the Aguirre visitor's center (☎ 787-853-4617 or 3569, fax 853-4618) for more information. Local fishermen say that the Mar Negro sometimes lights up with bioluminescence on a moonless night.

Boating

For less serene, but quicker, trips around the waters of **Parguera**, you can rent little Boston Whalers (about 12 feet) with chug-chug engines for about the same price as a kayak, letting you explore a much wider area without the muscle strain of kayaking. Try **Cancel Boats**, ☎ 787-899-5891, on the dock at La Parguera. This is a fun way to get around, even if you have little or no boating knowledge, although the sound of your motor will probably scare the birds that inhabit the mangrove. Cancel Boats also runs **Fondo de Cristal Glass Bottomed Boat**, ☎ 787-899-5891, which cruises offshore cays by day and the phosphorescent bay at night. It costs only $5 per person, but be warned the boat accommodates 150 people. Still, it's the best way to see underwater sea life without getting wet.

OOH, AHH – UNDERWATER FIREWORKS

After Mosquito Bay in Vieques, the **Bahía Fosforescente** (Phosphorescent Bay) in La Parguera is one of the best places in the Americas to witness the strange phenomenon of millions of saltwater microorganisms erupting in an eerie, green lightshow when disturbed. Scholarly study of these delicate, tiny creatures, known as dynoflagellates, is scarce, and scientists can only postulate that the flashes of bioluminescence are a defense mechanism against predators. Moonless nights are the best time to see this living light show. From the dock in Parguera, find a boat guide who will let you swim (bring your own mask and snorkel). After a short ride to the phosphorescent bay, jump in the waters and move your limbs vigorously to see the trails of light left in your motion's wake. You'll find yourself covered in sparkles. Even trailing your hand in the water from a moving boat will stir up a swirl of alien light, with luminescent green water dripping from your fingertips. The best charter to go with is **Alelí Tours**, La Parguera, ☎ 787-899-6086, which allows guests unlimited time in the water (most operators give you 10 minutes max before rushing you back to shore). Most of the tours cost $5 per person.

Just a few hundred yards off the **Caña Gorda** peninsula in Guánica, the deserted little cay known as **Gilligan's Island** is hardly the kind of place on which you'll find yourself marooned for months or years. And there's no Ginger or Mary Ann either! You will find little sandy beaches on either side of the main cay, mangrove sprouting from the water all around and, on weekends (and holidays and during summer vacations), up to a dozen or more other would-be castaways. A ferry runs daily from a little dock at the Restaurante San Jacinto, just past the Copamarina on Carr. 333. Otherwise, rent a kayak or other vessel from Copamarina or Paul Julien to give yourself more mobility. The ferry dumps passengers on the near side of Gilligan's Island, and the far side is often deserted. Relaxing here on a weekday, with your eyes closed, you might even find yourself dreamily imagining you hear Gilligan pestering the Skipper, or spot the Professor and Mary Ann emerging from the bushes.

If you've got your own boat, the slips at **Marina de Salinas**, ☎ 787-824-3185, fax 768-7676, cost $6.25 per foot, with electricity meter, free-running water, a laundromat, gas/diesel facilities and harbormaster on channel 16. **Payless Rent-A-Car**, ☎ 787-864-8351, will collect and deliver from here. Even more helpful is **Coquí Express**, ☎ 787-824-6985, run by an enterprising woman named Sara, who provides a "taxi" service, helps out with Customs and Immigration and generally troubleshoots for sailors. There are also plenty of offshore moorings here.

Diving & Snorkeling

Several miles off the south coast, the shallow waters of the Puerto Rican shelf drop to depths of 2,000 feet and more, in a dramatic wall that stretches for more than 20 miles from Cabo Rojo to Guánica. Here is some of the best diving on the island, and one of the only spots near land to do a deep dive of up to 130 feet (for intermediate divers). Generally, visibility averages about 80 feet, but rough seas sometimes hamper the diving schedule. Steep underwater faces are forested by elkhorn corals, the skeletons of deep-water gorgonians and, on the **Black Wall**, an abundant crop of the seriously-endangered Caribbean black coral – a treat for marine botanists.

The **Parguera Wall**, with a sharp drop to 2,000 feet and visibility of up to 120 feet on a perfect day, is one of the most dramatic offshores sites, and teems with aquatic life large and small. If you're lucky, you may see nurse sharks, dolphins, moray eels, barracudas and sea turtles. Other great dives include **Trench Alley** – a series of spur and groove formations where you may descend to 110 feet. A gigantic, blue, vase-shaped formation marks the entrance to the site, and as you enter the surreal imagery includes a thick wallpapering of psychedelic sponges, a resident six-foot moray and schools of Atlantic spadefish. Nearby, **Pináculos** has some of the best conical coral formations in the world, and at **Hole in the Wall,** a dramatic channel pierces a half-mile of vertical cliff face.

East of here, the **Guánica Wall** edges its way closer to the mainland, accessible within 20 minutes by boat – a plus for anyone who suffers from seasickness. Starting at 50 feet, this section of the Puerto Rican trench is a secret garden gouged with canyons where cuts in the rock reveal sea fans and multicolored corals – boulder, star, brain and finger specimens glitter like jewels against the sand bottom. Close by, a ring of barrier reefs slathered in hard and soft corals provides refuge for plentiful crabs and lobsters, nurse sharks and barracuda. Vestiges of the buccaneers and pirates that once sailed these waters have recently been uncovered in the form of muskets, cannons and gold coins.

Just five minutes from the San Jacinto area of Guánica, **The Aquarium** is a kaleidoscope of life with three distinct underwater types of ecology: a sandy bottom, a spectacular coral head system – one of which is 10 feet tall, 12 feet wide and estimated to be more than 1,000 years old – and a sponge colony. Tropical fish swarm the reef in their various Technicolor dreamcoats, at times so abundant you can barely make out the reef. Expect to see sergeant majors, butterfly and goatfish along with brown garden eels, cleaner shrimp and arrowhead crabs. This site is magical for night diving. Beginners, or those who haven't dived for some time, might request a checkout dive at **Las Pozas**. With a maximum depth of 55-feet, this rarely visited reef has some impressive rock formations, vast coral gardens and, like The Aquarium, an abundance of tropical fish, particularly grunts, doctor fish, soldiers, queen angels and, if you peer closely under ledges and let your eyes get accustomed to the dark, nurse sharks dozing in the shade. A couple of nice dives near Ponce at the Caja De Muertos nature reserve are listed under *Eco-Travel*, below.

DIVE SHOPS

The best dive team on the south coast, **Paradise Scuba Center**, ☎ 787-899-7611, next to Hotel Casa Blanca in La Parguera, keeps a close eye on conditions and visibility before making a dive trip. Their knowledge of the area is excellent, and they cover most of the 50 or so sites around La Parguera. A two-tank dive usually costs $80, a one-tank night dive is $50, and snorkeling trips start at $35. Prices for scuba certification courses begin at $150 if you have three weeks to do it in, and are still very reasonable at $250 for a five-day course.

Dive Copamarina, ☎ 787-821-0505, ext. 729, fax 821-0070, is on Carr. 333, Guánica, and is part of the Copamarina Beach and Dive Resort (see *Where To Stay*). With two dive boats, it offers six-day diving certification programs, including accommodations (based on two people sharing a room), for $760 per person – a great package deal. Otherwise, PADI Open Water certification costs around $400. Two-tank dives and night dives are fairly standard at $80/$50, respectively. Also, check out **Paul Julien's Caribbean Vacation Villa**, ☎ 787-821-5364, fax 821-0681, for off-the-beach eco-dives and unique kayaking dives.

Fishing Charters

Marine scientist Mickey Amador of **Parguera Fishing Charters**, ☎ 787-899-4698 or 382-4698, at the dock in La Parguera, e-mail mareja@aol.com, http://members.aol.com/mareja, offers customized trips (maximum six persons) aboard his 31-foot Bertram, *Mareja*. He regularly hooks up some of the speediest fish in the sea – marlin, wahoo, dorado and tuna – for his clients. A full day of fishing for four costs $650, including bait, tackle and lunch (the price rises for six people), and $400 for a half-day, including bait and tackle. If Mickey is booked, try the crew at **Pull The Hook Fishing Charters**, ☎ 787-899-6657 or 721-9096, cell 383-0102, La Parguera, who specialize in deep-sea fishing daily, and also make their 31-foot Bertram available for tournaments and special trips.

Surfing

There are occasional breaks off **Bahía de la Ballena** (Guánica), but here you'll have the advantage that when it does break you'll likely have the take-off to yourself. Few people know about or have the inclination to drag themselves to this spot (be prepared to hike, unless you catch a fishing boat from San Jacinto). Otherwise, the only other place on the south coast for wave riders is on the eastern side of the south coast near Patillas. **Inches** is named after the usual diminutive size of its waves. Add to this the menace of fire coral lurking under the surface, and it's not the most encouraging surf report. Nevertheless, some locals claim that Inches has the best left-break on the island during rare occasions when winds push the swell up three to six feet. In general, conditions are better in the afternoon when trade winds build momentum. It gets crowded on weekends.

Beaches

Despite comprising most of Puerto Rico's Caribbean coastline, the south coast will be a disappointment to hardcore *playeros* intent on finding a different white-sand beach every day. Two of the best stretches of sand are **Playa Santa** and **Balneario Manglillos**, at the end of Carr. 325 in the Guánica Forest Reserve. Packed during weekends and usually deserted during the week, both feature calm waters and mangroves that give way to soft sand. If you do show up on a weekend, prepare to endure the insect whine of personal watercraft swarming the bay. On Carr. 333, access to **Playa Jaboncillo** involves a short hike down a cliff-side path, creating a more tranquil atmosphere.

The public beach at **Caña Gorda** is another mob scene at weekends, but like all other beaches in the area, you can pretty much have the run of the place during the week. The same is true of the tiny offshore cays of **Gilligan's Island** and **Isla Ballena**. Ferries run every half-hour on weekends and only twice a day during the week (except Mondays), from the San Jacinto café, just past the Copamarina resort on Carr. 333. If you're energetic and independent-minded, get here under your own steam by renting a kayak (see *Kayaking*, above). A short hike from the end of Carr. 333, **Bahía de la Ballena** is probably the least visited of all beaches in Guánica. It is also a nesting ground for endangered green and leatherback turtles, and occasionally the elusive manatee can be spotted wallowing in the shallow waters of the mangrove forest. Nearby, the endangered Puerto Rican *bufo lemur* crested toad lays eggs on Tamarindo Beach. Tread carefully!

Coamo Hot Springs

Used since the time of the Taino Indians, the mineral-rich thermal waters of Coamo rise from as deep as two kilometers below the earth's surface. Aficionados believe one can heal almost any ailment by soaking long enough in the magic "fountain of youth," where the water temperature averages 110° Fahrenheit. The public pools have been dug out and lined with concrete, with pools of different depths and temperatures. Wade in the upper pool until you resemble a prune, then wallow in the shallows of the lower pool. Unfortunately, there is no cold-water pool in which to get a refreshing shock to the system. An adjacent hotel includes a shallow wading pool of the same water for guests or visitors who care to pay $5. The public pools are free. Be sure to bring plenty of drinking water, and take it easy if you have a heart condition, irregular blood pressure or other medical concern. The public pools are open 8 a.m. to 6 p.m. daily. Our recommendation is to come either first thing in the morning or late in the evening, when the air is pleasantly cool and the crowds thin. As with other tourist attractions in Puerto Rico, the Coamo baths can get crowded during weekends and holidays. If you have visited the volcanic springs of Ecuador or Patagonia, or are used to natural hot springs of California or elsewhere, Coamo may seem somewhat puny yet overdeveloped by comparison. If you've never been to hot springs before, however, check it out – it's an experience, and you're sure to leave feeling relaxed and rejuvenated. Carr. 546; ☎ 787-825-2186.

Eco-Travel

■ The Dry Tropical Forest of Guánica

Despite the rugged terrain, searing heat and scant rainfall, the Guánica forest flourishes with an astonishing number of plants and cacti that burst with desert-like blooms, 245 species of trees and over 1,000 insects, including the yellow, black and red orb-weaving spider and so-called crazy ants, which form endless columns along the trails. Walking the trails (see pages 237-240 for trail descriptions), you'll likely come across hermit crabs, geckos and lizards including, if you're lucky, the extremely rare *ameiva* lizard, identified by its speckled black body with two narrow racing stripes and its long, iridescent tail. Guánica is also widely considered the best bird-watching spot in Puerto Rico (see *Watch The Birdie!*, below). Designated by the United Nations as a "world biosphere reserve" in 1981, the 9,900-acre Guánica forest is considered one of the largest and best-preserved tracts of subtropical dry forest anywhere. Consider the rarity: scientists estimate that only one percent of the world's subtropical dry forest remains.

WHAT'S A BIOSPHERE RESERVE?

According to UNESCO, a biosphere reserve "conserves examples of characteristic ecosystems... in which people are an integral component." Bringing together a diverse team of scientists, biologists, farmers and local residents, the biosphere program manages land and water to protect the natural resources while taking into consideration human needs. Guánica is one of 285 biosphere reserves in 110 countries.

Entry to the Guánica reserve is free. If you visit in the middle of the week, the only other humans you are likely to come across are the odd jogger and possibly an organized tour group of binocular-toting bird watchers. For those without their own transport, *públicos* from the Guánica town center run to Playa Santa, where you can make arrangements for transportation to and from the ranger station, open 9 a.m. to 5 p.m., Tuesday through Sunday. For more information, call ☎ 787-821-5706, 724-3724 or 721-5495, or write to Miguel Canals, PO Box 985, Guánica, PR 00653. You can set out on your own to explore the forest trails (see *On Foot*, page 237), or take advantage of eco-tour charters in the area (listed on page 254).

WATCH THE BIRDIE!

Half of all bird species found in Puerto Rico dwell in the Guánica subtropical dry forest, and 11 of the island's 14 endemic species can be seen, especially around sunrise or sunset. Keen ornithologists from all over the world visit Guánica just to get a glimpse or a photograph of a particularly rare bird. Less dedicated birders can be sure of seeing at least some of the common residents and seasonal visitors, such as Puerto Rican todies, troupials, mangrove cuckoos, Adelaide's warblers and Puerto Rican bullfinches.

If you spot any of the following rare or endangered birds, consider yourself lucky. **Puerto Rican emerald-breasted hummingbirds** can often be seen in the dry scrub forest where they pollinate many of the cacti flowers. The **yellow-shouldered blackbird** is increasingly threatened, because its traditional nesting site – in the branches of the *ucar* tree (distinguished by whorled leaves unfolding from pincer like spikes, and white flowers) – has been cut extensively for use as fence posts. Reforestation is slowly helping to increase their numbers.

Hard to spot due to its nocturnal habits and mottled-gray, brown and black plumage, the **whippoorwill** may be noticed by the keen observer, usually resting lengthwise on a branch or camouflaged among dead brush on the ground. The **Puerto Rican nightjar** – an endemic species – was believed extinct until a few years ago. Numbers have now risen to approximately 1,000, and if you're lucky you will spot one camouflaged to blend in with dry leaf litter on the ground, where it remains in hiding most of the day. Endemic to Guánica, the **lizard cuckoo** (named after its favorite food) claims the title of largest Caribbean cuckoo – nearly two feet long! If you don't get to see one, you may at least hear its obnoxious squawking as it roams the tree tops terrifying small reptiles far and wide.

> **RECOMMENDED READING:** *For an in-depth book to the natural aviary of Guánica, pick up a copy of Herbert A. Raffaele's excellent book,* **A Guide to the Birds of Puerto Rico and the Virgin Islands** *(Princeton University Press).*

■ A Day (or Two) at Caja de Muertos

This tiny island nature reserve has something for almost everyone. But unless you have your own boat, the only way to get here is on a single charter, Island Ventures, which departs from the Ponce dock on weekends (or weekdays for groups of eight or more). Thankfully, this helps keep the island a tranquil habitat for endangered species and a great place for eco-tourists to escape the hordes. Rafi Vega at **Island Ventures**, ☎/fax 787-842-8546, e-mail iventure@caribe.net, offers a $20 "day at the beach," with passage to and from the island and a light lunch, or $35 for the same including snorkeling. The same trip with a two-tank dive on the eastern reef is a reasonable $65.

You'll approach the island from the northwest, passing the smaller lighthouse cay of Cardona to the right, and then either dock or drop anchor in front of the ranger station on the southern end of Caja de Muertos. It's about a 45-minute trip. The waters here are usually crystalline, and reef and sand patches fathoms below the surface appear to be just feet away. Roughly shaped like an exclamation point, the thick end of the island rises to a peak where a Spanish-era (now solar-powered) lighthouse warns passing ships at night. At the low, thin end, the ranger station is sandwiched on a stretch of grass between two beaches. A rock outcropping on the southern tip is off-limits to visitors, since it's a nesting ground for boobies, frigate birds and tropicbirds that wheel overhead.

Head up to the ranger station and ask for the resident biologist, who is usually happy to show visitors around the island. With luck, you'll be shown the beach to the east of the ranger station where, between June and December, endangered hawksbill turtle females crawl up the sand by night to lay their eggs (the beach is closed to visitors otherwise). Because these ancient creatures are still dwindling in number, biologists patrol the sand in season to rescue wayward newborns and help them into the sea.

A smooth trail leads from the ranger station through the dry tropical forest at the center of the island. Among the prominent species of flora, you'll see dramatic columnar cactus, with night-blooming flowers. And, our favorite, the gumbo limbo – a.k.a. the "tourist tree" because its reddish bark resembles the peeling, sunburned skin of a gringo. With luck, you'll glimpse the endangered *lucia* lizard, with its shiny aquamarine tail, or the harmless brown Puerto Rican garden snake.

> **CAUTION:** *Look at, but don't touch, the manzanillo plant, with broad leaves, small apple-like fruit and sap that irritates the skin.*

A short, rocky incline takes you past the cave where Portuguese pirate José Almeida supposedly buried his bride in a glass-and-copper coffin (see page 233 for the story). You can descend into the cave from the right-hand side of the small lookout platform, then head up to the lighthouse at the island's highest point. Before enjoying the view, head to the back of the lighthouse to scoop bucketfuls of water from a well over your head (just do it, you'll thank us!). Upon descending back to the beach, you'll find the light-blue water of the bay just cool enough to refresh, and white sand on which to bake in the sun.

There's a snorkeling spot with unspectacular shallows and a nice reef in 20-25 feet of water, about 200 yards north of the beach on the west side. A good diving reef is found about two miles off the east coast of the island, though the water can get choppy here.

For a truly relaxing nature (or beach) experience, try camping on the island. Though rarely done, it is possible if you present your case right. Call Robert Matos, director of reserves and refuges for the Dept. of Natural Resources in San Juan, ☎ 787-724-3640, and tell of your interest in dry tropical forested cays, hawksbill turtles or whatever. Or offer to spend a couple of hours picking up trash on the island. Call at least a week before your intended stay. It's also possible to just show up on the island with your overnight gear, and then speak directly to the resident biologist. If you're interested in nature (or if you bring a 12-pack of beer), they'll usually let you pitch a tent on their lawn.

■ Jobos Bay National Estuarine Research Reserve

Opportunities for hiking, bird-watching, and kayaking (see pages 241 and 245) abound at this underexplored area, which includes the **Bosque Estatal de Aguirre**, **Jobos Bay** itself and the **Guayama Cays**, also known as the **Los Cayos Caribes**, which wrap themselves around the bay like a string of pearls. Considering that relatively few people visit the Guánica reserve, you'll be nearly alone in the Jobos Bay area, making it a true "at one with nature" experience. Eco-travelers will be delighted to find such diverse types of ecosystems in such a small area, including subtropical dry forest, fringe and basin mangroves, salt flats, sea grass beds and coral reefs. It's also one of the best spots on the island for a chance meeting with a manatee.

At Bosque Estatal de Aguirre, a boardwalk (under construction when we visited) should make it easier to go birding among the tangle of roots and vines. Aguirre attracts a fairly dense population of migratory birds, so be sure to bring a pair of binoculars. The haughty **great blue heron** with its indigo plumes, maintains a royal composure. Also keep your eyes peeled for the **snowy egret, clapper rail** and **yellow warbler**.

Guided interpretive tours of the research reserve began in 2001, and include hiking and kayak eco-trips through this fascinating 2,883-acre area. Call ahead for prices, availablility and camping reservations. Make arrangements through the Aguirre visitor's center, ☎ 787-853-3569 or 4617, Reserva Nacional de Investigación, Estuarina de Bahia de Jobos, Call Box B, Aguirre, Puerto Rico 00704. You can also contact José Delgado in Caguas, ☎ 787-739-0380, or Marina de Salinas, ☎ 787-824-3185, who rent out kayaks on behalf of the reserve.

RESEARCH PROJECTS WANTED

Officials at Jobos Bay Natural Estuarine Research Reserve have asked us to help put out the word: they invite proposals for research by marine biologists and other scientists, as well as students. The on-site center can even provide accommodations for those involved in approved projects. Contact the research laboratory at the Aguirre visitor's center, ☎ 787-853-3569 or 4617, fax 853-4618, for information on submitting a proposal.

■ Eco-Tour Charters

We highly recommend taking advantage of a guided expedition (guides are usually marine biologists or others with a cross-disciplinary science background) in order to learn about the natural environment you're exploring. **Alelí Tours**, ☎ 787-899-6086, at the dock in Parguera, takes visitors via sailboat or kayak through the mangroves and the habitat they sustain. Victor Lopez operates **Tropix Wellness Outings**, ☎ 787-405-9036 (cell), offering what he calls "Wet and Dry Tours," which combine hiking and kayaking adventures in two- to three-day packages. **Encantos Ecotours**, ☎ 787-272-0005, fax 789-1730, e-mail ecotours@caribe.net, in Piñones, offers a range of eco-educational adventures – including bird, turtle and whale watching, hiking and kayaking – on the South Coast.

Where To Stay

ACCOMMODATIONS PRICE KEY

Rates are per room, per night, double occupancy. Single occupancy may or may not get you a discount, so ask when making a reservation. Breakfast included where noted.

$	Up to $50
$$	$50 to $100
$$$	$101 to $150
$$$$	$150 and up

■ San Germán

Sadly, the only guest house in San Germán has seen better times. At least, we hope it has seen better times. The **Parador Oasis & Restaurant**, Calle Luna, ☎ 787-892-1175, smells of something musty and forgotten (and possibly dead) and desperately needs a thorough cleaning. Cramped rooms are grim and appear furnished with items rejected by the Salvation Army. Pigeon droppings litter the outdoor seating area, and the passage around the swimming pool is so narrow you have to walk sideways like a crab. The highlight is an orange-and-black mural of a bowling alley – almost worth stopping by just to gape at it. This is another poor reflection on the government-run *parador* system. $$

For long-term visitors (especially exchange students at the university) try the **Hospedaje Casa Real**, also on Calle Luna, ☎ 787-899-4213. Tucked away in an old colonial home, it has basic rooms, a shared bathroom and kitchen, and a swimming pool. At around $200 a month you are unlikely to find anything cheaper.

For a budget option, also especially good for students, the **Universidad Interamericana de Puerto Rico**, Carr. 102, offers air-conditioned rooms in its hostel, with TV, VCR, mini-fridge, private bath and laundry; $. Even cheaper, short-term stays at the "annex" – dormitory rooms unused during the semester – cost $21.40 with bedsheets, $16.75 without (prices include 7% sales tax) for one person per night. Add about $5 per additional person for up to four occupants in a dorm room. ☎ 787-264-1912, ext. 7300 or 7301, Ask to speak to Muriel Pacheco Martínez, or send e-mail to muriel@sg.inter.edu.

■ La Parguera

About a dozen guest houses and hotels around the town center are all a short walk from the restaurants and the pier. The largest and most luxurious is **Villa Parguera**, ☎ 787-899-7777 or 3975, www.elshop.com. One of the government-run paradores, it has 70 rooms, most of which have sea views. The sundeck and gardens overlook the water, and are perfect for lounging with a cocktail and watching the water thwap against the pier. Villa Parguera has its own pool, playroom for kids, seafood restaurant and live cabaret (in Spanish) every Saturday night. Unsurprisingly, it gets extremely busy on weekends and public holidays. With cable TV, air conditioning and telephone in all rooms, the rates are reasonable. $$

Inspired by the many "floating" houses that hover on stilts above the Parguera bay, **Posada Porlamar Parador**, ☎ 787-899-4015 or 800-223-6530, is almost hidden by mangroves and, flanked by rolling hills, it's perfect for anyone seeking peace and privacy. This quintessential waterfront property also has a private dock, with a dive boat offering trips to the phosphorescent bay for $5 (**Parguera Divers**, ☎ 787-899-4171, cell 380-9424, fax 899-5558, e-mail divepr@caribe.net). All rooms have air conditioning. $$

The cheapest place in town is **Sinda's Guest House**, ☎ 787-899-5540/ 4582, Calle 7 (toward Playa Rosada), a quiet, family-run place just outside of the town center. It has 11 small but comfortable rooms, and gets busy at weekends so it's best to make a reservation. Sinda also has a small apart-

One of the floating houses in La Parguera bay.
(PRTC)

ment for self-catering. All rooms have air conditioning, but no credit cards are accepted, just cash. $

Right in the center of the action, **Hostal Casablanca**, ☎ 787-899-4250, is slightly more up-market and very popular with German travelers. In a town with no beach, its swimming pool is a welcome bonus. $$

■ Guánica

The lonely drive along Carr. 333 winds above the Caribbean in a series of hairpin bends until you feel far removed from the rest of Puerto Rico. Quiet even by day, it's completely devoid of nightlife (except for one or two restaurants), but has some of the best accommodations on the island, all with private docks and boats for getting you out onto the water (these cost about $5). A great escape, **Mary Lee's By The Sea** (turn right just after passing the Copamarina Beach Resort on Carr. 333), ☎/fax 787-821-3600, transports visitors to another time and place. During the past 40 years, Mary Lee has slowly created a secret village of unique *casas* and *casitas* between the subtropical dry forest to the north and the Caribbean Sea. Her gardens gurgle with water and are full of exotic plants and treasures gathered over decades of beachcombing. Accommodating two to eight people, each unit is named rather than numbered, painted bright Caribbean colors and softly lit at night by old-fashioned Chinese hanging lanterns. Haitian grass mats carpet the floors and each has something that makes it special: an indoor waterfall in "Ruthie" (named after Mary Lee's mother), a four-poster bed in "Tranquila" and an oval courtyard in "Pacifica." All come with a fully equipped kitchen, barbecue and access to washer/dryer (TV is an extra charge). $$$-$$$$

For "adventure accommodations" in the best sense of the term, look no further than **Paul Julien's Caribbean Vacation Villa**, ☎ 787-821-5364, fax 821-0681, on Carr. 333, San Jacinto, Guánica, www.viewthis.com/caribbean, e-mail julienpr@yahoo.com. Located right on the water overlooking Gilligan's Island, the villa has two studio apartments ($$$), immaculately furnished with every gadget you can imagine, cable television, sundecks and barbecues, as well as a blissful family-sized unit up top ($$$$). Prices include unlimited use of all sports equipment, and for an additional fee Paul also gives lessons in windsurfing and other adventure skills, as well as guided tours of the area (see *Adventures On Water*, page 243).

The cheapest accommodations in the area, **Gilligan View Apartments**, ☎ 787-821-4901, on the same turn as Mary Lee's (above), features peeling paint and dripping taps; a strangely depressing atmosphere. All it has going for it is the location. $$

For a typical resort-type experience, try **The Copamarina Beach Resort**, Carr. 333, ☎ 787-821-0505 ext. 729, fax 821-0070, www.copamarina.com, e-mail copamar@coqui.net. It is something of an oasis in the desert, with lush palm gardens and lots of water features, including an outdoor Jacuzzi, its own beach and boat dock, and two swimming pools. Copamarina also has two restaurants, tennis courts, a spa and a diving center. Rooms are spacious and bright, with handy extras like coffee makers and hairdryers, and all have views of either the sea or the gardens. When booking, ask about package deals such as the American Breakfast Plan or Dive Package, $$$; or the more decadent Spa Package, which includes massage, mud wrap, manicure and pedicure. $$$$

Guayanilla

Though there's little to do in Guayanilla itself, **Parador Pichi's**, ☎ 787-835-3335, fax 835-3272, on Carr. 132 (off Hwy. 2), www.pichis.com, is a good choice for families on a budget and a convenient base for exploring the southwest corner of the island. Halfway between the museums and restaurants of Ponce and the subtropical dry forest of Guánica (about 20 minutes from both), just off Hwy. 2, Pichi's has all modern conveniences; games rooms, swimming pools, a fast-food diner, a steak and seafood restaurant and spacious motel-style rooms with air conditioning, cable TV and telephone. A double can sleep two adults and a child, and includes continental breakfast. $$

Ponce

Ponce's oldest hotel is the **Meliá**, ☎ 787-842-0260 or 800-742-4276, fax 841-3602, between Plaza Degetau Plaza Las Delicias, http://home.coqui.net/melia, e-mail melia@coqui.net. It is still owned and run by the Meliá family that built it in 1908. This was once the chosen (or only) haunt of Ponce society, and although some of the original grandeur is gone, you can almost hear ghosts attending long-ago champagne parties still echoing off the walls. Check out the grainy photographs in the lobby of the Meliá clan dating back to 1906. Bedrooms on the ground and first floors have maintained all of their original features, vaulted ceilings and mint-condition original ceramic tiles. Though small, these rooms have a lot more charm than the newer rooms on the second to fourth floors, doubly so because they are the cheapest. Ask for the room featured in the Meliá brochure, which has a small balcony. Two rooms in the newest part of the hotel also have balconies overlooking the plaza, with a great view of the central mountains. Complimentary continental breakfast is served on the terrace. $$-$$$

The **Hotel Begica**, ☎ 787-844-3255, fax 844-6149, on Calle Villa, is located in another lovely colonial building. An excellent base for the sights and a great bargain, its large bedrooms have high ceilings, filigreed airvents and other details that lend it a Spanish-era feel. Two of the rooms have balconies opening onto the street. $$

Just outside of town, the **Ponce Inn Hotel**, ☎ 787-841-1000 or 800-329-7466, fax 841-2560, on Carr. 1, in the Mercedita *barrio*, has the advantage of a large swimming pool and courtyard, and modest resort-type facilities (it used to be Days Inn). The proximity to the main road is a bit off-putting, but it's modern, comfortable and a good choice for families who need a few extra amenities to keep the kids from getting bored. $$

Big chain hotels are scattered around the outskirts of town. The **Hilton Ponce & Casino**, ☎ 787-259-7676 or 800-HILTONS, www.ponce-hilton.com, e-mail poncehil@conqui.net, is on the road to La Guancha (follow signs to Playa Ponce or Paseos) just off Carr. 14. It has commanding views of a black sand beach, but unfortunately no access to it. The Hilton compensates with faux waterfalls, a tropical pool, tennis courts and practice range for golf. Room service and baby-sitting are added bonuses. $$$$

The less luxurious **Holiday Inn & Tropical Casino**, ☎ 787-844-1200, on Hwy. 2, is convenient for getting in and out of the city quickly, and is basically geared for business travelers. $$$

■ Coamo Hot Springs

The **Parador Baños de Coamo**, ☎ 787-825-2239 or 2186, fax 825-4739, is a spa-type guest house built as close to the springs as possible without physically covering them over. Its own pool of thermal spring water dates back to 1847, when the parador served as luxury retreat for dignitaries in need of rejuvenation. President Franklin D. Roosevelt stayed here in 1933. The chances of sharing the hot spring next to such luminaries today is remote, although the owners of the parador have made brave attempt at restoring the place to its former glory. The Café Puertorriqueño – a large barn-style structure – serves up international and Creole fare (steaks and seafood). Rooms are comfortable, with private terraces overlooking a courtyard shaded almost entirely by a lone samán tree that's about 500 years old. As paradores go, this is one of the better ones, especially if you come mid-week when the springs are less crowded. $$

■ Salinas

Located at the prettiest marina in Puerto Rico, **Marina de Salinas & Posada El Náutico**, ☎ 787-824-3185 or 752-8484, fax 768-7676, at Playa de Salinas, has spartan but comfortable rooms, waterfront terraces, a swimming pool, on-site kayak rental and a good nautical-style restaurant. Even if you're not a yachter, there is plenty to do in the area. The hotel provides free (but somewhat erratic) transportation to nearby cays. Kids under 11 sharing a room with their parents stay for free. $-$$$

■ Guayama & Arroyo

In Guayama, the **Molino Inn and Restaurant**, ☎ 787-866-1515, fax 866-1510, is located just off Hwy. 54, but nine acres of grounds seem to absorb much of the traffic noise. With swimming pool, tennis and basketball courts, a good restaurant and live music on weekends, it's the best Guayama has to offer. All rooms have air conditioning, cable TV and phones. $$$

For something a little more removed, try **Hotel Brandemar**, ☎ 787-864-5124, located about halfway between Guayama and Arroyo in Barrio Branderi (it's well signposted from Hwy. 3). A long, curving sand beach where locals cast for fish from the crumbling concrete pier overlooks a bay lined with colorful homes, and it's a pleasant walk to El Malecón (the boardwalk) in Arroyo. The beach gets few visitors and the water is extremely still. Brandemar also has a shallow pool and a patio with a view of the mountains. Rooms are simple, clean and good value. $$

Another good bet for budget travelers is the **Punta Guilarte Centro Vacacional**, ☎ 787-839-3565, on Carr. 3 in Arroyo. Its 28 cabañas and 32 villas, set in beautiful palm groves with a sand beach, sleep six to eight people, but are bunched too close together for much privacy. Facilities include a swimming pool, games rooms, basketball and volleyball courts. Remember to bring your own bedding, plates, knives, forks and cooking equipment, etc. Like other *centros vacacionales*, it's completely bare-bones style. $$

■ Patillas

If you're looking for a peaceful spot that has the best of the mountains and of the sea Patillas is preferable to either Luquillo or Fajardo. There are only two guest houses in the neighborhood, both small and comfortable with a family atmosphere. Within walking distance from the sea, **The Caribbean Paradise Hotel**, ☎ 787-839-5885, fax 271-0069, on Carr. 3, is owned by sisters Carmen and Maria Diaz who were born and grew up in Patillas and can tell you pretty much anything you might want to know about the area – like visiting the palm nursery or an old man in the hills who has a small vineyard. Patillas beaches aren't great for swimming, but there's a man-made tide pool within walking distance and the hotel has a pleasant swimming pool of its own. Guests also have use of new tennis courts and an international/*criollo* restaurant. Activities include horseback riding at the local farm, boat trips, and scuba diving. Bedrooms are brand new, light and airy with air conditioning, television and coffee maker. $$$, including a welcome drink.

If you want to be closer to the water, **Caribe Playa Beach Resort**, Carr. 3, ☎ 787-839-6339 or 7719, fax 839-1817, www.caribeplaya.com, was built in the shade of a coconut grove where the waves are practically knocking at your door. In terms of beachfront locations, few places can beat it, especially if you like to swing in a hammock and watch the surfers. Trade winds can turn this beach into a non-stop set for surfers, so previous owners also built a tide-pool for year-round swimming – the reef is good for snorkeling when you get a calm day – but there's a swimming pool and open-air Jacuzzi for those who don't like choppy water. Bedrooms are painted in desert colors, with cable TV, telephones and barbecue area. The menu at the oceanfront restaurant changes daily but always includes some type of meat and seafood. Ask about boat trips, fishing, diving and massage. $$-$$$

> **TIP:** *You quite often see oceanfront houses for rent along this stretch of Carr. 3, worth checking out if you're in for the long haul.*

■ Camping

In the foothills above Guánica, the **Bosque Estatal de Susúa** has two campsites located on Carr. 368, Km. 2.1, both fully equipped with campfire areas, basketball courts, running water and bathrooms. A river for swimming flows nearby. Called Almácigo I and Almácigo II, ☎ 787-833-3700, the campsites have a combined capacity for 165 people. Nearby, the **Lago Lucchetti Wildlife Refuge**, ☎ 787-844-4660, on Carr. 128, is right on the banks of the lake and has bathrooms, showers, picnic gazebos and a boat ramp for those with their own vessel (unfortunately, no boat rentals are available onsite). Camping in Susúa and at Lago Lucchetti costs $4 per person per night, and you should obtain a permit from the Department of Natural and Environmental Resources, ☎ 787-724-3724 or 3647.

West of Ponce, the **Bosque Estatal De Aguirre** has begun to issue camping permits for the wilds nearby. Contact the National Estuarine Research Reserve, ☎ 787-853-4617, on Carr. 705, to find out how to organize this.

> **TIP:** *Although neither La Parguera nor Guánica has official campsites, we have "unofficially" pitched our tent on the deserted beaches around the dry forest.*

Where To Eat

■ San Germán

One of the island's top restaurants is **Cilantro's**, ☎ 787-264-2735, on Calle Luna 85 (parallel to the central plaza). It serves up *nuevo latino* cuisine in an elegant yet casual atmosphere of patios and artwork in the Casa Real – a replica of the home of the Barcelona-born

Gelpí brothers, who emigrated to San Germán in the late 19th century. During the Depression, *los hermanos* Gelpí opened their home to hungry locals and *campesinos*. But since Cilantro's opened in August 2000, the tiled patios have catered to a very different clientele that doesn't mind traveling for chef Carlos Rosario's inventive cuisine. Try starters such as *tostones rellonos de ceviche y guacamole*, the gourmet *chapín* (a sweet white fish with the appearance of a chicken drumstick), or the tropical lobster and fresh fruit salad with coconut-vinaigrette dressing, before moving on to mouth-watering duck, filet mignon or Caribbean-spiced seafood dishes. Most main dishes go for around $15. Open Mondays to Fridays, 11 a.m. to 4 p.m. and 6 to 10 p.m. (closed Wednesdays), Saturdays 2 to 11 p.m., Sundays 11 a.m. to 8 p.m. Reservations are a must, especially on weekends, because owner Pilar Torres ensures that patrons aren't rushed from their table and may spend hours lingering over their dinner and conversation.

The **Del Mar Bar & Restaurant**, ☎ 787-264-2715, on the central plaza, serves traditional seafood and meat dishes, and is favored by locals. Entrées range from $12 to $18. For light fare in a gallery owned by an art professor, head to **Galería Lubben**, ☎/fax 787-892-7420, on Calle Luna 9 in the student quarter. Expect to pay between $5 and $12. This brightly painted shack, half hidden under the roadside foliage, is a great place for a cup of Puerto Rican coffee, vegetarian food sprinkled with home-grown herbs and offbeat desserts such as fried ice cream. Artist Richard Lubben, who teaches at the university nearby, has hung the walls with an inspired collection of his own and local works. It's open from 4.30 to 9 p.m., Monday to Friday.

■ La Parguera

The most expensive but the best place to eat here is **Zoé en el Náutico**, ☎ 787-899-5237, Playita Rosada, e-mail restaurante-el-nautico@yahoo.com, well worth the extra trip from out of town (people come from all over the island) for sumptuous seafood with atmosphere. Entrées range from $14 to $25 here.

Of the many casual restaurants around town serving decent seafood, two of the best are **La Casita Seafood**, ☎ 787-899-1681, Calle Principal, (closed Mondays); and **La Palmita**, ☎ 787-899-4320, on Calle Principal (Friday through Sunday only). Most local restaurants charge from $10 to $20 for a main dish, depending on whether it involves shellfish.

For cheaper eats, head down to the pier where street vendors barbecue fish *pinchos* (meat on a stick) – dorado (mahi-mahi), *tiburón* (shark) and *chillo* (snapper) for no more than $2.50. For dinner and dancing, ☎ 787-899-7777, **Villa Parguera**, Calle Principal, has a reputation for good dinner buffets on Friday and Saturday nights, lunch buffet Sunday and lively cabaret acts (in Spanish) on Saturday night. Overlooking the water, it has an elegant atmosphere. Entrées from the menu generally cost between $20 and $30.

■ Guánica

This region is fairly isolated, but the few restaurants range from five-star dining to home-style *criollo* kitchen. **Café San Jacinto**, ☎ 787-821-4149, at Playa San Jacinto, Km. 66 on Carr. 333 (the first right-hand turn after the Copamarina), serves typical Puerto Rican fare, including a tasty lobster and shrimp *mofongo* served in bamboo stems. You'll probably hear this place before you see it, as the staff cranks up love songs and salsa music onto the patio area, while dining inside takes place in an atmosphere not unlike that of a smuggler's tavern. The ferry to Gilligan's Island leaves from here, and it's a pleasant place to have a beer in the evening under one of the miniature gazebos that are knitted together along the beach. Entrées cost between $7 and $12.

The other two dining options are at the Copamarina Beach Resort, ☎ 787-821-0505 ext. 766/716, Carr. 333. For light snacks, lunches and cocktails, the resort's **Las Palmas Café** serves up juicy burgers, club sandwiches and a couple of Puerto Rican staples, such as *mofongo*, with prices between $7 and $12. In the evening, diners feast on the gourmet creations of chef Wilo Benet at **Copamarina Coastal Cuisine**. Start with a half-dozen oysters or grilled duck sausages (appetizers range between $6 and $9) and follow up with a distinctly Caribbean main course such as plantain-crusted mahi mahi with pepper *escabeche*, or a rack of lamb served with *mamposteao* rice – a sort of Puerto Rican paella. Expect to pay between $30 and $40 a head, not including drinks, for a two-course meal.

■ Guayanilla

Between Guánica and Ponce, **Guardarraya**, ☎ 787-865-4222, Carr. 127 (not far from Yauco), is considered the home of Puerto Rico's famous *chuletas cancán* – "frilly" pork chops cooked three times. Open Tuesday through Sunday, 11 a.m. to 8 p.m., it serves entrées for less than $10.

■ Ponce

Although it lacks the endless choices of San Juan for fine dining, there are some good options scattered around the city. **Mark's at the Meliá**, ☎ 787-842-0260, Hotel Meliá, has become something of a South Coast institution and, according to some of Puerto Rico's best chefs, his creations are a must for gourmets. The changing menu may include appetizers such as smoked salmon with caramelized mango and risotto with saffron and lobster, for around $10. Entrées put a *criollo* twist on old-fashioned favorites, such as the roasted Cornish hen with *gandules* (pigeon peas) and *mofongo* and tamarind barbecue duck with *yuca mojo*. Expect to pay $25 and up for entrées. The **Ponce Hilton** also has a couple of up-market restaurants.

More casual diners head downtown for **Lupitas**, ☎ 787-848-8808, Calle Isabel, where a lovely Mexican-styled courtyard makes a perfect place for downing margaritas and tasty Mexican food. It doubles as a live music venue on weekends and draws a crowd. Fajitas, burritos and enchiladas cost between $7 and $15.

Many locals head outside the historic quarter to Ponce Playa, which was once one of the most desperate slums in the city but has transformed in the last decade into a colony of seafood restaurants. **El Ancla**, ☎ 787-840-2450, Avenida Hostos Final, is one of the best known, attracting customers from all over the island for its fresh *frutas del mar* cooked the Puerto Rican way. Main courses cost between $12 and $22. Serving similar fare, **Canda's**, ☎ 787-843-9223, on Calle Alfonso XII, is bedecked with Puerto Rican masks and paintings and also draws in a crowd. Carnivores can get their fix at **El Manegua Restaurant**, ☎ 787-259-3666, 28 Salmón Street, which serves Cuban classics for around $10 a plate.

Off the beaten track, try **Restaurante Casa Grande**, ☎ 787-841-6139, on Carr. 505 in Barrio La Yuca, for country cooking in a rustic setting. Specialties include island favorites like pork chops *kankán* (named for the filly battered edges that resemble the underskirts worn by cancan dancers in 19th-century Paris). Most dishes cost between $10 and $15.

Several places in Ponce do good lunch deals for little more than $5. For sandwiches and cheap *criollo* cooking and steaming cups of coffee, check out **Café Tomas**, ☎ 787-840-1965, on Calle Isabel. On the same street, near the plaza, **Olé Plena**, ☎ 787-841-6162, Calle Isabel, has become hugely popular among bohemian *Ponceños* and young professionals, who come for $5 lunchtime specials like pasta alfredo and pepper steak. Plates of authentic Spanish-style tapas go for about the same price in the evenings. On weekends, a wine guzzling, 30-something crowd lets loose as hot local musicians take the stage. Melissa, the owner, was planning to host tango sessions on Sunday evenings, so check up on that one. Open late.

Also a good value is the **Everyday Restaurant**, ☎ 787-284-4612, fax 284-4632, next door to the art museum on Ave. Las Americas, with a selection of wok, pasta and grill food all for less than $7 during lunch, served in a pleasant courtyard for dining al fresco. The evening entrées range from $10 to $20. Open 11 a.m. to 10 p.m., Monday to Thursday; 11 a.m. to 11 p.m. Friday and Saturday, and 2 p.m. to 10 p.m. Sunday.

Fox Delicias Mall, on Plaza Las Delicias, was Ponce's finest movie theater but is now a food hall. Inside, hole-in-the-wall eateries serve anything from pizza slices and burgers to stuffed pitas, Chinese noodles and, of course, the ubiquitous rice and beans, all cheap. We recommend taking your lunch outside to the courtyard, where large umbrellas shade cast iron tables and chairs.

Genesis 1:29, ☎ 787-844-5529, on Calle Marginal A-9 in Urbanización Constancia, is a bit of a trek, but offers veggie breakfasts and lunches every day, along with a good selection of fresh fruit *batidas*. It closes at 5 p.m.

■ Salinas

Several seafood restaurants lining the shore at Playa Salinas (follow Carr. 701) get so heaving on weekends that the queues spill out onto the pavements. You may be better off elsewhere. **Restaurant Costa Marina**, ☎ 787-824-6647, at Marina de Salinas, decorated with a sailing theme, is known for its quality seafood and steaks and gets busy with Puerto Rican boaters on weekends. Grilled lobster tail runs between $10 and $30. Also in the marina, a snack bar serves decent *sancocho* (Puerto Rican stew) and finger foods throughout the day. Back on Carr. 1, as you head toward the central plaza, **Los Jalapeños** is the place to stop for fajitas, tacos and other Mexican-style favorites.

■ Aguirre

Don't get hungry in Aguirre, unless you've brought your own picnic or are lucky enough to visit during the irregular opening hours of **Restaurant El Batey**, ☎ 787-853-3386 – the only game in town. If it is open, however, stop in for a chat with owner Nelson Santos, who is a veritable mine of information about the history of Aguirre. Something of a fanatic on the subject, he has adorned the walls of his establishment with photographs of sugar mills and plantations from all over Puerto Rico, which support his claim that Aguirre was, and always will be, the king of cane.

■ Guayama & Arroyo

Fast-food junkies will feel they've died and gone to heaven here, but if you're looking for cuisine the pickings are slim. The **Molino Inn and Restaurant**, ☎ 787-866-1515, fax 866-1510, on Hwy. 54, is the absolute best the area has to offer, with prices to match those in San Juan's finest eateries. House specials include châteaubriand – $41 for two people, $25 for one – and the restaurant's signature dish: lobster margarita style, a rich treat involving lashings of cheese and béchamel sauce, for $35.

For a sit-down lunch or dinner with local hospitality, the **Hotel & Restaurant Brandemar**, ☎ 787-864-5124, signposted off Hwy. 3 between Guayama and Arroyo, serves *criollo* and international food and is another popular weekend spot for families on driving trips. The surf and turf is probably the most impressive dish ($25), but you can eat for considerably less if you go for something more basic. Otherwise, several Chinese restaurants in the area offer cheap MSG specials, and you'll find a few ubiquitous snack bars serving *arroz con habichuelas* (rice and beans), etc.

Patillas

There are plenty of places to choose from (many weekends only) along the seaside strip that runs the whole distance from Patillas to Manaubo. But the undisputed favorite seems to be **El Mar de la Tranquilidad**, ☎ 787-839-6469, Carr. 3, Km. 118.9, specializing in all things seafood. Entrées are more pricey than you would expect of a casual out-of-the-way place (up to $20), but its position on the water, the possibility of a face-to-face encounter with a bashful manatee and good food makes the extra drive worth it. If you're looking for something a little more international, you'll need to go to **Frenesí**, ☎ 787-839-7388, at the Caribbean Paradise Hotel, Carr. 3, Km. 113.4. Entrées here are between $20 and $30.

Nightlife

San Germán

Since the imposition of a midnight curfew during the late 1990s, most bars and nightspots in San Germán have closed shop or moved out of town. Two exceptions, located near the plaza, are pretty seedy. **The Red Baron**, ☎ 787-892-5770, on the corner of Calle de la Cruz and Calle Dr. Santiago Veve, starts pumping techno tunes in the mid-afternoon, drawing wild-eyed creatures from the university and elsewhere into its smoke filled core. No doubt it gets pretty crazed on weekends. Across the street, **Copacabana** hosts occasional X-rated comedy shows and other entertainment during the weekend. Tamer adventures can be found in the student quarter at **Las Tigres**, Calle Luna (near the cluster of fast-food restaurants). It's a "happy hour" place, with cheap drinks catering to a student crowd.

Ponce

Since the waterfront became a cool hangout, many *Ponceños* have started heading to an area called **La Guancha** (Carr. 14; follow signs to La Playa from Hwy. 52) for an evening of music, dancing and cheap drinks. Come 5 p.m. on a Saturday, the party is already in full swing, with grown-ups undulating to booming salsa music, skateboarding teenagers menacing pedestrians, and young couples lurking around the parking lot to steal furtive kisses and sneak cans of Medalla beer. This is a place to strut, see and be seen.

Students from the Universidad Católica tend to hang out at the **Hollywood Café**, ☎ 787-843-6703, on Hwy. 1, which doles out bargain beer and burgers from its open-air café. Those who aren't out in the parking lot trying to increase the volume of their car stereos are inside hustling pool. You can have a lot of fun here if your eardrums are up to it.

Downtown, **Jazz Nicole**, ☎ 787-848-5474, Calle Isabel, has a cigar bar and live jazz on Fridays and Saturdays until the wee hours. Also open for lunch and dinner. **Olé Plena** and **Lupitas** (see above in *Where To Eat*) also have live music on weekends. Movers and shakers with Saturday night fever can choose from discos at both the Hilton and at the Holiday Inn. Also check Calle Isabel, where a funky disco was due to open.

NIGHTS OF ROMANCE

Ponce is known for many things: politics and journalism, art and architecture and *quenepas* – a lychee-like fruit that sticks to the roof of your mouth. More recently, business owners on Calle Isabel have promoted Ponce as the "city of lovers" – at least on the last Thursday of every month, when the street closes to traffic for a *noche romantica*. If you're in the mood for love, grab a table set out on the street and give yourselves up to the ballads of Puerto Rican *mariachi* under the stars.

Central Mountains

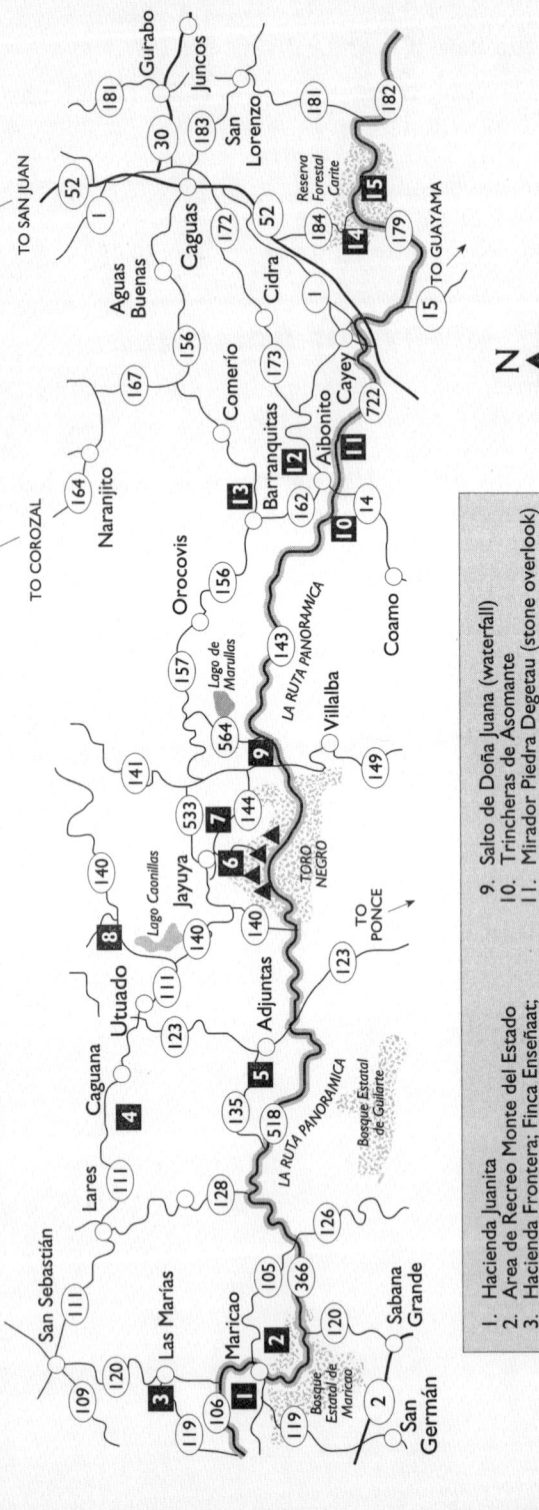

1. Hacienda Juanita
2. Area de Recreo Monte del Estado
3. Hacienda Frontera; Finca Enseñaat; Bill Birdsall's home
4. Parque Ceremonial Indígena Caguana
5. Sotomayor Resort Hotel & Country Club
6. Hacienda La Gripiñas
7. Museo Indígena Cemí; Casa Canales
8. Hotel La Casa Grande
9. Salto de Doña Juana (waterfall)
10. Trincheras de Asomante
11. Mirador Piedra Degetau (stone overlook)
12. San Cristóbal Canyon
13. Casa Natal Luis Muñoz Rivera; Casa Museo Joaquín de Rojas y Martínez & Tourist Office
14. Guavate Recreation Area
15. Charco Azul Recreation Area

© 2001 HUNTER PUBLISHING, INC

Central Mountains

To find the *real* Puerto Rico – the one that shopping malls and condos have yet to reach – head for the towns and villages of the **Cordillera Central**, or Central Mountains. Bisected by the Ruta Panoramica (Scenic Route), the mountains provide a relaxing getaway with an atmosphere so unlike the coast that it feels like an entirely different island. The Ruta Panorámica is a driving adventure covering more than a hundred miles of countryside, including coffee plantations, old *jíbaro* country and four forests: **Carite**, **Toro Negro**, **Guilarte** and **Maricao**. Along the route are valleys, canyons, wide-open terraces and views of the Atlantic and the Caribbean. Visitors who don't have time to do the whole Ruta Panorámica might consider a driving tour starting out from San Juan to the San Cristobal canyon in Aibonito, returning via Barranquitas – easily doable in a day if you start out early. Or take a few days to enjoy secluded swimming holes, hiking trails, cloud forest and the hospitality of the mountain locals.

IN THIS CHAPTER
- Canóvanas
- Luquillo
- Fajardo
- Ceiba
- Naguabo
- Humacao
- Jayuya
- Yabucoa & Maunabo

Getting Here & Getting Around

There is only one good way to explore the Cordillera Central – by car – and you'll need at least a full day or two (or more) to do it. A spellbinding drive, the **Ruta Panorámica** runs along the spine of the Central Mountains, and is extremely winding in many places. Although the entire island is only 100 miles long, this route takes a full day to complete in its entirety. *Públicos* connect all sizeable towns, but these mini-buses generally make short trips, and traveling in this manner will severely limit the amount of territory you can cover. If you plan to make short forays to specific locations in the mountains, choose your route carefully. Highways into the mountains (designated in red or yellow on roadmaps) are much faster than smaller roads. From San Juan, it takes roughly the same amount of time to reach most western mountain destinations via northern or southern highways.

> **AUTHORS' TIP:** *To enjoy your time in the mountains to the fullest, reserve a hotel room for a night or two, so you don't feel rushed.*

Communications

A sign of the modernity of today's Puerto Rico is that, even in the most remote mountain towns, public pay phones generally work as well as those in metropolitan San Juan. Mobile phone coverage, on the other hand, is extremely spotty in the mountains. Unless you're staying at one of the more upscale guest houses in the Cordillera Central, don't expect to be able to pick up your e-mail. Use the mountains an excuse to get away from the outside world!

Touring & Sightseeing

■ Punta Guavate & Carite Forest Reserve

Just to confuse you, this area has two names, which are often used interchangeably. To simplify: **Carite** officially refers to the forest; **Guavate** to the general area, which is best known for the 20 or 30 *lechoneras* that serve piping hot hunks of spit-roasted pork and chicken. From San Juan, it's a quick 30-minute trip. Take Hwy. 52 through the foothills of the Cordillera Central, then head southeast on Carr. 184, which marks the start of the pork-peddling district. This is a major gathering place on weekends, when families come from all over the island to literally pig out. During summer months, the *flamboyán* trees bloom fire-red and drop their petals on the ground, creating a carpet that one local resident jokingly described as "like driving through hell." Consider spending the night up here (or at least stopping in) at **La Casona de Guavate & Posada El Castillo** (see *Where To Stay*), a fantastical "medieval castle" and luxury campground.

Compared to nearby El Yunque, the smaller and fairly unknown **Reserva Forestal Carite** is less geared to visitors. For this reason, some nature lovers prefer it to El Yunque. The best trail starts out from the recreation area at **Charco Azul**, which is sometimes noted as Area Recreativa El Real on maps, at the southernmost part of the forest on Carr. 184. The highlight is a trek through **Hero Valley**, which you can organize through Cathy at Las Casas de la Selva (see page 292).

One of the many lechoneras in the Guavate area.
(Bob Krist, for the PRTC)

■ Aibonito

Meaning, "Ah, pretty!" in Spanish, Aibonito possesses a natural beauty that is marred by heavy traffic and one of the biggest chicken-processing plants in Puerto Rico. Creole architecture dating from the 1920s and 1930s is now painted in the garish primary hues of M&Ms and, from a distance, the town resembles a giant candy store spilled into a mountainous bowl. Unless you happen to be around for one of town's many festivals, you won't find too much going on here. The annual flower festival – **Festival de las Flores** – takes place for 10 days at the end of June. On the other hand, the nearby **San Cristóbal** canyon, a gaping, five-mile crevasse stretching from Aibonito to Barranquitas (see *On Foot*, page 281) is one of the most impressive natural sights on the island. Stop here for a picnic lunch.

There are two landmarks between Cayey and Aibonito. **Casa Manresa** on Carr. 162, a giant blue Catholic ceremonial center, is where Rome-educated local priests are ordained. **Mirador Piedra Degetau**, on Carr. 7718, is the "meditation site" of Federico Degetau y González, the first Puerto Rican national to enter US Congress. Despite magnificent views over the south coast and the town of Aibonito, the inspirational value of the site is all but destroyed by a concrete viewing platform and a stark picnic area. Nearby, a plaque commemorates the brief battle of **Trincheras del Asomante**, fought between Spanish soldiers armed with stones and a ragged American naval force on August 25, 1898. It was the last conflict in the Spanish-American War, ending when a few Spanish soldiers, apparently out of stones to throw, finally fled. To find this obscure footnote to military history, follow Carr. 723 to Tío Pepe's restaurant, then make a sharp left-hand turn into a residential area. Continue straight past the chicken slaughterhouse and park at the end of the road. A two-lane dirt track leads down the hill to the site.

> **DID YOU KNOW?** *One of the lowest-ever temperatures in Puerto Rico was recorded in Aibonito. On March 9, 1911, residents woke up shivering as temperatures dipped to (egad!) 40° Fahrenheit. Locals will say it was like "living in Canada," and the place has since been dubbed* la ciudad fria *(cold city).*

WEATHER FORECAST FROM THE GODS

Long before satellites or meteorologists, indigenous people had their own methods of predicting the weather. When the leaves of cecropia trees flipped over, giving the whole mountainside a silvery sheen, Taino Indians knew that storms would ravage the Cordillera the next day. Local residents still swear by this sign.

■ Barranquitas

Birthplace of perhaps the greatest Puerto Rican national hero, Barranquitas is the primary source for anyone interested in the origin of democracy on the island, and is full of sites of historical interest. Politician, poet and newspaperman Luis Muñoz Rivera was born and died here. His birthplace, **Casa Natal Luis Muñoz Rivera**, ☎ 787-857-0203, is a small *criollo* house with a corrugated roof, a block from the plaza on Calle Muñoz Rivera, which has been converted into a museum documenting the life history of this George Washington of Puerto Rican history. One block away, the **Casa Museo Joaquín de Rojas y Martínez & Tourist Office**, ☎ 787-857-2065, is another interesting example of turn-of-the-century Creole architecture. The woodwork and Spanish tiles are all original, and it's so tiny and perfect that you may feel a bit like Gulliver in a Lilliputian home, clumsily examining to-scale bronze bedposts, dining table and chairs, family portraits, and heirlooms that include two thumb-size ceramic dolls dating from 1900, a cigar roller from 1922 and an etching of the Día de San Antonio festivities in 1895.

Another highlight in town is the **Mausoleo Familia Muñoz Rivera**, ☎ 787-857-0203, at the bottom of Calle Padre Berrios, the family mausoleum, where both Muñoz Rivera and his son, Luis Muñoz Marín, are buried. The mural on the interior of the mausoleum tells the story of the Muñoz politicians as well as any written text. Call for hours.

> **FOR MUSIC-LOVERS:** *Travelers interested in jíbaro folk music should visit father-and-son team* **Ramón Luis and Luis Angel Colón**, ☎ *787-857-0117/4394/1513, who carve exquisite stringed instruments called* cuatros *from their workshop in Sector La Torre.*

■ Toro Negro

Situated nearly in the middle of the island, Toro Negro is accessible via either Carr. 143 (La Ruta Panorámica), which bisects the forest, or via Carr. 139, from Ponce. Forest layers are comprised mainly of palo colorado, tabonuco and cecropia trees that survived the clearing of land during the first half of the 20th century. On the highest mountains, sierra palm and dwarf forest are often spookily shrouded in clouds, which part to reveal great views of the seas far below on either side. Toro Negro is one of the finest examples of cloud forests in the Caribbean, and the temperamental weather patterns add to the thrill of being here. A typical day involves passing from torrential rain and unforgiving mist, high winds and (relatively) chilly temperatures to eye-aching sunlight reflecting from the sea and sky.

One of the more dramatic roadside attractions is the **Salto de Doña Juana**, a waterfall plummeting 120 feet into an irresistible pool of turquoise water right on the edge of Carr. 149. The **Río Toro Negro** is perfect for river hiking, with smooth, egg-shaped boulders and many private swimming holes, but be wary of flash floods. The western section of the Toro Negro forest is home to the highest peaks in Puerto Rico. **Cerro Punta**, the zenith of the island at 4,388 feet, **Cerro Maravillas** and **Cerro Jayuya** are all covered in radio transmitters and other communication equipment, and accessible from Carr. 143. To reach Cerro Punta, head westbound on Carr. 143 past Carr. 577 (which is signposted, but not listed on most roadmaps). A steep paved road leads up to the summit, where you can climb a set of stairs overgrown by weeds to what feels like the top of the world. As the clouds blow past you from the east (there are usually fewer clouds in the mornings), you may catch 360° views of the island and surrounding sea.

Basic information about forest features and attractions are available from the visitor center just west of the **Recreo Doña Juana**, ☎ 787-724-3724 (Monday through Friday 8 a.m. to 4 p.m.), on Carr. 143.

TWO GRAVES THAT TOPPLED A GOVERNMENT

Drive or hike up to the Cerro Maravillas peak (from Carr. 143, turn at the sign for Carr. 577), and you'll see two small concrete crosses dwarfed by all the communication equipment. On July 25, 1978, two young pro-independence radicals, Arnaldo Dario Rodado, 23, and Carlos Soto Arriví, 18, were murdered on this site, allegedly by undercover government agents who lured them to the peak in a plot to vandalize the communications tower. Although some details of the case remain murky, the controversy and public outcry helped bring down the government of Gov. Carlos Romero Barceló in 1984. Ten policemen were sentenced to long prison terms the next year for second-degree murder and other crimes in the case, which continues to stir controversy.

Graves of two pro-Independence youths slain in 1978.
(©2000, Tara Stephens)

Jayuya & Environs

For some metropolitan Puerto Ricans, the remote town of Jayuya is something of an inside joke, synonymous with crude country behavior, backwardness and hillbilly attitudes. If someone enters a fine restaurant in San Juan wearing rough clothes and speaking in a loud voice, for example, *sanjuaneros* might giggle and whisper among themselves, "Go back to

Jayuya!" Most of these people have never been to Jayuya, however, and although the mountain town is one of the most cloistered spots in the mountainous interior, it's no more backward than most small towns in the US. Those who have been here appreciate the lush tropical mountain landscape around Jayuya, the hospitality of its inhabitants and the town's rich history as former strongholds of *jíbaro* and Taino culture.

Tightly packed in a mountain pass, the small downtown area of Jayuya is worth visiting mostly for a quick lunch en route to surrounding attractions, a couple of nearby accommodations, or as an anthropological foray into the highland heart of Puerto Rico. The town was named for the Taino chief Hayuya, who presided over the area when the Spanish arrived. And some of the best sights in the area are related to Jayuya's Indian heritage.

A TAINO THEME PARTY

Every year in late November, Jayuya hosts **La Festival Indígena**, with music, arts & crafts and "living history" events, dedicated to the heritage of the Taino Indians who once populated this mountain region. For more information, contact the local tourism office, ☎ 787-828-1241, or the Jayuya City Hall, ☎ 787-828-0900.

The **Mural Indígeno de Zamas**, a hidden historical treasure in Barrio Zamas (southwest of the town center from Carr. 528), is the largest mural of petroglyphs in the Caribbean, and is rarely visited. Some scholars believe that its location on a massive rock of Cerro Punta, the highest peak in Puerto Rico, shows that this was an altar to the supreme Taino god, Yocahú Vagua Maorociti (akin to Zeus in Greek mythology). The alphabet soup of petroglyphs includes one symbol, called El Sol de Jayuya, that is unique to the island. Some experts say it represents the sun, while others believe it is a stylized drawing of a turtle, a sacred animal to the Tainos. If you stay in the Jayuya area long enough, you are bound to see this symbol on stamps, posters or bottles of local wine, even though many residents are unaware of its origins. To find the rock, follow Carr. 528 and then ask directions to the private finca (plantation) of Luis Reyes, on which you'll find the stone.

Following Carr. 144 westward from the Jayuya town center, you'll find some more impressive petroglyphs at the **Piedra Escrita** (signposted from the road). This is a monolith-type rock in the middle of the Río Saliente, as covered in petroglyphs as a graffiti-scrawled freeway underpass in Los Angeles. The *piedra* forms a natural swimming hole in the river, so bring a bathing suit. About half a mile upstream, a smaller rock called Piedra Tibe has fewer, but larger, petroglyphs.

Farther southwest on Carr. 144, you can't miss the incredible, cone-shaped **Museo Indigena Cemí**, ☎ 787-828-1241, built to resemble the form of a Taino idol (or, to the uninitiated, a giant, hunchbacked snail).

Built in 1989, this peculiar museum houses a small but fascinating collection of actual *cemí* icons, shell jewelry worn by Taino women and a complete photographic documentation of Taino petroglyphs found in Puerto Rico, displayed municipality by municipality. Notice the ceremonial spatulas, used by Taino mystics to induce vomiting before they took a mildly hallucinogenic herb known as *cojoba* – an expressway to the gods. The museum is open intermittently but, if you arrive on a weekday and the doors are closed, head for the office behind the cafeteria to seek out the friendly staff members, who will likely give you a spontaneous tour of the place.

WHAT'S A CEMÍ?

Tainos used the same word – *cemíes* – to describe both the gods that ruled their everyday world and the fetishistic idols carved to represent them. The god was embodied in the icon, and the icon imbued with the god. Most *cemí* talismans were carved in a rough dome or triangular shape, with animal or human faces and abstract designs. Other than that, clues to the meaning of *cemíes* died out with the Tainos, and today scholars still disagree on the significance of the form. Some say the rising shape represents a plant, or symbol of agriculture. Others suggest that it might suggest the sacred peak of El Yunque. Other academics argue that the pointy shape symbolizes fertility, in the form of a phallus or the female breast.

Casa Canales

Next to the *cemí* museum, an old plantation house known as **Casa Canales**, ☎ 787-828-4094, captures a very different epoch. Built in the late 19th century by the first mayor of Jayuya, this formerly successful coffee plantation was, for decades, the seat of local bigwigs and intellectuals. They gathered here to socialize, sip java and, at times, plot protests against centralized island government. During the early 20th century, nationalists used Casa Canales as a base, and it became a focal point in the struggle between freedom-minded locals and supporters of US control of the island. On Oct. 30, 1950, a woman named Blanca Canales (sister of famous columnist Nemesio R. Canales) led a group of nationalists from this house to declare the independent Republic of Jayuya, a largely symbolic gesture that lasted for only a few hours. The movement was quickly quashed by the US National Guard, and the Casa Canales afterward fell into ruins until its restoration in 1991. The museum is open to the public Saturday and Sunday, 12 p.m. to 4 p.m., for tours.

IN SEARCH OF THE JÍBARO

Their passion for storytelling, music making and the simple life of a country peasant was legendary in our minds. So, determined to find a living *jíbaro*, we asked friends in San Juan to point us in the right direction. "*Jíbaros* don't exist anymore," we were told. "However, you *could* try Jayuya." The long drive into town was not encouraging. Late-model sedans and sports cars whizzed past our Mazda. A group of young skateboarders on a street corner blasted alternative rock music from a boom box. Professionals in business suits ducked in and out of the cafés. Where were the peasant folk of yore – described by a 19th-century Spanish colonel as hammock-swinging, cigar-smoking, guitar-scraping do-nothings? The place seemed as modern as any suburb in the US. Even the older men tended to wear discount designer clothing and baseball caps, not the garb of yesterday's subsistence farmers.

"Where can we find a *jíbaro*?" we naively asked one shopkeeper. He stared at us disapprovingly, as though we'd asked the whereabouts of the tooth fairy. Many inquiries later, having entertained a number of locals with the same, apparently ridiculous, question, we gave up, and headed out of town on Carr. 144 toward the Toro Negro forest. Here were signs of a much older culture. Taino petroglyphs suggested a storytelling tradition that predated *jíbaros* by many centuries.

Farther on, a little museum housed relics of indigenous stone amulets that hinted at how the island's earliest indigenous farmers had spent their spare time – carving devotional totems. Sprawled under some of Puerto Rico's highest peaks, the overgrown former coffee- and sugar-growing fields around us seemed to sparkle in the cooler air of the highlands. On a little side road, we stopped to ask directions from an elderly man shaping a block of wood in an open-air workshop next to his home. His name was Pepito, his hands more gnarled and old than the wood with which he worked. What are you making? "It's called a *cuatro*," he said. "It's a traditional Puerto Rican instrument. Like a guitar, but with 10 strings." Pepito explained that he made a living from making and selling *cuatros* for hundreds of dollars to wealthy collectors from San Juan and Ponce. What does it sound like? "It's very pretty," he said, fetching a finished instrument. "Listen." Sitting on an old wooden stool, he plucked out a few lively chords. Then, glancing up at his impromptu audience, Pepito began to sing:

Sale loco de contento
Con su cargamento
Para la ciudad, sí
Para la ciudad.

We asked Pepito the same naïve question we had asked in Jayuya, but he didn't laugh. "The *jíbaro* has always been an image," he said. "A myth. And like a myth, it cannot die. All Puerto Ricans have a little bit of *jíbaro* inside us. This is our culture." Strung between two trees in front of Pepito's home, an empty hammock swung impatiently in the breeze. The only thing missing was the cigar.

Utuado

When Hwy. 10 cut the drive from the north coast into the mountains to less than 25 minutes, it helped transform Utuado from a quiet provincial town into a somewhat gritty suburb. The two-story buildings of the old town center now house a Payless shoe store, cheap fashion outlets and a Burger King. Outlying *barrios* retain more of the old country charm. East of town, Caonillas Lake feeds into Lago Dos Bocas and leads to **Casa Grande**, one of our favorite guest houses on the island. About five miles west of town on Carr. 111, the **Parque Ceremonial Indigena Caguana,** with excavated *batey* courts, and several ancient trails once traveled by Taino Indians make excellent day-trip excursions into the past (see *On Foot*).

A DROWNED CHURCH

After the construction of the Dos Bocas and Caonillas reservoirs, flood waters submerged a church that had been built in the Caonillas valley in the 1930s. During times of extreme drought, the water level has been observed to sink low enough that the bell tower of the church rises mysteriously from the lake's surface. Miracle seekers flock to the spectacle, hoping for some divine event, but have so far been disappointed.

Maricao

Called the "Ciudad de Café," Maricao is probably best known for its three-day **coffee festival** (in February), during which, traditionally, the farm with the best local coffee is chosen and locals celebrate the end of the harvest and invite good fortune for the next. Hurricane Georges wrought so much damage to the area in 1998, however, that the local coffee-growing industry may never fully recover. Recent festivals have conspicuously lacked the coffee tasting, and even the two local cafeterias in this small town serve imported (or instant!) java.

THE LEGEND OF MARICAO

According to legend, Maricao gets its name from a Taino woman who fell in love with a Spanish settler in this area and warned him of an impending attack by her people. The Spanish launched a preemptive strike, but during the battle the Indians captured their betrayer (whom the Spanish had renamed María). Afterward, the story goes, surviving Indians tied María to a tree and executed her for the act of treachery. Grateful Spanish colonists named the area Maricao, a contraction of Mari(a) and the suffix *cao*, signifying sacrifice or martyrdom.

Las Marías

Another former agricultural stronghold is Las Marías, which calls itself the "home of the sweet orange." Tucked between picturesque hills surrounded by coffee, bananas and, of course, orange trees (which generally grow at higher elevations than their California and Florida cousins), the town itself is small and rather dull. It was founded in the latter half of the 19th century. The small pueblo has a meager plaza, a few crumbling buildings from a century ago, a modern town hall and a pizzeria and two rice-and-beans cafeterias amidst featureless modern structures.

Hacienda Frontera, Carr. 124, Km. 6.8 in the direction of Lares, is a relic from the town's agricultural past, a colonial wood and zinc structure with period furnishings and coffee processing equipment on display. Opening hours are sporadic, so before visiting check with the mayor's office, ☎ 787-827-2280 or 2940. The more modern **Finca Enseñat**, Carr. 124, Km. 10.7, has facilities capable of producing two million coffee beans per year and grows more than 200,000 citrus trees. A working farm, it is not open to the public. The **"Las Marías Festival Honoring The Sweet Orange"** takes place in late March every year, with thousands enjoying the party atmosphere of three days of music, booze and orange juice.

Also in the direction of Lares, you'll find (with determination) one of the more fantastical homes ever conceived. It was built during the past 25 years by artist **Bill Birdsall**, out of discarded tuna fishnets, a cement-and-plaster mix and non-biodegradable garbage, and its hobbit-like shape consists of domes, grottos, staircases and sinkholes and a giant tunnel burrowed into the heart of the hillside. Open-minded visitors, especially musicians and drummers, are welcome (Bill has a one-room "guest house") to stop by for a jam session. Ask to see his homemade instruments, including the "Secretary's Nightmare" – a musical ball studded with old-fashioned typewriter keys, played with a ping-pong ball and heard through a stethoscope. To get here, follow Carr. 124 toward Lares, then turn left at Carr. 370. When you see the little Capilla Catolíca La Milagrosa, turn right and drive along a spectacular ridge. Bear right at the fork in the road, park where it ends, and follow the tractor path to, as Bill calls it, "another planet."

Adventures

■ On Foot

Hiking

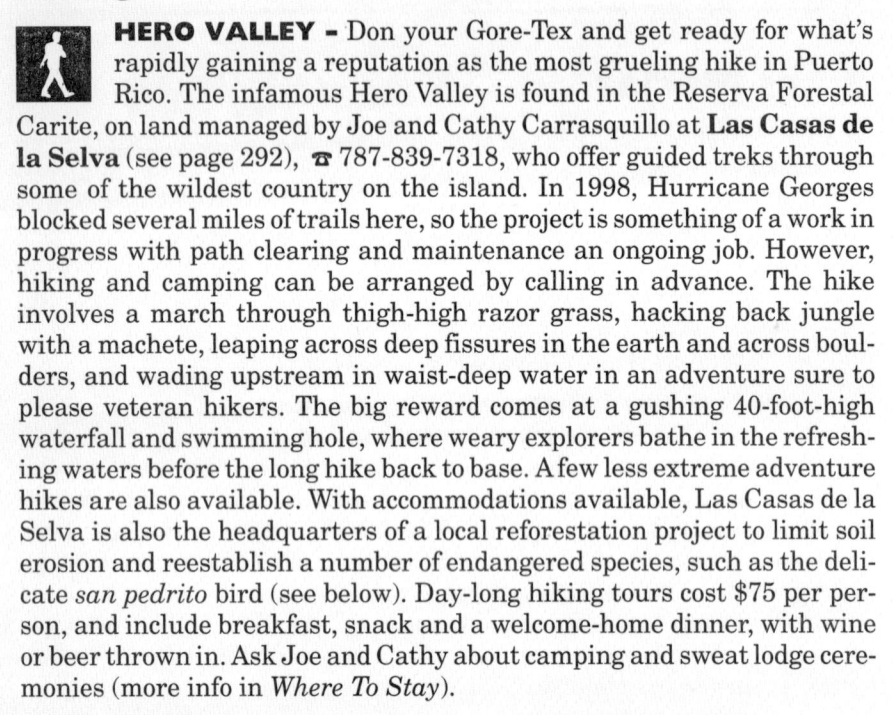

HERO VALLEY - Don your Gore-Tex and get ready for what's rapidly gaining a reputation as the most grueling hike in Puerto Rico. The infamous Hero Valley is found in the Reserva Forestal Carite, on land managed by Joe and Cathy Carrasquillo at **Las Casas de la Selva** (see page 292), ☎ 787-839-7318, who offer guided treks through some of the wildest country on the island. In 1998, Hurricane Georges blocked several miles of trails here, so the project is something of a work in progress with path clearing and maintenance an ongoing job. However, hiking and camping can be arranged by calling in advance. The hike involves a march through thigh-high razor grass, hacking back jungle with a machete, leaping across deep fissures in the earth and across boulders, and wading upstream in waist-deep water in an adventure sure to please veteran hikers. The big reward comes at a gushing 40-foot-high waterfall and swimming hole, where weary explorers bathe in the refreshing waters before the long hike back to base. A few less extreme adventure hikes are also available. With accommodations available, Las Casas de la Selva is also the headquarters of a local reforestation project to limit soil erosion and reestablish a number of endangered species, such as the delicate *san pedrito* bird (see below). Day-long hiking tours cost $75 per person, and include breakfast, snack and a welcome-home dinner, with wine or beer thrown in. Ask Joe and Cathy about camping and sweat lodge ceremonies (more info in *Where To Stay*).

THE SUN-SENSITIVE SAN PEDRITO

The endangered *san pedrito*, a petite, bright green and yellow bird, suffers from an unfortunate genetic glitch that prevents its pores from closing, making it completely reliant on shaded areas of forest canopy. If a *san pedrito* attempts to fly in direct sunlight for more than 30 yards, it is likely to collapse and die of dehydration.

CHARCO AZUL - Also in the Carite Forest area, and sometimes signposted as Area Recreativa El Real on maps, Charco Azul has trails that wind through thickets of bamboo and umbrella-like tree ferns to a sizeable natural swimming hole. Green mango hummingbirds, Puerto Rican woodpeckers, stripe-headed tanagers and sharp-shinned hawks, among others, inhabit the 6,000-acre reserve, along with six species of the coquí frog and two species of snakes; the Puerto Rican racer and the nocturnal Puerto Rican boa, both shy and not dangerous. Find trailheads at the southernmost part of the forest, on Carr. 184. The recreation area is open 9 a.m. to 4 p.m. weekdays, and 8 a.m. to 5 p.m. weekends and holidays. Just inside the north forest entrance, the ranger station, also on Carr. 184, provides excellent advice on where to hike and what to see in the forest, but has limited opening hours: Monday, Thursday and Friday between 8 and 10 a.m. Otherwise, contact the **Department of Natural Resources** in San Juan, ☎ 787-747-4545, for more information and camping permits.

> **GEARING UP:** *For most hikes in the Cordillera Central, we recommend boots (or good sports shoes) and some measure of protective clothing. Although the forests are free of the most dangerous types of tropical menaces, you may encounter fire ants, mosquitoes and a few stinging, clinging plants. Bring plenty of bug repellent, preferably in environmentally friendly lotion form.*

THE GRAND CANYON OF SAN CRISTÓBAL - Rarely hiked by outsiders, Aibonito boasts the widest, deepest canyon in Puerto Rico. Access is limited to two or three places (unless you rappel in) known only to a handful of local guides. Just over five miles long, the San Cristóbal Canyon may not compare to the vastness of the Grand Canyon or possess the surreal rock structures of Utah's Bryce, but it is one of the greatest natural splendors of Puerto Rico.

If the canyon floor seems unnaturally deformed, it is. Until the mid-1970s, San Cristóbal was used as a landfill by the municipalities of Aibonito and Barranquitas. Topped by more than a quarter-century of fast-growing jungle vegetation, the graveyard of old electrical appliances and garbage forms a bizarre environment. Here, Puerto Rico's highest waterfall – **Salto Usabón** – drops 500 feet and is fed by the Barranquitas and Usabón rivers.

Be aware that torrential afternoon downpours can turn steep earthen paths to mush. In 1993, civil defense workers had to haul 27 hikers out of the canyon after a flash flood trapped them at the bottom. Adventuring in this canyon during rainy season is best done with a guide. Contact Joe Esteras of the **Restaurante La Piedra,** ☎ 787-735-1034, for information on guided tours. During the dry season, guides meet at Restaurante La Piedra at 8.30 a.m. and take all comers on hikes into the canyon and out again by lunchtime.

For a more tailored adventure, groups of five or more should call local canyon expert **Felix Rivera**, ☎ 787-735-8721. The Barranquitas Tourist Office recommends as a guide **Miguel Angel de Jesús**, ☎ 787-875-3657. If you decide to go it alone, one trailhead can be found next to Carr. 725, but it involves a transaction with the "gatekeeper," Edildo, a real-life troll who is best approached with an introduction from Frank Charriez of the Casa Alcaldía, ☎ 787-735-8181, in Aibonito. Charriez is a civil defense veteran, and was part of the 1993 rescue team mentioned above. After gaining Edildo's blessing, we found the trail exhilarating; it's easily one of the most rewarding hikes on the island. To find the trailhead, turn right at Km. 5.1. on Carr. 725. Edildo's place is the aqua-blue one-story house on the corner. The trail starts from here.

> **CAUTION:** *Hiking unguided in the San Cristóbal Canyon should be done only by experienced hikers, who travel with a buddy and respect the potential effects of heavy rainfall. Schedule your hike to start early in the morning and be aware that darkness falls around 4 p.m. at the bottom of the canyon.*

THE "ENCHANTED FOREST" OF TORO NEGRO – Because a good portion of the Reserva Forestal Toro Negro is cloud forest, the best time for exploring is the morning, before clouds envelop the upper canopy in a thick mist. On the lower slopes of the eastern portion of the forest, however, short, well-maintained trails (some are even paved, and have handrails) around the **Recreo Doña Juana** lead to destinations such as a lookout platform, a picnic area or a swimming hole. Unfortunately, the swimming hole has been surrounded by concrete, presumably to make it safer for children, and what might have been a lovely river-fed recreation site more closely resembles a water treatment plant. The pool is open daily between April and September, 9 a.m. to 5 p.m; the entrance fee is $1.

The best trail in the area is probably along **Camino El Bolo**, a decent three-mile hike through palo colorado trees slashed with bright streaks of color – pink *miramelindas,* birds of paradise and lobster claw flowers that look good enough to eat. Rangers at the station just west of the Recreo Doña Juana area and campsite, ☎ 787-724-3724, (open Monday through Friday 8 a.m. to 4 p.m.), seem to know extremely little about most of the forest and are relatively useless to the traveler, except in an emergency. In the higher, western portion of the Toro Negro forest, sierra palms and gnarled cloud forest turn the slopes into an enchanting realm. However, the 1998 hurricane made the few independently charted trails in this area impassable, and no group has stepped up to maintain them. We've been told that the best contact for hiking in this area is DNR ranger René Román ☎ 787-867-3040, who is a keen hiker himself. A fairly well defined trail to the summit of **Cerro Punta** (the highest peak in Puerto Rico) begins at **Hacienda Gripiñas**, ☎ 787-828-1717, in Jayuya. Ask at the front desk how to get to the trailhead.

TRACKING TAINO PATHS IN ANGELES – Follow ancient Taino Indian trails in the karstic uplands through riverbeds and subtropical forest, and visit caves with petroglyphs that few humans have ever seen. Summit to a lookout over some of the most remote landscape on the island. Far from any road, the Tanamá River cuts the limestone rock into hills that seem to belong to another world. At **Expediciones Tanamá**, ☎ 787-894-7685, http://home.coqui.net/albite/albite/index.html/, eco-guide Roberto Bonilla takes visitors on some of the island's greatest and least discovered adventures, routes rediscovered by Bonilla and a few island anthropologists. Two of the routes are detailed below.

> **DID YOU KNOW?** *Tanamá is the Taino word for "butterfly." In Spanish, it's "mariposa."*

Toro Negro Hiking Trails

NOT TO SCALE
Trail locations are approximate

1. Camino Ortolaza
2. Camino El Bolo
3. La Piscina (Swimming Pool)
4. La Torre
5. Vega Grande
6. Camino Doña Petra
7. Las Cuarentas
8. Camino El Tabonuco
9. Recro Doña Juana and Camping Area
10. Ranger Station

© 2001 HUNTER PUBLISHING, INC

Although Roberto prefers to speak Spanish, he is accustomed to receiving gringo visitors and, if you cannot speak Spanish, he will quite amiably communicate in English (or Spanglish). At least one of his younger guides is bilingual. If you're in good physical condition, it's possible to do both routes in the same day. Arrive early with hiking boots or sturdy sports shoes and a willingness to get a little bit wet and dirty. To get here, from Utuado head west on Carr. 111 past the Parque Ceremonial Indigena Caguana to Carr. 602. Here you'll start to see some of Roberto's handmade signs, which lead to his hillside home. You'll find him on his humble coffee- and fruit-growing finca, usually wearing camouflage pants and an eco-warrior T-shirt, with his feet propped up among fossils and Indian artifacts collected during more than a half-century exploring the greater Angeles area.

> **TIP:** *A day-trip with Expediciones Tanamá is one of the best bargain adventures on the island, at $58 per person. Guests who take advantage of Roberto Bonilla's tour are welcome to pitch a tent, free of charge, on the lawn next to his little coffee finca. There is access to an outdoor shower and a bathroom.*

- **Ruta Fray Bartolomé de las Casas** – Trek into a deep canyon on an overgrown trail, named for the Spanish friar who, 500 years ago, came to live with the Tainos and learn about their culture. As you cut your way through the tropical underbrush with a machete, notice the rich diversity of plant life that tells its own version of the island's history, such as wild ginger first discovered in Puerto Rico by the French, who used it for cooking, various species of native orchid, delicate live-and-die plants, which temporarily shrivel up when touched, pink clover-shaped *mirame linda* flowers, two types of mimosas, Colombian plantains and coffee bushes planted more than three centuries ago by the Spanish. En route, you'll climb over the corpses of trees toppled by Hurricane Georges in 1998, and get a glimpse of a wooden shack – the only sign of human life in the area – inhabited by a hermit named Felix who subsists on his home-grown corn, tobacco and moonshine rum.

The path ends at Cueva del Arco, a cave the size of a football field and nearly the height of a stadium, where thousands of bats squeak high in the fissures of the stalactites above and drop their dark guano on the rocks of the cave floor. Limestone formations approximately 60 million years old open out onto the Tanamá River below. A chamber about 200 feet above the river was apparently used as a living space many centuries ago, as pieces of Indian ceramics have been found there. Behind you, notice a square hole where a chunk of rock etched with a petroglyph was recently cut out and shipped to the Museo del Indio in Old San Juan. From the cave, descend to the river, where you'll jump in up to your thighs and wade downstream through a glorious, untouched canyon that leads through a towering rock arch. Under the arch, a Jurassic-era shelf washed clear during the 1998 hurricane reveals perfectly preserved fossils, shells and sand dollars embedded there 150 million years ago.

CALLING ALL CACIQUES

After relations with the conquistadors had soured, the powerful Taino Cacique Guarionex sent messengers along this same route to request the support of other Indian chiefs in the first major uprising against the Spanish.

- **Ruta Cacique Uruyoán** – Named for the Taino chief who ordered the experimental drowning of a young Spanish settler in Añasco, this path was used by Uruyoán's messenger to bring news to Cacique Guarionex and others that the white man was, in fact, mortal. Bonilla or one of his young guides will lead you through pastureland and then grassy valleys walled by dense jungle and towering karstic rock. Keep an eye out for the knobby trunks of the rare white pine tree, a species endemic to Puerto Rico, the wood of which has been used for centuries to create *cuatro* and *tiple* string instruments. Taking a side trip to a hilltop lookout, you'll be able to see the tips of the Arecibo Observatory superstructure rising incongruously behind the haystack-shaped limestone rocks in the distance. After a 45-minute hike (depending on your pace), you reach Cueva Urubú, a sacred site for Taino spiritual leaders, who for centuries met here to sniff a leafy, coca-type substance in order to enter a trance and communicate with their gods, the *cemíes*. This small, amphitheater-shaped opening contains 41 Taino petroglyphs – one of the most marked caves in Puerto Rico – which have been outlined in black by contemporary anthropologists. Recent excavations of the burial remains of several Taino Indians have left indentations in the cave floor. Some visitors find the experience of visiting this cave incredibly moving, and according to Bonilla several people have spontaneously begun meditating upon entering it. At least one university professor has reverently collected a few grains of sand to take back to the United States, as a memento of the Taino spirit that he felt still lives here.

EXPLORING TAINO BATEY GROUNDS – Although the Tainos disappeared long ago, a sense of their culture, rituals and beliefs lives on at the **Parque Ceremonial Indigena Caguana**, ☎ 787-894-7325, Carr. 111 at

Km. 12.3, west of Caguana. The park is open daily from 9 a.m. to 4:30 p.m., but is occasionally closed for some holidays and special occasions, such as elections. Entrance costs $2 for adults, $1 for children.

Discovered and excavated during the 1950s by archeologist J. Alden Mason, the Caguana site is generally regarded as the most important Taino ceremonial grounds in the Antilles. It contains 12 ball courts, known as *bateyes*, each surrounded by small monoliths that have been dated back to at least AD 1200. Many of the monoliths are carved with petroglyphs depicting *cemíes*, the protective gods of the Tainos.

> **DID YOU KNOW?** Batey *is the name given to both the soccer-like ceremony practiced by Tainos and the court on which the sport was played. Archeologists have found the remains of* bateyes *in many mountain areas of Puerto Rico, usually at a bucolic spot near a river, including Lares, Adjuntas, Hatillo, Jayuya, Orocovis and Barranquitas. At least 30 courts have been discovered in the area around Utuado, however, and the concentration of* bateyes *at Caguana suggest that this site was the Taino equivalent of Rome's Coliseum, and that this remote region may have been the ultimate seat of Taino influence.*

Start your tour at the small museum full of Indian artifacts and interpretative displays in Spanish and English, then pass a small forest and botanical garden planted with typical Taino crops of *yautía* (a mild-tasting root), sweet potatoes, corn, tobacco, and materials used for building, such as ceiba, ausubo, tabonuco and royal palm trees. Spreading southward toward the Río Tanamá, a well-kept lawn surrounds the principal *batey* court, an adjacent circular court and 10 smaller courts, as well as replicas of *bohíos* (gazebo-like Indian homes) and a *cacique* hut. Strolling around takes only about half an hour, unless you request a guided tour, which we recommend, with bilingual guide Michael Guzmán. His family owns a Taíno-inspired gift shop, **Artesanías Indígenas**, just west of the Parque Ceremonial Indigena Caguana on Carr. 111, where you can pick up various souvenirs of this lost civilization.

Unfortunately, because the Spanish colonists put much more effort into indenturing and killing off Taino Indians than into learning about their culture, little is known about the exact significance of the game of *batey*. Caciques presided over the ceremony, and may have acted as judges. Although the ceremonial *batey* areas were usually uninhabited, it is estimated that during ceremonial events, hundreds, if not thousands, of Tainos came from surrounding areas to attend the matches in Caguana. The courts range in dimension from roughly half the size of a football field to slightly larger than a trampoline, suggesting different versions of the game. Certain basic rules are agreed upon: somewhat like a warm-up exercise for a soccer match, the game of *batey* may have been like a hybrid between a ball-juggling competition and a game of volleyball without the net.

HOW TO PLAY BATEY

- Teams of up to 10 may include players of either sex.
- The ball, made of rubber tree strips, should measure about 16 inches in diameter.
- The court is divided in half, and neither team shall cross into the competitor's area.
- Before play begins, teams agree on wagers (food or other items of value) and the number of points needed to win.
- Teams take turns launching the ball into the air and keeping it aloft using elbows, knees, shoulders, head, hips, etc., but never the hands or (unlike soccer) the feet.
- The ball is juggled by one team a varying number of times before it is lofted to the other team.
- One team gains a point when the opposing side commits a foul, such as when the ball drops to the ground.
- The first team to reach the agreed-upon number of points wins.

By slowly wandering around the ancient courts, you can begin to imagine how sport and spirituality combined to turn a Taino soccer- or volleyball-like game into an event of great socio-religious significance. Scholars believe that, for the indigenous people, matches took on an importance that went well beyond mere entertainment and were, in fact, an exercise in devotion. Sound familiar? It almost forces you to stop and imagine what archeologists of a future civilization might think, were they to someday unearth the remains of Yankee Stadium, the Rose Bowl or Wembley and speculate on the strange, ritualistic games practiced by the primitive people of the 21st century.

On Wheels

The Ruta Panorámica

Designated in green on most roadmaps, the Ruta Panorámica (Scenic Route) runs the entire length of Puerto Rico in a series of connecting mountainous roads between Maunabo to Mayagüez. If possible, allow time to drive the whole route, which passes through much of the island's prettiest country. Clearly signposted throughout, *la ruta* has enough detours to keep you busy for a week or more. In the eastern sections around the **Reserva Forestal Carite and Guavate** area, red-blooming *flamboyán* trees and African violets blaze against the intense greens of the forest. Past Cayey, take the detour to Aibonito and the gaping Cañon San Cristóbal for killer views. As you continue westward on Carr. 723, the island rolls out below like a rumpled carpet. You'll pass the **Trincheras de Asomate**, where rock-throwing Spanish soldiers briefly held advancing Americans at bay during the war of 1898. Make a brief detour north on Carr. 149 for a dip under the **Salto de Doña Juana** waterfall or to visit the sights around **Jayuya**. Two of the world's finest coffees (Alto Grande and Yauco Selecto) are grown in the mountains in western Puerto Rico, and in **Maricao** yellow mangos pile up in heaps along the roadside during summer. Explore odd byroads. The few travelers who drive the Ruta Panorámica experience one of the best adventures in Puerto Rico.

■ In The Air

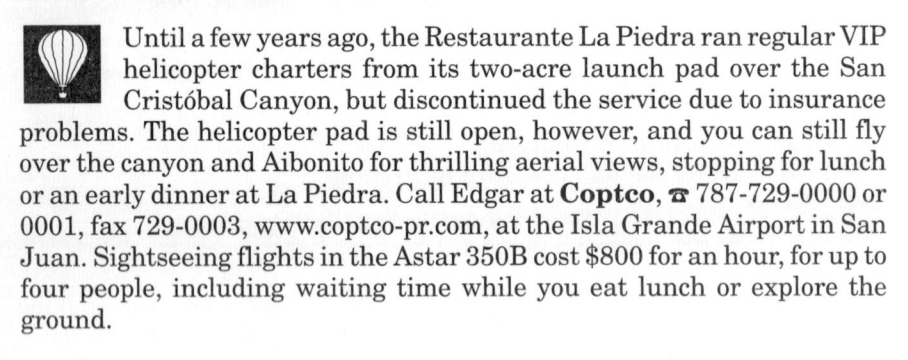

Until a few years ago, the Restaurante La Piedra ran regular VIP helicopter charters from its two-acre launch pad over the San Cristóbal Canyon, but discontinued the service due to insurance problems. The helicopter pad is still open, however, and you can still fly over the canyon and Aibonito for thrilling aerial views, stopping for lunch or an early dinner at La Piedra. Call Edgar at **Coptco**, ☎ 787-729-0000 or 0001, fax 729-0003, www.coptco-pr.com, at the Isla Grande Airport in San Juan. Sightseeing flights in the Astar 350B cost $800 for an hour, for up to four people, including waiting time while you eat lunch or explore the ground.

Where To Stay

ACCOMMODATIONS PRICE KEY

Rates are per room, per night, double occupancy. Single occupancy may or may not get you a discount, so ask when making a reservation. Breakfast included where noted.

$	Up to $50
$$	$50 to $100
$$$	$101 to $150
$$$$	$150 and up

Punta Guavate & Carite Forest Reserve

La Casona de Guavate & Posada El Castillo, ☎ 787-747-5533, Carr. 184, Km. 28 (about 10 minutes after you leave Hwy. 52 at Exit 32), is one of the wackiest places you could ever hope to stay, a combination of luxury campground and eccentric theme lodge. Nine family-sized tents each include two queen-sized beds, Astroturf carpeting and electric lanterns. Facilities include a Swiss chalet-style restaurant (see *Where To Eat*) and a living area decorated to resemble a medieval castle, with chessboard, TV and video and reading area. Built in 1993, the "castle" is illuminated by flaming torches at night. Statues of Greek gods and goddesses, and a few of Jesus for good measure, are placed around the grounds and on the roof. This is the labor of love of an elderly Puerto Rican couple, and it's a bargain. An unlimited breakfast of ham and eggs, coffee and juice costs just $3. Tents are less than $20 per person, per night. $

At Lago de Carite, the economical **Carite Lake Village**, ☎ 787-763-4004/866-2991, on Carr. 742 (on the south side, off Carr. 7741), has lakeside villas of up to three bedrooms, a small shop, restaurant, swimming pool, games room and ball courts, but so far has done little to provide opportunities for kayaking or boating on the lake. $$

Cayey

The Sand and The Sea restaurant and guest house, ☎ 787-738-9086, is perched high on a remote ridge in the Cayey Mountains, and nowhere near the sand or the sea. Heady views southward overlook the Caribbean Sea in the distance and a string of cays around Jobos Bay, which lights up like a Christmas tree at night. This is not a fancy place but a rustic lodge, with a few simple wooden rooms above the restaurant, with private baths, hammocks on the wide balcony and a peaceful air. To get here, follow signs to a restaurant called Siempre Vida off Carr. 715. The Sand and The Sea is next door. $$

Aibonito

El Coquí Posada Familiar; ☎ 787-735-3150, Carr. 722, Km. 7.3, has clean, comfortable rooms with air conditioning, kitchenettes, wheelchair access and a small cafeteria; $$. Likewise, the **Swiss Inn Guest House**, ☎ 787-735-8500, Carr. 14, is a motel right on the road; $$. When we visited, people in town were lamenting the closure of **Las Casitas Cabañas**, ☎ 787-735-7608, Carr. 162, Km. 4.8, but it is expected to reopen in the near future.

Barranquitas

Ex-Governor Pedro Rosselló presided over the re-opening of **Hacienda Margarita**, ☎ 787-857-0414, signposted from Carr.152, which has recovered after the 1998 hurricane smashed it to pieces. With views extending all the way from the Cayey Mountains to the distant peaks of El Yunque, spacious terraces, a large swimming pool, pool tables and an intimate restaurant, it has again become the most desirable place to stay in the Aibonito and Barranquitas area. Standard rooms have a queen-size bed and small balcony. Cabañas are more spacious, with two queen size-beds and terraces. All rooms have cable TV; $$. Also available are a deluxe room with Jacuzzi (call for rates) and the original farmhouse, which sleeps eight comfortably, for a bargain rate of $300 for a weekend. Hacienda Margarita is so popular that reservations should be made weeks in advance.

Toro Negro

A number of area residents rent cabins or rooms out to weekend travelers, but since few advertise their telephone numbers it's a matter of turning up and asking around. Several are signposted on Carr. 143 and Carr. 149. **Villa Eva Lourdes Mary**, ☎ 787-847-0849, Carr. 149, has a few cabañas near the Salto de Doña Juana waterfall and a shrine to Jesus in the garden; $$. **Terraza y Gasolinera Divisoria**, ☎ 787-847-1073, at the intersection of Carr. 149 and Carr. 143, is another good source for what's available locally, and rents out a small guest house of its own (often full on weekends), with a swimming pool that is filled during summer months. $

Jayuya

Originally built in 1853, **Hacienda Gripiñas**, ☎ 787-828-1717, fax 828-1718, Carr. 527, has 19 simple rooms in the restored former coffee plantation of Don Eusebio Pérez del Castillo, the richest and most powerful man in the region during the coffee heyday of the late 19th and early 20th century. In 1904, the Gripiñas coffee won the Gold Medal at the Louisiana Fair in St. Louis. The hotel prides itself on offering a genuine "Old World experience" and has become a favorite haunt of Puerto Rican and foreign visitors alike, especially couples. Facilities include a restaurant and swimming pool. $$$, including breakfast and dinner.

The **Parador Posada Jayuya**, ☎ 787-828-7250/1466, on Calle Guillermo Esteves 49 in the center of town, is nothing fancy. It has 27 rooms with air conditioning, refrigerator and cable TV, as well as a small terrace with swimming pool, barbecue facilities and a rather dull piano bar. For groups, the parador also offers excursions in a 27-seat, air-conditioned tour van for $20 per person, running to the town, the ruins of Hacienda Santa Bárbara, the Museo El Cemi, Casa Canales, an artisan's workshop and other sites. $$-$$$.

■ Lake Caonillas

A bargain retreat in an unbeatable setting, **Hotel La Casa Grande**, ☎ 787-894-3939, 894-3900, or 888-343-2272, on Carr. 612 just off Carr. 140, www.hotelcasagrande.com, can soothe even the most high-strung guest. Twenty clean, simple rooms, each with a private bath, balcony and hammock, perch on a steep hillside bursting with tropical vegetation. Picturesque walkways (romantically lit at night) are landscaped with fruit-bearing trees such as papaya, banana, pineapple, citrus and mangos that inevitably find their way onto the menu of Jungle Jane's Restaurant in the main building (see *Where To Eat*). Use of electronic devices at La Casa Grande is discouraged, and there's little to do here but chill out, swing in your hammock with a good book and gaze across the gushing river valley at a wall of jungle greenery. A pretty, freshwater swimming pool provides a perfect spot for soaking up sun and cooling off, and nearby hiking trails lead into the lush hills. Owner Steven Weingarten, an escaped New York lawyer, leads interested guests in morning yoga practice inside a 1,200-square-foot room that opens up to the cool mountain air. $$.

■ Adjuntas

The sprawling **Sotomayor Resort Hotel & Country Club**, ☎ 787-829-1717, 829-1774, 829-1730, fax 829-5105, on Carr. 522 north of Adjuntas, www.villassotomayor.com, has the only resort-style accommodations in the central mountains. Its 34 villas accommodate two, four and six people; most have kitchen facilities and all have modern conveniences. There are swimming pools for adults and children, courts for tennis, basketball and volleyball, indoor games, a restaurant and bar. Sotomayor attracts mostly Puerto Rican families from the middle and upper classes, as well as newlyweds and eco-travelers looking for a comfortable spot right in the middle of the Cordillera Central mountains. Hiking in the surrounding woods leads to the Garzas Waterfall, river pools and a mountain reservoir. The resort is graced with wide lawns and barbecue areas, and includes short pony rides for kids and a putting green for golf addicts. Only 20 minutes by car from Ponce, Sotomayor sometimes fills up on weekends and holidays despite its size, so it's best to book ahead of time. $$-$$$$.

■ Maricao

Converted to a hotel in 1976, the lovely **Hacienda Juanita**, ☎ 787-838-2550, fax 838-2551, on Carr. 105, Km. 23.5, www.haciendajuanita.com, reigned for decades as one of the region's most prosperous coffee plantations after its construction in 1834. Twenty-one rooms feature wooden ceilings and old-fashioned stable doors that open directly onto the courtyard or private balconies. Carved bedposts and white bed linen edged with *mundillo* lace grace the beds. Facilities include a restaurant and bar (see *Where To Eat*), swimming pool, gift shop and large tropical gardens. $$

Budget accommodations are available at the **Area De Recreo Monte Del Estado**, ☎ 787-873-5652, on Carr. 120. This is part of the *centro vacacionales* system, so you'll need to bring your own bedding, towels, kitchen items, toiletries, etc. Individual stone cottages have private barbecues and open fireplaces, and sleep up to six people. Designed with families in mind, there is a shallow swimming pool, basketball and volleyball courts and plenty of room to roam. $$

■ Camping

With enough sites to lay down your head every 25 miles or so, camping in the Cordillera Central is an economical and rewarding way to travel the mountains. There's nothing like falling asleep under the stars in the tropics.

Department of Natural Resources Campsites

Permits are required to camp at any sites administered by the Puerto Rico Department of Natural and Environmental Resources (DNER), and park officials insist that you request them 15 days before your planned arrival. We've found rangers to be often more flexible than they pretend, however, especially if you plan to camp on a non-holiday weekday. Be aware that campsites in the mountains often fill up on weekends. All sites have toilets, showers, picnic tables and barbecue facilities. Permits are issued by the DNER Forest Permit Division, ☎ 787-724-3724, on Fernández Juncos Avenue (next to Club Nautico) in San Juan. For more information, you can also call the regional office in Ponce, ☎ 787-852-4440. Rates are $4 per day, per person.

The **Reserva Forestal Carite**, ☎ 787-864-8903, has two campsites, one in its northern section (**Guavate**, with space for 30 people) and one in its southern section (**Charco Azul**, with capacity for 50 people), both on Carr. 184. Visitors can enjoy 25 miles of hiking trails and natural swimming holes throughout the forest.

In Toro Negro, the **Los Viveros** campsite is the first turnoff west of the ranger station of the Recreo Doña Juana. With capacity for just 35 people, it is usually full every weekend of the year and during Puerto Rican holidays, but often empty during the week.

Near Adjuntas, the **Bosque Estatal De Guilarte** has five wood cabins for $20 a night. Each sleeps six. Call the regional office in Humacao, ☎ 787-852-4440, for more information.

Alternative Campsites

Laid-back nature lovers will get a kick out of **Las Casas de la Selva**, ☎ 787-839-7318, on Carr. 184 in the Carite area, where days are spent hiking, basking in mountain streams, and nights usually involve singing around a campfire. Set in 1,000 acres of pine, teak, mahogany and eucalyptus forest, accommodations consist of covered, four-person tents with beds for $25 a night, including electric light and fan. Many of the more permanent facilities were destroyed in the 1998 hurricane. Communal kitchen facilities (bring your own bottled water) and hot showers are available (you may be asked to contribute $5-$10 for the use of showers, and/or water, which is difficult to manage on the farm) and you can pitch your own tent more or less where you like for a $10 donation. The profits fund the Las Casas de la Selva reforestation project, which has planted about 45,000 trees and welcomes volunteers. Cathy and Joe also offer courses in woodcarving, gourmet vegetarian cooking and jewelry making.

Tune in, turn on, and drop by **Baba's Retreat**. For a two-hour hike through the Carite forest into the middle of nowhere and a night of sharing outlandish travel stories, visit Baba in his mountain hideaway. This California rover moved to the tropics 30 years ago and now lives self-sufficiently off the land. Though by no means an official hotelier, Baba welcomes guests (bring your own tent and some food). There is no road, hot water, electricity or telephone. But you can shower under waterfalls and dine on fruits and vegetables plucked straight from the earth and cooked on a smoldering wood fire. Stop by Casas de la Selva (see above) for information and directions.

Another alternative campsite is at a working farm, **Magali and Andre's Agri-Tur**, ☎ 787-864-2956, Carr. 179, Km. 104, just south of the Reserva Forestal Carite near Lago Carite. There are 20 acres of fruit trees, pasture and woodland. For $25 a night, you can use all of Magali and Andre's facilities, including sleeping area, bedding and kitchen privileges. Accommodations are basic, with a cold shower and outdoor latrine. Pitching your own tent here costs $10 per night. One-day introductory workshops in massage, reflexology, Tai chi, shiatsu, naturopathy and healing with herbs are available for around $10 a head, including lunch. The owners also have a sweat lodge (see below).

SWEATY AQUARIANS

Since ancient times, some Native Americans have used sweat lodges as a purifying, healing and self-enlightening ritual. New Age seekers have adopted the practice, with varying interpretations. According to Magali, Agri-Tur's "lodge" – a crude, dome-like shelter heated with hot stones like a sauna – represents a sort of universal mother's womb, in which participants sing, pray and sweat out toxins from their skins and souls.

Where To Eat

■ Punta Guavate & Carite Forest Reserve

This little piggy went.... Generally regarded as the island center of spit-roasted pork, with a couple dozen *lechoneras*, the Guavate area is a meat-lover's paradise. Especially on weekends, Carr. 184 is lined with open-pit barbecues slow-roasting whole pigs and serving up melt-in-mouth heaps of pork, *morcilla* (blood sausage), tubers, vegetables and *arroz con gandules* (yellow rice and pigeon peas), for as little as $5. The best *lechoneras* are reportedly those past Km. 27 near the forest entrance. Open for more than 30 years, **Lechonera El Rancho Original** is the longest established. Better views are enjoyed at **Los Gemelos**, ☎ 787-286-3220. If this pigging out is too much for you, check out the menu at the odd Swiss chalet-style **La Casona de Guavate & Posada El Castillo**, ☎ 787-747-5533, Carr. 184, Km. 28, where poultry, steaks and seafood are all served with a "jam" made on the premises. The owners are very proud of this jam, which is a sweet sauce that goes well with many meats. Specials include filet *gallego* (sausage and jam), filet rings (medallions with "turkey jam") and various fish, shrimp and lobster combos all for around $15. But the pièce de résistance is a terrifying mountain of food, called "The Castle," sampling everything on the menu. Not for lightweights, this dish could feed a family of four, and costs $27.

■ Cayey

Great views, a casual atmosphere and "interesting" Puerto Rican food are found at **Jájome Terrace**, ☎ 787-738-4016, Carr. 15, Km. 18.6. Main courses cost $12 to $20. More glamorous, **Siempre Viva**, ☎ 787-738-0512 and **The Sand and The Sea**, ☎ 787-738-9086, are located next door to each other on a ridge on Carr. 715, with awesome views over the southeast corner of the island. Siempre Viva is a favorite for romance, with an intimate dining room designed by owners Joanne Romanacce and Luis Lavergie, a gourmet Puerto Rican menu and live music on a Sunday afternoon. It's a natural setting for wedding receptions, which are often held here. The Sand and The Sea (see also *Where To Stay*) is more rustic, but with the same excellent views, and on weekend nights diners and guests often gather around the baby grand piano to sing Puerto Rican classics. The great atmosphere outweighs the solid yet predictable menu on which filet mignon and garlic shrimp top the bill. Entrées at both restaurants are between $15 and $20.

■ Aibonito

Restaurante La Piedra, ☎ 787-735-1034, Carr. 7718 (next to the landmark Mirador Piedra Degetau), is extremely popular among weekend visitors, including hikers, due to its proximity to the "Grand Canyon of Puerto Rico," San Cristóbal. Hiking parties leave Saturday mornings 8 a.m. during the summer, and by the time they return at lunchtime, chef and owner Joe Esteras will have turned out creative *criollo* dishes with lots of fresh garden herbs and vegetables (Esteras also hosts a popular Saturday morning gardening show on the radio). Main dishes cost between $12 and $20. Opening hours are Monday and Tuesday, 11.30 a.m. to 6 p.m., Wednesday, Thursday and Sunday 11.30 p.m. to 8 p.m., and Friday and Saturday from 11.30 a.m. to midnight. Live music on weekends.

Downtown, **El Rincón Familiar**, Carr. 14 (no phone), is the local eatery, where a generously portioned *pechuga milanesa* (chicken breast Milanese) costs around $12. **Tío Pepe's**, ☎ 787-735-7425, Carr. 14, is another popular place for *comida criollo* with a bit more atmosphere. The local "pub" **La Selva**, Carr. 725 (no phone), has an interesting jungle-farmyard atmosphere with a small zoo of snakes, tropical birds, horses and other beasts.

■ Barranquitas

Everyone in town will recommend **El Mofongo Criollo**, ☎ 787-857-0480, a wooden shack halfway up the mountain on Carr. 152. Specializing in *mofongo relleno*, the "mixto" is a seafood extravaganza for a reasonable $13. Our favorite was seafood-stuffed *tostones* slathered in a thick garlic sauce – six of them for $6, and you won't need to eat for the rest of the day.

The restaurant at **Hacienda Margarita**, ☎ 787-857-0414 (first right after El Mofongo Criollo), is *the* spot for fine dining in Barranquitas, with an extensive menu and tables spread throughout a wood-paneled dining room, balcony and roof terrace, with fabulous views. Country classics such as *asopao de pollo* (chicken gumbo) cost as little as $5, while others like *mar y tierra* (surf and turf) cost upwards of $35. Live music on weekends could be anything from *cuatro* players to salsa or rock and roll. Otherwise, around the plaza, several cafés offer burgers, *medianoches* (toasted Cuban-style sandwiches) and sticky buns for a couple of bucks. Or, you can get burritos, slices of pizza and baked potatoes from a hole-in-the-wall eatery on Carr. 156 north of town.

■ Jayuya

El Dujo, ☎ 787-828-1143, Carr. 140, Km. 7.8, offers one of the island's greatest culinary adventures, specializing in good, old-fashioned Creole cooking the way *abuela* used to make it. But it's not just the excellent food that sets this place apart. Apparently inspired by a desert oasis fantasy, the restaurant has the décor and atmosphere of a Bedouin tent. Main courses costing $12 to $20 are worth making the trip for.

Closer to town than El Dujo, **Hacienda Gripiñas**, ☎ 787-828-1717, while a lovely place to stay, unfortunately features inconsistent cooking. Excellent French onion soup costs just $3, but the shrimp salad, *dorado* filet and steak were little better than frozen microwave meals (perhaps we caught the kitchen on an off night). Entrées cost between $16 and $22 ($35 for lobster).

■ Toro Negro

The cloud forest area is not known for food, but if you're desperate for a snack up here, try **Terraza y Gasolinera Divisoria**, ☎ 787-847-1073, Carr. 149 at the intersection with Carr. 143, for basic provisions and a few hot staples like rice and beans, between 7 a.m. and 8 p.m. On weekends, **Las Cabañas Doña Juana** (near the ranger station at Recreo Doña Juana) is packed with campers eating their fill of specials, such as white beans and rice. If you plan to survive for any length of time, bring supplies.

■ Utuado & Environs

Jungle Jane's Restaurant, ☎ 787-894-3939 or 3900, part of the Hotel La Casa Grande near Lake Caonillas, caters to hotel guests, gastronomically minded locals and travelers seeking probably the best dining in the central mountains. Try the salmon baked in a mango sauce, handmade pasta with shrimp in a creamy vodka sauce, or dorado (mahi-mahi) in *chimichurri*, as well as luncheon sandwiches and American breakfasts served with heaping portions of tropical fruits. A small, shaded patio and terrace face across a deep river valley, to a sheer, eye-popping green wall of subtropical forest on the other side. The isolation of the spot makes it a 40-minute drive from either Jayuya or Utuado. And the only sound you'll hear, besides the rush of the stream below, is the occasional bird or coquí chirping in the distance. Jungle Jane's is open daily for breakfast (8 to 10 a.m.) and dinner (6 to 9 p.m.), and most dinner entrées cost well under $20.

In the Caguana (Carr. 111) area, several roadside cafés and restaurants are open on weekends and intermittently during the week. **Restaurant La Familia** offers hearty Puerto Rican food such as chicken, rice and beans, just east of the Parque Indígena. Otherwise, try **El Indio** or **El Cemí** along the same stretch of road for *criollo* fare and pizza. You'll find a glut of fast-food restaurants just outside downtown Utuado, near the intersection of Carr. 111 and Carr. 123.

■ Adjuntas

At the Sotomayor Resort Hotel & Country Club, **Restaurant Las Garzas**, ☎ 787-829-1717 or 1774, serves reasonably priced *criollo* and international dishes, including chicken, steak, seafood and five types of *mofongo relleno*. It's one of the rare restaurants on the island that serves rabbit, either fried or fricassee style. Appetizers cost $3.50, and most main dishes (except lobster) will set you back $15 or less. On the south end of town on Carr. 123, **Playita Café** is a bar that retains a country-style atmosphere, with often as many horses in the parking lot as cars. Stop in for a beer and a chat with the local men, and you are guaranteed to make a few friends.

■ Maricao

Apart from a KFC-type cafeteria downtown and a couple of snack bars selling *empanadillas* kept warm in glass cases under heat lamps, the only place to dine in this area is the restaurant at **Hacienda Juanita,** ☎ 787-838-2550, fax 838-2551, Carr. 105, Km. 23.5, www.haciendajuanita.com. Remarkable mostly for the great atmosphere of terrace dining in lush surroundings, this is a great place to kick back and listen to the chirp of coquí frogs and soak up a hundred years of history in the restored living room of this famous coffee hacienda. The food, by contrast, is consistent but forgettable, and the watery coffee was disappointing considering Maricao calls itself the "city of coffee." Entrées cost between $10 and $20.

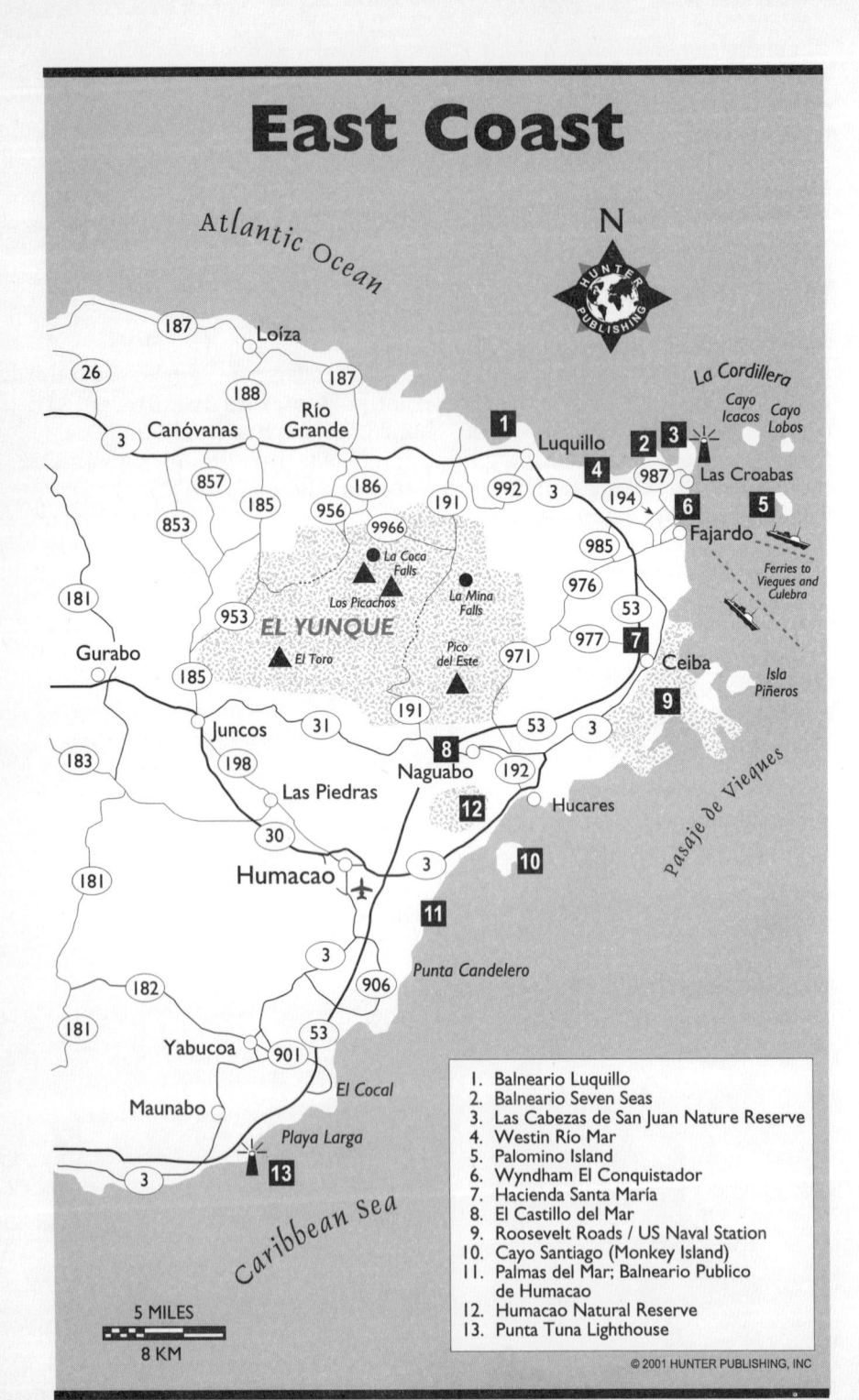

East Coast

1. Balneario Luquillo
2. Balneario Seven Seas
3. Las Cabezas de San Juan Nature Reserve
4. Westin Río Mar
5. Palomino Island
6. Wyndham El Conquistador
7. Hacienda Santa María
8. El Castillo del Mar
9. Roosevelt Roads / US Naval Station
10. Cayo Santiago (Monkey Island)
11. Palmas del Mar; Balneario Publico de Humacao
12. Humacao Natural Reserve
13. Punta Tuna Lighthouse

© 2001 HUNTER PUBLISHING, INC

East Coast

Most travelers to eastern Puerto Rico come to see and hike **El Yunque**, the island's second-most-visited tourist destination after Old San Juan, and probably the world's most user-friendly rain forest. Others come for the east coast's three sprawling resort hotels, half a dozen excellent golf courses, the US Navy base, and one of the biggest yachting and sailing charter ports in the Caribbean. But this side of the island has much to offer that eludes most visitors to Puerto Rico, from a glorious, six-mile stretch of deserted beach between Luquillo and Las Cabezas de San Juan, to the red cliffs and lonely lighthouse in the southeast. As with most places, you have to scratch the surface to find the hidden rewards here. Spend a day or two wandering around Loíza Aldea and talking to locals (or attending their *fiestas patronales* in late July) to get a deeper understanding of Afro-Caribbean culture. One of the old fishermen of Las Croabas may take you cay-hopping in his wooden sloop, setting you down on some deserted islet to swim in opaque waters. Local surfers gather at a few little-known breaks. Or visit one of the two other nature reserves on the east coast – Las Cabezas to San Juan and Humacao – where exotic waterfowl, mangrove and dry tropical forest ecosystems and a bioluminescent lagoon await.

IN THIS CHAPTER
- Loíza Aldea
- Canóvanas
- El Yunque
- Luquillo
- Las Croabas
- Fajardo
- Ceiba
- Naguabo
- Humacao
- Yabucoa & Maunabo

Getting Here & Getting Around

■ By Land

In the north, **Hwy. 3** runs from Río Piedras in the San Juan area to Fajardo. The easiest way to join Hwy. 3 from Old San Juan, Condado and Isla Verde, though, is via **Carr. 26**.

> **TIP:** Beware of **Hwy. 3**, which is studded with traffic lights and often congested. The drive from San Juan to Fajardo can take an hour or more on this route. Avoid traveling eastward during rush hour (4 p.m. to 7 p.m. on weekdays) and, unless you're game for a stop-and-start road rally, avoid the westbound side on Sunday afternoons.

A longer but infinitely more scenic route from San Juan to Hwy. 3 is via **Carr. 187** through Piñones and Loíza. At least you can stop amid palm groves for a dip in the sea here, if the driving gets you down. Unfortunately, plans for a toll highway (Route 66) along the northeast have stalled due to a political spat over funding. So for now, get used to the stop and go.

If you're headed from San Juan to Humacao or points south on the east coast, take Carr. 18 to Hwy. 52 and then **Hwy. 30** from Caguas, skirting El Yunque rain forest. And if you arrive from the south, **Hwy. 53** and **Carr. 3** alternately sweep you along a photogenic stretch of coastline. Hwy. 53, from Fajardo south to Yabucoa, is the only toll road on the east coast – a rare, open speedway, navigable in 30 minutes or less.

Rental Car Agencies & Taxis

Local rental car options include the following companies:

- **Avis Rent A Car** has offices on site at both the Westin Río Mar Hotel, Río Grande, ☎ 787-888-6638, and the Wyndham El Conquistador Hotel, Fajardo, ☎ 787-863-2735 ext. 2015; and in Ceiba, ☎ 787-885-0505.

- **Hertz** has offices at the Naval Station Roosevelt Roads, Ceiba, ☎ 787-885-3580 or 3660.

- **L&M Car Rental**, ☎ 787-865-4495 or 2655, also has an office at the Roosevelt Roads Naval Station, and another off Hwy. 3 in Fajardo, ☎ 787-860-6868, fax 860-6800.

- **Popular Leasing & Rental Inc.** has franchises at **Ramar Auto Inc.**, Humacao, ☎ 787-852-0015, and at **Sardinera Rent A Car**, Fajardo, ☎ 787-863-1098.

Taxi services are relatively scarce on this side of the island, but try **Fajardo Taxi Service**, ☎ 787-860-1112 – good for getting to and from the ferry terminal; **Humacao Taxi**, ☎ 787-852-6880; or **Oriental Taxi**, ☎ 787-852-0000, also based in Humacao. The major hotels and many of the smaller *paradores* and guest houses listed provide transit to and from the airport. A taxi ride from San Juan to Fajardo usually costs about $55, and if you plan to do any exploring, you're much better off renting a car.

Públicos

Público stations can be found at the town centers of Loíza, Luquillo, Fajardo, Naguabo and Humacao, as well as the promenade at Playa Naguabo and the ferry terminal at Fajardo. *Público* service also runs frequently between Las Croabas and Fajardo. As on the rest of the island, travel by *público* may require some patience. But if you stand by the side of a major road long enough, you can usually flag down a *público* van. Generally, fares within the east coast cost less than $5. A trip from Fajardo station to Río Piedras in San Juan (or vice versa) should cost about $10.

■ By Air

At **Aeropuerto Diego Jiménez Torres** (☎ 787-860-3110), a little airstrip southwest of Fajardo (take Carr. 976 from Hwy. 3), **Vieques Air Link,** ☎ 787-722-3736, 741-8331, or 888-901-9247, has flights twice a day, to and from the islands of Vieques and Culebra. Rates to Vieques are about $18 one-way and $35 round-trip; and to Culebra $25 one-way and $45 round-trip. The planes are twin- or tri-motor craft that seat nine, and can usually be chartered for groups. Another company, **Isla Nena,** ☎ 787-863-3030, offers a Fajardo-to-Culebra flight, depending on demand, as well as charters to the Isla Grande airport in San Juan and other island destinations.

The **Aeropuerto Humacao** (☎ 787-852-8188), even smaller than Diego Jiménez Torres, has no commercial flights, although it is possible to charter a flight there from one of the airports in San Juan or elsewhere. Try **Air Borinquen,** ☎ 787-253-1400, or **Icarus Caribbean,** ☎ 787-729-0001.

■ By Sea

Ferries between Fajardo and the islands of Vieques and Culebra are an uncommon bargain, at $2 and $2.25 one-way respectively. The boat from Fajardo to Vieques and back operates three times daily, with twice-daily service to and from Culebra. The **Port Authority** terminal, ☎ 787-863-4560, or ☎ 800-981-2005 (daytime hours), is located at the end of the dingy Playa Fajardo area (Carr. 195 from Hwy. 3). For more information, see the chapter on *Vieques & Culebra*, pages 349-351 and 376-377. If you're arriving by yacht or chartered boat, **Puerto del Rey** is the home port of the Nautical Federation of Puerto Rico and an official US port of entry. The multilingual harbormaster monitors VHF channels 16 and 71 around the clock, and is available by phone, ☎ 787-860-1000.

TRAVEL AGENCIES

For travel to and from St. Thomas and St. John, try **Transportation Services Virgin Islands**, 11 Unión, Fajardo, ☎ 787-863-0582 or 860-8809, who specialize in mini-cruises to the Virgin Islands. **Rosita's Travel & Tours**, Calle Calderón Mújica, Canóvanas, ☎ 787-876-2860, 6314 or 0210, fax 886-2560, and Calle San Patricio 66, Loíza, ☎ 787-876-8020, have good deals for students and group travelers, and may be able to help get a better deal on car rental. For 24-hour service, **Nell Travel Agency**, I-9 Calle Principal, Urb. Baralt, Fajardo, ☎ 787-860-1088, 6502, or 6503 (office hours), ☎ 800-981-4752 ext. 8363 (after hours), should be able to help. Both offer cruise packages to other Caribbean islands.

Communications

Ricky's Cyber Pizza at the Villa Marina shopping center, Fajardo, ☎ 787-860-4230, has two Internet connections for $5 per hour. He's open 11 a.m. to 11 p.m. every day. You can also access e-mail at a store named **Peek-a-Boo** at the Wyndham El Conquistador. It costs $8 for every half-hour spent on-line.

Post offices are located in **Loíza** at 64 Calle San Patricio, Suite 1; in **Fajardo** at 102 Calle Garrido Morales, Suite E, and in all other major towns. Private mail and fax services can be found at most shopping centers.

Touring & Sightseeing

■ Loíza Aldea

Commonly referred to simply as Loíza, this small coastal town began as a slave-trading center during the 16th century, due to its position at the mouth of the island's largest river, the **Río Grande de Loíza**. For centuries, plantation owners and European slave traders bought and sold African men, women and children at the town plaza here. Excavations nearby have uncovered iron chains and other implements of captivity from bygone days. And, if you dig deeper into this township's rich cultural life, other clues to African influence begin to emerge. The congregation at the **Iglesia de San Patricio**, the oldest active church in Puerto Rico (founded in 1729), spices up sermons with drumming and a more lively, upbeat atmosphere than the Catholic norm. A few roadside shacks still serve up the only African-style cuisine on the island, such as yucca with coconut and cassava bread cooked on a crude iron plate called the *burén*. The local *bomba* music is infused with rhythms more purely African than that of the rest of the island. *Espiritismo* – a blend of Catholicism, New Age spiritual ritual and herbal healing – thrives here. And the *Fiestas de Loíza*, a festival in July that brings together street-theater clowning, freakishly painted masks and dancing, descends from roots more African than Spanish.

The region still suffers the abusive legacy of its past, however. One of the three poorest municipalities of Puerto Rico, it fights probably losing battles against large-scale developers eager to build resorts and condominium complexes along the mangrove-dotted coastline around **Piñones** (see *San Juan & Environs*, page 94). The struggle pits the increasingly politically savvy descendents of slaves against the powerful and development-minded machinery based in San Juan.

BEACH LITTER

The curving beaches of Loíza receive little trash-disposal service, and taking a dip in the sea involves stepping over worn glass, cola and beer cans blanched by the sun and pieces of every imaginable type of plastic container. Better beaches abound to the east and west.

The town takes its name from a different sort of cultural struggle. Soon after the Spaniards arrived on the island, a young settler named Pedro Mejías seduced and married the local Taino chief, a woman named Yuisa. He converted this Caribbean Pocahontas (nominally, at least) to Christianity, an act that outraged the Carib and Taino locals. They united to attack the Mejías settlement twice, and in 1573 temporarily sacked the fledgling town, burning everything in sight and killing both Yuisa and Pedro Majías. The Spanish soon retook the area and re-established a booming slave market, using Yuisa's corrupted name for their township.

To get a sense of Loíza's insular culture, we suggest a quick visit to the **Centro Cultural**, just east of the main plaza (which displays the few local relics not snapped up by the university museum). Behind the cultural center, you'll find the banks of the Loíza river where, until the mid-1980s, traffic between Piñones and Loíza was conducted by ferry. The daughter of Señor Cotijo, the original ferryman, lives next to the abandoned cement dock, and has vague plans to turn part of her residence into a small museum. The best way to truly get into Loíza culture, though, is to attend the **town festival** in July.

Loiza festival masks.
(PRTC)

Fiestas De Loíza Aldea

The fiestas of Loíza, which take place during the last week of July each year, are widely considered the best in Puerto Rico, with wild street celebrations that mix Catholic miracle worship and Afro-Caribbean culture in an explosion of color and music. The festival honors Santiago Apóstol (Saint James), patron of Spanish crusaders against the pagan hordes. But the history behind this event is as tangled as Puerto Rico's own.

SAINT JAMES THE MOOR-KILLER

Santiago (Saint James) became the patron saint of Spanish crusaders circa the 11th century after he allegedly descended from the heavens and appeared to the motley Christian armies astride a great steed and dressed in white. *"Santiago, cierra España!"* ("Saint James, close off Spain!") became the rallying cry of the Reconquest of the Moors, who had developed modern medicine, algebra, glassmaking and a progressive culture in Spain, but had become militarily lax. In 1492, the same year Columbus stumbled upon the Americas, the Spanish retook Granada, the last Muslim stronghold in Spain, and began purging the country of all non-Catholics. Since this year of "glory," Santiago, aka "Matamoros" ("Moor killer") has been the most patriotic Hispanic saint.

The festival celebrates the mysterious (it is said, miraculous) appearance long ago of a tiny wooden statue of Santiago in the lower branches of a cork tree, in the Medianía neighborhood of Loíza. A fisherman found it, according to the story, and reverently brought it to the town church. The statue of Santiago disappeared, however, and was later found again in the branches of the same cork tree. Three times the statue was removed from the tree; and three times it reappeared there. Today, the central event of the Loíza festival is the transportation of the idol back to the cork tree, in honor of Santiago and the victory of the Spanish Reconquest against the Muslims. This statue and two others later brought from Spain represent divine protection of men, women and children.

The festivities culminate in three days (usually July 26-28), honoring the statues of *Santiago de los hombres, mujeres* and *niños*, in that order, with fireworks, *bomba* music and dance and processions to Las Carreras, the street where the cork tree stands (the original was destroyed during Hurricane Hugo in 1989, and has been replaced by a small sapling). Traditionally, participants dress as one of five characters. Spanish crusaders ostensibly represent the heroes of the story. Their enemies, the Moors, are depicted using bright costumes and fantastic, devilish *vejigante* (pronounced ve-hee-GAN-tay) masks (see the box on the next page). The "townsfolk" disguises are divided into three types – old beggar men in rags; crazy women who wash everything in sight; and mules.

Beneath the surface of this Catholic feast, however, you'll find interesting undercurrents of irony. Before his tiny statue was found in a cork tree, Santiago became the patron saint of Loíza not because he inspired Spanish crusaders, but due to his resemblance to the African god Changó, whom the Yoruba slaves were forbidden to worship. Like many peoples forced to adopt Christianity worldwide, the slaves simply changed the name of their god to that of a Christian saint, and carried on with as many of their traditions as they could get away with. There was also perhaps a latent sense of kinship between the ancestors of Loíza and the Moors. Notice that the *vejigante* masks representing the Muslims are the brightest and most fussed-over of the costumes. In fact, they have become the symbol of Loíza. Note, too, the extensive use of red, gold and green in the costumes, the complex rhythms of the *bomba* drums and the clownish street theater – all African, not Spanish, customs.

HOME OF THE VEJIGANTE

In their current form, the Loíza *vejigante* masks – one of the most recognizable examples of Puerto Rican folk art – were stylized in the early 1960s by the late Don Castor Ayala. The Ayala family still makes the masks out of coconut and bamboo at their home near Las Carreras in Loíza. You can buy masks at the family shop on Carr. 187 in the Medianía neighborhood, or visit the Ayalas (they're always willing to talk about their craft to outsiders, especially in Spanish) at home. From Carr. 187, turn left between two pink buildings at the Chique Liquor Store. Then turn left at the Lolin Bicycle Shop, make your first right and look for the peach-colored home with salsa music blaring from the open-air, ground-floor workshop. Give our *saludos* to Raúl and Beatríz.

Unfortunately, much of the original meaning of the festival has been lost through the generations, and many newcomers and tourists who attend are unaware of even the basic story behind the event. Most wear no costume, or worse. Responding to inappropriate dress of past interlopers, the Loíza municipality has forbidden the wearing of "Halloween-style disguises," such as "robots, nymphomaniacs or gorillas," in order to protect the tradition.

Prepare for an all-night affair of rum and dancing in the street. And if you can muster the resources, you'll be a big hit with the locals if you wear any of the following costumes:

- **The Spanish Crusader** – Wear shiny, colorful pants and a cape, cut to resemble, as closely as possible, the garb of a medieval Iberian knight, as well as a straw hat with ribbons, small mirrors and bells. The mask is made by painting heroic, masculine features (hint: include a moustache) on a wire screen. Your demeanor should be stately and chivalrous, restrained yet authoritative.

- **The Moor** – The outfit should be brightly colored and baggy, with dangling, bat-like sleeves. Cover your hands with old socks. Pick up a *vejigante* mask, complete with horns and buck teeth, from Ayala family shop on Carr. 187, and ask the proprietor for materials to affix it to your head. You can let loose in this outfit – blood-curdling screams and mumbled incantations are recommended. It's okay to lunge at strangers and carry a doll or other object with which to scare children.

- ***El Viejo*** (The Old Man) – This character represents the poor guy who can't afford a costume. Wear old, mutilated clothing and a pathetic cardboard-box mask of your own devising. Bring an instrument, as music groups often consist of *viejos*. Beg for money. Act senile and witless.

- ***La Loca*** (The Crazy Woman) – Often cross-dressing men, the crazy women roam the streets wearing outlandish colors, stage makeup and huge artificial breasts. Carry a broom and make an extravagant effort to clean everything (and anyone) you see. Along with the *viejos*, *las locas* find themselves frequently caught up in impromptu street dances.
- ***La Mula*** (The Mule) – Use burlap sacks and bamboo "legs" to approximate a donkey. This can be done tandem. Wander aimlessly and act dumb as a donkey.

Canóvanas

This uninteresting town calls itself "City of the Indians" because it was named for a powerful Taino chief. But any history here has left little visible trace. The entrance to the city on Hwy. 3, as well as a statue in the town plaza, depict stylized versions of Chief Canóvanas, along with plaques that mention "petroglyphs" and "bronze artifacts," none of which can be seen here. One kilometer north of town, on the road to Juncos, it's possible to see the sparse ruins of a Spanish colonial castle. Otherwise, the only cultural sight in Canóvanas is of teenagers practicing skateboard tricks around a statue of a long-forgotten cacique.

El Yunque

The only rain forest in the United States forest system, El Yunque sweats, slithers and breathes beneath a muggy cloud ceiling. Dozens of strange and endangered species live within the vine-clad tropical woods, under dewy ferns and high in the forest canopy. None of the plant or animal life is particularly threatening or poisonous, though, and compared to a hazard-filled trek through the Amazon or Congo, El Yunque (pronounced JOON-kay) is as tame as Disneyland. Its manageable size (about 28,000 acres) and proximity to San Juan (less than an hour's drive) make this a popular day-trip for more than a million visitors per year, who come to hike well-maintained trails, bathe in ancient river pools and get a sense of being in a primitive jungle atmosphere without months of planning and vaccinations.

Some of the longer hiking trails are little used and lead into the wilder forest depths, and those visitors who climb to the upper reaches of the mountains find their reward. When the mists part from the cloud forest, views from the 3,500-foot peaks reveal the eastern curve of Puerto Rico – tiny beaches, specks of coastal towns, and the wraparound sea that, from this height, seems almost close enough to leap into. Those who don't care to summit the peaks will also find plenty to do. Roadside lookout points, mellow walking paths and wheelchair-friendly facilities with information for all ages make El Yunque probably the most accessible rain forest in the world. It is also one of the best understood. Researchers from many countries use several off-limits sites within its boundaries to study everything from the maintenance of forest ecosystems to the preservation of the extremely endangered Puerto Rican parrot. Get here by taking Hwy. 3 from San Juan to Carr. 191 south. See *Eco-Travel*, page 325, for more information.

■ Luquillo

Inaccurately dubbed the "Puerto Rican Riviera," Luquillo is most famous for its public beach. Don't believe the hype. Once glorious, the place has gone to pot. The beach is often overcrowded and dirty, particularly near the food stands at the western end, where visitors seem to think nothing of chucking their trash in the bushes – a heartbreaking sight on an otherwise idyllic stretch of shore. On weekends the crowd feeds on itself, as thousands throng several-dozen food kiosks on the north side of the public beach and then cram themselves towel-to-towel on the sand. If your main goal at the beach is to meet people, check it out. Otherwise, you'll find more unspoiled shoreline farther east.

As for the town of Luquillo, it has strangely little to offer considering it abuts Playa Azul and the surfing area around La Pared. A waterfront area that seems like it should be pumping with sea-facing cafés, groovy hostels and surf culture is instead dominated by characterless apartment towers. The few hangout spots here are scattered on a couple of street corners. The redeeming features of Luquillo are the excellent **Alpha Scuba** and **La Selva Surf Shop** (see pages 319 and 322), with gear and access to watersports along these shores. Also, the beaches east of La Pared offer miles of deserted shoreline where you can walk, swim and sunbathe for hours without seeing a soul.

■ Fajardo & Environs

Often overlooked by land-based visitors to Puerto Rico, the Fajardo (pronounced fa-HAR-doe) area is extremely popular with local tourists and seafarers. This former fishing village has become one of the busiest yachting regions in the Caribbean in the past quarter-century, with sometimes more than 1,000 boats moored at three nearby marinas. The largest, **Puerto del Rey**, ☎ 787-860-1000, has more than 700 slips and offers services for all boating needs, including hauling and maintenance, equipment, banking, laundry, shops and a few good restaurants. If you're looking to find a job as crew on a sailboat, this is a good place to start. A number of charter boats for day/week sailing, fishing and diving trips operate here. It is also near the embarcation point for the ferry to the Puerto Rican islands of Vieques and Culebra. Puerto del Rey is signposted from Hwy. 3, about two miles south of the town of Fajardo.

Downtown Fajardo is a relatively charmless maze of pockmarked streets, inelegant shops and commercial buildings, among which it's easy to get lost in one-way traffic. The charming peninsula of **Las Croabas** to the north, however, presents a number of attractions for the adventurous traveler. The 300-slip **Villa Marina**, on a turnoff from Carr. 987, has some of the better bargains for catamaran sailing and snorkeling trips to the nearby cays, diving, kayaking and other charters. Farther north on Carr. 987, you'll find reasonably priced hotels and a slew of seafood restaurants as you wind your way onto a small, hilly cape with tropical dry forest, mangrove lagoons and views of the island-dotted sea. Depending on when you come (during the summer and on weekends, the place can get packed), you may find the area nearly deserted.

Near the end of Carr. 987, the crescent-shaped Playa Seven Seas marks the beginning of the **Cabezas de San Juan** nature reserve, with about 500 acres containing four distinct ecosystems and a restored 19th-century lighthouse. You'll find excellent shallow-water snorkeling here, as well as a decent bioluminescent bay. Again, the area will be crowded or nearly empty, depending on your timing. Snack bars selling fried fish, beer, *pinchos* and other Puerto Rican fast food crowd the roadside across from Playa Seven Seas, and stretch all the way to **Bahía Las Croabas**, which abuts a rundown seaside plaza. Las Croabas Bay is the place to hook up with fishermen for bargain-rate trips to the local cays. Unfortunately, it is also pervaded by a nauseating stink from the sulfurous seaside mud.

> **DRIVING TIP:** *To avoid downtown Fajardo en route to Las Croabas and the surrounding peninsula, take the exit marked "Avenida Conquistador" north from Hwy. 3. Follow it to the second traffic light (just past the Amigo supermarket and Burger King), turn right, and continue about a mile until you reach Carr. 987. Turn left and you're on your way.*

One of the better resorts on the island – the 918-room **Wyndham El Conquistador**, which has a commanding, cliff-top view to the east – can be reached by turning south on a spur road from the southeastern corner of the Bahía Las Croabas plaza. This isn't the main entrance, but allows non-guests access to the pricey hotel amenities, including the excellent Bally-Hoo restaurant/bar at the marina, casino and restaurants, diving and sailing charters.

The hotel and Las Croabas marinas are also the best places to find portage to **Palomino Island**, which is leased by El Conquistador and offers horseback riding, parasailing, kayaking and other adventures to guests. The secluded western end of Palomino has Puerto Rico's only two designated clothing-optional beaches. Although access to the private island is officially limited to those registered at El Conquistador, it is not difficult for non-guests to show up, blend in and get a trip there (see page 316).

PALOMINO ISLAND HISTORY

In May 1649, the Swedish ship *Katt*, loaded with settlers and supplies for the short-lived colony of New Sweden (present-day Delaware), ran aground on the shallow reef near the northeast corner of Puerto Rico. Most crew and passengers – including a large number of women – made it ashore to the deserted Palomino Island, where they languished for days. According to one chronicler, the thirsty Swedes licked dew from rocks to survive. This was only the beginning of their troubles, however. Two Spanish military vessels arrived and, despite peaceful relations between the two nations at the time, soldiers confiscated what was left of value, burned the hull of the *Katt* and took crew and passengers to San Juan as prisoners. Many became agricultural laborers or worse, ruing the day they left their homeland. Nearly two years later, 24 of the survivors bought a small boat in Puerto Rico and sailed for St. Kitts, hoping to find passage back to Sweden from there, but were intercepted by French pirates who raped at least one woman and sold the others into slavery. Three more years passed before a Swedish emissary, with the blessing of the Spanish crown, arrived at San Juan to demand the release of the remaining Swedish settlers and valuables (ironically, the colonists who remained in New Sweden had already given up the New World and returned to Scandinavia). Only 13 of crew and passengers of the *Katt* had survived in Puerto Rico. Most were, by then, happily married to local men and women, or otherwise integrated, and all 13 declined the offer of passage to their former home.

The highlight of the northeastern coast is undoubtedly **La Cordillera** – a series of cays that lie just offshore. A couple of them are privately owned and off-limits to the public, while others are nothing more than hazardous rocks sticking out of the sea. The surrounding shallows, however, are gorgeous and aquarium-like, and you can land hassle-free at **Cayo Icacos** and **Palominitos** (next to Palomino) for a deserted-island feel, mere minutes from the Puerto Rican mainland. You'll also find snorkeling and diving around **Cayo Lobos** (Wolf Cay) and **Cayo Diablo** (Devil Cay).

■ Ceiba

South of Fajardo on Carr. 3, Ceiba was named for the giant indigenous tree of the same name. And that's about as interesting as it gets. Apparently, a small grove of *ceiba* trees existed when the town was founded, but was later cut down. Just outside of town, you may see the ruins of a brick chimney – the only remains of the sugarcane plantation **Hacienda Santa María**, built more than 150 years ago. Scant remnants of several other sugar plantations are scattered around the municipality. Today, the local economy relies on several factories that produce, among other things, electronics and women's undergarments. Otherwise, the town is probably best known these days for its proximity to the **Roosevelt Roads Naval Base**. Built in 1940 by President Franklin D. Roosevelt for the defense of the Caribbean, Roosevelt Roads, which includes land on Vieques, is the largest naval base in the US, with an 11,000-foot-long runway and 29,000 acres of land – 1,000 acres more than El Yunque.

■ Naguabo

Southwest of Roosevelt Roads, downtown Naguabo is lined with various derelict businesses, bland architecture and a one-way road system that is truly impossible to navigate. Take Carr. 192 southeast to avoid it, and visit instead the outlying barrio of **Playa Húcares** (follow signs to Ceiba). Contrary to what the name might suggest, there is no beach here! Playa Húcares is built on a buttress of rock that separates land from sea. But this cute little bay, watched over by the hillside *barrio* of **Punta Lima**, with its slowed-down lifestyle, colorful fishing sloops and two or three dilapidated Victorian mansions, is worth a stop. Its star features include the renovated Malecón Arturo Corsino boardwalk and the impressive ruins of a beautiful Victorian building, **El Castillo Villa del Mar** (painted pink, on your right as you come in). In the past, it housed a restaurant and an art gallery where local painters showed their work. Sadly, today it is nothing but a crumbling, though still magnificent looking, structure, despite the graffiti that belies its position on the National Registry of Historic Places. This is also the only local spot to catch a sloop bound for the waters around Cayo Santiago. On weekends, Húcares explodes as locals come to promenade, kiss their paramours and gorge on fried *chillo* (snapper) and *sierra* (kingfish) steaks in one of the seafront cafés that line the waterfront. But during the week, it is the kind of place where toothless old geezers smile and wave from their slumber spots in the shade, and a solitary beer takes a couple of hours to enjoy. For foreigners, at least, this tiny bay remains one of the east coast's least discovered places.

Driving south from Naguabo on Hwy. 3 will take you past the so-called **Tropical Beach**, a pleasant drive, but with its grubby-looking sand and murky water, an unlikely place to stop for a dip. Continue to **Playa Punta Santiago**, a still less inspiring place to sun worship, but a great spot from which to see Cayo Santiago – almost swimming distance away – and to watch the fishermen wade to and from their boats. A small ferry strictly for scientists and students crosses from the pier to the islet every 30 minutes or so.

■ Humacao

Continuing south on either Carr. 3 or Hwy. 53 leads you to Humacao (pronounced ooh-ma-COW), with several large shopping plazas, a glut of fast-food restaurants and a cinema showing the same Hollywood blockbusters as other theaters on the island. Just outside town, **Casa Roig** is the former home of sugar plantation owners. Designed by a student of Frank Lloyd Wright, it now serves as a museum to local history, the Roig family and the sugar industry that built Puerto Rico and much of the Caribbean.

■ Yabucoa & Maunabo

After passing the Sunoco oil refinery complex on Hwy. 52 south, you'll end up at the junction of Carr. 3 and Carr. 901. This loop connecting Yabucoa and Maunabo marks the easternmost end of the Ruta Panorámica – a great drive with cliff-top views and access to secluded surfing beaches. At the southernmost tip of the loop, Carr. 760 and Carr. 7760 whisk you through a steep neighborhood of dizzying streets to the **Punta Tuna lighthouse**. The lighthouse was built in 1892 and is still active; it is open intermittently on weekdays. Hike down a short path to the left of the front gate, to the beach – a secluded arc of sand hidden by cliffs, with the old lighthouse towering overhead.

Adventures

■ On Foot

Hiking & Walking

Some of the best hiking snakes through the rain forest of **El Yunque** (trail descriptions are given under *Eco-Travel*, page 331), and there are a few idyllic seaside walks along beaches. For hikers seeking on- and off-trail adventures, we highly recommend spending a day or more with guide Richard Druitt (of La Casa Vida Natural) and his brother John "Rubio," who run **Island Walkers**, PO Box 1916, Río Grande, ☎ 787-887-4359, www.islandwalkers.com. If anyone can get you off the beaten track, it's this pair of consciousness-expanding nature nuts. You'll enjoy not only their limitless expertise about local plants and animals, but also their hilarious take on island history and personalities, as well as stories from their formative years managing El Yunque rain forest, participating in the Amazon's Biosphere project and hanging out with the likes of Timothy Leary. Of the many hikes they offer, we suggest "The Windward Trail," a 10-hour hike for serious walkers only, which meanders ever upwards to the dramatic and barren El Toro peak. A more forgiving ascent to Río Blanco Falls still requires six hours of hiking on the approach from Mt. Britton. The trail takes you along an old railway gauge, now barely discernable from the encroaching jungle, skirts a reservoir and ultimately reaches the falls, which can be scaled thanks to a ladder left by a past hiker.

At the **Naguabo Gold Mine**, which is nearly impossible to find without a knowledgeable guide, you'll meet up with the ghosts of colonial gold seekers. A shaft that tunnels 300 yards into the hillside is Puerto Rico's only remaining testament to an obsession with gold and the riches that mostly evaded colonists. Be sure to ask Richard and John about expeditions to other parts of the island, too. Half-day tours cost $100 for four people, $200 for the full day, with a surcharge of $25 or $50 per person, respectively.

Golf

Six courses on the east side of the island have the some of the most spectacular golfing terrain in the Caribbean, according to local aficionados. **The Berwind Country Club**, Carr. 187, Río Grande, ☎ 787-876-3056, fax 256-5030, is best known for "water hazards in all the wrong places" and three of the toughest finishing holes around. Visitors can enjoy this torturous course, weekdays from dawn till dusk (Weds. before 11 a.m.), for $65, including cart. Nearby, the **Bahía Beach Plantation**, Carr. 187, Río Grande, ☎ 787-256-5600, fax 256-1035, www.golfbahia.com, e-mail prgolfer@aol.com, seems to have been designed with a fashion shoot in mind, with abundant flora and fauna and views of the sea making it as appropriate for photography as golfing. Open daily from 6.30 a.m. to 7 p.m., it costs $75 before 1 p.m., $50 after 1 p.m. and $30 after 3 p.m., including cart.

The **Westin Río Mar** has more great views, a ludicrous number of bunkers around the 16th hole and (especially if you find yourself in the rough) bird watching along the Río Mameyes. Bring binoculars and you can enjoy two hobbies at the same time! Open weekdays, 6.30 a.m. to 6.30 p.m.

Set on a bluff overlooking the Atlantic, the **Wyndham El Conquistador Resort & Country Club**, Las Croabas, ☎ 787-863-6784, fax 863-1144, has cliff-top elevations of up to 200 feet and a number of water features and bunkers to get the blood pumping. The 18-hole championship course was designed by Arthur Hill. Not for the faint of heart nor pocket, a round of golf during peak season at El Conquistador costs $185 ($115 after 2 p.m.). Hotel guests can expect a discount of around $20.

The **Doral Resort at Palmas del Mar**, Hwy. 3, Humacao, ☎ 787-285-2256, fax 852-6273, describes itself, somewhat suspiciously, as the "last paradise on earth," with two designer courses – the Palm and the Flamboyán. Take this sugary brochure poetry with a pinch of salt, but both courses have innovative designs, great play and plenty of snob appeal. Morning play costs $100 on the Palm, $110 on the Flamboyán. Play during "twilight" hours (after 2 p.m.), drops to $65 on either. It's open to the public daily from 7 a.m. to 5 p.m.

■ On Horseback

Gallop headlong through the lower reaches of El Yunque, trot around a pasture track or navigate a stallion through the hills of a dry tropical cay. Two ranches on the east coast offer excellent rides – one from a sprawling farm through the foothills of the rain forest and to the beach in Luquillo, the other around Palomino Island, with views of dozens of islets and the surrounding shallow reef.

At **Hacienda Carabalí**, Carr. 992, Luquillo, ☎ 787-889-5820 or 4954, e-mail hcarabal@coqui.net, choose from 45 Paso Fino horses, ranging from slow, comfortable ponies for novices to spirited steeds for more experienced riders. The most basic ride – a brief introduction to stop and go and a quick plod around the farm for beginners – costs $20 an hour ($10 for kids). A more scintillating two-hour trek into the foothills of the rain forest costs $40 for adults/$25 for kids. For the whole enchilada – rain forest, river and beach – expect to pay $60 adults/$50 kids, plus pocket money for snacks.

Palominos Ranch on Palomino Island is ideal for novice riders or people who want to explore the cay without overexerting themselves. The ride is hilly, though relatively short, and you'll stop at a tiny wedding chapel and enjoy wrap-around views of surrounding cays, opaque waters and the distant islands of Culebra, Vieques and St. Thomas. Booking a ride in advance is a good excuse to use the island, which is normally reserved for guests of the Wyndham El Conquistador. Catch the water taxi running to Palomino Island from El Conquistador's marina. The horse treks start at 10 a.m., noon and 2 p.m., cost $55 per person and last about an hour. Contact José Melendez, ☎ 787-760-8585 (unit 123-1047), for more information.

■ On Wheels

Driving the Punta Tuna Loop

The southeastern towns of **Yabucoa** and **Maunabo**, generally unappealing in themselves, mark the end points of a great half-day driving loop (depending on how often you stop), especially for visitors who don't have time to do the whole of the Ruta Panorámica. From the north, the easiest way to get on course is to follow signs to the *parador*, which will get you onto Carr. 901 (ignore the misleading road signs where Hwy. 53 ends at Yabucoa). From here, the road traces the spectacular outline of Puerto Rico's southeast corner and delves into some of the island's most secret nooks. With plunging cliffs, coves the color of rust, seas whipped by trade winds and salt strong in your nostrils, this is a more rugged Caribbean than usually presented in postcards.

You'll find several roadside seafood restaurants with killer views along the way, and a number of access roads to red-sand coves. Follow signs on Carr. 901 for the depressing guest house Lunny Mar. About 200 yards beyond the guest house is **La Cocal**, one of the most hidden beaches on this side of the coast and a good spot for surfer spotting and a picnic in the sun. It marks the beginning of several miles of hidden coves and inlets to the south, which usually involve a steep descent to shore.

When you reach the southeastern tip of the island, take Carr. 9901 through a hilly little neighborhood to the lovingly restored **Punta Tuna lighthouse**. For lonely appeal, the lighthouse and the beach below is our favorite spot on this side of the island. Park next to the lighthouse gate and follow a narrow trail to the left to **Playa Larga**. It seems incredible that this wide-open stretch of sand, sheltered by cliffs and thick sweep of jungle, is frequented by so few.

At Maunabo, turn inland along Carr. 3. As the road rises above the town and heads north, the 515-meter peak of **Cerro La Pandura** has thrust itself up from the earth, leaving in its wake giant egg-shaped boulders, blackened with age. Keep an eye out for La Piedra, or **Eagle Rock**, a 100-foot shot of volcanic stone considered sacred by the island's first inhabitants for the imprint of an eagle's profile ingrained upon it.

Mountain biking enthusiasts will enjoy areas around El Yunque (see page 334).

■ On Water

Cay-Hopping on La Cordillera

With transparent waters and shallow reefs, abundant marine life, gorgeous stretches of white sand and gentle trade winds, boating around the ridge of islets just off Puerto Rico's northeast corner (known as La Cordillera, not to be confused with the mountain range) is one of the best adventures the east coast has to offer. The northernmost cay, **Icacos**, is a popular destination for sunseekers. A long stretch of sand gives way to several decent snorkeling spots on the south side of the island. Your deserted island fantasy may be interrupted in the late morning, however, as several catamaran charters regularly dump dozens of other would-be Robinson Crusoes on the beach. This is a good time to hike around to the rugged north side of the island, where crested iguanas can sometimes be spotted in a landscape of lava rock carved with blowholes. Charter boats usually pull anchor by 2 p.m., restoring tranquility to the southern side. Check out camping possibilities here by calling the Department of Natural Resources in San Juan, ☎ 787-724-3724. Disembarking on the neighboring, privately owned **Cayo Lobos** (Wolf's Cay) is strictly prohibited, and you'll notice ominous *Peligro* ("danger") signs along the beach. Nevertheless, visitors are welcome to enjoy the surrounding waters – the best snorkeling spot on the east coast, with schools of *balao*, bright tropicals and other life swarming around giant brain corals and a living reef that drops down to about 25 feet. Near-perfect visibility provides a glimpse of the submarine food chain, with resident gobies operating a kind of "car wash" for larger fish like grouper, blue tang and French angels, by eating parasites while the beneficiaries snack on silver fish and reef scum. As a result, the area is as busy as a school canteen at lunchtime. Beyond, **Cayo Diablo** (Devil's Cay) looms menacingly out of the water, with no place to land. Diving around Diablo is still popular, although the reef was largely covered over by sand after Hurricane Georges. Bird enthusiasts will enjoy traveling between Lobos and Diablo, as both islands are popular nesting and feeding grounds for sooty, royal, bridle and roseate terns from May to September. Tropicbirds come for the October-to-April season, and brown pelicans, brown boobies and frigate birds can be seen all year.

The most visited cay of La Cordillera, **Palomino Island,** is under a 99-year lease to the hotel El Conquistador, and the beach area has been developed with picnicking families in mind. Teenagers lounge on floating rafts close to shore, parents slap sun lotion on their young children, a few loners hunker around the bar, but few venture to the secluded, clothing-optional coves (see *Swimming & Beaches*) on the east side of the island, or hike the ridge of the cay for a 360° sea view.

Although hotel guests officially have exclusive access, there are ways to use Palomino without paying the high hotel rates. The easiest and most legitimate is aboard the **Palominos Water Taxi**, which leaves the Conquistador marina daily, every half-hour between 9 a.m. and 3 p.m. Don your most charming smile and have a valid excuse ready, such as having booked an activity (horseback riding, windsurfing, parasailing, etc.), and the ferry staff will usually give you a plastic access bracelet. It takes about 45 minutes to reach Palomino from Fajardo. Swimming distance from Palomino is **Palominitos**, the quintessential deserted island – a flat, round fringe of powdery white sand around a clump of palm trees. Get there early on a weekday morning in the spring or fall. Otherwise, the serenity is likely to be broken by zooming personal watercraft drivers and other motor-crazed jackals. The closest and most visible cay from Fajardo is **Isleta Marina**. It is something of a blot on the landscape, with a hideous pink condo taking up nearly a third of the landmass. There is little reason to visit unless you are staying there (see *Where To Stay*).

Getting a Boat

Perhaps the most romantic way to day-trip around the cays is to hire one of the rapidly vanishing *nativos*, or native sloops, from the fishing marina at **Bahía Las Croabas** (look for the signs saying *paseo en bote* and *a los cayos* near the end of Carr. 9987). Old-timer Raymundo Hernandez and his family still operate one or two of these colorful, sail-driven fishing boats (the younger fishermen prefer motorized craft), and will take groups up to six people out for a day for $150. It's best to book in advance with him or his son Freddy, ☎ 787-863-2471, cell 642-3116. Or just show up at the dingy marina and try your luck. You can't miss the marina, due to the unfortunate stench of sulfur surrounding it. A gang of jolly mariners (expect music and dancing) plays dominoes and drinks beer here from the morning hours. Even the motorboat fishermen will usually agree to drop you off and pick you up at Icacos for $10 to $20 a head, or take you island-hopping. It pays to ask around and negotiate the price, especially if you speak Spanish. Remember to bring your own food, drink and plenty of sunscreen.

Several catamaran charters to the cays are good value, and they're nearly indistinguishable from each other. Most hold 25-30 people and follow the same circuit: Cayo Icacos in the morning for a swim, beachcombing, lunch and beginner-level snorkeling (instruction provided), then to the reef of Cayo Lobos for more interesting snorkeling. They universally charge $55 per person for the day, including lunch buffet and snorkel equipment. Rum punch doled out from massive coolers lubricates the experience and helps ensure you'll disembark at the end of the day with newfound friends. **Castillo Tours**, ☎ 787-791-6195, 725-7970, or 726-5752, fax 268-0740, has two catamarans – *Stampede* and *Barefoot* – which makes them a good bet for last-minute reservations. The **Fun Cat**, ☎ 787-728-6606, cell ☎ 787-383-5700, is the only catamaran designed and built in Puerto Rico, by Capt. Greg Korwek. VIP sailing excursions, $495 for six passengers, and diving trips, $125 per person, are also available. Try **East Wind**, ☎ 787-860-3434, cell 409-2485, for kids, who will no doubt delight in its glass bottom and water slide, or, the **Spread Eagle II**, ☎ 787-887-8821, which gives out brand-new snorkels to use and keep.

Independent-minded explorers can hire their own motorboat from **Club Náutico International** at Fajardo's Villa Marina, and head to the cays or beyond. The most basic four-person boats cost $249 a day, while 10-person crafts with walk-around cabins go for $495 and up. The cruise director will supply navigational charts and tips on the area's best boating destinations. You'll need to show some proof of your nautical skills, depending on the type of boat you want to rent. Villa Marina is on Carr. 987 just north of the town of Fajardo, ☎ 787-863-5131; US 800-NAUTICO; Florida ☎ 800-BOAT-RENT.

Yachting

During the past 20 years or so, the Fajardo area has become the undisputed yachting capital of Puerto Rico, and one of the biggest boating centers of the Caribbean. Near-constant trade winds averaging 10 to 15 knots make sailing a breeze in Puerto Rican waters and to neighboring islands, and modern, protected marinas have attracted private yachters and charter companies alike. Here you can embark on sailing vessels from half-day trips to local cays to several week charters to Vieques, Culebra, the Virgin Islands and beyond. Of the four marinas in the Fajardo area, by far the largest is **Puerto del Rey**.

The 50-foot sailing ketch *Erin Go Bragh*, ☎ 787-860-4401 or 409-2511, www.egbc.net, e-mail egbc@coqui.net, featured in the *Swiss Family Robinson* movie, specializes in day-trips but also offers fully crewed charters for overnight and longer trips. Daily and term charters are also available on the 43-foot *Ventajero 3*, ☎ 787-645-9129, www.sailpuertorico.com. From Villa Marina, check out the *Fun Cat*, ☎ 787-728-6606, cell 383-5700 for a crewed, six-person catamaran charter for $495 per day.

MONKEY ISLAND

If you sail near the coast of Naguabo, you'll pass **Cayo Santiago** – a.k.a. Cayo de los Monos (Monkey Island) – a sort of biosphere-cum-Alcatraz for the rhesus monkey. Since just before WWII, when the University of Puerto Rico brought a clan of rhesus to the deserted islet for behavioral experiments, students and researchers have written innumerable papers about the social interaction of the group and the reaction of individuals to diseases such as arthritis and diabetes. Tagged, numbered and logged, the 600-plus rhesus monkeys are not allowed off the island, and the public is not allowed to visit. However, if you get close enough to the shore, you may catch a glimpse of our misplaced distant cousin engaged in some primal act. **Frank "Paquito" Lopez**, ☎ 787-850-7881, beeper 402-2337, takes visitors to the waters around the cay in his boat, *Mi Paseadora*. You'll find him at Playa Húcares in Naguabo, weekends only. Expect to pay $20 and up per head, depending on the size of the group, including snorkeling gear. For a kayaking trip that will take you right up to the island's shore, try Gary Horne at **Tortuga Kayak** in San Juan, ☎ 787-725-5169, www.kayak-pr.com, e-mail kayakpr@worldnet.att.net.

Kayaking

Timed right, a kayak venture through the mangrove of Las Cabezas de San Juan will put you in the middle of the **Laguna Grande** on a moonless night, when the warm shallow pond metamorphoses into a bioluminescent light show. Expect water that sparkles alien green when disturbed, and lots of mosquitoes. For best hallucinogenic effect, get in the water wearing a mask and snorkel and then splash around. In Las Croabas, Mark and Monica at **Caribe Kayak**, ☎ 787-889-7734, run night trips around the time of a new moon for $35 per person, as well as a steamy day kayak trip around the mangroves for $55 a head, lunch included.

At the public beach in Luquillo, when you finally tire of sun basking and eating fried fish, you can rent a kayak hourly for $10 (single) or $15 (double). The couple who owns the kayaks (you'll see them on the beach, more or less daily) runs nighttime trips to the Laguna Grande, when bioluminescence can be seen. On Playa Azul, at the east end of Luquillo, weekend kayak rentals are about the same hourly price, but if you can negotiate a good daily rate, we suggest paddling east to the wonderfully isolated virgin beaches of **La Selva** and **El Convento**.

Diving

Though visibility is usually well below 100 feet, and some divers complain that much of the reef is dead or covered by sand, several dive sites on the east coast remain popular. Because of its convenient location and heavy tourist traffic, **Palomino Island** is one of the most-visited local dive sites, with a double barrier reef system and sand channels, home to the curious band-tailed puffer fish and parrot fish colonies, among other things. A two-tank dive here should include the **Palominitos Wall**, with its submarine garden of star, mushroom and stony flower corals. Off **Cayo Diablo**, the reef plunges down a 60-foot slope where stingrays and hawksbill turtles often loiter. A dive off **Cayo Jureles** can take you to depths of 80-90 feet, a favorite among locals with the best "underwater mountaineering" on this side of the island. Near Naguabo, **The Barrels** is popular for its maze of giant vase corals at depths of 80-90 feet. Unfortunately, no Spanish galleons or pirate ships lurk beneath the waves. If you must do a wreck dive here, the hull of a 20th-century craft, the *Barcelona*, rests in about 60 feet of water off Luquillo, and there's a sunken barge at Naguabo as well as a contemporary wreck near Palominito. Finally, if you're after a cheap two-tank dive for beginners, check out the **offshore caverns** at Playa Azul in Luquillo. With maximum depths of about 30 feet, it's perfect for less-confident divers, and possibly a little dull for more experienced subaquatic creatures.

DIVE SHOPS

At **Alpha Scuba** in Luquillo, Calle Fernandez Garcia, ☎ 787-327-5108/3990, e-mail alphascuba@hotmail.com, owner Carlos Soltero runs snorkeling and diving trips on the East Coast and the rest of the island. His rate of $45 for a two-tank dive from Playa Azul is one of the cheapest on the island. Experienced and personable, with more than 20 years in operation in Puerto Rico, he usually offers SSI Open Water Diver certification for $99 (plus $65 for books and about $150 for the purchase of snorkel, mask, fins and weight belt). He also runs overnight trips to Mona Island, Culebra, Cerro Gordo and Sail Rock (the sail-shaped monolith between Culebra and St. Thomas).

In the Fajardo area, **La Casa del Mar Dive Shop** at El Conquistador Resort, ☎ 787-863-1000 ext. 7917, fax 860-1604, e-mail lacasadelmar@hotmail.com, offers snorkeling and scuba diving trips that cost $69 for one tank and $85 for a night dive – expensive compared to many other island shops. They have a "discover scuba" program, an easy, chaperoned dive for beginners without certification, for $119; and PADI nitrox certification for $250, including two dives and a combined "sailing and scuba" course that teaches the basics of both skills in one trip, for about $750 for four people. One of the best deals is the "Bubblemaker" program, for kids between eight and 15 years old, at $49 for first-timers and $35 for each additional time. Ask about the Junior Certification Program for kids aged 10 years or older.

At Fajardo's Villa Marina, Capt. Greg Korwek of the *Fun Cat*, ☎ 787-728-6606, cell 383-5700, offers local diving trips for $125 per person, snorkelers also welcome.

At the the Doral Resort at Palmas del Mar in Humacao, **Coral Head Divers**, ☎ 787-850-7208 or 800-635-4529, fax 852-6602, offers dives off the east coast and beyond, plus NAUI and PADI diver certification courses.

At Playa Húcares, Eliezer Díaz of **Puerto Rico Scuba**, ☎/fax 787-874-4077, does SSI and PADI certification for around $200, including all equipment and five dives. Certified divers can get a two-tank dive, day or night, for $45 – usually around Palmas del Mar and Yabucoa.

TIP: *To play Jacques Cousteau for a day, you can rent underwater video and camera equipment from* **PeekABoo** *at El Conquistador,* ☎ *787-863-6828.*

Fishing

The nearby **Puerto Rican Trench**, where underwater cliffs drop to an eventual depth of 28,000 feet, makes the eastern part of the island ideal blue marlin country, especially in the months of July through October. The sight of one of these sleek, glittering giants breaking water at the end of a fishing line is something you're not likely to forget. Other billfish, as well as wahoo, tuna and dorado (mahi mahi) also frequent offshore waters.

A few inlets and freshwater lagoons are worth exploring, as well. A couple of reputable fishing charters operate out of the Hotel El Conquistador, but to avoid the hotel surcharge we recommend Capt. Bill Burleson of **Karolette Charters** in Humacao, ☎ 787-850-7442. He'll take your group for a full day over seamounts and deep water for $970, and for a half-day along the continental shelf and over offshore reefs for $570. Burleson also offers discounts for payment in cash, and a 50% discount if the boat does not catch fish.

Across from Villa Marina in Fajardo, Capt. Marcos Hanke a "marine biologist and fishing consultant" at **Light Tackle Paradise**, ☎ 787-874-2294 or 646-2585, offers fly-fishing classes and inshore trips to local reefs and freshwater lagoons (where you may find tarpon, snook, bonefish and jacks, among others). Half-day trips for up to four people on a 22-foot catamaran cost $350; two-person trips on a 17-foot skiff cost $250. Tackle, bait and refreshments are included.

Beaches & Swimming

It's not that we don't like people; we really do. But it's one of the persistent ironies of Puerto Rico that, in our opinion, the best beaches are usually the least frequented, and vice versa. For example, the lovely stretch of sand at Balneario Luquillo has lost much of its charm due to trash buildup, overcrowding (especially on weekends) and the construction of dreary concrete kiosks. On the east side of Luquillo, however, **Playa Azul** is nearly deserted. Climb over a small jetty of rocks and head eastward, and you'll find the beach *is* deserted – for about six miles! Abutted by dense foliage and an unofficial nature reserve, the swath of sand is known locally as La Selva (the western three miles) and El Convento (the eastern section). Though it seems inevitable the area will someday be developed, for now the only structure along the entire six miles of sand is a modest green house on El Convento end, used as a retreat for government officials and their families. Along Luquillo's **La Pared** beach, you may come across a few lean-tos made of branches and the remnants of campfires left by past solitude seekers. But along the rest of the way, countless idyllic bays invite you to strip down and plunge in the clear waters, completely unmindful of the island population of four million crammed onto more accessible beaches far, far away. A second way to reach these beaches is from Playa Seven Seas in Las Croabas to the east. Follow a trail through the bush at the extreme northwest end of Seven Seas to El Convento, then head west past the government house. Walking the entire beach would take about three hours non-stop, so be prepared with plenty of water and sunscreen. There is no official campsite, but you'll find a perfect spot to pitch a tent every 10 feet or so.

> **CAUTION:** *Most beaches on the east coast have no lifeguards and occasional moderate to strong currents. Novice swimmers should let more experienced companions test the waters before getting in.*

Playa Escondido, along the same path that takes you from Playa Seven Seas to El Convento, is a lovers' hideaway – a small cove heaped with thick reddish sand, hemmed in by high, rocky dunes. Be aware that there is no shade here, and usually no people, either. Because of its proximity to Seven Seas, it could be a nice spot for a surreptitious campout. To get here, walk west along Seven Seas toward the headland (away from Cabezas de San Juan) until you reach a well-worn trail leading into the dry forest. The path to Playa Escondido is about 10 minutes along that trail on the right-hand side.

On Palomino Island, the beach at the ferry landing is wide and often crowded, with concessions and shallow water appropriate for young children. **Sunrise Cove** and **Hidden Cove** (clothing-optional) are about a 20-minute hike from the ferry landing, on the east side of the cay. A hand-painted map near the concessions will point the way. The beaches are clean, with chaise lounges provided, though the rocky shallows make swimming a bit uncomfortable.

In **Humacao**, the public *balneario* (beach) is clean but essentially unremarkable. Farther south, the beach at **Palmas del Mar** resort is lovely, and with three miles of it, you should be able to get as near or far as you wish from the boogie boarders, coconut-bronzed golf widows and the cocktails-at-sunset crowd. Just tell the guards at the resort entrance that you're headed for the beach, and they'll give you a pass.

On the northern end of Carr. 901, **Balneario Palmas de Lucia** tends to be a local hangout for families and picnickers, with a huge, fenced-in swimming pool and plenty of palm trees between which to string a hammock. Farther south on Carr. 901, keep an eye out for byroads that dip down steep inclines to beaches with no official name. Finally, below the lighthouse at Punta Tuna, on the southeastern tip of Puerto Rico, cliffs and a thick sweep of jungle shelter **Playa Larga**.

Surfing

The East Coast has nothing on the tubes of the north or the giddying drops of the west, but it's not a total wipeout. In Luquillo, **La Pared** (look for the wall at east end of Playa Azul) usually has some small but rideable waves. Hop over the rocks at the eastern end of La Pared and you're at the beginning of **La Selva**, where locals go for longer breaks.

> **TIP:** *Check out **La Selva Surf Shop**, a couple of blocks from the beach on Fernandez Garcia, ☎ 787-889-6205, for gear, tips and nice people.*

Another break nearby is beneath the lighthouse at **Cabezas de San Juan,** with conditions for experienced surfers only. It's a bit of a gray area in terms of access, however. Since Cabezas is a nature reserve (see *Eco-Tourism*) officially you need to be involved in some sort of guided tour to be on the land. On the other hand, all beaches in Puerto Rico are public property and therefore you should have the right to access. If you're dead-set on surfing this spot, try to slip into Las Cabezas from the beach south of Playa Seven Seas and follow the paved single track out to the point. A lot of serious locals head south to **El Cocal**, one of the more hidden spots on the east coast, accessible by following signs for Guest House Lunny Mar from Carr. 901. Another coveted break is on **Sharkey's Beach**, just north of the Playa Emajaguas Guest House on Carr. 901, Emajaguas.

■ In The Air

Skydiving

Few activities provoke the eye-popping, sphincter-clenching rush of adrenaline that comes with willingly leaping out of a small plane thousands of feet in the air. The only private DZ (drop zone) in Puerto Rico is the **Puerto Rican Skydiving Center**, which operates from the airstrip in Humacao. They apparently offer tandem jumps for beginners (you're strapped in with an instructor, who dives with you and controls the parachute), as well as training and certification courses and advanced jumps for qualified daredevils. Beginner tandem jumps cost $189 ($179 on weekdays), with discounts for groups. This outfit seems somewhat disorganized, however. Half a dozen calls to their office went unreturned (though we've been assured that the founders – Butch and Eric Van Lewis – are still in business), and thus we're unable to vouch for the quality or safety of their business. The web site – www.skydive-pr.com – lets you know that the staff "love to party," which is nice to know but not the most relevant or reassuring piece of information from your skydive instructor. So, good luck! Try to track them down at the airport, or call ☎ 787-726-0326.

Parasailing

A parachuting/water-skiing hybrid, parasailing is both peaceful and exhilarating (if you're comfortable with heights). Basically, you're pulled behind a motorboat while strapped to a parachute. Depending on the acceleration of the boat, you either shoot up into the air or float gently toward the water. Both the **Wyndham El Conquistador** and the **Westin Río Mar** hotels offer parasailing (usually lasting about a half-hour at $75 for a single flyer, $60 each for a double).

Hang Gliding

You're standing on a mountainside of El Yunque rain forest, looking out over the Caribbean Sea far below, a pair of nylon wings strapped to your back. You run down a grassy slope. And jump. The thermal air currents push you up, and your heart skips a beat. You're living a dream as old as the human imagination. Flying! In Puerto Rico, the only certified hang gliding outfit and school, **Team Spirit**, serves everyone from novices eager to try flying for the first time to seasoned pilots. Tandem flights with an instructor, from 1,440 feet up in the mountains of El Yunque, last 10 minutes to half an hour, and cost $100, including some preliminary training. An introductory program, in which you'll learn to fly solo on a bunny hill, includes sessions of three to four hours (usually over five days or more), involves everything from basic mastery of the apparatus to increasing levels of solo flight. To get airborne, contact Keishya and Bob at Team Spirit, ☎ 787-850-0508, www.mailways.net/teamspirit, e-mail tshg@coqui.net.

Eco-Travel

■ Las Cabezas de San Juan

Tourists rarely hear about (and even more rarely visit) Las Cabezas de San Juan, which is understandably overshadowed by the splendor of El Yunque. Yet, after the rain forest, it is one of the most significant ecological environments on the island, preserving the natural habitat of several endangered species and providing important laboratory space for research in ecology, marine biology, geology and archaeology. The 316-acre reserve was plucked from the hands of developers in 1975 by the Conservation Trust of Puerto Rico and officially designated a nature reserve in 1986 by the Puerto Rican and United States governments. It contains one of the island's three impressive bioluminescent lagoons, as well as mangrove swamps, dry forest, palm groves and coral reef. The mangroves swarm with blue, mangrove and fiddler crabs. Coves thick with sea grass are favorite feeding grounds of brown pelicans and various gulls. Endangered species like the sea turtle and osprey use the beaches as a breeding ground; mongooses and green iguanas can sometimes be seen around the stubby bush of the dry forest; and red-tailed hawks soar above in search of prey.

> **WATCHABLE WILDLIFE:** *Like a rooftop view of the Blitz, sitting at the far end of the beach of Las Cabezas in the late afternoon gives you the chance to watch hundreds of brown pelicans dive-bombing the water's surface to gulp down fish. Weirder still, you may (as we did) spot snorkelers with a death wish, paddling around in the target zone.*

Recent excavations near the beach have unearthed a number of pre-Colombian artifacts belonging to the Igneri Indians and dating back to about 500 BC. But the next sign of human life in Las Cabezas dates from nearly two millennia later. In 1880, the Spanish built a **neoclassical lighthouse** in response to increasing ship traffic through the Vieques and Culebra passage. The second-oldest lighthouse on the island, it is now protected under the Natural Register of Historic Properties. In 1989 an extensive renovation using 19th-century techniques restored the interior woodwork, masonry façade and copper dome to their original state. The lighthouse is now used as a research and laboratory facility by departments of the University of Puerto Rico, for disciplines as diverse as marine biology, pharmacology, physiology and animal behavior. Research findings are exhibited at the lighthouse, and visitors can sometimes observe scientists and naturalists at work.

Las Cabezas de San Juan is open Friday to Sunday to the general public (Wednesdays and Thursdays to school groups) and closed on all major holidays. Admission is by reservation only, through the Conservation Trust of Puerto Rico, ☎ 787-722-5882, weekends ☎ 787-860-2560. They do, however, have a somewhat irritating requirement that visits be made aboard a tour trolley – at 9.30 a.m., 10.00 a.m., 10.30 a.m. and 2.00 p.m. – which rather negates the feeling of being at one with nature. You might try sneaking around the official entrance shack and wandering solo (claim ignorance if confronted, and never, ever say we suggested it!) by cutting through several well-worn short paths from the beach abutting the reserve.

■ Humacao Natural Reserve

Reportedly the best place to view waterfowl in Puerto Rico, the Humacao Natural Reserve is a special treat for ornithologists, both serious and amateur. From Fajardo, follow Hwy. 3 south past the entrance to the Balneario de Humacao. The reserve is marked on the left just past a small concrete bridge. Barely shown on maps and rarely mentioned in tourist literature, the reserve's 2,800 acres is open for hiking, fishing and camping. If you like birds, be sure to bring binoculars. The West Indian whistling duck can often be seen at dawn and dusk when it emerges hungry from its roost. This is also a good time to see the white-cheeked pintail, American and Caribbean coots and a variety of different herons and egrets. Migratory birds, including teals, scaups and ospreys, can often be seen fishing in the lagoons. A breeding population of yellow-crowned bishops – a bird introduced to Puerto Rico from Africa – can be spotted in the marshy ground around the lagoons. The upland forest of the refuge also provides home to the Puerto Rican woodpecker, cave swallows and warblers. For more information on visiting the reserve, contact the Puerto Rico Department of Natural and Environmental Resources (DNER), ☎ 787-852-6088.

■ El Yunque

History

Before European colonists arrived to Puerto Rico, 90% of the island's mountains, hills and coasts were covered in forest. Settlers cleared most of the land down to bare dirt between 1493 and 1875, taming the island for military, construction and agricultural purposes. They rarely ventured, however, into the upper reaches of the rain forest, which remained a mysterious mountain zone shrouded in mist, and one of the last hideouts for Taino Indians.

Some of the lush foliage in El Yunque.
(© 2000 Tara Stevens)

El Yunque, meaning "The Anvil" in Spanish, is the name both for the rain forest and the highest peak visible from the north. Many guidebooks and travel journals flatly state that this is because the peak looks like an anvil, but you may notice that it doesn't. For the Taino people, the forested peaks were a sacred place and the home of their benevolent deity Yukiyú. The north-facing peak they simply called *yuke*, meaning "mountain" in their language. The early slaves called the area *Furidí*, meaning "mountain in white cloud" in the Yoruba tongue. All of this apparently confused the Spanish colonists, who translated the name of the enigmatic place to the closest-sounding word in their language.

In the following centuries, though, the Spanish began to appreciate the beauty of El Yunque, even as they logged away the woods of its lower sections. In 1876, King Alfonso XII of Spain set aside about half of the current forest area for protection – the first such designation in the Spanish New World, making El Yunque one of the oldest forest reserves in the Western Hemisphere. In 1903, five years after the United States gained possession of the island, the US Forest Service adopted El Yunque, and eventually doubled the size of the area under protection. In 1976, it was designated as the only national forest outside the continental United States, and as a "biosphere reserve" by the United Nations. This has made it one of the most studied and best understood forests in the tropics, and helped save it from the fate of the rest of the island, where more than 90% of native trees have been felled. It contains three-quarters of Puerto Rico's remaining virgin forest, as well as many sections that have reforested either naturally or with human help. Today, El Yunque is truly a natural museum piece, where one may get a sense of the ancient, Eden-like state of the island. It has also gained 21st-century strategic importance. About 200 different communications functions – from civilian telephone service to military transmissions – depend on towers located on El Yunque's peaks.

Getting Here & Getting Away

El Yunque forms a 43-square-mile section of the Sierra de Luquillo mountains, about an hour's drive from San Juan. Most visitors use the main entrance on the north side of the forest, taking Hwy. 3 to Carr. 191, which leads to the visitor centers, lookout towers and most trailheads. Carr. 191 once continued all the way through El Yunque to the south side, but a section inside the protected area was closed due to landslides, and the Forest Service has fought to keep it closed to through traffic, to minimize human impact. You can enter El Yunque from the south on Carr. 191, via Carr. 31 from Hwy. 53, but the road is closed a short way into the forest proper. Carr. 186 dips into El Yunque, connecting Río Grande to the west side of the forest. Although maps show the middle section of the road closed, many locals use this route by driving carefully around the concrete barriers and past a large sinkhole just within the forest limits. This is a pretty drive, and the easiest way to access the beginning of El Toro trail is by following Carr. 186 south from Río Grande. Unfortunately, no public transport serves El Yunque, so the best way to get here is with your own car. Many of the larger hotels and a few independent operators in the San Juan area offer organized bus tours, but these follow preset itineraries and usually involve little hiking or time to explore the forest on your own.

Flora & Fauna

With more than 200 inches of rainfall falling on much of El Yunque each year, the forest is a fantasyland of vegetation. Rare species of tree, such as the tabonuco and palo colorado, some of which date back 1,000 years, give way to dozens of variety of palms, more than 200 types of fern and a gnarled miniature forest on the mountain peaks. Technicolor flowers bloom from more than 80 varieties of orchids, as well as hibiscus, lilies, ginger and dozens of other tropical species. Many people who visit El Yunque remark afterwards that, while the flora was stunning, they didn't see much animal life. But these are usually the same people who hiked the trails at breakneck speed and failed to stop longer than to catch their breath. Viewing the rich diversity of life in the forest requires a willingness to stay in one place for a while, patiently focusing on one small area with your eyes and ears. Most of the species are non-mammalian (no monkeys jabbering in the treetops, no wild cats prowling the forest floor), and many are small, shy or well camouflaged. Patience may reward you with glimpses of birds, amphibians, reptiles, insects and types of vegetation

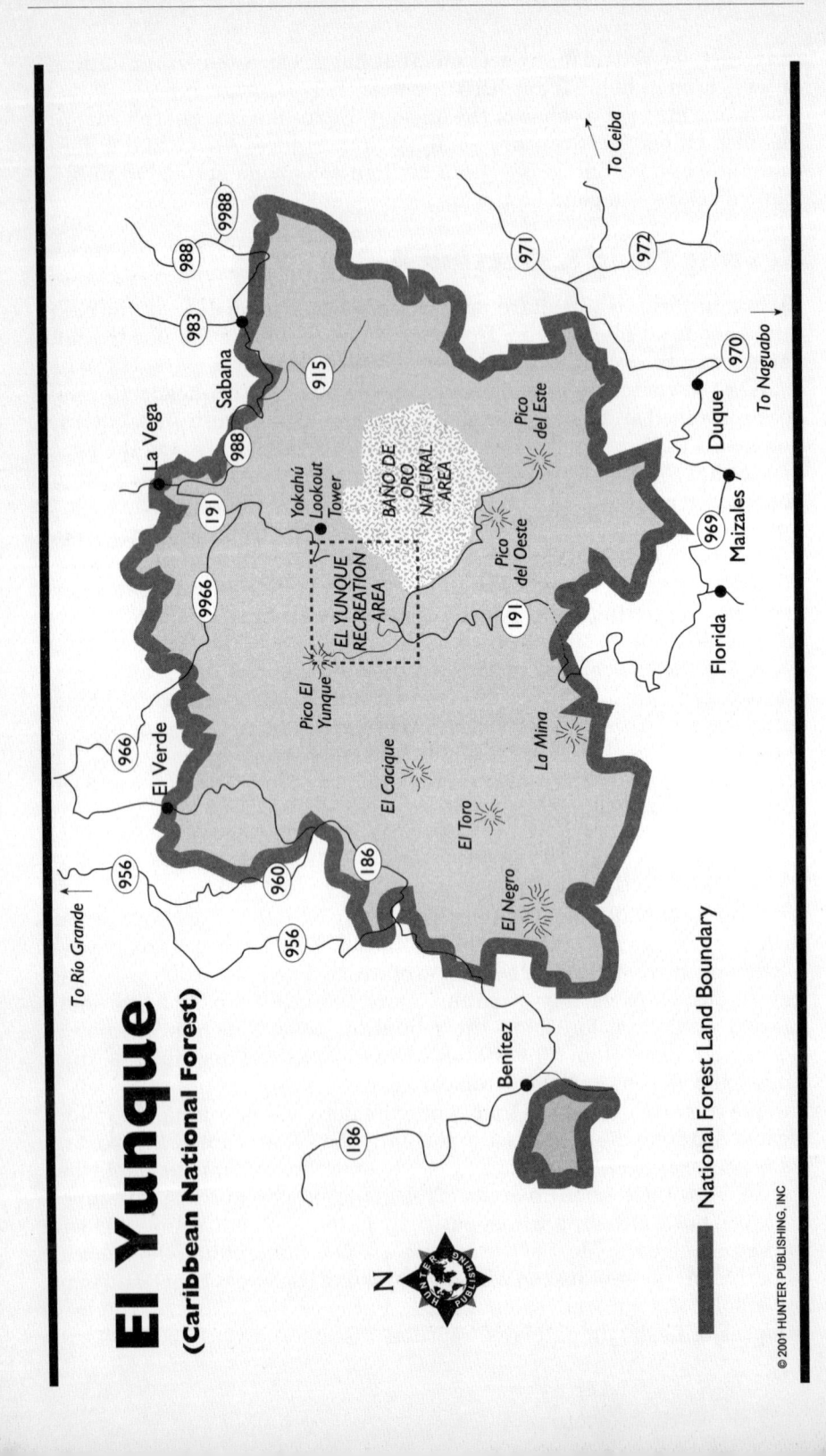

El Yunque
(Caribbean National Forest)

that exist nowhere else on earth. We recommend bringing a pair of binoculars or a camera with a good zoom lens.

El Yunque can be broken down into four distinct ecological zones. The lowest (below 2000 feet) is the **tabonuco forest**, with 225 native tree species, 23 of which can be found nowhere else in the world, including the **tabonuco tree**. Birdlife here includes **red-tailed** and **Puerto Rican broad-winged hawks** circling above the canopy (often seen from the Yokahú Tower), as well as **black-whiskered vireos**, **scaly-naped pigeons** and **stripe-headed tanagers**. A close inspection of the undergrowth will usually reveal large **forest snails** and **walking sticks**, one of the best-disguised insects in the animal kingdom.

Around and above the 2,000-foot elevation, the **palo colorado forest** is characterized by gentle sloping valleys and the ancient **palo colorado tree** (colored stick tree), which is the favored home of the **Puerto Rican parrot** (see below). Amid the thick vines and epiphytes hanging like dreadlocks from the trees, look for the **pearly-eyed thrasher**, several species of **anole lizards** and their main predator, the **lizard cuckoo**.

IT'S NOT EASY BEING GREEN

The little Puerto Rican parrot is one of the most endangered birds in the world and is rarely seen. Characterized by bright green plumage, with a splash of red at the bridge of its nose and white eye feathers, its timid personality has made it disastrously vulnerable to environmental changes. Researchers estimate that, before Columbus, about a million Puerto Rican parrots lived on the island. As the natural habitat shrank due to deforestation, however, the smaller but more-aggressive pearly-eyed thrasher intimidated the reclusive green parrot out of the few surviving nesting areas. When the parrot did manage to nest, often in less secure areas, its eggs often fell prey to red-tails hawks, boa constrictors, mongooses, forest rats and fly larvae. By the early 1970s, a mere 13 parrots were left in the wild, all in El Yunque. The Puerto Rican Parrot Cooperative Recovery Program, founded in 1968, has pulled off a near-miracle in their quest to save the beloved bird, through captive breeding and building alternative habitats for both for the parrot and its rival, the pearly-eyed thrasher. Today, more than 40 Puerto Rican parrots live wild in El Yunque, and more than 110 more have been bred in aviaries in El Yunque and Utuado. Newly released parrots are implanted with microchips, to track their whereabouts. Researchers hope to increase the number in El Yunque to 200 within the next decade, so that the green Puerto Rican parrot may begin to repopulate itself.

Above 2,500 feet, the **sierra palm forest** has much steeper terrain, with tall, slender palms growing out of a carpet of mosses and ferns. These areas are often enveloped in mist, creating an eerie, haunted atmosphere. At higher elevations up to above 3,500 feet, the **cloud forest**, also known as the **dwarf forest**, is so buffeted by trade winds that trees rarely grow higher than 12 feet and are often gnarled into freakish shapes. The lichens, moss and scarlet bromeliad flowers echo with the songs of many types of frog, including the endemic **burro coquí**, whose call sounds like a fingernail being run along the teeth of a comb. This is also the only known habitat for the elfin **woods warbler**, a species undiscovered until 1971.

Facilities

Operated by the Forest Service, part of the US Department of Agriculture, El Yunque is well equipped for all types of visitors, with rest and picnic areas, public toilets and visitor centers along or near many of the major trails. For information via phone, in Spanish or English, ☎ 787-888-1810, weekdays, from 8 a.m. to 4:30 p.m.

El Portal Visitor Center, located at the forest entrance on Carr. 191, Km. 4.3, provides information on the forest and maps, as well as pavilions with basic exhibits. A small theater shows a 12-minute film, alternating in Spanish and English, which gives an armchair traveler's tour of the forest. The forest rangers here are extremely friendly and helpful, and can help you plan your visit. Open since 1996, the center is wheelchair-accessible, with a paved sidewalk designed for viewing of tree ferns, cecropia trees and other rain forest plants, as well as birds and reptiles. There is a $3 entrance fee per person ($1.50 for kids under 12 and seniors).

The **Palo Colorado Visitor Center**, at the trailhead of La Mina Falls route, has a decent bookshop and friendly attendants who are generally better informed than those at El Portal. It's free of charge, and this is the place to request camping permits. Other visitor centers are located on Carr. 191 at Km. 8.9, 11.6 and 11.8, with information, restrooms and picnic spots. All open every day from 9 a.m. to 5 p.m.

Ranger-Guided Trips

Rangers run **Forest Adventure Tours** from the Palo Colorado Visitor Center, between 10:30 a.m. and 3:30 p.m., assuming at least five or six visitors are up for it. They'll tailor a guided introduction to highlights of El Yunque, depending on your area of interest (bird-watching, parrot trails, general flora and fauna, etc.). For more personal attention to your group, avoid going on weekends. The one- to two-hour tour costs a reasonable $5 per person for adults; $2.50 for young children and seniors.

El Yunque's Hiking Trails

Thirteen official trails – a few paved and most extremely well maintained – lead into El Yunque. Many have shelters to duck into during frequent deluges of rain, as well as commodities such as drinking fountains, parking lots and visitor centers. Only a few trails are semi-treacherous, with slippery mud slopes that usually pay off at the end with stunning peak-top views.

> **CAUTION:** *Going off-trail or off-road in El Yunque is not advised, both for environmental and personal safety reasons. It's easy to get lost.*

BIG TREE TRAIL: This moderate trail (.9 mile) descends from Carr. 191 through a prime example of tabonuco forest to La Mina Falls, with child-oriented descriptions of the flora and fauna on plaques along the way.

LA MINA FALLS TRAIL: At the falls, you can pick up La Mina Falls Trail (1.1 miles), which climbs up to Carr. 191 again, less than a mile south of the Big Tree trailhead. La Mina Falls is a popular swimming and picnic area, and both of these trails can get crowded. If you want a bit more privacy for bathing, hop off La Mina Trail above the falls and you'll find a number of relatively secluded river pools

LA COCA TRAIL: If you continue east from the falls, you will reach La Coca Trail (1.8 miles), which descends into a wild valley of El Yunque from Carr. 191. This is a more rugged, muddy trail, but rewards the extra effort with a true sense being in a thick jungle wilderness. La Coca Trail twice crosses the Quebrada La Coca river and, at its lowest point, meets the Río de la Mina. Look for good swimming holes up and down these rivers.

CARRILLO TRAIL: Hook up with this 1.9-mile trail at the end of La Coca, and you can follow it eastward into an isolated section of the forest.

FLASH-FLOOD WARNING

Most rivers in El Yunque are prone to flash floods. Although it is fine to bathe in any of them, use common sense. If it starts to rain heavily, get out of the river and head for higher ground. During rains, a slow rise in the water level usually precedes a flash flood, which can come barreling down a riverbed in a deadly wall of water. Every year, careless bathers are swept away and drowned.

CAIMITILLO TRAIL: Less than a half-mile long, the Caimitillo Trail is an easy walk on a concrete trail. It starts across the street from the Sierra Palm Visitor Center, through vine-clad trees and fern growth, crosses one stream and ascends a short set of steps. Along the way, you'll see examples of structures used in the Puerto Rican Parrot Recovery program.

BANO DE ORO TRAIL: From Caimitillo Trail, you end up at the crossroads of the Baño de Oro Trail (.2 mile), a mild concrete-and-gravel path that leads back to Carr. 191 through the habitat of the Puerto Rican parrot, via the ancient (and often crowded) Baño de Oro swimming hole.

EL YUNQUE TRAIL: El Yunque Trail (2.6 miles) can also be accessed from Caimitillo. It ascends to spectacular views (cloud cover permitting)

El Yunque Recreation Area

1. El Portal Visitor Center
2. Angelito Trail
3. La Coca Trail
4. La Coca Falls
5. Carrillo Trail
6. Yokahú Lookout Center
7. Big Tree Trail
8. La Mina Trail
9. La Mina Falls
10. Sierra Palma Visitor Center
11. Palo Colorado Visitor Center
12. Caimitillo Trail
13. Los Pichachos Trail
14. Los Pichachos Lookout Tower
15. El Yunque Trail
16. Mount Britton Spur
17. Mount Britton Lookout Tower
18. Mount Britton Trail
19. Trade Winds (to El Toro Trail)
20. Baño de Oro Trail
21. Baño de Oro

© 2001 HUNTER PUBLISHING, INC

from El Yunque peak. This slightly more strenuous trail (the one-way trip takes about an hour, rather than a matter of minutes) climbs to 3,496 feet, where an observation deck offers intermittent views of the Atlantic coast and the city of San Juan.

LOS PICACHOS TRAIL: From El Yunque Trail, you can pick up the short Los Picachos (.2 mile), an unpaved, muddy track that leads to a 1930s-era lookout post, with more great views.

MT. BRITTON TRAIL: Hook up with the Mt. Britton Trail (.8 mile) via the "high-altitude" Mt. Britton Spur (.9 mile). To find the trailhead of Mt. Britton, take Carr. 9938 from Carr. 191, just before the gate that blocks vehicular access. This mostly paved access road ascends through tabonuco and sierra palm forests to the cloud forest. You'll cross a couple of streams and the rutted Carr. 10, and then climb to the Mt. Britton Tower. Circular stairs lead up to the turret, where fierce trade winds will whip your face as you peer through the clouds at the southern, eastern and northern shores of Puerto Rico. Don't forget your camera!

El Yunque ferns grow before your eyes. (©2000, Tara Stevens)

EL TORO TRAIL: The most adventurous and remote hikes in these parts lead to **El Toro peak**, the highest point in the forest at 3,533 feet. The easiest access is via Carr. 186 on the west side of El Yunque, from El Toro Trail. This 2.2-mile hike is mostly on an unmaintained trail, which can turn muddy. When you reach El Toro peak, you'll be rewarded with wraparound views of the island perimeter (again, clouds permitting).

TRADEWINDS NATIONAL RECREATION TRAIL: From El Toro Peak, the sometimes-slippery walkway connects to the Tradewinds National Recreation Trail, the longest in El Yunque area (3.9 miles). Hiked together, the two connecting trails provide about seven hours of wilderness trekking that can make you feel lost in a world apart. To access the relatively strenuous Tradewinds Trail, drive to the locked gate on Carr. 191, then backtrack a quarter-mile to the trailhead.

ANGELITO TRAIL: On Carr. 988, you'll find the short Angelito Trail (.4 mile), an easy walk along a clay and gravel path, with access to the natural Las Damas Pool in the Mameyes River.

One of our favorite hiking areas is on the southern side of El Yunque, just outside the official rain forest border, around **Río Cubuy**. This requires entering the forest on the south spur of Carr. 191 via Carr. 31. Some trails blazed by past hikers lead to swimming holes, many of which are easily accessible from the road. The best access is via the lovely Casa Cubuy (see *Where To Stay*), but you can also park your car along the upper reaches of Carr. 191 (before the roadblock) and look for openings in the bush. Lonely waterfalls and wild river pools await.

Mountain Biking

For the sake and safety of hikers, keep any mountain biking to roads and trails outside the Forest Service system. One of the best biking adventures is on a section of Carr. 191 where a landslide cut off road access years ago. Some cars do edge their way around the roadblock but, for the most part, cyclists will find the route free of traffic and more tranquil than other sections of the rain forest. From Carr. 31 on the south side of El Yunque, take Carr. 191 north into the rain forest until you reach the roadblock, park and gear up. Follow your ears, and you'll find plenty of virgin streambeds to cool off in as you pedal your way through virgin rain forest.

Driving

If hiking isn't your thing, the rain forest can be experienced with a driving tour (for wheelchair adventurers, the main visitor center is wheelchair-friendly and, if you call ahead, the staff is helpful in recommending tours that can get you into the forest on buses designed for your needs). Follow Carr. 191 to El Portal Visitor Center for an introduction to rain forest study, then continue north to **La Coca Falls**, an 85-foot cascade of water that crashes onto boulders at the highway's edge. Less than a half-mile south, the **Yohakú Tower** provides a striking roadside observation point of the eastern coastline and the lower hills of El Yunque. Farther north, you'll find a couple of roadside stands with souvenirs and local snacks. By the side of the road, a couple of stick-your-head-through painted billboards provide ops for cheesy photos of you with the legendary goat-sucking *chupacabra* or dressed as a guitar-strumming *jíbaro*.

> **CAUTION:** *El Yunque is not immune to car thievery. If you park by the side of the road or at one of the more remote trailheads, leave nothing of value in your car – including packs of cigarettes, sunglasses and loose change – and lock it up.*

Where To Stay

ACCOMMODATIONS PRICE KEY

Rates are per room, per night, double occupancy. Single occupancy may or may not get you a discount, so ask when making a reservation. Breakfast included where noted.

$	Up to $50
$$	$50 to $100
$$$	$101 to $150
$$$$	$150 and up

■ El Yunque & Environs

It's one thing to spend the day hiking the trails of El Yunque, but quite another to spend the night noticing the forest come to life with the unrelenting chirp of the coquí, mist drifting in and out of the canopy as waterfalls rumble in the distance. For a little rain forest rejuvenation, **La Casa Vida Natural**, Carr. 186, Ramal 9960, Río Grande, ☎ 787-887-4359, e-mail elfspring@cs.com, is run by an English/South American pair – Richard and Eleanor – who offer room and board and a range of spa-type treatments, from "Yunque" mud wraps and herbal steams, to four-handed massage, Chinese medicine and Qi Gong and Tai Chi Chuan movement classes. You can also learn about live foods, sprouting and vegetarian cooking (the food is excellent). Combined with hiking trails, freshwater bathing in ancient Taino swimming holes and a landscape of fruit trees, ylang-ylang and tropical flowers, the "Casa Experience" will leave you completely rejuvenated and ready to face the rat race once more. $$

The sprawling **Río Grande Plantation & Eco-Resort**, Carr. 956, ☎ 787-887-2779 or 722-8665, fax 888-3239, operated as a sugar plantation until the 1940s. Today it specializes mostly in corporate retreats and wacky team-building exercises; if you poke around, you may see the grounds scattered with the Universal Studios-worthy props, such as mechanized *chupacabras*, flying pterodactyls and other dinosaurs, that somehow aid white-collar teamwork. However, Río Grande does have rooms for individuals. They're large with all modern conveniences, nothing special, but surrounded by tropical gardens, shady terraces, two swimming pools and a couple of easy hiking trails. Great for kids. $$$

■ El Yunque Southside

On the south side of El Yunque, the excellent **Casa Cubuy**, Carr. 191, ☎ 787-874-6221, fax 874-4316, e-mail cubuy@east-net.net, is another eco-hideaway with more traditional guest house callings. Most rooms have stunning views across a valley to the rain forest mountain wall. Owner Matthew maintains a small but interesting library and plenty of hammocks on the terrace in which to curl up and read when the afternoon rain comes. There is a self-serve bar and a kitchen for his inventive home cooking (breakfast included, dinner on demand). A hiking trail he maintains leads to three rivers with isolated swimming holes and waterfalls. Look out for giant single-clawed shrimp and other river delicacies, bananas, mangos and other fruits in season. Be sure to ask Matthew about nearby Taino petroglyphs and his Caribbean recipes. $$

Cheap, super-basic digs are available at **Cabañas de Yunque**, which is also on the south side of the forest on Carr. 191, ☎ 787-874-2138. $

■ Luquillo

The **Westin Río Mar Beach and Country Club**, Carr. 968, ☎ 787-888-6000, fax 888-6600, is everything one would expect of an expensive resort. Impeccably groomed grounds, golf, tennis and luxury swimming pools are presided over by an immense and sprawling seaside hotel. Vacation packages will save you cash. Otherwise expect to spend loads-a-money! $$$$

Located a block from Playa Azul, **Luquillo Beach Inn**, 701 Ocean Drive St., ☎ 787-889-1063 or 3333, fax 889-1966, http://home.coqui.net/jcdiaz, has one- and two-bedroom villas; $$$. On the same block is **Trinidad Guest House**, ☎ 787-889-2710, fax 889-0640, e-mail Trinidad51@aol.com, www.trinidadguesthouse.com. Trinidad has simple rooms and is a good choice for budget travelers. $$

■ Las Croabas

Wyndham El Conquistador Resort & Country Club, Carr. 987, ☎ 787-863-1000 or 800-468-8365, fax 863-6500, is one of the finest all-encompassing resorts in the Caribbean. Perched eagle-like on the cliffs surrounding Cabezas de San Juan, it looks over the world beyond and decides it doesn't need it; and, indeed it does not! There is literally nothing it does not have. With 918 guestrooms, 109 suites, a five-diamond private village in decadent Spanish colonial style, a more modest yet still dramatic cliffside village and a private 25-slip marina, 11 restaurants, a casino, disco, Golden Door spa and fitness center, 18-hole championship golf course, shopping malls and every imaginable watersport (check the Marina Activities desk), one hardly even needs to visit the hotel's private island – Palomino (which offers horseback riding along the 100-acre island's pristine beaches). Whether this pleasure powerhouse retains any vibes from its spiritual past, you be the judge. Previously, the site was used for 10 years by the Maharishi Mahesh Yogi; before that, by the Evangelical Christian Mission. Plans are in the works for a dolphin park at El Conquistador. $$$$+

A few large leaps down the price scale, **Hotel La Familia**, Carr. 987, ☎ 787-863-1193 or 1140, fax 860-5345, is a great value. Within walking distance of local restaurants and Playa Seven Seas, it's an excellent base for exploring the area, and if you can't afford to stay at El Conquistador, you can at least admire the view of its golf course from the swimming pool and sundeck. $$

For self-catering, **Anchors Inn**, Carr. 987, ☎ 787-863-7200, fax 860-6934, has a guest house with all-amenities rooms, but even nicer are the nine rooms of its auxiliary in Las Croabas. Each comes with a small kitchen, cable television, private parking, with no extra charge for the swimming pool and chilled-out ambience. $$

LONG-TERM RENTALS

Longer-term visitors can save some cash by going local. The fishing village of Las Croabas has many houses and apartments for rent if you ask around. The hillside overlooking the marina and El Conquistador is a particularly good spot, with monthly rents between $300 and $600.

■ Fajardo

Within walking distance from the terminal for the ferry to Culebra and Vieques, the **Fajardo Inn**, Parcelas Beltran #52, ☎ 787-860-6000, www.fajardoinn.com, has 75 air-conditioned rooms, a seafood and Creole restaurant, tapas bar, swimming pool and terraces with sea views. It's on a hill and removed from the crowded port area; $$. There are about a half-dozen relatively cheap, semi-clean, barebones hostels on the street leading to the ferry terminal.

If you're into self-catering and don't mind being surrounded by high-rise condominiums, **B.V. Real Estate**, ☎ 787-863-3687, www.bvrealty.com, has properties in and around Fajardo, including some on Isleta Marina. Prices vary wildly depending on where and how long you stay.

■ Ceiba

If you want to stay close to the Roosevelt Roads Naval Base, the **Ceiba Country Inn**, Carr. 977, ☎ 787-885-0471, comes highly recommended. With clean, comfortable rooms, it offers sea views, barbecue facilities for guests, a small cocktail lounge and continental breakfast thrown in. $$

▪ Humacao

Another mega-resort, **Doral Resort at Palmas del Mar**, is a 2,630-acre, self-contained paradise for retired millionaires and wannabes, golfers and high-rolling vacationers. The exclusive Palmas has all the trappings of a world-class resort: two golf courses, the largest tennis complex center in the Caribbean, an equestrian center, private marina, a long sandy beach, casino, restaurants, shopping and facilities for children. Look for signs from Hwy. 53 to Candelero Drive, Palmas del Mar, ☎ 787-852-6000, ext 74, 800-PALMAS-3, or 800-752-6273, fax 852-6295, www.palmasdelmar.com. As with other resorts, you'll save a bundle by booking a package vacation from home. $$$$+

At the other end of the price scale, the **Centro Vacacionales Punta Santiago**, Hwy. 53, ☎ 787-852-1660, is one of the best self-catering accommodations, with modern villas and cabañas right on the beach. Each sleeps six comfortably, with a double room and two sets of bunk beds. Excellent for independent families or groups, the only downside is the proximity of the cabins. $$

▪ Yabucoa, Maunabo & Environs

The **Hotel Parador Palmas de Lucia**, Carr. 901, ☎ 787-893-4423, fax 893-0291, is more or less on the beach, within spitting distance of the Ruta Panorámica. The plain, faded atmosphere of the place does little to inspire, however; $$. The lesser-known and smaller **Hotel Campo Viejo**, ☎ 787-266-1294, wins points for its cliff-top pool with a stunning view of the big blue. Ask for a room with a balcony facing the sea. $$

Surfers wanting to hang out on El Cocal beach may be tempted by the **Guest House Lunny Mar**, signposted from Carr. 901, ☎ 787-893-8996, but it's expensive for what it is: dreary; $$. A few miles away, **Playa Emajaguas Guest House**, ☎ 787-861-6023, is set behind an avenue of palms that leads to a garden filled with bougainvillea and jasmine, and a totally laid-back family atmosphere (you may have to coax the owner out of his sleeping cot). Access to a beach is a few steps away from this Caribbean hideaway. $$

▪ Camping

There's only one designated camping area in **El Yunque**. It's situated at the end of La Coca trail and marked simply by a green clearing in the thick of the jungle. Other campsites have been closed due to environmental concerns. It's a good hour and a half steep descent to get to the camping area, but it's free. Reservations are a must; contact the US Forest Service in El Yunque, ☎ 787-888-1810.

Camping at the public beaches **Balneario Luquillo** and **Seven Seas** in Las Croabas can get crowded during weekends and summer months, but on weekdays and during winter months you may find a haven of tranquility by the sea. Tent space for both costs $10 a night, to be paid upon arrival. If no one is around to collect the fee, go ahead and pitch your tent and eventually an official should come around.

Camping in unofficial areas can be well worth the extra trek – especially on **El Convento**, east of Playa Azul in Luquillo, and the beach locals call **Playa Escondido**, a 20-minute walk from Seven Seas (see *Beaches*, page 321).

Where To Eat

■ Loíza Aldea

The closes thing you'll get to authentic African cooking in Puerto Rico is at one of Loíza's **Buréns,** named for the long, flat iron skillet used from the time of Yoruba slaves until the present. Don't expect fine dining – some have dirt floors and grubby furniture. But you can find authentic *yucca* and *cassava empanadas* and *rociao* – a kind of yucca and coconut milk omelet – at bargain prices. Two or three are located at the beach end of Las Carreras (see *Touring* section). More conventional *criollo* dishes are served up at the local favorite, **El Parrilla**, ☎ 787-876-3191, Carr. 187 toward Río Grande. The covered terrace is a nice spot to enjoy a piña colada and a dish of crab. The "Chef's Special" serves it all ways: stewed, boiled, with rice, and as a fritter, for $16, and two people could easily share one plate.

■ Río Grande

Río Grande is not known for dining, and rain forest residents practically fell on their knees in thanks when the tiny **Mirabueno**, ☎ 787-809-5809, Carr. 3, Int. 967, opened. Pastry chef Blanca González Relaño turns out a limited but inventive dinner menu, with dishes like roast duck with apples, chicken baked in pastry with cheese and mandarins, among others. Ask her about awards she's won in her native Madrid for desserts such as coffee and Sambuca pie. A main course, drinks and a slice of pie will set you back no more than $25 a head. For lunch, **Villa Pesquera Sea Food**, ☎ 787-887-0140, signposted from Carr. 187 (near the Bahia Beach Golf Course), has a great spot on the muddy banks of the Río Espíritu Santo. Apparently few people finish the *filete a lo macho*, a monstrous steak topped with shrimp and octopus. Afterwards ask if river boater **Papo Dones** is around. If he's in the mood he'll give you a boat trip up the river for a negotiable few bucks. Villa Pesquera is open 10 a.m. to 7 p.m., closed Mondays.

> **TIP:** *For picnic supplies in the Fajardo area, the supermarket **Pueblo Xtra** on Carr. 3 has an excellent deli counter with criollo plates and pasta, salad, lasagna, etc.*

■ Luquillo

More than 30 food stalls at the western end of the public beach serve different fried meats and fish, of origins both identifiable and obscure, along with beer, every day of the week. It's cheap and, as far as we know, harmless.

In town, **The Brass Cactus**, ☎ 787-889-5735, Carr. 193, is reportedly run by the owners of The Landing in Rincón, and has much the same menu – alligator bites (tastes like chicken), buffalo wings (is chicken), burgers, and fish that's, well, a bit like chicken! It doubles up as a sports bar and gets packed with Navy personnel from Roosevelt Roads and other US expats on weekends. Most entrées cost about $15. Next door, **El Flamboyán** is just as loud and lively, but caters to a more local crowd. They serve up basic snacks, with live salsa, African drumming and other music on weekends.

El Rincon de Sabor, Fernandez Garcia, is popular for *pinchos* (meat on a stick), tacos and baked potatoes, on which you can make a meal for $2 to $5. Also on Fernandez Garcia, near the underpass of Hwy. 3, **Erik's Gyros and Deli** does a lamb gyro and drink for $5.

Chef Wayne at Hacienda Carabalí, on a hilltop overlooking Luqillo, ☎ 787-889-1962 or 2911, Carr. 992 (look for signs on Hwy. 3), is a hearty ranch-style restaurant with an excellent 360° view of the ocean and the rain forest. Come on a Sunday afternoon for a buffet (noon to 5 p.m.) with four or five main dishes, salads and live music, for $16 a head. The à la carte menu includes porterhouse steak, filet mignon and red snapper with crabmeat, all for around $18. Ask about any weekend activities and parties.

Lolita's, ☎ 787-889-5770, Hwy. 3, (just south of Luquillo), has become something of an institution for good value Mexican food and potent margaritas. Most entrées are under $10.

At the Westin Río Mar Resort and Hotel, ☎ 787-888-6000, Chef Jeramie Cruz has won awards for his innovative Tex-Mex cooking at **Cactus Jack's**. Most entrées cost $15 to $20. A bit more up-market, **Shima's**, also at the Westin Río Mar, is a colorful Asian restaurant with plenty of ambiance. It's good for sushi lovers. Expect to spend close to $30 a head, not including drinks.

■ Fajardo & Las Croabas

Thanks to the **Wyndham El Conquistador** (☎ 787-863-1000), Las Croabas has some of the finest dining on the east side of the island. Eleven restaurants serve everything from sushi, Japanese, Chinese, lobster and seafood, steaks, gourmet Italian, pizza and Mediterranean. Think Las Vegas without the ersatz pyramids. A dinner for two with drinks will run well over $100 at their fine dining restaurants, but you're on vacation, aren't you?

KIDS IN THE KITCHEN

Las Brisas Terrace restaurant at the Wyndham El Conquistador opens its kitchen doors to young gourmets, allowing kids to assist master chefs. The fun starts every Saturday at 7 p.m., for $20 per person, including the fruits of their labor.

For more local flavor (and easier on the wallet), the strip between Fajardo and Las Croabas on Carr. 987 has several seafood restaurants. **Anchors Inn** is popular, and looks like it was lifted from a seaside town in England and dropped here by accident (white clapboard, with red and white decking). On weekend nights, the place has been known to get hopping with the local young crowd. Entrées range from $18 to $30.

Aficionados of Jack Daniel's should take note that **Tropical Paradise**, at the Hotel La Familia, ☎ 787-863-1193, has won an award from the Kentucky whiskey maker for their baby back ribs – $20 full / $15 half.

La Conquista, closer to Seven Seas beach on Carr. 987, serves the same seafood platters as neighboring restaurants, with the advantage that the furniture is made of wood and wicker, rather than plastic. Conch fritters and lobster *arepas* cost about $5. Entrées range from $12 to $30. Nearby, at Villa Marina, **Ricky's Cyber Pizza**, ☎ 787-860-4230, is the only place for miles where you can check your e-mail and get a pizza or sub sandwich, for $5 to $10.

Puerto del Rey has several dining options, the best of which is probably **A La Banda**, ☎ 787-860-9162, where you can choose a live lobster from the aquarium for around $20, or go for Italian fare such as eggplant Parmesan. Stingy side dishes may leave your steak feeling lonely, however. Entrées between $8 and $28.

Vegetarians and fellow travelers will enjoy **Eden Vegetarian Restaurant**, 57S Muñoz Rivera St, ☎ 787-863-7060, where lunch costs less than $10. Eden closes at 5 p.m.

■ Playa Húcares

The *malecón* is lined with seafood cafés. One of the better ones is **Tacomiqueo**, ☎ 787-643-7168, famed locally for its *mojito criollo* sauce. You can eat your fill for $10 to $15.

Fans of *empanadillas* should check out the **rooftop café** above the dock at the north end of town. Stuffed *chapín pastillos* cost just $3 each, and the view from the dining room is wonderful.

■ Humacao & Environs

Aside from malls of fast-food outlets, try **Alo**, ☎ 787-648-5647, Calle BA-3 #26, for a healthy veggie lunch that costs less than $10. Like many vegetarian restaurants, it closes at 5 p.m. At Palmas del Mar, the seaside **El Chinchorro** serves fresh-off-the-boat catch for a pittance. Rickety tables and chairs under the trees and excellent fish give it a rare old Caribbean ambiance. At the other end of the spectrum, **Chez Daniel**, ☎ 787-852-6000, Ext. 17785, fax 850-4865, at Anchor's Village in Palmas del Mar, has one of the best reputations on the east coast for fine French cooking and exquisite seafood dishes. Perfect for a romantic dinner on the waterfront, it's open for dinner every night except Tuesday, and for lunch Friday through Sunday. Most entrées cost about $20.

SIRLOIN IN THE OLD RUM HOUSE

A favorite dining excursion for *sanjuaneros* is **El Tenedor**, ☎ 787-734-6573, located at the old Ron Carey distillery in Juncos. Owner Julio Mantero presides over a unique restaurant featuring excellent service by uniformed staff, who dart across the Spanish tile floor carrying huge portions of steak from the room's centerpiece, a giant hooded grill. The sounds of guitar trios often fill the high-ceilinged main dining room, which features black grillwork and elegantly casual high-backed chairs. Steak ranging in portion size from eight ounces to two pounds is the star feature of the menu, but seafood, veal and game birds are also served with a flourish. Mantero has been attracting regular crowds of city folk for 25 years. Built in the 19th century, the distillery produced rum until 1942, when Mantero's father in law was forced to close for business due to WWII. For fine dining in a lovely historic setting, El Tenedor is open seven days a week for lunch and dinner. Sandwiches and salads start at less than $5, and an eight-ounce sirloin costs a reasonable $16.

■ Yabucoa & Maunabo

On Carr. 901, you'll find a few good seafood restaurants with excellent sea views from the cliff tops. **El Nuevo Horizonte**, ☎ 787-839-6173, is popular for *dorado* and marlin. Come on a Sunday when local musicians stir up the crowd. Entrées range between $15 and $25. Farther along Carr. 901 toward Maunabo, the **Bella Vista Restaurant**, ☎ 787-861-1501, has dining on a terrace teetering over the cliff top, for a spectacularly windswept dinner experience. Finally, if you're visiting the lighthouse at Punta Tuna, continue along Carr. 760 to **Playa Los Bohíos**, where you can get Puerto Rican finger food from the seaside bar.

Vieques Island & Culebra Island

Travelers who have spent time on the main island of Puerto Rico may have a "eureka!" moment upon arriving on the fantasy islands of Vieques or Culebra. The brightly colored cottages, tranquility and timeless feel of the so-called Spanish Virgin Islands immediately set them apart from the overpopulated *borinquen* (Puerto Rican) mainland, and the friendly local vibe is contagious. After just a day or two on either island, you'll find yourself exchanging smiles and waves with each passerby as though you'd spent your whole life here. And why not? Once you step on shore, the exact details of your life before arrival begin to seem fuzzy and indistinct.

IN THIS CHAPTER
- Isabel Segunda
- Esperanza
- Dewey

Overview

Geologically, Vieques and Culebra are part of the island chain that includes the Virgin Islands, not the landmass of Puerto Rico proper. It's more than a symbolic difference. Both islands are refreshingly free of the strip malls, franchise outlets and concrete that characterize what locals refer to (with a vague wave of the hand westward) as Puerto Rico. Neither island has even a single stoplight. Keep an eye out for hybrid characters we call *boricua* Rastafarians, who speak Spanish slowly and wear dreadlocks tucked beneath oversize knitted caps. Things are definitely more laid-back here. At the exact spot where the Greater and Lesser Antilles meet, steel drums and reggae music are heard nearly as often as salsa and merengue.

Sometimes referred to as "The Last Virgins," Vieques and Culebra nevertheless lost some of their maidenhood at the hands of the US Navy, which has used both islands as target ranges for its gunners. On the other hand, Navy presence may have helped keep Vieques free of large-scale development and commercial use. So far, Vieques and Culebra have registered only the smallest blip on the editorial radar screens of glossy travel magazines. Quietly, though, gringo influence has steadily trickled in during the past 25 years, making a big, and largely positive, impact on both islands. The *norteamericano* immigrants tend to be ex-pat escapists looking for a laid-back lifestyle, not a portfolio-expanding investment. Most have been content to build a small guest house, eco-dwelling or tropical hideaway bar, and then kick back and watch daily sunsets through the warm glow of a rum buzz, to the soundtrack of Jimmy Buffett's *Cheeseburger in Paradise*. Vieques and Culebra are still quiet getaways meant for those seeking natural splendor and a desolate beach, not busy nightlife or the pampering of a luxury resort. Kayaking or boating to more than two dozen uninhabited cays, exploring mangroves and subtropical dry forests, snorkeling and diving through unearthly submarine gardens and relaxing in the sun keep most people "busy." If a romantic stroll along miles of deserted, sugary sand is your fantasy, get here fast! The virginity of Vieques and Culebra won't last forever.

Vieques

From the Taino word *bieque*, meaning "small island," Vieques is often referred to by mainland Puerto Ricans as *la isla nena,* or "little girl island." The term of endearment strikes a nostalgic chord among those who see in Vieques an innocence that Puerto Rico has in some senses lost. Just seven miles from eastern Puerto Rico, Vieques feels worlds apart. Wild horses are more common on the roads than cars. *Viequenses* still spend their days in an unhurried manner. For many Puerto Ricans, Vieques is a magical place where they spent – and continue to spend – childhood summer vacations, camping and picnicking on the beach with their families.

Vieques is also squarely in the public eye at the beginning of the 21st century. The continuing presence of the US Navy, which took over more than two-thirds of the island at the start of the Cold War, is an emotional issue that has united a majority of mainland Puerto Ricans and *viequenses* in calling for the military to leave. Don't let this controversy dissuade you from visiting, however. Aside from a few bumper stickers and the occasional rally at the gate to Camp García, the highly publicized protests against the Navy could easily pass unnoticed to travelers.

The island has a number of stunningly beautiful – and often empty – beaches, many wonderful guest houses, snorkeling and possibly the best bioluminescent bay in the world (a must-see). Renowned for its tolerance and open-minded populace, Vieques has also become a favorite destination for gay and lesbian travelers, as well as others who appreciate an atmosphere in which conformist pressure seems melted away by open spaces and Caribbean sunshine.

History

■ Indians & Pirates

An aura of mystery surrounds the earliest settlers of the Caribbean, including the remains left by Stone Age humans who, according to some historians, inhabited Vieques more than 3,500 years ago. A group of fisher-gatherers of the archaic people apparently spent about two centuries on the island, before disappearing altogether (see *Stonehenge on Vieques?*, page 356). As many as 2,000 years passed before Arawak people arrived on the island, and on mainland Puerto Rico, before being decimated by conquistadors. Spanish conquest of Puerto Rico caused many Taino families to flee to Vieques, and for a brief moment the island was an important center of Indian resistance against the invaders. Historical accounts differ slightly, but all agree that in 1513, the Taino chief of Vieques, Cacimar, joined forces with mainland chiefs to attack a Spanish settlement on the west coast of Puerto Rico. On the way home, Cacimar and his forces, armed with clubs made of sharpened palm wood and heavy four-foot bows, stopped to fight settlers near present day Loíza, and the chief was slain. Shortly afterward, 70 well-armed Spanish soldiers arrived in Vieques and killed or took prisoner the remaining Indian population of Vieques.

During the following three centuries, nonconformist European settlers trickled in, and Vieques existed as a wild outpost and supply station for pirates, who visited its shores to buy supplies and recruit malcontents and castaways into their ranks. One of the last great Caribbean pirates, Roberto Cofresí, a.k.a. The Robin Hood of Puerto Rico (see page 181), stopped in Vieques in 1824 to recruit the crew that the next year accompanied him to the firing squad in San Juan.

> **TIP:** *For more on the history of Vieques, pick up the well-written, 88-page* **Vieques: History of a Small Island**, *by Elizabeth Langhorne, available from the Vieques Conservation and Historical Trust in Esperanza.*

■ French Coffee & Spanish Sugar

The same year that Cofresí arrived to recruit his luckless crew, the island of Vieques received a call from a visitor with longer-term plans – a French plantation owner named Don Teófilo Jaime María Le Guillou forced to flee Haiti during a slave revolt. After convincing the authorities in San Juan that he could turn Vieques into an economic asset, the charismatic Le Guillou was named governor of Vieques and managed (with funding from

France and plenty of slave labor) to convert several hundred unruly island residents into members of a thriving coffee-growing community. With a keen sense of personnel management, he both attracted European aristocrats (Le Guillou banned "uninvited guests" from upper-class dances for the gentry) and appeased peasant urges (he quickly retracted his ban on cockfighting due to popular pressure), creating an unlikely microcosm of a class-driven society on a rogue island. By the time he died in an apparent drunken fall from his carriage in 1843, he left a legacy of foreign influence and absentee ownership that continues today. After Le Guillou's death, the English, Spanish and Danish governments made halfhearted claims to the isolated island. The issue resolved itself with local help. On Vieques, the sugarcane-producing Benitez family emerged as the economic prime mover, tipping the scales of influence to Spain. Hacienda life reached a peak mid-century on Vieques – with ladies promenading in white gloves and idle gentlemen raising horses – on a plantation called Playa Grande in western Vieques, since destroyed by the US Navy. By this time, however, Spanish rule was already a lost cause. Most of Latin America had already gained independence. In a desperate act to preserve its last holdings in the Americas, the Spanish government built the final Caribbean fort of its empire on a hill overlooking the bay of Isabel Segunda.

■ US Guns & Vieques Bumper Stickers

In 1898, when the US Navy stepped ashore to take control of Vieques after the Spanish-American War, the commander of the Fortín de Vieques made one request: that he be allowed to fire a volley of gunfire into the air so that, for honor's sake, he could never be accused of surrendering the fort "without firing a shot." Since then, relations between locals and the Navy have continued in an atmosphere of political wrangling and patriotism. When Word War II hit, shipping lanes around the island nearly shut down due to the threat of Nazi submarines, which dominated the waters. In response, in 1941 the US Navy appropriated 70% of Vieques (the eastern and western ends) to use as a base and training ground. The move surprised and alienated islanders – who then numbered more than 10,000 – many of whom were displaced into the strip of land in central Vieques. For decades, local protests were generally appeased by military investment on the island. But on April 19, 1999, the accidental killing of local security guard David Sanes Rodriguez by a stray bomb unleashed pent-up feelings of resentment against the Navy. Since then, residents of the island – and Puerto Ricans in general – have been nearly unanimous in calling for the Navy to leave. Large-scale protests on the bombing range in eastern Vieques led to mass arrests of citizens, clergy and politicians who participated, and made news headlines in the US and other countries. Although the US government has promised to hold a referendum on the issue in Vieques, the Navy has resumed military exercises and the future of Camp Garcia and Roosevelt Roads, which the Navy considers a vital base, is in doubt. Meanwhile, the emotional issue was widely credited with aiding the sweeping victory of the Popular Democratic Party in the 2000 elections. Visitors to Vieques are sure to note bumper stickers and T-shirts that read *"Ni una bomba mas!"* (Not one more bomb!) and *"Fuera la Marina!"* (Navy out!). Otherwise, protests center on the gate to Camp Garcia, which leads to half the *viequense* landmass to the east.

Getting Here

■ By Air

The flight between Fajardo and Vieques lasts only seven to 10 minutes, and includes an inspiring aerial view of the island, making it well worth the fare – $18 one-way, $35 round-trip. Arrival is at **Antonio Rivera Rodriguez Airport**, ☎ 787-741-8358, on Carr. 200 on the northwest side of the island, about 10 minutes by car from the town of Isabel Segunda. Flights from San Juan to Vieques leave from both **Luis Muñoz Marín International Airport** (☎ 787-791-3840) and **Aeropuerto de Isla Grande** (☎ 787-722-3736 or 888-901-9247), and cost about $125 round-trip.

Vieques Air Link, ☎ 787-741-8211 or 8331 (in Vieques), or 888-901-9247, and **Isla Nena Air Service**, ☎ 800-263-6213, usually have frequent flights between Fajardo and Vieques during the season (November-April), and run trips at least six times daily during the off-season. Vieques Air Link also has flights to and from the airport in Isla Grande, as well as St. Croix in the US Virgin Islands. Planes are small craft (twin- or tri-motor) that often seat fewer than eight people. On Vieques, pilot **Tony Bennett** (not the singer), ☎ 787-741-0292, tony@mangovieques.com, will fly you to and from the main island, Culebra, the Virgin Islands or just up in the air for fun and great views, for negotiable rates.

■ By Sea

A real bargain at $4 per person, one way, the one-hour (less in calm water) **ferry ride** between Fajardo and Vieques, ☎ 787-863-0705 or 0852, is usually smooth, with air-conditioned indoor seating areas. You'll find the ferry terminal signposted from Hwy. 3 in Fajardo. Parking at an attended lot near the terminal costs $5 per day. On weekends only, the cargo ferry takes a limited number of private cars back and forth, by reservation only.

> **TIP:** *Berths for private cars fill up early, so travelers should book their vehicle onto the ferry at least two weeks in advance.*

350 ■ Vieques

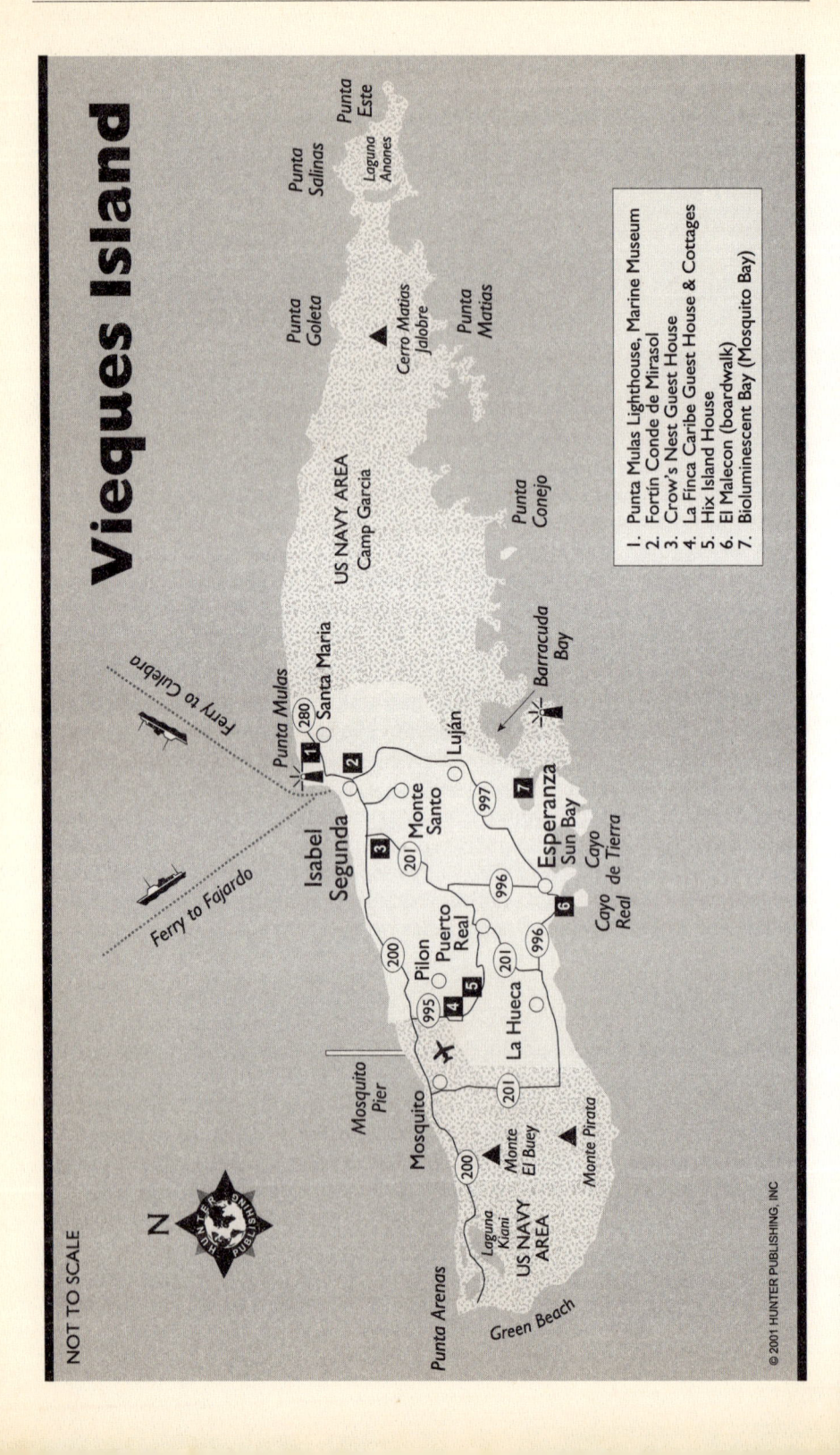

PASSENGER FERRY SCHEDULE

It's always best to call ahead to ask about changes in schedules.

WEEKDAYS

Fajardo to Vieques . . . . 9:30 a.m., 1 p.m. and 4:30 p.m.
Vieques to Fajardo . . . . 7 a.m., 11 a.m. and 3 p.m.

SATURDAYS & SUNDAYS

Fajardo to Vieques. . . . . 9 a.m., 3 p.m. and 6 p.m.
Vieques to Fajardo . . . . 7 a.m., 1 p.m. and 4:30 p.m.

CARGO FERRY (weekends only)

Fajardo to Vieques . . . . 4 a.m., 9:30 a.m. and 4:30 p.m.
Vieques to Fajardo. . . . . 6 a.m., 1:30 p.m. and 6:30 p.m.

BETWEEN VIEQUES & CULEBRA   (see *Culebra* section, pages 376-377)

Getting Around

Think of the island as being split into three sections. The **western and eastern** ends are owned by the US Navy and, except for the northwest corner of the island, are unfortunately off-limits to the public at this time. There were no immediate plans to reopen Navy areas in 2001 or 2002 although, considering popular pressure, it does seem inevitable that local residents will someday reclaim the island. The **middle section** is a strip of land about five miles wide that runs from the north coast to the south coast. This is where civilians reside. The highest concentration of people is in and around the north coast town of **Isabel Segunda** (also known as **Isabel II**), which is home to the ferry port, government services and most of the island's limited commerce, such as supermarkets, banks and car rental agencies.

From Isabel II, **Carr. 200** runs west to the airport, the mile-long Mosquito Pier and the remote northwest corner, which includes the island's longest stretch of sand, **Green Beach. Carr. 201** runs south to the Caribbean Sea and **Carr. 996**, which circumnavigates the tiny, largely gringo getaway community of **Esperanza** on the south coast. Although the town is little more than a pretty boardwalk cluttered with Caribbean cocktail bars and a few budget guest houses, visitors will find practical amenities here such as a bank, post office, supermarket, ferry terminal, and car rental agencies. Those in search of luxury accommodations should head west from Esperanza along **Carr. 996**, while the best beaches are east of the town, past Sun Bay.

Most visitors to the island rent a Jeep because it is the easiest way to get around and gives you more freedom and flexibility than relying on other forms of island transport (taxis and públicos). Although you can drive around the whole island in little more than an hour, many people clock up a surprising number of miles exploring small interior roads and having fun off-roading along the coast.

■ Rental Cars

Upon arrival, most visitors rent a vehicle in order to see Vieques to its fullest. Jeep rentals are a standard $45 to $50 a day, including insurance. Be wary of driving down the most obscure dirt roads during or after a heavy rain, or you may get stuck in the mud (Jeeps are usually small, with two-wheel drive only). Most rental agencies are located in and around Isabel II along Carr. 200, and *públicos* waiting at the airport outside of Isabel II and the ferry terminal on the northeast end of town will take you there for $2 per person. During peak season, it's essential to reserve a car in advance.

VIEQUES RENTAL CAR COMPANIES

Acevedo's Rent-A-Car . . . . ☎ 787-741-4380 or 8397
Fonsin Rent-a-Car . . . . ☎ 787-741-8163
Island Car Rentals Inc. . . . . ☎ 787-741-1666
Marcos Car Rental . . . . ☎ 787-741-1388
Martineau Car Rental . . . . ☎ 787-741-0087
Steve's Car Rental . . . . ☎ 787-741-8135, cell 319-8524

■ Taxis

Taxi operators serving all of Vieques include **Ana. L. Robles**, ☎ 787-741-2318, 313-0599 or 382-8565; **Fast Eddie**, ☎ 787-741-8621; and **Pepe Car Service**, ☎ 787-741-3392. All are radio dispatched.

Communications & Information

You'll find the **Vieques Tourism Office**, ☎ 787-741-5000, on the corner of the town plaza at Calle Carlos Lebrún and Calle Benítez Guzman. The staff are very pleasant and willing to help, but it's unlikely you will get more out of them than this book can provide. By all means go ahead and pay them a visit, as you never know what new information they may have.

The island's bilingual newspaper – the ***Vieques Times***, ☎ 787-741-8508, www.viequestimes.com – is published every couple of weeks or so, and is largely a sound-off board for locals and gringo residents. The August 2000 edition ran a feature about a new "cow crossing" sign as one of the important events, to give an idea of island "news."

There is no official map of Vieques. However, a little island outfit called Whizzbang Designs publishes a cartoon-style map with details of Isabel II and Esperanza, and includes things like where and how to snorkel, useful phone numbers, and classified ads. Pick up a copy at most hotels and guest houses, as well as at many island shops, bars and restaurants.

Two useful Web sites are www.enchanted-isle.com and www.vieques-island.com, which give information on island events, dining, accommodations and travel options.

E-mail connection service is available at the **Vieques Conservation & Historical Trust**, ☎ 787-741-8850, on the main strip in Esperanza, open Tuesday to Saturday, 10 a.m. to 3 p.m., and Sundays, 11 a.m. to 3 p.m. For an up-to-date listing on weekly happenings, including who's open for dinner and who's not, check out the message board at **The Crow's Nest**, ☎ 787-741-0033, Carr. 201. The **Colberg Travel Agency**, ☎ 787-741-0945, on Calle Antonio G. Mellado in Isabel Segunda, can arrange air, land and sea travel, as well as car rental and hotel reservations, between 9 a.m. and 5 p.m. weekdays, and Saturday mornings.

Mr. Coconut Man, Vieques.
(© 2000, Kurt Pitzer)

The **post office**, as well as the island's only bank with an **ATM**, is on Calle Luis Muñoz Rivera, Isabel II.

Touring & Sightseeing

Begin your tour in **Isabel Segunda**, where some local characters are so friendly they'll cross the street or leap from the backs of trucks to shake your hand and say, "Hello!" The majority of the population of Vieques lives around this five-block port town, and it has the feel of what Puerto Rico must have been like 50 years ago, before large-scale commercial development hit. School children in uniforms crowd the candy store. Elderly men repose on benches in the sunny central plaza. The coconut man rides his custom-made bicycle, machete at his hip, with a goat and a pig in tow.

Up the hill east of the ferry terminal, past **Siddhia Hutchinson's Fine Art Studio & Gallery**, ☎ 787-741-8780, you'll find **Punta Mulas Lighthouse**, ☎ 787-741-0060. Built in 1896 by the Spanish, using a French lamp, it is still an active aid to navigation and is also home to a small maritime museum. Beyond the Water's Edge Guest House, small, architecturally masterful homes along the north shore road inspire envious glances from all passersby.

Circling back toward town, pass the art gallery of **Helen Davis**, ☎ 787-741-4451, en route to a historical jewel, **Fortín Conde de Mirasol**, ☎ 787-741-1717. It was the last Spanish fort built in the Americas, but was never fully completed. Inside, displays include the first human remains found on Vieques and quite good exhibits chronicling the history of the island. The fort is open Wednesday to Sunday from 10 a.m. to 4 p.m., and admission is free.

> **TIP:** When leaving Isabel Segunda, drive carefully to avoid the many wild horses that roam the island and often run freely in the roads.

South of Isabel Segunda on Carr. 997, **Camp Garcia Gate**, previously the portal to Navy land, is closed to the public. A half-dozen strong-looking young women wearing the dark blue of military police uniforms, shiny boots and sunglasses usually guard this flashpoint of the protests against the Navy. Protesters, meanwhile, have rented out the property across the road and often hold demonstrations. Farther along Carr. 997, history in the making gives way to mysterious traces of antiquity, at a signposted dirt road on the right that leads to the **Area Arqueologica Hombre de Puerto Rico**.

Touring & Sightseeing ■ 355

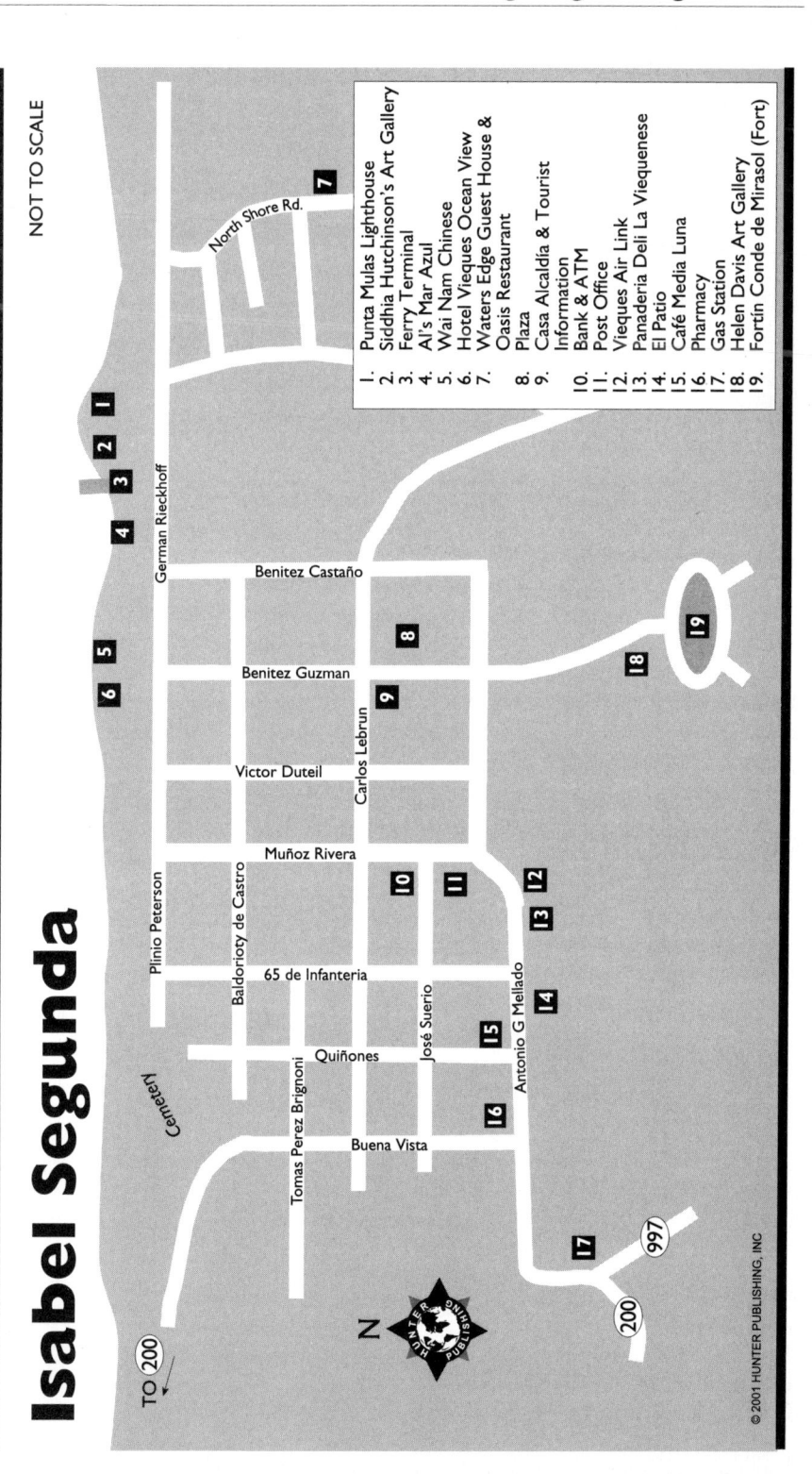

Isabel Segunda

NOT TO SCALE

1. Punta Mulas Lighthouse
2. Siddhia Hutchinson's Art Gallery
3. Ferry Terminal
4. Al's Mar Azul
5. Wai Nam Chinese
6. Hotel Vieques Ocean View
7. Waters Edge Guest House & Oasis Restaurant
8. Casa Alcaldia & Tourist Information
9. Plaza
10. Bank & ATM
11. Post Office
12. Vieques Air Link
13. Panaderia Deli La Viequense
14. El Patio
15. Café Media Luna
16. Pharmacy
17. Gas Station
18. Helen Davis Art Gallery
19. Fortin Conde de Mirasol (Fort)

Vieques & Culebra

© 2001 HUNTER PUBLISHING, INC

STONEHENGE ON VIEQUES?

Though some have dubbed the otherworldly looking circle of smooth boulders at Area Arqueologica Hombre de Puerto Rico as Vieques' Stonehenge, it is a natural formation. Unlike its counterpart on Salisbury Plain, the area was created by erosion around hard mounds of volcanic rock. The discovery on this site of a skeleton that dates back about 3,500 years prompted scientists to re-evaluate their estimate of when the first humans arrived in Puerto Rico – by well over a millennium! Researchers are unclear about what these archaic people did at this site, but it is believed they were a pre-ceramic people who lived in camps rather than established villages, engaged in only the most primitive form of cooking if at all, ate mangrove oysters, conch and raw fruits, and used crude stone tools. The skeleton is on display at the Fortín. The only humans using the site today are locals who often visit for meditation and to soak up the spiritual ambiance of one of the oldest inhabitations in the Antilles. If you ask around you might be invited to join one of the latter-day full moon ceremonies that take place here.

At the end of Carr. 997, stop at one of the charming eateries along the waterfront **Esperanza strip** (see *Where To Eat*, page 368) for lunch, a late-afternoon beer, or just to listen to reggae or classic rock and take in the sparkling Caribbean view. Between songs, the only sound you'll hear is the clanking of sailboat halyards in the breeze and the lapping of the waves against the shore. The **Esperanza Pier** – once an important loading dock for the island's now-defunct sugar industry – is also a great snorkeling site on calm days. Esperanza is considered Vieques' second town, and this side of the island is more heavily influenced by the *norteamericanos* who arrived during the past 20 years.

The little **Esperanza Museum** displays a collection of butterflies and some local artifacts and crafts, and is also home to the Vieques Conservation and Historical Trust and gift shop (donations welcome). The museum is open 10 a.m. to 3 p.m., Tuesday to Saturday. For local lore and gossip, stop in on Lou at **18 Degrees North**, Carr. 996 in Esperanza (no phone), who sells T-shirts, island souvenirs and secondhand novels. Next door, **Kim's Cabin**, ☎ 787-741-3145, is full of tropical dresses and swimwear, and **Balai Lama**, ☎ 787-741-0490 or 0520, has resort rags designed by New York ex-pat Patricia Herman.

East of the Esperanza strip, you'll find the public beach, **Playa Sun Bay**, and, farther east, a labyrinth of sandy roads through forests of mesquite. Stick to the wider passageways around here, because those along the coast are deeply pitted. All roads lead to access to **Media Luna** and **Navio** beaches. Farther east, just before the border of Navy land, **Mosquito Bay**

Esperanza

1. La Dulce Vida (Bikes) & Eco-Center (Mosquito Bay)
2. Hacienda Tamarindo
3. Inn on the Blue Horizon & Café Blue
4. The Crab Walk Café
5. Trade Winds
6. Bali Llama; 18 Degrees North; Kim's Cabin
7. Vieques Conservation & Historic Trust
8. Bananas
9. Captain Richard's Underwater Eco-Tours
10. Amapol
11. Blue Caribe Dive Center
12. La Casa del Frances

is possibly the finest bioluminescent bay in the world. (See information about excursions to it on page 363.)

West of the Esperanza Strip on Carr. 996, **La Campesina** is a jungle hideaway serving excellent grill food just east of a Navy roadblock. The quickest route back to Isabel Segunda is via Carr. 201, which ends at Carr 200. Head west here toward **Green Beach**, the only section of Navy land currently open to the public. You may hear the Navy checkpoint before you see it – the sociable guards are usually blaring salsa music. You'll need to show a driver's license or some other form of identification in order to be waved through. Stretching just over a mile into the Atlantic, the military appendage **Mosquito Pier** seems to reach almost to mainland Puerto Rico. Farther west, the road to Green Beach is a microcosmic tour of tropical ecosystems – subtropical dry forest gives way to the mangrove colonies of **Laguna Kiani**, which may be toured via a new boardwalk, palm groves, and finally sandy dunes, coves, shell grounds and the 987-foot peak of **Mt. Pirata**, the highest point on Vieques.

BLUE MONDAY

Remember that most sights and many restaurants are closed on Mondays. During the off-peak season in the summer months, many tourist-oriented establishments are closed much of the time.

Adventures

■ On Foot

Hiking

For guided adventure hikes, get in touch with Mark, Jason, Owen or Mary Alice at the **Water's Edge Guest House**, North Shore Road in Isabel Segunda, ☎ 787-741-1128, fax 741-3918, e-mail rehillism@aol.com. They specialize in outdoor mayhem and eco-fun. They can also hook you up with off-the-beaten-path trips into the rain forest and mountains of the main island of Puerto Rico. In Esperanza, you can hike along a rocky outcropping (wear sturdy shoes) to **Cayo Tierra**, with great views and a couple of little desolate beaches.

■ On Wheels

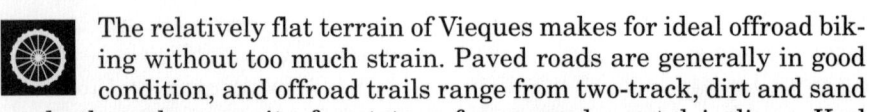

The relatively flat terrain of Vieques makes for ideal offroad biking without too much strain. Paved roads are generally in good condition, and offroad trails range from two-track, dirt and sand roads through mesquite forest to a few rugged coastal inclines. Karl Husson of **La Dulce Vida**, ☎ 787-617-2453 (BIKE), www.bikevieques.com, has spent the past couple of years exploring trails and developing mountain biking challenges suitable for novice to intermediate bikers. His bikes are top of the line, and come with 24-hour roadside repair service. Find him at the bottom of the lane leading up to Hacienda Tamarindo (see *Where To Stay*) on Carr. 996. The intermediate course starts near Camp Garcia at **Shanklin Farms**, for a smooth ride along a ridge, with photogenic views of the south coast and the Caribbean Sea. If you didn't fly to Vieques, this is the next best thing for aerial views of Barracuda and Mosquito bays. At **Los Chivos**, a fun downhill through mesquite forest leads back toward the coast. This ride finishes with a choice of two routes: an easy one along sand roads leading to Navio Beach, or a lovely but kidney-punching ride along an eroded coastal track. After a three-hour ride through the wilderness, the trail ends at Navio Beach where Karl will have left his truck prepared with a picnic lunch, soft drinks and beer, and sweaty riders can take a refreshing swim in the sea. The easier ride starts with the same loop from Shanklin Farms to Los Chivos, but then follows Carr. 997 to the archeological site Area Arqueologica Hombre de Puerto Rico, sometimes called the Vieques Stonehenge. This flat track gives a good first-time experience of offroading, and ends at the circle of stones with a picnic lunch and an exploration of the area before heading back to Esperanza. Guided tours cost $35, with an additional $5 to $7 for lunch. Renting a bike for the day to head out on your own costs $25, including lock, helmet and 24-hour roadside repair.

■ On Horseback

A horseback-riding operation called Billy the Kid closed in 2000, but with so many horses and good riding trails on the island it's probably only a matter of time before it reopens or someone else picks up where Billy the Kid left off. If so, most people on the island will know about it. News travels fast on Vieques.

■ On Water

Beaches

Most people come to Vieques to relax and enjoy miles of unspoiled, white sand beaches, and there are plenty among which to choose. Unfortunately, the Navy has indefinitely closed off access to some of the island's best beaches, including Caracas (Red Beach), Manuel Key (Blue Beach), Playa Secreta (Secret Beach) and other, even more secluded, spots. However, most visitors agree that the remaining beaches provide enough options for seekers of sun and isolation.

> **TIP:** *Bring plenty of water and sunscreen when you visit beaches on Vieques, because none of them has places to buy either.*

The most popular is the public beach at **Sun Bay**, a two-mile crescent of white sand and glassy water. If you come during the week, chances are you will share it with no more than a few distant silhouettes on the horizon. But it can get busy on weekends, as evidenced by the size of the parking lot. Camping is allowed here, by permission (see *Where To Stay*).

Accessed by continuing on the dirt road next to Sun Bay, **Media Luna** gets its name from its shape – a half moon of sand fringed by almond trees. You may see the remains of a few illicit campfires here, but usually few signs of life. Farther east, sink into the thick drifts of sand and the aquamarine surf at **Playa Navio**. With high rock formations at either end, it's short by comparison to the other beaches, and gorgeous. On Sundays, this is the *viequense* version of the town park or the local pub. The waves are speckled with body surfers, locals show off their endless summer tans, and impromptu beach volleyball games continue throughout the day on the eastern end. It's the quickest possible introduction to the population of Vieques. As with other beaches, Navio is often deserted during the week.

> **DID YOU KNOW?** *Shooting for the original 1960 film version of* Lord of the Flies, *including several of the dramatic final scenes, took place at Navio Beach.*

At the far northwestern tip of the island **Green Beach** runs nearly the length of the west coast, making it the longest accessible beach on the island. Millions of tiny seashell fragments add an interesting luster to the sand, and empty queen conch shells by the thousands expose their glossy pink interiors to the sun. Fringing palm groves provide some shade, and the rising peak of Mt. Pirata (at 987 feet, the highest on the mountain) forms a buffer against trade winds. This is a great place to watch the sun go down over Puerto Rico, and almost completely deserted even on weekends.

Fishing

Captain Franco González of the **Caribbean Fly Fishing Co.**, ☎ 787-741-1337, runs charters from the shallow flats to the big blue. His specialty is fly-casting for bonefish – pound for pound one of the fastest, strongest fish in existence. A four-hour trip starts with a journey in his 28-foot Bertram to the flats around Ensenada Honda, which he has permission to fish from the US Navy; casting is done wading in knee-deep water. This trip costs $250 for one or two people. Franco also offers deep-sea fishing charters to a ledge about 10 miles south of Vieques that drops from 200 to more than 1,000 feet. Here you're likely to find wahoo, tuna, dorado and plenty of barracuda. Half-day charters cost $350, full days are $500, with a maximum of four people, including beverages (bring your own lunch). Jorge Gavino-Medina of **El Malcriao**, ☎ 787-741-5012, cell 510-0430, with 10 years' experience as a commercial fisherman, runs charters for fishing around Vieques and Culebra, as well as diving and shorkeling trips. Also, **Lowell's Bait and Tackle**, ☎ 787-741-1344, rents out rods, reels and tackle for $15 a day, with a $25 deposit for equipment. They have lures and bait for sale, and guided trips by appointment. Delivery and pickup can be arranged.

Kayaking

The most impressive kayaking trail on the island is an easy paddle on a moonless night through **Mosquito Bay** (see *Eco-Travel*, page 363). For more adventurous daytime kayaking, Dan Moreau and Virgina Kozur at **Aqua Frenzy**, ☎ 787-741-0913, offer eco-tours of the Vieques coastline – either in the north or south, depending on the wind. Unfortunately, access to many lagoons has been restricted since the Navy closed most of its land to the public. Kayaks are put in at Puerto Mosquito (Laguna Kiani), where mangrove estuaries serve as nurseries for young marine life and birds, before paddling out to sea and along the coast. All kayaks are ocean-going with rudder steering, and private instruction is provided for ambitious adventurers who want to paddle off on their own (this costs $20 per hour). Groups are small (maximum six), reservations must be made by phone and a good level of fitness is required. The eco-tour lasts about 3½ hours and costs $55 per person. Morning, afternoon and sunset kayak cruises are also available.

Diving

Vieques has about 10 easy to intermediate dive sites, all off the southern shore. Don't center your entire vacation on diving in Vieques, however. High winds have been known to chop up the water for days, causing poor visibility and strong surge, leaving divers high and dry onshore.

- Submarine courtship is a daily occurrence at **Patti's Reef II**, where sergeant majors favor the flat boulder corals of this site as a nursery for their eggs. Males vigorously guard slick patches of purple eggs against the hungry advances of parrotfish, butterflyfish and rock beauties. Whiskered goatfish and sea cucumbers are common here, and southern stingrays can often be seen muzzling through the sand.

- Right off the shore, **Cayo Real** and the **Esperanza** form a shallow aquarium full of sea life, including fairy-like seahorses, great for divers and snorkelers alike.

SWIMMING WITH SEAHORSES

Often no bigger than a human finger, these delicate creatures are so well camouflaged and shy that seeing one requires patience and a keen eye. Using the chameleon nature of their scales, they make themselves nearly invisible at the first sign of danger. Look for them in shady hiding places under Esperanza and Mosquito piers, and around Cayo Real. The secret is to stay very still in the water and keep your eyes focused on a small area.

- **Horseshoe Reef** is an aptly named coral formation that rises from 60 feet to about 15 feet of water all around the horseshoe. Communication cable to the island lies across this reef, providing a good navigational tool, and following it leads to a Spanish-era cannon on the upper portion of a small ledge. Green and moray eels, spiny lobster and nurse sharks are common in this area.

- **Castle Reef** and **Anchor Reef** are good novice dives, with large amounts of sea life and, on the latter, a coral encrusted anchor, presumably from a Spanish galleon centuries ago.

- East of Esperanza and two miles out to sea, **Blue Reef** stretches for about two miles and is still largely unexplored. Depths range from 60 to 80 feet. Due to strong east-west currents, Blue Reef is usually done as a drift dive. Just assume the neutral buoyant position and watch the reef pass before your eyes, including giant barrel and vase sponges and plenty of marine life.

DIVE OPERATORS

Blue Caribe Dive Center, ☎/fax 787-741-2522, bluecaribe@aol.com, www.enchanted-isle.com/bluecaribe, faces the bay in Esperanza. It has the only offshore diving and snorkeling operation in Vieques. A typical day of diving begins with equipment fitting at 8:30 a.m., followed by a boat ride of no more than 20 minutes to most sites. Blue Caribe takes a maximum of six divers and usually returns to the dock around noon. A two-tank dive, including all equipment, costs a reasonable $70, or $50 for a one-tank dive during the day. Night dives, including equipment and lights, cost $70. Blue Caribe offers full PADI open water certification courses for $300 or, for those who have completed the classroom instruction and confined-water training before arriving, $225. It's also possible to rent full scuba equipment, including unlimited air, for offshore or pier dives, for $40 per day, or $50 per day with mask and fins. Snorkeling trips to a fringe reef known as Blue Tang Reef usually begin in the early afternoon and end by 4:30 or 5 p.m. You'll circle 10-foot coral heads in search of octopus, turtles, rays, blue tangs and other sea life, with the help of a knowledgeable guide. The snorkeling trips cost $30 per person.

Eco-Snorkeling with Captain Richard

Native son Captain Richard Barone, a passionate *viequense* naturalist, educates islanders and visitors alike on the underwater wonders of his birthplace. If you have any interest in sea life whatsoever, don't miss his three-hour eco-snorkeling tour, **Vieques Nature Tours**, ☎ 787-741-1980, in Esperanza. The tour starts right off the Esperanza pier, in Captain Richard's glass-bottom pontoon boat, the Sea View, which he designed himself. With a natural capacity for storytelling, he explains the life-and-death drama taking place a few feet away, as the boat's glass-bottomed viewing area passes over several distinct ecosystems. Sea grass beds, with dark, noodle-like turtle grass and green strands of manatee grass, are thick with queen conch, which start life as a male and undergo a sex change about midway through life. Here you're likely to see mackerel, jacks, cowfish and, with luck, a green or hawksbill turtle. So-called blow-out zones – sandy patches between sea grass beds and the coral reef – are thriving with life, if you know how to look for it. Creatures such as urchins, jawfish, burrowing eels and big hermit crabs all leave the relative safety of the reef to graze the sand for algae. Southern stingrays and diamond-shaped spotted eagle rays burrow in these sands to suck down hidden clams or worms.

Before visiting the reef, Richard will take the boat past the *tambolos* – submerged sand bars – between Cayo Tierra and the mainland, which are home to, among other things, two curious species of seahorses: the lined and the long-snout seahorse. Passing over the coral reef in a glass-bottom boat is an excellent way to observe coral heads and the life around them, sometimes no more than inches from the viewing area. Star coral, finger coral, gorgonian soft coral, fans and giant candelabras form unearthly cities made up of millions of individual polyps, which look like tiny glass flowers with algae photosynthesizing within their tissues. Here you'll begin your snorkel tour, with coaching from Captain Richard for anyone timid in the water. Look for lizard fish prowling the bottom, snappers and grunts, rainbow-colored parrot fish, schools of whiskered goatfish, queen angels and rock beauties. Focus on small amounts of underwater territory and you may see strange creatures emerge from their camouflage, such as the long-lure frogfish, which possesses a horn sticking out from its nose like a fishing pole, and actually fishes with a little white ball dangling in front of it like a lure. Unlucky fish attracted to the ball find themselves quickly gobbled into the giant mouth of the frogfish. The three-hour trip usually begins at 11 a.m. to accommodate day-trippers from the main island and costs $30 per person, including the use of top-quality snorkel gear.

SHARING IT WITH LOCAL KIDS

The son of a local fisherman, Captain Richard learned about marine biology from experience, library books and a few mentors, not by earning university diplomas. He sets aside 10% of all tour fees to pay for trips he regularly runs for low-income families and children, mostly from Vieques. "Everyone should have the chance to appreciate the magic of the nature around them, and this is one way we can all give back to the people who live here," Richard says. "It makes everybody feel good. Tips go in that jar, too."

Sunset Cruising

Captain Richard also runs a sunset **Rum & Rhythms Cruise** on his boat, the *Sea View*, Saturdays from 5 p.m. to 7 p.m., with a capacity for more than three dozen people. Complimentary piña coladas and rum punches (or beers) loosen up the dancing feet, as a live steel band plays on deck and guests boogie the sun down into the water. Costs $25 per person.

■ Eco-Travel

Mosquito Bay

Bahía Mosquito is perhaps the most shining example of a bioluminescent bay in the world, and is one of the must-do adventures here. With 60 acres of waist-deep water surrounded by mangrove forest and protected from tides by a slanting inlet, the bay is home to trillions of single-celled creatures called **dinoflagellates**, which produce a luminous blue-green glow when disturbed. Though not completely understood by scientists, bioluminescence is assumed to be a natural defense mechanism, attracting larger fish to feed on the dinoflagellates' predators (akin to a bird calling a dog to chase away the cat). A chemical stored in the organism's single cell produces the light when combined with oxygen. Production of the chemical, luciferin, is controlled by an internal clock and may be the result of the fact that dinoflagellates get energy both from photosynthesis and the vitamin B12-rich nutrients of mangrove leaves decomposing in the warm, shallow waters. Since vitamin B12 is also good for human skin, jump in for a free spa treatment!

Unlike the bioluminescent bay in Parguera, and many others around the world that have fallen victim to water pollution, ambient light, coastal development or invasion by predator organisms, Mosquito Bay remains stunning for its sheer concentration and brightness of dinoflagellates. A single gallon of the bay's water contains between 500,000 and a million of them, and a researcher from Johns Hopkins University who studies the bay says it is just as luminescent as it was 30 years ago, when he first visited the site. The best time to view the bioluminescence is on a moonless or cloudy night. As you enter the bay, you'll begin to see glowing tracers zipping off in all directions – the electric-green wakes left by fish fleeing the boat or kayak. With your hand, scoop up handfuls of water, which glimmers with tiny diamonds of light as it trickles down your arm. Jump into the warm water and see how your every move is bathed in an aura of color that seems borrowed from a science fiction movie. You will not soon forget this adventure!

PROTECTING MOSQUITO BAY

The federal government is considering designating Mosquito Bay a National Park, which would help protect it from the uncertain future of development in the area. Already, efforts by Sharon Grasso of Island Adventures, the Vieques Conservation and Historical Trust and others have helped preserve the bay, convincing local authorities to shield the water from ambient light and make it off-limits to boats with gasoline motors. To join efforts to preserve Mosquito Bay, visit the VCHT at the Esperanza Museum or log onto www.vieques-island.com/biobay.html.

Most trips to Mosquito Bay leave right after sundown. **Island Adventures**, ☎ 787-741-0720, takes visitors aboard an electric boat, guided by a naturalist. The two-hour trip includes a short ride on a rickety old bus to the electric boat, which glides almost silently across the water to the bay. Sharon Grasso, former seventh-grade biology teacher who has dedicated most of her adult life to Mosquito Bay, provides an informative lecture on the dinoflagellates and ecosystem of Mosquito Bay. After you plunge into the waters and swim for as long as you wish, Sharon directs the attention of guests skyward, for a constellation-by-constellation tour of the heavens.

A great trip, it costs $20 per person. You'll find Island Adventures at their new headquarters near Hacienda Tamarindo on Carr. 996. For a more intimate trip to Bahía Mosquito, **Blue Caribe Dive Center**, ☎ 787-741-2522, take groups of two to 10 to the bay by kayak. Guides Tom and Kevin are also knowledgeable about the ecology of the bay, and provide an in-depth explanation to their guests. The trip costs $20, plus a $3 donation to save-the-bay efforts.

Where To Stay

ACCOMMODATIONS PRICE KEY

Rates are per room, per night, double occupancy. Single occupancy may or may not get you a discount, so ask when making a reservation. Breakfast included where noted.

$	Up to $50
$$	$50 to $100
$$$	$101 to $150
$$$$	$150 and up

■ High-End

It's nearly impossible to find a room in Vieques that doesn't have a view – if not of the sea, then of a vibrant tropical garden or of the rolling hillsides. Guest houses are generally small and most have something special or unique about them, whether it's their location, design or history.

Martineau Bay, run by Rosewood Hotels & Resorts, ☎ 787-741-4100, 888-ROSEWOOD (888-767-3966), may be open by the time you read this. The five-star luxury resort is on the north shore, between Isabel Segunda and the airport. It will have 155 rooms, including 20 suites. $$$$+

The Inn on the Blue Horizon, ☎ 787-741-3318, fax 741-0522, on Carr. 996, west of Esperanza, www.innonthebluehorizon.com, is perched on a bluff of savannah grass overlooking the sea. Easily one of our favorite places to stay anywhere, it has six ocean-facing casita rooms well-spaced along pathways that run parallel to the cliff, and three rooms in the charming main house. Owners James Weis and Billy Knight have turned a once-rundown house on a prime location into one of the classiest, most tasteful accommodations in the Caribbean. The details speak volumes. Easy chairs, antiques and ornaments from around the world turn an open area under a Polynesian-style roof into a breezy sitting room. Beyond the freshwater swimming pool, a small lawn stretches toward the cliff top, where white lounge chairs face the, well, the blue horizon. Bedrooms include nice touches such as antique reading lamps, well-chosen hardback classics and handmade soaps wrapped in handmade paper. Giant pillows, cool cotton bedsheets and parachute-silk drapes soften paintwork deliberately mottled to give the impression of age. Such attention to detail has caught the eye of several top magazines. Paul Theroux raved about Blue Horizon in *Architectural Digest*, which featured the inn in its November 2000 issue, saying that guests enjoy "the sense of being part of a voluptuous landscape rather than of being trapped in an air-conditioned room." Make reservations early and often. No children under 12 allowed. $$$$

Two hundred yards inland, Linda and Burr Vail run **Hacienda Tamarindo**, Carr. 996 west of Esperanza, ☎ 787-741-8525, fax 741-3215, www.enchanted-isle.com/tamarindo, which also gets rave reviews from guests. Sixteen rooms are intriguingly decorated with a collection of art, antiques and curios, and some have stunning sea views. The library appears lifted from an English manor house. Outside, hammocks swing in the breeze under mahogany trees, and a stone griffin spews water into a beautiful freshwater swimming pool. Complimentary American breakfast is served on a rooftop terrace shaded by a giant tamarindo tree. No children under 15 allowed here either; $$$-$$$$

Another unique and elegant high-end guest house is **Hix Island House**, ☎ 787-741-2302, Carr. 995, (near the junction with Carr. 201), Barrio Pilón, www.hixislandhouse.com, e-mail hixisle@coqui.net. Naked concrete walls and strong lines cut into hillsides of elephant grass make this an architectural gem, with a freshwater infinity swimming pool overlooking the sea far below. Roll-up metal gates open the large rooms to great vistas, with interiors designed in strict Scandinavian minimalism. Hix Island House has become a Caribbean darling of design and fashion photographers, who have shot features here for *Travel & Leisure*, *Metropolitan Home*, *Elle* and *Vogue*, among others. Includes stylish kitchens for self-catering. Yoga classes available on Tuesday and Friday mornings or by reservation; $$$$

■ Mid-Range

For fun-loving travelers with a taste for adventure, check out **Water's Edge**, ☎ 787-741-1128, fax 741-3918, on North Shore Road in Isabel Segunda, www.villagloria.com, e-mail rehillism@aol.com. Built around a perpetually flowering courtyard, rooms here are good value, spacious and have cable TV and views of the Atlantic Ocean. A sea-facing pool, bar and excellent restaurant are added bonuses. The youthful crowd that runs the place treats visitors like family, so don't be surprised to find yourself invited to volleyball on the beach, hiking on back-road trails or whatever else they're up to. Prices are $$ for courtyard and ocean-view rooms, $$$

for honeymoon suites and $$$$ for a three-bedroom villa with its own pool, gardens and screened-in deck.

Formerly known as the New Dawn Caribbean Retreat, **La Fínca Caribe**, ☎ 787-741-0495 (Corky and David, 206-567-5656), Carr. 995, www.lafinca.com, e-mail lafinca@merwincreative.com, is a tropical hideaway for people who enjoy going barefoot and showering outdoors. Set in several acres of rolling hills and colorful gardens, with swimming pool, the décor is rustic, the atmosphere laid back. Wide wooden swings, farmhouse tables, grill and a huge open living and kitchen space make it a home away from home. The house can sleep six to 20. A family-sized cabaña and casita are also available by the week. $$-$$$

La Casa del Francés, ☎ 787-741-3751, fax 741-2330, north of Esperanza on Carr. 996, www.enchanted-isle.com/lacasa, e-mail fceleste@worldnet.att.net, was built by French sugar plantation owner Don Teófilo Le Guillou, who governed the island in the 19th century. It is by far the oldest hotel on the island. Built around a large interior courtyard, cavernous rooms could easily sleep a football team, but most are furnished simply with two queen-size beds. According to staff, the ghost of Le Guillou's wife haunts room number 12. Used as an officers' club for the Navy in the middle of the century, it is now an eccentric hotel with a swimming pool in a lush backyard and a small restaurant catering to guests with breakfast items such as "eggistential omelet – whatever, who cares" and "eggspose – naked eggs served by waiter in raincoat," as well as dinner. $$-$$$$

The Crow's Nest, ☎ 787-741-0033/0993, fax 741-1294, on Carr. 201, www.crowsnestvieques.com, e-mail thenest@coqui.net, is a farm-style guest house in the hills above Isabel Segunda, with views over the Atlantic in the distance. Painted buttercup yellow, it includes shady gardens, a good-sized pool, restaurant and bar. Rooms, some with TV and telephone, all with kitchenettes, are a good deal for self-caterers, and the upstairs two-bedroom suite makes a comfortable home for a family or group of friends. The gift shop offers Internet access, $4 for 20 minutes; $$-$$$$

An excellent option for a weekly rental is **Mango Vieques**, ☎ 787-741-0292, Isabel Segunda, www.mangovieques.com. Accommodations are a second-floor, two-bedroom apartment above the home of pilot Tony Bennett. Situated on the Monte Santo ridge in the middle of the island, it has a large and fully equipped kitchen and dining room, plus a rooftop deck with Jacuzzi and wraparound views of the Atlantic to the north and the Caribbean to the south. $$$

Budget

Three guest houses right on the Esperanza strip offer more basic, budget accommodations in a great location. All are above or behind shorefront restaurants. The best deal is at **Bananas**, Calle Flamboyán, ☎ 787-741-8700, fax 741-0790 where some of the rooms have screened porches, living areas and air conditioning. Smaller rooms with fans are cheaper, and guests have use of a small shady courtyard lined with bright pink ginger flowers. $-$$

Amapola Inn & Tavern, on the Esperanza strip, ☎ 787-741-1382 or 3704, has clean, simple, fan-cooled rooms, all with private bathrooms, off a small communal living room; $$. The rooms at **Trade Winds**, also on Esperanza strip, ☎ 787-741-8666, fax 741-2964, tradewns@coqui.net, look somewhat hospital-like, but clean. Daily maid service keeps the beach sand from accumulating in your sheets. Beach towels provided. $$

A desperate option for slumming it in Isabel Segunda is **Hotel Ocean View**, ☎ 787-741-3696, next to the ferry dock and right on the Atlantic. Obviously having seen better days, the hallways smell of industrial cleaning fluid, and when we visited the swimming pool was choked with algae, its water the color of bile. $$

Camping

The only official camping area on Vieques – and a great option for budget travelers – is on the gorgeous **Sun Bay Beach**, east of Esperanza, ☎ 787-741-8198, (reservations recommended, but not necessary). Facilities under construction include showers, bathrooms and a *bohío* with cafeteria. A second renovation phase, which should be complete by 2002, will organize camping spaces into 50 areas complete with picnic tables and barbecue pits.

Where To Eat

Surprisingly for an isolated island, Vieques has some top-rate eating establishments and a good variety of culinary experiences from which to choose. Chefs at the finer restaurants resourcefully tap food sources from all over the United States and Puerto Rico, and typically spend at least one day a week on the main island shopping for delicacies.

■ Around Esperanza

Chef Michael at **Café Blu**, ☎ 787-741-3318, at the Inn on the Blue Horizon, is praised internationally by gourmets and critics for artfully blending Caribbean and continental flavors into an imaginative menu that tastes as good as it reads. Appetizers, priced from $6 and $14, range from blue corn chips and a tangy homemade salsa to oyster stew with caramelized leeks, in which oysters are poached just long enough to turn them to velvet on the outside, warm but raw in the middle. The delicious chanterelle and blue-foot oyster mushrooms on polenta, normally a starter, could make a good main dish for vegetarians. Entrées cover the gamut from bar favorites – gourmet burgers and Bloody Mary steaks – to rosemary-scented roast pork tenderloin, accompanied by a *risolé* of potato, butternut squash and portobello; or cornmeal-crusted sea bass filet on a toss of gingered beets, fresh spinach leaves and black-eyed peas. A must for foodies, entrées cost $12-$30 (closed Mondays).

Tucked away in the woods of Barrio La Hueca, **La Campesina**, ☎ 787-741-1239, on Carr. 201, serves up grill food and gourmet fish platters that many locals say is as magical as the setting itself. Entrées are $25 to $30.

Something of an institution, **Chez Shack**, ☎ 787-741-2175, on Carr. 995, is owned by Hugh Duffy, one of the first gringos to settle on Vieques during the early 1970s. His latest enterprise mixes Caribbean shack vibe with inventive homemade décor (Japanese-style lamps made of plastic plant pots, etc.), excellent grill food and a live steel band on Monday and Thursday nights. Choose from whole or half lobster, lamb kebabs marinated in orange, ribs and Cajun chicken all cooked to perfection and served with a buffet salad for less than $20 a head. Asian nights are in the works, so call ahead to Duffy, who closes Tuesdays or any other night he chooses.

THE MAMAS, THE PAPAS & DUFFY

Born in 1921, the colorful proprietor of Chez Shack – known to friends as "Duffy" – had already left careers as a merchant seaman, WWII military escort, New York fashion photographer and liquor salesman by the time he caused the formation of one of the most influential rock 'n roll bands of the 1960s. As seen on a recent VH1 documentary, Duffy was running a shack of a restaurant in St. Thomas, on a little street called Creeque Alley, when he received a visit from a group of free-wheeling hippies, including John Phillips, Cass Elliot, Dennis Doherty and Holly Michelle Gilham. "They were camping out at my place," he remembers. "We were doing a lot of acid, and one day I said, 'Hey, you guys play guitar and sing, why don't you be the band for my bar this season?' So they made some funny costumes and started calling themselves The Mamas and The Papas." The rest is history. The impromptu group failed as a cover band in the Caribbean, but the next year moved to L.A. and recorded *Monday Monday* and *California Dreamin'* and became a legend. Stop by Chez Shack for more of Duffy's stories about wild times with Mama Cass and the rest.

La Casa del Francés, Carr. 996, Esperanza (if you get to "the strip" you've gone too far), ☎ 787-741-3751, is good for reasonably priced pasta dishes, nothing costs more than $10. The seafood pasta special and vampire-proof spinach lasagna are recommended. Open 6.30 p.m. to 9.30 p.m.

Nearly all of the bars and restaurants on the Esperanza strip serve decent food, and the area attracts a young crowd. The cool breeze through **Trade Winds**, ☎ 787-741-8666, is one reason to stop in for a drink after a long day of work at the beach. Another is the nautical-themed restaurant, with pirate posters, maps and satellite images of the Caribbean islands. Appetizers include creamy seafood chowder ($6), Caribbean fish cakes and conch fritters ($7) and lively Latino main courses like grilled chicken with black beans and sweet corn, *mofongo* ($12 to $18), and Caribbean lobster spiced with rum and butter (priced according to weight).

Bananas, Calle Flamboyán, ☎ 787-741-8700, fax 741-0790, www.enchanted-isle.com/bananas, is a cool little joint with palm thatched lanterns, iguana-green tables and a head-on view of the bay. It's often the first place visitors stop in Esperanza, either for a cold beer or a plate of good, hearty fare like jerk chicken, homemade chili and salads for less than $10.

The Crabwalk Café, Carr. 996 (Esperanza strip), doesn't look like much during the day – just a covered patio – but you'll see people at the bar the minute it opens, and by the time the sun goes down it resembles a Serengeti watering hole during drought season. Wednesday is Thai Night, from 5 p.m. to 10 p.m., the rest of the time it's Mexican (entrées $10 to $15).

Visitors missing the Puerto Rican touch should track down Olga at **Posada Vistamar**, ☎ 787-741-8716, on the Esperanza strip, who cooks up the meanest fish stew and rice and beans on this side of the island for less than $10.

■ Around Isabel Segunda

Café Media Luna, ☎ 787-741-2594, on Calle Luis Muñoz Rivera, brings different jazz acts over from San Juan once a month, and local residents tell us this is a great night out. The Indian-inspired menu is very popular among ex-pats. Entrées around $30, call for opening hours.

Healthy portions of inventive dishes are on the menu created by chef Owen Tilley at **Oasis** at Water's Edge, ☎ 787-741-0655. A veteran of the East Coast Grill in Boston, famed for its "hotter than hell" nights, Tilley is capable of providing an endorphin rush to blow your mind. If you don't do "hot," he'll keep it mellow. The menu changes often, but expect to see tasty appetizers like cumin-seared scallops ($10) and chilled *calabaza* soup with avocado purée ($5). House specials include ostrich breast in a port glaze and seafood hotpot – a Thai-inspired stew of tender seafood. Most entrées cost less than $20. Look for live music at Water's Edge on weekends.

For cheap eats, **El Patio**, ☎ 787-741-6381, is guaranteed for mountainous *criollo* lunches, such as roast chicken with rice, beans and creamy *amarillos* (fried ripe plantains) for around $8. Likewise, **Gaby's BBQ**, ☎ 787-741-6336, has chicken, ribs and Puerto Rican side dishes, as does **Clarky's Barbecue Palace**, under a palm-thatched gazebo east of town.

Sandwiches, cakes and pastries are available from **Panaderia Deli La Viequenese**, ☎ 787-741-8213, and **Wai Nam Chinese**, ☎ 787-741-0622, serves basic Chinese fast food and noodles.

Nightlife

Vieques is not particularly a party island, although weekend nights can be fun along the Esperanza strip until 1 a.m. or so. In Isabel Segunda, the surest bet is **Al's Mar Azul**, ☎ 787-741-3400, just west of the ferry dock. Al prides himself on "same-day service and sometimes food," and has been known to buy rounds of tequila for patrons when the evening starts to get going. It's everything one could hope for in a seaport drinking den full of withered old sea dogs, wild-eyed gringos and a few local lushes. Open 11 a.m. to 1 a.m. on weekdays, 2 a.m. on weekends.

Culebra

Whether by land or by sea, arrival to Culebra cheers the soul. Straight from an Impressionist's paintbrush, fanciful cottages, dockside eateries and brightly painted waterfront guest houses dot the Ensenada Honda cove. Reflections of sailboats and hills ripple on the water. Bulging hammocks suggest the forms of residents locked in a contest for longest-running siesta. Relax, and slip into the picture.

Don't come to Culebra unless you enjoy digging your toes into sun-bleached sands on some of the emptiest and best beaches in the Caribbean or scuba diving and snorkeling with Technicolor fish on pristine reefs. This crab-shaped island, halfway between Puerto Rico and St. Thomas of the US Virgin Islands, is so tranquil it too might as well be underwater. And locals would prefer it stays that way, locked in a time capsule. At City Hall, municipal officials still use typewriters. One of the island's major exports seems to be shark-tooth jewelry. The main feature of the post office is a second-floor balcony with rocking chairs.

There is only one town on Culebra – the little village of **Dewey**, which residents call *El Pueblo*, meaning "the town." With only about 2,000 inhabitants on the entire island, the social scene gives new meaning to the word "cozy." By the time you've waved to the same person four times within an hour, you'll know what we mean. For example, locals motivated enough to go jogging have printed "I'm exercising" T-shirts to ward off passing motorists who inevitably stop to ask, "What's the hurry?" and offer a ride. "Your personal business is not private here," jokes Jerry Beaubein, owner of

372 ■ **Culebra**

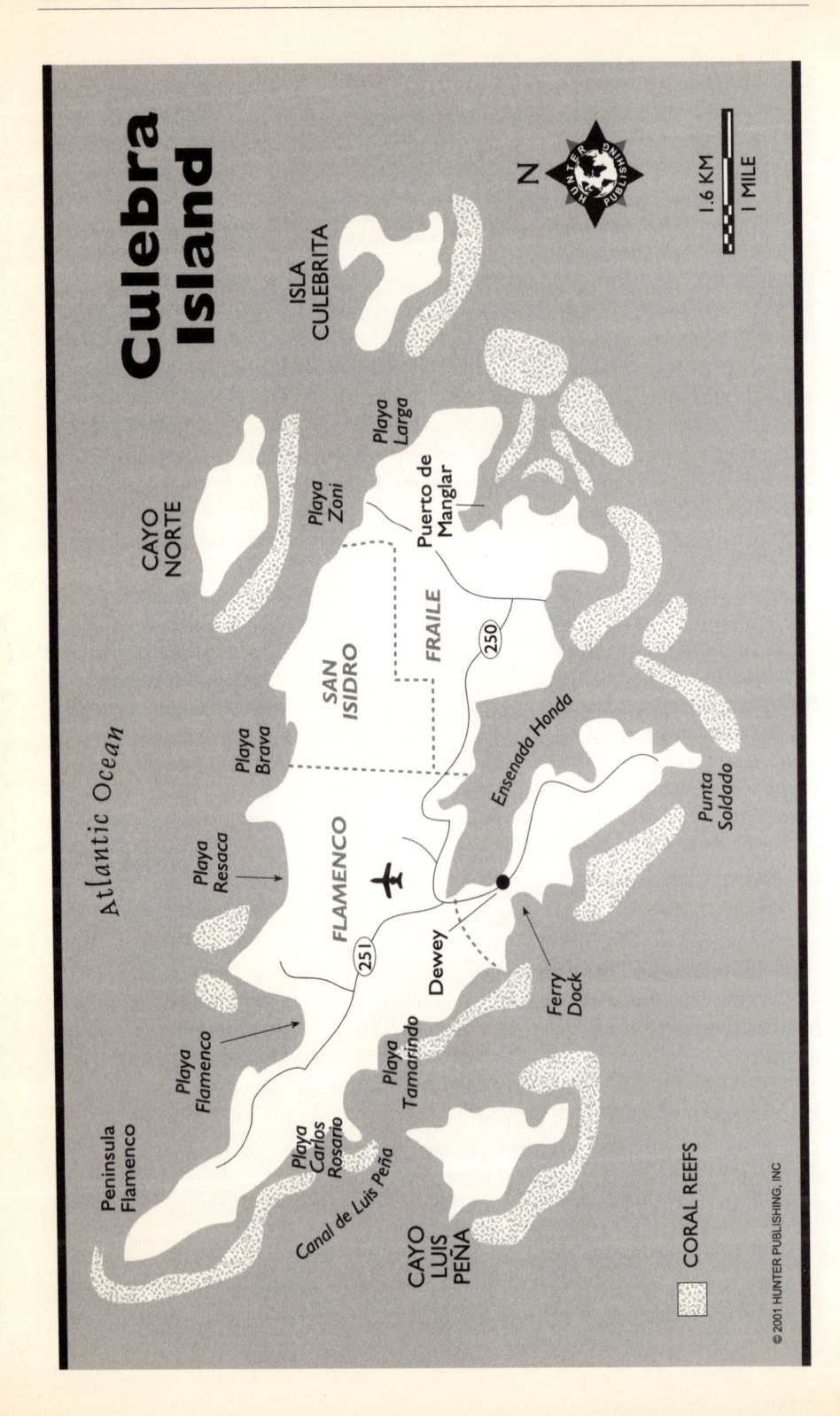

The town of Dewey.
(Bob Krist, for the PRTC)

Jerry's Jeeps. "If someone catches you cheating on your wife, she's bound to know about it before you get home."

History

Recorded history of Culebra begins with a bang in 1875, with the appointment of a "governor," a black Englishman named Stevens, who was given the task of keeping the waters around the desolate isle free of foreigners. He was brutally killed the same year by unknown assassins. Before that, inhabitants of Culebra apparently consisted of waves of transients, from Arawak Indians to pirates to European settlers, who used the island as a way station for shelter and hunting sea turtles. Lacking a natural source of fresh water, Culebra failed to attract long-term settlers until 1880, when Spain ordered it colonized in an effort to boost its fast-fading power in the region. By 1891, however, only seven years before Spain lost all her Caribbean holdings to the United States, the settlement in Culebra was described as no more than "a few houses made of straw, a church, a government house and a water tank."

During the next 10 years, several hundred people moved to the island and began exporting small quantities of wood, agricultural goods and the oil and shells of sea turtles. The tranquility of this little agricultural and fishing community was shattered in 1901, however, when in the wake of its victory over the Spanish the US Navy declared its intention to use Culebra

Tank used for bombing practice during Naval occupation of the island.
(© 2000, Kurt Pitzer)

as a training site. In defiance of the 1898 Treaty of Paris, the Navy removed the central settlement of San Ildefonso to its present location, and christened it Dewey, in honor of Admiral George Dewey, who had defeated the Spanish in the Philippines and became the first US Naval commander of the Caribbean. Although it set up a headquarters on the island, Navy exercises were minimal and low impact. In 1909, President Theodore Roosevelt designated Culebra as a wildlife refuge.

Navy occupation of Culebra had little local effect until WWII, when ships began using it for target practice before going into combat. After the war, responding to the pressures of the Cold War and Vietnam, Navy gunners continued to hone their skills by firing at pristine beaches on Culebra, especially Playa Flamenco (the corpse of a tank once used for target practice can still be seen there). Paralleling the US anti-war movement in the 1960s, *culebrenses* began demanding an end to Naval bombardment of their island. As it would in Vieques years later, the Partido Independentista Puertorriqueño (PIP) mobilized large numbers of protesters to block Navy access to Playa Flamenco with fishing boats, and to occupy the beach with a peaceful encampment and a hastily built chapel. In 1975, in an agreement brokered by Secretary of State Henry Kissinger, the Navy agreed to leave the island. More than a quarter-century later, with animosity toward the military faded, native *culebrenses* and immigrant *norteamericanos* live on an island that enjoys tourism, but is still a virgin to large-scale development.

Flora & Fauna

For the most part, Culebra is a semi-arid island, with a few moist areas of greenery on the difficult-to-reach upper slopes of Monte Resaca. Severe deforestation during the past 130 years at the hands of first settlers and then the US Navy has stripped many hillsides to wild grasses, and soil erosion is now one of the biggest threats to the island. Introduced species such as mesquite and thorny acacia – a yellow-flowered species imported from Mexico – have spread like wildfire, but a few pockets of **mangroves** and excellent examples of **subtropical dry forest** remain. Of 373 indigenous plants, 33 are rare or unique to Culebra. A visit to the little garden in front of the Fish and Wildlife Service (Carr. 250, just past the cemetery) provides a snapshot of botanical highlights, including the organ pipe cactus, the **snow cactus**, with spiny, white-skinned orbs for flowers, the pink-helmeted **Turks cap cactus**, the **night-blooming cereus** and the **jumping cactus**. On Monte Resaca, you may see examples of so-called **"boulder forest,"** where smooth round boulders are surrounded by eye-catching orchids, bromeliads and the endemic peperromia – a phenomenon seen only on Culebra and Virgin Gorda in the British Virgin Islands. The tallest tree on the island, the fan-leafed palm, can be found on Monte Resaca and a few coastal areas.

DON'T FEEL THE MANCHINEEL

Found throughout Culebra, the nasty manchineel tree is distinguished by a prominent yellow mid-vein, milky sap and bullet-like green fruit that somewhat resemble small limes. The fruit are highly poisonous, and contact with the rest of the tree can produce a poison ivy-like skin rash. Avoid sitting under these trees and eating, burning or touching any part of them.

With an exception or two, the celebrities of Culebra's animal kingdom reside in the sea. As early as 1909, the area around the island was designated a **wildlife preserve** in order to protect the vast colonies of seabirds that nest here – and with 1,568 acres today it remains one of the most important refuges in the Caribbean. More than 50,000 seabirds of 13 different species find their way to Culebra and its cays every year, including **laughing gulls**, **white-tailed** and **red-billed tropicbirds**, **terns** and three species of **boobies**. The largest concentration is a colony of more than 15,000 sooty terns around the Flamenco peninsula. Migratory foul, particularly **masked** and **ruddy ducks**, thrive in the marshy mangrove nurseries of the island that also protect fringe and barrier reefs from run-off. Aside from birds, Culebra is also the nesting ground of four endangered species of **sea turtles**: the **hawksbill, leatherback** and **green sea turtles** (see *Eco-Travel*, page 392, for more information).

On the remote beaches of Resaca and Brava, you may see a **green tree iguana**, a non-indigenous species, which can grow to four feet or more in length.

NOT SO DEAR DEER

Don't be surprised if you see a white-tailed deer while visiting Culebra, a recently introduced species that has become an ecopest. During the 1970s, the mayor of Culebra brought five deer from Georgia in the US, and since then the population has mushroomed to more than 200. However, they pose a threat to the environment – trampling turtle eggs, damaging seabird nests and further spreading acacia and mesquite with their droppings.

Getting Here

■ By Air

Flying into Culebra is an unforgettable experience, with the cays and reefs clustered around the main island like bridesmaids. The flight path crosses over the crescent sands of Playa Flamenco, and you'll undoubtedly crane your neck at the window for a view of her heartbreakingly beautiful hemline before dipping into the little **Aeropuerto Benjamin Rivera Noriega**, just north of Dewey. **Isla Nena Air Service**, ☎ 800-263-6213, usually has at least four flights a day between Culebra and San Juan (both the International and Isla Grande airports), for $60 one way and $115 round-trip. Schedules and fares are subject to change, so call for more info. **Vieques Air Link**, ☎ 787-741-8211 or 8331 (in Vieques), 888-901-9247, flies between Culebra and Fajardo on demand, with comparable rates. The company often schedules flights the same day, and during the tourist season there may be regular flights. At least two charter companies fly between Culebra and the main island of Puerto Rico on demand: **Air Flamenco**, ☎ 787-801-8256 (in Fajardo), 742-1040 (in Culebra), or 724-6464 (in Isla Grande); and **Air Culebra**, ☎ 787-268-6951, 379-4466, or 888-967-6623 (pager).

■ By Sea

The ferry between Culebra and Fajardo, ☎ 787-863-0705 or 0852, costs just $2.25 per person one way, and takes about an hour. The ferry terminal and pier in Fajardo is the same one used for Vieques, and the trip is similar, except that on weekends the boats are often crammed full of Puerto Ricans heading for Playa Flamenco to camp and party. Passengers alight in the town plaza on the southwest side of Dewey.

A cargo ferry takes a limited number of cars to and from Culebra, but is often fully booked weeks in advance, and bringing a car to the island is truly more hassle than it's worth. Passengers may take the cargo ferry, but be warned that the ride is considerably rougher. The schedule is subject to change, so call ahead.

FERRY SCHEDULE

It's always best to call ahead to ask about changes in schedules.

PASSENGER FERRY

WEEKDAYS

Fajardo to Culebra . . . . 9:30 a.m. and 3 p.m.
Culebra to Fajardo . . . . 11 a.m. and 4:30 p.m.

SATURDAYS AND SUNDAYS

Fajardo to Culebra . . . . 9 a.m. and 4 p.m.
Culebra to Fajardo . . . . 7 a.m., 2 p.m. and 5:30 p.m.

CARGO FERRY

WEEKDAYS

Fajardo to Culebra . . . . 10 a.m. (and 4 p.m. Wednesday and Friday)
Culebra to Fajardo . . . . 1 p.m. (and 7 a.m. Wednesday and Friday)

SATURDAY (no service on Sunday)

Fajardo to Culebra . . . . 4:30 a.m. and 4 p.m.
Culebra to Fajardo . . . . 7 a.m. and 6 p.m.

■ Travel Between Vieques & Culebra

There is no official and published passenger route between Vieques and Culebra (a once-monthly ferry was recently discontinued), which unfortunately discourages many travelers from visiting both islands. However, the **Isla Nena Air Service**, ☎ 787-741-6362 or 888-263-6213, flies mail and newspapers from Isabel Segunda in Vieques to Culebra each morning – sometimes twice, at 6:30 and 8:30 a.m. – and will take passengers for $20 each, one way, if they have room. Most charter companies fly between the two islands, too, but the prices are usually higher. Try calling pilot **Tony Bennett** on Vieques, ☎ 787-741-0292, tony@mangovieques.com, who offers negotiable rates, or the charter companies listed above. For hardy adventurers hoping to reach Culebra directly from Vieques, head to the fishing docks in Isabel Segunda at about 5 a.m. and ask one of the fishermen to drop you at Culebra on their way to fishing grounds. They'll usually charge $20 or so, and if the seas are rough you may get soaked. Otherwise, you can catch connecting ferries by returning to Fajardo, but it may cost you an extra two to three hours.

Getting Around

Shaped like a crab claw, Culebra is small enough (roughly five miles long and three miles wide) that many people choose to bike around the island. The most popular spots on the island are **Playa Flamenco** (a wide cove of sand on the north coast), **Playa Tamarindo** and **Playa Carlos Rosario** on the west coast, and **Playa Larga** and **Playa Zoni** on the east coast. The offshore cays of **Culebrita**, to the east, and **Luis Peña**, to the west, are also favorites. The town of **Dewey**, where you'll find most guest houses, restaurants and what passes for activity, is located on the "thumb" of the claw, on the the southwest side of the island.

■ Rental Cars

Most rental car agencies are located near the airport, just north of Dewey on Carr. 251, within easy walking distance if you arrive by plane. Visitors arriving on the ferry should allow 15 minutes to walk through town toward the airport, or arrange with the rental agency to be picked up at the plaza. Most rental agents are happy to do so. One rental agency, **Tamarindo Car Rental**, ☎ 787-742-0550, is located within the airport terminal, and for this reason is usually the first to run out of cars. **Jerry's Jeeps**, ☎ 787-742-0587 or 0526, is right across the street, detected by an open doorway and lots of mechanical endeavor going on. Added bonuses of renting through Jerry are his own hand-drawn map of the island, detailed information on the best spots, and lots of interesting anecdotes on what it's like to live in Culebra. If you're nice, he might even give you a quick 15-minute tour just to get you started. If Jerry's all out of Jeeps, try Willy, a plumber, Jeep rental guy, water taxi and snorkel equipment provider. He's just down the block at **Willy's Jeep Rentals**, ☎ 787-742-3537.

ON THE BEATEN TRACK

Rental agencies will ask you to keep your vehicles on paved roads. On the back roads are acacia bushes with talon-like thorns, which regularly puncture car tires.

■ Públicos & Taxis

A *público* runs from the ferry dock across the island to **Playa Flamenco** for those coming for a day-trip who do not wish to rent a Jeep. It leaves the dock shortly after the ferries arrive, and stops by Playa Flamenco in time to pick up beachgoers to catch every departing ferry. Otherwise, unless you rent your own wheels or hitchhike, you'll need to call a taxi: try **Romero**, ☎ 787-742-0250; **Willy**, ☎ 787-742-3537; or **Tony**, ☎ 787-742-0148, cell 512-3334.

■ Mountain Bikes

An excellent, invigorating and more economical way to get around the island is by bike. The **Culebra Bike Shop**, ☎ 787-742-2209, has 20 mountain bikes for rent at $15 a day or $80 a week. The shop is usually open Monday-Thursday mornings, 9 a.m. to noon (closed Tuesdays), and Friday- Sunday, 9 a.m. to noon and 4:30 to 7:30 p.m. If they're booked, some of the guest house and boat owners in town occasionally rent out bikes, too, so ask around.

TOO FEW WHEELS

During the height of tourist season (holiday weekends and between February and April), car and bike rentals are sometimes fully booked. Make reservations early!

Communications & Information

Rather than wasting your time at the useless tourist office near the ferry dock, head straight to Leslie Alteri at **eXcétera**, Calle Sallisberry (opposite the Hotel Puerto Rico), ☎ 787-742-0844, fax 742-0826, who (like many locals) keeps her finger on the daily pulse of Culebra. If you've arranged to meet friends on the island and can't locate them, there's a good chance Leslie will know where they're staying. If you get sick, she's a trained pharmacist and can fax a prescription to San Juan and have medication shipped back to Culebra within 24 hours (weekdays). You can check and send e-mail ($5 for 15 minutes, $15 an hour), make long distance phone calls, send faxes, rent a mailbox, use eXcétera as a temporary phone number for incoming calls or take advantage of the message board. The little shop also has nautical charts, a small but good selection of English language magazines and books, and useful information about Culebra, including a full directory of businesses and individuals on the island, the Culebra Calendar and the Tourist Times. It's also home to the only travel agent on Culebra, **4 Seasons Travel**, ☎ 787-742-0231, where M.J. Mattson can help you organize everything from island hopping to flights to Japan.

Also extremely helpful are Bruce and Kathie Goble at **La Loma Gift Shop**, Calle Escudero in Dewey, ☎ 787-742-3565, who publish the Isla de Culebra *Tourist Guide*, which costs $2.50 and is chock-full of information.

Touring & Sightseeing

■ In Town

Start your tour of Culebra in the "pulsing metropolis" of **Dewey** – known to locals simply as *el pueblo* – a few streets lined with colorful cottages, guest houses, restaurants, boat charters and gift shops. It offers waterfront sunshine and an easygoing vibe. From the ferry dock, walk along the waterfront past Culebra Divers and Hotel Kokomo to the **freight dock**. A little plaza here with a mahogany tree comes alive every day at 5:30 p.m., when the cargo ferry – still the island's lifeline – arrives with supplies from Fajardo. You'll see a sign for a tourist office, but ignore it. You'll get much better information from local guesthouse and business owners.

Descending Calle Pedro Marquez, past the blue concrete City Hall on the left and the post office on the right, you'll come to a triangle of one-way streets, where you'll see the run-down Hotel Puerto Rico, a school library, the Culebra Dive Shop and **Colmado Esperanza**, known to locals as Rafy's, the oldest building in town. Built in 1903, shortly after the Navy established Dewey, it is one of only four buildings that survived the devastation of Hurricane San Ciprián in 1932. You'll also pass the home of a local character who has turned his small front yard into a "garden" of irreverently painted Navy bomb shells, as well as old buoys, tractor tires, ceramic geese and other wacky items.

Across the street from Citibank, a curving road along the lagoon leads past **Mamacitas**, a restaurant and happy hour hangout, and **Paradise Gift Shop**, one of several places to buy handmade tropical crafts, spices, Caribbean clothing and wraps, straw hats, etc., and the only place in town to pick up copies of the *San Juan Star* newspaper. Turn right at the end of this road to cross the "drawbridge" between Laguna Lobina and Ensenada Honda. Originally built to maintain boat passage through the narrow channel, the drawbridge lost its draw when the government ran electrical lines underneath it, making the opening too shallow to allow passage of deeper and V-hulled craft, such as most sailboats. The channel is now filled with enough silt to allow passage of only the smallest boats, and the municipal government has immobilized the useless drawbridge by weld-

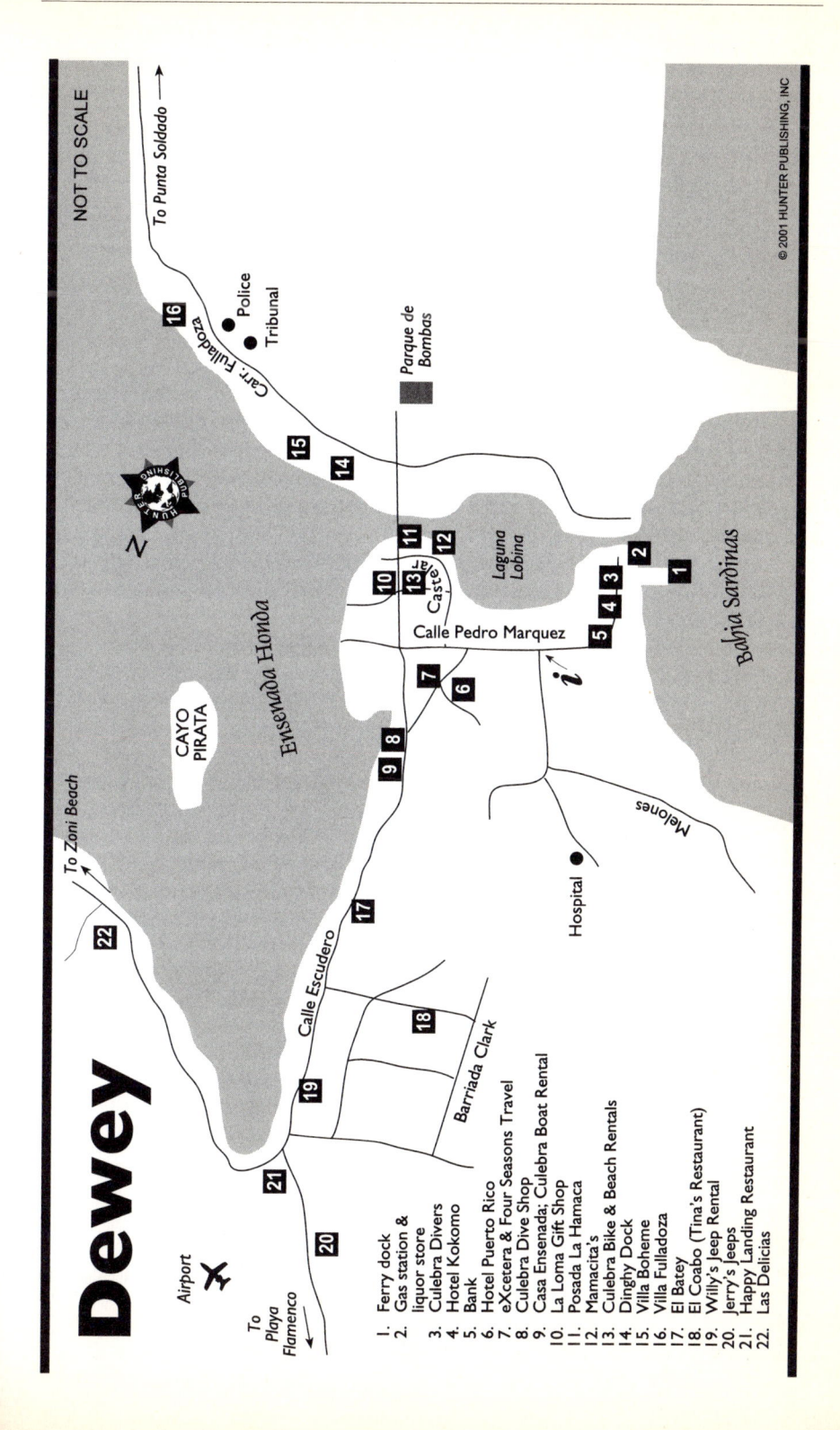

Dewey

NOT TO SCALE

1. Ferry dock
2. Gas station & liquor store
3. Culebra Divers
4. Hotel Kokomo
5. Bank
6. Hotel Puerto Rico
7. eXcetera & Four Seasons Travel
8. Culebra Dive Shop
9. Casa Ensenada; Culebra Boat Rental
10. La Loma Gift Shop
11. Posada La Hamaca
12. Mamacita's
13. Culebra Bike & Beach Rentals
14. Dinghy Dock
15. Villa Boheme
16. Villa Fulladoza
17. El Batey
18. El Coabo (Tina's Restaurant)
19. Willy's Jeep Rental
20. Jerry's Jeeps
21. Happy Landing Restaurant
22. Las Delicias

ing it fast. Turn left past the bridge and find the **Dinghy Dock** (restaurant and dock), **Reef Link Divers**, and some of the best guest houses in town en route to Punta Soldado (Soldier's Point).

> **TIP:** *Although Culebra may be a laid-back tropical isle, downtown areas are not Miami Beach or Ibiza. Local ordinances stipulate against wearing only swimwear around town – this means shirts are required for men and bathing suit cover-ups for women.*

If you re-cross the bridge and head toward the airport, look for **El Batey** on the left, a popular local hangout and burger joint, and the municipal baseball stadium behind it. Because all air and sea transport between Culebra and the main island of Puerto Rico shuts down after dark, visiting baseball teams spend Saturday nights in a dormitory behind the stadium and enjoy the hospitality of their opponents and local restaurant owners. This area marks the beginning of **Barriada Clark**, the first housing subdivision built after the Navy left the island, characterized by tiny cottages. Few gringos hang out in this part of the island; here you can get a good feel for purely *culebrense* culture. Residents sell sweets and vegetables from small stands outside their homes, and in the late afternoon the little roads are thick with children playing in their school uniforms and their parents standing in groups to socialize and gossip. Practice your Spanish and joke with the locals. To reach the center of the action, take the first left after El Batey to Colmado Romero and Restaurant El Caobo, better known as Tina's. Another popular hangout is **Happy Landings Restaurant & Bar**, located just east of the airport.

■ Around Culebra

From the airport, Carr. 251 leads northwest through thorny acacias and other scrub toward **Playa Flamenco**, the most popular spot on the island, which also has the only camping ground. About halfway to the beach, an overgrown Spanish well is one of the only signs that Iberian settlers ever set foot on Culebra. Reaching Playa Flamenco, depending on whether it's a weekday or weekend, you'll find either a nearly deserted paradise or a heaving campground on the sand where, as one resident put it, "people come over from Puerto Rico to stand testicle-deep in water and knock back Finlandia and orange juice all day." Park and walk west to reach **Tamarindo Grande** beach and the island's best snorkeling site, **Playa Carlos Rosario**. Another path leads to **Peninsula Flamenco**, but in order to hike into this protected seabird nesting area you must first request permission from the US Fish and Wildlife Service, ☎ 787-742-0115.

Backtrack on Carr. 251 and turn left onto the dirt road just before the airport to reach the old **Navy helipad**, with spectacular views of the island, including Flamenco and Resaca beaches. From the turnoff, pass the Flamenco lagoon until the road forks at a former Navy lookout post, then bear right up an old concrete road. Keep left at the next fork until you reach another Navy observation post (this one's red and yellow). Park here and hike a quarter mile up to the helipad.

Heading in the opposite direction from the airport, Carr. 250 skirts the northern side of **Ensenada Honda** (Deep Cove), dotted with mangrove and dry scrub, on the road toward **Playa Zoni**. The first left-hand turnoff past the airport leads to the **Playa Resaca** trailhead. Continuing on Carr. 250 affords great views of the cove, **Punta Soldado** (Soldier's Point) and **Cayo Pirata** (Pirate's Cay). Just past the small, pretty town cemetery that rises up the side of a hill, you'll notice an old desalination plant that stands unused on the right-hand side of the road – once the island's main source of water. Plans are in the works to repair it for use as a backup for the pipeline that now brings water from mainland Puerto Rico via Vieques.

Just past the desalination plant, a right-hand turnoff leads to the Department of Natural and Environmental Resources and the US Fish and Wildlife Service. In general, the DNER are friendly, but less helpful or informed than Teresa Tallevast at the Fish and Wildlife Service, who is both a font of information about the ecosystems of Culebra and a community activist. From here, Carr. 250 winds up to a bluff overlooking Zoni Beach, with commanding views of Isla Culebrita, surrounding cays and, in the distance, St. Thomas of the US Virgin Islands.

■ Touring The Cays

Ensenada Honda

Cayo Pirata is in the middle of Ensenada Honda, and gets its name from pirates such as Captain Henry Morgan, who apparently used the deep, protected waters of the cove as a hiding place back in the buccaneer days. Don't expect to find hidden treasure, though, or much else for that matter. A well-intentioned picnic spot, with *bohíos* (huts), tables and a boat landing, has succumbed to overgrowth and mosquitoes, and few boaters venture here. Before leaving Ensenada Honda by boat and heading northeast, you'll pass two little mangrove-covered cays in Bahía Manglar, a safe haven for boaters during hurricanes. Though neither cay has a beachhead, they attract a few adventurous kayakers.

Isla Culebrita

East of Playa Zoni, the uninhabited island of Culebrita forms roughly the same crab-claw shape as Culebra, in a smaller version. Towering over the little island's highest point, the Culebrita lighthouse – built of reddish-brown stone by the Spanish – is claimed to be the oldest lighthouse in the Caribbean. Unfortunately, its poor state of repair has prompted the DNER to let the trails leading to it become overgrown to discourage visitors.

Approaching Culebrita by boat, you'll see the outlines of St. Thomas and, midway, Sail Rock, which sticks out of the water like an enormous shark fin. Most water taxis to Culebrita drop passengers on the westernmost beach, from which a trailhead leads to an easy 15-minute walk on a well-maintained trail northeast to **Playa Tortuga**, the main attraction of Culebrita. Nearly a mile long, Playa Tortuga was "discovered" by the masses in the late 1990s, and on weekends you may find up to two dozen pleasure craft moored here, making it seem more like a drive-in than a deserted isle. On weekdays, though, there may be just one or two (or zero) boats here, and you can walk along its luxurious sandy beach and swim in relative privacy. In the same bay, two tide pools known as **The Baths** – smaller versions of the baths of Virgin Gorda – are incredible swimming areas, where you may wade in chest-high water with angelfish, sergeant majors and other large tropical fish that get stuck here between high tides. The clear water reveals underwater white-sand flats, turtle grass and, often, turtles that feed on the grass (hence the name Playa Tortuga), making it an idyllic spot for a day-trip by boat.

From Playa Tortuga, a five-minute walk along a trail to the eastern side of the island ends at a less-inspiring strip of sand known as **Trash Beach**, because the rough waves send debris ashore from St. Thomas and the sea at large.

Just north of Culebrita are **Cayo Botella**, **Cayo Henike** and **Cayo Ballena**, which are all bird sanctuaries (with no beachheads). They are the protected nesting grounds of sooty terns and other seabirds. The large, snail-shaped **Cayo Norte** is the only cay around Culebra with private structures on it (a couple of small, forlorn houses). Owned by members of an extended family who can't agree what to do with the lovely cay, it is populated mostly by goats, brought long ago by a would-be herdsman and now run wild.

AMPHIBIOUS DEER

If you see what looks like a deer on Culebrita, don't pinch yourself – you're not dreaming. About half a dozen white-tailed deer now live on the cay, having swum over from the main island of Culebra.

Cayo Luis Peña

Named for the second owner of this cay, Cayo Luis Peña has a few excellent snorkeling spots and isolated beaches, and is now a nature reserve. Palm trees, dense foliage and rocky terrain fringe Playa Norte on the northeastern side of the cay, making it inaccessible from other parts of the cay. A single boat mooring just offshore ensures that if you land here, you'll be the only castaway on this gorgeous stretch of deserted shoreline. The bluff on the western end of the cay serves as a breeding ground for the long-tailed tropicbird, so named because during its summer breeding season it grows dual tail feathers that may reach two feet or more in length. At the lower neck of the cay, a short sand path connects two opposing beaches. Protected from the wind and waves, the west-facing beach is cleaner with some great snorkeling around live coral heads. Just west of Cayo Luis Peña, you'll see the wishbone-shaped Cayo Lobo, with two long-abandoned Navy observation decks sprouting from either side. Rumor has it that the Navy used this relatively flat cay as a dumping ground for Agent Orange during the early 1970s and, although it's still pretty green, many locals are wary of going near it.

Adventures

■ On Wheels

Culebra is the perfect size for getting around by pedal power. Most beaches and attractions are no more than 30 minutes away by bike, the roads are often empty of traffic and a couple of hills on the north and east side of the island (along Carr. 250) challenge even in-shape bikers. A few curving downs on the road to Playa Resaca and around Playa Zoni will get the adrenaline pumping. The rest of the island is a breeze, and recent road paving makes things easier for bikers. Locals recommend against riding on many of the dirt roads because it's easy to run over a thorny acacia twig and puncture a tire. Also, be sure to lock up bikes when you hit the beach, especially when tourists flood in on weekends. "Bikes don't get stolen," says Culebra Bike Shop owner Steve Harding. "But they do get borrowed." **Culebra Bike Shop**, ☎ 787-742-2209 (shop), 742-0434 (home), has 20 front- and full-suspension mountain bikes available for $15/$80 per day/week, as well as beach chairs, towels and coolers for $5 per day.

■ On Water

Beaches

Culebra is blessed with a few of the best beaches in the Caribbean – wide stretches of sand the color and texture of icing sugar – with virtually no one on them. Although nude and topless sunbathing is generally frowned upon in mainland Puerto Rico, Culebra has a more laid-back attitude, and on the lonelier stretches of sand you may encounter sun worshippers seeking to erase all tan lines. The following four beaches are attractive more for their sunbathing and solitude. Other beaches with reef-oriented attractions are listed below (see *Snorkeling*).

PLAYA FLAMENCO – This beach, named after the pink flamingo birds that used to occupy the adjacent lagoon, is practically deserted during the week, even though it's the most popular beach. By Saturday morning, however, hundreds and sometimes thousands of weekend warriors from mainland Puerto Rico dog-pile onto Playa Flamenco, turning it into a standing-room-only party. A two-mile horseshoe of sand at least 20 yards wide slopes gently into electric blue waters, making this a perfect swimming beach. Two innocuous reminders of naval occupation bookend Playa Flamenco. To the east, an abandoned tank, once a bombing target, sinks into sand and has been painted with cool graffiti designs. To the west, two rock jetties designate the spot where Navy Seals once tested repellents and sonar devices on caged sharks before venturing into the deep. Neither of these oddities detracts from the natural beauty of Flamenco, which remains one of the best and most photographed beaches in the Caribbean. From the southeast corner of the parking lot, a trail leads to **Playa Carlos Rosario** (see *Snorkeling*).

LUNCHBOX REQUIRED

Coconuts Café at Culebra Beach Villas on Playa Flamenco is the only beach bar on the island, and is open intermittently. So pack a lunch, cold drinks and plenty of water before heading to the sand.

PLAYA ZONI – On the sunrise side of Culebra, Zoni Beach was named for a lone Englishman who once lived here. Today a few millionaire playpens command the cliff top over two miles of unspoiled beach, which never gets crowded. A highlight here is the view of neighboring Cayo Norte, Culebrita and St. Thomas. To get here, follow Carr. 250 from the airport for about 20 minutes until you reach a steep hill, dug up in places. Pass a castle-scale set of private villas on your right, park near the bottom of the hill near three green-roofed cabañas, then walk down about three minutes to the beach. Do not attempt to drive all the way down to the beach, or you may get stuck.

PLAYAS RESACA & BRAVA – If you're intent on finding a completely isolated stretch of sand, these two beaches are rarely visited by anyone except mother turtles laying their eggs. The more remote of the two, Playa Resaca involves a steep, 30-minute hike through the dry forest scrub. Despite voracious mosquitoes, prickly brush, razor grass, boulders and holes in the ground, the hike is well worth it to get to a mile of golden sand and solitude, surrounded by vacant hills and sky. Wear bug repellent, reef-sandals or hiking shoes and protective clothing, and then strip down once you reach the bottom.

> **CAUTION:** *Resaca is Spanish for undertow (and hangover), so check currents before heading into water higher than your shins. The flip side of absolute solitude is that no one will see you if you get pulled out to sea. Also, tread carefully and close to the water during springtime, as this is a nesting ground for leatherback turtles.*

To reach Playa Resaca, follow Carr. 250 out of town and take the first left turn after the airstrip. A concrete road winds steeply up a hill and ends in a circular parking space. Look for an opening in the bushes on the ocean side of the parking area (not the well-worn two-track path leading up the hill to the radio tower).

The route to Playa Brava involves kindlier, flatter terrain, with no evil vegetative claws tugging at your clothing or slashing your legs (this also increases the chances of having to share the beach, of course). The second half of the hike – a "butterfly trail" with lovely *Mariposas amarillas* flitting though the air – passes a water well constructed in the 1900s for cattle. The beach is very similar to Playa Resaca, with a wide swath of sunset yellow sand and slightly more shade. With the biggest waves on Culebra, Playa Brava also suffers from a riptide that can easily sweep you out to sea. Don't go out of your depth here, no matter how good a swimmer you think you are. Follow Carr. 250 past the cemetery until you reach a Danish-built structure with the date 1905 over the doorway. Turn left and follow the road through a grove of mesquite trees until you get to two small farmsteads. Park in front of the signs marked "private property" and walk straight north. Property owners must allow beach access by law, and the signs are mostly for show.

Water Taxis

Part of the magic of Culebra is the chance to visit its surrounding cays – often deserted islets with hidden sandy coves, rocky and coral baths and some of the best snorkeling in the Caribbean. A number of "water taxis" will ferry you to Isla Culebrita or Cayo Luis Peña in the morning and pick you up in the afternoon. There are several to choose from, and most charge roughly the same per person: $25 round-trip to Cayo Luis Peña and $40 round-trip to Isla Culebrita. Check out *Tanamá*, ☎ 787-501-0011, hand-built by a late Culebra legend named Lana, and now run by Captain Pat. A six-by-two-foot glass bottom lets you peek at shallow reefs along the way. She also offers snorkeling trips. **Guilín**, ☎ 787-742-1061 (after 4.30 p.m.), cell 314-6163, goes everywhere, and also offers snorkeling, diving and fishing charters. Or try Willy of **Willy's Water Taxi**, ☎ 787-742-3537, who knows all the good snorkeling spots (he also rents out Jeeps and runs a ground taxi service).

Sailing & Powerboat Charters

For a more intimate, daylong tour of the local cays, we highly recommend heading out to sea with **Bayhunter Charters**, ☎ 787-742-0559, www.bayhunter.com. Instead of simply dumping you on a cay to fend for yourself, guides Barry Trexler and (his "better half") M.J. Mattson provide several day-trip tour options, ranging in price from $45 to $80 per person. He operates a powerboat with cabin, and she handles the sailing. Both prefer groups of fewer than six.

Dan Gilmore at **Club Seabourne**, ☎ 787-742-3169, and Chris Goldmark, ☎ 787-742-0412, can also help organize a guided trip to the cays, including lunch and guidance to the best snorkel spots, for $45 per person for a six- or seven-hour day out. Ask Chris about adding a "turtle tour" to your trip.

A SKIFF OF YOUR OWN

Visitors wanting to do some exploring solo can rent a motorboat from **Casa Ensenada & Culebra Boat Rental**, ☎ 787-742-3559, cell 309-1122. Depending on the size and type of boat you get, it will cost between $150 and $175 for the first day, $100 and $125 for additional days. You will need to demonstrate motorboat and coastal navigation experience and be 25 or older. A 14-foot Sunfish is also available for the day ($75) and half-day ($50). You need to be over 15 years and have some previous sailing experience. In both cases you need to assure the owners you can swim, just in case!

Kayaking

Kayaking along the coast or in the coves and lagoons of Culebra is a great adventure, and on days when the sea is calm you may even be able to reach Cayo Luis Peña or Isla Culebrita. Chances are, if you're staying at one of the guest houses facing Ensenada Honda or Laguna Lobina, your hosts will rent out kayaks (sometimes they're included with the price of the room). Jim and Barbara at **Ocean Safari**, ☎ 787-379-1973, will deliver and collect kayaks wherever and whenever. Also try **Culebra Dive Shop**, ☎ 787-742-0566, or **Casa Ensenada & Culebra Boat Rental**, ☎ 787-742-3559, cell 309-1122. Kayak rental is a standard $40 per day on the island.

WHALE WATCHING

Although you may not find "whale-watching tours" listed as attractions in Culebra, anyone heading into the channel between Culebra and Isla Culebrita between December and April has a good chance of seeing a magnificent humpback whale break the water's surface as it travels to the warm breeding grounds of the Caribbean.

Deep-Sea & Fly-Fishing

Anyone who loves fly-fishing should contact **Chris Goldmark**, ☎ 787-742-0412, who will take you out wading in knee-deep flats of sand and grass and help you hook up a bonefish, one of the fastest sea creatures in the world. They average about eight pounds in the shallows on the eastern side of Culebra. You'll find yourself sight casting in transparent water with stunning surroundings. Ask about tarpon fishing in the area, too. If you bring a camera, have it ready at hand when you've finally brought in your quarry. Favoring a quick release, Chris always errs on the side of the safety of the fish rather than a good photo op. He prefers to take clients individually, but will take two people to a site if you insist, for $35 an hour, all equipment included. At **Culebra Dive Shop**, ☎ 787-742-0566, cell 501-4656, fax 742-1953, www.culebradiveshop.com, e-mail divecul@coqui.net, Captain Richard Cantwell offers deep-sea fishing for tuna, dorado, wahoo and other game fish for $400 (half-day) or $600 (full day).

Diving

With more than 50 excellent sites, Culebra is one of the hottest dive destinations in the Virgin Islands. Unlike Vieques, Culebra is protected by two barrier reefs on the west coast and is relatively unaffected by strong trade winds that can sometimes shut down diving on its southern neighbor for days at a time. Off limits as a Navy training ground until 1975, and protected by the US Fish and Wildlife Service since then, nearly all of the reefs are still in excellent condition. Flourishing marine life includes stingrays, turtles, barracuda, blue tang and several species of angelfish, many of which are seen on a typical dive. Although runoff from increasing island development is beginning to cause a buildup of sediment that kills both coral and turtle grass, Culebra still has some of the healthiest offshore reefs around. With many sites to choose from, one could easily spend a two-week diving holiday in Culebra and never hit the same spot twice. Highlights include:

- A mile-long **reef** sweeps south of Culebrita, with a maximum depth of about 90 feet. Noted for an intact tugboat wreck 30 feet down with its stacks just 12 feet below the surface, this is also a popular spot for adventurous snorkelers. The tugboat went down in 1989 and is overgrown with fiery-colored corals and blooming polyps, in an area full of popular dive sites. Nearby, in November 2000, two locals lost a sailboat in about 100 feet of water not far from the tugboat wreck. The victims (and their cat) survived, thankfully, and the intact wreck may soon be explored by more advanced divers.
- On the other side of Culebra, sharks occasionally roam the reef around **Punta Soldado**, which is a popular spot on a calm day.
- East of Cayo Luis Peña is a beautiful single pinnacle dive called **Las Hermanas**, which has intricate stuccoes of hard and soft corals, giant sea fans and sponges creating a tapestry of blinding color.
- For exceptional sea life, don't miss a trip to **Sail Rock**. This is the one destination where dive masters practically guarantee you'll see turtles. Underwater, the "rock" includes six or seven awesome pinnacles, all about 60 feet in diameter, dropping from about 30 feet at their highest points to 125 feet at the bottom. This is also a good destination for spotting spiny lobster and large schools of iridescent barracuda.
- For fairy-tale underwater architecture, check out **Arch Dive** – a series of large boulders worn smooth over time into the shape of an arch, and **Amberjack Hole**, a "cleaning station" where large fish congregate to allow smaller fish and shrimp to relieve them of microscopic parasites. The water sometimes gets stew thick with French angels, grunts, triggerfish and blue tangs.
- Until 1975, the Navy used **Anchor Reef** for mooring their ships and it's a good place for spotting rogue naval artifacts, including a massive chain and anchor in the process of becoming a living thing.

DIVE OPERATORS

The oldest diving operator on the island is **Culebra Dive Shop**, ☎ 787-742-0566, cell 501-4656, fax 742-1953, a good bet for anyone interested in underwater photography (check out their album of photos, many of which are available as postcards in town). Captain Richard Cantwell, a keen underwater photographer, is happy to advise beginning and advanced underwater shooters. This is also the only shop in town that specializes in drift dives, which, according to dive master Carlos, is excellent in the channel between Culebra and Cayo Norte and Culebrita. One- and two-tank dives are $45 and $85 respectively. A night dive costs $60 and a discovery dive costs $90 (all equipment included on both). Open-water PADI or PDIC certification cost $450. Boat guests can come along and enjoy the ride for $25 per person. Snorkelers get a full day at sea for $45, including gear, lunch and refreshments. Call for dive and hotel packages.

Swiss couple Monika Frei and Walter Rieder also have a sterling reputation, and run **Culebra Divers**, ☎/fax 787-742-0803, located across from the ferry dock, www.culebradivers.com. Morning dive trips cost $75 for two tanks, $60 for a night dive, and $80 for an "easy scuba experience," which lets you try scuba diving without committing to the certification process. If you decide to go for it, Walter and Monika offer full NAUI certification for $450. If you've done register dives (basic training) at home, completion of open water training costs $250. Many islanders say Culebra Divers is the best operation for snorkeling. Monika and Walter cover Punta Soldado, Cayo Luis Peña and Carlos Rosario, where marine life and coral is absolutely pristine and hugely varied. Snorkel lessons for cautious first-timers costs $45 and includes two sites. Snorkeling gear rents for $12.50 a day, $10 a day for two to four days, and $7.50 a day for five to seven days.

Snorkeling Sites

CARLOS ROSARIO AND THE WALL – Probably the best snorkeling site in Puerto Rico, the reef begins about 100 yards north of the path to Flamenco Beach, surrounding a white sandy bottom and beach, with eels and tropical abundance feeding on wide coral that dips to 18 feet and deeper. Just north of here, The Wall shoots along the Peninsula Flamenco in a mile-long reef that drops from exposed coral to 40 feet in kaleidoscope bursts of color. With rays, nurse sharks, barracuda and teeming sea life common here, this site draws dive boats all the way from Fajardo.

TAMARINDO AND LITTLE TAMARINDO – Just south of Carlos Rosario, the shores are rockier and the snorkeling impressive around coral heads about 10 feet under water. Nice, but not as awe-inspiring as The Wall.

PLAYA MELONES – The closest beach and snorkeling to town features live coral heads about 10 feet underwater, especially at either end of the beach.

PUNTA SOLDADO – Just offshore from a coral beach on the western edge of the point, the reef eventually drops off to 50 feet. In late summer, walk behind the point to Bahía Tiburón, where nurse sharks come to breed, and you may swim freely with these bottom feeders, especially in the early morning or just before dusk.

WESTERN CULEBRITA - On the sunset-facing beach, look for a small nipple of coral sticking out of the water, called **Dragon's Head**, about 100 yards off the old concrete dock. Good snorkeling all around here. It's popular with novice divers.

PLAYA TORTUGA TIDE POOLS - Perfect for novice snorkelers, these swimming pool-sized baths are rarely deeper than chest height, with a grab bag of sea life trapped between high tides. Don't be surprised to find yourself among big grouper, angelfish, sergeant majors and other fish you'd ordinarily have to go looking for – suddenly you're sharing a bath with them! Climb over boulders at the northeast corner of Playa Tortuga for access.

CAYO NORTE - On the southeastern tip of the cay, along the stretch of beach, a favorite snorkeling site is thick with a forest of sea fans and tropical fish.

Eco-Travel

■ Volunteer For Turtle Watch

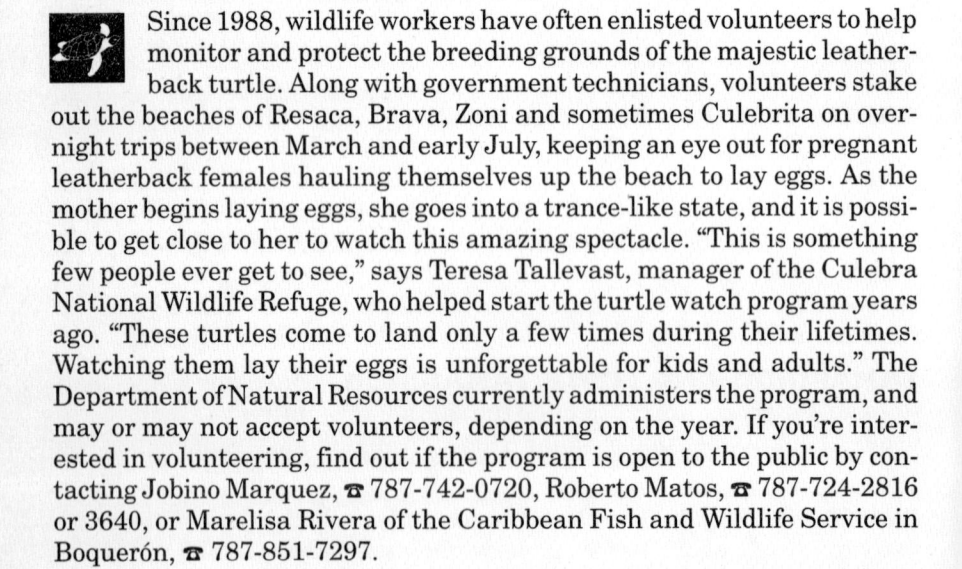

Since 1988, wildlife workers have often enlisted volunteers to help monitor and protect the breeding grounds of the majestic leatherback turtle. Along with government technicians, volunteers stake out the beaches of Resaca, Brava, Zoni and sometimes Culebrita on overnight trips between March and early July, keeping an eye out for pregnant leatherback females hauling themselves up the beach to lay eggs. As the mother begins laying eggs, she goes into a trance-like state, and it is possible to get close to her to watch this amazing spectacle. "This is something few people ever get to see," says Teresa Tallevast, manager of the Culebra National Wildlife Refuge, who helped start the turtle watch program years ago. "These turtles come to land only a few times during their lifetimes. Watching them lay their eggs is unforgettable for kids and adults." The Department of Natural Resources currently administers the program, and may or may not accept volunteers, depending on the year. If you're interested in volunteering, find out if the program is open to the public by contacting Jobino Marquez, ☎ 787-742-0720, Roberto Matos, ☎ 787-724-2816 or 3640, or Marelisa Rivera of the Caribbean Fish and Wildlife Service in Boquerón, ☎ 787-851-7297.

QUEEN OF THE TURTLES

By far the largest living sea turtle, leatherbacks can weigh up to 1,400 pounds and measure as long as seven feet. Unlike many turtles, the leatherback does not have a hard shell but a black leathery skin, covered by white blotches and seven longitudinal ridges. A friend to all swimmers, it feeds on jellyfish. Females typically nest on the same sandy beach on which they were born, between March and July. During nesting period, the mother-to-be heaves herself onto the beach every 10 days or so (three to eight times during the season), and lays about 100 eggs. Fewer than one in 1,000 hatchlings survive to adulthood, due to nest poaching, predators and the disposal of plastics in or near the water.

Where To Stay

Thumbing through a list of Culebra guest houses, you'll no doubt be amazed at how many there are – close to 30 on an island of just 2,000 inhabitants. Yet Culebra doesn't feel crowded, because most of the guest houses are small, with 10 rooms or fewer, and blend in with the Caribbean cottage feel of the island. This will undoubtedly change in the years and decades to come, especially when a planned sewage system makes way for larger developments. For now, though, Culebra remains (as residents here like to say) "the last virgin" in the Virgin Islands.

ACCOMMODATIONS PRICE KEY

Rates are per room, per night, double occupancy. Single occupancy may or may not get you a discount, so ask when making a reservation. Breakfast included where noted.

$	Up to $50
$$	$50 to $100
$$$	$101 to $150
$$$$	$150 and up

■ Dewey

Next door to the Dinghy Dock, **Villa Boheme**, ☎ 787-742-3508, www.villaboheme.com, has been recently acquired by Rico, a gregarious *sanjuanero*, who is renovating it with panache. It promises to be a good place for social families and couples, with plenty of outdoor space, barbecue, hammocks and a communal kitchen for rooms that don't have kitchenettes. Rooms come in all shapes and sizes, some with sea views, others with decks or balconies. Rico provides guests with beach chairs, umbrellas and coolers, and rents out sports equipment from the property. Ask him about romantic champagne and moonlight cruises, for $75 a couple. $$-$$$

In what might be called "downtown," **Mamacitas**, ☎ 787-742-0090, Calle Castelar, has a couple of double rooms and two fully equipped apartments for longer stays above a funky Caribbean bar and restaurant; $$. Next door at **Posada La Hamaca**, basic rooms and less than attentive service (as in, where's the toilet paper?) can be found, ☎ 787-742-3516, fax 742-0181, www.posada.com; $$. Both places have patios that overlook the canal.

Overlooking the ferry dock, the bright pink **Hotel Kokomo**, ☎ 787-742-0719, in the plaza, has small, slightly dingy rooms that are expensive for what you get compared other Culebra guest houses. $$

With its own dock on the road to the airport, **Casa Ensenada & Culebra Boat Rental**, ☎ 787-742-3559, cell 309-1122, Calle Escudero (near the baseball field), www.choice1.com/censenada.htm, is small and unspectacular, but includes the use of kayaks with the price of rooms. All three rooms have TV and VCR, if you need to escape the sunshine. Choose from a double, studio with kitchen or a one-bedroom apartment and kitchen (the only one with a sea view). $$-$$$

For total budget accommodations, try **Hotel Puerto Rico**, ☎ 787-742-3372, Calle Pedro Marquez. It's the rundown mint green-colored building as you come into town along Calle Escudero from the airport. $

If you're interested in long-term rentals or property for sale, call **Culebra Island Realty**, ☎ 787-742-0227.

■ Near Town

Culebra Island Villas, ☎ 787-742-0333, on the road to Playa Melones, west of the ferry dock in Dewey, has three unusual villas with a funky California design, overlooking Cayo Luis Peña. Available on a weekly basis for about $1,000.

The newest guest house on the hilltops overlooking Ensenada Honda Bay, the super-modern facilities at **Bahía Marina**, ☎ 787-742-0366, are an excellent choice for groups, as all double rooms can be converted into two-bedroom suites. Front units include balconies with a view of the cove, and there's a small swimming pool. None have cooking facilities. Ask about package deals, especially in low season. Bahía Marina is at the tail end of Carr. Fulladoza just before you reach Punta Soldado. Rates include breakfast. $$$

On the adjacent hill, also with postcard-perfect views of Ensenada Honda, **Club Seabourne**, ☎ 787-742-3169, fax 742-3178, Carr. Fulladoza, www.culebra-island.com (click on Places To Stay), e-mail seabourn@coqui.net, has long enjoyed a reputation as the best place to stay on Culebra. Eight cotton-candy-colored villas and cottages perch on the hillside, each with a private balcony, patio table and chairs. Clean rooms include air conditioning and large, comfortable beds. Surrounding the main house below, an outdoor bar, restaurant, freshwater swimming pool and living area with a small library make the Club Seabourne a favorite gathering place for happy hour. Cheaper rooms are available in the main house and the laid-back owners are happy to pick guests up at the airport or ferry dock. $$-$$$

Within walking distance from town, **Villa Fulladoza**, ☎ 787-742-3576, Carr. Fulladoza, is fun, frivolous and a good deal. Painted pastel pink, with bougainvillea and other tropical flowers spilling over its walls and a buxom nautical figurehead over the entrance, Fulladoza has a surprise around every corner. Within the gated walls, comfortable studio apartments overlook the bay and a garden filled with mariners' treasures and greenery, with hand-painted slogans such as "geck off" and "US Turd Snapper" painted in odd places throughout. $$

■ Flamenco Beach

One of the best guest houses in the Caribbean (and beyond) in terms of location, **Culebra Beach Villas**, ☎ 787-767-7575 or 643-1479, www.culebrabeachrental.com, is right on Playa Flamenco. With 33 units, it's one of the biggest ventures on the island, but remains classy and low-key with carved oak furniture and doors straight off the boat from Mexico, bright ceramic details and tiled floors. All have fully equipped kitchens for self-catering (there's no restaurant anywhere in the area) and giant beds. Choose from efficiency apartments for couples ($$$), three-bedroom villas sleeping up to eight people ($$$$), and beachfront penthouse suites ($$$$), and call well in advance for weekend or in-season reservations.

Next door, the little **Villa Flamenco Beach**, ☎ 787-742-0023, run by the friendly Gutierrez family, is slightly cheaper and also just a few steps away from Playa Flamenco. Four upstairs studios (two of which face the beach) have fully equipped kitchens and queen-sized beds. Downstairs, a family apartment with king-sized bed and rollout beds for the kids also includes a full kitchen. Bring your own beach towels, suntan lotion and basic groceries for the barbecue on the lawn. $$$

■ Camping

For $10 per night, you can pitch a tent at one of the choicest beaches in the Caribbean: **Playa Flamenco**. To get here, follow Carr. 251 northwest of the airport. It's clearly signposted and is an easy cycle ride for visitors traveling on two wheels. Tent spaces each have a picnic table, a barbecue and a trashcan, about 15 yards from the sugary sands and glittering water. Showers and bathrooms are available nearby. You'll no doubt find one of two extremes: on weekdays, you might have the place to yourself; on weekends and holidays (and during late summer), the campground is overrun with partiers from mainland Puerto Rico. Call ahead for reservations: ☎ 787-742-0600.

Where To Eat

Dining on Culebra is a matter of food, not cuisine. Eateries tend to be casual, serving simple items, with opening hours often in flux, depending on whether the cook or owner is around. For lunch on the beach, **Coconuts Beach Grill** (no phone), next to Culebra Beach Villas on Playa Flamenco, has barbecue and local appetizers, piña coladas and other fruity cocktails. Open weekends and intermittently during the week.

In Barriada Clark, **Restaurante el Caobo**, better known as Tina's, ☎ 787-742-3235, is the best spot on the island for old-style Puerto Rican fare, including beefsteak, barbecued chicken, pork chops or whole *chillo* (red snapper) served with rice, beans and *tostones*. The atmosphere is familiar and friendly, and on busy nights patrons pack themselves in around plastic tables for giant main courses that cost about $8-$10. Tina and Mirita serve food as long as the customers keep coming, which can be as late as 10 p.m. or as early as 8 p.m.

On Carr. 250 toward Playa Zoni, **Las Delicias** (no phone) is another island favorite for seafood, usually open weekends only. The signature dish is commonly, if not crudely, called *pescado en vagina*, a puff pastry that envelops a mound of marinated octopus, fish or conch. Dining takes place in an interior patio that formerly served as the island's cockfighting arena. As with many other restaurants, opening times are erratic, but Saturday and Sunday nights are usually a good bet. Dishes cost between $15 and $20.

For the best burgers on the island, head to **El Batey**, ☎ 787-742-3828, next to the municipal baseball field on Calle Escudero, and just say *seis onzas* (or go for a four-ounce *pequeño* burger if you don't need to prove yourself a rabid carnivore). Burgers and other sandwiches cost $4-$6, and there's plenty of cold beer in the fridge. On Friday nights, El Batey is the place to dance salsa and merengue, play pool and hang out with a wild mix of *culebrenses* and newer arrivals.

Right next to the airport on Carr. 250, **Happy Landing**, ☎ 787-742-0135, is a little bar and restaurant serving basic Puerto Rican food, as well as breakfast to workers who gather here to catch rides to construction sites and other jobs. Next to it, **Panadería El Patio**, ☎ 787-742-0374, is the place to order $3 sandwiches for a picnic on the beach. In town near the ferry dock, you'll also find a few cheap eats, such as pizza and Chinese food.

Restaurants opened by *norteamericanos* tend to be more expensive, and a few have made mixed-result stabs at fine dining. Most, however, offer basic fish and meat plates and good appetizers. And chefs may change almost monthly! One of the best eateries is the **Dinghy Dock**, ☎ 787-742-0233, on the left-hand side of Carr. Fulladoza just after the drawbridge, a colorful, dockside restaurant with a view across Ensenada Honda. Breakfasts include eggs benedict, smoked salmon on bagels, homemade quiche of the day and home baked fruit breads – rare treats on a tiny island – for $8 or less. In the evenings, the chefs wisely stick to grill food, using quality ingredients, and a couple of pasta dishes. The most expensive dish is around $20 but most are less than $15. In an admirable show of gastronomic assertion, the menu clearly states: "We cannot be responsible for the quality of dinners/burgers ordered well done."

Mamacitas, ☎ 787-742-0090, overlooking the water on Calle Castelar, is another colorful happy-hour hangout on the water, with holiday lights blinking perpetually and steel drum and reggae music pumping from the sound system. Popular with travelers, Mamacitas serves a respectable octopus salad and other appetizers. A whole fish of the day for two costs $30, steaks between $15 and $20, lasagna and pastelons (ripe plantains stuffed with meat or chicken) $12. The bar sometimes stays open until 11:30 p.m. or so for weekend parties.

The chef at **Club Seabourne Restaurant**, ☎ 787-742-3169, offers a lobster special, steaks and, for the homesick Brit, excellent fish and chips from $12 to $20 a head. The restaurant is about a mile south of Dewey, on Carr. Fulladoza toward Punta Soldado.

Also at the tail end of Carr. Fulladoza (near Punta Soldado), newcomer **Bahía Marina**, ☎ 787-742-0366, has a pleasant cliff-top restaurant with food by a San Juan chef who has previously cooked for both Café Matisse and the Caribe Hilton. Tipped to offer the best "cuisine" in Culebra, the menu reads well with shrimp in sherry for $18, Black Angus steaks for $18 and seafood dishes upwards of $20. The view over the bay is among the best on the island.

Spanish Phrases

Here are some basic words and phrases, as well as some expressions you won't find in most dictionaries. One note on usage: As a general rule, older people are more likely to use the formal *usted* form for "you" and young people usually use the informal *tu* form between each other. If in doubt, use *usted*, especially when first meeting someone.

■ Directions

Where is... ?	*¿Donde está el/la... ?*
How do you get to... ?	*¿Como llegar al/a la... ?*
hotel	*hotel*
guest house	*casa de huéspedes*
bathroom	*baño*
public telephone	*teléfono público*
restaurant	*restaurante*
museum	*museo*
airport	*aeropuerto*
bus/minibus	*guagua/público*
post office	*correo*
entrance/exit	*entrada/salida*
ticket office	*taquilla*
bank	*banco*
station	*estación*
Please write it down	*Escríbalo, por favor*
this way (over here)	*por aquí*
that way (over there)	*por allí*
continue	*sigue*
straight	*directo*
ahead	*adelante*
until you get to	*hasta que llegue a*
avenue	*avenida*
street	*calle*
road/path	*camino*
highway (toll)	*autopista*
road/highway	*carretera*
curve	*curva*
corner	*esquina*
bend/corner	*vuelta*
turn to	*dobla a*
to the left	*a mano izquierda*
to the right	*a mano derecha*
near	*cerca*
far	*lejos*

north . . . . *norte*
south . . . . *sur*
east . . . . *este*
west . . . . *oeste*

■ Accommodations

Is there a room (available)?. . *¿Hay una habitación / cuarto (disponible)?*
single . . . . *sencillo*
double . . . . *doble*
for one/two person/s. . . . . *para una / dos persona / s*
tonight. . . . . *esta noche*
the weekend. . . . . *el fin de semana*
It's full (no vacancy) . . . . *Está lleno*
How much does it cost? . . . . *¿Cuanto cuesta?*
Does it have a bathroom/shower? . . . . *¿Tiene baño / ducha?*
towels . . . . *toallas*
blanket . . . . *frisa*
sheets . . . . *sábanas*
air conditioning . . . . *aire acondicionado*
toilet paper . . . . *papel de inodoro*
soap . . . . *jabón*
Where can one change money? . . . . *¿Donde se puede cambiar dinero?*

■ Shopping

Are you open/closed? . . . . *¿están abiertos?*
Do you have... ? . . . . *¿Tienen... ?*
How much does it cost? . . . . *¿Cuanto cuesta?*
I would like two of those . . . . *Quisiera dos de ellos*
size/clothing size . . . . *tamaño / talla*
Do you have something smaller? . . . . *¿Tienen algo mas pequeño?*
less expensive? . . . . *¿mas barato?*
bigger? . . . . *¿mas grande?*
Give me one . . . . *Deme uno*
market . . . . *mercado*
deli/corner store . . . . *colmado*
dollar . . . . *peso*
quarter . . . . *peseta*
dime . . . . *vellón de diez*
nickel . . . . *vellón* or (in Ponce) *ficha*
penny . . . . *chavo*

■ Food & Eating Out

Foods are listed with the Spanish name first, in alphabetical order.

Seafood

almejas .... clams
atún .... tuna
bacalao .... codfish
calamares .... squid
cangrejo/jueyes .... crab/land crab
chapín .... trunkfish
chillo .... snapper
gambas/guábaras .... shrimp/freshwater shrimp
langosta .... lobster
mejillones .... mussels
ostras .... oysters
pez espada .... swordfish
pulpo .... octopus
sardinas .... sardines
trucha .... trout

Meats

albondigas .... meatballs
bistec .... beefsteak
callos .... tripe
caracoles .... snails
cerdo .... pork
cordero .... lamb
costillas .... chops
hígado .... liver
jamon .... ham
lechón .... barbecued pork
lengua .... tongue
pato .... duck
pavo .... turkey
pollo .... chicken

Fruits & Vegetables, Etc.

aceitunas/olivas .... olives
aguacate .... avocado
amarillo .... fried sweet plantain
arroz .... rice
cebolla .... onion
china .... orange
ensalada .... salad
espárragos .... asparagus
espinacas .... spinach
fresa .... strawberry
guineo .... banana

guisado .... stew
habichuelas .... beans
hongos .... mushroom
jugo .... juice
lechuga .... lettuce
limón .... lemon
manzana .... apple
melocotón .... peach
mofongo .... baked mashed plantain
papas .... potatoes
pera .... pear
piña .... pineapple
plátano .... plantain
pepinillo .... cucumber
sopa .... soup
tomate .... tomato
toronja .... grapefruit
uva .... grape
zanahorias .... carrots

Utensils, Condiments & Basics

knife .... *cuchillo*
fork .... *tenedor*
spoon .... *cuchara*
plate .... *plato*
bowl .... *tazón*
cup .... *taza*
glass .... *vaso/copa*
salt .... *sal*
pepper .... *pimienta*
oil .... *aceite*
vinegar .... *vinagre*
bread .... *pan*
butter .... *mantequilla*
sugar .... *azúcar*
honey .... *miel*
coffee .... *café*
milk .... *leche*
mustard .... *mostaza*
ketchup .... *catsup*
garlic .... *ajo*
hot sauce .... *pique*

■ Numbers

one .... *uno/a*

two . . . . *dos*
three . . . . *tres*
four . . . . *cuatro*
five . . . . *cinco*
six . . . . *seis*
seven . . . . *siete*
eight . . . . *ocho*
nine . . . . *nueve*
ten . . . . *diez*
eleven . . . . *once*
twelve . . . . *doce*
thirteen . . . . *trece*
fourteen . . . . *catorce*
fifteen . . . . *quince*
sixteen . . . . *dieciséis*
seventeen . . . . *diecisiete*
eighteen . . . . *dieciocho*
nineteen . . . . *diecinueve*
twenty . . . . *veinte*
twenty-one . . . . *veintiuno*
thirty . . . . *treinta*
thirty-one . . . . *treinta y uno*
forty . . . . *cuarenta*
fifty . . . . *cincuenta*
sixty . . . . *sesenta*
seventy . . . . *setenta*
eighty . . . . *ochenta*
ninety . . . . *noventa*
one hundred . . . . *cien*
one hundred-one . . . . *ciento uno*
one hundred-seventy-six . . . . *ciento setenta y seis*
two hundred . . . . *doscientos*
five hundred . . . . *quinientos*
nine hundred . . . . *novecientos*
one thousand . . . . *mil*
two thousand . . . . *dos mil*
one million . . . . *un million*

■ Dates & Times

Monday . . . . *lunes*
Tuesday . . . . *martes*
Wednesday . . . . *miércoles*
Thursday . . . . *jueves*
Friday . . . . *viernes*
Saturday . . . . *sabado*
Sunday . . . . *domingo*

today .... *hoy*
yesterday .... *ayer*
tomorrow .... *mañana*
tomorrow morning .... *mañana por la mañana*
tomorrow afternoon .... *mañana por la tarde*
tomorrow night .... *mañana por la noche*
noon .... *mediodía*
midnight .... *medianoche*
the wee hours .... *la madrugada*
What time is it? .... *¿Que hora es?*
It's 6:30 .... *Son las seis y media*
It's 3:15 .... *Son las tres y cuarto*
It's a quarter to five. .... *Son las cinco menos cuarto*
It's 2:10 .... *Son las dos y diez*

■ Conversation

Hello .... *Hola*
Good morning/afternoon/night .... *Buenos días*
Good afternoon .... *Buenas tardes*
Good night .... *Buenas noches*
How are you? .... *¿Como está/s usted/tu?*
Well. Everything is well .... *Bien, todo bien*
My name is... .... *Me llamo...*
I'm... .... *Soy...*
What's your name? .... *¿Como se llama usted?*
Glad to meet you .... *Mucho gusto de conocerle*
Enchanted .... *Encantado/a*
Thank you .... *Gracias*
Thank you (in reply) .... *A usted/ti*
You're welcome .... *De nada*
Excuse me .... *Con su permiso*
Oh, pardon me! .... *¡Ay perdone!*
I'm sorry .... *Lo siento*
What? .... *¿Como?*
Speak a little slower, please ..... *Hable un poco mas despacio, por favor*
I don't understand .... *No le entiendo*
I'm American .... *Soy norteamericano/a*
I'm Canadian .... *Soy canadiense*
I'm English .... *Soy inglés/esa*
I'm Australian .... *Soy australiano/a*
I'm Welsh .... *Soy galés/esa*
I'm Irish .... *Soy irlandés/esa*
I'm Scottish .... *Soy escosés/esa*
I'm a New Zealander .... *Soy neozelandés/esa*
I like Puerto Rico very much .... *A mí me gusta mucho Puerto Rico*
How old are you? .... *¿Cuantos años tiene/s?*

I am 28 . . . . *Tengo vienti ocho*
May I sit here? . . . . *¿Me deja sentar aquí?*
Want to dance? . . . . *¿Quiere/s bailar?*
I'd like to learn. . . . . *Quisiera aprender*
It's been a pleasure. . . . . *Ha sido un placer*
Goodbye. . . . . *Adiós*
(Until) Later . . . . *Hasta luego*
See you. . . . . *Nos vemos*

■ Puerto Rican Slang

baba, *nf*, literally meaning "spittle," used for boring or meaningless talk.

bacalao, *nm*, cod fish, also used as a vulgar term for female sexual organs

bañar el caballo, *phr*, literally "to bathe the horse," a humorous and archaic (male) term for having sex.

batey, *nm*, from the Taino word, meaning a yard in the country.

bellaco/a, *adj*, horny, hot.

bicho, *nm*, literally "bug," the most common vulgar term for the male sexual organ.

bohío, *nm*, from Taino language, meaning a hut, usually without walls.

boricua, *n*, also from Taino language, meaning Puerto Rican. Also **borinqueño/a**.

buena gente, *phr*, "good people," used to describe a nice person, as in *"El es muy buena gente."*

cagar (se), *v*, Literally to defecate, also to screw up, or blow it. *¡La cagó!* He blew it!

¡carajo!, *nm*, an expletive used like the English "damn!" "hell!" or "shit!" Also, **¡puñeta!**

chévere, *adj*, "cool" or great. Also **chuchín**.

chicar, *v*, vulgar term for the act of love.

chichaito, *nm*, a Puerto Rican drink of rum and anise (suggesting *chicar*)

chisme, *nm*, gossip.

chocha, *nf*, vulgar term for the female sexual organs (as are *"papaya," "montón," "cueva"* and a host of other terms).

chulo, *nm*, literally a "pimp", used as an adjective for something really cool, especially an object.

cocopelao, *adj*, literally "peeled coconut", it means bald.

coño, a well-accepted term expressing surprise, displeasure and a range of other feelings. Originally meaning female genitals.

dolorosa, *nf*, literally "the painful," a cute way of saying *la cuenta*, or "the check."

friquear, *v*, to freak out.

gufear, *v*, to goof around.

janguear, *v*, to hang out.

jebo/a, *n*, an extremely attractive person of either sex. Also used for the person you are dating. Also *jevo/a*.

jíbaro/a, *n* or *adj*, hillbilly. Can be derogative like "hick" or complimentary as in "country-style."

joya, *nf*, literally a jewel, also used for a pond or swimming hole.

lechón/ona, *n*, roast pig. In the feminine form, the word has been used to describe a big old car or a woman with an especially wide fanny.

mano, *nm*, Bro or buddy. From the word "*hermano*," meaning "brother," an extremely popular greeting between friends, as in ¿*Como estás, mano?*

mijo/a, *n*, dear, darling, sweetie. Contraction of *mi hijo/a* ("my child").

palmolive, *nm*, a green bottle of Heineken beer.

palo, *nm*, an alcoholic drink, usually a shot. Literally, "a stick."

pendejo, *nm*, loser or coward.

peo, *nm*, fart.

picao, *adj*, tipsy.

pipón/a, *n*, a person with a protruding belly or paunch.

piropo, *n*, sexually aggressive flattery, as in cat calls.

pitorro, *nm*, moonshine rum.

playero/a, *n*, a beach bum.

pon, *nm*, a lift or ride in a vehicle. *Dar pon:* to give a lift; *pedir pon:* to hitchhike.

puta, *nf*, whore, a conjunction of "prostituta."

quemao, *nm*, hangover.

quemar, *v*, literally "to burn," refers to smoking marijuana.

rajar(se), *v*, literally "to split", this flexible verb can mean to leave a place, to get drunk, to wear oneself out fornicating or to quit a job.

relajar(se), *v*, from the verb for "relax," meaning to have fun, joke around or engage in wild behavior at a party.

rumba, *nf*, party. Also, **pachanga** (usually with music and dancing).

salsero / salsera, *n*, a person who loves salsa music and dance.

sanjuanero/a, *n*, someone from San Juan.

suave, *adj*, smooth, easy. *Cogerlo suave*: to take it easy.

taco, *nm*, an uncommon way of referring to a nice, easy-going person. Literally, a pool cue, the heel of a shoe or a Mexican snack.

tapón, *nm*, a traffic jam or a short person (literally, a cork or a stopper). *Hora de tapón:* rush hour.

teta, *nf*, vulgar term meaning "tit," also used for the end slice of French bread.

tipo, *nm*, a guy (usually complimentary). *Tipo raro:* weirdo.

trigueño, *adj*, having bronzed, medium-dark skin, the desired suntan.

¡Wepa!, *exp*, informal Puerto Rican greeting, (like "Hey!"), also used to express surprise, like "Wow!" or "You don't say!" Sometimes it's pronounced ¡*Jepa*!

yerba, *nf*, marijuana. Also *pasto*.

Bibliography

Suggested Further Reading

■ Flora & Fauna

Silva Lee, Alfonso. *Coquí y Sus Amigos / Coquí and His Friends*. Pangaea Press, 2000. A fun book for young nature lovers, it stars Puerto Rico's mascot, the coquí frog, and 40 of his friends from land and sea.

Benedetti, María Verde Luz. *Earth and Spirit: Medicinal Plants and Healing Lore from Puerto Rico*. 1998. Puerto Rican healers and herbalists offer a series of interviews and discussions on natural health.

Raffaele, Herbert A., Cindy J. House and John Wiessinger. *A Guide to the Birds of Puerto Rico and the Virgin Islands*. Princeton University Press, 1989. A must for ornithologists and bird enthusiasts in the Caribbean.

Silva Lee, Alfonso. *Natural Puerto Rico / Puerto Rico Natural*. Pangaea Press, 1998. Presented in Spanish and English, colorful photos and clearly written text provide an in-depth look at the islands' wildlife including useful anecdotes on the natural history of insects, birds and reptiles.

Nellis, David W. *Puerto Rico and Virgin Islands Wildlife Viewing Guide*. Falcon Publishing Company, 1999. A concise overview of the different nature reserves and ecosystems of Puerto Rico.

Robinson, Kathryn. *Where Dwarfs Reign*. University of Puerto Rico Press, 1997. A tramp through the Caribbean rain forest of El Yunque without leaving the sofa.

■ History & Culture

Baralt, Guillerma A. and Andrey Hurley (Translator). *Buena Vista: Life and Work on a Puerto Rican Hacienda: 1833-1904*. University of North Carolina Press, 1999. Depicts life on a Puerto Rican hacienda at the turn of the century, with detailed illustrations. Good info about the history of Ponce.

Corrales, Scott and Marc Davenport. *Chupacabras and Other Mysteries*. Greenleaf Publications, 1997. An investigation into the mysterious "goat sucker" and other paranormal curiosities.

Flores, Juan. *Divided Borders: Essays on Puerto Rican Identity*. Arte Publico Press, 1993.

Dietz, James L. *Economic History of Puerto Rico*. Princeton University Press, 1987.

Schmidt-Nowara, Christopher. *Empire and Antislavery: Spain, Cuba and Puerto Rico, 1833-1874*. University of Pittsburgh Press (Pitt Latin American Series), 1999. An excellent analysis of the abolition of slavery in the Spanish colonies.

Suarez-Findlay, Eileen J. *Imposing Decency: The Politics of Sexuality and Race in Puerto Rico, 1870-1920*. Duke University Press (American Encounters/Global Interactions), 2000. A feminist perspective on the racial and sexual issues that confronted Puerto Rican society as it shifted from Spanish to US sovereignty.

Fuson, Robert H. *Juan Ponce De León and the Spanish Discovery of Puerto Rico and Florida*. McDonald & Woodward Publishing Company, 2000. A well-researched biography of Ponce de León that argues the man ridiculed for his obsession with the fountain of youth was an unusually humane conquistador.

Bernier-Grand, Carmen T. *Poet and Politician of Puerto Rico: Don Luis Muñoz Marin*. Orchard Books, 1995. A biography of the man, his writing and his politics.

Wagenheim, Kal and Olga Jiménez Wagenheim, eds. *The Puerto Ricans: A Documentary History*. Markus Wiener Publishers, Princeton, 1994. Called "an essential sourcebook" by *The New York Times*, it's a great collection of primary-source documents from conquistador letters to modern musings.

Carrión, Arturo Morales. *Puerto Rico: A Political and Cultural History*. W.W. Norton & Company, 1984. A valuable, in-depth analysis of the makings of modern-day Puerto Rico.

Delano, Jack. *Puerto Rico Mío: Four Decades of Change*. Smithsonian Institution Press, 1990. A collection of photographs that captures the spirit of Puerto Rico and its people, generation by generation.

Monge, José Trias. *Puerto Rico: The Trials of the Oldest Colony in the World*. Yale University Press, 1999. A discussion of the tribulations of Puerto Rican politics.

Ronald Fernandez, Serafin Mendez Mendez, and Gail Cueto y Mendez Mendez. *Puerto Rico Past and Present*. Greenwood Publishing Group, 1998. An encyclopedic overview of the past 500 years, with special attention to the 19th and 20th centuries.

Ramirez, Rafael L., Rosa E. Casper (translator) and Peter J. Guarnaccia. *What It Means to Be a Man: Reflections on Puerto Rican Masculinity*. Rutgers University Press, 1999. A fresh approach to masculinity and masochism in Puerto Rico and beyond.

Langhorne, Elizabeth. *Vieques: History of a Small Island*. The Vieques Conservation and Historical Trust, 1987. A great little history of Vieques.

■ Music, Dance & Food

Flores, Juan. *From Bomba to Hip-Hop (Popular Cultures, Everyday Lives)*. Columbia University Press, 2000. A study of the Latino identity; past, present and future.

Aparicio, Frances R. *Listening to Salsa: Gender, Latin Popular Music, and Puerto Rican Cultures*. Wesleyan University Press, 1997. Widely regarded as a landmark publication for all students of Latin music, gender and popular culture.

Thompson, Donald and Annie F. Thompson. *Music and Dance in Puerto Rico from the Age of Columbus to Modern Times: An Annotated Bibliography*. Scarecrow Press (Studies in Latin American Music, No 1), 1991.

Ortiz, Yvonne. *A Taste of Puerto Rico: Traditional and New Dishes from the Puerto Rican Community*. Plume, 1997. More than 200 recipes with cultural history make this a great buy for travelers interested in Puerto Rican cooking.

■ Fiction, Poetry & Prose

Ferré, Rosario. *The House on the Lagoon*. Plume, 1996. The daughter of former Governor Luis. A Ferré delivers a family saga with all the magic, mayhem and drama of Isabel Allende.

Lewis, Oscar. *La Vida*. Irington, 1982. An illuminating account of survival in the Caribbean's most notorious slum, La Perla.

Santiago, Roberto (editor). *Boricuas: Influential Puerto Rican Writings, An Anthology*. Ballantine Books, 1995. Poems, fiction, plays, essays and speeches from some of Puerto Rico's most important and original writers.

Santiago, Esmeralda. *When I Was Puerto Rican*. Vintage Books, 1994. A compelling autobiographical story of a young girl growing up in Puerto Rico.

Santiago, Esmeralda. *Almost a Woman*. Vintage Books, 1999. This sequel to her memoir includes Santiago's memories of adolescence in New York City.

Zeno-Gandía, Manuel, Kal Wagenhem (translator). *The Pond / La Charca*. Markus Wiener Publishing, 1999. A first-rate translation of the classic 19th-century Latin American novel, which was widely recognized as the first major novel to emerge from Puerto Rico.

Index

Accommodations, 44-48; bargains, 46; Central Mountains, 288-292; Culebra, 393-395; East Coast, 335-338; guest houses, 45; North Coast, 156-159; paradores, 45-46; price key, 44; San Juan area, 105-111; South Coast, 255-261; top ten, 46-47; types of, 45-46; Vieques, 365-368; West Coast, 204-209
Adjuntas: accommodations, 291; where to eat, 296-297
Adventures, 50-59; Central Mountains, 280-288; Culebra, 385-392; East Coast, 312-324; Isla Mona, 203-204; North Coast, 143-153; San Juan area, 97-104; South Coast, 237-250; top ten, 52-53; Vieques, 358-363; West Coast, 182-197
Aguada: accommodations, 205; touring and sightseeing, 171
Aguadilla: accommodations, 205; camping, 209; diving, 189; surfing, 54, 192; touring and sightseeing, 168-169; where to eat, 210
Aguirre: biking, 53, 242; golf, 241; kayaking, 55; touring and sightseeing, 234-236; where to eat, 265
Aibonito: accommodations, 289; touring and sightseeing, 271-272; where to eat, 295
Air adventures: Central Mountains, 288; East Coast, 323-324
Amphibians and reptiles, 18-19, 104
Añasco: touring and sightseeing, 175-176; where to eat, 211
Animals, 15, 17-22; feral, 201; zoo, 186
Ann Wigmore Institute, Aguada, 205
Archaeology, Vieques, 354, 356
Arecibo: accommodations, 156; diving and snorkeling, 153; fishing, 150; surfing, 54, 152; touring and sightseeing, 137
Arecibo Observatory, 138-139
Arroyo: accommodations, 260; touring and sightseeing, 236-237; where to eat, 265
Art and culture, 31-33; Dorado, 133-134; folk art, 61; Ponce, 225-228, 231-232; Río Piedras, 95; San Germán, 219-220; San Juan area, 87-92, 121, 127-128; Vieques, 354, 356-357
ATMs (ATHs), 68

Bacardi Rum distillery, Cataño, 96
Bahía Fosforescente, 220, 246
Baino Batey Grounds, 285-287
Ballaja Barracks and Museo, San Juan, 88
Balneario de Guajataca, 141
Balneario los Tubos, 136, 150-151; surfing, 152
Banana boat rides, San Juan, 101-102
Barceloneta, touring and sightseeing, 136-137
Barranquitas: accommodations, 290; touring and sightseeing, 272-273; where to eat, 295
Barrio Isolde, beach, 151
Beaches, 54; Culebra, 100-101, 385-387; East Coast, 321-322; San Juan area, 100-101; South Coast, 249; Vieques, 359-360; walks, 51, 182; West Coast, 168, 182; *see also* Swimming
Biking, 53; Culebra, 385; Paseo Tablado, 99; San Juan area, 99-100; South Coast, 241-242; West Coast, 187
Bioluminescent waters: Bahía Fosforescente, 220, 246; by glass-bottomed boat, 245; Laguna

Torrecilla, 94; Piñones State Forest, 104
Biosphere reserves, UNESCO, 15-16, 250
Birds, 19-20, 252; Boquerón, 197-198; Bosque Río Abajo, 155; Cabo Rojo Refuge, 198; Culebra, 375; El Yunque, 329; Guánica, 251; Humacao, 325; Jobos Bay, 253-254; Mona Island, 200-201; Piñones State Forest, 104; *see also* Eco-travel
Birdsall house, Las Marías, 279
Blackjack ("21"), 127
Boating: Culebra, 388; East Coast, 316-318; San Juan area, 101-102; South Coast, 245-246
BONUS (nuclear power plant), 174
Boquerón: accommodations, 208; beach walks, 182; bird refuge, 184, 197-198; swimming, 194; touring and sightseeing, 179; on wheels, 187-188; where to eat, 213
Bosque Estatal de Aguirre, 241, 253; camping, 261
Bosque Estatal de Guilarte, camping, 292
Bosque Estatal de Susúa, 222; camping, 261
Bosque Jagueyes, 241
Bosque Río Abajo: camping, 159; eco-travel, 137-138, 154-155; hiking, 145
Botanical gardens: Mayagüez, 198; Río Piedras, 95
Botanica San Miguel, San Germán, 220
Brazo gitano (jelly roll), 212
Bugs, 19
Butterflies and moths, 19
Buye, beach walks, 182

Cabo Rojo (town): accommodations, 209; biking, 187; camping, 209; swimming, 194; touring and sightseeing, 178-179
Cabo Rojo Lighthouse, 180, 184
Cabo Rojo National Refuge, 198
Cabo Rojo Peninsula, touring and sightseeing, 180
Caimans, 136
Caja de Muertos, 252-253
Calendar, festivals and events, 37-40
Cambalache State Forest: camping, 159; eco-travel, 153-154; hiking, 145; mountain biking, 146-147; touring and sightseeing, 53, 136
Camping, 47-48; administrative offices, 48; Central Mountains, 292-293; Culebra, 395-396; Dept. of Natural Resources, 292; East Coast, 338-339; North Coast, 157, 159-160; South Coast, 261; Vieques, 368; West Coast, 209
Camuy: accommodations, 157; caving, 51, 141, 143-145; touring and sightseeing, 141
Canóvanas, touring and sightseeing, 307
Caparra, sightseeing, 97
Capilla de Cristo, Old San Juan, 85-86
Capilla de San José, San Juan, 88-89
Caribbean, map, viii
Caribbean stud, 126-127
Carite Forest Reserve: accommodations, 289; camping, 292; touring and sightseeing, 270, 288; where to eat, 294
Carnival masks, 61
Casa Armstong Poventud, Ponce, 226
Casa Bavaria, Manatí, 161
Casa Blanca, San Juan, 89-90
Casa Canales, Jayuya, 276
Casa Cautiño, Guayama, 236
Casa de Don Juan Serralés, Ponce, 225
Casa del Rey, Dorado, 133
Casa de Ponce de León, San Germán, 219-220
Casa de Ramón y Giralt, Old San Juan, 92
Casa Labadie, Moca, 183-184
Casa Morales Lugo, San Germán, 219
Casa Museo Joaquín de Rojas y Martínez, Barranquitas, 272

Casa Natal Luis Muñoz Rivera, Barranquitas, 272
Casa Roig, Humacao, 312
Casa Rosada, Old San Juan, 87
Casinos, 126-127
Castillo Serrallés, Ponce, 229
Cataño, sightseeing, 95-96
Catedral de San Germán de Auxerre, 219
Catedral de San Juan, 85
Catedral Nuestra Señora de la Guadalupe, Ponce, 226
Catholicism, 25
Caving, 51; Camuy, 51, 141, 143-145; Indio, 136-137, 149; Isla Mona, 203-204; Luquillo, 319
Cayey: accommodations, 289; where to eat, 294
Cayo Caribe Trail, kayaking, 245
Cayo Luis Peña, 384-385
Cayo Pirata, 383
Cayo Ratones, 178
Cayo Ron, diving, 189
Cayo Santiago, 318
Ceiba: accommodations, 337; touring and sightseeing, 310-311
Cementerio de San Juan, 87
Cemíes, 276
Centipedes, poisonous, 19, 201
Central Mountains, 268-297; accommodations, 288-292; adventures, 280-288; camping, 292-293; communications, 270; getting here and getting around, 269; hiking, 50-51; map, 268; touring and sightseeing, 270-280; where to eat, 294-297
Centro Historico y Turistico del Cibuco, 134
Cerro Gordo: camping, 159; diving, 153
Cerro La Pandura, 315
Cerro Punta, 273, 282-283
Charco Azul, hiking, 280-281
Chupacabras, 26-27
Churches, 25-26; *see also specific sites*
Ciales, touring and sightseeing, 135
Cigars, shopping for, 60

Climate, 14
Cloud forest, 15
Club Deportivo del Oeste, golf, 186
Club Gallistico de Puerto Rico, 58-59
Club Jibarito, 60
Coamo Hot Springs, 249-250; accommodations, 259; touring and sightseeing, 233-234
Cockfighting, 58-59
Coconut husks, painted, 61
Coffee, shopping for, 59
Cofresí (pirate), 181
Communications, 68-69
Condado: accommodations, 107-108; entertainment, 123; kayaking, 55; map, 92; sightseeing, 92; surfing and windsurfing, 103; swimming and sunbathing, 100-101; where to eat, 115-117
Convento de los Dominicos, San Juan, 90
Coral reef protection, 202
Coral reefs, 21-22
Cordillera Central, *see* Central Mountains
Cordillera Jaicoa, scenic drive, 150
Corozal, touring and sightseeing, 134-135
Corozo Salt Flats, 195
Corsega, swimming, 194
Costs, 67-68
Crime, 42, 62-63; Piñones, 101; tourist police, 63, 70
Cuatros (stringed instruments), 273
Cueva del Indio, 136-137, 149
Cuevas de Camuy, 141, 143-145
Culebra Island, 345, 371-397; accommodations, 393-395; adventures, 55, 385-392; beaches, 100-101, 385-387; camping, 395-396; cays, 383-385; communication and information, 379-380; eco-travel, 392-393; flora and fauna, 375-376; getting around, 378-379; getting here, 376-378; history, 373-374; map, 372; mountain bikes, 379; overview, 345-346; touring and sightseeing, 380-385; travel be-

tween Vieques and, 377-378; water taxis, 387; whale watching, 56; where to eat, 396-397
Customs regulations, 68
Cycling, *see* Biking

Decompression chamber, 55
Deep-sea fishing, *see* Fishing
Dewey, 371; accommodations, 393-394; map, 381; touring and information, 380-382
Dining, *see* Where to eat
Disabilities, travelers with, 66-67
Diving, 54-55; choosing a dive shop, 190-191; Culebra, 55, 389-391; decompression chamber, 55; East Coast, 319-320; Isla Mona, 55, 204; for kids, 189; North Coast, 153; San Juan area, 102-103; South Coast, 247-248; Vieques, 55, 361-363; West Coast, 188-191
Dorado: accommodations, 156; touring and sightseeing, 133-134; where to eat, 160-161
Doral Resort at Palmas del Mar, 338
Driving, 42-43; car theft, 42; caution, 166; El Yunque, 334; Guajataca Lake, 150; mileage chart, 43; North Coast, 148-150; Punta Tuna loop, 314-315; Ruta Panorámica, 54, 269, 287-288; West Coast, 188

East Coast, 298-343; accommodations, 335-338; adventures, 312-324; camping, 338-339; communications, 302; eco-travel, 324-334; getting here and getting around, 299-302; map, 298; touring and sightseeing, 302-312; where to eat, 339-343
Eco-travel, 59; call for research proposals, 254; Cambalache State Forest, 153-154; Culebra, 392-393; East Coast, 324-334; North Coast, 137-138, 141-142, 153-155; phone numbers, 70; Piñones State Forest, 104-105; reef protection, 202;

South Coast, 250-254; Vieques, 363-365; West Coast, 197-198
El Cañuelo, sightseeing, 96-97
El Castillo Villa del Mar, Naguabo, 311
El Combate, beach, 54, 181-182
El Convento, camping, 339
El Convento Hotel, 46, 98, 106, 114
El Morro, San Juan, 86-87
El Tenedor, Juncos, 342
El Yunque, 15, 325-334; accommodations, 335-336; camping, 338; driving, 334; facilities, 330; flash-flood warning, 331; flora and fauna, 327, 329-330; getting here and getting away, 327; hang gliding, 323-324; hiking, 50-51, 312-313, 331-334; history, 325-327; maps, 328, 332; mountain biking, 334; ranger-guided trips, 330; touring and sightseeing, 307-308
E-mail and Internet access, 69, 71
Emergencies, phone numbers, 70
EMV International House of Cigars, 60
Ensenada Honda, 383
Entertainment: Rincón, 214; San Juan area, 121-127; South Coast, 266-267; Vieques, 371
Esperanza, 356; map, 357; where to eat, 368-370
Estación Experimental Agrícola Federal, 177
Evangelical churches, 25-26
Extra-terrestrial intelligence, search for, 27, 139, 179, 184, 185

Fajardo: accommodations, 337; diving, 319-320; fishing, 320-321; picnic supplies, 340; sailing, 57; snorkeling, 55; touring and sightseeing, 308-310; where to eat, 341
Faro el Vigia, 149
Festivals and events, 37-40; Ponce, 231-232
Finca Enseñat, Las Marías, 279
Fishing, 56-57; Culebra, 389; East Coast, 320-321; Guajataca Lake,

150; San Juan area, 102; seasonal catches, 56, 57; South Coast, 248; Vieques, 360; West Coast, 195-196
Flamenco Beach, accommodations, 395
Folk art, 61
Food, 34-37; African, 339; *brazo gitano*, 212; *hojaldre* cakes, 176; oysters, 213; plantains, 135; shopping for, 59
On foot, 50-52; Central Mountains, 280-287; East Coast, 312-313; North Coast, 143-146; San Juan area, 97-99; South Coast, 237-241; Vieques, 358; West Coast, 182-186
Forests, 15-16; waterfalls, 151; *see also* El Yunque
Fruit, 17
Fuerte San Cristóbal, 91; San Juan, 91

Galería Doctor Marcelino Canino, Dorado, 133-134
Gallery Inn, Old San Juan, 105
Gambling, casinos, 126-127
Gays and lesbians: entertainment, 126; information for, 65-66
Ghost town, Aguirre, 234-236
Gilligan's Island, 221, 246, 249
Golf, 51-52; East Coast, 313; North Coast, 145-146; South Coast, 241; West Coast, 186
Grand Canyon, San Cristóbal, 281-282
Green tree iguanas, 104
Guajataca: camping, 159; eco-travel, 141-142; forest waterfalls, 151; hiking, 145; touring and sightseeing, 141-142; where to eat, 163
Guajataca Lake: accommodations, 158; fishing, 150; scenic drive, 150
Guánica: accommodations, 257-258; beaches, 249; biking, 241; birding, 251; diving, 247-248; eco-travel, 250-252; hiking, 237-240; islands, 221; kayaking, 244; map, 239; surfing, 248-249; touring and sightseeing, 221; UN Biosphere Reserve, 15-16, 250; where to eat, 263
Guayama: accommodations, 260; touring and sightseeing, 236; where to eat, 265
Guayama Cays, 241, 253
Guayanilla: accommodations, 258; biking, 242; where to eat, 263

Hacienda Buena Vista, Ponce, 230
Hacienda Frontera, Las Marías, 279
Hacienda Gripiñas, Jayuya, 290, 296
Hacienda Juanita, Maricao, 291, 297
Hacienda Las Marias, biking, 148
Hacienda Margarita, Barranquitas, 290, 295
Hacienda Santa María, Ceiba, 310-311
Hang gliding, East Coast, 323-324
Hatillo: accommodations, 157; surfing, 140; touring and sightseeing, 140; where to eat, 162-163
Hato Rey: sightseeing, 95; where to eat, 120
Hero Valley, hiking, 280
Hiking, 50-51; Central Mountains, 280-287; East Coast, 312-313; El Yunque, 50-51, 312-313, 331-334; Isla Mona, 203; North Coast, 145; protective clothing, 281; Vieques, 358
Hojaldre cakes, 176
Hormigueros, touring and sightseeing, 177-178
Horned Dorset Primavera, Rincón, 206-207, 211
On horseback, 53; East Coast, 314; North Coast, 146; Paso Fino horses, 58; Vieques, 359; West Coast, 186
Hot sauce, shopping for, 59
Humacao: accommodations, 338; beaches, 322; fishing, 320; touring and sightseeing, 311-312; where to eat, 342
Humacao Natural Reserve, 325
Humpbacks, endangered species, 196-197

Hyatt Dorado Beach Resort, 156; golf, 145-146
Hyatt Regency Cerromar Beach Resort, 156; golf, 146
Hyperbaric Medical Facility, 55

Icacos, on water, 315
Iglesia de San Patricio, Loíza Aldea, 302-303
Iguanas, 104, 201
Information, 62-71; South Coast, 216
Insects, 19, 201
Instituto de Cultura Puertorriqueña, San Juan, 88
Instituto de Cultura Puertorriqueña Sur, Ponce, 226
Internet and e-mail access, 69, 71
Isabela: accommodations, 158; surfing, 54, 152; touring and sightseeing, 142
Isabel Segunda: map, 355; touring and sightseeing, 354; where to eat, 370-371
Isla Ballena: beaches, 249; touring and sightseeing, 221
Isla Caja de Muertos, 232-233, 252-253
Isla Culebrita, 383-384
Isla de Cabras peninsula: biking, 53; sightseeing, 96-97
Isla Desecheo, diving, 55, 188
Isla Mona, 198-204; adventures, 203-204; caving, 51; diving, 55, 188-189; flora and fauna, 200-201; getting here, 202-203; history, 199-200; map, 199; stargazing, 204; touring and sightseeing, 182; travel solo, 203; what to bring, 203
Isla Verde: accommodations, 109-111; entertainment, 123, 125; sightseeing, 94; surfing and windsurfing, 103; swimming and sunbathing, 54, 101; tennis, 98-99; where to eat, 119-120

Jardín Botánico, Río Piedras, 95
Jarealito, 149

Jayuya: accommodations, 290; touring and sightseeing, 274-278, 288; where to eat, 295-296
Jíbaros, 277-278
Jobos: accommodations, 158-159; call for research proposals, 254; camping (crashing on the beach), 160; crime warning, 152; diving and snorkeling, 153; horseback rides, 146; surfing, 152, 192; swimming, 151; touring and sightseeing, 142; where to eat, 163
Jobos Bay National Estuarine Research Reserve: eco-travel, 253-254; hiking, 241; kayaking, 245; manatees, 20
Joyuda: accommodations, 208; fishing, 196; touring and sightseeing, 178; where to eat, 212-213
Julien, Paul: accommodations, 257; water adventures, 243
Juncos, where to eat, 342

Kayaking, 55; Culebra, 388; East Coast, 318-319; South Coast, 244-245; Vieques, 360; West Coast, 195, 197
Kids: in the kitchen, 341; scuba for, 189; traveling with, 63-64
Kite surfing, San Juan area, 103

La Casa del Libro, Old San Juan, 86
La Casa Labadie, Moca, 170
Lace, 61, 170-171
La Coca Falls, 334
La Cordillera, cay-hopping, 315-322
La Cueva del Indio, 136-137
La Fortaleza, San Juan, 90
Lago Dos Bocas: touring and sightseeing, 138; where to eat, 162
Lago Lucchetti Wildlife Refuge, camping, 261
Laguna Cartagena: on foot, 184-185; touring and sightseeing, 179-180
Laguna Grande, kayaking, 318
Laguna Torrecilla (bioluminescent), 94

Laguna Tortuguero, touring and sightseeing, 136
Lake Caonillas, accommodations, 291
La Parguera, *see* Parguera
La Perla, San Juan, 87
La Playa de Dorado, 134
Las Cabezas de San Juan nature reserve: eco-travel, 324-325; snorkeling, 55, 309; surfing, 322
Las Casas de la Selva, hiking, 280
Las Coronas, diving, 189
Las Croabas: accommodations, 336-337; boating, 316; camping, 339; touring and sightseeing, 308-309; where to eat, 341
Las Marías, touring and sightseeing, 279-280
Las Salinas de Cabo Rojo, saltworks, 180
Lesbians and gays: entertainment, 126; information, 65-66
Lighthouses: Cabo Rojo, 180, 184; Faro el Vigia, 149; Las Cabezas de San Juan, 324-325; Punta Higüero, 173; Punta Mulos, 354; Punta Tuna, 312, 315
Loíza Aldea: touring and sightseeing, 302-307; where to eat, 339
Los Castillos Meléndez, Moca, 183
Los Cayos Caribes, 241, 253
Luquillo: accommodations, 336; beaches, 54, 321; camping, 339; diving, 319; horseback riding, 314; kayaking, 318-319; offshore caverns, 319; surfing, 54, 322; touring and sightseeing, 308; where to eat, 340

Magazines and newspapers, 69
Mail system, 69
Mammals, 17-18
Manatees, 20
Manatí: accommodations, 156; touring and sightseeing, 135-136; where to eat, 161-162
Mangroves, 16
Manzanillo plant, poisonous, 253

Maricao: accommodations, 291-292; touring and sightseeing, 278-279, 288; where to eat, 297
Marine life, 20-22
Mary Lee's By the Sea, Guánica, 257
Masks, carnival, 61
Maunabo: accommodations, 338; driving, 314; touring and sightseeing, 312; where to eat, 343
Mayagüez: accommodations, 207-208; botanical garden/research station, 198; getting to, 177; touring and sightseeing, 176-177; where to eat, 212
Medical emergencies, phone numbers, 70
Meliá, Ponce, 258-259, 263
Mercado de Río Piedras, 95
Moca: lace making, 61, 170-171; plantations, 183-184; touring and sightseeing, 169-171
Mona Passage: lighthouse, 184; whale watching, 56, 196
Money, 67-68; ATM/ATHs, 68; tipping, 68; Western Union, 68
Monkey Island, 318
Montañas Guarionex, scenic drive, 150
Morovis, touring and sightseeing, 135
Mosquito Bay, 356-357; eco-travel, 363-365; kayaking, 360
Moths and butterflies, 19
Mountain biking, 53; Culebra, 379; El Yunque, 334; Isla Mona, 204; North Coast, 146-148; South Coast, 241-242; Vieques, 358; West Coast, 187
Mundillo lace, 61, 170-171
Mural Indígeno de Zamas, 275
Museo de Antropología, Historia y Arte, Río Piedras, 95
Museo de Arte de Ponce, 228
Museo de Arte de Puerto Rico, 93
Museo de Arte e Historia de San Juan, 90
Museo de Arte Religioso Porta Coeli, San Germán, 219

Museo de la Historia de Ponce, 226, 228
Museo de la Masacre de Ponce, 224
Museo de la Música Puertorriqueña, Ponce, 228
Museo de Las Américas, San Juan, 88
Museo del Indio, San Juan, 90
Museo del Niño de Puerto Rico, Old San Juan, 85
Museo de los Proceres, Cabo Rojo, 178
Museo de Nuestra Raíz Africana, San Juan, 89
Museo Felisa Rincón de Gautier, Old San Juan, 84
Museo Indigena Cemí, Jayuya, 275-276
Museo Pablo Casals, San Juan, 89
Museo y Escuela de Arte Marcos Juan Alegría, Dorado, 133
Music and dance, 28-31
Mystical apothecary healing, 220

Naguabo, touring and sightseeing, 311
Naguabo Gold Mine, 313
Naranjito, touring and sightseeing, 134
Narcotics Anonymous, 67
Natural Resources Dept. Campsites, 292
Newspapers and magazines, 69, 216
Nightlife, see Entertainment
North Coast, 131-163; accommodations, 156-159; adventures, 143-153; camping, 157, 159-160; ecotravel, 137-138, 141-142, 153-155; getting here and getting around, 131-133; map, 132; touring and sightseeing, 133-142; where to eat, 160-163

Occult, 26
Ocean Park, 93; accommodations, 108-109; entertainment, 123; swimming and sunbathing, 54, 101; where to eat, 118

Old San Juan, 82-92; accommodations, 105-106; biking, 99-100; entertainment and nightlife, 121-122, 124-125; map, 83; walking tours, 97-98; where to eat, 111-115; see also San Juan
Oysters, 213

Pai gow poker, 126
Palacete Los Moureau, Moca, 183-184
Palomino Island, 309, 310; cay-hopping, 316; diving, 319; horseback riding, 314
Panadería La Patria, Morovis, 135
Panama hats, shopping for, 60
Parador Baños de Coamo, 259
Parasailing: East Coast, 323; San Juan area, 101-102
Parguera: accommodations, 256-257; boating, 245; diving, 55, 247-248; fishing, 248; kayaking, 55, 244; sailing, 57; touring and sightseeing, 220-222; where to eat, 262-263; windsurfing, 244
Parque Ceremonial Indigena Caguana, 278, 285-287
Parque de Bombas, Ponce, 226
Parque el Sueño de los Niños, Añasco, 176
Parque Lineal Martí Coll, San Juan, 99-100
Parrots, 155
Paseo Tablado, biking, 99
Paso Fino horses, 58
Patillas: accommodations, 260-261; surfing, 249; touring and sightseeing, 237; where to eat, 266
Patronato del Museo Antigua Aduana, Arroyo, 236
Petroglyphs: Camuy Caves, 143; Jayuya, 275
Piedra Escrita, Jayuya, 275
Piñones: biking, 53, 99; crime warning, 101; entertainment, 123; getting here, 94; sightseeing, 94-95; surfing and windsurfing, 103; swimming and sunbathing, 101

Piñones State Forest, eco-travel, 104-105
Pirates, 181
Plantains, 135
Plantations, Moca, 183-184
Plant life, 15-17, 253
Playa Buye: camping, 209; swimming, 179, 194
Playa Escondido, camping, 339
Playa Húcares, where to eat, 342
Playa Jaboncillo, 249
Playa Larga, 315, 322
Playa Montones, 142
Plaza Colón, Old San Juan, 91
Plaza de Armas, Old San Juan, 90
Plaza del Quinto Centenario, San Juan, 88
Plaza de San José, San Juan, 88
Plaza Mercado, San Juan, 93, 124
Police, 63, 70
Ponce, 222-232; accommodations, 258-259; festivals and events, 231-232; history, 222-225; map, 227; market, 228; nightlife, 266-267; shopping, 232; sightseeing, 225-230; where to eat, 263-265
Porta Coeli, San Germán, 218, 219
Protestant churches, 25-26
Public transportation/*públicos*, 43-44
Puerta de Tierra: accommodations, 106; entertainment, 125
Puerto Real: sailing, 57; touring and sightseeing, 179
Puerto Rican Skydiving Center, 323
Puerto Rican Trench, fishing, 56
Puerto Rico: accommodations, 44-48; adventures, 50-59; art and culture, 31-33; camping, 47-48; climate, 14; communications, 68-69; customs regulations, 68; directory/phone numbers/Web sites, 70-71; economy, 13-14; eco-travel, 59; festivals and events, 37-40; flora and fauna, 15-22; food, 34-37; getting around, 42-44; getting here, 40-42; government, 11-13; history, 3-11; the land, 1-3; language, 24-25; map, 2; money and costs, 67-68; music and dance, 28-31; newspapers and magazines, 69; people, 22-24; religion and spirituality, 25-27; shopping, 59-62; travel information, 62-71; UFO sightings, 27, 185; where to eat, 49-50
Puerto Rico International Speedway, 243
Puerto Rico Zoo, 186
Punta Borinquen Golf Course, 186
Punta Cerro Gordo, Dorado, 134; surfing, 151-152
Punta Guavate: accommodations, 289; touring and sightseeing, 270; where to eat, 294-297
Punta Higüero lighthouse, 173
Punta Las Marias, surfing and windsurfing, 101, 103-104
Punta Las Tunas, surfing, 152
Punta Mulos lighthouse, 354
Punta Palmas Altas, scenic drive, 148
Punta Tuna lighthouse, 312, 315
Punta Tuna loop, driving, 314-315

Quebradillas: accommodations, 157; biking, 147; where to eat, 163

Rain forest, *see* El Yunque
Recinto Universitario Mayagüez, 177
Reef protection, 202
Religion, 25-27
Reptiles and amphibians, 18-19, 164
Research proposals, call for, 254
Rincón: accommodations, 206-207; beach walk, 182; driving in, 173; fishing, 195-196; horseback rides, 186; information, 175; map, 172; nightlife, 214; snorkeling, 191; surfing, 193; swimming, 194-195; touring and sightseeing, 171-175; where to eat, 210-211
Río Camuy, 143
Río Grande de Loíza: touring and sightseeing, 302; where to eat, 339-343
Río Grande Plantation and Eco-Resort, 335

Río Piedras: sightseeing, 95; where to eat, 120
Río Tanamá, 145, 283
Roman Catholicism, 25
Roulette, 127
Rum, 37, 59; Bacardi distillery, 96
Ruta Panorámica, 54, 269, 287-288

Sailing, 57; Culebra, 388
Salinas: accommodations, 259; kayaking, 245; sailing, 57; touring and sightseeing, 234; where to eat, 265
Salto de Doña Juana, 273, 288
San Cristóbal, Grand Canyon, 271, 281-282
San Germán: accommodations, 255; history, 218; nightlife, 220, 266; touring and sightseeing, 218-220; where to eat, 220, 261-262
San Juan, 72-129; accommodations, 105-111; adventures, 97-104; art and culture, 87-92, 121, 127-128; city walls, 75-76, 84; eco-travel, 104-105; entertainment and nightlife, 121-127; folk art, 61; gay and lesbian spots, 126; getting around, 78-81; getting here, 77-78; history, 74-77; leisure and shopping, 127-129; mail and communications, 81-82; maps, 72, 83; renaissance, 76-77; rentals, 111; sailing, 57; shopping, 128-129; spas, 128; touring and sightseeing, 82-97; where to eat, 111-120, 160
Santa Catalina Palace, San Juan, 90
Santos, 61
Santurce, 93; entertainment, 125; where to eat, 115-117
Scenic drives, see Driving; On Wheels
Scooters, Boquerón, 187-188
Scorpions, 201
Scuba, see Diving
Seahorses, 361
Sharks, 201
Shopping, 59-62; Ponce, 232; San Juan area, 128-129

Shrine of Our Lady of Montserrat, 177-178
Skydiving, East Coast, 323
Snorkeling, 54-55; Culebra, 391-392; North Coast, 153; Vieques, 362-363; West Coast, 191; see also Diving
Sotomayor Resort Hotel and Country Club, Adjuntas, 291, 296-297
South Coast, 215-267; accommodations, 255-261; adventures, 237-250; camping, 261; communications and information, 216; eco-travel, 250-254; getting here and getting around, 215-216; map, 217; touring and sightseeing, 218-237; where to eat, 261-266
Spanish phrases, 399-407
Spas, San Juan, 128
Spectator sports, 58-59
Spiders, black widow, 201
Spirituality, 26
Stargazing: Arecibo, 138-139; Isla Mona, 204
Stock car racing, 243
Street food, 36-37
Sugar Train, 242
Sunbathing, 54; see also Beaches; Swimming
Sunset cruising, Vieques, 363
Surf biking, 55; West Coast, 195
Surfing, 54; East Coast, 322; North Coast, 151-152; San Juan area, 101, 103-104; South Coast, 248-249; West Coast, 191-194
Sweat lodges, 293
Swimming, 54; East Coast, 321-322; North Coast, 150-151; San Juan area, 100-101; warnings, 84, 101, 321; West Coast, 194-195

Taino Indian trails, hiking, 283-285
Tarantulas, 19
Teatro La Perla, Ponce, 226
Teatro Tapia, Old San Juan, 91-92
Telephone numbers, 70
Telephones, 68-69
Tennis, Isla Verde, 98-99

Tibes Indian Ceremonial Park, 225, 229-230
Tipping, 68
Toro Negro: accommodations, 290; camping, 292; hiking, 282-283; touring and sightseeing, 273; where to eat, 296
Tourist police, 63, 70
Travel information, 62-71; crime, 62-63; for disabled, 66-67; for gays and lesbians, 65-66; medical emergencies, 70; money, 67-68; travel with kids, 63-64; useful phone numbers, 70; Web sites, 71; when to go, 62; for women, 64-65
Trees, 16-17
Tres Hermanos: camping, 209; swimming, 194
Tropical Agriculture Research Station, 198
Turtles, 21, 202, 376, 392-393

UFO sightings, 27, 139, 179, 184, 185
UNESCO biosphere reserves, 15-16, 250
Utuado: touring and sightseeing, 278; where to eat, 296

Vieques Island, 345-371; accommodations, 365-368; adventures, 55, 358-363; archaeology, 354, 356; camping, 368; communications and information, 352-353; eco-travel, 363-365; getting around, 351-352; getting here, 349-351; history, 347-349; map, 350; nightlife, 371; overview, 345-346; touring and sightseeing, 354-357; travel between Culebra and, 377-378; whale watching, 56; where to eat, 368-371; wild horses, 354

Walking tours, *see* On foot
On water, 54-57; Culebra, 385-392; East Coast, 315-322; North Coast, 150-152; San Juan area, 100-104; South Coast, 243-250; Vieques, 359-363; West Coast, 188-197

Watercraft: personal, 55; and whales as endangered species, 196-197
Web sites, helpful, 71
West Coast, 164-214; accommodations, 204-209; adventures, 182-197; eco-travel, 197-198; getting here and getting around, 165-168; Isla Mona, 198-204; mail and communications, 168; map, 164; touring and sightseeing, 168-182; where to eat, 210-213
Western Union, 68
Whales, 20, 56; Culebra, 389; endangered species, 196-197; Isla Mona, 201; West Coast, 196-197
On wheels, 53-54; Central Mountains, 287-288; Culebra, 385; East Coast, 314-315; North Coast, 146-150; San Juan area, 99-100, 160; South Coast, 241-243; Vieques, 358; West Coast, 187-188
Where to eat, 49-50; Central Mountains, 294-297; Culebra, 396-397; East Coast, 339-343; *Mesones Gastronómicas*, 50; North Coast, 160-163; San Juan area, 111-120; South Coast, 261-266; top ten restaurants, 49-50; Vieques, 368-371; West Coast, 210-213
Where to stay, *see* Accommodations
Wigmore Institute, Aguada, 205
Windsurfing: San Juan area, 101, 103-104; South Coast, 243-244
Women, harassment of, 64-65
Wreck diving, West Coast, 189-190
Wyndham El Conquistador, Las Croabas, 309; accommodations, 336-337; golf, 313; parasailing, 323; where to eat, 341

Yabucoa: accommodations, 338; driving, 314; touring and sightseeing, 312; where to eat, 343
Yachting, East Coast, 317-318

Zoorico Zoológico de Puerto Rico, 186

www.hunterpublishing.com

Hunter's full range of travel guides to all corners of the globe is featured on our exciting Web site. You'll find guidebooks to suit every type of traveler, no matter what their budget, lifestyle, or idea of fun. Full descriptions are given for each book, along with reviewers' comments, a sample chapter and table of contents, and a cover image. Books may be purchased on-line using a credit card via our secure transaction system. All online orders receive 20% discount.

Alive! guides are a refreshing change from the "same-old" guidebooks. They are written for the savvy traveler who is looking for quality and value in accommodations and dining, with a selection of activities to fill the days and nights.

Check out our *Adventure Guides*, a series aimed at the independent traveler who enjoys outdoor activities (rafting, hiking, biking, skiing, canoeing, etc.). All books in this signature series cover places to stay and eat, sightseeing, in-town attractions, transportation and more!

Hunter's *Romantic Weekends* series offers myriad things to do for couples of all ages and lifestyles. Quaint places to stay and restaurants where the ambiance will take your breath away are included, along with fun activities that you and your partner will remember forever.

Hunter-Rivages Hotel Guides have become the best-selling guides of their kind in both Europe and America. Originating in Paris, they set the standards for excellence with their fabulous color photographs, superb maps and candid descriptions of the most remarkable hotels of Europe. Italy, Spain and Portugal books contain restaurant guides to the country. All have a color atlas pinpointing the location of every hotel and inn. Previous editions published by Fodor's.